The
Yorkshire County
Cricket Club Limited

Registered Number 28929R

YEARBOOK
2015

117th EDITION

Sponsors of

THE YORKSHIRE COUNTY CRICKET CLUB

Editor:
DAVID WARNER

Production Editor:
JAMES M GREENFIELD

Records and Statistics
Yorkshire First Eleven:
JOHN T POTTER
Yorkshire Second Eleven:
HOWARD CLAYTON

Official Photographers:
SIMON WILKINSON, ALEX WHITEHEAD
and ALLAN MCKENZIE *SWpix.com*

Published by
THE YORKSHIRE COUNTY CRICKET CLUB LTD
HEADINGLEY CRICKET GROUND
LEEDS LS6 3BU
Tel: 0843 504 3099   Fax: 0113 278 4099
Internet: http://www.yorkshireccc.com
e-mail: cricket@yorkshireccc.com

Solicitors: *Auditors:*
DLA PIPER UK LLP   KPMG Audit plc
Medical Officer: Dr NIGEL MAYERS, MBChB, MRCGP
Burley Park Medical Centre, 273 Burley Road, Leeds LS4 2EL

The opinions expressed by contributors are not necessarily those of the Board.

TELEPHONE AND FAX NUMBERS

HEADINGLEY CRICKET GROUND	**Tel: 0843 504 3099** Fax: 0113 278 4099
NORTH MARINE ROAD, SCARBOROUGH	**Tel: 01723 365625** Fax: 01723 364287
BURNLEY ROAD, TODMORDEN	**Tel: 01706 813140**
SHIPTON ROAD, YORK	**Tel: 01904 623602**
BRADFORD & BINGLEY Wagon Lane, Bingley	**Tel: 01274 775441**
STAMFORD BRIDGE Low Catton Road	**Tel: 01759 371545**

© The Yorkshire County Cricket Club Ltd 2015

Produced by:

Great Northern Books
PO Box 213, Ilkley LS29 9WS
www.greatnorthernbooks.co.uk

ISBN: 978-0-9928193-9-2

CONTENTS

Officers for 2015

THE BOARD

Mr C J GRAVES (Executive Chairman)
Mr R A SMITH TD, DL (Director)
Mr S DENISON (Director)
Mr M FARRINGTON (Leeds City Council)
Mr S WILLIS (Leeds Metropolitan University)
Mr M P VAUGHAN OBE

MEMBERS' COMMITTEE

Chairman: Mr S J MANN

ELECTED MEMBERS

Ms C EVERS   Mr R LEVIN
Mr S J MANN   Mr E STEPHENS

APPOINTED MEMBERS

Mr A KILBURN   Ms K MATHEWS
          Mr R W STOTT

MUSEUM DIRECTOR

Mr D S HALL CBE, TD

ARCHIVES COMMITTEE

Chairman: Mr J C D ALLAN

Mr J C D ALLAN   Mr P E DYSON
Mr J M GREENFIELD   Mr B SANDERSON
Mr D WARNER   Mr R D WILKINSON

Changes announced after February 16 will be recorded in the 2016 edition of the Yorkshire County Cricket Club Yearbook

5

MAGICAL MOMENTS MAKE FOR AN UNFORGETTABLE SEASON

By 'Dickie' Bird

When I was elected President of Yorkshire County Cricket Club last March it was one of the proudest moments of my life, because Yorkshire cricket has been such a big part of me for as long as I can remember.

To be elected President by the Yorkshire members was an honour and a privilege, regardless of what the team would go on to do on the field in the 2014 season. But for them to lift the LV-County Championship title made the Presidency extra special for me, and I will never forget that magical moment against Nottinghamshire at Trent Bridge when Richard Pyrah took the catch that sealed our success.

Moments later the Trophy was being passed from player to player amid joyous cheers from all of our supporters, and these scenes were repeated at the end of the final day of the season at Headingley when the team was applauded by an even larger crowd of loyal fans. One of the most pleasing aspects of our title triumph was that all of our opponents and their followers were quick to acknowledge that Yorkshire thoroughly deserved to be crowned Champions, and had proved themselves in no uncertain terms to be the best county side in the competition.

I will be 82 soon after the start of the 2015 season, and when I first walked through the gates at Headingley as a 16-year-old for net practices I never dreamt that I would become President of this great Club. I can honestly say that the Presidency has given me a new lease of life. People were telling me around the beginning of last year that I seemed to be fading away, but after I became President they were coming up to me and saying how well I looked.

I have enjoyed every minute of my 12 months in office and I was just as honoured a few months ago when the Yorkshire Board told me that I had been nominated by a unanimous vote to serve a second term as President in 2015. I can promise you all that if elected at the annual meeting I will serve the Club just as conscientiously over the next year as I have over the previous one. It was amazing that Yorkshire should win the Championship during my first term, and it goes without saying that I hope they can retain the greatest Trophy in domestic cricket — and add others to it for good measure.

I went to every Championship match last season, and it was not long before I was telling everyone that Yorkshire would win because I could see what a strong squad they had.

It was not only the first team I followed, but I watched the Second Eleven and the Academy whenever possible, and I was delighted with the progress that I saw our younger players were making. The Academy

That's my boy! President Bird congratulates captain Gale as he kisses the County Championship Trophy.

deserve great credit for their tremendous achievement in pulling off a splendid double by winning both the Yorkshire League title and the Cup competition, and all this augurs well for future of the county side.

We have a marvellous set of lads, and I think that at least six who are still below regular first-team level will go on to play for England. They are as good as that. I have seen them play so much that I have every confidence in their ability. There were many outstanding individual performances by Yorkshire players throughout the season, but cricket is a team game, and they became Champions not just because of what they themselves did but because of how well they knitted together as a side.

Everyone connected with the Club, from the office staff right through to our courageous captain, Andrew Gale, and his players, deserve the rewards which their hard work and devoted attention to detail have brought. All of our coaching staff have been brilliant and I must say how especially pleased I am for our Director of Cricket, Martyn Moxon, who, like me, is a Barnsley lad. He and Coach Jason Gillespie work so well together, and they have made the players successful while still allowing them to enjoy their cricket to the full.

Finally, I would like to pay a special tribute to groundsman Andy Fogarty and his staff. Often, no one gives the groundstaff a second thought, but Andy and his team have done a superb job in preparing pitches that last four days and bring a positive result towards the end of the fourth day. Every credit to them — and to everyone else who has played a part in our memorable season.

Officials of the Yorkshire County Cricket Club

President	Treasurer	Captain	Captain (Contd)
T R Barker 1863	M J Ellison 1863-1893	R Iddison 1863-1872	P Carrick 1987-1989
M J Ellison 1864-97	M Ellison, jun 1894-1898	J Rowbotham 1873	M D Moxon 1990-1995
Lord Hawke 1898-1938	Chas Stokes 1899-1912	L Greenwood 1874	D Byas 1996-2001
Rt Hon Sir F S Jackson 1939-1947	R T Heselton 1913-1931	J Rowbotham 1875	D S Lehmann 2002
T L Taylor 1948-1960	A Wyndham Heselton 1932-1962	E Lockwood 1876-1877	A McGrath 2003
Sir W A Worsley Bart 1961-1973	M G Crawford 1963-1979	T Emmett 1878-1882	C White 2004-6
Sir K Parkinson 1974-1981	J D Welch 1980-1984	Hon M B (Lord) Hawke 1883-1910	D Gough 2007-8
N W D Yardley 1981-1983	P W Townend 1984-2002	E J R H Radcliffe 1911	A McGrath 2009
The Viscount Mountgarret 1984-1989	*Chairman*	Sir A W White 1912-1918	A W Gale 2010-
Sir Leonard Hutton 1989-1990	A H Connell, DL 1971-1979	D C F Burton 1919-1921	*Secretary*
Sir Lawrence Byford QPM, LLD, DL 1991-1999	M G Crawford 1980-1984	Geoff Wilson 1922-1924	Geo Padley 1863
R A Smith TD, LLB, DL 1999-2004	H R Kirk 1984-1985	A W Lupton 1925-1927	J B Wostinholm 1864-1902
David Jones CBE 2004-6	B Walsh, QC 1986-1991	W A Worsley 1928-1929	F C (Sir Fredk.) Toone 1903-1930
Robert Appleyard 2006-8	Sir Lawrence Byford CBE, QPM, LLD, DL 1991-1998	A T Barber 1930	J H Nash 1931-1971
Brian Close CBE 2008-10	K H Moss MBE 1998-2002	F E Greenwood 1931-1932	J Lister 1972-1991
Raymond Illingworth CBE 2010-12	GA Cope 2002	A B Sellers 1933-1947	D M Ryder 1991-2002
Geoffrey Boycott OBE 2012-13	R A Smith TD, LLB, DL 2002-5	N W D Yardley 1948-1955	*Company Secretary*
Harold 'Dickie' Bird OBE 2014-15	Colin J Graves 2005-	W H H Sutcliffe 1956-1957	B Bouttell 2002-5
		J R Burnet 1958-1959	C Hartwell 2011-14
		J V Wilson 1960-1962	P Hudson 2014-
		D B Close 1963-1970	*Chief Executive*
		G Boycott 1971-1978	C D Hassell 1991-2002
		J H Hampshire 1979-1980	Colin J Graves 2002-5
		C M Old 1981-1982	Stewart Regan 2006-10
		R Illingworth 1982-1983	Colin J Graves 2012-13
		D L Bairstow 1984-1986	Mark Arthur 2013-

ENGLAND '15
AT HEADINGLEY

2nd Investec Test Match

England vs New Zealand

29 May - 2 June 2015

4th Royal London One-Day International

England vs Australia

11 September 2015

9

COUNTY FIXTURES — 2015

PRE-SEASON FIRST CLASS

Date			*Opponents*	*Venue*
Sun	22-25	March	MCC XI ....Zayed Cricket Stadium, Abu Dhabi

LV COUNTY CHAMPIONSHIP — Division 1

(All four-day matches)

Sun	12-15	April	Worcestershire ....Worcester
Sun	19-22	April	Nottinghamshire ....Trent Bridge
SUN	**26-29**	**APRIL**	**WARWICKSHIRE** ....**HEADINGLEY**
SUN	**10-13**	**MAY**	**HAMPSHIRE** ....**HEADINGLEY**
Sun	24-27	May	Somerset ....Taunton
SUN	**7-10**	**JUNE**	**MIDDLESEX** ....**HEADINGLEY**
MON	**22-25**	**JUNE**	**NOTTINGHAMSHIRE** ....**HEADINGLEY**
Sun	28-1	June/July	Durham ....Riverside
Sun	5-8	July	Warwickshire ....Edgbaston
SUN	**19-22**	**JULY**	**WORCESTERSHIRE** ....**SCARBOROUGH**
FRI	**7-10**	**AUGUST**	**DURHAM** ....**SCARBOROUGH**
Fri	21-24	August	Sussex ....Hove
TUE	**1-4**	**SEPTEMBER**	**SOMERSET** ....**HEADINGLEY**
Wed	9-12	September	Middlesex ....Lord's
Mon	14-17	September	Hampshire ....Southampton
TUE	**22-25**	**SEPTEMBER**	**SEPTEMBER** ....**HEADINGLEY**

ROYAL LONDON 50-OVER CUP

SUN	**26**	**JULY**	**GLOUCESTERSHIRE** ....**SCARBOROUGH**
Mon	27	July	Derbyshire ....Derby
Wed	29	July	Surrey ....The Oval
Thu	30	July	Worcestershire ....Worcester
Sun	2	August	Durham ....Riverside
MON	**3**	**AUGUST**	**LEICESTERSHIRE** ....**HEADINGLEY**
WED	**5**	**AUGUST**	**SOMERSET** ....**SCARBOROUGH**
TUE	**18**	**AUGUST**	**NORTHAMPTONSHIRE** ....**HEADINGLEY**
Tue	25-27	August	Quarter-Finals ....TBC
Sun	6-7	September	Semi-Finals ....TBC
Sat	19	September	Final ....Lord's

NATWEST T20 BLAST CUP

FRI	**15**	**MAY**	**DERBYSHIRE** ....**HEADINGLEY**
Fri	22	May	Nottinghamshire ....Trent Bridge
Fri	29	May	Durham ....Riverside
FRI	**5**	**JUNE**	**LANCASHIRE** ....**HEADINGLEY**
SUN	**14**	**JUNE**	**NORTHAMPTONSHIRE** ....**HEADINGLEY**
FRI	**19**	**JUNE**	**NOTTINGHAMSHIRE** ....**HEADINGLEY**
Sun	21	June	Warwickshire ....Edgbaston
Fri	26	June	Leicestershire ....Leicester
Fri	3	July	Lancashire ....Old Trafford
FRI	**10**	**JULY**	**DURHAM** ....**HEADINGLEY**
Sun	12	July	Derbyshire ....Chesterfield
TUE	**14**	**JULY**	**WORCESTERSHIRE** ....**HEADINGLEY**
Fri	17	July	Northamptonshire ....Northampton
FRI	**24**	**JULY**	**WARWICKSHIRE** ....**HEADINGLEY**
Wed	12-15	August	Quarter-Finals ....TBC
Sat	29	August	Semi-Finals and Final ....Edgbaston

OTHER MATCHES

TUE	**7-9**	**APRIL**	**LEEDS/BRADFORD MCCU** ....**HEADINGLEY**

INVESTEC TEST MATCHES

(All five-day matches)

ENGLAND v. NEW ZEALAND

Thu May 21 . . . . Lord's   **FRI MAY 29 . . . . HEADINGLEY**

ENGLAND v. AUSTRALIA

Wed July 8 . . . . Cardiff   Thu July 16 . . . . Lord's
Wed July 29 . . . . Edgbaston   Thu August 6 . . . . Trent Bridge
Thu August 20 . . . . The Oval

ROYAL LONDON ONE-DAY INTERNATIONALS

Tue	9	June	England v. New Zealand . . . . Edgbaston (Day/Night)
Fri	12	June	England v. New Zealand . . . . The Oval (Day/Night)
Sun	14	June	England v. New Zealand . . . . Southampton
Wed	17	June	England v. New Zealand . . . . Trent Bridge (Day/Night)
Sat	20	June	England v. New Zealand . . . . Riverside
Thu	3	September	England v. Australia . . . . Southampton (Day/Night)
Sat	5	September	England v. Australia . . . . Lord's
Tue	8	September	England v. Australia . . . . Old Trafford (Day/Night)
FRI	**11**	**SEPTEMBER**	**ENGLAND V. AUSTRALIA . . . . HEADINGLEY**
Sun	13	September	England v. Australia . . . . Old Trafford

NATWEST INTERNATIONAL T20

Sun	7	September	England v. India . . . . Edgbaston
Mon	31	August	England v. Australia . . . . Cardiff

SECOND ELEVEN CHAMPIONSHIP

Tue	28-30	April	Leicestershire . . . . Away (TBC)
MON	**8-10**	**JUNE**	**NORTHAMPTONSHIRE . . . . YORK**
TUE	**16-18**	**JUNE**	**DERBYSHIRE . . . . SCARBOROUGH**
MON	**6-9**	**JULY**	**LANCASHIRE . . . . HEADINGLEY**
TUE	**21-23**	**JULY**	**WARWICKSHIRE . . . . HARROGATE**
Tue	11-13	August	Durham . . . . Riverside
MON	**17-19**	**AUGUST**	**MCC UNIVERSITIES . . . . WEETWOOD**
MON	**24-26**	**AUGUST**	**NOTTINGHAMSHIRE . . . . . . STAMFORD BRIDGE**
Mon	7-10	September	Final . . . . TBC

SECOND ELEVEN TROPHY

Mon	27	April	Leicestershire . . . . Away (TBC)
MON	**15**	**JUNE**	**DERBYSHIRE . . . . MARSKE**
Mon	22	June	Worcestershire . . . . Away (TBC)
THU	**9**	**JULY**	**LANCASHIRE . . . . PUDSEY CONGS**
Wed	15	July	Unicorns . . . . Long Marston
MON	**20**	**JULY**	**WARWICKSHIRE . . . . YORK**
Mon	10	August	Durham . . . . Riverside
Fri	21	August	Semi-Finals . . . . TBC
Thu	27	August	Final . . . . TBC

SECOND ELEVEN TWENTY20 (TWO MATCHES IN THE SAME DAY)

Fri	8	May	Lancashire . . . . Away (TBC)
Tue	19	May	Derbyshire . . . . Away (TBC)
THU	**21**	**MAY**	**NOTTINGHAMSHIRE . . . . HARROGATE**
TUE	**26**	**MAY**	**DURHAM . . . . YORK**
THU	**11**	**JUNE**	**NORTHAMPTONSHIRE . . . . BARNSLEY**
Thu	25	June	Worcestershire . . . . Away (TBC)
Thu	16	July	Semi-Finals and Final . . . . Arundel

SECOND ELEVEN FRIENDLIES

TUE	14-16	APRIL	GLAMORGAN ....HEADINGLEY
Mon	20-22	April	Gloucestershire ....Bristol
Tue	12-15	May	Kent ....Polo Farm, Canterbury
Tue	4-7	August	Sussex ....Hove
Wed	2-4	September	Somerset ....Taunton Vale
TUE	15-17	SEPTEMBER	LANCASHIRE ....SCARBOROUGH

YORKSHIRE ACADEMY IN THE YORKSHIRE LEAGUE

Sat	18	April	Doncaster Town ....Doncaster Town CC
Sat	25	April	Cleethorpes ....Cleethorpes CC
Sat	2	May	Hull ....Hull CC
Mon	4	May	York ....York CC
	9	MAY	HARROGATE ....WEETWOOD
Sat	16	May	Sheffield United ....Sheffield United CC
Sat	23	May	Sheffield Collegiate ....Sheffield Collegiate CC
MON	25	MAY	DONCASTER TOWN ....WEETWOOD
Sat	6	June	Barnsley ....Barnsley CC
SAT	13	JUNE	DRIFFIELD ....WEETWOOD
SAT	20	JUNE	APPLEBY FRODINGHAM ....WEETWOOD
SAT	27	JUNE	CASTLEFORD ....WEETWOOD
Sat	4	July	Rotherham Town ....Rotherham Town CC
SAT	11	JULY	CLEETHORPES ....WEETWOOD
SAT	18	JULY	HULL ....WEETWOOD
Sat	25	July	Harrogate ....Harrogate CC
SAT	1	AUGUST	SHEFFIELD UNITED ....WEETWOOD
SAT	8	AUGUST	COLLEGIATE ....WEETWOOD
SUN	9	AUGUST	YORK ....WEETWOOD
SAT	22	AUGUST	BARNSLEY ....WEETWOOD
Sat	29	August	Driffield Town ....Driffield Town CC
Mon	31	August	Rotherham Town ....Rotherham Town CC
Sat	5	September	Appleby Frodingham ....Appleby Frodingham CC
Sat	12	September	Castleford ....Castleford CC

YORKSHIRE ACADEMY IN THE YORKSHIRE LEAGUE CUP

Sun	28	June	(Round 2) Appleby Frodingham or Driffield Town . .TBC

YORKSHIRE ACADEMY IN THE YORKSHIRE LEAGUE T20

Sun	7	June	Hull ....Sheffield Collegiate CC

YORKSHIRE ACADEMY FRIENDLIES

Sat	11	April	Sheriff Hutton Bridge ....Sheriff Hutton Bridge
Wed	15	April	Durham ....Richmondshire CC
Thu	16	April	Durham ....Richmondshire CC
Wed	29	April	Sedbergh School ....Sedbergh School
Tue	28	July	Scotland Development Squad ....TBC

YORKSHIRE UNDER-17s in TWO-DAY NATIONAL CHAMPIONSHIP

Tue	7-8	July	Cheshire ....TBC
Tue	14-15	July	Lancashire ....TBC
Tue	21-22	July	Durham ....TBC
Tue	4-5	August	Derbyshire ....TBC

YORKSHIRE UNDER-17s in ONE-DAY NATIONAL CHAMPIONSHIP

Sun	31	May	Durham ....TBC
Thu	9	July	Cheshire ....TBC
Thu	16	July	Lancashire ....TBC
Thu	6	August	Derbyshire ....TBC

ANDREW GALE AND HIS MEN GET COUNTY CRICKET'S HOLY GRAIL

By Graham Hardcastle

The summer of 2014 will not be forgotten in a hurry as Yorkshire's exciting squad delivered the ultimate prize.

There is still plenty of work to do in limited-overs cricket, but that can wait for now after Andrew Gale's side secured the Holy Grail, the LV= County Championship title.

The *White Rose* wrestled the title from Durham in ruthless fashion, winning eight out of 16 matches and

Out in front: Will Yorkshire's opening pair of Alex Lees, left, and Adam Lyth cross over into the Test arena?

losing only once — against Middlesex at Lord's early in the season. They finished 17 points clear of second-placed Warwickshire, although Nottinghamshire were their closest challengers throughout much of the campaign. Nottinghamshire finished fourth, losing their last three matches to Durham, Yorkshire and Sussex — who crept up to third place after thoughts of relegation in August when they lost at Scarborough.

Gale's players learned from the mistakes of the previous season when, with the title in their sights going into the last quarter of the summer, they took their eye off the ball and, to a degree, believed the suggestion that glory was theirs. Starting their 13th match at Scarborough in August 2013, they were 25.5 points clear of opponents Durham, who had five to play. They lost. Durham went on to win their last five games and claim the crown.

"Going through that year, we learned," Gale admitted. "I think we got caught up too much in trying to win the Championship. We got carried away with the big goal as opposed to just focusing on the process. It wasn't a subject we approached as a team, but as a management group we knew. We just concentrated on getting the message across: 'Do the processes right, don't get caught up in the hype'.

"I think the players knew that we got carried away. They must be sick of hearing me say 'process, process, process'. But they've been saying it, too, so it's sunk in."

Gale wanted the players to concentrate on each session and not to look too far ahead.

Yorkshire won five matches by an innings in 2014, and they won four of their last five fixtures to stamp their authority all over the league. It was a run which included a first *Roses* win at the 16th attempt at Emirates Old Trafford at the start of September and a title-clinching victory against Nottinghamshire at Trent Bridge nearly a fortnight later.

Yorkshire's dominance is highlighted by these three statistics:

***ADAM LYTH** was the Division's leading run-scorer with 1,489

***JACK BROOKS** was the Division's second most prolific bowler with 68 wickets

***ADAM LYTH** was Division's most prolific outfield catcher with 35

While Lyth moved to the verge of an England Test call-up, Adil Rashid's resurgence with bat and ball, especially in the second half of the season, also helped him to reignite his international ambitions.

It is surprising to look down the county's batting averages and see only Lyth with more than 1,000 runs to his name, but six others passed 500 for the season, including his opening partner Alex Lees (971).

Lyth and Lees were far and away the country's best opening partnership, and Gale compared them to the great Australian duo of Justin Langer and Matthew Hayden: "They're both very much in a similar mode to Langer and Hayden," he said. "They're quite aggressive in how they play, looking to put pressure on the bowlers and to dominate. Those are good values to have as an opener.

"It's certainly not out of the question that they could open together for England. I can see a day when four of the top five in England's order are Yorkshire batsmen."

Although Yorkshire had to do without Joe Root and Gary Ballance for large parts of the season they were boosted by the prolonged availability of Jonny Bairstow and Tim Bresnan, and when they needed somebody to step in because of injury or unavailability it happened. The contributions of young batsman Jack Leaning in his breakthrough season and experienced all-rounder Richard Pyrah should not be forgotten.

Batting duo Kane Williamson and Aaron Finch, who split the overseas duties, also impressed in their different ways, scoring hundreds against Sussex at Scarborough and Warwickshire at Edgbaston.

Finch played two stunning *T20* knocks — against Lancashire at Old Trafford, where he hit The Point Conference facility with two mighty blows to set tongues wagging, and Nottinghamshire at Headingley.

JACK LEANING: Breaking through

There were also two *T20* catches to remember — both involving Finch and Lyth — against Lancashire and Leicestershire. Both were similar — flicked backed acrobatically by Lyth at long-off and long-on before his body went over the ropes, and the ball was caught by Finch.

The ridiculous racism controversy surrounding captain Gale at the end of the season should not detract from the part he played. He was one of those to pass 500 Championship runs, while leaving himself out early in the season at Lord's proved a brave call to make, one which earned him the respect of the dressing room in an instant.

Coach Jason Gillespie said: "That was one massive moment in our season. He felt that Lees and Lyth were going to play a big part in our season to strive for a top-three finish. He backed our opening combination to get off to some really good, solid starts. He felt it was really important that the captain showed them support and backing."

That brings us nicely on to Gillespie and the rest of the coaching team. All must take credit — Richard Dawson with the Second Eleven and Ian Dews and Richard Damms with Academy and age groups. The Academy won the ECB Yorkshire County Premier League and Cup double, which was a tremendous achievement.

Most notably, the relationship forged between Gillespie and Director of Cricket Martyn Moxon was a crucial factor in creating a relaxed environment in which the players could flourish.

Yorkshire have the ability and depth to defend their title this year, although they will also be keen for success in limited-overs cricket. In spite of improving on their performances in 2013 they still under-achieved again last summer.

Top-order batsman Lees, who arguably was Yorkshire's standout per-former against the white ball, was rewarded with a call-up to the England Lions one-day squad for the New Year winter tour of South Africa to face their A side. No fewer than seven Yorkshire players were picked for that tour, which included one-day and first-class matches. Bairstow, Ballance, Brooks, Lees, Lyth, Plunkett and Rashid were all recognised.

Gillespie said of Yorkshire's limited-overs performance: "We seek to play as well as we can in each game. Some people have questioned our selections, especially when we've been out of competitions, but we want to try and do as well as we can.

"We were really disappointed not to go further in 50-over cricket. We felt that we had the team to really challenge and get to Lord's. To lose against Durham in a home quarter-final was bitterly disappointing. There were some good, honest chats in the dressing room after that. We know we need to be better.

"Individuals need to improve their games. In that game we had three out of the top six who got ducks. Coming in on a slow wicket that's tak-ing a bit of turn, we need to find ways of overcoming those situations. We did that on the majority of occasions. It was just that game we did-n't do it, and it cost us."

The last word on a fantastic campaign shall be left to Moxon, a man who has worked hard for Championship glory for more than 30 years as player and coach. "I've been in the game a long time," he said. "So it's a big moment for me to be part of a Championship-winning team. I've been close a couple of times, and I've been involved with others in developing teams. But to finally finish it off is certainly the highlight of my cricketing career.

"Playing for England is a fantastic feeling and achievement. But the background to this, the hard work that goes into it and everything that's involved in winning a Championship – for me, it feels the best thing for sure."

Graham Hardcastle is Yorkshire Cricket Correspondent for the Bradford Telegraph & Argus, The Press, York, and The Northern Echo.

WERE YOU AN 'I WUZ THERE' AT THESE PREVIOUS TITLE WINS?

By Nigel Pullan

What have Eastbourne, Newport (Mon), Hove, Harrogate, Harrogate, Leicester, Harrogate, Harrogate, Hull, Scarborough and Nottingham in common? They are the venues on which Yorkshire won the Championship on 11 occasions since the Second World War.

Many of our senior members will have been counting up their *I Wuz Theres*. I wuz there five times, and the family pet was photographed at Harrogate in 1962. She would not have gone on her own, so my parents must have been there. So I am going to claim five-and-a-half *I wuz Theres*. I assume that the best record is held among the players in that successful decade of the 1960s who actually scored the runs and took the wickets and catches.

Championship cricket resumed in 1946, and Yorkshire sustained their pre-war dominance for one more season. Success came on the beautiful Saffrons ground at Eastbourne, when they beat Sussex who finished bottom. It was a very close match. Sussex made 91, but bowled Yorkshire out for 82. Harry Parks carried his bat for 49 when Sussex made 105, and Yorkshire at one time were 26-4. Then Frank Smailes, 67*, and Maurice Leyland in his final season, 21*, saw Yorkshire home. Middlesex were Yorkshire's closest rivals, but were heavily beaten by Kent. I imagine the Yorkshire team would have celebrated with an invigorating walk along the cliffs to Beachy Head.

In 1949 Yorkshire shared the Championship with Middlesex, who had beaten Derbyshire on August 26 and would take the title unless Yorkshire got full points at Newport. Middlesex had had a hard fight against Derbyshire, but made 196-7 off Jackson, Copson and Gladwin, thanks to Denis Compton's 97*. *Wisden* records: "The equanimity of the Lord's pavilion was disturbed when Gladwin, after being run out by his partner, accidentally put his bat through the dressing-room window."

Yorkshire beat Glamorgan at Rodney Parade in two days, bowling them out a second time at 7.14 on Monday evening as Wardle took 5-15 and Coxon 5-17. Rodney Parade, once the home of Newport RUFC, now hosts Newport County AFC, and cricket has moved elsewhere. Some of us in June 1990 spent a drizzly day outside the gates waiting for a Refuge Assurance League 40-over game against Yorkshire that never started. It knows how to drizzle in Newport. That was the last scheduled Glamorgan match on the ground.

There followed a decade of Surrey dominance in the 1950s. In fact, Surrey were very much the favourites in 1959. Yorkshire lost twice on their West Country tour at Bath and Bristol, while Surrey won at Cheltenham to end Gloucestershire's challenge. Yorkshire won their next two games at Worcester and Hove, and when Surrey met Middlesex concurrently with Hove a Yorkshireman, Don Bennett, was instrumental in Middlesex winning. Yorkshire made 215 in 105 minutes to win at Hove with seven minutes to spare: they took 15 off the first over, and reached 50 in 20 minutes, 100 in 43, 150 in 63, and 200 in 85. Bryan Stott and Doug Padgett were outstanding, but the winning hit, actually a deflection to the fine-leg boundary, came from Brian Bolus to end a decade without a Championship.

Vic Wilson, who took over the captaincy from Ronnie Burnet in 1960, would lead the team to first, second and first again. In 1960 came the first of four Harrogate title wins, each of them threatened by bad weather. There was a heavy storm at the end of the first day against Worcestershire, but Yorkshire won fairly easily as Fred Trueman hit 56 in half-an-hour with five sixes and three fours. Lancashire were our main challengers, but they had a bad time in late August, losing at Southport and just failing to beat Sussex at Blackpool when rain washed out the last day.

Hampshire won in 1961, with Yorkshire a close second, and in 1962 Vic Wilson again had to win at Harrogate. Worcestershire had finished their fixtures, and were 10 points ahead of Yorkshire who had to get 14 for a win against Glamorgan. All went well at first as Glamorgan were all out for 65, Don Wilson taking 6-24, although Yorkshire managed only 101 with 67 from Ken Taylor – possibly his best-ever innings. With Glamorgan 13-0 it rained and rained. There was no play next day, but 5,000 were present and over 10,000 on Wednesday and Friday. Once play started on the last day Raymond Illingworth and Wilson bowled Glamorgan out for 101, so Yorkshire needed only 66. Jeff Jones bowled Taylor first ball — thus completing prolonged a hat-trick which had included Mel Ryan and Don Wilson two days before.

In 1963 Yorkshire under Brian Close beat Leicestershire twice to be sure of first place: they outplayed them at Scarborough, when Jimmy Binks made his 300th consecutive appearance for Yorkshire, and the Championship was confirmed at Grace Road. Warwickshire were the other contenders and, as usual, weather was a factor. Yorkshire were dominant, and at the end of the second day had Leicestershire 61-5. It took only 15 minutes on the last day to win — 20 minutes less than Trent Bridge 2014 — Illingworth taking 6-13. Meanwhile, at Edgbaston Warwickshire lost two-and-a-half hours to rain and Brian Reynolds hit a century, so they could not catch Yorkshire.

Harrogate was another exciting, tense and damp three days in 1966. As the season ended Yorkshire only drew with Surrey, lost to Warwickshire at Hull and again at Northampton. Worcestershire kept winning, and had the incentive of a third Championship. Yorkshire arrived at Harrogate to play Kent with Worcestershire only six points behind and playing Sussex at Worcester. Yorkshire made 210 with 80 from Geoff Boycott, and Trueman and Tony Nicholson dismissed Kent for 109. Then a young Derek Underwood took 7-30, so the visitors had to get 200. At lunch on the last day they were well placed at 143-3, but a strong drying wind and the spin of Illingworth and Wilson reduced them to 176 all out. Wilson took a hat-trick comprising Brian Luckhurst, Alan Ealham and Alan Knott, while John Snow and Tony Buss bowled Worcestershire out for 77. Colin Cowdrey made a speech of congratulation to members assembled in the Harrogate dining room.

The fourth Harrogate title-winner was against Gloucestershire in 1967. Yorkshire's win at Middlesbrough against Warwickshire, Wilson taking 7-21, put them in a strong position and they only required a first-innings lead. Philip Sharpe made 75 and Boycott 74 in a first-innings total of 309. At lunch on the second day Gloucestershire were 64-0, but the wet pitch was drying, and they had lost all 20 wickets by 6.45, Illingworth taking 7-58 and a remarkable 7-6. How often have we mentioned the names of Illingworth and Don Wilson in this narrative?

Hull in 1968 saw the most exciting finish of all. Kent had two more games, but if Yorkshire won Kent could not catch them. Yorkshire controlled the game, but the problem would be bowling Surrey out to win. It was going well enough until Arnold Long joined Younis Ahmed: they batted for one-and-three-quarter hours, so with about 15 minutes to go all seemed lost. Then Younis pulled Wilson firmly to short-leg, where it hit Brian Close on the shoulder and rebounded to wicket-keeper Binks, who caught it. Robin Jackman, usually a doughty opponent, was out second ball. In the next over Long was caught by Binks, standing up to Nicholson, on his home ground. Never had there been such drama at Anlaby Circle, but it was to be the last Championship until 2001.

In 2001 Yorkshire won at Scarborough for the first time post-war. It would be interesting if someone went back to all the Championships to see where they were decided. It was Yorkshire's first two-division Championship, and they won on August 24 with two games to play, both of which they lost — at The Oval and here against Essex. David Byas led a side at the top for most of the summer, and Australians Darren Lehmann and Wayne Clark had important roles. Again the result depended on weather, and Yorkshire won just before the rain came when Simon Jones was caught by Byas. It had been 33 years...and 12 more were to elapse before Ryan Sidebottom took the crucial last wicket at Trent Bridge. Let us hope that we can emulate the 60s.

CHALLENGE FOR HONOURS AGAIN HINDERED BY ENGLAND CALLS

By Howard Clayton

RYAN GIBSON: Attacking all-rounder who showed his mettle at the helm

The season saw improvement in some areas and a standstill in others. The team again finished fourth in the northern section of the Championship, but moved up to third in the Trophy.

As usual the *T20* matches saw the weakest performances, with only two wins out of eight games arranged, but one of these — against Nottinghamshire at Trent College — saw a remarkable turnaround in fortunes engineered by Jack Leaning, who went onwards and upwards in the second half of the season as he made his mark in first-class cricket.

The action began in South Wales in early April with Trophy and Championship games against Glamorgan at the SWALEC. The Trophy game was lost on the *Duckworth-Lewis* calculation, but the Championship match ended with Yorkshire having five overs at the last pair. They could not find the ball that mattered, and it was drawn.

Next, it was to Nottingham and Lady Bay or Nottinghamshire Sports Ground or Boots. Whatever you call it the batting showed what it could do as Jonathan Tattersall and Eliot Callis put on 146 for the first wicket in a successful chase for 249. This was followed by the Championship encounter and a battling draw to save the game on the last day.

Unspoken hopes had been that Nottinghamshire would declare their first innings to set up an interesting fourth-innings chase, but they batted on well into the last day to establish a substantial lead. Yorkshire rightly showed no interest in making a match of it, and skipper Azeem

Rafiq helped himself to an unbeaten 87 to ensure safety. He declared on the stroke of 5pm to end the game when 13 runs away from his century, a very sporting consideration.

Attentions turned to the *T20*, and some very mixed performances. They began against Durham at York with two heavy defeats. In the first game Calum MacLeod, a Scottish international on trial with Durham, hammered the bowling around Clifton Park for an unbeaten 103 to see his side home by seven wickets. The second game followed a similar path as Durham triumphed by six wickets.

The two games against Lancashire at Abbeydale Park were abandoned an hour before the scheduled start after a torrential day-long downpour, and the remaining two games saw a return to the Midlands at Trent College for two fixtures against Nottinghamshire. The first brought the first victory of the campaign by 43 runs as Richard Pyrah top-scored with 44 and added a splendid return of 4-13, but that was nothing to what happened next. Steven Mullaney made an unbeaten 103 for Nottinghamshire as they totalled 195-5 in 20 overs, and Yorkshire were in disarray at 97-6 after 13.3 overs, with 99 still needed.

Leaning cut loose. He completed the first century for Yorkshire in the Second Eleven *T20* format, falling to the first delivery of the final over for 102, made from 54 deliveries with five fours and seven maximums. This innings won him the Second Eleven Performance of the Year Trophy. Moin Ashraf and Karl Carver needed to score 12 in five balls, and they did so with a scampered two from the last delivery. It was the first time in the three years that the format has been extended to second teams that two centuries have been scored in the same game.

Denby CC was the venue for the final two games against Derbyshire, and both were lost. Yorkshire were dismissed for 91 in the first, their lowest total against Derbyshire in this format and only two better than their lowest ever in the *T20*.

The remaining games in the Championship ended in draw after draw, six in all, as neither side was able to establish a final advantage. At Stamford Bridge the Warwickshire visitors included Jonathan Trott as part of his recuperation after his problems in Australia the previous winter. No play was possible on either the second or third days, but Yorkshire passed the magic 300 total for the first time, although certainly not the last, in 2014. The Lancashire game at Todmorden saw a similar result as all three days were severely interrupted by the weather.

The next two games against Worcestershire and Durham brought the best cricket of the season as both teams of visitors were beaten by an innings. Worcestershire were bowled out for 153 at York as left-armer James Wainman, looking fitter and stronger then he has ever done, took 3-45 and worked up a fair pace. Leaning then made 74 and Ryan Gibson, the Academy Player of the Year, 54 as the hosts established a healthy first-innings lead of 145. It was enough as Worcestershire were dis-

Getting ahead: Yorkshire captain Andrew Gale takes time out on Royal London Cup Quarter-Final Day to present Matthew Fisher with his Second Eleven cap

missed for 135 second time around, so Yorkshire won by an innings and 10 runs. Matt Fisher led the way with 5-31, ably supported by Wainman's 3-35.

Durham were the visitors for the return to Harrogate after a gap of two years. They reached 224, Josh Shaw (5-31) recording his maiden five-wicket haul, before a splendid 113 by Dan Hodgson and a blistering 79 from Gibson saw the home side to 416. Durham trailed by 192, and it was over before lunch on the third day as Shaw did it again — this time with 5-28 to finish with match figures of 10-71, a testament to his improvement. He left after this game to join England Under-19s, and promptly took 6-103 against the South Africans at Northampton.

Yorkshire bumped down to earth at York after the euphoria of these two successes as the eventual Champions, Leicestershire, triumphed by eight wickets. Yorkshire were virtually level after first innings, but the visitors' all-round experience carried the day as they completed the first leg of their Second Eleven treble, the first time it has been achieved.

The Championship season continued with a visit to Shenley in Hertfordshire to take on MCC Young Cricketers. Rain on the final afternoon ensured another draw — but not before a monumental performance by Matthew Waite and Nathan Firn, two Academy players who came in to cover for Yorkshire's international calls.

The score was 149-7 as the pair came together in what turned out to be the highest eighth-wicket stand of the season by any side in the Championship. They began slowly, but gradually accelerated, and were parted only after they had added 158. Waite finished undefeated on 112, a maiden century in his first Championship innings, and Firn reached 64 to follow his equally steely performances. The possibility of a close run-chase disappeared under grey skies and drizzle on the final afternoon.

Back to Denby CC for a flat anti-climax. Trailing by 23 on first innings, Yorkshire were set a target of 265, but at 25-1 the rain ended it.

For the second successive season any chance Yorkshire might have had of progressing in either the Championship or the Trophy was lost as five players left for England Under-19s. When a side loses players of the calibre of Will Rhodes, Jonathan Tattersall, Shaw, Fisher and Carver the spine has gone, and although those who came in performed well at times they were not yet of the standard of the five departees.

The loss of Rhodes and Tattersall opened the door for Gibson to try his hand at captaincy. He showed an immediate liking for permanent slips, a move that wins the vote of this traditionalist.

The one-day Trophy *Roses* dual at Todmorden was abandoned without a ball bowled, and there was a surprising defeat at Swarkestone CC to Derbyshire. Sitting pretty at 171-2, requiring 65 more to win, Yorkshire's wheels came off as they fizzled out to 206-9. The last overs were a particular disappointment as batsmen failed to force the pace.

There were bright spots as Warwickshire, Worcestershire and Durham were all beaten. The game at Pudsey Congs against Warwickshire saw the second appearance in as many days of Trott, who top-scored as they chased 302-5. Andrew Hodd led the way with 112, and Tattersall chipped in with 65. The visitors had a chance with Trott there, but once he had been dismissed joyously by Fisher the end was nigh.

The next game against Worcestershire saw Yorkshire pile on the runs to record 332-5, Rhodes 124 and Gibson 66. Worcestershire chased well, but succumbed for 289 as Fisher and Wainman took three wickets apiece. Then it was on to Marske-by-the Sea and the aptly named Windy Hill Lane, where Yorkshire reached their highest-ever total in the competition of 383-5. It was also the second-highest total by any team in the 2014 competition. Yet another century provided the backbone of the innings as Richard Pyrah made 128 from 73 deliveries with five fours and 13 sixes. Hodgson made 77 with one six, but this would have expensive consequences for the owners of the house over the wall who would return from holiday to a smashed greenhouse.

That was the final appearance of the strongest XI, and Yorkshire ended with successive defeats by Leicestershire and MCC Young

Cricketers. The Leicestershire game was played at Barnsley CC before one of the best crowds I have seen in my short time in post, the receipts topping £300. A scorecard reprint was necessary in mid-afternoon. The young side struggled against Leicestershire's 258, but James Logan and Firn cheered the crowd with a 10th-wicket stand of 56, the highest in the 2014 competition by any side. Finally, it was the Young Cricketers and a nine-wicket defeat at Shenley. The least said about that the better.

Yorkshire had 14 friendly games in 2014, the highlight being the *T20* at Malton and Old Malton CC to raise money to replace Old Malton's fire-damaged pavilion. Yorkshire Chief Executive Mark Arthur attended a dinner at the Club in late 2013, and promised a Yorkshire visit for a fund-raising event. This was fulfilment of that promise.

The weather was kind and the crowd huge. Tents were set up by local butchers as well as Betty's of Harrogate and Black Sheep Ale, and all were well supported. Takings towards the rebuilding funds amounted to £5,000, but the benefit of such a successful public-relations campaign is incalculable. Wainman starred with the bat, making 61 from 25 deliveries including seven sixes on a very large ground, and Yorkshire won by 58 runs as Hodgson nabbed his first wicket for the county in any format.

The team travelled to Sleaford in Lincolnshire for a drawn two-dayer against England Under-19s, Callis remaining unbeaten on 124 in the first innings. Other *T20* games took place at Headingley in early May against Lancashire, with one won and one lost.

A one-day outing was staged against Gloucestershire at Bristol with a five-wicket defeat under the *Duckworth-Lewis* system, but not before Tattersall had registered 102 not out in his team's 305-6. In the three-day game that followed he struck 137 out of 468-8 declared, but the pitch died and Gloucestershire replied with a first-wicket stand of 256 before Carver took three quick wickets to finish the proceedings.

The rest of the programme concentrated on three-day cricket. Three of these games were against Lancashire, with one victory, one hard-fought draw in North Wales and defeat by 11 runs at Headingley as Yorkshire were put out for 351 chasing 363.

Nottinghamshire were beaten by two runs at Harrogate in a marvellous match of four hundreds as Andrew Hodd, 166, and Gibson with his maiden Second Eleven century of 127 starred for Yorkshire. There were two games at Scarborough. One against Scotland ended in a draw as the visitors totalled 400-6 in their second innings to kill it, and the other was against Kent: it lasted 9.2 overs before the rain came and never left.

The season finished at Taunton Vale with a 10-wicket defeat in a three-day game that lasted a day and a half. Two years earlier Yorkshire had lost by an innings with the same amount of time remaining.

*Howard Clayton is the Yorkshire CCC Second Eleven Scorer

TEAM REACH THE STARS AFTER DEWSY LAUNCHES 'ROCKET'

As Mosun Hussain hit the winning runs with a six against Cleethorpes on the last-but-one day of the season it was a moment in which we created history.

Topping the League is talked about every year in the Academy

A special article by captain Will Rhodes, right, whose Colts Academy made Yorkshire history in 2014 when they did the ECB Yorkshire County Premier League double by lifting both the Cup and League titles.

side, but for the previous 20 years we had fallen short each time. In 2014 it was different. Each person in the squad genuinely believed that this was the year we could create our own bit of history.

I think both Dewsy (Ian Dews) and Dammsy (Richard Damms) believed we could, too. At least Dewsy did until we had an absolute shocker away at Appleby Frodingham. Not often does he get Sir Alex Ferguson's "hair-dryer" treatment out, but this time we deserved it! His words after the game have stayed with me ever since: "You can forget about winning the League. You never have and you never will!"

Whether this was him trying to motivate us or him being serious I'll never know, but what happened four months later at the end of the season is history. Our side, which looked good on paper, was an impressive one. We had six players on the England books, two lads who had played first-team cricket and a host of talented youngsters coming through — although having this side did have its problems.

For 90 per cent of the team there were exams during the summer, and England could be away for four to five weeks at a time. That's not taking into account injuries and fatigue that occur from playing all week in Second Eleven cricket.

For Dewsy and Dammsy it can be nightmare picking the side. Credit goes to those two for bringing in players with quality when lads were missing. When we played Rotherham away in the League towards the end of August we had seven games left — five in the League and two in the Cup. Our team talk from Dewsy was simple: "Win seven games and you win two cups. Easy." It wasn't until that point that we really believed we could make our own history.

From the start of the year — from our convincing win at Clifton Park against York to the end of the year at Shaw Lane in the Cup final against Barnsley — our season can only be described as successful bar two minor slip-ups in the League. In the Cup we played some really impressive cricket. We had beaten Rotherham, York and Castleford on our way to the final...which was a strange one.

The first half of our innings was a disaster, and if it had not been for Barney Gibson and Eliot Callis we would have been bowled out for 60. Then Barnsley's innings followed the same pattern. For the first 10 overs we bowled poorly, and even when Karl Carver removed their overseas opener the game was still theirs to lose. We needed a miracle or an act of genius to win us that game. Josh Shaw provided that piece of genius: his hat-trick was the master stroke that ended a superb season.

During a double-winning campaign there were moments that stood out — Eliot Callis's century on the opening day of the season against York and his innings in the Cup final, Matthew Fisher's hat-trick on the last day of the League season against Harrogate and Shaw's hat-trick in the Cup final against Barnsley. Ryan Gibson picking up the Junior and Senior League batting awards remains fresh in my memory.

*   *   *

Academy Scorer Harold Galley writes: Victory by 127 runs in the first Yorkshire League match of the season at York heralded what was to be a superb season for the Academy. Two further League victories followed over both Sheffield clubs before a cup victory by 243 runs against Rotherham. The Academy had never experienced such an excellent start.

A warning not to be complacent came with the visit to Appleby Frodingham: the side performed poorly, both in the field and at the wicket, so suffering one of the two League defeats of the season.

Early-season weather was poor, and five matches had to be cancelled. A trip to Scarborough brought a League victory, and a Cup win over York followed. Eliot Callis, Ryan Gibson and Will Rhodes each scored three centuries, Gibson's 160 off 108 balls at Weetwood making Scarborough suffer. A League hiccup came when the batting was not good on a difficult pitch at Castleford, resulting in a five-wicket loss.

Victory in the Cup semi-final over Castleford at Weetwood saw the Academy through to the final against Barnsley at Shaw Lane, but before that came further League victories, and the long trip to Cleethorpes saw

CUP THAT CHEERS: Academy skipper Will Rhodes receives the ECB Yorkshire County Premier League Cup from League President and former Yorkshire captain David Byas. *(Photo: Richard Damms. More of Richard's pictures appear in our colour pages.)*

Yorkshire return as Champions with one match still to be played. Losing players to the England Under-19s and Under-17 squads did not affect the strength of the side. Indeed, it gave younger players the chance to shine and show off their talents.

The last match of the season, the Cup final at Barnsley, saw opener Callis play yet another fine innings, and the Academy reached 191 in their 45 overs. An opening partnership of 88 by Barnsley gave the South Yorkshire team hope, but a hat-trick by Josh Shaw — all lbw decisions — saw the Academy back in control. Three wickets by Jared Warner confirmed this, and the Barnsley middle-order failed to rise to the occasion. The Academy were home by 33 runs.

A magnificent year for the team...and a wonderful double!

FINE CRICKET IN ENJOYABLE AND SUCCESSFUL SEASON

By Chris Hassell

There were exciting performances at all age groups in another successful and enjoyable season for Yorkshire Schools' Cricket Association.

The 15s battled their way through to the ECB finals at Kibworth, and beat Derbyshire for third place; the 13s experienced a very good summer, beating Lancashire convincingly in the Northern Counties final as well as lifting the Taunton Festival Trophy for the second year; the 12B team won the Oundle Festival; the 11s recorded a clean sweep with 18 victories, including the Taunton Festival for the third year, and the first season for U10B was a great success with enormous interest shown.

A total of 200 matches were played at county level, and for the first time a junior presentation evening was held at Headingley for the U10, 11 and 12 teams.

15A: P 15, W 10, L 4, Ab 1. An indifferent start to the season with two early defeats against Lancashire and Derbyshire was retrieved to enable the side to reach the quarter-final and then the national finals. The squad contained some talented individuals, but a lack of consistency and an inability to perform under pressure exposed many frailties, although the depth of talent ensured that a good measure of success was still achieved. The county was again well represented at the Bunbury Festival with six boys in the North team. Team manager Andy Rowsell; coaches Andrew Chadwick, Bob Wincer and Peter Hepworth.

15B: P 18, W 10, D 1, L 3, Ab 4. A generally good season, particularly so with a number of players progressing through to the A team. Some excellent cricket was played against a number of very good sides. The trial matches and early games were rain-affected, but the season finished in fine style with victories in eight of the last nine games. Team manager Bob Wincer; coach Peter Hepworth.

14A: P 21, W 8, L 7, Ab 6: A fluctuating and disappointing season, but not without some good performances. A number of players failed to achieve their full potential, and it is hoped that improvements will be forthcoming this season. Team manager/coach Tony Pickersgill; assistant manager/coach Jack Bethel.

14B: P 20, W 13, L 4, D 1, Ab 2: A rather average season, where questions remained unanswered in respect of fielding and fitness. The value of B teams was evident with a number of players promoted to the A side. Team manager/coach Tony Pickersgill; coach Bren Terry.

13A: P 19, W 17, L 2: A remarkable season with no weather interference. All matches were played to a conclusion, giving players plenty of opportunity to make their mark. The two narrow defeats to Lancashire were avenged in the final of the ESCA Northern Counties Cup with a resounding nine-wicket victory. There was success, too, at the Taunton Festival for a second successive year. Team manager Keith Dickson; coaches Ghulam Rafique and Chris Marsden.

13B: P 19, W 13, L 5, Ab 1: Early season trials were hampered by the weather, but it was a good year, the highlight being the Taunton Festival with a close finish on the last day against Kent resulting in a six-run defeat to take third place. The festival gives boys valuable experience against county A teams and the opportunity to develop team spirit. Team manager/coach Dick Whaley; assistant manager Linda Whaley.

12A: P 16, W 10, L 4, Ab 2: A good season, although not without disappointments with some difficulty chasing targets. Team manager Simon Horkin; coach Tom Smith.

12B: P 15, W 13, L 1, Ab 1: A really impressive season with only one defeat against a strong North Yorkshire team containing four A players. Team manager Phil Chapman; coach Roy Chapman.

U11: P 18, W 18. Another wonderful season, unbeaten again with a third consecutive victory at the Taunton Festival and retention of the Tony Hemingway Roses Trophy for the fourth year with victories against Lancashire home and away. There was a willingness to learn and a determination to succeed. The Taunton week was successful due to the depth of batting and strength in bowling with great variety and diversity. Team manager Dick Whaley; assistant manager Linda Whaley.

11B: P 13, W 8, L 3, Ab 2: Early predictions were impossible, but with commitment to a team ethic a measure of success was achieved and valuable lessons learned. The one blip was a couple of defeats to the "old enemy" which will be a target for the boys to redress at 12B. Team manager Mark Loker; coaches Mark Welford and George Saville).

10A: P 9, W 5, L 2, Ab 2: Another good season and a big learning curve for the team moving from pairs cricket to 40-over matches. There were good wins over Lancashire, Leicestershire (twice) as well as Sussex and Surrey on the Southern tour. Team manager Steve Holliday; coaches Phil Chapman and Chris Holliday.

10B: P 11, W 5, L 4, Ab 2: The first season for this new group was most rewarding, with some excellent performances from all of the boys, who will be looking to improve with winter nets of the new season. The Repton Festival was a great experience and will help them in their transition from pairs to 40-over matches. Team manager John Green; coaches Roy Chapman and Haydon Jackson.

19: P 6, W 3, L 2, D 1: The 45th festival at St Peter's School was another enjoyable week with mixed success against Lincolnshire (lost), Northumberland (drawn, rain), Lancashire (won), MCC (lost) and Durham (won). Team manager Ian Frost (Woodhouse Grove); coach Glenn Roberts Silcoates School.

This award for outstanding service to Yorkshire County Cricket Club was inaugurated in 2008, and last year it went to BOB STOTT, an appointed representative of the Members' Committee and the man who chaired the committee set up to organise the special events to mark Yorkshire CCC's 150th anniversary celebrations in 2013. Here Bob tells how his keen interest in *White Rose* cricket developed over the years.

FROM SCHOOL YARD TO HEADINGLEY STADIUM

BOB STOTT

So my cricket journey began — with the dustbin as stumps in the Paddock County School yard during the Easter, Whitsuntide and Summer holidays.

The ball was a much-used tennis ball and the bat the best any of us had managed not to break. We started after breakfast, and continued until the street lamps no longer gave the batsman enough light to have any chance.

The biggest disappointment was not being bowled out but being caught, one-handed, off the tall building opposite when you had really hit a great six — but you had to go, as that was the rule.

I graduated at 12 years old to Paddock Cricket & Bowling Club, who had first and second XIs in the Huddersfield & District League but, more importantly for me, they had a junior side which was then "under 18" and played on Wednesday evenings. I struggled to get a game, but always turned up in case someone was missing, and in my first season I twice managed to make the team this way. Both times down to bat at No. 11, but I never reached the wicket — not in an innings of 20 overs per side — and "little" boys didn't bowl. So was *T20* cricket invented in the 1950s?

However, I was now playing cricket with the big boys, and no one bigger than Chris Balderstone, who was our star man – yes that very same Chris Balderstone, the Yorkshire, Leicestershire and England cricketer and Huddersfield Town and Carlisle United footballer. No four overs for Chris: he bowled his 10 from one end, and was usually still in the middle when we knocked off the runs. I believe it was 1956 when I started taking an interest in the County Club, and I later learned it was one of the worst seasons up to that time in terms of where we finished in the Championship table.

I certainly didn't know that at the time as I was just in awe of Trueman, Appleyard, Wardle and Illingworth — not to mention Mr Platt. You've got it, I was going to bowl for England, or so I thought. The only batsman who came into my full view was Vic Wilson: he took catches for "my bowlers" as though he were shelling proverbial peas. In spite of the team's relatively poor season the 2006 *Yearbook*, reviewing 1956, tells me that 66,000 attended the *Roses* game at Headingley and I was one — or should I say three? — of them, being there on all three days!

The other ground I was allowed to visit on my own that season was Bradford — a bus from Huddersfield dropped you at the Listers Arms, and Park Avenue was but a short walk from there. I also bowled regularly in the Paddock CC nets that summer, and my left-arm seamers occasionally seemed to trouble the lesser batsmen!

We moved home in 1959 — from Huddersfield to Bradford — and on inquiring about the nearest cricket club I found out that it was Thornbury, who played in the Bradford Central League, albeit their ground was just inside the Pudsey boundary. Pudsey's Bear hadn't been born, and the borough wasn't even part of Leeds back then. Off I went to Thornbury Cricket Club, and there I stayed for 28 seasons until my wife and I moved home from Pudsey to deepest Lincolnshire.

Thornbury CC became my relaxation from career building, initially with Mars and then with Morrisons — as it became obvious that I was never going to bowl for England. I did make the first team at Thornbury, opening the bowling most weeks for the best part of 20 years, and I even represented the Bradford Central League once. The club became a way of life — on a weekly basis grass-cutting on Saturday morning, playing in the afternoon and socialising in The Farmers pub post match...and being secretary, treasurer and captain on a more variable basis.

Margaret, my wife, helped to make the teas; our daughter met her husband there; my son captained the juniors to league and cup success — and we did what all dads want to do, we played in the first XI together, even if only for a season. Life moved on and deepest Lincolnshire called. I left Thornbury CC with my life-membership award and a mounted match ball — this for my claim-to-fame moment, a hat-trick against Pudsey St Lawrence in the Pudsey Jubilee Cup, a competition for those clubs with their grounds in, by then, the old Pudsey Borough.

All things Yorkshire CCC continued in the background, of course, but were more of a passing interest to me, being as involved as I was elsewhere — until 2006, when I retired and wrote to Robin Smith, asking

TO THE VICTOR, THE SPOILS: Captain Andrew Gale shows off the LV=County Championship Trophy to ecstatic fans at Headingley immediately after the final day's play of the season had come to an end. Gale guided his team to county cricket's most coveted prize 13 years after Yorkshire's previous success under David Byas in 2001.

CHAMPIONS 2014: Back Row, left to right: Daniel Hodgson, Azeem Rafiq, Ben Coad, James Wainman, Andrew Hodd, Alex Lees, Moin Ashraf, Will Rhodes, Karl Carver and Jonathan Tattersall. Front Row: Jack Brooks, Gary Ballance, Steven Patterson, Jonathan Bairstow, Richard Pyrah, Tim Bresnan, Andrew Gale (captain), Joe Root, Ryan Sidebottom, Adam Lyth, Liam Plunkett, Adil Rashid and Jack Leaning.

YORKSHIRE AT THE PALACE

ROYAL DAY OUT: All those available from Yorkshire's LV=County Championship-winning team visited Buckingham Palace in October to receive the Trophy from Prince Philip, the Duke of Edinburgh. It was presented to the captain, Andrew Gale, and the Duke presented each player with their own medal. Our top picture shows the Duke chatting with, from left, Karl Carver, Jonny Bairstow and Yorkshire President Dickie Bird.

CHAMPION CHAIRMAN: One of the happiest moments for Yorkshire Chairman Colin Graves in 2014 came when he was able to hold aloft the LV=County Championship Trophy which his team had won so convincingly. Colin has been nominated to become ECB Chairman in May, and if elected he can look back with great pride on all he achieved at the helm for Yorkshire. Without Colin's close involvement with Yorkshire since joining the new Management Board as Chief Executive in August, 2002, and later becoming Chairman, the Club could now be struggling to exist instead of riding the crest of a wave.

CHAMPIONSHIP CHAMPAGNE MOMENT

WE'VE DONE IT! Ryan Sidebottom captures the final wicket against Nottinghamshire at Trent Bridge to bring Yorkshire the title and below, he is then mobbed by his delighted team-mates.

CONGRATULATIONS: Captain Andrew Gale, closely followed by Tim Bresnan, leads the way as Yorkshire receive a standing ovation at Headingley upon winning the LV=County Championship Trophy which Gale shows to the fans. Below: Wicketkeeper-batsman Jonny Bairstow gets a handshake from a happy supporter.

TWIN ATTRACTIONS: Yorkshire's Alex Lees, above left, and Adam Lyth were tagged the most successful pair of opening batsmen in the country last summer, picking up a host of awards, including Alex being named The Cricket Writers' Club Young Cricketer Of The Year and Adam the CWC's County Championship Player Of The Year. All-rounder Richard Pyrah, below, enjoys the Headingley lap of honour with two-and-a-half-year-old twin daughters Tilly, left, and Mollie.

THE BIG THREE: Yorkshire first-team coach Jason Gillespie, left, and Director of Cricket Martyn Moxon congratulate skipper Andrew Gale on a job well done. Without their top coaching and backroom team who can say how long members and supporters might have had to wait to witness the scene below?

whether I could be of any use to the Club. I had never met Robin, but Margaret, my wife, knew his wife, Jennifer, and I therefore understood Robin's role(s) at YCCC. So, a little like at Thornbury CC, willing hands were welcomed. I became involved with the Yorkshire Pride Appeal, and some time later I was invited by Steve Mann and the YCCC Board to join the Members' Committee as a Board nominee. I was asked by the Board in 2010 to chair a committee to organise the 2013 celebrations to mark the Club's 150th Anniversary. Wow, what a responsibility, and I hesitated before accepting the appointment.

I had learned in business that you are only as good as the team around you – and with Rachael Boycott, David O'Kelly, David Hall, Steve Mann, Robin Smith, Andy Dawson, Simon Pixsley and Charles Hartwell how could we fail to have a successful sesquicentennial celebration? People were kind enough to say that we did indeed succeed — if we did, it certainly was "we".

The team were magnificent. and we even made some useful money. To be awarded the President's Medal for the small part I played and to be the recipient of the first presentation made by our newly elected President, Dickie Bird, was probably an award too far. However, I was incredibly proud and pleased to accept the award at the 2014 Annual General Meeting of the most famous cricket club in the world, Yorkshire County Cricket Club. Thornbury CC being the second greatest for me, of course, given the part it played in my life.

Four from overseas

Yorkshire give a clear indication of their intentions to scoop one-day trophies as well as attempting to retain the LV=County Championship title by announcing four overseas signings.

They first re-signed Aaron Finch along with fellow Australian Glenn Maxwell, and in February clinched a deal with Pakistan Test batsman Younus Khan, who played for them in 2007, and brought back for a third term Kiwi star batsman Kane Williamson. He will be available for the last month of the season when Finch joins Australia's one-day squad to play England.

Younus in 2007 became the only Yorkshire batsman to score a century and a double century in the same match (v. Hampshire at the Rose Bowl, 106 and 202 not out). He will be available for the start of the Championship programme, remaining at Headingley until the end of Finch's Indian Premier League commitments.

Maxwell, named Australia's *T20* player-of-the-year in the winter, comes as a specialist *T20* batsman, having had spells with Surrey and Hampshire.

AZEEM RAFIQ MOVES ON — WITH GOOD WISHES ALL ROUND

By David Warner

AZEEM RAFIQ: First Yorkshire Asian to lead an England side

Amicable discussions between player and Club ended with Yorkshire's announcement in mid-August that Azeem Rafiq would not be offered a new contract at the end of the 2014 season, so ending a *White Rose* career of high promise never consistently fulfilled, and which included moments of well-documented controversy.

Limited first-team chances was the main reason given for his release, along with the expressed hope that his departure would allow him to explore opportunities elsewhere in search of regular first-team cricket.

Although Rafiq did not play for Yorkshire again during the remainder of the summer both parties remained on friendly terms, and the 23-year-old off-spinner-batsman was included in all of the first-team celebrations upon clinching the LV-County Championship title.

In the end, however, it was a disappointment to Rafiq and all Yorkshire followers that he was unable to nurture a talent that on occasions looked as if it would take him to the very top.

Born in Karachi, Rafiq came to England with his family at a young age, and attended Holgate School near his home town of Barnsley. He developed his game at Barnsley Cricket Club, and went on to captain England Under-15s and England Under-19s, the first Yorkshire cricketer from an Asian background to lead an England side at any level. Rafiq continued to show exceptional promise at Yorkshire Academy, and his first senior appearance for Yorkshire came aged 17 when he was included in the *Twenty20* Cup game against Nottinghamshire at Trent Bridge in 2008. It was to become a debut shrouded in controversy through little fault of his own.

Yorkshire stormed to victory by nine wickets to gain a quarter-final tie with Durham at Riverside, but the match had to be abandoned shortly before it was due to start when it was discovered that Rafiq had not been registered properly by his county, an oversight which led to the two points gained against Nottinghamshire being deducted and Glamorgan replacing them as quarter-finalists.

Happier days were just around the corner, and on June 6, 2009, he made his first-class debut against Sussex at Headingley, emerging from the drawn encounter with match figures of 5-89. He was not included in the next fixture, but he returned against Worcestershire at New Road. This time he shone with the bat, completing a magnificent century in another weather-hit draw.

The following year Rafiq returned to the Championship side in the *Roses* clash at Old Trafford, where he claimed 4-92 in the first innings, but the spotlight was soon on him again for all the wrong reasons. Captaining England Under-19s, he was dropped for the second Test against Sri Lanka for disciplinary reasons, and this prompted him to launch a tirade on Twitter against manager John Abrahams. He apologised unreservedly for his actions but was banned by the ECB from all cricket under their jurisdiction for a month, Yorkshire already having banned him while they carried out their own investigation which found his behaviour "totally unacceptable".

With this youthful indiscretion behind him, Rafiq worked cheerfully and hard upon his game and, after a short-term loan spell with Derbyshire in 2011, he gained the right headlines in 2012 when he took over as captain from the injured Andrew Gale for a batch of *Twenty20* matches. It was an inspired choice by the cricket management. Not only did Rafiq become the youngest player to captain Yorkshire in competition, but he showed real flair for the job and piloted his team to the top of the North Group, from where they earned a home quarter-final draw. Gale then returned, but Rafiq continued to play a key part in taking Yorkshire through to their first — and so far only — Finals Day.

As in *Twenty20* cricket Rafiq and Adil Rashid proved a lethal spin combination in the Clydesdale Bank 40 Cup, capturing 22 wickets between them, while Rafiq's all-round heroics in the final LV-County Championship match of 2012 against Essex was a major factor in gaining promotion. He contributed invaluable scores of 53 and 75 not out, and emerged with bowling figures of 3-65 and a career-best 5-50 as

Yorkshire crushed their opponents at Chelmsford by 239 runs.

Rafiq was effective again in the *Twenty20* arena in 2013, he and Jack Brooks topping the wickets table with 13 apiece, but a knee injury kept him out of contention for much of the Championship programme.

He maintained his effectiveness in the shortest form of the game last summer, and this time he shared top place among the wicket-takers with fellow-spinner Rashid, the pair each bagging 14.

Rafiq, now 24, still has many years of cricket left in him, and everyone hopes that he can rebuild his career and go on to achieve outstanding success.

OLIVER ROBINSON
Death bowler and
hard-hitting batsman

Oliver Robinson

Oliver Robinson's ability to bowl yorkers in the crucial final overs made him a valuable asset in *Twenty20* cricket last summer, but a potentially promising career with Yorkshire was cut short in late July when the Club announced that his contract had been terminated with immediate effect due to "a number of unprofessional actions".

Born in Margate and educated at King's School, Canterbury, he played second-team cricket for Kent in 2011 and 2012, and joined Yorkshire the following season, turning out also for Lightcliffe in the Bradford League. He soon showed plenty of ability in Yorkshire Second Eleven Championship and one-day matches as a quick bowler and hard-hitting batsman.

He came second that summer in both the Second Eleven Championship batting and bowling averages, being the leading wicket-taking with 15 dismissals at 18.26. He scored 329 runs at an average of 36.55, with a top score of 90 not out against Warwickshire at Coventry, when he also struck an unbeaten 30 in the second innings.

Robinson also made his Yorkshire first-team debut in 2013 in the Yorkshire Bank 40 encounter with Leicestershire at Leicester, but he did not take a wicket in three appearances.

Last season, however, he made valuable contributions in Yorkshire's *Twenty20* campaign, earning particular praise for his bowling at the death in tight situations. He put a brake on the runs with his well-directed yorkers, which proved difficult to get away.

Robinson played for Hampshire on August 14 in a List A match against Sri Lanka after leaving Yorkshire.

AZEEM RAFIQ

FIRST-CLASS CRICKET FOR YORKSHIRE

Right-hand Batsman   Right-arm off-break bowler
Born: Karachi, Pakistan   February 27, 1991
Debut: v. Sussex at Leeds   June 6, 2009
Last played: v. Sussex at Arundel   June 16, 2014

BATTING AND FIELDING

Seasons	M	I	NO	Runs	HS	Avge	100s	50s	Ct
2009-14	22	25	2	511	100	22.21	1	2	9

BOWLING

Seasons	Matches	Overs	Mdns	Runs	Wkts	Avge	Best	5wI
2009-14	22	537.2	100	1717	47	36.53	5-50	1

ALL FIRST-CLASS MATCHES

BATTING AND FIELDING

M	I	NO	Runs	HS	Avge	100s	50s	Ct
25	29	3	563	100	21.65	1	2	9

BOWLING

Seasons	Matches	Overs	Mdns	Runs	Wkts	Avge	Best	5wI
	25	636.2	125	2010	55	36.54	5-50	1

LIST A CRICKET FOR YORKSHIRE

Debut: NatWest Pro 40   v. Sussex   at Scarborough   August 30, 2009
Last played: Yorkshire Bank 40   v. Somerset   at Taunton   August 15, 2013

BATTING AND FIELDING

Seasons	M	I	NO	Runs	HS	Avge	100s	50s	Ct
2009-13	15	11	4	116	34*	16.57	0	0	4

BOWLING

Seasons	Matches	Overs	Mdns	Runs	Wkts	Avge	Best	4wI
2009-13	15	89.5	4	483	17	28.41	5-30	1

ALL LIST A CRICKET

BATTING AND FIELDING

Matches	Innings	Not Out	Runs	Highest Score	Avge	100s	50s	Ct
20	14	6	146	34*	18.25	0	0	7

BOWLING

Overs	Maidens	Runs	Wickets	Average	Best	4wI
115	4	598	19	31.47	5-30	1

T20 CRICKET FOR YORKSHIRE

Debut: v. Nottinghamshire   at Nottingham   June 27, 2008
Last played: v. Nottinghamshire   at Leeds   July 25, 2014

BATTING AND FIELDING

Seasons	M	I	NO	Runs	HS	Avge	100s	50s	Ct
2008-14	60	27	17	131	21*	13.10	0	0	27

BOWLING

Overs	Maidens	Runs	Wickets	Average	Best	4wI
202.4	0	1510	62	24.35	3-15	0

OLIVER EDWARD ROBINSON

Right-hand Batsman.　　Right-arm medium-pace bowler
Born: Margate　　　　　December 1, 1993

LIST A CRICKET FOR YORKSHIRE

Debut:	Yorkshire Bank 40	v. Leicestershire	at Leicester	August 1, 2013
Last played:	Yorkshire Bank 40	v. Glamorgan	at Leeds	August 26, 2013
Last List A:	for Hampshire	v. Sri Lanka A	at Southampton	August 14, 2014

BATTING, FIELDING AND BOWLING

Season	M	I	NO	Runs	HS	Avge	100s	50s	Ct	O	Mdns	Runs	Wkts	Avge
2013	3	2	2	16	12*	—	0	0	4	10	0	66	0	—

ALL LIST A CRICKET

Seasons	M	I	NO	Runs	HS	Avge	100s	50s	Ct	O	Mdns	Runs	Wkts	Avge
2013-14	4	2	2	16	12*	—	0	0	4	14	0	83	0	—

T20 CRICKET FOR YORKSHIRE

| Debut: | NatWest T20 Blast | v. Derbyshire | at Leeds | May 30, 2014 |
| Last played: | NatWest T20 Blast | v. Durham | at Leeds | July 11, 2014 |

Season	M	I	NO	Runs	HS	Avge	100s	50s	Ct	O	Mdns	Runs	Wkts	Avge	Best
2014	7	3	0	5	3	1.66	0	0	3	17	0	162	6	27.00	2-25

Richard moves on

Second Team coach Richard Dawson, right, left Yorkshire at the end of January to take over as Club coach at Gloucestershire after spending one season in his role with his native county.

The former Yorkshire and England off-spinner, who went on to have spells with Northamptonshire and Gloucestershire, captured 199 first-class wickets in all, 157 of them for Yorkshire. His move means that six former Yorkshire Schools' Cricket Association and Humberside boys will hold similar roles in county cricket in 2015. The other five are Martyn Moxon (Yorkshire), Steven Rhodes (Worcestershire), David Ripley (Northamptonshire), Mark Robinson (Sussex) and Paul Grayson (Essex).

BRADFORD LEAGUE WAR-TIME HOME FOR COUNTY PLAYERS

By David Swallow

Millions of emotional words and as many pictures and images were produced to mark the 100th anniversary of the start of the Great War.

Now, in 2015 we can look back at another aspect of the conflict — to a time when the Bradford League became *Cricket's Wartime Sanctuary*, the evocative title of a book which has become a minor classic.

Tony Barker, who followed me at Bradford Grammar School, indulged a labour of love in a masterpiece of research to tell of what he called *The First-Class Flight to Bradford*.

One appendix revealed that there were 53 men who had played first-class cricket before turning out in the Bradford League in the five seasons from 1915 to 1919, ranging from S F Barnes — was he the greatest bowler of all time? —to H Wrathall and F E Woolley, with names like J B Hobbs and G E Tyldesley interspersed.

SYDNEY F BARNES
Was he the greatest?
(Photo: Ron Deaton Archive)

Not everyone, as Barker relates, agreed with cricket continuing on a competitive level. Lord Hawke forcefully argued that the game should be called off for the duration, and the Football League was shamed into reversing its own policy, suspending the competition in April 1915.

Bradford League president John James Booth, a pharmacist from Idle, became ever more strident in his insistence that they were providing a vital war-time service. The arrival of Barnes and Hobbs boosted his case, and crowds turned up in their hundreds every Saturday. There are still stories of queues waiting to see The Master bat, only for many spec-

Home fires burning: Bowling Old Lane, who won the Bradford League and the Priestley Cup in 1915. Seated centre is E F Holdsworth, who was to become Yorkshire's highly regarded Second Eleven captain.
(Photo: Ron Deaton Archive)

tators to leave when he was out early. Presumably they were old men or children as the flower of the area's youth had died on the Somme or in other futile fighting.

Infantry soldiers in the trenches had a miserable time during the winter of 1914-15. Lice, fleas and other vermin were rife, and a new disease called trench foot affected up to 30,000, who had to be taken out of the fighting. Poison gas was first used on April 22, 1915, presumably as the cricket season was getting under way in Bradford. It was released from canisters, and hundreds died as the white fog swept over them in the area of Ypres.

Cricket went on in Bradford, league president Booth having won the arguments and having a major fallout with his younger brother. Headlines in the truncated Press of 1915 would talk of the failure of Gallipoli, the beginning of the war-changing tank as a weapon and battles in the air. Nurse Edith Cavell was executed by the Germans.

It seemed to matter little as crowds turned out in their hundreds for Bradford League games every Saturday. Bowling Old Lane won both the league and the Priestley Cup in that first year of the county professionals coming to earn a few bob.

THE GENTLEMAN CAPTAIN OF YORKSHIRE AND ENGLAND

By Martin Howe

Norman Walter Dransfield Yardley, left, was born in Barnsley 100 years ago on March 19, 1915 "while the guns of the preliminary bombardment were thundering at the entrance to the Dardanelles," as he later put it.

He made his debut for Yorkshire in 1936 while in his second year at Cambridge, and went on to play in 302 matches for the Club before retiring in 1955 after losing six years of his career to the Second World War.

Yardley scored 11,632 runs for Yorkshire at 31.95, made 17 hundreds and took 195 wickets at 29.83. He is most remembered as the captain of England in 10 of his 14 Tests and as captain of Yorkshire from 1948 until 1955.

Norman Yardley was an amateur, of course, a perquisite for captaincy in his time. He could, one writer said, "be trusted to pass the port the correct way". The writer is Australian. The quip suggests a man from a privileged and cosseted background, immured from the daily grind of earning a living, but this was not the case. He was no toff, no snob. He grew up in Royston, a town in the heart of the South Yorkshire coalfield. He knew well the hardships of the miners and their families during the General Strike and subsequent miners' strike and of working people generally in the depressed 1930s.

Norman always said that his family were not wealthy. This is disingenuous. His grandfather began a successful retailing business, and also made money from shrewd investment in property. He built himself a grand house, The Grove, with extensive gardens which became Norman's family home. Norman's father, Percy, fanatically keen on cricket (and racing), described himself as a master grocer, but he did not need to work. He was able to send Norman to St Peter's School, York, and to Cambridge, in which institutions Yardley did outstandingly well

41

at sport, especially squash and cricket, but less well academically. At Cambridge he no doubt also learnt how to pass the port.

Yardley's time at Cambridge was crowned in 1938 with the captaincy, although his team were to win none of their matches. Since 1936 he had appeared increasingly for Yorkshire in the vacation, and by 1938 he was already spoken of as the successor to Brian Sellers as captain of Yorkshire. He was twice 12th man for England against Australia in 1938, and his international prospects were underlined when he was selected as Wally Hammond's vice-captain on the tour of South Africa in 1938-39. He was widely tipped as a future captain of England, and both honours came to pass, but only after the war when Yardley, like his colleagues in the Yorkshire team of 1939, served in the armed forces. The war changed much in British society but little in cricket. When the first-class game resumed in 1946 the anachronistic distinction between professionals and amateurs and the social divisions that went with it continued. Soon he was to become the first Yorkshire amateur since Lord Hawke to captain both the county and his country.

The captaincy of England came first. He deputised for Hammond in the last Test of the 1946-47 series in Australia, as he had in a number of non-Test matches, and he made a good impression in the role. With Hammond retired, Yardley was the obvious choice to captain England against South Africa in 1947. It was a summer forever remembered for the batting exploits of Bill Edrich and Denis Compton, and England won the series, played in the best of spirits, by three Tests to none. Yardley, now married and with a baby daughter, had to find some source of income if he were to continue playing regularly, and he was offered winter employment first by a paper company and then a paint firm.

While both were prepared for him to play full-time in the summer, he was not available for any further winter tours. This led to some chopping and changing of the England captaincy. Yardley next took charge against Bradman's Australians in 1948. In Ray Lindwall, Keith Miller and Bill Johnston the Australians had a pace attack England could not match, and there was little Yardley could do to counteract that advantage. Australia won the series by four Tests to none.

England had one great chance of victory in the Fourth Test at Headingley when Yardley set Australia 404 to win in 345 minutes on a wicket helpful to spinners. With Laker out of sorts and no other regular spinner in the side, Yardley had to rely heavily on Compton and even give four overs to Len Hutton, overs that went for 30 runs. Yardley had to gamble to have any chance of winning: he gambled and lost, and was pilloried for it. Bradman had been determined that Australia should finish the summer unbeaten, and the ruthless manner in which he pursued his objective was completely foreign to the way Yardley played his cricket. Sportsmanship was part of Yardley's DNA. One of the best-known images in cricket is of him doffing his cap and calling for three cheers from his team as Bradman came to the wicket for the last time at The Oval — and was bowled second ball by an Eric Hollies googly for nought.

FG Mann was captain against New Zealand in 1949, but in 1950 Yardley was back in charge for the first three Tests of a four-Test series against the West Indies, who won two of those three and also the last one when FR Brown took over the captaincy with the 1950-51 tour of Australia in the selectors' minds.

The West Indies win at Lord's by 326 runs, with "those little pals of mine" Ramadhin and Valentine taking 18 wickets between them, was particularly embarrassing. Yardley's final Test as captain went little better, the West Indies winning by 10 wickets, mainly as a result of some pulverising batting by Frank Worrell and Everton Weekes.

A courteous, fair-minded and charming man, Yardley had none of the ruthlessness of a Bradman or a Jardine, but he had many of the attributes a good captain needs on the field. He was an excellent judge of a pitch; he read a game well, and was tactically astute. He knew the

YARDLEY THE BATSMAN

strengths and weaknesses of his and his opponents' players. Not one to bluster and harangue, quiet encouragement was how Yardley sought to get the best out of his men. His captaincy skills were to be fully tested when he took over from Brian Sellers as captain of Yorkshire in 1948.

Yorkshire were still in the process of rebuilding, and 1947 had been the last season for Bill Bowes. Frank Smailes would have gone by the end of 1948, leaving only Hutton and Yardley of the great Yorkshire side of the late 1930s. Such players as Willie Watson, Harry Halliday, Vic

43

Wilson and Alex Coxon, who would very likely have been first-team players after 1939 but for the war, and a number of untried young hopefuls had to be welded into an effective unit. It could not be done overnight, but in 1948 Yorkshire finished fourth in the championship, a considerable improvement on the previous season.

Then in 1949, when Yardley had none of the responsibilities of the England captaincy to worry about, Yorkshire were joint champions with Middlesex. All was looking rosy for Yardley and his team. They fell back to third in 1950, and then were second in all but one of Yardley's remaining five seasons in charge — the exception was 1953, when Yorkshire sank to 13th. These were reasonable performances but, to Sellers and most Yorkshire followers, second was not good enough.

It was in 1952 that Surrey began their seven-year period of domination of the County Championship. While Yorkshire in Yardley's years could call on such outstanding players as Hutton, Frank Lowson, Wilson, Watson, Ted Lester, Brian Close, Don Brennan, Johnny Wardle, Bob Appleyard, Fred Trueman and Raymond Illingworth. Hutton thought the Surrey attack of Alec Bedser, Peter Loader, Jim Laker and Tony Lock gave them the edge even over the Yorkshire side of the 1930s. Surrey also had a charismatic captain in Stuart Surridge.

Questions have been raised about the quality of Yardley's captaincy in these years. Many have said he was "too nice", that is too soft, and that a stronger personality was needed to deal with the jealousies and backbiting that apparently began to erode team spirit in the 1950s.

Ted Lester, as loyal a Yorkshire player as there ever was, said the dressing-room atmosphere was so bad that he wished he played for another county. Bob Appleyard believes that much of the problem was that those (like him) who had lost six years of their career to the war were unwilling to concede their place in the side to up-and-coming players like Close, Trueman and later Illingworth. These three are among those who have written that Yardley should have taken a stronger line with players who, they said, put their own interests before those of the side. Illingworth went so far as to claim that the Championship could have been won in 1954 and 1955 with firmer leadership. Illingworth's assertion cannot be tested.

To Yardley cricket was a team game in which all needed to pull together for the common good. He imagined this to be ingrained in any Yorkshire player, as it was in the 1930s, and was distressed to find that not all of his players had that attitude. In retirement Yardley admitted that he could have been firmer: "I really appreciated the toughness of men like Coxon, Wardle and Appleyard. The only problem was getting the ball off them. I think, following Sellers, they regarded me as rather soft and perhaps friendly, but they'd learnt their cricket under a man who was a holy terror for discipline."

If there was dressing-room unrest, an interesting question is why Sellers, Cricket Committee chairman, did not intervene.

By 1955 Yardley, increasingly troubled by lumbago and wearying of the stresses and strains of captaincy, retired. He then ran a wine and spirits business in Sheffield, was employed by the BBC as a Test match summariser, played lots of golf and kept in touch with cricket at Headingley and at a local level.

In 1981 he was elected President of Yorkshire CCC, an honour of which he was extremely proud and which (then) was held for life. He was appalled by the long-simmering and highly public rumpus over Geoffrey Boycott and the methods used on Boycott's behalf by the Reform Group, later renamed the Yorkshire Members 1984 Group.

YARDLEY THE BOWLER

When, at a general meeting in Harrogate on January 21,1984, votes of no confidence in the cricket and general committees were passed, Yardley resigned as President. His family say that Norman was deeply hurt by this experience, and vowed never to visit Headingley again. It was a bitter end to a long relationship

Yardley played in 446 first-class matches in all. He scored 18,173 runs at 30.48 with 27 hundreds, took 279 wickets at 30.48 and held 328 catches.

It it is for his captaincy and his personal charm, not these statistics, that Yardley should be remembered in this his anniversary year.

YARDLEY AND THE DON: Bradman congratulates the England captain on the birth of a son during the Fourth Test at Headingley in 1948

BOYCOTT DAZZLES IN TEAM'S FIRST CUP FINAL TRIUMPH

By Anthony Bradbury

Yorkshire won the County Championship seven times in the 10-year period from 1959 to 1968, but 1965 was not one of them. It was regarded as one of their poorest seasons. They came fourth in the Championship, well behind Worcestershire, Northamptonshire and Glamorgan, and on only eight occasions since 1900 had they finished lower. Bad weather was a factor, since several winning situations were thwarted by rain, and some fine players who were later in that decade to win a hat-trick of Championships were not always in their best form.

Though the bowling sparkled, with five of the regular players each taking more than 40 wickets at an average of less than 19.00, the batting was a grave disappointment. The rising star of two previous years, Geoffrey Boycott, still headed the county averages, but at only 34.88, and he failed to score a Championship century. He may, however, have achieved one unique record in being twice run out in the Yorkshire game v. the South African tourists at Sheffield.

The next highest average was John Hampshire's 27.55, and of only five Championship centuries from the entire squad one was by Fred Trueman, a very fine 101 against Middlesex at Scarborough, batting at No. 9. His partner for most of his innings was Peter Chadwick, playing in his last season for Yorkshire and a notable all-rounder in league cricket. In 2013 Chadwick was to be elected President of the Yorkshire Players' Association.

The batting horribilis was a second-innings team score of 23 at Middlesbrough in mid-May, a match then lost to Hampshire by 10 wickets. The Middlesbrough pitch was certainly lively — 22 wickets had fallen on the first day, and the last eight fell before lunch on the second. In their second innings Yorkshire were soon 13-8, decimated by 'Butch' White, who at one stage took five wickets without a run in response. White finished with 6-10, and no Yorkshire player reached double figures. That 23, which thankfully 50 years on remains Yorkshire's lowest total, crept under the previous lowest of 26 all out v. Surrey at The Oval in 1909. Middlesbrough's reward was to be given the first home Championship match of the 1966 season, when Gloucestershire were bowled out twice for 204.

The bowling provided compensation for the batting. Trueman in 1965 was in his 16th season as a Yorkshire player, and in his last season for England — though he would not have accepted that at the time.

The fast bowlers who played in the Headingley Test against New Zealand were Fred Rumsey and David Larter. While England played in Leeds — and John Edrich plundered an unbeaten 310 — Yorkshire visited Hove where Trueman's response was to take 13 Sussex wickets, 8-36 and 5-41.

His 115 Championship wickets were taken at 11.36 runs each. Alas, he also had a contretemps with Brian Sellers, the Yorkshire cricket chairman, and was suspended for one match allegedly for not making a better attempt at a run-out during a *Roses* game.

Fred was understandably furious, and within a few years Sellers was to create a greater furore with the dismissal of Brian Close.

The other bowlers who had great success were Raymond Illingworth, with 71 wickets at 16.19, Don Wilson, Richard Hutton, Tony Nicholson and Close. All obtained more than 45 Championship wickets in the season of 28 fixtures. A

BOYCOTT BLITZ: Geoffrey's 146 in Yorkshire's Gillette Cup final triumph against Surrey at Lord's will be remembered as one of the greatest innings ever played for the county. Here he savages David Sydenham.

47

YORKSHIRE 1965. Back row, left to right: Philip Sharpe, Doug Padgett, Don Wilson, Tony Nicholson, John Hampshire and Geoffrey Boycott. Front row: Jimmy Binks, Freddie Trueman, Brian Close (captain) Raymond Illingworth and Ken Taylor.

(Photo: Ron Deaton Archive)

most remarkable analysis was obtained by Illingworth at Headingley against Worcestershire in a rainy May when in the only completed Worcestershire innings he bowled 30 overs, with 20 maidens, and took 8-20. That must rank as one of the most astonishing of all bowling analyses. His control was immaculate. In a match against Sussex he bowled 29 overs for 21 runs. No side had to consider batting points.

Close's best match was perhaps the one against Kent at the now forgotten Gillingham ground, where as captain he first scored 44, then took 5-67, and followed with 21 not out to make an attacking declaration. In the Kent second innings he took 6-49 as Yorkshire won by 82 runs. A tremendous match with Close to the fore in every aspect of the game.

For one young bowler 1965 saw the start and end of a first-class career. David Ash played three games as a slow left-armer, but was given only 11 overs and took no wickets. In three innings he scored 22 runs. He went on to play for Cumberland, and was professional at Penrith, taking 512 wickets at 10.14. Another who retired in 1965 was the estimable Mel Ryan, who for business reasons finished a first-class career that extended to 150 matches, starting in 1954, and in which he took 413 wickets. He had been a valiant Yorkshire servant.

48

Caught Trueman: Yorkshire beat the New Zealanders by an innings and 77 runs at Bradford, and Vic Pollard, batting above, was caught by Fred Trueman both times. Brian Close hit 115 and took 5-69 in the tourists' second innings. *(Photo: Adelphi Archive)*

Mention must be made of the performance by two opponents, the unsung Jim Pressdee and the better known Don Shepherd, both of Glamorgan. At Swansea in early June these two spin bowlers each captured nine wickets in an innings, and for once had the better of Illingworth and Don Wilson. The other wicket to fall when Pressdee was doing so well was a run-out. Has the nine-wicket-times-two performance of the Glamorgan duo ever been matched in another game? Glamorgan won that thriller by 31 runs.

The season had started with Yorkshire bowling out Gloucestershire for 74 and 65 to win by an innings. In the next match Sussex clung on for a draw with nine second-innings wickets down. Northamptonshire were beaten, and Worcestershire were struggling when rain came to their aid. Then came a sequence of eight matches with five draws and three defeats. Yorkshire could not recover from that run, but there was still a Gillette Cup to play for, with Yorkshire having not achieved much in the first two seasons of such cricket.

It was a true knockout competition from start to finish. Some minor counties played in the first round, and Yorkshire entered only for the second round. They eliminated Leicestershire easily enough, and swamped Somerset at Taunton, bowling out the home side for 63. Yorkshire were in the semi-finals, with three days allocated in case of rain. Play began on the third day. Each side could bat for 60 overs, the hours of play being up to 7.30pm. Yorkshire struggled to 177, so Warwickshire from start to finish needed less than three runs per over. They failed to reach the target, committing suicide as five batsmen were run out including Dennis Amiss for a duck. Yorkshire won by 20 runs.

Now came the Lord's final in front of a full house of 25,000 on

MEL RYAN
Valiant servant

DAVID ASH
Start and finish

PETER CHADWICK
Players' President

September 4, 1965. The writer was one of them. The match started late because of overnight rain, the ground strewn with sawdust. Surrey won the toss, inserted Yorkshire, and the *White Rose* started slowly. Taylor went early; Close came in and spoke to Boycott...who changed gear. His 146 was for years the most outstanding score in one-day cricket. He hit three sixes and 15 fours in an innings that those who were there will never forget. It showed Boycott's abilities in an astonishing new light.

Close was no slouch in hitting 79, and Yorkshire closed on 317-4. Surrey had no chance. Trueman soon snared Edrich and Barrington, and Illingworth took three wickets in an over. Surrey were bowled out in 41 overs for 142, and Yorkshire were home by 175 runs. Yorkshire supporters had seen one of the great matches in their county's history and their one-day cricket was now certainly on its way.

The Yorkshire Annual Report proudly reported: "Your Committee was pleased to grant the players £25 each for their performances in the Cup Final." In 2014 that £25 would equate to just £450.

The Annual Report also recorded "with sincere gratitude the munificent gift of £10,000 from Mrs F Frazer to be used to provide an indoor cricket shed at Headingley in memory of her late husband." Mrs Frazer was also made an Honorary Life Member and joined a select group of six others, of whom four were Sir Donald Bradman, Maurice Leyland, Wilfred Rhodes and Herbert Sutcliffe. Even Sir Leonard Hutton was not an Honorary Life Member.

Mrs Frazer's indoor cricket shed has long gone, but the spirit of Yorkshire cricket epitomised by its players and supporters in 1965 is still present on great days in the modern era, and the 1965 side would have gladly saluted the Championship winners of 2014.

YORKSHIRE'S FIRST-CLASS HIGHLIGHTS OF 1965

Win by an innings (4)

Yorkshire (419) defeated New Zealand (134 and 208) by an innings and 77 runs at Bradford

Cambridge University (130 and 99) lost to Yorkshire (295-9 dec) by an innings and 66 runs at Cambridge

Somerset (89 and 90) lost to Yorkshire (240) by an innings and 61 runs at Taunton

Gloucestershire (74 and 65) lost to Yorkshire (191) by an innings and 52 runs at Harrogate

Win by over 200 runs (1)

Yorkshire (320 and 153-7 dec) defeated Nottinghamshire (122 and 144) by 207 runs at Nottingham

Totals of 400 and over (1)

419   v. New Zealanders at Bradford

Opponents dismissed for under 100 (8)

65	Gloucestershire at Harrogate		87	Gloucestershire at Lydney
		2nd innings	89	Somerset at Taunton 1st innings
74	Gloucestershire at Harrogate		90	Somerset at Taunton 2nd innings
		1st innings	94	Somerset at Hull
74	Lancashire at Sheffield		99	Cambridge University at Cambridge

Century Partnerships (8)

For the 1st wicket (1)

116   G Boycott and J H Hampshire   v. Cambridge University at Cambridge

For the 3rd wicket (1)

180   D E V Padgett and J H Hampshire v. Lancashire at Sheffield

For the 4th wicket (1)

201*   J H Hampshire and D B Close   v. Surrey at Bradford

For the 6th wicket (2)

140   R Illingworth and R A Hutton   v. Leicestershire at Leeds

113   D B Close and R A Hutton   v. New Zealanders at Bradford

For the 7th wicket (2)

141   J H Hampshire and J G Binks   v. MCC at Scarborough

107   J C Balderstone and J G Binks   v. Sussex at Bradford

For the 8th wicket (1)

147   J P G Chadwick and F S Trueman   v. Middlesex at Scarborough

Centuries (8)

D B Close (3)

117*   v. South Africans at Sheffield

115   v. New Zealanders at Bradford

101*   v. Surrey at Bradford

Centuries *(Continued)*

J H Hampshire (3))

    149* v. MCC at Scarborough
    110* v. Lancashire at Sheffield
    105* v. Surrey at Bradford

P J Sharpe (1)

    100 v. Warwickshire at Sheffield

F S Trueman (1)

    101 v. Middlesex at Scarborough

5 wickets in an innings (26)

F S Trueman (10)

    8-36 v. Sussex at Hove 1st innings
    6-34 v. Nottinghamshire at Nottingham
    6-50 v Leicestershire at Leeds
    5-23 v. Derbyshire at Scarborough
    5-32 v. Middlesex at Scarborough
    5-34 v. Gloucestershire at Harrogate
    5-41 v. Nottinghamshire at Sheffield
    5-41 v. Sussex at Hove 2nd innings
    5-47 v. Lancashire at Sheffield
    5-49 v. Hampshire at Portsmouth

R Illingworth (6)

    8-20 v. Worcestershire at Leeds
    6-27 v. Cambridge University at Cambridge
    6-39 v. Northamptonshire at Northampton
    5-39 v. Nottinghamshire at Nottingham
    5-52 v. Leicestershire at Leeds
    5-62 v. Warwickshire at Sheffield

D B Close (4)

    6-49 v. Kent at Gillingham 2nd innings
    6-52 v. Glamorgan at Swansea
    5-67 v. Kent at Gillingham 1st innings
    5-69 v. New Zealanders at Bradford

R A Hutton (3)

    5-28 v. Somerset at Hull
    5-31 v. Somerset at Taunton
    5-50 v. Essex at Leyton

D Wilson (2)

    5-37 v. Glamorgan at Swansea
    5-80 v. MCC at Scarborough

A G Nicholson (1)

    5-19 v. Gloucestershire at Harrogate

10 wickets in a match (2)

D B Close (1)

    11-116 (5-67 and 6-49) v. Kent at Gillingham

F S Trueman

    13-77 (8-36 and 5-41) v. Sussex at Hove

3 catches in an innings (11)

J G Binks (6)

5	v. Lancashire at Sheffield
4	v. Somerset at Hull
3	v. Gloucestershire at Harrogate
3	v. Lancashire at Manchester
3	v. Nottinghamshire at Nottingham
3	v. Essex at Leyton

D B Close (3)

3	v. Gloucestershire at Harrogate
3	v. Derbyshire at Chesterfield
3	v. New Zealand at Bradford

P J Sharpe (1)

4	v Sussex at Bradford

A G Nicholson (1)

3	v. MCC at Scarborough

3 dismissals in an innings (2)

J G Binks (2)

5 (4ct, 1st)	v Somerset at Hull
4 (3ct, 1st)	v. Nottinghamshire at Nottingham

5 catches in a match (3)

J G Binks (2)

6 (5 + 1)	v. Lancashire at Sheffield
5 (3 + 2)	v. Nottinghamshire at Nottingham

P J Sharpe (1)

6 (4 + 2)	v. Sussex at Bradford

5 dismissals in a match (2)

J G Binks (2)

6 (5ct, 1st)	v. Nottinghamshire at Nottingham
5 (4ct, 1st)	v. Somerset at Hull

Debut (1)
In first-class cricket: D L Ash

New coaching structure

Following the departure of Second Eleven coach Richard Dawson for Gloucestershire the Yorkshire Director of Cricket Development, Ian Dews, has been put in charge of the Seconds, and Richard Damms becomes Academy Head Coach with the responsibility of coaching and developing the successful Academy squad.

Former Yorkshire captain Anthony McGrath has been appointed Coaching Consultant to work with players across all age categories. Over the previous year McGrath has been employed by Yorkshire as a player mentor, and he will continue to offer his expertise and experience across a number of areas associated with player development.

LIST A HIGHLIGHTS OF 1965

Total of 250 and over (1)

   317-4   v. Surrey at Lord's

Match aggregate of 450 and over (1)

   459   Yorkshire (317-4) defeated Surrey (142) by 175 runs at Lord's

Opponents dismissed for under 100 (1)

   63 Somerset at Taunton

Century Partnerships (1)

For the 2nd wicket (1)

   192   G Boycott and D B Close   v. Surrey at Lord's

Century (1)

   G Boycott (1)

     146   v. Surrey at Lord's

4 wickets in an innings (2)

   R Illingworth (1)

     5-29   v. Surrey at Lord's

   F S Trueman (1)

     6-15   v. Somerset at Taunton

Debuts (2)

List A cricket: R A Hutton and J S Waring

£100,000 bookstall pair honoured

Geoff Holmes and Vivien Stone, who run the second-hand bookstall at Headingley, have been made honorary life members of Yorkshire Schools' Cricket Association in recognition of the £43,000 they have raised for the association over the years. The only other honorary life member is Tony Bowes, son of former Yorkshire and England fast bowler Bill Bowes.

The stall, which is manned by Geoff, Vivien and Jeremy Wimbush, raised £6,121 in 2014 for the John Featherstone Foundation, resulting in a £6,000 donation to the association. The stall will pass a special milestone early in the 2015 season, because when the first £125 has been raised it will take total sales since it started up 16 years ago to £100,000.

Geoff said: "Jeremy joined our small team in 2014, and he and Vivien are now the driving force behind the operation."

YORKSHIRE AVERAGES 1965

ALL FIRST-CLASS MATCHES

Played 33   Won 12   Lost 4   Drawn 17

County Championship: Played 28   Won 9   Lost 4   Drawn 15

BATTING AND FIELDING *(Qualification 10 completed innings)*

Player	M.	I.	N.O.	Runs	H.S.	Avge	100s	50s	ct/st
G Boycott	22	36	2	1215	95	35.73	0	9	14
J H Hampshire	30	49	4	1424	149*	31.64	3	7	32
D B Close	30	46	7	1127	117*	28.89	3	2	31
R Illingworth	31	47	8	916	90	23.48	0	3	25
D E V Padgett	32	55	2	1220	91	23.01	0	5	15
P J Sharpe	31	53	5	1091	100	22.72	1	3	42
J G Binks	33	42	8	732	72	21.52	0	5	65/10
K Taylor	20	36	2	729	86	21.44	0	3	7
R A Hutton	25	35	6	579	91	19.96	0	3	16
F S Trueman	28	37	2	630	101	18.00	1	2	16
J C Balderstone	11	14	1	213	51	16.38	0	1	5
D Wilson	30	39	10	300	37	10.34	0	0	22
Also batted									
J P G Chadwick	3	5	2	72	59	24.00	0	1	1
J S Waring	8	7	5	18	6*	9.00	0	0	5
D L Ash	3	3	0	22	12	7.33	0	0	0
A G Nicholson	23	25	16	65	12	7.22	0	0	10
M Ryan	3	3	1	12	11	6.00	0	0	0

BOWLING *(Qualification 10 wickets)*

Player	Overs	Mdns	Runs	Wkts	Avge	Best	5wI	10wM
F S Truman	658.1	157	1574	121	13.00	8-36	10	1
R Illingworth	819	346	1560	94	16.59	8-20	6	0
D Wilson	697	271	1486	82	18.12	5-37	2	0
A G Nicholson	536.2	177	1093	57	19.17	5-19	1	0
R A Hutton	460.1	107	1202	62	19.38	5-28	3	0
D B Close	527.2	202	1217	58	20.98	6-49	4	1
J S Waring	128	33	348	15	23.20	3-30	0	0
Also bowled								
D E V Padgett	6	4	6	1	6.00	1-6	0	0
G Boycott	46.1	20	74	4	18.50	1-0	0	0
J C Balderstone	94	43	172	9	19.11	4-31	0	0
M Ryan	44	10	118	6	19.66	2-28	0	0
K Taylor	47	15	109	4	27.25	1-10	0	0
J H Hampshire	12	0	56	0	—	—	0	0
D L Ash	11	7	22	0	—	—	0	0
P J Sharpe	4	1	17	0	—	—	0	0
J P G Chadwick	2	0	9	0	—	—	0	0
J G Binks	2	0	12	0	—	—	0	0

50 YEARS AGO

YORKSHIRE AVERAGES 1965

LIST A KNOCKOUT COMPETITION — GILLETTE CUP

Played 4   Won 4   Abandoned 1

BATTING AND FIELDING

Player	M.	I.	N.O.	Runs	H.S.	Avge	100s	50s	ct/st
G Boycott	3	3	1	225	146	112.50	1	1	0
J H Hampshire	4	3	2	60	38*	60.00	0	0	0
R Illingworth	4	2	1	51	45	51.00	0	0	3
D B Close	4	4	1	128	79	42.66	0	1	1
F S Trueman	4	2	0	52	28	26.00	0	0	1
J G Binks	4	1	0	21	21	21.00	0	0	4/2
D E V Padgett	4	3	0	56	31	18.66	0	0	0
P J Sharpe	4	3	1	28	21	14.00	0	0	2
D Wilson	2	2	1	13	11*	13.00	0	0	1
K Taylor	4	4	0	51	18	12.75	0	0	0
R A Hutton	3	1	0	8	8	8.00	0	0	0
J S Waring	1	1	1	1	1*	—	0	0	0
A G Nicholson	2	0	0	0	—	—	0	0	3
J C Balderstone	1	0	0	0	—	—	0	0	0

BOWLING

Player	Overs	Mdns	Runs	Wkts	Avge	Best	4wI	RPO
F S Trueman	40.2	7	108	12	9.00	6-15	1	2.67
K Taylor	11	3	32	3	10.66	1- 0	0	2.90
R Illingworth	24.4	2	58	5	11.60	5-29	1	2.35
A G Nicholson	24.4	7	56	3	18.66	2-23	0	2.27
D Wilson	22	6	60	3	20.00	2-15	0	2.72
D B Close	17	6	47	2	23.50	1-12	0	2.76
R A Hutton	28	5	101	4	25.25	3-50	0	3.60
G Boycott	10	1	33	1	33.00	1-33	0	3.30
J S Waring	4	1	11	0	—	—	0	2.75

NO HEAD IN THE SAND AS BATES OSTRICH TROPHY IS ACQUIRED

By J C David Allan

The receipt on loan of a unique trophy presented to Yorkshire and England all-rounder Billy Bates in Australia in 1883 and the purchase of one of Hedley Verity's *White Rose* county caps were among the main features of a busy and varied year for the Yorkshire Cricket Foundation Archives Committee.

The magnificent Bates Trophy, reputed to be an ostrich egg mounted on a silver and black plinth, was presented to Bates in Melbourne by the Australian team after England's innings victory in the Second Test in which the Lascelles-born cricketer played a substantial part. He returned the astounding figures of 7-28 and 7-74, including his country's first ever hat-trick in the first innings, and scored 55 to become the first player to claim at least 10 wickets and make a half-century in the same Test.

Bates, known as ''The Duke' for his dapper looks, made his debut for Yorkshire in 1887 and played for 11 seasons, ending with 6,499 runs at 20.37 and 637 wickets at 16.78. He toured Australia on five occasions, playing all of his 15 Tests there, and scoring 646 runs at 27.33 with 50 wickets at 16.42. The family have kindly loaned the trophy to the Foundation, and it has been on permanent display in the museum since it was handed over at Headingley in January 2014. Among those present were Trevor Bates, the great-great nephew of Billy, and Linda Riley, whose mother, Brenda Pearson (nee Bates) is Billy's great-great niece.

Another key feature of the year involved contact with the family of the late Gerald Smithson, the former Yorkshire, Leicestershire and England left-hand batsman, and discussions over the future of memorabilia from his playing days. Born in Spofforth, near Harrogate, Smithson played in 39 matches for Yorkshire between 1946 and 1950 before moving on to Leicestershire. He represented England in two Test matches.

The Archives Committee arranged in the summer for his widow, Anne Smithson, and daughter, Jacqueline Burrows, to be entertained at Headingley on the day of a Championship match, and they were also escorted around the museum.

Brian Sanderson attended several cricket auctions on behalf of the committee, and it was at one of these that he was able to purchase one of Hedley Verity's Yorkshire caps which will be professionally restored.

Verity, the Yorkshire and England left-arm bowler who died of wounds in Italy in the Second World War, twice took all 10 wickets for his county.

A copy of Chris Waters' book on Verity, *10 for 10*, published last year, was kindly donated by the author to the Archives which also received copies of Joe Sayers's *Rose-Tinted Summer*, Anthony Bradbury's *Frank Mitchell* and Myles Hodgson's and Graham Hardcastle's *Yorkshire A Champion Year* which details last season's glorious journey to the Championship title.

Items acquired in 2014 included a postcard of the 1905 England team which played Australia and was captained by the great Yorkshire all-rounder, F S Jackson. The England team at Headingley included Yorkshire's Schofield Haigh, David Denton, Wilfred Rhodes and George Hirst.

BILLY BATES
Hat-trick first

Among other items were: A letter by Norman Yardley to James P Coldham who had written a book about F S Jackson; Press cuttings donated by David Thorpe of George Hirst's funeral, attended by Wilfred Rhodes; the centenary brochures of Huddersfield League sides Golcar (1860-1960) and Hall Bower (1876-1976); a letter from Hedley Verity to a friend in Rawdon while Verity was on the MCC tour to South Africa in 1938; a White Rose emblem from Yorkshire's tour of North America and Bermuda in 1964 when Garfield Sobers was in their side; the original sepia photograph of Joseph Rowbotham, Yorkshire captain from 1871 to 1875, inscribed in ink by E R Wilson, Yorkshire 1899-1923.

The committee dealt with numerous enquiries during the year and these included matters on lesser known players such as Harry Green, H E Hartington, Alex Morris and Charles Oyston as well as an interview with Sir Leonard Hutton in Mombasa in 1987. There were queries concerning signed bats, cricket during the Second World War and the old Savile Town Ground at Dewsbury.

Archives Open Days were held on two occasions at Headingley during the summer, and it is hoped to organise them more frequently during 2015.

I would like to thank Mick Pope, Dennis Smith and Howard Clayton (secretary) for their services on the Archives Committee until standing down, and to thank Paul Dyson, James Greenfield, Brian Sanderson, David Warner and Roy Wilkinson, who remain on the committee and continue to give much valued support and expertise.

* David Allan is Chairman of the Yorkshire
Foundation Cricket Archives Committee

PHILIP SHARPE

By Felicity McCormick

Philip Sharpe, right, who was the finest slip fielder ever to play cricket for Yorkshire and England and arguably the best in the world, died in May 2014, aged 77.

He had the rare distinction of being picked for England against the West Indies in 1963 specifically for his slip catching after they had dropped so many, but he was an accomplished middle-order batsman — not bad for someone who was told at school that he was too small to be a cricketer.

He had the safest pair of hands in any team through a combination of lightning reflexes, relaxed hands and, being short in stature, a low centre of gravity. His confidence in his catching ability from any position was such that on one memorable occasion, in the 1969 Headingley Test against the West Indies, he called for a catch that others would have left to the wicket-keeper. Vanburn Holder skied the ball behind himself and three fielders, including Sharpe from first slip and wicket-keeper Alan Knott, ran back towards the boundary. Instead of leaving it to the man with the gloves Sharpe called "mine", and held it in front of the Main Stand.

For all that confidence in his ability he was modest and unassuming, genial, with a wonderfully dry wit, excellent company and a very contented man. Yorkshire have never played cricket for fun, but they had fun off the field with Sharpe, along with Don Wilson, leading the singing in the dressing room or when they were travelling.

His county career spanned nearly 20 years, and he was part of the team in 1959 and through the 1960s that won seven County Championships and the Gillette Cup twice.

Philip John Sharpe was born in Shipley, the only son of Bert and Winifred Sharpe. His father was in the wool trade and passionate about cricket, which meant that when someone offered to sponsor his natural ly talented son to play either tennis or cricket he guided him towards the bat rather than the racquet.

Philip played hockey for Ben Rhydding, represented the North of England, and had Olympic trials. He competed annually at Folkestone Hockey Festival with a team of celebrities and professionals called The Ladykillers.

As an accomplished tennis player he once won at the annual Ilkley tournament, but being modest he did not tell his parents. It only emerged later. In later years he was a member of Ilkley Golf Club with a handicap of nine.

The family lived at Bolton Old Hall, Wrose, near Shipley, which they bought from a wealthy author, but she so loved the house that she eventually wanted to buy it back.

They moved to Pudsey. The sale paid for Philip to leave Bradford Grammar School when he was 12 to

ACE OF SLIPS: England chose Philip Sharpe against the West Indies in 1963 for his catching, but he scored 85 not out in his first Test. *(Photo: Yorkshire Post)*

be educated at Worksop College where he excelled at sport. In 1955 he made 240 not out against Wrekin, a batting record which still stands.

He had a passion for music and a wonderful singing voice. As a treble he was chosen to sing the opening of *O for the Wings of a Dove* on a recording, but having sung it with perfect clarity at the rehearsal he was so overcome with nerves for the recording that his voice was too sharp and another boy was chosen to take his place.

Philip John Sharpe

Born: December 27, 1936
Died: May 19, 2014

Reproduced by kind permission of The Yorkshire Post

PHILIP JOHN SHARPE

FIRST-CLASS CRICKET FOR YORKSHIRE 1958 TO 1974

Right-hand batsman   Right-arm off-break bowler

Born: Shipley   December 27, 1936

First Class Debut: for Combined Services	v. Warwickshire	June 13, 1956
First Class Debut for Yorkshire	v. Sussex at Worthing	July 23, 1958
Last played for Yorkshire	v. Lancashire at Manchester	August 3, 1974
Final First Class: for Derbyshire	v. Hampshire at Chesterfield	September 8, 1976

Capped: September 21, 1960

FIRST-CLASS MATCHES FOR YORKSHIRE

BATTING AND FIELDING

Season	M	I	NO	Runs	HS	Avge	100s	50s	Ct
1958	12	23	2	461	141	21.95	1	2	10
1959	17	27	1	642	73	24.69	0	5	24
1960	24	37	5	1039	203*	32.46	2	2	36
1961	35	55	7	1240	87	25.83	0	7	45
1962	36	62	8	2201	138	40.75	7	7	70
1963	26	41	5	994	138*	27.61	2	6	37
1964	30	49	8	1273	79*	31.04	0	9	28
1965	31	53	5	1091	100	22.72	1	3	42
1966	32	49	5	988	72	22.45	0	3	45
1967	29	46	5	1352	197	32.97	1	10	39
1968	30	46	8	1256	143*	33.05	3	3	29
1969	18	29	2	1012	101	37.48	1	4	21
1970	24	38	1	1149	120	31.05	2	7	33
1971	17	27	3	823	172*	34.29	1	4	18
1972	11	17	0	370	53	21.76	0	1	10
1973	22	38	4	1320	133	38.82	2	10	22
1974	17	29	2	474	83	17.55	0	2	17
	411	666	71	17685	203*	29.72	23	85	526

Centuries (23)

1958	141	v. Somerset	at Sheffield
1960	203*	v. Cambridge University	at Cambridge
	152	v. Kent	at Sheffield
1962	108*	v. Lancashire	at Leeds
	104	v. Nottinghamshire	at Worksop
	138	v. Somerset	at Taunton
	132	v. Surrey	at Sheffield
	110	v. Northamptonshire	at Sheffield
	112	v. Lancashire	at Manchester
	136*	v. Pakistan	at Bradford
1963	138*	v. Derbyshire	at Chesterfield
	106	v. Lancashire	at Manchester
1965	100	v. Warwickshire	at Sheffield
1967	197	v. Pakistan	at Leeds
1968	143*	v. Nottinghamshire	
	125	v. Surrey	at The Oval
	114	v. Glamorgan	at Cardiff
1969	101	v. MCC	at Lord's
1970	108	v. Kent	at Sheffield
	120	v. Middlesex	at Scarborough
1971	172*	v. Glamorgan	at Swansea
1973	133	v. Somerset	at Sheffield
	110	v. Derbyshire	at Chesterfield

TEST MATCHES

BATTING AND FIELDING

Season	Versus	M	I	NO	Runs	HS	Avge	100s	50s	Ct
1963	West Indies	3	6	1	267	85*	53.40	0	3	4
1963/64	India	1	2	1	58	31*	58.00	0	0	0
1964	Australia	2	3	1	71	35*	35.50	0	0	0
1969	West Indies	3	5	0	120	86	24.00	0	1	8
1969	New Zealand	3	5	1	270	111	67.50	1	0	5
		12	21	4	786	111	46.23	1	4	17

ALL FIRST-CLASS MATCHES

BATTING, FIELDING AND BOWLING

M	I	NO	Runs	HS	Avge	100s	50s	Ct	Overs	M	Runs	Wkts	Avge	Best
493	811	78	22530	228	30.73	29	111	618	50.2	7	197	3	65.66	1-1

DOMESTIC LIST A MATCHES FOR YORKSHIRE 1963 TO 1974

Debut: Gillette Cup v. Nottinghamshire at Middlesbrough   May 22, 1963
Last played: John Player League v. Hampshire at Portsmouth   September 1, 1974
Final List A: NatWest Trophy for Norfolk v. Leicestershire at Leicester July 3, 1982

BATTING AND FIELDING

Season	M	I	NO	Runs	HS	Avge	100s	50s	Ct
1963	2	2	0	39	29	19.50	0	0	1
1964	1	1	0	0	0	0.00	0	0	3
1965	4	3	1	28	21	14.00	0	0	2
1966	1	1	0	10	10	10.00	0	0	1
1967	2	1	0	33	33	33.00	0	0	3
1968	1	1	0	38	38	38.00	0	0	1
1969	13	13	0	452	81	34.76	0	5	7
1970	15	14	0	234	60	16.71	0	1	6
1971	10	9	0	77	22	8.55	0	0	5
1972	17	17	2	256	89*	17.06	0	1	8
1973	7	6	0	90	40	15.00	0	0	3
1974	18	18	1	258	50	15.17	0	1	13
	91	86	4	1515	89*	18.47	0	8	53

ALL LIST A MATCHES

BATTING, FIELDING AND BOWLING

M	I	NO	Runs	HS	Avge	100s	50s	Ct	Overs	M	Runs	Wkts	Avge	Best
134	129	7	2619	114*	21.46	2	13	77	0.4	0	11	0	—	0-11

RICHARD HUTTON'S TRIBUTE
TO TEAMMATE AND FRIEND

A service of thanksgiving for the life of Philip Sharpe was held in St Joseph's Church, Wetherby, on May 30, 2014, attended by his widow, Sue, and their family, his many friends from the world of cricket and beyond and former teammates. The text of Richard Hutton's eulogy is:

Although he achieved great fame as a cricketer, Philip Sharpe was a man of many parts, not the least of which were enacted on the stage of the Theatre Royal in the company of the York Light Opera Society...to the considerable amusement and enjoyment of his many friends and associates – but more of that anon.

Above all, Philip was a devoted husband to Sue in a marriage lasting into its 44th year, a doting father to Catherine and grandfather to four-year-old Sam. Sadly, his death denies his knowing a second grandchild to be born in October.

Through his broad spread of interests Philip came into contact with many people, from which he developed a wide circle of friends and acquaintances. His easygoing manner, natural modesty, amiability and good humour made him a popular and endearing figure to all who knew him. He was the perfect companion, whether as a colleague in many of the teams that he played in or just sharing a drink in the corner of a bar.

I counted him as a close friend for over 50 years. Luckily, I had more opportunity than most get to know him very well as we stood next to each other in the slips for several seasons. We made an odd combination — Philip short and stocky at 5ft 7in, and myself tall and gangling at 6ft 4in. Nevertheless, Philip thought the arrangement worked well for, as he put it, "you take the high balls and I'll take the low balls". We were never short of things to say to each other as we stood together for all that time. An idiosyncrasy of his was the tuning fork he kept in the pocket of his flannels, which he would occasionally bring out and ping, presumably when he thought the bowlers were not hitting the right notes.

Philip had been a schoolboy prodigy as a cricketer, although early prognostications were not favourable. The headmaster of his first school wrote in one report to his father: "The boy will never make a cricketer – he is too small". Philip confounded his headmaster and went on to Worksop College, where he was five years in the First Eleven and broke all the school's batting records. Among the vast number of runs he made were two innings of double centuries, feats then normally beyond the capability of any schoolboy.

He was a while getting started with Yorkshire. National service intervened, and he spent two years with the Royal Electrical and Mechanical Engineers as a craftsman. This did not go down too well with him, although giving him plenty of opportunity to play for the Combined Services. Drilling and square-bashing he found irksome, somewhat unsurprisingly given that 22 yards became his maximum range.

When I first played with him, in 1962, he was at the crease when I went out to bat in my first innings for Yorkshire, against Lancashire at Old Trafford. We were 52-4 and soon afterwards 57-5, but he held the innings together and went on to make a hundred. My initial feeling toward him was that of admiration.

He was at the height of his powers in what was probably his best season. In that year he scored 2,200 runs, which ought to have secured him selection for that winter's tour of Australia. His style of batting was well suited to the hard and fast pitches that were normal in the southern hemisphere, where the ball came on to bat and where he could make the best use of his acute sense of timing. He was a fine player of fast bowling with a technique that relied little on forward foot movement. He was a particularly effective cutter and puller of the ball.

In their wisdom the selectors overlooked him, and he was disappointed that they preferred the Rev. David Sheppard, who had engineered a sabbatical from his duties as a chaplain. Regrettably, when he put his hands together on that tour little stayed between them. Philip's chance came in the following season when the mighty West Indies with their battery of terrifyingly fast bowlers toured England. He was picked for the third Test after two below-par performances by England in the first two matches, in which Colin Cowdrey had his arm broken at Lord's. The worst of it was that England's fielding had been particularly disappointing, their slip fielders having an alarming propensity to grass everything.

On the face of it Philip became the first to be selected for England as a slip catcher. His ability derived from an exceptional eye-to-hand co-ordination, a lightning reaction combined with a natural relaxation. He remained perfectly still while the ball was being bowled, never making an anticipatory move. He let the ball come to him, and often appeared to let it go past him before he caught it. He was exceptional fielding to spin bowling, and caught catches from edged back-foot slashes when other fielders would not have had time to see which way the ball went. If I might paraphrase a remark of another departed but well-known Yorkshireman, he may not have been the greatest slip catcher the world has ever known but he was certainly in the top one!

Having said all that, it is disappointing to have to record that I am one of two people in this congregation to have suffered the infamy of having Philip drop two catches from two consecutive balls off their bowling.

Before he played his first Test match, allegedly someone in the

England management said to him that if he could get us 25 or so runs that would be great. Such low expectation of his batting prowess was not the sort of confidence booster he wanted.

Philip was the England batting success of the remainder of the 1963 series. In three matches he made 257 runs at an average of 53.4, caught several catches and was named as one of *Wisden's* Five Cricketers of the Year.

The selectors rewarded him with a tour of India, the least likely place where he might be seen to good effect on the low and slow-turning pitches of the subcontinent.

PADDED UP: Philip Sharpe and Geoffrey Boycott await the nod. *(Photo: Yorkshire Post)*

He was not alone in being struck down by one of the various and mystifying ailments all too prevalent in that country in those days, and he spent more of that tour than he would have liked in a hospital bed.

Thereafter, his Test career was somewhat intermittent and less than it should have been, because with his calm disposition he had the temperament for the big occasion. For Yorkshire he remained as committed as ever and was a vital component in the huge run of success in the 1960s. Aside of his runs and catches he put the interest of the team ahead of himself, and was a big contributor on and off the field to its spirit.

His involvement in cricket continued long after his career with Yorkshire ended. Two seasons with Derbyshire were followed by spells with Norfolk in the Minor Counties Championship, where he proved to be as equally popular as in Yorkshire. He also played in the Bradford League for Manningham Mills alongside his great friend and collaborator Don Wilson, who predeceased him by only 18 months. He also played regularly for the Courage Old England XI, a team sponsored by the brewery of the same name that toured the country playing a series of Sunday exhibition matches in the 1980s.

Throughout it all he conducted himself with a probity that, allied to his reputation as a sound judge of the game, made him much sought after. He won election to The Yorkshire County Cricket Club Committee as the representative for York, and in due course was the county's natural nomination to the panel of Test selectors, a duty he fulfilled with relish in the 1980s. Subsequently, he became a pitch liaison officer or PLO, as he liked to call it.

He was a great traveller, and indulged his passion by organising winter tours to the Test-playing countries of England's opponents for Yorkshire members and their friends. He and Sue were popular hosts and guides, and they were taking tours as recently as February, by when his health was already failing him.

Philip was a gifted all-round games player. He was a high-class hockey player, befitting someone of his hand-eye coordination and sense of timing. He was a member of Ben Rhydding Hockey Club for several years, a Yorkshire County player, and he played for the North of England. He was especially thrilled to become a member of the Ladykillers Hockey Club, hockey's equivalent of rugby's Barbarians, an itinerant club for many of the country's best players. He took great pleasure in playing alongside them each year at the Easter Hockey Festival in Folkestone.

Music was among his many accomplishments. He played the piano to a good standard, and was blessed with a fine baritone singing voice. He found the perfect outlet for this passion when he joined the York Light Opera Society in 1969 through his connection with Albert Marston, who was Scarborough CC's wicket-keeper. Each year following the Christmas season the society performs a musical. Philip appeared in 27 of these between 1970 and 2006. Apart from being a regular in the chorus he was often cast in cameo roles that essentially combined servility with a modicum of inebriation. Having a penchant for serving drinks, he was a natural as Drake, the butler in *Annie*, and as Charles in *Me and My Girl*. His playing of Njegus, the factotum in *The Merry Widow*, has been recorded for posterity.

He was a convincing portrayer of Americans, as:
Elisha J Whitney in *Anything Goes*
Senator Wingwood in *The Best Little Whorehouse In Texas*
Everett Baker in *Crazy For You*
Julius Goldschmidt in *Barnum*
and in his last part in 2006 as the minister, The Reverend Ed Parsley, in *The Witches of Eastwick*.

Philip did not confine his singing to the stage, particularly when he had had an opportunity to quench his thirst. His rendition of *How to Handle a Woman* was a masterpiece of four-part harmony. He felt greatly honoured to be named as the president of the society in 2009, which he would have remained until his death, but he withdrew within a year because deterioration of his eyesight had begun to restrict his mobility.

Nearer to home he joined the church choir of this basilica where Sue has worshipped for many years – an ideal preparation for the hereafter.

There was much more to Philip's life than it has been possible for me to recount here. His was a full life...well lived.

Thank you, Philip, for giving us so much to remember.

YORKSHIRE'S EPIC SEASON BROUGHT TO LIFE AGAIN

By David Warner

YORKSHIRE: A CHAMPION YEAR   **Myles Hodgson**
and Graham Hardcastle (Well Done Media, £30).

The sun did not set on Yorkshire's glorious season of Championship success until the evening of September 26, yet within weeks this splendid book was on the shelves, offering readers a permanent and detailed reminder of the *White Rose Club's* 31st outright title triumph — a number no other county can match.

In this age of rapidly changing technology any outstanding sporting achievement can appear on the web within seconds of it happening, but for a book of this sumptuous quality to be on the market in such a short passage of time since the final ball was bowled is an achievement for which all concerned with the publication can feel immensely proud.

Not all people involved in media work in the sporting world these days can be classed as experts in their field, but the team responsible for *Yorkshire A Champion Year* certainly can.

The authors, Graham Hardcastle and Myles Hodgson, are more than qualified to write about the twists and turns of Yorkshire's sensational season. Graham, an award-winning cricket journalist, was watching the *White Rose* story unfold in Press Boxes around the country on most days of the summer, and if he wasn't there the chances were that Myles, a former Press Association cricket correspondent and son of cricket writer and author Derek Hodgson, was acting as his backup.

After each day's Championship action one of them would be on hand to interview a key player about the drama that had unfolded in front of them, and quotes from these observations are liberally sprinkled throughout the book, so providing an insight from on the field as well as off it.

Equally deserving of praise for this lavish book is its publisher, Simon

Wilkinson, who runs Well Done Media and is head of SWpix.com, the official photographers for Yorkshire CCC. Simon has an uncanny knack of giving budding young photographers their chance and then seeing them blossom, as is the case with Alex Whitehead, who last year scooped three industry awards for his work and was the man behind the lens on most days at Headingley and often further afield. Alex is a man of few words, but his camera says it all for him.

Simon worked closely with Yorkshire CCC's head of media and marketing, Danny Reuben, on the project, and they must be delighted with the end result. The book is expertly edited by Neil Hanson, while designer Jonny Thynne has done a thoroughly splendid job.

As one would expect from this team the narrative and the pictures are simply superb, and as you turn the pages the season unfolds in glorious colour. An added bonus is that the detailed scorecard from every match is spread out over a whole page, and the Christian names of all opposing players, as well as the familiar Yorkshire ones, are given in every reference.

The book is expensive, but quality counts, and if kids cannot afford it their parents should buy it for them. If it finds a place on your coffee table guests are bound to pick it up — but make sure they put it back before bidding you a fond farewell.

WATERS SPINS A FINE TALE ON VERITY'S TEN FOR TEN

By Nigel Pullan

10 for 10: Hedley Verity And The Story Of Cricket's Greatest Bowling Feat   Chris Waters (Bloomsbury £10.99)

On July 12, 1932, Hedley Verity took 10-10 against Nottinghamshire at Headingley. It was a remarkable bowling performance that is likely to remain a first-class record for ever. Chris Waters of the *Yorkshire Post*, working in another incarnation at the *Nottingham Evening Post*, went to interview Frank Shipston, then the oldest first-class cricketer, who played in this match, and Chris was inspired to investigate further.

This excellent book deals not only with the details of Verity's bowling on that Tuesday. but describes his family background, his playing days with Yorkshire and his relationship with his good friend Bill Bowes, his Test career and duels with Don Bradman and his conspicuous bravery as a soldier ending with his death at Caserta. Chris acknowledges the help and support he received from Douglas Verity, Hedley's son, who encouraged him to write this book. Douglas died in 2012.

The author's contacts with Hedley's family and his researches in local papers in Leeds and Nottingham have produced many interesting details. For instance, Hedley's sister, Grace, whom he once tried to swap for a rabbit when he was little, became a primary-school teacher who taught both Bryan Stott and Brian Close in Rawdon.

I had not realised that the Football Stand at Headingley had been badly damaged by fire during a Rugby League match between Leeds and Halifax at Easter. Hedley took his wickets from the football end with rebuilding work in progress, and there is a photograph of the bleak structure among many interesting contemporary black-and-white illustrations. Members were moved into the 2s 4d seats, and everyone else had to occupy the 1s 6d seats!

Chris writes interestingly on the personalities of both sets of players, having been associated with both Nottinghamshire and Yorkshire. The imperious Herbert Sutcliffe had made his 100th century in the previous match at Park Avenue. He was out first ball here, but he won the match with his batting alongside Percy Holmes in the second innings. RC Robertson Glasgow described Sutcliffe as "the sort of man who would rather miss a train than run for it."

There is a portrait of Arthur Carr, the eccentric Nottinghamshire captain who instilled a drinking culture into his team and smoked three packets of cigarettes each day. Larwood and Voce both played here in the season before the bodyline tour. When someone takes all 10 wickets you speculate about the bowler at the other end. The ferocious and combative George Macaulay must have wondered why he went wicketless – Hedley thought he put on too much spin in his anxiety to succeed as Tony Lock is said to have done at Old Trafford in 1956.

This is the best and most detailed account of the match I have read. At about 4 pm on Monday, July 11, heavy rain arrived and an inch fell in four hours in the city centre, while a cinema in Dewsbury was struck by lightning. On Tuesday Brian Sellers took out his senior players to inspect the pitch at 12.30, and declared. The visitors apparently decided to play for a draw, and Verity bowled nine consecutive maiden overs without taking a wicket. Then, as his father had predicted, he brought up Percy Holmes to second slip as the ball began to turn. There is a detailed account of the fall of the wickets including Verity's hat-trick. George Geary's apparently unassailable 10-18 at Ynysangharad Park in Pontypridd — where I saw my shortest ever day's cricket of about 10 minutes — was surpassed. Then, remarkably, Sutcliffe and Holmes made an unbeaten 139 to win the match. Hedley, "never a man for the tap room", no doubt celebrated quietly, and next day took only two wickets when Yorkshire visited Macaulay's old school, Barnard Castle.

Chris gives a good account of Verity's England career, and particularly his encounters with Bradman. There was mutual respect between these two great players, and Verity dismissed Bradman eight times in Tests and 10 altogether. Chris describes the great day at Lord's in 1934 when Hedley took 14-80 on the third day and 15-104 in the match despite running over a black cat on the way to the ground – and stopping to apologise to the owner.

The most memorable chapter is "The Valiant End", which describes Hedley's military service with the Green Howards, his bravery on the battlefield, his terrible wounds and his death in hospital nine days later after an apparently successful operation. Bill Bowes, in his prisoner-of-war camp, heard the news from a casual remark by an American soldier.

This fine book leaves us in no doubt about the personal qualities of Verity as well as his achievements on the cricket field. What if he had survived? Would he have stayed in the army as he had intimated? Would he have gone into politics? Would he have played on with Yorkshire? He would have been 41, and Arthur Booth was 44 in 1946. Would he have served Yorkshire as a committee member or in some other capacity?

Douglas Jardine, after whom Douglas Verity was named, said "no captain could have a greater asset in his side than Hedley Verity." If Doctor Who offered me a spot of time travel I would have to decide whether to go around the grounds with Wilfred Rhodes in 1900 or Hedley Verity in 1932. After reading this excellent book I would have to choose Headingley on July 12, 1932, even if it was in the 1s 6d seats.

Frank Mitchell Imperial Cricketer   Anthony Bradbury
(Association Of Cricket Statisticians, £14)

One of the best series of books I have come across is *Lives in Cricket*. My old Bradford Grammar School friend Tony Barker wrote No. 26 about the Australian Keith Carmody, who devised the "umbrella" field and shook the game half-a-century ago. Now No. 34 is available, *Frank Mitchell Imperial Cricketer* by Anthony Bradbury, a prolific writer on the sport, particularly on off-beat or forgotten figures.

Mitchell was one of the few Yorkshire cricketers to be born in East Yorkshire. Just why that is so is hard to fathom, but he went on to become a superstar of the late Victorian and Edwardian eras. He played Test cricket for both England and South Africa, Rugby Union for England, scored 17 first-class centuries in a 20-year career and was no stranger to controversy.

Going late to Cambridge University, he captained the team in 1896 against Oxford at Lord's. Deciding that his bowlers were too tired to make the follow-on a proposition, he instructed EB Shine to gift runs to the opposition. The uproar which followed was unprecedented at the ground, with MCC members expressing their outrage. Letters to *The Times* followed, of course. Shades of Brian Close and Edgbaston 70 years later!

The incident seemed to have little impact on his subsequent career, as the author makes clear in his supremely researched book. There will be no-one left who saw Mitchell play, but even though we are talking about a century ago there is a wealth of interest for any lover of sport.

Mitchell did not have the backing of great wealth, but played as an amateur, perhaps living beyond his means at times. He was declared bankrupt in 1912 while in London with the South African team for a triangular tournament.

LIVES IN CRICKET
Frank Mitchell
Imperial Cricketer

ANTHONY BRADBURY

ACS PUBLICATIONS

A firm of Savile Row tailors served him a writ for £192 for clothing provided — equivalent to £15,000 today. Mitchell would not be the first sporting personality to find his personal affairs out of control, and certainly not the last.

Retired Judge Bradbury was born in Goole, some 20 miles from the birthplace of the man whose life and times he has documented in such readable fashion. Like Mitchell he left Yorkshire to live and work, but always retained his love for the county, and to his great credit he reveals that Leonard Hutton is his cricketing hero.

As a writer presumably aiming to boost his finances, Mitchell looked knowingly into a crystal ball expressing strong views about betting, bodyline, Sunday cricket and other matters of the day. As a soldier he fought in two wars, the Boer and in 1914-18, rising to high rank. That he did not become renowned in the manner of C B Fry or H K Rodd remains a mystery.

Mitchell's grave is in Charlton Cemetery, London. Pelham Warner wrote of him as a staunch and loyal friend, who had lived a full life and travelled in many countries.

There is no doubt that Anthony Bradbury has delivered a sympathetic verdict on a man who, had he been around now, would have been feted as a huge celebrity.

DAVID SWALLOW

20-YEAR MASTERPLAN WILL TRANSFORM HEADINGLEY

By David Warner

The Headingley Masterplan, unveiled last June, details the ambitious plans to transform Headingley Cricket Ground into one of the finest venues in the world. It will see Yorkshire CCC work in partnership with Leeds Rugby, Leeds City Council and DLA Architecture to prepare for the phased redevelopment of the ground over the next 20 years.

The scheme includes the installation of floodlights, work upon which went on during the winter in order to have them up and running for the 2015 season; the rebuilding of the North West Stand adjoining the rugby ground, which will become the centrepiece of the project; the addition of 915 seats to the upper tier of the North East Stand with the possibility of a cantilever roof from the side of the Carnegie Pavilion to the existing scoreboard; the erection of a new pavilion in the North West area of the stadium; the erection of a translucent cantilever roof to cover the White Rose Stand on the western side of the ground, and landscaping on the White Rose Stand and North East Stand concourses. The capacity of the cricket ground will increase from 17,000 to 20,000t.

Yorkshire Chairman Colin Graves said: "This is the most ambitious project the Club and the venue will have undertaken since the ground was first established 125 years ago. Our ambitions are clear. We want to create a stadium that is among the finest in the world and which will enable Yorkshire to continue to stage major international fixtures over the long term.

"It is vital that we don't lose sight of our objectives. As other venues around the country continue to invest in their facilities we cannot afford to stand still and expect that Headingley will always host international cricket. The stark reality is that if our stadium fails to evolve we will lose our Test match status, which would be a devastating blow to the region. The Masterplan has been designed to provide a framework to enable us to achieve our objectives of improving facilities over a period of time."

Drawings showing an aerial sketch of the proposed redevelopment, the new pavilion to be built next to the Carnegie Pavilion and the proposed North-South Stand overlooking the cricket ground can be viewed in the second colour-plates section of this YCCC Yearbook.

ILLUMUNATING VIEWS UPON HEADINGLEY UNDER LIGHTS

The construction of floodlights at Headingley gives an opportunity to reflect on how changes in technology influence the course of the game as well as spectators' enjoyment of it.

It will be 10 years this summer since floodlights first influenced Yorkshire's fortunes in the County Championship: they were playing at Derby, and on course for the win that would secure promotion when the dark September evening demanded the use of lights for play to continue. How generous of Derbyshire to pay for what would enable Yorkshire to win when not playing would increase the chances of a draw.

The game worked out very differently. A straightforward catch went begging with the home side one run ahead and only three second-innings wickets left, and Yorkshire ended up struggling to avoid defeat. They did, however, scrape the draw which was to ensure promotion. In a dismal 2012 Derbyshire did achieve two victories courtesy of the lights which probably secured them the Second Division title and promotion.

Unfortunately, ECB rules require counties to have floodlights available in all games or not at all to avoid picking and choosing. This is supposed to level the playing field between sides, but in my opinion it does not do that. More recently Derbyshire have reverted to playing Yorkshire at Chesterfield, the one home match per season where floodlights are not available. Were they to be available in the County Championship at Headingley the same would be true of the two Scarborough matches.

Yorkshire's lights, like those at Lord's, have permission for a limited number of matches. This makes sense in planning terms to protect the right of neighbours to be spared their visual intrusion, but unlike the issues of daylight and sunlight aroused by the recently constructed pavilion the planning concern is really limited to night-time use. Limits should be justified only for day-night matches, and even here a little give-and-take is needed to avoid the lights being turned off with two balls to go and three runs to win. Matches should be scheduled to finish well ahead of the agreed cut-off time to allow for unexpected delays.

Meanwhile, the ECB could review its all-or-nothing rule. If we are to play later and later into September — usually a lot warmer than early April — there is a strong case for stipulating that lights can be allowed on any ground which has them. Yorkshire could designate the four days of the last Championship match as part of the 16 on which lights can be

10 years ago: Yorkshire play Middlesex under lights at Headingley in the Totesport League

used. September 2014 was unseasonably sunny. For all that the last day at The Oval and the 50-over Final at Lord's required lights. Ironically, had the floodlights not been in place for the Final play would most probably have taken place at Lord's on a glorious bright and sunny Sunday, producing a very different game to the low-scoring thriller under lights.

There also needs to be a rethink of noon starts when there are day-night matches the previous evening. If we cannot play to the end on a sunny day in late-May we should not be starting after 11.30 or we should make up the lost hour on the second and third days.

Finally, consideration of another change to the conduct of the Championship is occasioned by the presence of TV cameras at a few key games. In the interests of a level playing field DRS is not used, but the cameras are brought into play when there is a possible run-out or — as in Yorkshire's match at Trent Bridge — a brilliant stumping. This is sound enough: lbw decisions have a degree of subjectivity, whereas line decisions are a matter of fact — but it has to be faced that Jonny Bairstow's stumping of Samit Patel at Trent Bridge may have been too close for the naked eye to discern from square-leg. And it may be that TV cameras put added pressure on the umpires, with a detrimental effect on the on-field decisions. If so, not resorting to DRS for lbw shouts prevents a levelling of the playing field.

Whereas floodlights are a boon to the spectator, providing play where previously there was none, prolonged scrutiny of TV frames which are out of our sight is not.

SCHEME WOULD SEE REVIVAL OF CRICKET AT PARK AVENUE

By David Warner

Eight new net artificial pitches and four net grass pitches could be up and running at Bradford Park Avenue by next year if an England and Wales Cricket Board plan to redevelop the famous old ground for the local community comes to fruition.

Yorkshire released details of the scheme last December, and said they were already in talks with the ECB and Bradford Metropolitan Council. The ECB are keen on helping and interacting with local communities, and Bradford Park Avenue is an ideally situated inner-city ground with the fastest growing population in the country. In addition five as yet to be identified sites could be developed in other areas of the city.

The County have not played at Park Avenue since 1996, after which they also stopped visiting other outgrounds apart from Scarborough, but if Park Avenue is fully redeveloped there could be occasions when the Club would be keen to use it again.

In 2019, for example, Headingley will host an *Ashes* Test, a one-day international against Australia and up to four ICC World Cup games. This could mean Yorkshire having to play much of their cricket elsewhere to avoid overloading. Other cricket could also be earmarked for Bradford as the redevelopment progresses, including Yorkshire Second Eleven and Academy matches and women's cricket.

Bradford has been identified as having a shortage of 18 cricket grounds, and this figure is set to rise to 25 in seven years' time. The ECB have given Bradford Council a five-figure sum to undertake a feasibility study to determine how this shortfall can be addressed.

Commenting on Headingley's busy cricket schedule in 2019, Yorkshire Chief Executive Mark Arthur, said: "I was aware that we might have this type of programme in Leeds for 2019, in which case we will probably need to schedule some of Yorkshire's cricket away from Headingley. What better place than Bradford Park Avenue if the ground and its facilities are up to scratch by then?"

A LIFE IN THE CHURCH — AFTER ONE OUTING FOR YORKSHIRE

By Michael Pulford

Charles Molesworth Sharpe, a native of Hertfordshire who made one appearance for Yorkshire in 1875, was the first southern-born cricketer to represent the Club. The summer of 1875 was Sharpe's only season in first-class cricket, but he had much success — taking 70 wickets and finishing sixth in the national bowling averages. No fewer than 69 of those wickets were taken in seven matches for Cambridge University.

Sharpe was born in 1851 in the village of Codicote, a pleasant settlement of timber-framed and chequered brick houses on the dip slope of the Chiltern Hills midway between Welwyn and Stevenage. He was a son of the Vicar, Thomas Sharpe, and his wife, Emma, who both hailed from the East Midlands.

Charles took naturally to sport. His cricketing skills — he was a right-handed batsman and slow round-arm bowler — were soon appreciated, for he played for Hertfordshire against I Zingari aged 17 in 1869. Two years later his father became Vicar of Holy Trinity, Huddersfield, and Charles moved with the family to Yorkshire, where he was to live and work, save for two years at Cambridge University, for the rest of his life.

Charles went to Cambridge to follow his father into the church. He quickly showed himself to be an all-round sportsman there, for though below average height and slim of build he represented the university at both soccer and rugby in the winter of 1874-5. He was to prove unlucky in varsity matches, Cambridge losing 0-1 in the first soccer game between the two universities, while injury frustrated his aim to play in the rugby fixture against Oxford. To add to Charles's disappointment only half blues were given for the soccer match because of complaints from the rugby section. In old age Charles remained vexed about that.

Charles did not break into Cambridge's cricket first team during the summer of 1874, yet the following season he was not only their best bowler but one of the country's leading performers. His first-class debut was against an England XI, and it was a momentous start as he managed to take the wicket of W G Grace. His best figures for Cambridge that summer were 7-43 against Surrey, but all his bowling was significant, and often prolific, for he took five wickets in an innings nine times in

seven matches. Sharpe took a total of 69 wickets for Cambridge at a cost of less than 13 runs each, and though the pitches of the time still favoured bowlers his place in the season's averages showed his worth.

His bad luck with varsity matches continued, for though he took 11 wickets in the match and top-scored with 29 in the second knock Cambridge lost by six runs.

Charles's record with Cambridge brought him to national attention, and in July he was selected to play for the North versus the South at his adopted home ground of Fartown.

Then he was chosen to play for Yorkshire at Bramall Lane against

Charles Sharpe: Devoted Vicar who might instead have been Yorkshire's first amateur captain before Lord Hawke. *(Photo: By kind permission of Elsecar History Society)*

Gloucestershire. Yorkshire were able to pick him because his family home and permanent address was in the county. He was not the first non-Yorkshire-born cricketer to play for the county — others had done so since the Club was formed 12 seasons earlier. In August a Cambridge teammate of Sharpe, Herbert Sims, who was resident in the county, played twice for Yorkshire despite having been born in Devon — making Sims the second southern-born player to represent Yorkshire a fortnight after Sharpe had become the first.

Charles did not have much opportunity to make an impression in the Yorkshire-Gloucestershire match, bowling only 12 overs. He did not take a wicket, but his 15 runs at number six in his only innings were a useful contribution. Grace had his revenge by having Charles caught and bowled. Charles was asked to play for Yorkshire again but, perhaps not expecting to have the opportunity with the county side, he had already agreed to work as a tutor in Scotland and, as a man of his word, told Yorkshire he was unavailable.

Sharpe was a committed Christian who was to dedicate the remainder of his working life to the church, so 1875 was his only season of first-class cricket and his appearance for Yorkshire against Gloucestershire his sole match for the county. He took a curacy in Sheffield the following year before returning to Huddersfield in 1880 to assist his father. Then in 1888, following his father's death, Charles became Vicar at Elsecar, a mining village in South Yorkshire, where he devoted the rest of his ministry.

Charles's all-round cricket talent and his amateur status begs the question: had he not been so committed to his Christian ministry, and had he made himself available for Yorkshire, would he have been asked to captain the team? The side was otherwise stocked with professionals, and most of the other counties were led by amateurs. A decade later another amateur born outside the county, the Hon. Martin Bladen Hawke, was immediately offered the captaincy.

Sharpe's work as a minister certainly suggested that he had the strength of character to succeed, but he considered sport a pastime, not a career, and he was determined to devote his entire life to his vocation.

Nevertheless, Charles continued to be involved with cricket whenever it did not interfere with his work, and he assisted the Elsecar club until 1895, when in his mid-40s. He played some more matches for his native Hertfordshire in 1890, presumably during his holidays, and doubtless made possible by his remaining a bachelor. One of the Hertfordshire fixtures was against an MCC side at Lord's, when he took six wickets in an innings. Later in life Charles became a keen supporter of the church bible-class cricket team, and he was known to show children in the village school how to play shots with his walking stick.

Charles was a much loved and respected priest in Elsecar over three decades until his retirement in 1922 after he had turned 70. He worked tirelessly and with great conviction, for he was a man of strong beliefs. Proof of the respect and esteem in which he was held was seen on his retirement, when a stained-glass window showing him baptising a baby was placed in Elsecar Church.

He then moved to Wharfedale to live in the hamlet of Nesfield, near Ilkley. He regularly helped at the local mission church until his death in 1935 aged 83, having lived and worked in Yorkshire for almost 60 of those years. Charles is buried in Ilkley, Yorkshire CCC's first southern-born cricketer who, had he not been so committed to the Church, might even have been Yorkshire's first amateur captain.

ENGLAND CAPTAIN *BEFORE* PLAYING FOR YORKSHIRE

By Martin Howe

It is a not unfamiliar quiz question: which Yorkshire cricketer captained England before he had played for the county — indeed for any county? The answer is Ronald Stanyforth. His name barely registers in the annals of Yorkshire cricket, for he played only three times for the county, all in 1928. But he had an interesting cricket career, and he was a distinguished soldier and a long-serving royal courtier.

Stanyforth was born in 1892 to wealthy parents who lived at Kirk Hammerton Hall, North Yorkshire. He was educated at Eton and Christ Church, Oxford, from where he graduated with a modest degree in 1914. He was already commissioned in the 17th Lancers when war broke out in August, 1914, and by that November he was in France with his regiment. As the cavalry soon proved to be no match for machine-guns and heavily defended trenches, the regiment served as dismounted infantry.

Lieutenant Stanyforth was wounded at Festubert in 1915, was awarded the Military Cross and was Mentioned in Despatches. He lacked nothing in bravery.

A spell with the Army in Ireland followed the war, and then Captain Stanyforth was appointed equerry to Prince Henry, third son of George V, and also a cavalry officer. Stanyforth accompanied the Prince at many royal functions, including the weddings of King George V's children, Princess Victoria and Prince Albert, the Duke of York. He left to resume normal regimental duties in 1924, but when he retired from the Army in 1930 with the rank of Major, Prince Henry, now Duke of Gloucester, chose him to be Comptroller of the Royal Household.

With this responsible position at Court he was a participant not just in the range of routine activities that fall to members of the Royal Family but also in glittering State occasions such as banquets for visiting royalty or Heads of State, the Silver Jubilee of George V, the King's funeral, and, after the Abdication of Edward VIII, the coronation of Prince Albert as George VI. He proved a loyal and completely trustworthy courtier, and he and the Duke of Gloucester became as close as their positions would allow. The Duke was a regular visitor to the Stanyforths'

Yorkshire home, where he was able to share in the family's passion for hunting and shooting. For services to the Crown he was appointed Commander of the Royal Victorian Order (CVO) in the Coronation Honours List.

Stanyforth rejoined his regiment on the outbreak of the Second World War, and served first as ADC to General Sir Alan Brooke, who had the task of organising the retreat to, and evacuation from, Dunkirk.

The two men, who became firm friends, were among the last officers to leave the beaches. They were soon back in France when General Brooke was sent to command the remaining British troops and help to shore up the collapsing French Army. Another hazardous evacuation had to be organised when France sued for an armistice, this time from St Nazaire.

Stanyforth was made a senior staff officer after these dangerous assignments, based in London in the Army Group charged with planning the Normandy landings and the liberation of Occupied Europe. He left the Army at the end of the war with the rank of Lieutenant Colonel.

From 1947 he had another spell

RONALD STANYFORTH
Courtier and cricketer

as equerry to the Duke of Gloucester, which included the period when the Duke was Senior Counsellor of State while King George VI and his family were on their tour of South Africa.

What about Ronald Stanyforth the cricketer? He was an amateur, of course. Of medium height and build with the agility of a natural games player — he was superb at racquets — Stanyforth was a fine wicket-keeper, who wrote an excellent short book on the art in 1935.

He made his first-class debut in 1914 for Oxford University against

80

MCC, but after the Great War most of his cricket was at club level with a few first-class matches each season, mainly for MCC and Army sides. In what was to prove a fillip to his cricket career Stanyforth was selected by MCC for an all-amateur tour of South America, mainly Argentina, where four "Test" matches were played, in the winter of 1926-27.

He much impressed his captain, the 53-year-old Pelham Warner, with his wicket-keeping and cricketing "nous", and after a handful more of first-class games he was chosen for the tour of South Africa in 1927-28 as vice-captain to G R Jackson, of Derbyshire. When Jackson had to withdraw at the last moment Stanyforth was elevated to the captaincy, a position he had yet to hold in any first-class match.

Indeed, he had yet to play in the County Championship.

It was on the voyage to South Africa that Herbert Sutcliffe heard of his own appointment as Yorkshire captain, an honour he tactfully declined after the controversy that followed the announcement. Yorkshire quickly appointed Sir William Worsley, who had all the credentials of background and class then thought essential for the captaincy of a first-class team. It is not known whether Sutcliffe consulted the captain of the tour party over his dilemma, but Stanyforth would have been aware of the controversy and of Yorkshire's *volte-face*.

The series in South Africa was squared, each country winning two Tests, with one drawn. Stanyforth had to miss the last through injury. Never much of a batsman, he scored 13 Test runs in six innings, though he kept competently enough, accounting for nine dismissals. He proved to be a capable and firm captain who won the respect of colleagues and opponents alike. There was much comment on the excellent spirit in which the matches were contested.

On his return MCC publicly acknowledged the valuable contribution of Stanyforth's captaincy, and he was elected to their main committee. This was to be the first of his three stints on this august body, and he served on other MCC committees including Finance and General Purposes and Cricket and Selection Committees. He was to prove as able a cricket administrator as he was a royal courtier.

Stanyforth was in his element at Lord's. He fitted easily into the exclusive, elitist, all-male club that MCC was at the time. The distinctions the cricket establishment made between amateurs and professionals were as natural to him as those between officers and other ranks in the Army, between members of Court and the man in the street, between the local gentry and the tenants on the family's Kirk Hammerton estate. To Ronald, as to others with his background, the class system was part of the natural order of things and, indeed, a system that bound British

One man and his dogs: Ronald Stanyforth at ease

society together, not one that divided it. He was apparently never at ease with people other than of his own class and background.

It seems that the Yorkshire Committee were also aware of the reputation Stanyforth had made in South America with his wicket-keeping and in South Africa with his captaincy. Certainly, Lord Hawke would have been. Yorkshire were looking for a wicket-keeper to take over from Arthur Dolphin, who had retired at the end of the 1927 season. Arthur Wood was one candidate, but before the new season had started the Committee invited Stanyforth to keep in three early-season matches against Warwickshire, Middlesex and Hampshire.

Ronald was born in the Stanyforths' Knightsbridge home in the London Borough of Kensington and Chelsea. It seems unlikely that no-one on the Yorkshire Committee, least of all Lord Hawke, whose London house in Belgravia was close to the Stanyforths' in Lowdnes Street, would not have known of Stanyforth's birthplace and therefore that his selection breached the long-standing convention that Yorkshire players must be born within the county. If they did turn a blind eye it seems unlikely that the motive was solely so that they could try another wicket-keeper to Arthur Wood.

Perhaps the possibility that Stanyforth might be suitable for the captaincy, should Captain Worsley decide that he did not want the post, was in their minds. In the event Stanyforth achieved little in his three matches. He was not selected for more games for Yorkshire, and Arthur Wood made the wicket-keeper position his own in the course of that 1928 season. When Worsley did stand down as captain after the 1929 season Alan Barber proved a most effective replacement if, sadly, for one season.

So after his match at Southampton he returned to club cricket and occasional first-class matches for MCC or the Army when these could be fitted in with his Army and, later, royal duties. He was able to accept MCC's invitation to tour the West Indies in 1930 in a party captained by the Hon "Freddie" Calthorpe, but he had played in only four matches, none of them Tests, when a damaged hand forced an early return home. Thereafter his first-class cricket career ran down, and he played his last match, for Free Foresters, in 1933.

Ronald Stanyforth married late in life in 1941. It was only after the Second World War that the couple chose to live at Kirk Hammerton Hall, which Ronald had inherited on the death of his father in 1939 and which had been taken over by the military during the war. He interested himself in the activities of the Kirk Hammerton Cricket Club, whose ground was built by Ronald's father in 1907 when Ronald began to show interest in the game, and he became involved in the Scarborough Cricket Festival. In 1960 he was elected president of the Scarborough Club, and in 1961 he was invited to be a Patron of Yorkshire County Cricket Club, although it is not known how active he became in its deliberations.

Stanyforth died at Kirk Hammerton in 1964 after a long illness. The couple had no children. Ronald's widow sold the Hall and its contents, and returned to live in London.

He was the epitome of the gentleman cricketer. It is hard to see how Stanyforth would have fitted in with the hard-nosed professionals who made up the Yorkshire sides — other than the captains — of the 1920s had he been offered more than the three games he had in 1928, but we should not demean his ability. He played 61 first-class matches in a career extending intermittently from 1914 to 1933, scoring 1,092 runs at 17.33 and making 93 dismissals. There can be no doubt that had he played more regularly and enjoyed the benefit of the coaching and advice that goes with regular cricket his record would have been more noteworthy. The Ronald Stanyforth story, in and beyond cricket, deserves to be more widely known.

Editor's Note: Martin Howe has written a 15,000-word monograph, *Ronald Thomas Stanyforth: Cricketer, Soldier, Courtier*, which tells Stanyforth's story in detail. Anyone interested in procuring a copy should contact Martin at martinhowe1@sky.com or telephone 01582-792074.

Price £10 to cover printing and postage. This is not a commercial venture.

The Players

Andrew William GALE

Left-hand batsman
Born: Dewsbury, November 28, 1983
First-Class cricket:
Debut: v. Somerset at Scarborough, 2004
Highest score: 272 v. Nottinghamshire
at Scarborough, 2013
Best bowling: 1-33 v. Loughborough UCCE
at Leeds, 2007
One-Day:
Highest score: 125* v. Essex at Chelmsford, 2010
t20:
Highest score: 91 v. Nottinghamshire
at Leeds, 2009

Joe Edward ROOT

Right-hand batsman, right-arm off-spin bowler
Born: Sheffield, December 30, 1990
First-Class cricket:
Debut: v. Loughborough MCCU at Leeds, 2010
Highest Score: 236 v. Derbyshire at Leeds, 2013
Best bowling: 3-33 v. Warwickshire
at Birmingham, 2011
One-Day:
Highest Score: 113 for England v. v. India
at Leeds, 2014
Hiighest for Yorkshire: 63 v. Essex at Leeds, 2009
Best bowling: 2-10 for England Lions v. Bangladesh A
at Sylhet, 2011/12
For Yorkshire: 2-14 v. Kent at Leeds, 2012
t20:
Highest score: 90* for England v. Australia
at Southampton, 2013
For Yorkshire: 65 v. Worcestershire at Leeds, 2012
Best bowling: 1-12 v.Warwickshire at Leeds, 2011

Gary Simon BALLANCE

Left-hand batsman, leg-break bowler
Born: Harare, Zimbabwe, November 22, 1989
First-Class Cricket:
Debut: v Kent at Canterbury, 2008
Highest score: 210 for Mid-West Rhinos v.
Southern Rocks at Masvingo, Zimbabwe, 2011-12
For Yorkshire: 174 v. Northamptonshire
at Leeds, 2014
One-Day:
Highest score: 139 v. Unicorns at Leeds, 2013
t20:
Highest score: 68 v Durham
at Chester-le-Street, 2013

Ryan Jay SIDEBOTTOM

Left-hand bat, left-arm fast-medium bowler
Born: Huddersfield, January 15, 1978
First-Class cricket:
Debut: v. Leicestershire at Leicester, 1997
Highest score: 61 v. Worcestershire
at Worcester, 2011
Best bowling: 7-37 v. Somerset at Leeds 2011
One-Day:
Highest score: 32 for Nottinghamshire v. Middlesex
at Nottingham, 2005
Highest score for Yorkshire: 30* v. Glamorgan
at Leeds, 2002
Best bowling: 6-40 v. Glamorgan at Cardiff, 1998
t20:
Highest score for Yorkshire: 16* v. Worcestershire
at Worcester, 2011
Best bowling: 4-25 v. Durham
at Chester-le-Street, 2012

Adam LYTH

Left-hand batsman, right-arm medium bowler
Born: Whitby, September 25, 1987
First-Class cricket:
Debut: v. Loughborough UCCE at Leeds, 2007
Highest score: 251 v. Lancashire
at Manchester, 2014
Best bowling: 2-15 v. Somerset at Taunton, 2013
One-Day:
Highest score: 109* v. Sussex
at Scarborough, 2009
Best bowling: 1-6 v Middlesex at Leeds, 2013
t20:
Highest score: 78 v. Derbyshire at Leeds, 2012
Best bowling: 2-5 v. Derbyshire
at Chesterfield, 2014

Jonathan Marc BAIRSTOW

Right-hand batsman, wicket-keeper
Born: Bradford, September 26, 1989
First-Class Cricket:
Debut: v Somerset at Leeds, 2009
Highest score: 205 v. Nottinghamshire
at Nottingham, 2011
One-Day:
Highest score: 123 for England Lions
v. New Zealand A at Bristol, 2014
Highest score: 114 v. Middlesex at Lord's, 2011
t20:
Highest score: 102* v. Durham
at Chester-le-Street, 2014

Kane Stuart WILLIAMSON
Right-hand batsman, right-arm off-break bowler
Born: Tauranga, August 8, 1990
First-Class cricket:
Debut: Northern Districts v. Auckland
at Auckland, 2007/8
Debut for Yorkshire: Nottinghamshire
at Nottingham, 2013
Highest score: 284* for Northern Districts
v. Wellington at Lincoln, 2011/12

For Yorkshire: 189 v. Sussex at Scarborough, 2014
Best bowling: 5-75 for Northern Districts
v. Canterbury at Christchurch, 2008-9
For Yorkshire: 2-44 v. Sussex at Hove, 2013
One-Day:
Highest score: 145* for New Zealand
v. South Africa at Kimberley, 2012/13
For Yorkshire: 70 v. Lancashire at Manchester, 2014
Best bowling: 5-51 for Northern Districts v. Auckland at Auckland, 2009/10
For Yorkshire: 1-42 v Glamorgan at Leeds, 2013
t20:
Highest score: 101* for Northern Districts v. Cape Cobras at Raipur, India, 2014
For Yorkshire: 41 v. Derbyshire at Chesterfield, 2014
Best bowling: 3-33 for Northern Districts v. Wellington at Wellington, 2011/12
For Yorkshire: 2-26 v. Derbyshire at Chesterfield, 2014

Liam Edward PLUNKETT
Right-hand batsman, right-arm fast-medium bowler
Born: Middlesbrough, April 6, 1985
First-Class cricket:
Debut: For Durham v. Durham UCCE
at Durham, 2003
Yorkshire Debut: v. Leeds/Bradford MCCU
at Leeds, 2013
Highest score: 114 for England Lions v. S Lanka A
Emerging Players at Colombo, 2013/14
For Yorkshire: 86 v. Warwickshire at Leeds, 2014
Best bowling: 6-33 v. Leeds/Bradford MCCU
at Leeds, 2013
One-Day:
Highest score: 72 for Durham v. Somerset
at Chester-le-Street, 2008
For Yorkshire: 53 v. Leicestershire
at Scarborough, 2013

Best bowling: 4-15 for Durham v. Essex at Chester-le-Street, 2007
For Yorkshire: 2-38 v. Unicorns at Leeds, 2013
t20:
Highest score: 41 for Durham v. Lancashire at Manchester, 2011
For Yorkshire: 36 v. Northamptonshire at Leeds, 2014
Best bowling: 5-31 for Durham v. Lancashire at Chester-le-Street, 2011
For Yorkshire: 2-20 v. Leicestershire at Scarborough, 2013, and 2-20 v. Northamptonshire
at Leeds, 2014

Jack Alexander BROOKS

Right-hand batsman, right-arm medium-fast bowler
Born: Oxford, June 4, 1984
First-Class Cricket:
Debut: For Northamptonshire v. Australia
at Northampton, 2009
Debut for Yorkshire: v. Leeds/Bradford MCCU
at Leeds, 2013
Highest score: 53 for Northamptonshire
v. Gloucestershire at Bristol, 2010
For Yorkshire: 33* v Somerset at Leeds, 2013
Best bowling: 5-23 for Northamptonshire
v. Leicestershire at Leicester, 2011
For Yorkshire: 5-36 v. Northamptonshire
at Leeds, 2014
One-Day:
Highest score: 10 for Northamptonshire v. Middlesex at Uxbridge, 2009
Highest score for Yorkshire: 0 v. Gloucestershire and v. Durham at Leeds, 2014
Best bowling: 3-30 v. Hampshire at Southampton, 2014
t20:
Highest score: 33* for Northamptonshire v. Warwickshire at Birmingham, 2011
For Yorkshire: Has not batted
Best bowling: 5-21 v Leicestershire at Leeds, 2013

Timothy Thomas BRESNAN

Right-hand batsman, right-arm medium-fast bowler
Born: Pontefract, February 28, 1985
First-Class cricket:
Debut: v. Northamptonshire at Northampton, 2003
Highest score: 126* for England Lions v. Indians
at Chelmsford, 2007
Highest for Yorkshire: 116 v. Surrey
at The Oval, 2007
Best bowling: 5-42 v. Worcestershire
at Worcester, 2005
One-Day:
Highest score: 80 for England v. Australia
at Centurion Park, 2009
For Yorkshire: 61 v. Leicestershire at Leeds, 2003
Best bowling: 4-25 v. Somerset at Leeds, 2005

t20:
Highest score: 42 v. Leicestershire at Leeds, 2004
Best bowling: 3-10 England v. Pakistan at Cardiff, 2010
Best bowling for Yorkshire: 3-21 v. Durham at Chester-le-Street, 2006

Adil Usman RASHID

Right-hand batsman, leg-break bowler
Born: Bradford, February 17, 1988
First-Class cricket:
Debut: v. Warwickshire at Scarborough, 2006
Highest score: 180 v Somerset at Leeds, 2013
Best bowling: 7-107 v. Hampshire
at Southampton, 2008

One-Day:
Highest score: 71 v. Gloucestershire at Leeds, 2014
Best bowling: 5-33 v. Hampshire
at Southampton, 2014

t20:
Highest score: 36* v Uva Next
at Johannesburg, 2012/3
Best bowling: 4-20 v. Leicestershire at Leeds, 2010

Alexander Zak LEES

Left-hand batsman
Born: Halifax, April 14, 1993
First-Class Cricket:
Debut: India A at Leeds, 2010
Highest score: 275* v Derbyshire
at Chesterfield, 2013
Best bowling: 0-14 v. Nottinghamshire
at Scarborough 2013
One-Day:
Highest score: 102 v. Northamptonshire
at Northampton, 2014
t20:
Highest score: 67* v. Derbyshire
at Chesterfield ,2014

Steven Andrew PATTERSON

Right-hand batsman, right-arm medium-fast bowler
Born: Beverley, October 3, 1983
First-Class cricket:
Debut: v. Bangladesh 'A' at Leeds, 2005
Highest score: 53 v. Sussex at Hove, 2011
Best bowling: 5-43 v. Nottinghamshire
at Nottingham, 2013

One-Day:
Highest score: 25* v. Worcestershire at Leeds, 2006
Best bowling: 6-32 v. Derbyshire at Leeds, 2010

t20:
Highest score: 3* v. Derbyshire at Leeds, 2010
Best bowling: 4-30 v. Lancashire at Leeds, 2010

Richard Michael PYRAH

Right-hand batsman, right-arm medium bowler
Born: Dewsbury, November 1, 1982
First-Class cricket:
Debut: v. Glamorgan at Colwyn Bay, 2004
Highest score: 134* Loughborough v. MCCU
at Leeds, 2010
Best bowling: 5-58 v. Nottinghamshire
at Leeds, 2011
One-Day:
Highest score: 69 v. Netherlands at Leeds, 2011
Best bowling: 5-50 for Yorkshire Cricket Board
v. Somerset at Scarborough, 2002
Best bowling for Yorkshire: 4 for 24 v. Netherlands
at Rotterdam, 2010
t20:
Highest score: 42 v Nottinghamshire
at Nottingham, 2013
Best bowling: 5-16 v. Durham at Scarborough, 2011

Andrew John HODD

Right-hand batsman, wicket keeper
Born: Chichester, January 12, 1984
First-Class cricket:
Debut: Sussex v. Zimbabwe at Hove, 2003
Debut for Yorkshire: v. Derbyshire at Leeds, 2012
Highest score: 123 for Sussex v. Yorkshire
at Hove, 2007
Highest score for Yorkshire: 68* v. Somerset
at Taunton, 2013
One-Day:
Highest score: 91 for Sussex v. Lancashire
at Hove, 2010
For Yorkshire: 69* v. Leicestershire
at Leicester, 2014
t20:
Highest score: 26 for Sussex v. Kent at Hove, 2010
For Yorkshire: 11 v Durham
at Chester-le-Street, 2013

Jack Andrew LEANING

Right-hand batsman, right-arm medium
and off-break bowler
Born: Bristol, October 18, 1993

First-Class cricket:
Debut: v. Surrey at Leeds, 2013
Highest score: 99 v. Sussex at Arundel, 2014
Best bowling: 0- 4 v Surrey at Leeds, 2013

One-Day:
Highest score: 111* v. Essex at Scarborough, 2014
Best bowling: 5-22 v Unicorns at Leeds, 2013

t20:
Highest score: 8 v. Leicestershire at Leicester, 2013
Best bowling: 0-12 v. Derbyshire at Leeds, 2014

Aaron James FINCH

Right-hand batsman, left-arm medium-pace bowler
Born: Colac, Victoria, November 17, 1986
First-Class cricket:
Debut: Victoria v Indians at Melbourne, 2007
Debut for Yorkshire: v Northamptonshire
at Northampton, 2014
Highest score: 122 v. Zimbabwe XI at Harare, 2011
Highest score for Yorkshire: 110 v. Warwickshire
at Birmingham, 2014
Best bowling for Yorkshire: 1-20 v. Sussex
at Arundel, 2014
One-Day:
Highest score: 154 for Victoria v. Queensland
at Brisbane, 2007
Has not played List A for Yorkshire
t20:

Highest score: 156 for Australia v. England at Southampton, 2014
For Yorkshire: 89 v. Nottinghamshire at Leeds, 2014

Glenn James MAXWELL

Right-hand batsman, right-arm off-break bowler
Born: Kew, Melbourne, Victoria, Australia,
October 14, 1988
First-Class cricket:
Debut: Victoria v. New South Wales at Melbourne,
February 18, 2011
Highest score: 155* for Australia A v South Africa
A
at Pretoria, 2013
Best bowling: 4-42 for Victoria v South Australia
at Melbourne 2012-13
One-Day:
Highest score: 146 for Hampshire v. Lancashire
at Manchester, 2014
Best bowling: 4-63 for Australia v West Indies
at Perth 2012-13
t20:

Highest score: 95 for Kings XI Punjab v. Chennai Super Kings at Abu Dhabi, 2014
Best bowling: 3-13 for Australia v. Pakistan at Dubai 2014-15

Moin Aqeeb ASHRAF

Left-hand batsman, right-arm fast-medium bowler
Born: Bradford, January 5, 1992
First-Class cricket:
Debut: v. Loughborough MCCU at Leeds, 2010
Highest score: 10 v. Kent at Leeds, 2010
Best bowling: 5-32 v. Kent at Leeds, 2010
One-Day:
Highest Score: 3* v. Kent at Leeds, 2012
Best bowling: 3-38 v Glamorgan at Leeds, 2013
t20:
Highest score: 4 v Leicestershire at Leicester, 2013
Best bowling: 4-18 v. Derbyshire at Derby, 2012

Younus KHAN
Right-hand batsman, right-arm medium, leg-break
Born: Marden, North West Frontier Province,
Pakistan on November 29, 1977
First-Class cricket:
Debut: For Peshawar v. Hyderabad
at Peshawar 1998-99
*Debut for Yorkshire:*v Surrey at The Oval, 2007
Highest score: 313 for Pakistan v Sri Lanka
at Karachi 2008-9
Highest score for Yorkshire: 217* v. Kent
at Scarborough, 2007
Best bowling for Yorkshire: 4-52 v. Hampshire
at Southampton, 2007
List A:
Debut: For Peshawar v. Water and Power
Development at Peshawar 1998-99

Debut for Yorkshire: v. Nottinghamshire at Nottingham, 2007
Highest score for Yorkshire: 100 v. Nottinghamshire at Nottingham, 2007
Best bowling: 3-5 for Nottinghamshire v. Gloucestershire at Cheltenham, 2005
Best bowling for Yorkshire: 2-43 v. Durham at Leeds, 2007
t20:
Debut for Yorkshire: v. Leicestershire at Leicester, 2007
Highest score: 71* for Abbottabad Falcons v. Bahawalpur Stags at Islamabad, 2013-14
Highest score for Yorkshire: 40 v. Sussex at Hove, 2007
Best bowling: 3-18 for Pakistan v Kenya at Nairobi, 2007-8
Best bowling for Yorkshire: 2-32 v. Sussex at Hove 2007-5

Daniel Mark HODGSON
Right-hand batsman, wicket-keeper
Born: Northallerton, February 22, 1990
First-Class cricket:
Debut: For Leeds-Bradford MCCU v. Surrey
at The Oval, 2012
Debut for Yorkshire: v. Leeds-Bradford MCCU
at Leeds 2014
Highest score: 94* for Mountaineers
v Southern Rocks at Mutare, 2012/13
Highest score for Yorkshire: 18 v. Leeds-Bradford
MCCU at Leeds, 2014
One-Day:
Highest score: 90 v Glamorgan at Leeds, 2013
t20:
Highest score: 52* v Leicestershire at Leeds, 2013

Karl CARVER
Left-hand batsman, slow left-arm orthodox bowler
Born: Northallerton, March 26, 1996
First-Class Cricket:
Debut for Yorkshire: v. Warwickshire
at Birmingham, 2014
Highest score: 2* v. Warwickshire
at Birmingham, 2014
Best bowling: 2-27 v. Warwickshire
at Birmingham, 2014
One-Day:
Awaiting Debut
t20:
Awaiting Debut

YORKSHIRE'S FIRST-CLASS HIGHLIGHTS OF 2014

Wins by an innings (5)

Yorkshire (444) defeated Warwickshire (200 and 89) by an innings and 155 runs at Leeds

Yorkshire (532-9 dec) defeated Nottinghamshire (203 and 177) by an innings and 152 runs at Nottingham

Yorkshire (459-9 dec) defeated Northamptonshire (94 and 245) by an innings and 120 runs at Leeds

Lancashire (278 and 314) lost to Yorkshire (610-6 dec) by an innings and 18 runs at Manchester

Warwickshire (228 and 186) lost to Yorkshire (422) by an innings and 8 runs at Birmingham

Wins by over 200 runs (2)

Yorkshire (136 and 546-3 dec) defeated Northamptonshire (251 and 160) by 271 runs at Northampton

Yorkshire (253 and 400-5 dec) defeated Middlesex (232 and 201) by 220 runs at Scarborough

Totals of 400 and over (14)

610-6 dec	v. Lancashire at Manchester
589-8 dec	v. Durham at Chester-le-Street
546-3 dec	v. Northamptonshire at Northampton
532-9 dec	v. Nottinghamshire at Nottingham
493	v. Sussex at Scarborough
470-7 dec	v. Sussex at Arundel
459-9 dec	v Northamptonshire at Leeds
454	v. Leeds/Bradford MCCU at Leeds
450	v. Somerset at Taunton
444	v. Warwickshire at Leeds
426	v. Durham at Leeds
422	v. Warwickshire at Birmingham
416	v. Middlesex at Lord's
400-5 dec	v. Middlesex at Scarborough

Opponents dismissed for under 100 (2)

89   v. Warwickshire at Leeds   94   v. Northamptonshire at Leeds

Century Partnerships (22)
For the 1st wicket (4)

375	A Lyth and A Z Lees	v. Northamptonshire at Northampton
270	A Lyth and A Z Lees	v. Durham at Leeds
176	A Lyth and A Z Lees	v. Nottinghamshire at Nottingham
100	A Lyth and A Z Lees	v. Somerset at Taunton

For the 2nd wicket (2)

179	A Lyth and K S Williamson	v. Durham at Chester-le-Street
132	A Z Lees and K S Williamson	v. Middlesex at Scarborough

For the 3rd wicket (1)

149	A Lyth and G S Ballance	v. Leeds/Bradford MCCU at Leeds

Century Partnerships *(Continued)*

For the 4th wicket (6)

198	A W Gale and J M Bairstow	v. Durham at Chester-le-Street
156	A Z Lees and G S Ballance	v. Northamptonshire at Leeds
149	K S Williamson and J M Bairstow	v. Sussex at Scarborough
125	J A Leaning and J M Bairstow	v. Sussex at Arundel
110	J E Root and J M Bairstow	v. Somerset at Leeds
103	A Lyth and J M Bairstow	v. Lancashire at Manchester

For the 5th wicket (2)

182	A W Gale and J A Leaning	v. Middlesex at Scarborough
115	G S Ballance and A U Rashid	v. Somerset at Taunton

For the 6th wicket (4)

296	A Lyth and A U Rashid	v. Lancashire at Manchester
	(New Yorkshire record)	
138	J M Bairstow and T T Bresnan	v. Sussex at Arundel
123	A J Finch and R M Pyrah	v. Warwickshire at Birmingham
108	A U Rashid and A J Hodd	v. Somerset at Taunton

For the 7th wicket (2)

157	K S Williamson and T T Bresnan	v. Sussex at Scarborough
113	K S Williamson and T T Bresnan	v. Warwickshire at Leeds

For the 9th wicket (1)

106	L E Plunkett and S A Patterson	v. Warwickshire at Leeds

Centuries (20)

A Lyth (7)

251	v. Lancashire at Manchester
230	v. Northamptonshire at Northampton
143	v. Durham at Leeds
130	v. Leeds/Bradford MCCU at Leeds
122	v. Nottinghamshire at Nottingham
117	v. Middlesex at Scarborough
104	v. Durham at Chester-le-Street

G S Ballance (3)

174	v. Northamptonshire at Leeds
130	v. Middlesex at Lord's
101	v. Leeds/Bradford MCCU

J M Bairstow (2)

161*	v. Sussex at Arundel
123	v. Leeds/Bradford MCCU at Leeds

A W Gale (2)

126*	v Middlesex at Scarborough
124	v. Durham at Chester-le-Street

A Z Lees (2)

138	v. Northamptonshire at Northampton
108	v. Durham at Leeds

A U Rashid (2)

108	v. Somerset at Taunton
159*	v. Lancashire at Manchester

A J Finch (1)

110	v. Warwickshire at Birmingham

K S Williamson (1)

189	v. Sussex at Scarborough

5 wickets in an innings (5)

J A Brooks (2)

    5-36   v. Northamptonshire at Leeds
    5-90   v. Lancashire at Leeds

R J Sidebottom (2)

    7-44   v. Middlesex at Scarborough
    6-30   v. Nottinghamshire at Nottingham

A U Rashid (1)

    5-117 v. Lancashire at Manchester

3 catches in an innings (11)

J M Bairstow (3)

    6   v. Sussex at Arundel
    3   v. Northamptonshire at Northampton
    3   v. Lancashire at Manchester

A J Hodd (3)

    5   v. Northamptonshire at Leeds
    3   v. Somerset at Taunton
    3   v. Durham at Chester-le-Street

A Lyth (3)

    4   v. Middlesex 2nd innings at Scarborough
    3   v. Middlesex 1st innings at Scarborough
    3   v. Somerset at Leeds

A Finch (1)

    4   v. Warwickshire at Birmingham

A U Rashid (1)

    3   v. Nottinghamshire at Leeds

5 catches in a match (5)

J M Bairstow (2)

    6 (6 + 0) v. Sussex at Arundel
    5 (2 + 3) v. Lancashire at Manchester

A J Hodd (2)

    7 (2 + 5) v. Northamptonshire at Leeds
    5 (3 + 2) v. Durham at Chester-le-Street

A Lyth (1)

    7 (3 + 4) v. Middlesex at Scarborough

5 dismissals in a match (2)

J M Bairstow (1)

    6 (5ct + 1st) v. Lancashire at Manchester

A J Hodd (1)

    6 (4ct +1st) v. Durham at Chester-le-Street

Debuts (3)

In first-class cricket: K Carver
In first-class cricket for Yorkshire: D M Hodgson and A J Finch

Capped (1)

A Z Lees on September 23, 2014

LV CHAMPIONSHIP FACTFILE

Compiled by John T Potter

Versus LEEDS/BRADFORD MCCU at Headingley

1. Yorkshire First Class debut for D M Hodgson
2. First Class debuts for C A L Davis, A R Laws and P A Ross
3. Yorkshire's 454 was their highest against Leeds/Bradford MCCU
4. G S Ballance scored his third century in consecutive innings, the third Yorkshire player to do this in the last two seasons
5. Yorkshire had three centurions in their innings for the 22nd time. The last was at The Oval in 2007 against Surrey

Versus SOMERSET at Taunton

1. A U Rashid scored his third century against Somerset in consecutive matches
2. Six Somerset players scored half-centuries in their innings of 553, the 33rd time a team had achieved this. Somerset also did it in 2008 at Scarborough and in 2010 at Taunton
3. A Lyth passed 5,000 First Class career runs

Versus NORTHAMPTONSHIRE at Headingley

1. G S Ballance's 174 was his highest score for Yorkshire
2. Northamptonshire's first-innings total of 94 was the fourth time they had failed to pass three figures at Headingley, the others being 63 in 1933 and 69 (first innings) and 88 (second innings) in 1922.
3. J A Brooks's 5-36 was his best analysis for Yorkshire. His match figures of 8-112 were his First Class career best
4. R J Sidebottom took his 500th Championship wicket when he dismissed S D Peters in Northamptonshire's first innings
5. Yorkshire achieved consecutive Championship wins at Headingley for the first time since 2007, when the Durham match began on April 25 and Worcestershire on May 9

LV CHAMPIONSHIP FACTFILE *(Continued)*

Versus Middlesex at Lord's

1. R J Sidebottom played his 100th First Class match for Yorkshire
2. T J Murtagh took his 500th First Class wicket when he dismissed G S Ballance in Yorkshire's second innings
3. C J L Rogers passed his career aggregate of 10,000 Championship runs when he reached 168
4. His 241* equalled the highest score by an Australian for Middlesex — J L Langer against Kent in 1999 at Lord's was the other
5. Middlesex's second-innings total of 472-3 was their highest fourth-innings winning total at Lord's. It was their second highest in all matches, their highest being 502-6 at Trent Bridge in 1926 against Nottinghamshire
6. It was the third highest fourth-innings winning total in all Championship matches. The first was as above, and the second was Somerset's 479-6 at Taunton in 2009 against Yorkshire
7. It was only the third time Yorkshire had lost a match when over 400 runs were scored in the fourth innings. Two have already been mentioned, and the third was Hampshire's 404-5 at Headingley in 2006

Versus DURHAM at Chester-le-Street

1. A Lyth passed an aggregate of 5,000 First Class runs for Yorkshire during his first innings
2. Yorkshire became the first visiting team at Chester-le-Street to take more than one batting point since Somerset on May 12, 2012
3. Lancashire were the last visiting team to pass 300 in their first innings on June 1, 2011, but they still lost by an innings
4. Yorkshire's 589-8 dec was the third highest total on this ground. The two higher were 648-5 dec by Durham in 2009 and 610-6 dec by Somerset in 2011
5. M D Stoneman's 131 and M J Richardson's 148 were both First Class career bests
6. P D Collingwood was A U Rashid's 300th First Class wicket for Yorkshire

LV CHAMPIONSHIP FACTFILE *(Continued)*

Versus WARWICKSHIRE at Headingley

1. Yorkshire's ninth-wicket partnership of 106 by L E Plunkett and S A Patterson was the highest against Warwickshire in Yorkshire
2. L E Plunkett's 86 was his highest for Yorkshire
3. S A Patterson's first wicket (L J Evans) in the match was his 200th First Class wicket for Yorkshire
4. This was the third time Warwickshire had been bowled out at Headingley for a total in the 80s
5. The last time this happened was in 1998 (84 all out), H D Bird's final First Class match as an umpire. He was Yorkshire's President in 2014-15
6. Yorkshire's innings victory was their 27th against Warwickshire and their fifth at Headingley, the last time at Headingley being 1998
7. Yorkshire's victory was their third in a row in Championship matches at Headingley. The last time they did this was in 2001, when they won four consecutive matches: Northamptonshire on May 25, Kent on June 6, Leicestershire on June 29 and Lancashire on July 27

Versus LANCASHIRE at Headingley

1. J M Bairstow passed 5,500 First Class career runs
2. S J Croft passed 4,000 Championship runs
3. Yorkshire's run of victories at Headingley came to an end

Versus NORTHAMPTONSHIRE at Northampton

1. A J Finch made his First Class debut for Yorkshire
2. Yorkshire's second-innings total of 546-3 dec was their highest in Northamptonshire
3. A Lyth's 230 was the highest by a Yorkshire player at The County Ground, Northampton. It was also the highest individual score at this venue in a match between the two counties, P A Jaques's 222 for Northamptonshire in 2003 being the previous highest
4. Yorkshire's second-innings opening partnership of 375 by A Lyth and A Z Lees was the highest against Northamptonshire by any team. It equalled the highest opening partnership on the ground by R A White and M J Powell for Northamptonshire against Gloucestershire in 2002. It was the fourth-highest opening stand for Yorkshire, and was the best since P Holmes and H Sutcliffe's record of 555 against Essex at Leyton in 1932
5. Yorkshire's 271-run win was their second highest by runs against Northamptonshire. The 351-run victory in 1947 was the highest
6. Yorkshire's last double over Northamptonshire was in 1981

LV CHAMPIONSHIP FACTFILE *(Continued)*

Versus NOTTINGHAMSHIRE at Headingley

1. A J Finch passed 2,000 First Class career runs
2. M J Lumb passed 9,000 Championship runs
3. A R Adams took his 400th Championship wicket

Versus SUSSEX at Arundel Castle

1. Sussex's tenth-wicket partnership of 68 between J Lewis and L J Hatchett was the highest at this venue
2. J M Bairstow's six catches in Sussex's first innings was the best by a wicket-keeper in a First Class innings at this venue. It was only the second time that a Yorkshire wicket-keeper had taken six against Sussex, R J Blakey at Eastbourne in 1990 being the first. This was the second time Bairstow had taken six catches in an innings, the match against Middlesex at Headingley in 2013 being the other
3. Yorkshire's sixth-wicket partnership of 138 by J M Bairstow and T T Bresnan was Yorkshire's highest for this wicket against Sussex
4. This was Yorkshire's third First Class visit to this ground, and they are still awaiting a victory

Versus WARWICKSHIRE at Birmingham

1. First Class debut for K Carver
2. A J Finch's 110 was his maiden First Class century for Yorkshire
3. J A Brooks took his 200th First Class career wicket when his dismissed K H D Barker in Warwickshire's second innings
4. This was the third time Yorkshire had achieved two innings victories in the same season against Warwickshire, 1919 and 1922 being the other seasons

Versus DURHAM at Headingley

1. Yorkshire's first-innings opening partnership of 270 was their highest against Durham. It was the third best for Yorkshire at Headingley: above it are 290 by P Holmes and H Sutcliffe against Middlesex in 1928 and 272 by M J Wood and J J Sayers against Bangladesh A in 2005
2. A Lyth passed 1,000 First Class runs for the season

LV CHAMPIONSHIP FACTFILE *(Continued)*

Versus MIDDLESEX at Scarborough

1. A Lyth passed 1,000 Championship runs for the season during his first innings
2. S A Patterson took his 200th Championship wicket when he dismissed N R T Gubbins in Middlesex's first innings
3. K S Williamson's dismissal in Yorkshire's second innings was T J Murtagh's 500th Championship wicket
4. J A Brooks took his 50th First Class wicket of the season
5. A U Rashid took his 350th First Class career wicket
6. Yorkshire's second-innings fifth-wicket partnership of 182 by A W Gale and J A Leaning was Yorkshire's highest for this wicket against Middlesex
7. A Lyth, with seven catches in the match, became only the fourth Yorkshire fielder to achieve this feat, J T Tunnicliffe twice — against Leicestershire at Leeds in 1897 and at Leicester in 1900 — A B Sellers against Essex at Leyton in 1933 and E P Robinson against Leicestershire at Bradford in 1938 being the others.

Versus SUSSEX at Scarborough

1. J A Brooks took his 50th Championship wicket of the season with his first dismissal in the match
2. K S Williamson scored his maiden century for Yorkshire
3. Yorkshire's seventh-wicket stand of 157 by K S Williamson and T T Bresnan was Yorkshire's highest for this wicket against Sussex
4. This was Yorkshire's 100th First Class victory at Scarborough and their first home win against Sussex since 1997.

LV CHAMPIONSHIP FACTFILE *(Continued)*

Versus LANCASHIRE at Manchester

1. R J Sidebottom played his 200th First Class match and took his 650th First class wicket, U T Khawaja, his second victim, who fell to the third ball of the match
2. A Lyth hit his career-best score of 251 and passed 6,000 First Class career runs. His innings was the highest by a player batting at No. 1 against Lancashire
3. A U Rashid passed 5,000 First Class career runs in his 159*
4. Yorkshire's sixth-wicket partnership of 296 by A Lyth and A U Rashid was their highest for this wicket against any team. It was also a record partnership for this wicket by any team against Lancashire and at Old Trafford
5. Yorkshire's 610-6 dec was their highest total against Lancashire, and was the fourth highest against Lancashire. Above it are 707-9 dec by Surrey at The Oval in 1990; 634 by Surrey at The Oval in 1989 and 615 by Kent at Tunbridge Wells in 2004. It was the eighth highest total at Old Trafford
6. Yorkshire made three visits to Old Trafford in 2014 in different competitions, and enjoyed three victories.

Versus NOTTINGHAMSHIRE at Nottingham

1. J M Bairstow played his 100th First Class match
2. A Lyth was G Keedy's 650th Championship wicket
3. G S Ballance passed 6,000 First Class career runs
4. T T Bresnan passed 3,000 Championship runs
5. J A Brooks took his 200th Championship wicket with his first of the match
6. 11-37 am on Friday, September 12, 2014: Yorkshire win the County Championship with their fourth victory in a row
7. The last time Yorkshire had four wins in a row was with a run of six victories — five at the end of 1998: Glamorgan at Cardiff, Essex at Scarborough, Surrey and Warwickshire at Leeds and Sussex at Hove followed by Gloucestershire at Leeds in 1999. A loss at Taunton against Somerset ended the run.

Versus SOMERSET at Headingley

1. A Z Lees passed 1,000 First Class runs in a season for Yorkshire
.2. J E Root also passed 1,000 First Class runs for the season split between Yorkshire and England
3. J M Bairstow passed 6,000 First Class career runs
4. 6-15pm on Friday, September 26, 2014, brought Yorkshire's Championship winning season to a close, with Somerset hanging on for a draw and once again ending a winning sequence.

LV Championship Division 1, 2014

Captain: A W Gale

*Captain

§ Wicket-Keeper

Figures in brackets ( ) indicate position in 2nd Innings batting order,
where different from 1st Innings.

DETAILS OF PLAYERS WHO APPEARED FOR YORKSHIRE IN 2014
(ALL FIRST-CLASS MATCHES)

Player	Date of Birth	Birthplace	First-Class debut for Yorkshire	Date Capped
A W Gale	November 28, 1983	Dewsbury	July 21, 2004	Sept. 18, 2008
R J Sidebottom	January 15, 1978	Huddersfield	July 2, 1997	July 23, 2000
T T Bresnan	February 28, 1985	Pontefract	May 14, 2003	July 19, 2006
A U Rashid	February 17, 1988	Bradford	July 19, 2006	Sept. 18, 2008
A Lyth	September 25, 1987	Whitby	May 16, 2007	Aug. 22, 2010
R M Pyrah	November 1, 1982	Dewsbury	August 24, 2004	Aug. 22, 2010
J M Bairstow	September 26, 1989	Bradford	June 11, 2009	Aug. 17, 2011
S A Patterson	October 3, 1983	Beverley	August 3, 2005	May 16, 2012
G S Ballance	November 22, 1989	Harare, Zim	July 11, 2008	Sept. 4, 2012
J E Root	December 30, 1990	Sheffield	May 10, 2010	Sept. 4, 2012
J A Brooks	June 4, 1984	Oxford	April 5, 2013	Aug 2, 2013
L E Plunkett	April 6, 1985	Middlesbrough	April 5, 2013	Aug 2, 2013
K S Williamson	August 8, 1990	Tauranga, N Zealand	August 21, 2013	Aug 21, 2013
A Z Lees	April 14, 1993	Halifax	June 5, 1990	Sept 23, 2014
A J Finch	November 17, 1986	Colac, Australia	May 31, 2014	May 31, 2014
Azeem Rafiq	February 27, 1991	Karachi, Pak	June 5, 2009	—
A J Hodd	January 12, 1984	Chichester	August 15, 2012	—
J A Leaning	October 18, 1993	Bristol	June 21, 2013	—
D M Hodgson	February 26, 1990	Northallerton	April 1, 2014	—
K Carver	March 26, 1996	Northallerton	June 22, 2014	—

Match-By-Match Reports   **NIGEL PULLAN**

LV County Championship Division 1
Somerset v. Yorkshire

Played at The County Ground, Taunton, on April 13, 14, 15 and 16, 2014
Match drawn at 4.51pm on the Fourth Day

Toss won by Somerset — Yorkshire 11 points, Somerset 9 points

Close of play: First Day, Yorkshire 342-5 (Rashid 84*, Hodd 22*); Second Day, Somerset
166-3 (Petersen 12*, Hildreth 16*); Third Day, Somerset 530-9 (Mescehde 45*, Overton 7*)

YORKSHIRE

First Innings		Second innings	
A Lyth, c Gregory b Overton	85	c sub (J H Davey) b Hildreth	54
A Z Lees, b Meschede	34	c Kieswetter b Meschede	47
K S Williamson, c Jones b Meschede	0	not out	57
* A W Gale, lbw b Meschede	24	c Kieswetter b Petersen	11
G S Ballance, lbw b Gregory	77	c sub (G H Dockrell) b Myburgh	5
A U Rashid, c Kieswetter b Overton	108	not out	8
§ A J Hodd, c Trescothick b Overton	55		
L E Plunkett, not out	19		
R J Sidebottom, c Trescothick b Myburgh	13		
S A Patterson, b Thomas	7		
J A Brooks, lbw b Myburgh	6		
Extras lb 10, w 2, nb 10	22	Extras b 5, lb 1, w 1, nb 4	11
Total	450	Total (4 wkts dec)	193

Bonus points — Yorkshire 5, Somerset 1   Score at 110 overs: 401-5

FoW:
1st   1-69 (Lees), 2-71 (Williamson), 3-133 (Gale), 4-179 (Lyth), 5-294 (Ballance)
       6-402 (Hodd), 7-403 (Rashid), 8-430 (Sidebottom), 9-441 (Patterson), 10-450 (Brooks)
2nd   1-100 (Lees), 2-120 (Lyth), 3-150 (Gale), 4-163 (Ballance)

	O	M	R	W		O	M	R	W
Thomas	29	5	80	1	Gregory	14	5	44	0
Gregory	30	7	113	1	Meschede	11	5	31	1
Meschede	28	5	105	3	Myburgh	25	7	54	1
Overton	24	6	72	3	Petersen	15	2	37	1
Myburgh	21.5	0	70	2	Hildreth	6	0	21	1

SOMERSET

* M E Trescothick, b Sidebottom	20
C R Jones, c Lees b Plunkett	75
N R D Compton, b Plunkett	32
A N Petersen, c Hodd b Williamson	24
J C Hildreth, lbw b Brooks	67
§ C Kieswetter, c Lyth b Williamson	63
J G Myburgh, lbw b Rashid	91
L Gregory, c Hodd b Plunkett	69
C A J Meschede, not out	59
A C Thomas, c Hodd b Plunkett	1
C Overton, lbw b Patterson	15
Extras b 14, lb 7, nb 16	37
Total	553

Bonus points — Somerset 3, Yorkshire 1   Score at 110 overs: 342-6

FoW: 1-36 (Trescothick), 2-127 (Compton), 3-136 (Jones), 4-208 (Petersen), 5-252 (Hildreth),
       6-364 (Kieswetter), 7-464 (Myburgh), 8-490 (Gregory), 9-496 (Thomas), 10-553 (Overton)

	O	M	R	W
Sidebottom	27	11	54	1
Brooks	23	4	92	1
Patterson	31.5	10	74	1
Plunkett	28	1	117	4
Rashid	27	2	127	1
Lyth	6	1	23	0
Williamson	15	3	45	2

Umpires: N G C Cowley and M J Saggers   Scorers: J T Potter and G A Stickley

Early wake-up call for bowlers

Yorkshire's season began with their longest journey, unexpected spring sunshine and a placid wicket where bowlers struggled to make any impact.

Put in to bat, and without the injured Root and Bairstow, Yorkshire batted well, although the lower order disappointed.

Meschede took the first three wickets, including New Zealand overseas player Kane Williamson for a duck, but Lyth made an attractive 85 before falling to a remarkable catch by Gregory at mid-wicket.

The partnership of Ballance and Rashid gave substance to the innings. Rashid hit his third hundred against Somerset in the last three Championship games, and looked an accomplished

ADIL RASHID: Fine hat-trick of hundreds v. same county

batsman, while Hodd gave sound support with 55. The last four wickets added only 48. Craig Overton, one of twins from Barnstaple on the Somerset staff, showed his potential as a fast bowler.

By the close of the second day with the home side on 166-3 Yorkshire were in a good position, and Trescothick and Compton were back in the pavilion. Chris Jones, last year's captain of Durham University, made a resolute 75. On Tuesday Somerset batted very well to reach 530-9, and ultimately 553 to lead by 103. No one made a century, but Myburgh, having moved from Durham, made 91 and there were 60s for Hildreth, Gregory and Kieswetter — whose 63 included two big sixes. Plunkett was particularly sharp, and took four wickets. Patterson and Sidebottom were economical, but found little help from this unresponsive wicket.

It is a concern that Yorkshire conceded too many runs as Somerset reached 553. A similar situation occurred at Scarborough last year with Durham, but here there was insufficient time for Somerset to exploit their superiority. If Yorkshire had lost early wickets it could have been difficult, but Lees, Lyth and Williamson steered them to safety. Bowling Championship sides out twice, as Yorkshire did last year, remains a priority. They left this first match at Taunton on April 16 and meet Somerset again at Headingley as late as September 23. Is this a record?

LV County Championship Division 1
Yorkshire v. Northamptonshire

Played at Headingley, Leeds, on April 20, 21, 22 and 23, 2014

Yorkshire won by an innings and 120 runs at 12.54pm on the Fourth Day

Toss won by Yorkshire — Yorkshire 23 points, Northamptonshire 2 points

Close of play: First Day, Yorkshire 328-7 (Ballance 117*, Sidebottom 4*); Second Day, Northamptonshire 94 all out; Third Day, Northamptonshire 149-4 (Newton 11*, Chambers 0*)

YORKSHIRE

A Lyth, c Murphy b Azharullah		11
A Lees, lbw b Hall		90
K S Williamson, lbw b Hall		3
* A W Gale, lbw b Azharullah		13
G S Ballance, lbw b Hall		174
A U Rashid, lbw b Crook		33
§ A J Hodd, lbw b Chambers		21
L E Plunkett, lbw b Hall		11
R J Sidebottom, lbw b Middlebrook		15
S A Patterson, not out		17
J A Brooks, not out		37
Extras b 13, lb 11, nb 10		34
Total (9 wkts dec)		459

Bonus points — Yorkshire 4, Northamptonshire 2

Score at 110 overs: 384-7

FoW: 1-15 (Lyth), 2-21 (Williamson), 3-57 (Gale), 4-213 (Lees), 5-275 (Rashid) 6-309 (Hodd), 7-324 (Plunkett), 8-396 (Sidebottom), 9-398 (Ballance)

	O	M	R	W
Chambers	22	4	77	1
Azharullah	25	7	78	2
Hall	28	3	103	4
Crook	24	2	93	1
Middlebrook	23	8	68	1
Spriegel	3	0	16	0

NORTHAMPTONSHIRE

First Innings			Second innings	
* S D Peters, lbw b Sidebottom	9	c Hodd b Sidebottom	11
J D Middlebrook, b Brooks	6	c Hodd b Brooks	63
K J Coetzer, c Lyth b Sidebottom	10	c Hodd b Sidebottom	39
M N W Spriegel, not out	29	lbw b Brooks	7
R I Newton, c Hodd b Brooks	2	c Lees b Williamson	11
A J Hall, c Williamson b Brooks	6	(7) c and b Plunkett	12
D J Willey, c Plunkett b Brooks	0	(8) c Hodd b Patterson	20
S P Crook, c Rashid b Brooks	8	(9) c Rashid b Patterson	5
§ D Murphy, c Hodd b Plunkett	0	(10) not out	23
M A Chambers, b Sidebottom	10	(6) c Lyth b Brooks	1
M Azharullah, c Ballance b Sidebottom	0	c Hodd b Rashid	23
Extras b 4, lb 8, nb 2	14	Extras b 20, lb 2, nb 8	30
Total	94	Total	245

Bonus points — Yorkshire 3

FoW:	1st	1-16 (Middlebrook), 2-16 (Peters), 3-27 (Coetzer), 4-39 (Newton), 5-45 (Hall) 6-55 (Willey), 7-65 (Crook), 8-68 (Murphy), 9-94 (Chambers), 10-94 (Azharullah)
FoW:	2nd	1-24 (Peters), 2-113 (Coetzer), 3-132 (Spriegel), 4-145 (Middlebrook), 5-149 (Newton) 6-151 (Chambers), 7-181 (Hall), 8-190 (Crook), 9-195 (Willey), 10-245 (Azharullah)

	O	M	R	W		O	M	R	W
Sidebottom	9	2	16	4	Sidebottom	18	4	34	3
Brooks	12	2	36	5	Brooks	21	3	76	3
Patterson	4	1	10	0	Williamson	3	1	5	0
Plunkett	5	1	20	1	Rashid	7.4	2	18	1
					Patterson	14	3	28	2
					Plunkett	15	2	62	1

Umpires: M R Benson and I J Gould

Scorers: J T Potter and A C Kingston

Easter parade for the pacemen

GARY BALLANCE: His 173 showed international class

The home season began with a convincing win after Yorkshire had elected to bat despite doubts on an overcast, showery Easter Day morning.

Ballance and Lees justified the decision after the loss of three wickets. Lees was a watchful opener, who played some fine drives through extra-cover, but lost impetus after reaching 50 when he was dropped at slip and survived a stumping chance.

Ballance hit his Championship best 173 of considerable quality to emphasise his growing international stature. Each of the remaining batsmen contributed, and there was a carefree last-wicket stand by Patterson and Brooks before Gale declared.

There were eight lbw dismissals, equalling a world record; if Patterson or Brooks had chosen self sacrifice Yorkshire could have made it nine.

Northamptonshire's batting was very disappointing as Sidebottom and Brooks bowled them out for an abject 94. Some of the middle-order appeared to lack application, and no one stayed with Spriegel. Sidebottom conceded only 16 runs in nine overs, removing Peters and Coetzer. Brooks dominated proceedings on Easter Monday, bowling Middlebrook with an excellent delivery and taking four more wickets from the Rugby Stand end. He bowls off a relatively short run, but gains pace from a good body action, a quick arm and some inspired extra energy when things are going right. He can move the ball both ways, and his 5-36 added a Yorkshire best bowling analysis to a top score of 37.

Northamptonshire showed greater resolution in the second innings as Middlebrook and Coetzer put on 89 and Middlebrook had a creditable 63. There was an inevitability as Sidebottom and Brooks again took wickets and Patterson claimed two. Both sides had players unavailable, but the visitors' injured batsmen and Willey's inability to bowl were the greater handicap. Yorkshire gave an exemplary display of aggressive and skilful cricket, their catching and outfielding a joy to behold.

LV County Championship Division 1
Middlesex v. Yorkshire

Played at Lord's on April 27, 28, 29 and 30, 2014
Middlesex won by 7 wickets at 2.56pm on the Fourth Day

Toss won by Middlesex   Middlesex 19 points, Yorkshire 3 points

Close of play: First Day, Middlesex 64-3 (Morgan 24*, Dexter 0*); Second Day, Yorkshire 213-4 (Ballance 10*, Patterson 4*); Third Day, Middlesex 230-1 (Rogers 122*, Malan 28*)

First Innings	YORKSHIRE		Second innings	
A Lyth, c Simpson b Finn		34	c Rayner b Finn	54
A Z Lees, c Simpson b Murtagh		2	b Rayner	33
K S Williamson, c Rayner b Harris		30	c Robson b Finn	37
* J E Root, lbw b Finn		0	lbw b Finn	63
G S Ballance, c Robson b Harris		20	c Finn b Murtagh	130
A U Rashid, c Rayner b Murtagh		6	(7) c Simpson b Murtagh	43
§ A J Hodd, c Robson b Harris		5	(8) c Harris b Finn	22
L E Plunkett, not out		56	(9) b Dexter	0
R J Sidebottom, c Robson b Finn		12	(10) c Simpson b Rayner	5
S A Patterson, b Finn		2	(6) c Malan b Dexter	6
J A Brooks, b Murtagh		1	not out	10
Extras b 5, lb 1, nb 4		10	Extras lb 13	13
Total		178	Total	416

Bonus points — Middlesex 3

FoW: 1-3 (Lees), 2-55 (Lyth), 3-55 (Root), 4-74 (Williamson), 5-93 (Rashid)
1st   6-98 (Hodd), 7-113 (Ballance), 8-161 (Sidebottom), 9-173 (Patterson), 10-178 (Brooks)
FoW: 1-82 (Lees), 2-96 (Lyth), 3-194 (Williamson), 4-199 (Root), 5-216 (Patterson)
2nd   6-288 (Rashid), 7-333 (Hodd), 8-333 (Plunkett), 9-350 (Sidebottom), 10-416 (Ballance)

	O	M	R	W		O	M	R	W
Murtagh	18.2	5	48	3	Murtagh	21.5	6	77	2
Harris	15	4	42	3	Harris	25	7	62	0
Finn	17	5	50	4	Finn	22	3	89	4
Dexter	5	2	21	0	Dexter	26	1	108	2
Rayner	3	0	11	0	Rayner	16	2	67	2

First Innings	MIDDLESEX		Second innings	
* C J L Rogers, c Lyth b Brooks		1	not out	241
S D Robson, c Hodd b Brooks		7	c Ballance b Brook	77
D J Malan, b Sidebottom		31	lbw b Williamson	35
E J G Morgan, c Lyth b Sidebottom		33	c Lyth b Williamson	27
N J Dexter, c Hodd b Sidebottom		0	not out	72
J L Denly, lbw b Sidebottom		7		
§ J A Simpson, b Plunkett		6		
O P Rayner, b Brooks		15		
J A R Harris, not out		7		
T J Murtagh, b Plunkett		3		
S T Finn, c Plunkett b Patterson		7		
Extras lb 5, w1		6	Extras b 8, lb 4, nb 8	20
Total		123	Total (3 wkts)	472

Bonus points — Yorkshire 3

FoW: 1-1 (Rogers), 2-20 (Robson), 3-57 (Malan), 4-70 (Dexter), 5-80 (Denly)
1st   6-83 (Morgan), 7-95 (Simpson), 8-107 (Rayner), 9-110 (Murtagh), 10-123 (Finn)
2nd   1-181 (Robson), 2-257 (Malan), 3-327 (Morgan)

	O	M	R	W		O	M	R	W
Sidebottom	16	6	34	4	Sidebottom	20	3	80	1
Brooks	16	3	47	3	Brooks	22	3	134	1
Patterson	4.5	2	21	1	Patterson	11	2	40	0
Plunkett	9	2	16	2	Plunkett	13	2	57	0
					Root	3	0	11	0
					Rashid	18	0	69	0
					Williamson	14.4	3	69	1

Umpires: R J Bailey and S J O'Shaughnessy   Scorers: J T Potter and D K Shelley

Magnificence destroys hope

The visitors were in control until mid-way through the third day when skipper Rogers played an innings of exceptional quality. Middlesex ran to a remarkable victory with the third-highest winning total in the fourth innings of a Championship match.

Gale left himself out of the side, conceding the captaincy to Root, who had recovered from his broken thumb. Root lost the toss, Yorkshire were invited to bat and struggled all day against a three-man seam attack with Finn, in rehabilitation from his problems in Australia, maintaining his encouraging start to the season with three wickets.

Had it not been for Plunkett's assertive 56 not out Yorkshire would have had a meagre total.

Middlesex fared even less well, losing three wickets on the first evening and collapsing to 123 all out next morning. Sidebottom, in his 100th first-class game for Yorkshire, destroyed the middle-order, and Morgan, ambitious to play Test cricket, was brilliantly caught by Lyth high above his head. Brooks took early wickets, and Patterson and Plunkett contributed at the end.

The match now changed character.

**RYAN SIDEBOTTOM
Century celebration**

Most pitches no longer deteriorate, and batting actually becomes easier as Yorkshire demonstrated by making 416. Ballance, who made his fifth century in eight Yorkshire innings, was on 74 when Brooks arrived but cut loose to finish with 130 — including six sixes, four of them conceded by Rayner. Root's 63 was some consolation for his first innings duck. Set a formidable 472 to win, Middlesex were well placed on 230-1 at the close. On Wednesday Rogers almost doubled his 122 to reach 241 not out — in his opinion his best-ever innings despite two Test centuries in Melbourne and Sydney during the winter. He hit 37 fours and gave no chance. Dexter put on an unbroken 145 for the fourth wicket with Rogers, who was magnificent and won a match that had appeared well beyond Middlesex. Yorkshire bowlers did lose line and length and should have made more progress against the other batsmen.

LV County Championship Division 1
Durham v. Yorkshire

Played at Durham ICG, Chester-le-Street, on May 4, 5, 6 and 7, 2014

Match drawn at 5.32pm on the Fourth Day

Toss won by Yorkshire   Yorkshire 11 points, Durham 9 points

Close of play: First Day, Yorkshire 299-3 (Gale 35*, Bairstow 22*); Second Day, Durham 62-1 (Stoneman 48*, Borthwick 1*); Third Day, Durham 361-8 (Harrison 15*, Onions 12*)

YORKSHIRE

A Lyth, c Borthwick b Harrison	....	104
A Z Lees, c Mustard b Harrison	....	9
K S Williamson, b Rushworth	....	97
* A W Gale, c Mustard b Jennings	....	124
J M Bairstow, lbw b Rushworth	....	95
A U Rashid, c Sangakkara b Rushworth	....	68
§ A J Hodd, not out	....	41
T T Bresnan, c Mustard b Onions	....	1
L E Plunkett, lbw b Onions	....	0
R J Sidebottom		
J A Brooks	Did not bat	
Extras b 7, lb 13, w 5, nb 25	....	50
Total (8 wkts dec)		589

Bonus points — Yorkshire 4, Durham 1   Score at 110 overs: 385-3

FoW: 1-29 (Lees), 2-208 (Lyth), 3-257 (Williamson), 4-455 (Bairstow), 5-501 (Gale), 6-588 (Rashid), 7-589 (Bresnan), 8-589 (Plunkett)

	O	M	R	W
Onions	32.2	7	83	2
Rushworth	29	6	113	3
Harrison	25	2	110	2
Wood	30	5	90	0
Jennings	13	2	39	1
Collingwood	14	2	62	0
Stoneman	20	0	72	0

DURHAM

First Innings			Second Innings	
M D Stoneman, lbw b Plunkett	131		run out (Plunkett)	4
K K Jennings, c Hodd b Sidebottom	9		not out	54
S G Borthwick, lbw b Bresnan	2		c Hodd b Brooks	0
K C Sangakkara, c Lyth b Sidebottom	0		c Lyth b Sidebottom	14
M J Richardson, st Hodd b Rashid	148		c Hodd b Rashid	7
* P D Collinwood, b Rashid	10		not out	14
§ P Mustard, c Hodd b Plunkett	3			
M A Wood, b Rashid	7			
J Harrison, b Williamson	3			
G Onions, c Hodd b Plunkett	2			
C Rushworth, not out	2			
Extras b 4, lb 10, nb 10	24		Extras b 2, lb 2, w 1, nb 2	7
Total	388		Total (4 wkts)	100

Bonus points — Durham 3, Yorkshire 2   Score at 110 overs: 343-8

FoW: 1st 1-48 (Jennings), 2-69 (Borthwick), 3-70 (Sangakkara), 4-206 (Stoneman), 5-256 (Collingwood), 6-278 (Mustard), 7-314 (Wood), 8-339 (Richardson), 9-384 (Harrison), 10-388 (Onions)

2nd 1-10 (Stoneman), 2-10 (Borthwick), 3-35 (Sangakkara), 4-42 (Richardson)

	O	M	R	W		O	M	R	W
Sidebottom	30	7	69	2	Brooks	14	6	25	1
Brooks	21	9	94	0	Plunkett	8	4	18	0
Bresnan	30	14	59	1	Sidebottom	5	2	18	1
Williamson	9	6	5	1	Bresnan	7	6	2	0
Plunkett	25	6	74	3	Rashid	14	6	22	1
Rashid	23	7	73	3	Williamson	4	1	10	0
					Bairstow	1	0	1	0

Umpires: J W Lloyds and A G Wharf   Scorers: J T Potter and B Hunt

Third: M J Saggers

Durham v. Yorkshire
Winning, but not winners

Yorkshire won the toss, batted on an overcast day, and were justified as they compiled a large score over most of two days on a ground where high scoring recently has been infrequent.

Root and Ballance were on an England training session for the One-Day International with Scotland, and so missed one of the most important matches of the season.

The batsmen chosen proved more than equal to the task. Lyth and Williamson gradually

ANDREW GALE: Showed his true fighting qualities in top-score 124

took control, and Lyth played his attacking strokes on a sunny afternoon before succumbing to the left-arm Harrison, who had been Durham's best bowler. Williamson again just missed his first Yorkshire hundred. Next day Gale and Bairstow took over, Gale having been dropped by Sangakkara, playing for Durham prior to Sri Lanka's tour of England.

They made 152 runs in two hours before lunch to emphasise the dominance of bat over ball on a benign pitch. Bairstow played with freedom and confidence until he received what TV replays indicated was a dubious lbw decision. Gale, who had dropped himself at Lord's, showed his fighting qualities to make an enterprising 124, while Rashid and Hodd contributed to the formidable total. The last two wickets fell in two balls but a declaration precluded an Onions hat-trick.

It proved impossible to bowl Durham out twice, although weather interruptions played a part. Stoneman and Richardson enabled Durham to reach a respectable total, both scoring centuries as they had last year at Scarborough. Stoneman made a dominant 131 while Richardson stayed in to guide Durham towards 388 before being stumped by Hodd off Rashid for 148. Rashid and Plunkett deserved their three wickets apiece, and the follow-on was enforced. Durham then lost four wickets for 50, including Sangakkara whose hesitant 14 followed his first-innings duck. Yorkshire were in a winning position, but were thwarted by Jennings with 54 not out and a resolute Collingwood, who stayed two hours for 14 to save his side from any possibility of defeat.

LV County Championship Division 1
Yorkshire v. Warwickshire

Played at Headingley, Leeds, on May 11, 12 and 13, 2014
Yorkshire won by an innings and 155 runs at 6.28pm on the Third Day

Toss won by Warwickshire   Yorkshire 23 points, Warwickshire 3 points

Close of play: First Day, Yorkshire 310-8 (Plunkett 4*, Patterson 12*); Second Day, Warwickshire 136-6 (Bell 58*, Barker 4*)

YORKSHIRE

A Lyth, c and b Woakes	32
J E Root, b Barker	69
K S Williamson, lbw b Barker	75
* A W Gale, b Woakes	5
G S Ballance, lbw b Barker	4
§ J M Bairstow, b Wright	15
A U Rashid, c Porterfield b Wright	10
T T Bresnan, b Woakes	61
L E Plunkett, c Porterfield b Woakes	86
S A Patterson, c Bell b Patel	43
J A Brooks, not out	14
Extras b 12, lb 14, nb 4	30
Total	444

Bonus points — Yorkshire 4, Warwickshire 2   Score at 110 overs: 363-8

FoW: 1-91 (Lyth), 2-111 (Root), 3-128 (Gale), 4-137 (Ballance), 5-159 (Bairstow), 6-181 (Rashid), 7-294 (Williamson), 8-294 (Bresnan), 9-400 (Patterson), 10-444 (Plunkett)

	O	M	R	W
Barker	29	8	82	3
Wright	26	3	101	2
Jones	18	1	86	0
Woakes	27.3	7	68	4
Patel	22	3	78	1
Javid	2	0	3	0

WARWICKSHIRE

	First Innings		Second Innings	
V Chopra, b Brooks	3	lbw b Bresnan	13
W T S Porterfield, c Bresnan b Plunkett	11	c Lyth b Brooks	6
L J Evans, c Ballance b Patterson	14	b Brooks	0
* I R Bell, c Bairstow b Brooks	97	c Williamson b Bresnan	4
A Javid, lbw b Brooks	6	lbw b Brooks	5
§ T R Ambrose, c Ballance b Bresnan	21	b Patterson	28
C R Woakes, b Williamson	15	not out	25
K H D Barker, c Bairstow b Plunkett	20	c Bairstow b Patterson	4
J S Patel, b Patterson	0	c Lyth b Brooks	0
R A Jones, lbw b Rashid	5	lbw b Plunkett	0
C J C Wright, not out	0	c Bresnan b Plunkett	0
Extras b 1, w 1, nb 6	8	Extras b 1, lb 3	4
Total	200	Total	89

Bonus points — Warwickshire 1, Yorkshire 3

FoW: 1st: 1-3 (Chopra), 2-25 (Evans), 3-37 (Porterfield), 4-49 (Javid), 5-88 (Ambrose), 6-128 (Woakes), 7-178 (Barker), 8-181 (Patel), 9-198 (Jones), 10-200 (Bell)

FoW: 2nd: 1-21 (Porterfield), 2-21 (Chopra), 3-25 (Evans), 4-25 (Bell), 5-31 (Javid), 6-80 (Ambrose), 7-84 (Barker), 8-89 (Jones), 9-89 (Wright)

	O	M	R	W		O	M	R	W
Bresnan	18	5	33	1	Brooks	12	5	37	4
Brooks	11.1	2	39	4	Bresnan	9	1	26	2
Plunkett	13	4	34	2	Plunkett	5.2	1	12	2
Patterson	19	3	44	2	Patterson	4	0	10	2
Rashid	16	5	42	1	Williamson	1	1	0	0
Williamson	4	0	7	1					

Umpires: G D Lloyd and R T Robinson   Scorers: J T Potter and M D Smith

Master class from the quicks

Dominant Yorkshire won in three days. Rain threatened throughout the game, but disruption from showers was remarkably short.

Bell put Yorkshire in on a blustery morning, but by lunchtime his decision seemed unwise as Root, Lyth and Williamson put on 105.

Warwickshire's bowlers were more accurate after lunch,

Safe as houses: Kane Williamson holds Ian Bell in Warwickshire's second innings as fellow slips Adam Lyth and Gary Ballance look on.

reducing Yorkshire to 181-6 with left-armer Barker taking three wickets. They could not dismiss Williamson, whose concentration and resolution in a four-and-a-half hour 75 sustained the innings. He was well supported by Bresnan in a stand of 113 until both were out at 294. Two partnerships followed around Plunkett: first he and Patterson added 106, then Brooks joined him for a last-wicket assault. Plunkett's 86 was his highest score for Yorkshire, and one of his four sixes threatened the glass front of the East Stand.

Yorkshire now had to dismiss Warwickshire twice. This Headingley pitch had pace and bounce, and the four quick bowlers worked as a team — Brooks and Plunkett fast and hostile, Bresnan and Patterson steady and accurate. Gale could utilise them strategically in short spells. The benefits of Coach Jason Gillespie's advice and encouragement as an experienced Test Match bowler were apparent. Wickets fell regularly, but Bell played an impeccable innings. Correct and assured with a classical technique, he missed a deserved century when last out for 97.

In their second innings the visitors were soon 31-5, including Bell caught by Williamson off Bresnan (see above), and after a two-hour rain delay the last three wickets fell in four overs. Perhaps Brooks should receive the accolade of outstanding bowler, but all four pacemen were very good, and spinners Rashid and Williamson played their part. The bowlers were assisted by some excellent fielding, with Ballance, Williamson and Lyth taking impressive slip catches, but none better than Bresnan's dive at fourth slip to despatch Wright off Plunkett and send us all home late on Tuesday with a three-day win.

LV County Championship Division 1
Yorkshire v. Lancashire

Played at Headingley, Leeds, on May 25, 26, 27 and 28, 2014
Match drawn at 11.30am on the Fourth Day

Toss won by Yorkshire   Lancashire 11 points, Yorkshire 9 points
Close of play: First Day, Lancashire 87-2 (Horton 48*, Prince 0*); Second Day, Yorkshire 29-0 (Lyth 15*, Lees 8*); Third Day, Lancashire 48-3 (Croft 23*, Smith 5*)

First Innings — LANCASHIRE

			Second innings	
P J Horton, b Brooks	66		c Lyth b Bresnan	6
L M Reece, c Sidebottom b Plunkett	23		lbw b Bresnan	10
K R Brown, lbw b Bresnan	3		lbw b Bresnan	0
A G Prince, lbw b Plunkett	29		not out	23
S J Croft, c Bairstow b Plunkett	5		not out	5
T C Smith, b Brooks	54			
§ A L Davies, c Lyth b Brooks	17			
* G Chapple, b Brooks	33			
K W Hogg, not out	47			
Kabir Ali, c Hodd b Bresnan	12			
S C Kerrigan, lbw b Plunkett	6			
Extras b 5, lb1 7, nb 8	30		Extras b 4	4
Total	325		Total (3 wkts)	48

Bonus points — Lancashire 3, Yorkshire 3

FoW: 1-70 (Reece), 2-86 (Brown), 3-123 (Horton). 4-136 (Croft), 5-155 (Prince)
1st 6-183 (Davies), 7-251 (Chapple), 8-267 (Smith), 7-298 (Ali), 10-325 (Kerrigan)
2nd 1-10 (Horton), 2-10 (Brown), 3-31 (Reece)

	O	M	R	W		O	M	R	W
Sidebottom	14	1	39	0	Bresnan	7	3	9	3
Brooks	31	9	90	5	Brooks	4	0	11	0
Bresnan	27	7	69	1	Plunkett	2	0	15	0
Plunkett	21.3	2	74	4	Rashid	2	0	4	0
Williamson	6	4	2	0	Williamson	2	1	5	0
Rashid	5	0	29	0					

YORKSHIRE

A Lyth, c Reece b Smith		50
A Z Lees, c Davies b Smith		21
K S Williamson, c Croft b Smith		4
* A W Gale, not out		95
§ J M Bairstow, lbw b Hogg		20
A U Rashid, c Davies b Smith		12
A J Hodd, b Kabir Ali		0
T T Bresnan, c Horton b Kabir Ali		1
L E Plunkett, lbw b Smith		12
R J Sidebottom, c Smith b Kerrigan		9
J A Brooks, c and b Chapple		0
S A Patterson	Did not bat	
Extras b 2, lb 8, w 3, nb 6		19
Total		243

T T Bresnan replaced S A Patterson after tea on the first day

Bonus points — Yorkshire1, Lancashire 3

FoW: 1-66 (Lees), 2-82 (Williamson), 3-97 (Lyth), 4-136 (Bairstow), 5-178 (Rashid)
6-179 (Hodd), 7-183 (Bresnan), 8-196 (Plunkett), 9-234 (Sidebottom), 10-243 (Brooks)

	O	M	R	W
Hogg	15	2	69	1
Chapple	20	6	56	1
Kabir Ali	15	4	35	2
Smith	13	3	49	5
Kerrigan	8	0	24	1

Umpires: I J Gould and P Willey   Scorers: J T Potter and D M White

Red Rose on top before storm

TIM BRESNAN: 3-9 burst before weather closed in

The first *Roses* Championship match for three seasons, in which Lancashire were marginally the better side, was one of the least distinguished as a potentially interesting last day was entirely lost to rain.

On Sunday there was a minute's silence in memory of the late Philip Sharpe. Yorkshire won the toss, invited Lancashire to bat and rain came to delay proceedings for nearly six hours.

Horton and Reece made a good start. Horton is now an experienced opener, inclined to caution and resolute against Yorkshire. Reece is a graduate of the successful Leeds/Bradford MCCU side.

Yorkshire took two wickets on the curtailed first day, but the prospect of a big innings from Prince was ended by Plunkett, who also dismissed Croft. Smith, who usually does well in *Roses* matches, made a valuable 54 before being bowled by Brooks.

At 183-6 Yorkshire were in a strong position, but the last four wickets added 142 runs. Lancashire's Skipton-born skipper, Chapple, made 33, and Sonny Ramadhin's grandson, Hogg, 47 not out. Kabir Ali, who made his Test debut at Headingley, batted at No 10. Brooks and Plunkett took the wickets, but perhaps at too great a cost.

Yorkshire's batting on the third day was disappointing apart from Gale and Lyth. Smith had more to contribute, as his medium-pace bowling accounted for the top three. Lyth made 50, but fell straight afterwards, and so much depended on Gale. There was an unusual incident when Gale, given out caught behind, made a visible and no doubt verbal protest, and umpire Peter Willey called him back, later reporting him with consequences to follow. Gale made an undefeated 95 and deserved his hundred. Yorkshire were 82 behind, but Bresnan set about the Lancashire openers, claiming 3-9 before bad light ended play. The *Roses* fixture saw more play than Middlesex and Sussex, who lost all four days at Merchant Taylors' School, Northwood.

LV County Championship Division 1
Northamptonshire v. Yorkshire

Played at The County Ground, Northampton, on May 31 and June 1, 2 and 3, 2014
Yorkshire won by 271 runs at 2.45pm on the Fourth Day

Toss won by Northamptonshire — Yorkshire 19 points, Northamptonshire 5 points

Close of play: First Day, Northamptonshire 191-7 (Duckett 19*, Butler 13*); Second Day, Yorkshire 237-0 (Lyth 116*, Lees 105*); Third Day, Northamptonshire 66-3 (Spriegel 14*; Keogh 19*)

YORKSHIRE

	First Innings		Second innings	
A Lyth, lbw b Chambers	0	c Duckett b Hall	230
A Z Lees, c Duckett b Azharullah	15	c Chambers b Spriegel	138
J A Leaning, c Middlebrook b Hall	15	(4) not out	52
* A W Gale, c Hall b Butler	0		
§ J M Bairstow, b Butler	9	not out	25
A J Finch, b Azharullah	34	(3) c Peters b Chambers	63
A U Rashid, c Duckett b Butler	11		
T T Bresnan, b Butler	0		
L E Plunkett, c Duckett b Chambers	25		
S A Patterson, c Duckett b Azharullah	4		
J A Brooks, not out	8		
R M Pyrah Did not bat			
Extras b 9, lb 6	15	Extras b13, lb10, w7, nb8	38
Total	136	Total (3 wkts dec)	546

Bonus points — Northamptonshire 3

T T Bresnan replaced R M Pyrah after lunch on the First Day

FoW: 1-4 (Lyth), 2-8 (Lees), 3-29 (Gale), 4-41 (Leaning), 5-45 (Bairstow),
1st 6-87 (Rashid), 7-95 (Finch), 8-95 (Bresnan), 9-110 (Patterson), 10-136 (Plunkett)
2nd 1-375 (Lees), 3-424 (Lyth), 3-486 (Finch)

	O	M	R	W		O	M	R	W
Chambers	9.3	2	23	2	Chambers	27	3	100	1
Azharullah	14	4	41	3	Azharullah	27	3	102	0
Butler	11	3	41	4	Butler	16	4	77	0
Hall	6	0	16	1	Middlebrook	26	4	69	0
					Hall	26	4	96	1
					Spriegel	25	5	79	1

NORTHAMPTONSHIRE

	First Innings		Second innings	
* S D Peters, c Lees b Brooks	27	c Lyth b Bresnan	23
J D Middlebrook, c Finch b Bresnan	70	c Bairstow b Bresnan	6
D J G Sales, b Brooks	6	lbw b Brooks	0
M N W Spriegel, lbw b Brooks	8	lbw b Bresnan	14
R I Keogh, c and b Brooks	1	c Bairstow b Brooks	25
R I Newton, lbw b Bresnan	19	c Finch b Plunkett	33
A J Hall, lbw b Plunkett	16	c Lees b Plunkett	24
§ B M Duckett, b Rashid	51	c Bairstow b Plunkett	10
I G Butler, c Plunkett b Patterson	14	lbw b Rashid	0
M A Chambers, c Lees b Rashid	17	b Plunkett	10
M Azharullah, not out	9	not out	2
Extras b 5, lb 3, w 1, nb 4	13	Extras lb 7, nb 6	13
Total	251	Total	160

Bonus points — Northamptonshire 2, Yorkshire 3

FoW: 1-44 (Peters), 2-60 (Sales), 3-84 (Spriegel), 4-90 (Keogh), 5-129 (Newton);
1st 6-138 (Middlebrook), 7-173 (Hall), 8-200 (Butler), 9-242 (Duckett), 10-251 (Chambers)
FoW: 1-31 (Middlebrook), 2-32 (Peters), 3-32 (Sales), 4-66 (Spriegel), 5-78 (Keogh);
2nd 6-109 (Hall), 7-135 (Duckett), 8-148 (Newton), 9-158 (Butler), 10-160 (Chambers)

	O	M	R	W		O	M	R	W
Bresnan	19	2	67	2	Bresnan	16	2	46	3
Brooks	17	1	78	4	Brooks	16	4	41	2
Patterson	15	5	42	1	Patterson	9	4	18	0
Plunkett	8	0	55	1	Plunkett	14.1	2	42	4
Rashid	2	1	1	2	Rashid	9	4	6	1

Umpires: N G B Cook and P J Hartley — Scorers: J T Potter and A C Kingston

Lyth and Lees smash records

Yorkshire turned this match around after a first-innings deficit of 115 to win by 271 runs.

On a sullen, breezy Saturday morning, after perhaps too brief a respite from *T20* blasting, they were put in by the host.

No batsman played a major innings. Australian debutant Finch made 34, and there were three ducks. Chambers, Hall, Azharullah and especially New Zealand Test bowler Butler took advantage of the conditions and some indifferent batting.

By contrast Peters and Middlebrook added 44

ADAM LYTH: 230 without equal

before Brooks intervened against his former county to take four wickets in a characteristically inspired spell. By the close of a good day for the hosts they were 191-7, and Middlebrook had made an excellent 70, more than double anyone else's score. Thanks to a good innings by Duckett, a young wicket-keeper from Stowe, they eventually reached 251.

Now for the fightback: Lyth and Lees enjoyed a remarkable partnership of 375, breaking numerous records. This was Lyth at his fluent best, driving through his favourite extra-cover, hitting powerfully square on the off side, hooking and pulling to the leg boundary. Lyth in fine form and full concentration has no equal. Lees kept him company with a compact, responsible innings, more subdued than Lyth's but correct and patient, playing just as the situation required. When Lees succumbed to Spriegel's off-spin they had put on 375 for the first wicket – a record against Northamptonshire. Lyth went on to a career-best 230, made over eight hours. Finch and Leaning made runs to give Yorkshire time for a late assault on their opponents, who lost three wickets before the close.

After a delayed start on the last morning Spriegel unwisely padded up to Bresnan's first ball. Brooks and Plunkett were hostile, and no batsman was secure for long enough to save the game. Duckett and Newton showed some resolution, but Plunkett dismissed both and bowled Chambers to give Yorkshire their third Championship success.

LV County Championship Division 1
Yorkshire v. Nottinghamshire

Played at Headingley, Leeds, on June 8, 9, 10 and 11, 2014
Match drawn at 5.35pm on the Fourth Day

Toss won by Nottinghamshire   Yorkshire 9 points, Nottinghamshire 9 points

Close of play: First Day, Yorkshire 52-2 (Leaning 23*, Gale 16*); Second Day, Yorkshire 76-2 (Leaning 35*, Gale 23*); Third Day, Nottinghamshire 102-2 (Lumb 43*, Taylor 27*)

	First Innings		Second innings	
	NOTTINGHAMSHIRE			
P A Jaques, c Lyth b Bresnan	20	(2) c Bairstow b Patterson		20
A D Hales, b Patterson	12	(1) lbw b Bresnan		8
M J Lumb, c Bairstow b Bresnan	45	c Bairstow b Patterson		49
J W A Taylor, lbw b Brooks	3	c Rashid b Bresnan		96
S R Patel, c Rashid b Brooks	0	c Rashid b Patterson		0
M H Wessels, c Lyth b Brooks	24	lbw b Bresnan		18
* C M W Read, run out (Leaning)	30	c Rashid b Bresnan		75
P M Siddle, not out	39	not out		48
A Shahzad, lbw b Bresnan	0	(10) not out		12
L J Fletcher, c Bresnan b Rashid	29			
A R Adams, c Bresnan b Rashid	0	(9) c Finch b Patterson		0
Extras lb 3	3	Extras b 8, lb 1		9
Total	205	Total (8 wkts dec)		335

Bonus points — Nottinghamshire 1, Yorkshire 3

FoW: 1-32 (Hales), 2-36 (Jaques), 3-46 (Taylor), 4-46 (Patel), 5-90 (Wessels),
1st 6-135 (Lumb), 7-139 (Read), 8-139 (Shahzad), 9-204 (Fletcher), 10-205 (Adams)
FoW: 1-16 (Hales), 2-30 (Jaques), 3-125 (Lumb), 4-125 (Patel), 5-154 (Wessels),
2nd 6-269 (Taylor), 7-314 (Read), 8-316 (Adams)

	O	M	R	W		O	M	R	W
Bresnan	16	3	43	3	Bresnan	27	2	112	4
Brooks	16	3	74	3	Brooks	23	7	73	0
Patterson	15	6	44	1	Patterson	25	10	57	4
Pyrah	4	1	12	0	Pyrah	11	2	32	0
Rashid	5	0	29	2	Rashid	8	1	44	0
					Finch	4	1	8	0

	First Innings		Second innings	
	YORKSHIRE			
A Lyth, c Read b Siddle	0	c Adams b Patel		13
A Z Lees, c Read b Siddle	9	c Read b Adams		6
J A Leaning, b Fletcher	41	c Shahzad b Adams		15
* A W Gale, c Patel b Siddle	29	not out		5
§ J M Bairstow, c Siddle b Adams	18	not out		3
A J Finch, b Patel	45			
A U Rashid, c Wessels b Adams	3			
T T Bresnan, c Wessels b Siddle	25			
R M Pyrah, c Siddle b Patel	45			
S A Patterson, lbw b Patel	7			
J A Brooks, not out	0			
Extras b 4, lb 9, nb 12	25	Extras lb 5, nb 6		11
Total	247	Total (3 wkts)		53

Bonus points — Yorkshire 1, Nottinghamshire 3

FoW: 1-0 (Lyth), 2-21 (Lees), 3-83 (Leaning), 4-95 (Gale), 5-116 (Bairstow),
1st 6-128 (Rashid), 7-184 (Bresnan), 8-220 (Finch), 9-247 (Pyrah), 10-247 (Patterson)
2nd 1-19 (Lees), 2-41 (Leaning), 3-43 (Lyth)

	O	M	R	W		O	M	R	W
Siddle	23	3	65	4	Siddle	7	2	8	0
Fletcher	12	1	41	1	Shahzad	6	2	6	0
Adams	19	5	59	2	Adams	7	1	24	2
Shahzad	11	1	56	0	Patel	11	7	10	1
Patel	7	1	13	3					

Umpires: M J Saggers and A G Wharf   Scorers: J T Potter and R Marshall

What a difference a day makes

AARON FINCH: 45 runs, a bowl and a catch

Two of the stronger sides in the Championship had to be content with a draw after the loss of virtually all of the second day to rain.

It was a lively pitch and overcast, but Read chose to bat. Early wickets fell, including Test batsmen Jaques, Taylor and Patel, and when Lumb was caught behind by Bairstow off the persevering Bresnan the visitors were in real difficulty.

The controversial running out of Read came at a moment of crisis. It was controversial not only because he appeared to dispute the run-out from a direct hit by Leaning, but also because he had collided with the bowler in his follow-through.

Fletcher and Siddle took Nottinghamshire towards respectability before Rashid dismissed Fletcher and Adams, a surprising No. 11.

Nottinghamshire spirits were revived by the admirable Siddle. Bowling from the Kirkstall Lane End with a long run, easy action and commendable accuracy the Australian removed Lyth and Lees on Sunday, and bowled well again on Tuesday. Finch, another Victorian, made 45 as he seeks to gain experience of first-class cricket, and Pyrah made a contribution when it mattered, so Yorkshire had a lead of 42. Patel's left-arm spin claimed three wickets.

The visiting batsmen were more impressive in their second innings, although Patterson and Bresnan bowled well. Taylor, who played his first Test at Headingley, displayed considerable patience, yet when the fifth wicket fell Nottinghamshire's lead was only 112. Read now joined Taylor, and played with such self confidence that by lunchtime they were in a strong position. Taylor was caught down the leg side for 96, and Read hit 75 off 94 balls. Had Bresnan's throw not been deflected by hitting the stumps where both batsmen stood there might have been a run-out at the other end. Patel, who is having another good season, was dismissed twice without scoring, as he had been on his previous visit to Headingley. There was just time for Yorkshire to lose three wickets.

LV County Championship Division 1
Sussex v.Yorkshire

Played at Arundel Castle on June 16, 17, 18 and 19, 2014
Match drawn at 4.50pm on the Fourth Day

Toss won by Sussex   Yorkshire 10 points, Sussex 9 points

Close of play: First Day, Sussex 300-9 (Lewis 50*, Hatchett 10*); Second Day, Yorkshire 208-3 (Leaning 75*, Bairstow 33*); Third Day, Sussex 21-0 (Wells 4*, Nash 17*)

First Innings	SUSSEX		Second innings	
C D Nash, c Bairstow b Patterson	28		(2) c Lyth b Azeem Rafiq	53
L W P Wells, c Bairstow b Pyrah	74		(1) b Lyth	81
R J Hamilton-Brown, c Bairstow b Bresnan	45		c Azeem Rafiq b Lyth	62
* E C Joyce, c Bairstow b Bresnan	0			
L J Wright, c Bairstow b Brooks	21		(5) not out	11
M W Machan, c Pyrah b Patterson	3		(4) not out	13
§ B C Brown, c Bairstow b Pyrah	6			
J C Tredwell, lbw b Bresnan	45			
S J Magoffin, c Gale b Finch	12			
J Lewis, c Finch b Brooks	61			
L J Hatchett, not out	11			
Extras b 6, lb 2, nb 2	10		Extras w 1, nb 7	8
Total	316		Total (3 wkts dec)	228

Bonus points — Sussex 3, Yorkshire 3

FoW: 1-48 (Nash), 2-108 (Hamilton-Brown), 3-108 (Joyce), 4-138 (Wright), 5-145 (Machan),
1st   6-163 (Brown), 7-188 (Wells), 8-227 (Magoffin), 9-248 (Tredwell), 10-316 (Lewis)
2nd   1-66 (Nash), 2-176 (Hamilton-Brown), 3-212 (Wells)

	O	M	R	W		O	M	R	W
Bresnan	26	5	81	3	Bresnan	11	3	27	0
Brooks	23.5	2	67	2	Brooks	10	1	29	0
Pyrah	16	6	38	2	Patterson	7	3	13	0
Patterson	23	9	71	2	Azeem Rafiq	31	6	79	1
Azeem Rafiq	7	0	31	0	Pyrah	9	4	16	0
Finch	4	0	20	1	Leaning	6	1	13	0
					Finch	6	2	11	0
					Lyth	15	3	40	2

YORKSHIRE

A Lyth, c Lewis b Magoffin		66
A Z Lees, lbw b Magoffin		22
J A Leaning, c and b Tredwell		99
* A W Gale, b Tredwell		5
§ J M Bairstow, not out		161
A J Finch, lbw b Magoffin		3
T T Bresnan, b Magoffin		68
Azeem Rafiq, c Lewis b Tredwell		14
R M Pyrah, not out		20
S A Patterson		
J A Brooks	Did not bat	
Extras b 1, lb 5, w 1, nb 5		12
Total (7 wkts dec)		470

Bonus points — Yorkshire 2, Sussex 1   Score at 110 overs: 272-5

FoW: 1-56 (Lees), 2-129 (Lyth), 3-139 (Gale), 4-264 (Leaning), 5-267 (Finch),
6-405 (Bresnan), 7-428 (Rafiq)

	O	M	R	W
Magoffin	42	17	81	4
Hatchett	27	4	102	0
Lewis	25	4	56	0
Tredwell	59	12	158	3
Wright	8	0	31	0
Nash	10	1	27	0
Hamilton-Brown	2	0	9	0

Umpires: N L Bainton and R A Kettleborough   Scorers: J T Potter and M J Charman

Bairstow 161 and six catches

The warm sunny weather enhanced the beauty of the Arundel Castle ground, which in the opinion of many is the most attractive on the circuit.

Good crowds, especially on the second day, almost filled the ground, which was stewarded with cheerful efficiency.

JONATHAN BAIRSTOW: Best outing to the Castle by a first-class 'keeper

The problem was that a slow pitch with little bounce made bowling a penance, and only 11 wickets fell from the second day onwards. Sussex batted first, but did not make the most of this opportunity, although Wells battled on despite injury. Yorkshire bowled steadily, Bairstow taking six catches behind the stumps, so that when bad light intervened they were in a strong position. Play resumed after many spectators had departed, and Lewis and Hatchett enjoyed a late revival. Sussex had reached 300 by the close.

On Tuesday Yorkshire batted very slowly. Leaning in only his fourth match looked very secure and compact, made no discernable errors and moved inexorably towards a deserved century. On 99, however, he drove impetuously towards mid-on and Tredwell leapt to his right to take a smart catch off his own bowling. Leaning stood awhile in disbelief that he had been punished for one mistake.

Bairstow had another good day, hitting 161, yet there were only eight fours and two sixes on this slow surface. Lyth and Bresnan made good contributions. Magoffin, the tall Queenslander who is one of the best county bowlers, sent down 42 overs including 17 maidens with a remarkable analysis of 4-81. Tredwell, on loan from Kent, bowled 59 overs from the Castle End, where the Ducal flag flew, and took 3-158.

Yorkshire declared with a lead of 154 and a day to bowl the hosts out. There was never any prospect of doing so, as Wells was again imperturbable, and a range of bowlers enjoyed the chance to turn their arm. First-class cricket at venues like Arundel must be retained, but consideration must be given to providing faster. more competitive pitches.

LV County Championship Division 1
Warwickshire v. Yorkshire

Played at Edgbaston, Birmingham, on June 22, 23 and 24, 2014
Yorkshire won by an innings and 8 runs at 4.34pm on the Third Day

Toss won by Warwickshire — Yorkshire 24 points, Warwickshire 3 points
Close of play: First Day, Yorkshire 367-2 (Lees 171*, Gale 9*); Second Day, Derbyshire
Close of play: First Day, Yorkshire 82-2 (Lees 40*, Gale 31*); Second Day, Yorkshire 422 all out

WARWICKSHIRE

	First Innings			Second innings	
V Chopra,	c Bairstow b Pyrah	29		lbw b Sidebottom	5
W T S Porterfield,	c Finch b Patterson	13		c Bairstow b Sidebottom	43
* J O Troughton,	b Pyrah	23		c Carver b Brooks	9
S R Hain,	c Finch b Brooks	8		b Patterson	19
§ T R Ambrose,	c Lees b Pyrah	29		c Lyth b Sidebottom	14
C R Woakes,	c Finch b Brooks	0		c Lyth b Patterson	16
R Clarke,	c Lees b Patterson	0		c and b Patterson	20
K H D Barker,	c Finch b Carver	36		c Bairstow b Brooks	16
J S Patel,	not out	63		b Carver	11
C J C Wright,	b Brooks	6		not out	19
W B Rankin,	lbw b Sidebottom	11		lbw b Carver	1
	Extras lb 5, w 5	10		Extras b 4, lb 5, nb 4	13
	Total	228		Total	186

Bonus points — Warwickshire 1, Yorkshire 3

FoW: 1st 1-20 (Porterfield), 2-64 (Chopra), 3-65 (Troughton), 4-89 (Hain), 5-89 (Woakes)
6-90 (Clarke), 7-124 (Ambrose), 8-171 (Barker), 9-180 (Wright), 10-228 (Rankin)
FoW: 2nd 1-8 (Chopra), 2-19 (Troughton), 3-66 (Hain), 4-95 (Ambrose), 5-110 (Porterfield)
6-133 (Woakes), 7-136 (Clarke), 8-158 (Patel), 9-172 (Barker), 10-186 (Rankin)

	O	M	R	W		O	M	R	W
Sidebottom	15.3	4	35	1	Sidebottom	16	4	31	3
Brooks	16	4	63	3	Brooks	17	7	59	2
Patterson	17	4	50	2	Patterson	16	6	26	3
Pyrah	12	4	37	3	Pyrah	11	3	30	0
Carver	11	1	38	1	Carver	9	3	27	2
					Lyth	1	0	4	0

YORKSHIRE

A Lyth,	c Patel b Woakes	11
A Z Lees,	c Ambrose b Woakes	64
J A Leaning,	c Chopra b Woakes	0
* A W Gale,	c Ambrose b Wright	49
§ J M Bairstow,	b Rankin	68
A J Finch,	c Ambrose b Rankin	110
R M Pyrah,	lbw b Clarke	62
S A Patterson,	c Porterfield b Patel	32
R J Sidebottom,	c Ambrose b Wright	8
J A Brooks,	c Chopra b Barker	3
K Carver,	not out	2
	Extras b 1, lb 10, nb 2	13
	Total	422

Bonus points — Yorkshire 5, Warwickshire 2 — Score at 110 overs: 417-7

FoW: 1-31 (Lyth), 2-37 (Leaning), 3-112 (Gale), 4-150 (Lees), 5-242 (Bairstow),
6-365 (Finch), 7-387 (Pyrah), 8-417 (Patterson), 9-419 (Sidebottom), 10-422 (Brooks)

	O	M	R	W
Barker	15.3	2	68	1
Woakes	24	4	81	3
Clarke	20	1	61	1
Wright	23	2	94	2
Rankin	21	2	79	2
Patel	14	6	28	1

Umpires: J H Evans and N J Llong — Scorers: T R Owen and M D Smith

Bowlers in the driving seat

RICHARD PYRAH: So often a strong contributor

Yorkshire returned to winning ways with another convincing display, finishing the job just after tea on the third day.

Their attack is based on seam bowling and, in the absence of Bresnan and Plunkett, Pyrah was included. As so often before he made a strong contribution to his side's success. Carver, a young left-arm spinner, replaced Rashid, who was on paternity leave.

The quick bowlers broke through as Warwickshire lost wickets either side of lunch, and had it not been for Patel's determined 63 not out and Barker's solidity they would have been in real trouble. Barker gave Carver his first wicket as Yorkshire bowled them out for 228.

Yorkshire gained maximum batting points after the early loss of Lyth and Leaning to Woakes. Gale and Lees played aggressive cricket on Monday morning, and Bairstow and Pyrah also batted well, but the main scorer was Finch, who made his first century for Yorkshire. As a limited-overs batsman he has some exceptional performances to his credit, but he has been less impressive at first-class level. This was a mixture of sensible application with occasional outbursts of inspired aggression; Finch moved from 86 to his century in four balls, but was dismissed by an excellent catch from wicket-keeper Ambrose. No Warwickshire bowler stood out but Woakes, a contender for a Test place, took the first three wickets.

Warwickshire were not able to make much impact in their second innings. Again it was mainly the fast bowlers, pitching the ball up and moving it around, combined with some excellent catching, that brought about this decisive win and the full 24 points. Most notable were Sidebottom's dismissal of Chopra and Porterfield, who was in obdurate mood, Patterson's catch off his own bowling to account for Clarke and Lyth's slip catch from Woakes. Then Carver took the last two wickets.

121

LV County Championship Division 1
Yorkshire v. Durham

Played at Headingley, Leeds, on July, 7, 8, 9 and 10, 2014
Match drawn at 5.15pm on the Fourth Day

Toss won by Durham
Yorkshire 13 points, Durham 9 points

Close of play: First Day, Yorkshire 367-7 (Bresnan 6*, Patterson 14*); Second Day, Durham 50-1 (Jennings 25*, Borthwick 3*); Third Day, Durham 2nd 58-1 (Stoneman 35*, Borthwick 6*)

YORKSHIRE

A Lyth, lbw b Wood		143
A Z Lees, lbw b Borthwick		108
J A Leaning, b Wood		4
* A W Gale, lbw b Wood		5
§ J M Bairstow, b Wood		0
A J Finch, c Borthwick b Rushworth		36
A U Rashid, c Borthwick b Rushworth		15
T T Bresnan, c Borthwick b Hastings		6
S A Patterson, c Mustard b Wood		17
R J Sidebottom, c Coughlin b Borthwick		25
J A Brooks, not out		27
Extras b 4, lb 19, w 4, nb 13		40
Total		426

Bonus points — Yorkshire 5, Durham 3
Score at 110 overs: 403-9

FoW: 1-270 (Lees), 2-282 (Lyth), 3-288 (Gale), 3-288 (Bairstow), 5-291 (Leaning), 6-337 (Rashid), 7-344 (Finch), 8-367 (Bresnan), 9-380 (Patterson), 10-426 (Sidebottom)

	O	M	R	W
Rushworth	26	7	79	2
Hastings	26	6	89	1
Wood	24	3	87	5
Coughlin	13	1	57	0
Borthwick	17.4	1	69	2
Collingwood	8	1	21	0
Jennings	1	0	1	0

First Innings	DURHAM		Second innings	
M D Stoneman, c Bairstow b Bresnan	21	lbw b Lyth	86
K K Jennings, c Lyth b Patterson	56	b Lyth	16
S G Borthwick, c Bairstow b Sidebottom	10	lbw b Brooks	8
M J Richardson, c and b Rashid	23	b Brooks	95
G J Muchall, lbw b Bresnan	5	lbw b Rashid	5
* P D Collingwood, not out	64	c Bairstow b Rashid	17
§ P Mustard, c Leaning b Rashid	3	not out	57
J W Hastings, c Lyth b Rashid	3	c Bairstow b Brooks	11
P Coughlin, c Brooks b Rashid	11	lbw b Brooks	6
M A Wood, lbw b Patterson	13	not out	8
C Rushworth, lbw b Sidebottom	2		
Extras b 1, lb 3, nb 2	6	Extras b 6, lb 8	14
Total	217	Total (8 wkts)	323

Bonus points — Durham 1, Yorkshire 3

FoW: 1-39 (Stoneman), 2-60 (Borthwick), 3-109 (Jennings), 4-116 (Muchall), 5-119 (Richardson),
1st 6-170 (Mustard), 7-174 (Hastings), 8-194 (Coughlin), 9-228 (Wood), 10-231 (Rushworth)
FoW: 1-39 (Jennings), 2-64 (Borthwick), 3-150 (Stoneman), 4-166 (Muchall),
2nd 5-210 (Collingwood), 6-250 (Richardson), 7-276 (Hastings), 8-290 (Coughlin)

	O	M	R	W		O	M	R	W
Sidebottom	14.2	6	18	2	Sidebottom	11	1	41	0
Brooks	15	2	62	0	Patterson	17	3	58	0
Patterson	20	8	27	2	Brooks	23	7	66	4
Bresnan	19	3	47	2	Bresnan	17	6	41	0
Rashid	20	2	73	4	Rashid	33	10	85	2
					Lyth	11	3	18	2
					Finch	1	1	0	0

The victory that got away

ALEX LEES: 108 in opening stand of 270 with Adam Lyth

All the cyclists having departed, the match began on Monday with an outstanding batting display from Lyth and Lees.

They openers put on 270 after Collingwood had put Yorkshire in — it was Lyth's first Championship century at Headingley, and one of his best with 26 fours.

Lees batted equally well, although dropped on 91 by Mustard. Yorkshire hit 145 runs in the opening session, but only 85 in the afternoon.

After tea Wood transformed Durham's fortunes. Hitherto only ordinary, he now bowled over the wicket at considerable pace and with reverse swing to catch Lees and Gale lbw, bowl Leaning who offered no shot, and then bowl Bairstow neck and crop. Finch provided some resistance, and there was a last-wicket stand of 46. There was occasional pronounced lift at the Rugby Ground End and some variable bounce, yet over 400 had been made on a faster, more competitive pitch.

The second day was mostly lost to rain. Yorkshire dismissed Durham for 231 on Wednesday, and Rashid took four wickets. His first came when Richardson inexplicably tried to hit the last ball before lunch over the bowler's head, and Hastings was caught off a ball that lifted disconcertingly. Only Collingwood survived as Durham finished 195 behind and lost Jennings to Lyth, bowling at left-handers in the evening.

At the start of the fourth day Yorkshire had to take nine wickets, and Durham were still 136 behind. Stoneman and Richardson, and later an uncharacteristically subdued Mustard, proved resolute, and gradually took the visitors to safety. In a full day Sidebottom, Patterson and Bresnan took no wickets. Richardson was the best Durham batsman, effectively saving the game, but he was fortunate to be dropped by Bresnan at cover on 27. Yorkshire had a good spell around tea as Brooks took three wickets: Durham were then 290-8 with a lead of 95 and 24.1 overs remaining, but Mustard found a reliable partner in Wood, and they saved a game Yorkshire really should have won.

LV County Championship Division 1
Yorkshire v. Middlesex

Played at North Marine Road, Scarborough, on July 19, 20, 21 and 22, 2014
Yorkshire won by 220 runs at 5.06pm on the Fourth Day

Toss won by Middlesex

Yorkshire 21 points, Middlesex 4 points

Close of play: First Day, Yorkshire 211-6 (Rashid 3*, Bresnan *); Second Day, Yorkshire 2nd 29-1 (Lees 10*, Williamson 10*); Third Day, Yorkshire 400-5 (Gale 126*, Rashid 5*)

YORKSHIRE

First Innings		Second Innings	
A Lyth, c Malan b Helm	117	c Malan b Murtagh	9
A Z Lees, c Simpson b Roland - Jones	28	c Malan b Murtagh	67
K S Williamson, b Finn	14	c Rayner b Murtagh	62
* A W Gale, c Rogers b Finn	30	not out	126
§ J M Bairstow, b Helm	5	c Helm b Roland - Jones	32
J A Leaning, b Roland - Jones	2	st Simpson b Malan	76
A U Rashid, c Malan b Finn	15	not out	5
T T Bresnan, c Morgan b Finn	20		
S A Patterson, lbw b Murtagh	4		
R J Sidebottom, c Rogers b Murtagh	2		
J A Brooks, not out	0		
Extras b 4, lb 8, nb 4	16	Extras b 10, lb 10, w 1, nb 2	23
Total	253	Total (5 wkts dec)	400

Bonus points — Yorkshire 2, Middlesex 3

FoW: 1-49 (Lees), 1-92 (Williamson), 3-177 (Gale), 4-204 (Bairstow), 5-207 (Leaning),
1st: 6-211 (Lyth), 7-234 (Rashid), 8-241 (Patterson), 9-253 (Sidebottom), 10-253 (Bresnan)
2nd: 1-14 (Lyth), 2-146 (Williamson), 3-155 (Lees), 4-201 (Bairstow), 5-383 (Leaning)

	O	M	R	W		O	M	R	W
Murtagh	20	4	51	2	Murtagh	23	6	64	3
Finn	19.5	3	81	4	Finn	20	3	88	0
Helm	15	3	30	2	Roland-Jones	18	3	71	1
Roland-Jones	18	2	55	2	Rayner	27	2	94	0
Rayner	15	3	24	0	Helm	17	2	44	0
					Malan	4	1	19	1

MIDDLESEX

First Innings		Second innings	
* C J L Rogers, c Bairstow b Sidebottom	0	c Lyth b Patterson	44
N R T Gubbins, lbw b Patterson	0	c Lyth b Brooks	9
D J Malan, c Lyth b Sidebottom	78	c Lees b Bresnan	26
E J G Morgan, c Bairstow b Sidebottom	0	c Bairstow b Rashid	29
P R Sterling, c Williamson b Sidebottom	4	lbw b Patterson	0
§ J A Simpson, run out (Rashid/Bairstow)	110	c Williamson b Brooks	61
O P Rayner, lbw b Sidebottom	6	c Lyth b Rashid	9
T S Roland-Jones, c Lyth b Sidebottom	9	c Bairstow b Rashid	9
T G Helm, not out	11	c Williamson b Rashid	0
T J Murtagh, c Lyth b Sidebottom	2	c Lyth b Rashid	5
S T Finn, c Williamson b Rashid	9	not out	5
Extras lb 1, nb 2	3	Extras b 1, lb 1, nb 2	4
Total	232	Total	201

Bonus points — Middlesex 1, Yorkshire 3

FoW: 1-0 (Rogers), 2-4 (Gubbins), 3-7 (Morgan), 4-11 (Sterling), 5-179 (Malan),
1st: 6-195 (Rayner), 7-209 (Roland - Jones), 8-210 (Simpson), 9-217 (Murtagh), 10-232 (Finn)
FoW: 1-18 (Gubbins), 2-70 (Malan), 3-92 (Rogers), 4-92 (Stirling), 5-163 (Morgan),
2nd: 6-179 (Rayner), 7-190 (Roland - Jones), 8-191 (Helm), 9-191 (Simpson), 10-201 (Rashid)

	O	M	R	W		O	M	R	W
Sidebottom	17	3	44	7	Sidebottom	11	2	26	0
Brooks	15	6	53	0	Brooks	15	6	30	3
Patterson	14	7	41	1	Patterson	16	4	51	2
Bresnan	15	4	58	0	Bresnan	16	3	44	1
Williamson	2	1	5	0	Williamson	1	0	7	0
Rashid	4	0	30	1	Lyth	4	0	14	0
					Rashid	17.3	6	27	4

Umpires: S A Garratt and M J Saggers

Scorers: J T Potter and D K Shelley

7-44: Ryan Sidebottom after his first-innings triumph

White Rose top of the table

Yorkshire won comprehensively after parity on first innings and some excellent second-innings batting before they bowled Middlesex out on the last day. Lyth made his first Scarborough first-class century on the opening day in difficult conditions, and was first to 1,000 runs for the season. The Middlesex seam attack took advantage of pitch and weather, especially Finn, the Test bowler on rehabilitation, with four wickets.

On a hot, steamy Sunday morning Sidebottom bowled with great skill to take 7-44. He swung the ball late, and disconcerted an array of left-handers with away movement. Middlesex were 11-4 as both Rogers and Morgan failed to score and, but for a crucial miss by Bairstow, would have been 11-5. There followed an excellent recovery stand of 168 between the reprieved Malan and Lancastrian wicket-keeper Simpson, who hit a most valuable century. Once Sidebottom returned to the attack he broke through to take three more wickets, and Simpson ran himself out trying to keep the strike thanks to a straight throw by Rashid.

It was good to see Gale's return to form on a ground he favours, and his unbeaten 126 was the centrepiece of the second innings. Lees, Williamson, Bairstow and Leaning all contributed, but despite Murtagh's example the visitors were inclined to bowl too short. All depended on Yorkshire's bowlers after an overnight declaration.

It was not all seam this time as Rashid recalled Scarborough successes with four wickets to bring the match to an early conclusion. Middlesex took tea on 168-4. Rogers was a danger to Yorkshire before Lyth took a remarkable catch off Patterson, who bowled a long accurate spell. Simpson again top-scored, but received scant support from the lower order. He was one of Brooks's three victims on a good day for Yorkshire, who went top of the Championship Table by four points.

LV County Championship Division 1
Yorkshire v. Sussex

Played at North Marine road, Scarborough, on August 15, 16, 17 and 18, 2014
Yorkshire won by 9 wickets at 4.47pm on the Fourth Day

Toss won by Yorkshire   Yorkshire 24 points, Sussex 6 points

Close of play: First Day, Sussex 315-8 (Magoffin 7*); Second Day, Yorkshire 258-5 (Williamson 90*, Rashid 0*); Third Day, Sussex 98-4 (Wright 56*, Piolet 10*)

SUSSEX

First Innings		Second innings	
C D Nash, c Lyth b Sidebottom	35	(2) c Bairstow b Brooks	15
L W P Wells, b Sidebottom	10	(1) b Sidebottom	0
* E C Joyce, lbw b Rashid	130	b Sidebottom	5
C Cachopa, c Lyth b Bresnan	53	c Lyth b Bresnan	7
L J Wright, b Patterson	52	lbw b Bresnan	113
S A Piolet, lbw b Brooks	6	c Williamson b Patterson	32
§ B C Brown, c Williamson b Brooks	4	lbw b Patterson	0
J C Tredwell, c Williamson b Patterson	15	c Sidebottom b Bresnan	26
S J Magoffin, b Rashid	39	b Rashid	18
L J Hatchett, not out	20	c Gale b Rashid	4
M E Hobden, lbw b Rashid	0	not out	0
Extras lb 2, nb 2	4	Extras b 7, lb 2, w 1	10
Total	368	Total	230

Bonus points — Sussex 4, Yorkshire 3   Score at 110 overs: 364-9

FoW: 1-44 (Nash), 2-45 (Wells), 3-169 (Cachopa), 4-237 (Wright), 5-260 (Piolet), 6-268 (Brown),
1st 7-307 (Tredwell), 8-315 (Joyce), 8-315 (Joyce), 9-364 (Magoffin), 10-368 (Hobden)
FoW: 1-8 (Wells), 2-20 (Nash), 3-20 (Joyce), 4-48 (Cachopa), 5-175 (Piolet),
2nd 6-175 (Brown), 7-201 (Wright), 8-218 (Tredwell), 9-223 (Hatchett), 10-230 (Magoffin)

	O	M	R	W		O	M	R	W
Sidebottom	23	3	75	2	Sidebottom	11	2	26	2
Brooks	24	2	100	2	Brooks	15	2	68	1
Bresnan	19	1	87	1	Bresnan	17	2	60	3
Patterson	29	11	63	2	Patterson	16	8	24	2
Rashid	13.4	3	32	3	Rashid	19.1	6	40	2
Lyth	3	0	9	0	Lyth	1	0	3	0

YORKSHIRE

First Innings		Second Innings	
A Lyth, b Hatchett	3	not out	39
A Z Lees, c Joyce b Magoffin	0	c Hatchett b Hobden	46
K S Williamson, c and b Wells	189	not out	15
* A W Gale, c Brown b Magoffin	35		
§ J M Bairstow, lbw b Hobden	77		
J A Leaning, b Tredwell	33		
A U Rashid, b Hobden	28		
T T Bresnan, c and b Wells	61		
S A Patterson, lbw b Wells	5		
R J Sidebottom, not out	14		
J A Brooks, c Hatchett b Tredwell	15		
Extras b 3, lb 9, w 1, nb 20	33	Extras b 4, lb 2	6
Total	493	Total (1 wkt)	106

Bonus points — Yorkshire 5, Sussex 2   Score at 110 overs: 443-6

FoW: 1-3 (Lyth), 2-5 (Lees), 3-57 (Gale), 4-206 (Bairstow), 5-257 (Leaning), 6-429 (Rashid),
1st 7-449 (Bresnan), 8-459 (Patterson), 9-466 (Williamson), 10-493 (Brooks)
2nd 1-88 (Lees)

	O	M	R	W		O	M	R	W
Magoffin	37	12	102	2	Magoffin	5	2	13	0
Hatchett	23	1	116	1	Hatchett	7	0	31	0
Tredwell	19.2	1	76	2	Tredwell	4	0	32	0
Hobden	22	1	101	2	Hobden	3	0	22	1
Piolet	13	0	48	0	Wells	1.1	0	2	0
Wells	12	1	38	3					

Umpires: P J Hartley and G D Lloyd   Scorers: J T Potter and M J Charman

Just Williamson for 189

KANE WILLIAMSON
Quality and patience

Putting Sussex in seemed misconceived when they ended the first day on 315-8, but it may have been justified had Lyth caught Cachopa at 55-2.

Joyce played an excellent captain's innings, showing sound judgement outside off-stump and hitting some fine drives in his 130. Cachopa struggled to 54, but Wright also gave good support. In the final session Yorkshire took five wickets, but they allowed Sussex to add 53 next morning.

Williamson led the Yorkshire response with an innings of exceptional quality and patience. Compact and orthodox in technique, with sound judgement and impeccable timing, he batted eight hours to make his maiden century for Yorkshire with 22 fours, providing the essential backbone for a long innings and a lead of 125.

In a stand of 149 for the fourth wicket he kept pace with an exuberant Bairstow whose incisive stroke play ended with a dubious lbw decision. There had also been controversy over a possible catch at slip when Williamson was 16 that the umpires disallowed after discussion. Williamson was then involved in a partnership of 157 with Bresnan, who made a valuable 61, and the New Zealander was the ninth wicket to fall, just missing a well merited double-century. Magoffin bowled very well with considerable away swing but no luck, and Wells took three late wickets with his leg-spin.

By the close on Sunday Sussex had lost four wickets and were still 77 behind. Wright emerged from the pavilion playing shots on his way, and it seemed that every stroke he played in the middle went for runs and he might save Sussex. Piolet gave support almost to lunch, but Yorkshire soon took the last five wickets and, although Brooks conceded too many runs, credit must go to the bowling collective that dismissed a good side for 230. As rain clouds drifted past Lyth and Lees ensured the outcome.

LV County Championship Division 1
Lancashire v. Yorkshire

Played at Old Trafford, Manchester, on August 31 and September 1, 2 and 3, 2014
Yorkshire won by an innings and 18 runs at 3.05pm on the Fourth Day

Toss won by Lancashire   Yorkshire 23 points, Lancashire 3 points

Close of play: First Day, Yorkshire 61-0, Lyth 25*, Lees 36*; Second day, Yorkshire 396-5 (Lyth 182*, Rashid 44*); Third day, Lancashire 144-2 (Khawaja 69*, Prince 18*)

	First Innings	LANCASHIRE		Second innings	
P J Horton, lbw b Sidebottom		0	c and b Rashid		49
L M Reece, lbw b Sidebottom		53	b Sidebottom		4
U T Khawaja, c Bairstow b Sidebottom		0	st Bairstow b Rashid		117
A G Prince, b Rashid		53	c Bairstow b Rashid		40
S J Croft, lbw b Brooks		38	c Williamson b Rashid		16
§ A L Davies, c Leaning b Pyrah		35	c Lees b Brooks		7
T C Smith, c Bairstow b Brooks		57	c Bairstow b Brooks		2
S D Parry, lbw b Brooks		17	b Lyth		28
* G Chapple, b Rashid		9	b Brooks		3
S C Kerrigan, c Lees b Rashid		0	c Bairstow b Rashid		1
T E Bailey, not out		7	not out		25
Extras b 4, lb 5		9	Extras p 5, b 11, lb 1, nb 5		22
Total		278	Total		314

Bonus points — Lancashire 2, Yorkshire 3

FoW: 1-0 (Horton), 2-0 (Khawaja), 3-96 (Prince), 4-121 (Reece), 5-169 (Croft),
1st   6-194 (Davies), 7-240 (Parry), 8-265 (Smith), 9-271 (Chapple), 10-278 (Kerrigan)
FoW: 1-17 (Reece), 2-98 (Horton), 3-190 (Prince), 4-226 (Croft), 5-243 (Davies),
2nd   6-249 (Smith), 7-254 (Williamson), 8-259 (Chapple), 9-270 (Kerrigan), 10-314 (Parry)

	O	M	R	W		O	M	R	W
Sidebottom	14	3	42	3	Sidebottom	17	2	42	1
Brooks	16	3	64	3	Brooks	18	3	61	3
Patterson	15	2	47	0	Rashid	40	5	117	5
Rashid	17.3	1	77	3	Patterson	7	1	16	0
Pyrah	11	1	35	1	Pyrah	6	2	24	0
Lyth	1	0	4	0	Lyth	15.2	5	37	1

YORKSHIRE

A Lyth, c Kerrigan b Parry	251
A Z Lees, lbw b Bailey	40
K S Williamson, st Davies b Parry	46
* A W Gale, c Khawaja b Parry	6
§ J M Bairstow, b Croft	60
J A Leaning, lbw b Kerrigan	1
A U Rashid, not out	159
R M Pyrah, not out	21
S A Patterson	
R J Sidebottom Did not bat	
J A Brooks	
Extras b 7, lb 14, w 1, nb 4	26
Total (6 wkts dec)	610

Bonus points — Yorkshire 4, Lancashire 1   Score at 110 overs: 381-5

FoW: 1-72 (Lees), 2-149 (Williamson), 3-163 (Gale), 4-266 (Bairstow), 5-281 (Leaning)
     6-577 (Lyth)

	O	M	R	W
Chapple	31	8	92	0
Bailey	30	5	98	1
Kerrigan	28	1	115	1
Croft	26	1	96	1
Smith	12	1	56	0
Parry	33	3	109	3
Reece	4	0	23	0

Umpires: S A Garratt and S J O'Shaughnessy   Scorers: J T Potter and D M White

Lyth's 251 epic beyond praise

ADAM LYTH: Restraint and abundance of strokes over three days

An excellent all-round performance gave the *White Rose* their first Championship win over Lancashire since 2002.

The match began dramatically with two wickets to Sidebottom in the first over. The promising Reece batted until lunch alongside Prince, but he received another in- swinging yorker from Sidebottom shortly afterwards.

Yorkshire dismissed the hosts just before the close on Sunday despite some defiance from Prince and Smith.

Lyth played an outstanding innings of 251 over three days which enabled Yorkshire to build an impregnable lead, and Rashid contributed a fine 159 not out to take the score beyond 600. Lyth displayed an abundance of attacking strokes, but it was his restraint and self-discipline which made this such a significant long innings in Yorkshire's challenge for the Championship. When he was out for 251, one run behind Lehmann's record *Roses* score, he had been at the wicket while 577 runs were made. No praise can be too high for his endeavours. Rashid, who now appears a more effective bowler as well as a batsman of considerable accomplishment, participated in a record-breaking sixth-wicket partnership of 296 to establish a lead of 332. Chapple, Lancashire's captain, now 40 years old, bowled 31 overs with characteristic dedication but no reward. The two spinners, Kerrigan and Parry were unable to contain the batsmen, and Smith, probably their best bowler this season, suffered a back injury. An altercation between Gale and Prince at the close on Tuesday resulted in Gale's suspension for the last two matches.

Rashid made another significant contribution with his wrist spin by taking five Lancashire wickets, including that of Khawaja, who made a century to compensate for his first-ball dismissal in the first innings. Brooks had one of his inspired spells to run through the middle-order, so Yorkshire won with relative ease on their first visit to the reconstructed Old Trafford with its pitch turned around and a new players' pavilion.

LV County Championship Division 1
Nottinghamshire v. Yorkshire

Played at Trent Bridge, Nottingham, on September 9, 10, 11 and 12, 2014
Yorkshire won by an innings and 152 runs at 11.37am on the Fourth Day

Toss won by Yorkshire   Yorkshire 23 points, Nottinghamshire 2 points

Close of play: First Day, Yorkshire 319-4 (Ballance 82*, Leaning 8*); Second Day, Nottinghamshire 58-4 (Lumb 35*, Wessels 14*); Third Day, Nottinghamshire (following on) 149-5 (Taylor 56*, Keedy 0*)

YORKSHIRE

A Lyth, c and b Keedy		122
A Z Lees, c Wessels b Keedy		86
G S Ballance, lbw b Keedy		99
* J E Root, lbw b Gurney		11
§ J M Bairstow, c Lumb b Fletcher		2
J A Leaning, lbw b Keedy		42
A U Rashid, c Wessels b Fletcher		42
T T Bresnan, c Wessels b Mullaney		95
S A Patterson, lbw b Keedy		17
R J Sidebottom, not out		4
J A Brooks	Did not bat	
Extras b 4, lb 6, nb 2		12
Total (9 wkts dec)		532

Bonus points — Yorkshire 4, Nottinghamshire 1   Score at 110 overs: 357-4

FoW: 1-176 (Lees), 2-271 (Lyth), 3-289 (Root), 4-298 (Bairstow), 5-362 (Ballance), 6-387 (Leaning), 7-433 (Rashid), 8-490 (Patterson), 9-532 (Bresnan)

	O	M	R	W
Fletcher	30	11	73	2
Gurney	34	4	124	1
Ball	24	3	73	0
Keedy	50	2	163	5
Mullaney	16.2	4	37	1
Patel	20	3	52	0

NOTTINGHAMSHIRE

First Innings		Second innings	
S J Mullaney, c Lyth b Sidebottom	9	lbw b Sidebottom	0
A D Hales, c Bairstow b Brooks	0	c and b Brooks	43
M J Lumb, lbw b Brooks	41	c Ballance b Brooks	9
J W A Taylor, c Ballance b Sidebottom	0	c sub (R M Pyrah) b Sidebottom	75
S R Patel, c Ballance b Brooks	0	st Bairstow b Patterson	25
M H Wessels, c Bairstow b Sidebottom	21	b Sidebottom	10
* § C M W Read, not out	81	(8) c Bairstow b Sidebottom	2
L J Fletcher, c Brooks b Rashid	23	(9) c Lyth b Sidebottom)	5
J T Ball, lbw b Rashid	2	(10) lbw b Rashid	0
G Keedy, c Bresnan b Rashid	4	(7) b Sidebottom	0
H F Gurney, lbw b Brooks	15	not out	0
Extras lb 5, nb 2	7	Extras b 4, lb 3, w 1	8
Total	203	Total	177

Bonus points — Nottinghamshire 1, Yorkshire 3

FoW: 1-8 (Hales), 2-12 (Mullaney), 3-12 (Taylor), 4-25 (Patel), 5-68 (Lumb),
1st 6-82 (Wessels), 7-123 (Fletcher), 8-126 (Ball), 9-140 (Keedy), 10-203 (Gurney)
FoW: 1-0 (Mullaney), 2-9 (Lumb), 3-71 (Hales), 4-124 (Patel), 5-144 (Wessels),
2nd 6-154 (Keedy), 7-156 (Read), 8-172 (Fletcher), 9-177 (Ball), 10-177 (Taylor)

	O	M	R	W		O	M	R	W
Sidebottom	12	2	35	3	Sidebottom	18.2	7	30	6
Brooks	13.2	1	58	4	Brooks	12	1	64	2
Rashid	22	4	52	3	Rashid	9	2	33	1
Patterson	7	2	29	0	Bresnan	4	0	12	0
Bresnan	11	4	24	0	Patterson	10	5	28	1
Root	1	1	0	0	Root	3	0	3	0

TV Man of the Match: R J Sidebottom

Umpires: R J Bailey and M J Saggers   Scorers: J T Potter and R Marshall
Third Umpire: M R Benson

Yorkshire take the Gold

CHAMPION MOMENT: Yorkshire's dance of joy is led by Ryan Sidebottom, whose nine wickets in the match secured him the double of two titles with Yorkshire and two with their Trent Bridge opponents

Yorkshire nailed down the Championship on Friday, September 12, at 11.37am with one game still to play when they bowled out Nottinghamshire for 177 to register their eighth win of the season.

It was a performance which left no one in any doubt that the *White Rose* were worthy Champions and the best side by far in the country.

Captained by Root in the absence of Gale, who had been banned from taking part by the ECB following his altercation with Prince in the previous game at Old Trafford, Yorkshire built up a large total after winning the toss.

Lyth, who is in the best form of his career, made an excellent 122, but if he had been caught second ball by Read off Fletcher it might have been a different story. The left-handed partnership of Lyth and Lees continued their outstanding work together by putting on 176 before Lees was caught by Wessels, who had twice missed him at short-leg.

Ballance, like Root, was back with his county after a magnificent summer of Test cricket and, batting at No. 3, he made a solid 99. He was denied a well merited century when he fell lbw to Keedy, the Yorkshire-born left-arm spinner showing that he had lost none of his guile when the occasion demanded it.

Bresnan took over until he also lost his wicket in the 90s, but Leaning and Rashid chipped in nicely to ensure that Yorkshire's 532 made it

131

JACK BROOKS
Dynamic spell knocked
heart out of batsmen

highly improbable that the home side could achieve the victory necessary to maintain their own challenge for the Championship. Keedy, playing for his fourth county — his one match for Yorkshire was way back in 1994 — toiled for 50 overs, and obtained a very creditable 5-163 with his flighted orthodox spin.

Sidebottom and Brooks knocked the heart out of Nottinghamshire in the dynamic closing overs on Wednesday by taking two wickets each to reduce them to 25-4. It was high-class stuff and worthy of a side that had the Championship title almost within their grasp.

There was something of a recovery the following morning, led by Lumb and Read, but Yorkshire's two opening bowlers, assisted by some leg-breaks and googlies from Rashid, dismissed their struggling opponents for 203. The follow-on was enforced.

Five second-innings wickets fell on the third evening, and with nightwatchman Keedy at the crease Yorkshire were poised to win the match. A large crowd came to Trent Bridge for the final day, not surprisingly a good number travelling down the M1 in anticipation of the *White Rose* side lifting the Championship Trophy. They were not to be disappointed.

Sidebottom was in magnificent form again, and took four of the remaining wickets to finish with 6-30 and 9-65 in the match. It was his fourth Championship — two for each side — and he has served Yorkshire outstandingly since returning from Trent Bridge, losing none of his stamina and determination.

This was Yorkshire's first Championship title win since Scarborough in 2001, and only the second since Hull in 1968. It was especially pleasing to Yorkshire members and supporters that the majority of the team had come through the Academy — which was a tribute not only to all the age group coaches but also to the many grandparents, parents,

BEST FORM OF HIS LIFE: Opener Adam Lyth strokes his way to 122 as wicket-keeper Chris Read looks on

uncles, cousins and aunts who give so much encouragement and support to young players in the county. Much is owed to Jason Gillespie as coach, adviser and motivator, and to Martyn Moxon as Director of Cricket. It was achieved despite the loss of players to international duty.

It was an achievement to which all the team contributed under the captaincy of Gale. Yorkshire often bowled their opponents out twice, which is the essence of first-class cricket. The quick bowlers worked as a team, but special credit should go to Sidebottom for his consistency and skill, to Brooks for his inspired spells and 60 wickets so far with one match to play, and to Patterson for his reliability. Rashid has had a good season as an all-rounder.

The batting has been strong, and Lyth has had a wonderful year, forming an opening partnership with Lees that will almost certainly go on to make them among the most successful first-wicket combinations in the club's history if Test calls do not cut into their appearances together, as they almost certainly will.

Unsurprisingly, there were celebrations over lunchtime at Trent Bridge. The one big regret, of course, was that the ECB had ruled that Gale could not go on to the field to receive the Trophy, and he had to observe proceedings from the dressing-room balcony. When he eventually came down on to the field he received the enthusiastic reception that he so thoroughly deserved.

It was appropriate that Yorkshire's Executive Chairman Colin Graves presented the Championship Trophy, and all of us who were so pleased by the team's success were aware that without his support and leadership none of this might have happened.

LV County Championship Division 1
Yorkshire v. Somerset

Played at Headingley, Leeds, on September 23, 24, 25 and 26, 2014
Match drawn at 6.15pm on the Fourth Day

Toss won by Yorkshire   Yorkshire 9 points, Somerset 12 points

Close of play: First Day, Yorkshire 241-9 (Leaning 50*, Brooks 16*); Second Day, Somerset 319-3 (Abell 71*, Leach 10*); Third Day, Yorkshire 148-2 (Ballance 59*, Root 17*)

YORKSHIRE

First Innings			Second Innings	
A Lyth, c Hildreth b Thomas	10		c Groenewald b Trego	51
A Z Lees, c Kieswetter b Trego	83		c Kieswetter b Trego	23
G S Ballance, c Trescothick b Thomas	7		lbw b Trego	69
* J E Root, b Overton	35		b Leach	97
§ J M Bairstow, b Trego	8		c Kieswetter b Overton	49
J A Leaning, not out	57		c Hildreth b Trego	28
A U Rashid, c and b Groenewald	0		c Kieswetter b Trego	11
R M Pyrah, lbw b Groenewald	2		st Kieswetter b Leach	11
S A Patterson, c Kieswetter b Trego	13		b Trego	4
R J Sidebottom, b Leach	5		c Trescothick b Trego	0
J A Brooks, c Trescothick b Trego	21		not out	0
Extras b 4, lb 7, w 1	12		Extras b 4, lb 16, w 2	22
Total	253		Total	365

Bonus points — Yorkshire 2, Somerset 3

FoW: 1-24 (Lyth), 2-32 (Ballance), 3-95 (Root), 4-132 (Bairstow), 5-173 (Lees),
1st   6-177 (Rashid), 7-181 (Pyrah), 8-206 (Patterson), 9-213 (Sidebottom), 10-253 (Brooks)
FoW: 1-44 (Lees), 2-121 (Lyth), 3-178 (Ballance), 4-288 (Bairstow), 5-313 (Root), 6-330
2nd   (Rashid), 7-349 (Leaning), 8-353 (Patterson), 9-365 (Pyrah), 10-365 (Sidebottom)

	O	M	R	W		O	M	R	W
Thomas	13	5	33	2	Thomas	5	0	23	0
Trego	19.1	6	69	4	Trego	28.3	6	84	7
Groenewald	16	4	56	2	Overton	13	0	61	1
Overton	24	6	60	1	Groenewald	16	1	62	0
Leach	11	4	24	1	Leach	24	2	88	2
					Myburgh	8	2	27	0

SOMERSET

First Innings			Second innings	
* M E Trescothick, c Lyth b Root	66		c sub (J A Tattersall) b Rashid	44
J G Myburgh, c Lyth b Patterson	14		c Pyrah b Sidebottom	1
N R D Compton, b Patterson	156		b Brooks	18
T B Abell, c Lyth b Brooks	75		(6) c Rashid b Brooks	34
M J Leach, c Bairstow b Patterson	43		(9) st Bairstow b Rashid	8
J C Hildreth, b Patterson	4		(4) run out (Bairstow)	9
§ C Kieswetter, st Bairstow b Rashid	17		(5) lbw b Patterson	3
P D Trego, c Root b Rashid	41		(7) b Brooks	0
T D Groenewald, c Leaning b Rashid	4		(8) c Bairstow b Sidebottom	1
A C Thomas, c Leaning b Rashid	0		(11) not out	8
J Overton, not out	4		(10) not out	12
Extras b 4, lb 7, nb 2	13		Extras lb 13	13
Total	437		Total (9 wkts)	151

Bonus points — Somerset 4, Yorkshire 2   Score at 110 overs: 382-6

FoW: 1-42 (Myburgh), 2-150 (Trescothick), 3-304 (Compton), 4-335 (Abell), 5-364 (Leach),
1st   6-373 (Hildreth), 7-424 (Trego), 8-426 (Groenewald), 9-428 (Thomas), 10-437 (Kieswetter)
FoW: 1-7 (Myburgh), 2-62 (Trescothick), 3-74 (Compton), 4-83 (Kieswetter), 5-83 (Hildreth),
2nd   6-83 (Trego), 7-110 (Groenewald), 8-121 (Leach), 9-135 (Abell)

	O	M	R	W		O	M	R	W
Sidebottom	21	5	68	0	Sidebottom	11	4	24	2
Brooks	17	2	69	1	Brooks	14	4	46	3
Patterson	28	10	54	4	Patterson	9	4	15	1
Pyrah	19	3	85	0	Rashid	10	2	53	2
Rashid	27.1	2	116	4					
Root	6	0	26	1					
Lyth	2	0	8	0					

Umpires: P J Hartley and A G Wharf   Scorers: J T Potter and G A Stickley

Bowlers turn a gripping finale

JACK LEANING: Half-century as he slots seamlessly into the side

The hosts entered the final match of the season as Champions, but were out-played by Somerset on the first two days.

They batted well second time round, and then the bowlers provided an exciting climax when Yorkshire almost won.

Perhaps Root, not possessing hindsight, should not have batted first, because conditions were difficult on Tuesday but improved after that.

The innings of Lees, capped before play started after an excellent season, and Leaning stood out as batsmen struggled against a persistent seam attack led by Trego and Thomas, whose injury handicapped Somerset later in the match.

On the second day Somerset made 315-3. Trescothick, large and dominant, eventually succumbed to Root, but Compton hit a hard-working century with some attractive strokes, and his 156 ensured a large total for the visitors. Abell, *Wisden* Schools Cricketer of the Year in 2013 at Taunton School, showed an impressive technique and personal courage after an incapacitating injury.

Yorkshire hit back by bowling Somerset out, thanks mainly to Rashid, who took the last four wickets to add respectability to some wayward bowling earlier. Then they batted with greater resolution, Root just missing a century when he was bowled by left-arm spinner Leach, another Tauntonian. Trego was not to be denied, and his application and accuracy were rewarded with a career-best 7-84 and 11-153 altogether.

With Root and Ballance at the crease it looked as if Yorkshire would save the match, but Trego gave Somerset an attainable target of 182, especially when Trescothick began with such belligerence. After a steepling catch by substitute Tattersall wickets fell, including two Brooks specials to bowl Compton and Trego and a runner run-out mixup after Abell returned with a pronounced limp.

Yorkshire now expected to win. Finally, Overton and Thomas, also with a runner, played out the final overs. The season ended in late September sunshine and applause to both sides.

LV COUNTY CHAMPIONSHIP 2014

DIVISION 1

	P	W	L	D	BAT	BOWL	Pen.	Points
					Bonus Points			
1 Yorkshire (Div 1, 2)	**16**	**8**	**1**	**7**	**48**	**44**	**0.0**	**255.0**
2 Warwickshire (Div 1, 4)	16	8	4	4	47	43	0.0	238.0
3 Sussex (Div 1, 3)	16	6	4	6	44	40	0.0	210.0
4 Nottinghamshire (Div 1, 7)	16	6	6	4	50	40	0.0	206.0
5 Durham (Div 1, 1)	16	5	4	7	42	42	0.0	199.0
6 Somerset (Div1, 6)	16	4	2	10	42	42	0.0	198.0
7 Middlesex (Div 1, 5) *	16	4	5	7	35	38	2.0	170.0
8 Lancashire (Div 2, 1) *	16	3	6	7	30	41	0.0	154.0
9 Northamptonshire (Div 2, 2) *	16	0	12	4	27	32	0.0	79.0

Pen. 1 point deducted for each over short in a match based on a rate of 16 overs per hour

* Relegated to Division 2 for 2015

DIVISION 2

	P	W	L	D	BAT	BOWL	Pen.	Points
					Bonus Points			
1 Hampshire (Div 2, 4) *	16	7	1	8	50	38	0.0	240.0
2 Worcestershire (Div 2, 5) *	16	8	3	5	37	47	0.0	237.0
3 Essex (Div 2, 3)	16	7	2	7	37	45	0.0	229.0
4 Derbyshire (Div 1, 8)	16	6	5	5	26	41	0.0	188.0
5 Surrey (Div 1, 9)	16	4	5	7	43	44	3.0	183.0
6 Kent (Div 2, 7)	16	4	6	6	35	42	0.0	171.0
7 Gloucestershire (Div 2, 6)	16	4	5	7	28	36	0.0	163.0
8 Glamorgan (Div 2, 8)	16	3	6	7	29	41	0.0	153.0
9 Leicestershire (Div 2, 9)	16	0	10	6	36	42	0.0	108.0

Pen. 1 point deducted for each over short in a match based on a rate of 16 overs per hour

* Promoted to Division 1 for 2014.

(2013 positions in brackets)

YORKSHIRE AVERAGES 2014

LV COUNTY CHAMPIONSHIP

Played 16   Won 8   Lost 1   Drawn 7

BATTING AND FIELDING

(Qualification 10 completed innings)

Player	M.	I.	N.O.	Runs	H.S.	100s	50s	Avge	ct/st
A Lyth	16	23	1	1489	251	6	6	67.68	35
K S Williamson	9	13	2	629	189	1	4	57.18	10
J M Bairstow	13	17	3	647	161*	1	4	46.21	38/4
A Z Lees	15	22	0	971	138	2	5	44.13	10
A W Gale	13	16	3	562	126*	2	1	43.23	2
J A Leaning	10	14	2	465	99	0	4	38.75	4
A U Rashid	14	18	3	577	159*	2	1	38.46	9
T T Bresnan	10	10	0	338	95	0	4	33.80	5
S A Patterson	15	14	1	178	43	0	0	13.69	1
R J Sidebottom	12	12	2	112	25	0	0	11.20	2
Also played									
G S Ballance	6	9	0	585	174	2	3	65.00	7
A J Finch	5	6	0	291	110	1	1	48.50	8
J E Root	4	6	0	275	97	0	3	45.83	1
R M Pyrah	6	6	2	161	62	0	1	40.25	2
L E Plunkett	7	8	2	209	86	0	1	34.83	4
A J Hodd	5	6	1	144	55	0	1	28.80	18/1
J A Brooks	16	14	8	142	37*	0	0	23.66	4
Azeem Rafiq	1	1	0	14	14	0	0	14.00	1
K Carver	1	1	1	2	2*	0	0	—	1

BOWLING

(Qualification 10 wickets)

Player	Overs	Mdns	Runs	Wkts	Avge	Best	5wI	10wM
R J Sidebottom	351.1	84	881	48	18.35	7-44	2	0
L E Plunkett	167	27	596	24	24.83	4-42	0	0
A U Rashid	369.4	71	1199	46	26.06	5-117	1	0
S A Patterson	403.4	133	1001	36	27.80	4-54	0	0
J A Brooks	523.2	105	1906	68	28.02	5-36	2	0
T T Bresnan	331	76	947	30	31.56	4-112	0	0
Also bowled								
K Carver	20	4	65	3	21.66	2-27	0	0
A Lyth	59.2	12	160	5	32.00	2-18	0	0
K S Williamson	61.4	21	160	5	32.00	2-45	0	0
A J Finch	15	4	39	1	39.00	1-20	0	0
J E Root	13	1	40	1	40.00	1-26	0	0
R M Pyrah	99	26	309	6	51.50	3-37	0	0
Azeem Rafiq	38	6	110	1	110.00	1-79	0	0
J A Leaning	6	1	13	0	—	0-13	0	0
J M Bairstow	1	0	1	0	—	0-1	0	0

MCC University Match (First-Class)
Yorkshire v. Leeds/Bradford MCCU

Played at Headingley, Leeds, on April 1, 2 and 3, 2014
Match drawn at 5pm on the Third Day
Toss won by Yorkshire

Close of play: First Day, Yorkshire 94-1 (Lyth 45*); Second Day, Yorkshire 366-5 (Bairstow 61*, Hodgson 6*)

First Innings LEEDS/BRADFORD MCCU Second innings

D R Young, c Ballance b Plunkett	5	c Bairstow b Brooks	0
N R T Gubbins, c Bairstow b Sidebottom	0	not out	31
C A L Davis, lbw b Brooks	13	lbw b Patterson	1
* W G R Vanderspar, not out	60	not out	20
P A Ross, c Bairstow b Patterson	1		
A R Laws, lbw b Patterson	5		
H P Rouse, b Brooks	16		
A MacQueen, c Lyth b Plunkett	12		
§ C A R MacLeod, b Rashid	4		
Z R Patel, c Hodgson b Rashid	4		
I A A Thomas, lbw b Rashid	3		
Extras b 1, lb 10, w 5	16	Extras lb 8, w 1, nb 2	11
Total	139	Total (2 wkts)	63

FoW: 1-1 (Gubbins), 2-20 (Davis), 3-29 (Young), 4-30 (Ross), 5-50 (Laws)
1st 6-91 (Rouse), 7-122 (MacQueen), 8-129 (MacLeod), 9-136 (Patel), 10-139 (Thomas)
2nd 1-9 (Young), 2-16 (Davis)

	O	M	R	W		O	M	R	W
Sidebottom	10	2	20	1	Sidebottom	6	5	4	0
Brooks	11	5	30	2	Brooks	6	3	5	1
Patterson	13	5	25	2	Patterson	7	1	15	1
Plunkett	12	0	45	2	Plunkett	7	1	22	0
Rashid	7	2	8	3	Rashid	3	0	9	0

YORKSHIRE

A Lyth, c Ross b Laws	130
A Z Lees, b Thomas	47
J A Leaning, c Young b Patel	13
* G S Ballance, b Vanderspar	101
§ J M Bairstow, c Vanderspar b MacQueen	123
A U Rashid, c MacLeod b Vanderspar	0
D M Hodgson, run out (Patel)	18
L E Plunkett, c Ross b MacQueen	1
R J Sidebottom, c Thomas b MacQueen	2
S A Patterson, not out	5
J A Brooks, c Laws b MacQueen	6
Extras b 2, lb 2, w 4	8
Total	454

FoW: 1-94 (Lees), 2-123 (Leaning), 3-272 (Lyth), 4-328 (Ballance), 5-328 (Rashid), 6-392 (Hodgson), 7-409 (Plunkett), 8-437 (Sidebottom), 9-448 (Bairstow), 10-454 (Brooks)

	O	M	R	W
Thomas	19	5	43	1
Patel	29	3	102	1
Rouse	31	5	120	0
Vanderspar	14	2	52	2
MacQueen	34	5	116	4
Laws	5	0	17	1

Umpires: P J Hartley and G D Lloyd   Scorers: J T Potter and C N Rawson

Centuries for flannelled fools

First-class cricket started this year on April 1. The only April Fool surprise was that it was bright, sunny and warm, and after a short delay there was a full day's cricket.

All six MCC University sides were able to start the 2014 season. Oxford and Cambridge were at the Parks and Fenner's, where cricket has been played since the 19th Century.

Durham were at Derby, but will shortly appear at their University ground where our new life member, Sachin Tendulkar, made a century for Yorkshire.

Loughborough

The shape of things to come: Adam Lyth on his way to 140

University and cricket centre is now a first-class ground, but they were down at Hove, and there was an all-Welsh contest at Cardiff.

Yorkshire won the toss, and sent the visitors in. Four capped seam bowlers were playing, although Bresnan was absent, and they shared wickets as the University struggled. Then Rashid took the last three wickets for eight runs. Will Vanderspar, who made an undefeated 60 with a first 50 off 78 balls, was the fourth *Wisden* schoolboy cricketer of the year in 2010 when he made 1,286 runs for Eton College. Jonathan Bairstow was the first in 2007. Although Leeds/Bradford had seven players who appeared here last year Yorkshire's batsmen were predominant, both Lyth and Ballance scoring centuries as they had in 2013, and there were plenty of off-side boundaries to savour. Lyth, who hit 19 fours and a six, might have run himself out at 98, while Ballance was in good form in pursuit of an England place this summer. Bairstow was the third centurion with a sparkling 123 over two days.

The University bowlers worked hard and showed promise. Patel had a good action, but gained little reward. Thomas and Vanderspar were economical, and off-spinner McQueen's long spell was rewarded with four wickets on the last morning. The match ended at teatime with the Middlesex pair Gubbins and Vanderspar batting as the weather closed in.

YORKSHIRE AVERAGES 2014

ALL FIRST-CLASS MATCHES

Played 17　　　Won 8　　　Lost 1　　　Drawn 8

BATTING AND FIELDING

(Qualification 10 completed innings)

Player	M.	I.	N.O.	Runs	H.S.	100s	50s	Avge	ct/st
A Lyth	17	24	1	1619	251	7	6	70.39	36
G S Ballance	7	10	0	686	174	3	3	68.60	8
K S Williamson	9	13	2	629	189	1	4	57.18	10
J M Bairstow	14	18	3	770	161*	2	4	51.33	41/4
A Z Lees	16	23	0	1018	138	2	5	44.26	10
A W Gale	13	16	3	562	126*	2	1	43.23	2
J A Leaning	11	15	2	478	99	0	4	36.76	4
A U Rashid	15	19	3	577	159*	2	1	36.06	9
T T Bresnan	10	10	0	338	95	0	4	33.80	5
S A Patterson	16	15	2	183	43	0	0	14.07	1
R J Sidebottom	13	13	2	114	25	0	0	10.36	2

Also played

A J Finch	5	6	0	291	110	1	1	48.50	8
J E Root	4	6	0	275	97	0	3	45.83	1
R M Pyrah	6	6	2	161	62	0	1	40.25	2
L E Plunkett	8	9	2	210	86	0	2	30.00	4
A J Hodd	5	6	1	144	55	0	1	28.80	18/1
J A Brooks	17	15	8	148	37*	0	0	21.14	4
D M Hodgson	1	1	0	18	18	0	0	18.00	1/0
Azeem Rafiq	1	1	0	14	14	0	0	14.00	1
K Carver	1	1	1	2	2*	0	0	—	1

BOWLING

(Qualification 10 wickets)

Player	Overs	Mdns	Runs	Wkts	Avge	Best	5wI	10wM
R J Sidebottom	367.1	91	905	49	18.46	7-44	2	0
A U Rashid	379.4	73	1216	49	24.81	5-117	1	0
L E Plunkett	186	28	663	26	25.50	4-42	0	0
S A Patterson	423.4	139	1041	39	26.69	4-54	0	0
J A Brooks	540.2	113	1941	71	27.33	5-36	2	0
T T Bresnan	331	76	947	30	31.56	4-112	0	0

Also bowled

K Carver	20	4	65	3	21.66	2-27	0	0
A Lyth	59.2	12	160	5	32.00	2-18	0	0
K S Williamson	61.4	21	160	5	32.00	2-45	0	0
A J Finch	15	4	39	1	39.00	1-20	0	0
J E Root	13	1	40	1	40.00	1-26	0	0
R M Pyrah	99	26	309	6	51.50	3-37	0	0
Azeem Rafiq	38	6	110	1	110.00	1-79	0	0
J A Leaning	6	1	13	0	—	0-13	0	0
J M Bairstow	1	0	1	0	—	0-1	0	0

Second Investec Test Match
England v. Sri Lanka

Played at Headingley, Leeds, on June 20, 21, 22, 23 and 24, 2014
Sri Lanka won by 100 runs at 7.07pm on the Fifth day

Toss won by England

Close of play: First Day, England 36-0 (Cook 14*, Robson 21*); Second Day, England 320-6 (Prior 3*, Jordan 4*); Third Day, Sri Lanka 214-4 (Jayawardene 55*, Mathews 24*); Fourth Day, England 57-5 (Root 6*)

SRI LANKA

	First Innings		Second innings	
F D M Karunaratne, b Plunkett	28	c Prior b Plunkett	45
J K Silva, c Prior b Anderson	13	c Prior b Plunkett	13
K C Sangakkara, c Bell b Broad	79	lbw b Ali	55
D P M D Jayawardene, c Jordan b Plunkett	22	c Prior b Anderson	79
H D R L Thirimanne, c Robson b Plunkett	0	b Ali	0
* A D Mathews, c Ballance b Anderson	26	c Ali b Anderson	160
§ L D Chandimal, c Cook b Broad	45	c Ballance b Plunkett	7
K T G D Prasad, c Prior b Plunkett	22	c Root b Plunkett	0
H M R K B Herath, not out	14	run out (Root)	48
R M S Eranga, c Prior b Broad	0	not out	20
N Pradeep, c Prior b Plunkett	13	b Anderson	0
Extras b 8, lb 7, w 2	17	Extras b 5, lb 10, w 10, nb 5	30
Total	257	Total	457

FoW: 1-37 (Silva), 2-56 (Karunaratne), 3-108 (Jayawardene), 4-108 (Thirimanne), 5-161 (Mathews)
1st 6-228 (Sangakkara), 7-229 (Prasad), 8-229 (Chandimal), 9-229 (Eranga), 10-257 (Pradeep)
FoW: 1-40 (Silva), 2-93 (Karunaratne), 3-172 (Sangakkara), 4-176 (Thirimanne), 5-268
(Jayawardene), 6-277 (Chandimal), 7-277 (Prasad), 8-426 (Herath), 9-437 (Mathews), 10-457 (Pradeep)

	O	M	R	W		O	M	R	W
Anderson	19	5	49	2	Anderson	25.5	5	91	3
Broad	15	3	46	3	Broad	29	6	86	0
Jordan	16	4	58	0	Jordan	28	8	79	0
Plunkett	15.5	2	64	5	Plunkett	29	2	112	4
Ali	3	0	16	0	Ali	21	0	74	2
Root	1	0	9	0					

ENGLAND

	First Innings		Second innings	
* A N Cook, c Sangakkara b Prasad	17	(2) b Prasad	16
S D Robson, b Pradeep	127	(1) c Jayawardene b Prasad	24
G S Ballance, c Chandimal b Mathews	74	lbw b Prasad	0
I R Bell, c Chandimal b Eranga	64	b Prasad	8
J E Root, c Chandimal b Mathews	13	c Thirimanne b Pradeep	31
M M Ali, c Chandimal b Eranga	2	(7) not out	108
§ M J Prior, not out	27	(8) c Silva b Prasad	10
C J Jordan, c Jayawardene b Eranga	17	(9) lbw b Herath	21
S C J Broad, c Thirimanne b Mathews	4	(10) lbw b Herath	0
L E Plunkett, b Mathews	2	(6) c Pradeep b Herath	0
J M Anderson, c and b Eranga	0	c Herath b Eranga	0
Extras b 2, w 3, nb 13	18	Extras b 11, lb 7, w 4, nb 9	31
Total	365	Total	249

FoW: 1-49 (Cook), 2-191 (Ballance), 3-278 (Robson), 4-311 (Bell). 5-311 (Root)'
1st 6-313 (Ali), 7-338 (Jordan), 8-344 (Broad), 9-350 (Plunkett), 10-365 (Anderson)
FoW: 1-39 (Cook), 2-39 (Ballance), 3-50 (Robson), 4-52 (Bell), 5-57 (Plunkett)'
2nd 6-124 (Root), 7-160 (Prior), 8-212 (Jordan), 9-228 (Broad), 10-249 (Anderson)

	O	M	R	W		O	M	R	W
Pradeep	22	3	90	1	Pradeep	13	2	55	1
Eranga	32.5	10	93	4	Eranga	23.5	10	38	1
Herath	25	3	61	0	Herath	42	16	59	3
Prasad	20	3	75	1	Mathews	10	3	16	0
Mathews	16.4	4	44	4	Prasad	22	5	50	5
					Jayawardene	6	2	13	0

Man of the Match: A D Mathews

Umpires: B F Bowden and S J Davis
Third Umpire: P R Reiffel
Scorers: J T Potter and H Clayton
FourthUmpire: R T Robinson
A J Pycroft

142

ROYAL LONDON ONE-DAY CUP HIGHLIGHTS OF 2014

WINNERS

Durham, who defeated Warwickshire by 3 wickets

Wins by 10 wickets (1)

Derbyshire (151) lost to Yorkshire (155-0) by 10 wickets at Scarborough

Totals of 250 and over (2)

| 324-7 | v. Lancashire at Manchester (won) |
| 290-6 | v. Essex at Scarborough (lost) |

Match aggregates of 450 and over (3)

601	Yorkshire (324-7) defeated Lancashire (277) by 47 runs at Manchester
581	Yorkshire (290-6) lost to Essex (291-5) by 5 wickets at Scarborough
524	Sri Lanka A (275-9) defeated Yorkshire (249) by 26 runs at Leeds

Century Partnerships (4)

For the 1st wicket (2)

| 195 | A Lyth and A Z Lees | v. Northamptonshire at Northampton |
| 151* | A Lyth and A Z Lees | v. Derbyshire at Scarborough |

For the 6th wicket (2)

| 129 | J A Leaning and A U Rashid | v. Gloucestershire at Leeds |
| 109 | J A Leaning and A J Hodd | v. Essex at Scarborough |

Centuries (2)

J A Leaning (1)

   111* v. Essex at Scarborough

A Z Lees (1)

   102 v. Northamptonshire at Northampton

4 wickets in an innings (4)

A U Rashid (2)

   5-33 v. Hampshire at Southampton

   4-57 v. Sri Lanka A at Leeds

T T Bresnan (1)

   4-28 v. Worcestershire at Leeds

R M Pyrah (1)

   4-51 v. Durham at Leeds

3 catches in an innings (2)

J M Bairstow (1)

   4   v. Hampshire at Southampton

A J Hodd (1)

   3   v. Northamptonshire at Northampton

Debuts (4)

List A cricket: E Callis, J C Wainman and M E Waite
For Yorkshire: J A Brooks

Match-By-Match Reports **DAVE CALDWELL**

Royal London One-Day Cup — Group A
Lancashire v. Yorkshire

Played at Old Trafford, Manchester, on July 26, 2014
Yorkshire won by 47 runs

Toss won by Yorkshire

Yorkshire 2 points, Lancashire 0 points

YORKSHIRE

A Lyth, c Brown b Jarvis	46
A Z Lees, c Khawaja b Parry	66
K S Williamson, c Croft b Kabir Ali	70
* A W Gale, c Croft b Parry	38
§ J M Bairstow, c Croft b Clark	18
T T Bresnan, c Khawaja b Kabir Ali	32
J A Leaning, c Brown b Kabir Ali	18
R M Pyrah, not out	17
A U Rashid, not out	6
S A Patterson	
J A Brooks	Did not bat
Extras lb 4, w 5, nb 4	13
Total (7 wkts, 50 overs)	324

FoW: 1-69 (Lyth), 2-151 (Lees), 3-223 (Williamson), 4-230 (Gale), 5-256 (Bairstow), 6-290 (Bresnan), 7-303 (Leaning)

	O	M	R	W
Kabir Ali	10	0	77	3
Jarvis	5	1	33	1
Croft	10	0	53	0
White	10	0	66	0
Parry	10	0	58	2
Clark	5	0	33	1

LANCASHIRE

U T Khawaja, c Lyth b Bresnan	22
§ A L Davies, c Bresnan b Patterson	20
A G Prince, c Bresnan b Lyth	10
* P J Horton, run out (Pyrah)	38
K R Brown, b Brooks	129
S J Croft, run out (Brooks/Bairstow)	19
J Clark, c Lyth b Rashid	19
W A White, c Williamson b Rashid	3
Kabir Ali, c Bairstow b Bresnan	7
S D Parry, not out	0
K M Jarvis, run out (Brooks/Bairstow)	4
Extras b 1, lb 1, w 2, nb 2	6
Total ((46.4 overs)	277

FoW: 1-36 (Khawaja), 2-51 (Prince), 3-57 (Davies), 4-160 (Horton), 5-213 (Croft), 6-250 (Brown), 7-253 (White), 8-271 (Clark), 9-272 (Kabir), 10-277 (Jarvis)

	O	M	R	W
Brooks	10	0	61	1
Bresnan	7.4	0	40	2
Patterson	10	1	47	1
Lyth	3	0	24	1
Pyrah	6	0	33	0
Rashid	10	0	70	2

TV Man of the Match: K R Brown

Umpires: N G B Cook and M J Saggers   Scorers: J T Potter and D M White
Third Umpire: P K Baldwin

White Rose makes the hay

Suitably dusted down after the previous evening's exit from the *T20* competition, Yorkshire, recorded a 47-run victory against their arch-rivals.

They posted their top score against Lancashire in List A cricket of 324-7, the highest conceded by Lancashire at old Trafford, but the *Red Rose* still attempted a gallant run chase, led by Brown's scintillating 129.

It was no surprise to see skipper Gale opt for first use after winning the toss, and he was not let down by openers Lyth and Lees, who looked in sumptuous form on an excellent track.

Shots on both sides of the wicket came thick and fast as the pair closed in on seven per over in the initial 10-over powerplay. Lyth, having made 46 from 35 deliveries, picked out the only fielder on the leg-side boundary with the total on 69.

Williamson joined his junior partner as the runs continued to flow at a run a ball, Lees in particular striking the ball with gusto and timing. Lees passed his

KANE WILLIAMSON
Took flight with 70

highest List A score before perishing on the long-on fence. Williamson's circumspect innings began to take flight, a straight six signalling his intentions, but their partnership of 82 ended when the Kiwi international was taken at mid-on. Gale's 65-minute vigil ended in a catch to mid-off, but the lower order made hay, Bresnan smacking 32 in 18 balls.

Lancashire reached only 40 off the first 10 overs with Khawaja wonderfully taken by Lyth running back at mid-wicket. Opening partner Davies found it tough, and his innings came to an almost apologetic end when he was caught by Bresnan off Patterson for a 46-ball 20. With Prince also dismissed cheaply, Lancashire were staring down the barrel at 59-3 from 15 overs. Brown, in tandem with Horton, gave the *Red Rose* a sniff of victory. They put on 103 until Horton was run out when Pyrah deflected Brown's straight drive on to the stumps at the non-striker's end, but Brown raced to his century in 82 balls as the fielding became ragged with dropped catches. With 75 still needed the decisive wicket fell. Brown was deceived by a slower ball from Brooks, and the last five wickets fell in a flurry in a little over three overs.

Royal London One-Day Cup — Group A
Yorkshire v. Gloucestershire

Played at Headingley, Leeds, on July 29, 2014
Gloucestershire won by 3 wickets

Toss won by Yorkshire
Gloucestershire 2 points, Yorkshire 0 points

YORKSHIRE

A Lyth, lbw b Payne		6
A Z Lees, c Cockbain b Gidman		10
K S Williamson, c Rouse b Gidman		12
* A W Gale, c Rouse b Payne		16
§ J M Bairstow, c Klinger b Payne		0
J A Leaning, st Rouse b Taylor		56
A U Rashid, c Cockbain b Howell		71
T T Bresnan, run out (Dent)		0
R M Pyrah, run out (Rouse)		1
S A Patterson, not out		1
J A Brooks, lbw b Taylor		0
Extras b 5, lb 5, w 9		19
Total (41.4 overs)		192

FoW: 1-12 (Lees), 2-16 (Lyth), 3-45 (Gale), 4-45 (Williamson), 5-45 (Bairstow), 6-174 (Rashid), 7-181 (Bresnan), 8-186 (Pyrah), 9-192 (Leaning), 10-192 (Brooks)

	O	M	R	W
Payne	8	2	31	3
Gidman	8	2	28	2
Miles	8	1	39	0
Howell	10	0	45	1
Taylor	6.4	0	33	2
Smith	1	0	6	0

GLOUCESTERSHIRE

* M Klinger, c Bresnan b Pyrah		37
H J H Marshall, c Lyth b Bresnan		7
C D J Dent, c Bairstow b Bresnan		5
I A Cockbain, b Rashid		19
W R S Gidman, not out		71
B A C Howell, c Gale b Rashid		4
§ A P Rouse, c Bairstow b Pyrah		4
J M R Taylor, c Lyth b Rashid		38
J M J Smith, not out		4
C N Miles		
D A Payne	Did not bat	
Extras w 2, nb 2		4
Total (7 wkts, 45.2 overs)		193

FoW: 1-19 (Marshall), 2-27 (Dent), 3-69 (Klinger), 4-72 (Cockbain), 5-78 (Howell), 6-83 (Rouse), 9-152 (Taylor)

	O	M	R	W
Bresnan	9.2	0	51	2
Brooks	8	0	47	0
Patterson	7	0	24	0
Pyrah	10	2	22	2
Rashid	10	1	43	3
Lyth	1	0	6	0

Umpires: N G B Cook and S A Garratt
Scorers: J T Potter and A J Bull

Stop-go march of Gladiators

WELL HELD: Yorkshire's Adam Lyth catches Jack Taylor for 38

Yorkshire tried to find every conceivable way of losing before they went down in a game short on quality but high on incident.

They somewhat surprisingly opted to bat first under a cloudy sky with a 10.30am start.

Lees fell in the second over, slicing to point, and Lyth was trapped in front aiming to leg.

Williamson and Gale staged a recovery of sorts before three wickets were lost for no runs. Williamson edged a beauty to wicket-keeper Rouse; Gale flayed at one outside the off-stump, and Bairstow was taken smartly low down at first slip.

At 45-5 in 13 overs the Vikings were capitulating in spectacular fashion, but Leaning and Rashid set about rebuilding: watchful at first, they began to take a grip, and their stand reached three figures in 136 deliveries as Rashid brought up his first List A half-century at the 59th attempt. A rattled Gloucestershire began to make elementary errors in the field, and Leaning's regulation chance to third-man was shelled.

Leaning brought up his half-century from 73 balls, and Yorkshire were eyeing a total in excess of 250 with over 12 overs remaining. The sixth-wicket partnership reached 129 — a county record for List A — but Rashid skied Howell to Cockbain on the mid-wicket boundary for 71. Two needless run-outs and a stumping brought a grinding halt, and when Brooks was lbw first ball the Vikings had lost their last four wickets for 11 runs in 18 deliveries, with nearly nine overs unused.

The Gladiators were 34-2 at lunch, both scalps to Bresnan, and Yorkshire reduced the visitors to 82-6, Rashid and Pyrah causing chaos in the middle-order. It was the partnership of 69 between Gidman and Taylor that settled the issue, despite Rashid claiming Taylor's wicket for 38 (above). Pyrah finished with 2-22 from his 10 overs, but Gidman's career-best unbeaten 71 saw his side home with 28 balls remaining.

Royal London One-Day Cup — Group A
Northamptonshire v. Yorkshire

Played at Wantage Road, Northampton, on August 7, 2014
Yorkshire won by 6 wickets

Toss won by Yorkshire

Yorkshire 2 points, Northamptonshire 0 points

NORTHAMPTONSHIRE

R E Levi, c Hodd b Patterson		34
S D Peters, c Hodd b Bresnan		0
* K J Coetzer, c Hodd b Brooks		8
A M Rossington, c Brooks b Rashid		75
§ B M Duckett, c Leaning b Pyrah		45
M N W Spriegel, c Lyth b Pyrah		12
G G White, c Leaning b Pyrah		11
A J Hall, not out		9
J D Middlebrook, not out		5
M A Chambers		
M Azharullah	Did not bat	
Extras lb 4, w 4, nb 2		10
Total (7 wkts, 38 overs)		209

FoW: 1-1 (Peters), 2-17 (Coetzer), 3-90 (Levi), 4-163 (Rossington), 5-179 (Duckett), 6-194 (White), 7-194 (Spriegel)

	O	M	R	W
Bresnan	8	0	36	1
Brooks	8	0	36	1
Pyrah	7	0	50	3
Patterson	7	0	44	1
Rashid	8	0	39	1

YORKSHIRE

A Lyth, c Spriegel b Middlebrook		84
A Z Lees, c White b Spriegel		102
K S Williamson, b White		4
* A W Gale, not out		4
J A Leaning, c Spriegel b Middlebrook		0
A U Rashid, not out		0
§ A J Hodd		
T T Bresnan		
R M Pyrah	Did not bat	
S A Patterson		
J A Brooks		
Extras b 3, lb 6, w 6, nb 4		19
Total (4 wkts, 34 overs)		213

FoW: 1-195 (Lees), 2-205 (Williamson), 3-209 (Lyth), 4-209 (Leaning)

	O	M	R	W
Spriegel	8	0	35	1
Azharullah	4	0	52	0
Chambers	4	0	22	0
Hall	5	0	23	0
Middlebrook	5	0	26	2
White	8	1	36	1

Umpires: N G C Cowley and R T Robinson   Scorers: J T Potter and A C Kingston

Lees puts Steelbacks to sword

A maiden List A century for Lees helped Yorkshire to cruise to an emphatic victory after rain had reduced the match to 38 overs per side.

The Vikings unsurprisingly chose to field, and Peters was caught behind off Bresnan's first ball of the match. Coetzer was put down in the slips next ball, but he fell in the fourth over, Hodd taking the catch as Brooks found the edge.

From 17-2 Steelbacks recovered through a typically robust inning from South African Richard Levi and a dashing display from the promising Rossington.

ALEX LEES: A maiden List A century out of the top drawer

With the score advanced to 90 in the 17th over, Patterson tempted Levi and Hodd celebrated his third catch. Rossington continued to impress as Yorkshire's bowling became a little ragged, but on 75 he holed out to Brooks off Rashid. The total now was 163 with under 10 overs remaining. but Yorkshire closed the innings down in fine fashion, despite a 49-ball 45 from Duckett, who batted excellently with Rossington. The hosts looked below par at 209-7 from their revised allocation, only 50 runs coming in the last 10 overs.

Yorkshire's reply was straight out of the top drawer, Lyth and Lees bringing their Championship form into the shorter format in no uncertain terms. Lyth was first to his half century off 55 balls in the 16th over, and Lees followed soon afterwards at a shade over a run a ball. Then the acceleration really began. Lees was in no mood to stand on ceremony as the depleted attack was put to the sword: he blazed his way to a maiden List A century in 85 balls with 14 fours and a six before falling for 102, the total on 195 in the 29th over. With the game all but done, a late flurry of wickets went down, including Williamson for four and Lyth for a superb 84 that spanned 88 deliveries and contained nine boundaries. Leaning departed to his first ball, three wickets having tumbled for four runs, before Gale and Rashid saw Vikings home with 24 balls in hand.

Royal London One-Day Cup — Group A
Yorkshire v. Worcestershire

Played at Headingley, Leeds, on August 7, 2014
Yorkshire won by 6 wickets

Toss won by Worcestershire   Yorkshire 2 points, Worcestershire 0 points

WORCESTERSHIRE

* D K H Mitchell, lbw b Fisher		33
R K Oliver, lbw b Brooks		5
T C Fell, b Bresnan		10
A N Kervezee, c Lees b Bresnan		0
T Kohler-Cadmore, c Lyth b Bresnan		1
R A Whiteley, lbw b Rashid		13
§ O B Cox, b Rashid		10
J Leach, not out		43
S H Choudhry, c Hodd b Brooks		0
J D Shantry, st Hodd b Rashid		7
M J McClenaghan, b Bresnan		16
Extras w 1, nb 2		3
Total (43.2 overs)		141

FoW: 1-15 (Oliver), 2-42 (Fell), 3-42 (Kervezee), 4-48 (Kohler-Cadmore), 5-54 (Mitchell), 6-67 (Cox), 7-78 (Whiteley), 8-85 (Choudhry), 9-102 (Shantry), 10-141 (McClenaghan)

	O	M	R	W
Bresnan	7.2	2	28	4
Brooks	10	1	34	2
Fisher	9	1	29	1
Pyrah	7	1	29	0
Rashid	10	2	21	3

YORKSHIRE

A Lyth, c Cox b Leach		14
A Z Lees, c Fell b McClenaghan		3
K S Williamson, lbw b McClenaghan		43
* A W Gale, b McClenaghan		29
J A Leaning, not out		20
A U Rashid, not out		27
§ A J Hodd		
T T Bresnan		
R M Pyrah	Did not bat	
M D Fisher		
J A Brooks		
Extras lb 1, w 3, nb 4		8
Total (4 wkts, 30.2 overs)		144

FoW: 1-5 (Lees), 2-55 (Lyth), 3-77 (Williamson), 4-100 (Gale)

	O	M	R	W
Shantry	8	2	22	0
McClenaghan	8	0	57	3
Leach	6	1	30	1
Choudhry	6	0	16	0
Whiteley	2.2	0	18	0

Umpires: R J Bailey and G D Lloyd   Scorers: J T Potter and D E Pugh

Bowlers set up victory romp

Excellent bowling led by Bresnan and Rashid sent back the visitors for 141 with 40 balls remaining.

It would have been far worse but for brisk runs from Leach and McClenaghan, the final pair.

All-round triumph: Adil Rashid follows his fine bowling with the winning hit

After a tight opening burst Brooks took the first wicket of Oliver, who was lbw aiming to leg. The total advanced to 42, but Bresnan produced a double-wicket maiden, bowling Fell and finding the edge of Kervezee's bat for Lees to hold on at slip at the second attempt. Wickets continued to tumble, Bresnan again the bowler as Kohler-Cadmore was comfortably taken by Lyth at slip. Then came the key wicket of skipper Mitchell, 16-year-old Fisher trapping the in-form batsman in front for 33 as he aimed to mid-wicket.

Rashid turned the screw mid-innings with 3-21 in his 10 overs as Worcester subsided to 85-8 in the 30th over. Leach and Shantry showed some resistance, and the last wicket partnership of 39 gave Worcester some hope before Bresnan returned to claim his fourth victim, Leach remaining unbeaten with a pleasing 43 from 63 balls.

Yorkshire's reply was not without the odd blemish, Lees playing a curious inning in which a mixture of poor shot selection and perhaps over-confidence resulted in a fine catch running round from mid-on by Fell with only five on the board. Williamson was dropped at first slip on one, and after taking lunch on 38-1 Yorkshire restarted their reply in circumspect fashion. Lyth, in particular, was strangely subdued, and on 14 he feathered behind to Cox, leaving his side at 55-2.

The total reached 77 before Williamson was pinned on the back foot by McClenaghan, having contributed 43 from 63 balls. Gale appeared in positive mood, striking his first six scoring shots to the boundary before McClenaghan bowled him off an inside edge for 29 in 21 balls, and an unbeaten partnership of 44 in eight overs between Rashid and Leaning settled any nerves as the Vikings romped home.

Royal London One-Day Cup — Group A
Leicestershire v. Yorkshire

Played at Grace Road, Leicester, on August 8, 2014
Yorkshire won by 3 wickets (D/L method)

Toss won by Yorkshire

Yorkshire 2 points, Leicestershire 0 points

LEICESTERSHIRE

A J Robson, b Brooks		12
§ N J O'Brien, c Williamson b Rashid		34
G P Smith, b Brooks		4
M A G Boyce, not out		74
D J Redfern, st Hodd b Rashid		15
S J Thakor, b Pyrah		0
* S B Styris, c Hodd b Fisher		19
T J Wells, c Brooks b Pyrah		24
B A Raine, c Hodd b Bresnan		43
A J Ireland, not out		0
C E Shreck	Did not bat	
Extras b 1, lb 4, w 6		11
Total (8 wkts, 50 overs)		236

FoW: 1-24 (Robson), 2-34 (Smith), 3-68 (O'Brien), 4-90 (Redfern), 5-92 (Thakor), 6-118 (Styris), 7-172 (Wells), 8-234 (Raine).

	O	M	R	W
Bresnan	10	1	42	1
Brooks	10	1	26	2
Fisher	7	0	49	1
Lyth	1	0	8	0
Pyrah	9	0	43	2
Rashid	10	0	50	2
Leaning	3	0	13	0

YORKSHIRE

Revised target to win: 191 runs off 32 overs

A Lyth, c Styris b Oreland		13
A Z Lees, c O'Brien b Shreck		0
K S Williamson, c Shreck b Raine		20
* A W Gale, b Thakor		10
J A Leaning, c Wells b Styris		14
A U Rashid, c O'Brien b Styris		18
§ A J Hodd, not out		69
T T Bresnan, c Wells b Shreck		24
R M Pyrah, not out		10
M D Fisher		
J A Brooks	Did not bat	
Extras lb 4, w 11		15
Total (7 wkts, 31.3 overs)		193

FoW: 1-7 (Lees), 2-20 (Lyth), 3-47 (Gale), 4-54 (Williamson), 5-81 (Rashid), 6-91 (Leaning), 7-153 (Bresnan).

	O	M	R	W
Shreck	7	0	16	2
Ireland	7	1	31	1
Thakor	4.3	0	36	1
Raine	6	0	57	1
Styris	4	0	25	2
Redfern	3	0	24	0

Umpires: R J Bailey and G D Lloyd

Scorers: J T Potter and P J Rogers

Leicestershire v. Yorkshire

Hodd proves his winning worth

ANDY HODD: His career-best 69 not out snared the Foxes

Andy Hodd provided a timely reminder of his worth with a match-winning unbeaten 69 that dragged Yorkshire over the line in a rain-affected contest.

Chasing a revised target of 191 in 32 overs, Hodd's partnership with Bresnan for the seventh wicket proved pivotal when defeat looked very much on the cards.

Set an initial target of 237 from 50 overs, the visitors lost wickets at regular intervals: Lees was caught at the wicket for a duck, and Lyth contributed a strange innings of 13 from 37 deliveries, his departure reducing Yorkshire to 20-2.

After 11 overs and with only seven runs added a heavy shower drove the players from the field for more than an hour, *Duckworth-Lewis* prescribing a deduction of 18 overs and a revised target. Big wickets fell soon after the resumption — Gale cleaned up by Thakor for 10 and Williamson, looking set on 20, falling on his sword. Rashid and Leaning both departed within 10 runs, and at 91-6 the likelihood of a Yorkshire victory was remote. A stand of 62 between Hodd and Bresnan turned the tide completely, although a key chance was missed when Hodd on 41 was dropped at long-on by Ireland at 149.

Bresnan was taken in the deep for 24, but Hodd continued his assault on the Foxes' beleaguered attack along with Pyrah. This pair blasted a scintillating 32 from 15 deliveries to drive Yorkshire home with only three balls remaining — the winning runs coming from a huge six by Pyrah. Hodd finished with his Yorkshire career-best List A score of 69 in 43 balls with 10 fours and a maximum.

Leicestershire had found the going tough in their own innings, with wickets going down frequently, and only a steadfast unbeaten 74 in 94 balls from Boyce gave them a total worth defending. Brooks claimed two early wickets in a fine spell, clean bowling Robson and the dangerous Smith. The Foxes recovered from 118-6 in 30 overs, thanks to the patience of Boyce and some late fireworks from Raine who struck a brutal 43 as Yorkshire's fielding became sloppy.

Royal London One-Day Cup — Group A
Yorkshire v. Essex

Played at North Marine Road, Scarborough, on August 11, 2014
Essex won by 5 wickets

Toss won by Essex

Essex 2 points, Yorkshire 0 points

YORKSHIRE

A Lyth, run out (Velani)		38
A Z Lees, b Masters		8
K S Williamson, c Foster b Masters		2
* A W Gale, c Phillips b ten Doeschate		45
J A Leaning, not out		111
A U Rashid, c Pettini b Masters		14
§ A J Hodd, b Masters		42
T T Bresnan, not out		9
R M Pyrah		
S A Patterson	Did not bat	
J A Brooks		
Extras lb 4, w 17		21
Total (6 wkts, 50 overs)		290

FoW: 1-26 (Lees), 2-38 (Williamson), 3-55 (Lyth), 4-123 (Gale), 5-154 (Rashid), 6-263 (Hodd)

	O	M	R	W
Napier	10	0	84	0
Masters	10	2	34	4
Topley	10	0	54	0
Westley	5	0	14	0
Phillips	7	0	42	0
ten Doeschate	8	0	58	1

ESSEX

M L Pettini, c Hodd b Brooks		0
T Westley, not out		111
G M Smith, c Williamson b Bresnan		0
K S Velani, lbw b Bresnan		1
J D Ryder, c Lyth b Pyrah		36
* R N ten Doeschate, c Lyth b Patterson		119
§ J S Foster, not out		7
G R Napier		
D D Masters		
R J W Topley	Did not bat	
T J Phillips		
Extras b 1, lb 3, w 5, nb 8		17
Total (5 wkts, 45.5 overs)		291

FoW: 1-1 (Pettini), 2-11 (Smith), 3-15 (Velani), 4-68 (Ryder), 5-277 (ten Doeschate)

	O	M	R	W
Brooks	9	0	43	1
Bresnan	10	1	53	2
Patterson	8	0	44	1
Pyrah	7	0	51	1
Leaning	3	0	25	0
Rashid	8.5	0	71	0

Umpires: S C Gale and P J Hartley

Scorers: J T Potter and A E Choat

Yorkshire v. Essex

Quickfire Leaning outgunned

A maiden List A century for Jack Leaning proved in vain as Yorkshire were swept aside.

A stunning partnership between Westley and ten Doeschate saw both batsmen strike fine centuries in chasing a seemingly impossing score of 290.

JACK LEANING: His maiden century should have made mission impossible

The fifth-wicket pair put on 209 in 31 overs, only eight runs short of being the highest against Yorkshire for any wicket in one-day cricket. It was all the more impressive because Essex had slipped to 15-3 as Yorkshire got off to a flying start with the ball. Pettini went third ball of the innings for a duck, caught behind off Brooks, and then Bresnan bagged a brace of cheap wickets — Smith taken smartly by Williamson, also for nought, and Velani trapped in front for a single.

Westley held up one end while the dangerous Ryder hit six fours and a six in his breezy 36 before driving Pyrah to point. Attack proved the best defence as Westley and ten Doeschate launched a thrilling onslaught on the hapless bowling. They added 100 in 16 overs as fours and sixes became common place. The powerplay arrived on 34 overs as both batsmen seemed unstoppable. ten Doeschate reached his century in 86 balls, and Westley soon followed in a more sedate but no less impressive 120 deliveries. ten Doeschate finally failed to get hold of an attempted hook, and spooning a catch to Lyth off Patterson, but the damage was done. Essex reached their target with 25 balls remaining.

Yorkshire's innings had threatened to fall apart on a fine batting strip. Lees and Williamson succumbed to the nagging medium-pace of Masters, but Lyth looked in fine touch, reaching a run-a-ball 38 before he was run out by Velani's direct hit. Yorkshire were 55-3, and skipper Gale dropped anchor to let others flourish at the other end. Gale fell for 45, while Rashid's brief sojourn ended on 14, leaving the hosts 154-5.

Leaning was finding his feet, and he and Hodd blazed away freely as Essex attack began to lose control, 109 runs coming in a frantic 12 overs. Leaning reached 50 in 67 balls before Hodd tried one reverse-sweep too many and was cleaned up by Masters. Napier's last over cost 23 runs as Leaning brought up his landmark century with a six. He remained unbeaten on 111 from 99 balls with four fours and four sixes.

Royal London One-Day Cup — Group A
Yorkshire v. Derbyshire

Played at North Marine Road, Scarborough, on August 13, 2014
Yorkshire won by 10 wickets

Toss won by Yorkshire   Yorkshire 2 points, Derbyshire 0 points

DERBYSHIRE

W J Durston, c Rashid b Bresnan	1
B A Godleman, c Lyth b Pyrah	36
M J North, c Hodd b Bresnan	2
* W L Madsen, c Hodd b Pyrah	20
A L Hughes, c Leaning b Patterson	43
S L Elstone, c Lyth b Pyrah	0
§ G D Cross, c Bresnan b Rashid	11
D J Wainwright, c Leaning b Rashid	5
A P Palladino, lbw b Rashid	5
B D Cotton, not out	18
M H A Footitt, b Patterson	5
Extras lb 1, w 2, nb 2	5
Total (41 overs)	151

FoW: 1-1 (Durston), 2-4 (North), 3-52 (Madsen), 4-73 (Godleman), 5-73 (Elstone), 6-92 (Cross), 7-104 (Wainwright), 8-114 (Palladino), 9-138 (Hughes), 10-151 (Footitt)

	O	M	R	W
Patterson	8	0	27	2
Bresnan	8	2	30	2
Pyrah	7	0	25	3
Rashid	10	0	45	3
Fisher	8	0	23	0

YORKSHIRE

A Lyth, not out	67
A Z Lees, not out	69
K S Williamson	
* A W Gale	
J A Leaning	
A U Rashid	
§ A J Hodd	Did not bat
T T Bresnan	
R M Pyrah	
S A Patterson	
M D Fisher	
Extras b 8, lb 2, w 3, nb 6	19
Total (0 wkts, 29.3 overs)	155

	O	M	R	W
Footitt $	4.5	0	24	0
Cotton	8.3	1	39	0
North $	1.1	0	7	0
Palladino	6	0	22	0
Wainwright	3	0	20	0
Elstone	4	0	26	0
Hughes	2	0	7	0

$ Footitt was not allowed to complete his fifth over

Umpires: M R Benson and P J Hartley   Scorers: J T Potter and J M Brown

Yorkshire v. Derbyshire
A stroll into quarter-finals

An emphatic 10-wicket win took Yorkshire into the quarter-finals with a game to spare as they brushed Derbyshire aside with the minimum of fuss.

Lyth and Lees off their own bats raced to the well below-par target of 152 with a not insignificant 20 overs remaining.

Heels over head: A diving acrobatic save by paceman Steven Patterson

Yorkshire's pace took control from the off, Bresnan's opening delivery producing an indeterminate shot from Durston straight into the hands of Rashid at third-man. The same bowler found the edge of North's bat in his next over, Hodd taking a fine tumbling catch. Derbyshire struggled to find the fence in the initial powerplay overs, and it was not until the seventh over that Madsen was able to contribute his side's first boundary.

The score advanced past 50 as Madsen and Godleman dug in resolutely before the wheels came off rapidly, thanks to fine bowling by Pyrah, who dismissed the pair of them on his way to superb figures of 3-25 in seven overs. Alex Hughes offered some defiance to compile 43 from 76 balls, yet he found willing partners in short supply. Cross, Palladino and Wainwright all departed to Rashid. Hughes counterattacked until his demise at 138, and the innings fell away quietly in the 41st over.

A swift turnaround saw Yorkshire's openers in no mood to hang around as they raced to 64 from 12 overs before the interval. By this time Footitt had been ordered out of the attack by umpires Hartley and Benson: in one over the paceman bowled a beamer and three short-pitched deliveries, and his race was run for the day. Lees reached his half-century in 66 deliveries with a rasping cut off Elstone, and Lyth followed him to the landmark from 63 balls with two quickfire boundaries off the same bowler. With the weather closing in the pair accelerated through the gears, the game ending in almost routine fashion, with Lyth unbeaten on 67 and Lees 69.

Royal London One-Day Cup — Group A
Hampshire v. Yorkshire

Played at The Rose Bowl, West End, Southampton, on August 21, 2014
Yorkshire won by 6 wickets

Toss won by Yorkshire

Yorkshire 2 points, Hampshire 0 points

HAMPSHIRE

* M A Carberry, c Bairstow b Bresnan	0
S P Terry, c Bairstow b Brooks	0
J H K Adams, not out	91
L A Dawson, c Bairstow b Brooks	18
J S Gatting, lbw b Rashid	13
M T Coles, c Lees b Patterson	25
§ M D Bates, c Bairstow b Brooks	19
D R Briggs, lbw b Rashid	1
B M R Akram, b Rashid	1
T E Barber, lbw b Rashid	0
J A Tomlinson, lbw b Rashid	0
Extras w 2, nb 2	4
Total (39 overs)	172

FoW: 1-1 (Carberry), 2-5 (Terry), 3-31 (Dawson), 4-76 (Gatting), 5-122 (Coles), 6-161 (Bates), 7-162 (Briggs), 8-168 (Akram), 9-168 (Barber), 10-172 (Tomlinson)

	O	M	R	W
Bresnan	6	0	40	1
Brooks	8	2	30	3
Lyth	5	1	27	0
Rashid	10	1	33	5
Patterson	6	1	13	1
Pyrah	4	0	29	0

YORKSHIRE

A Lyth, c Carberry b Tomlinson		21
A Z Lees, c Gatting b Tomlinson		61
K S Williamson, c Bates b Barber		33
* A W Gale, c Bates b Barber		0
§ J M Bairstow, not out		45
J A Leaning, not out		1
A U Rashid		
T T Bresnan		
R M Pyrah	Did not bat	
S A Patterson		
J A Brooks		
Extras lb 1, w 9, nb 2		12
Total (4 wkts, 28.5 overs)		173

FoW: 1-31 (Lyth), 2-81 (Williamson), 3-81 (Gale), 4-159 (Lees)

	O	M	R	W
Coles	8.5	1	57	0
Tomlinson	5	0	25	2
Akram	2	0	24	0
Briggs	6	0	28	0
Barber	4	0	22	2
Dawson	3	0	16	0

Umpires: M J D Bodenham and D J Millns   Scorers: J T Potter and K R Baker

Questions without answers

A career-best display by wrist-spinner Adil Rashid helped to secure the points as already qualified Yorkshire continued their limited-overs form.

Rashid finished with 5-33, his last four wickets coming in only 15 balls as Hampshire, batting first, were sent back in 39 overs for 172.

Yorkshire still opted for full strength in stark contrast to their hosts, who chose to rest four players ahead of *T20* Finals Day.

Carberry, made skipper for the day, got off to a doubly bad start, losing the toss and lasting for only two balls before he edged Bresnan to Bairstow. Brooks found the edge of Terry's bat in the next over, and Hampshire were 5-2.

Only a stoic effort by Adams took Hampshire to a remotely challenging target. He shared a stand of 45 for the fourth wicket with Gatting and 46 for the next with

ADIL RASHID: Wrist-spin wizard in a purple patch

Coles. Despite the run rate being kept under control the wickets had dried up before Rashid's spell. The score crashed from 161-5 to 172 all out as the all-rounder's purple patch continued, Hampshire's tail having no answer to his searching questions. Adams remained resolute to finish with a fine unbeaten 91 from 110 balls.

Yorkshire made light work of their reply, reaching the target in the 29th over. Lees and Lyth struck 31 inside the first six overs before Lyth miscued Tomlinson into the hands of Carberry. Yorkshire were 79-1 at the interval, but a double strike upon the resumption threatened to scupper an excellent run chase. Williamson feathered one behind off debutant Barber for a sprightly 33, only for Gale to fall in identical fashion next ball. From 81-3 the game fell firmly back into the visitors' hands as Lees, 61, completed his fourth score of 50 or more. He and the typically industrious Bairstow, 45, added 78 for the fourth wicket, Lees falling with 14 runs required. Bairstow and Leaning completed the task with minimum fuss and 127 deliveries still to be bowled.

Royal London One-Day Cup — Quarter-Final
Yorkshire v. Durham

Played at Headingley, Leeds, on August 28, 2014
Durham won by 31 runs
Toss won by Yorkshire

DURHAM

* M D Stoneman, c Ballance b Pyrah	102
§ P Mustard, c Bairstow b Rashid	23
C S MacLeod, b Patterson	4
S G Borthwick, c Bresnan b Rashid	10
P D Collingwood, c Ballance b Brooks	38
K K Jennings, c and b Pyrah	2
G J Muchall, c Williamson b Pyrah	26
G R Breese, c Bresnan b Patterson	13
J W Hastings, b Patterson	6
P Coughlin, not out	2
C Rushworth, b Pyrah	3
Extras b 4, lb 2, w 2	8
Total (48.4 overs)	237

FoW: 1-57 (Mustard), 2-69 (MacLeod), 3-98 (Borthwick), 4-178 (Stoneman), 5-182 (Collingwood) 6-184 (Jennings). 7-208 (Breese), 8-223 (Muchall), 9-232 (Hastings), 10-237 (Rushworth)

	O	M	R	W
Bresnan	9	0	51	0
Brooks	9	1	46	1
Patterson	10	1	39	3
Pyrah	9.4	0	51	4
Rashid	10	0	37	2
Lyth	1	0	7	0

YORKSHIRE

A Lyth, c Mustard b Hastings	28
A Z Lees, c Stoneman b Rushworth	49
K S Williamson, c Mustard b Hastings	0
G S Ballance, c Coughlin b Borthwick	61
§ J M Bairstow, c Mustard b Rushworth	0
* A W Gale, st Mustard b Breese	0
A U Rashid, c Muchall b Collingwood	6
T T Bresnan, b Collingwood	12
R M Pyrah, not out	29
S A Patterson, b Rushworth	8
J A Brooks, run out (MacLeod/Rushworth)	0
Extras lb 6, w 7	13
Total (48.1 overs)	206

FoW: 1-58 (Lyth), 2-58 (Williamson), 3-133 (Lees), 4-133 (Bairstow), 5-138 (Gale), 6-147 (Rashid) 7-168 (Bresnan), 8-170 (Ballance), 9-204 (Patterson), 10-206 (Brooks)

	O	M	R	W
Coughlin	4	0	34	0
Rushworth	7.1	1	23	3
Breese	10	1	31	1
Hastings	9	0	38	2
Collingwood	10	0	29	2
Borthwick	8	0	45	1

Umpires: M J D Bodenham and N G C Cowley   Scorers: J T Potter and B Hunt

Bowlers pilot the Jets home

Yorkshire fell 31 runs short in a pulsating tie after both sides had wrestled for the initiative.

It was to be Durham's bowlers who struck the knockout blows.

Gale had no hesitation in inserting Durham with cloud cover around and the threat of rain in the afternoon.

Play was suspended for 30 min-

GARY BALLANCE: Looked set to take the game away with top-score 61

utes after only three overs when a spectator required emergency medical attention, but could not be saved. Durham began to play their strokes on the resumption, the ever dangerous Mustard in tandem with Stoneman feasting on some wayward bowling to rattle up 46 in the first nine overs.

The introduction of Patterson proved to be the fillip Yorkshire needed. The dependable medium-pacer bowled a miserly spell of seven overs for 15 runs to stall the Jets, the run-rate dipping under four per over. Rashid claimed the first scalp as Mustard let frustration get the better of him to reverse-sweep, the ball lobbing gently to Bairstow. Patterson bowled MacLeod for four, reducing the visitors to 69-2 in the 18th over, and Borthwick exited for 10 when a poor shot was taken superbly by a tumbling Bresnan at mid-on.

Stoneman was going to be the key wicket: the elegant left-hander

Thumb up: Andrew Gale puts the Dynamos on strike

enjoyed a partnership of 80 with Collingwood as Durham showed real intent in the middle overs, Stoneman going on to his century from 117 balls.

He perished two runs later, caught at deep square leg off Pyrah, the score 178-4 with 10 overs remaining. Collingwood followed in similar fashion, taken by the same fielder off

Quarter-Final: Yorkshire v. Durham

Brooks for 38, and this signalled the Jets' swift demise, the last seven wickets falling for 59 runs.

Only a breezy 26 from Muchall ensured that a semi-competitive total was posted. The last wicket went down in the 49th over as Durham reached a below-par 237, Pyrah finishing with 4-51 and Patterson 3-39.

Yorkshire's reply started in typically assured fashion, Lyth and Lees soon into their stride. The prolific opening pair had reached 58 in the ninth over before Lyth was caught at the wicket attempting an expansive drive of Hastings.

With his very next ball the Australian seamer struck again, Williamson tentatively prodding outside the off-stump. Durham now looked in control, spearheaded by Hastings who very nearly had Ballance without scoring as he spilled a sharp return catch.

RICHARD PYRAH: Topped the bowling and was still there at the end on 29

Ballance endured a scratchy start, but he began to show his quality as he and Lees started to take the game away from the visitors. Lees fell one short of a deserved half century, Rushworth getting one to climb on the batsmen, who could only lob it to short-extra-cover. Bairstow was caught behind two balls later, and Gale was stumped off Breese, both failing to score. The Vikings were in trouble on 138-5, requiring nearly six runs an over. Ballance brought up his half century off 68 balls, but at the other end Rashid picked out Muchall on the mid-wicket boundary. Yorkshire were now second favourites at 147-6.

The batting powerplay brought a mere 23 runs for the loss of two wickets after Bresnan was bowled by Collingwood. The innings had fallen apart, and once Ballance was taken on the square-leg boundary for 61 the game was effectively over. Pyrah provided some hope with a gutsy unbeaten 29 before he ran out of partners, but Yorkshire lost their last eight wickets for 73 runs. Collingwood, Breese and Hastings all turned in outstanding figures for the Jets.

Royal London One-Day Cup

FINAL TABLES 2014

GROUP A

		P	W	L	T	NR/A	PTS	NRR
1	Yorkshire Vikings (C 6) *	8	6	2	0	0	12.00	1.040
2	Essex Eagles (B 2) *	8	5	1	0	2	12.00	0.387
3	Gloucestershire (C 4) *	8	4	2	0	2	10.00	-0.016
4	Derbyshire Falcons (B 6) * + ...	8	4	2	0	2	8.00	0.045
5	Leicestershire Foxes (C 5)	8	3	4	0	1	7.00	-0.393
6	Northamptonshire Steelbacks (A 2)	8	2	4	0	2	6.00	-0.277
7	Worcestershire Rapids (A 5)	8	2	4	0	2	6.00	-0.328
8	Lancashire Lightning (B 3)	8	2	5	0	1	5.00	-0.279
9	Hampshire Royals (B 1)	8	1	5	0	2	4.00	-0.569

+ Deducted 2 points for a poor pitch in 2013

GROUP B

		P	W	L	T	NR/A	PTS	NRR
1	Nottinghamshire Outlaws (A 1) *	8	4	1	1	2	11.00	0.364
2	Kent Spitfires (A 4) *	8	4	1	1	2	11.00	0.245
3	Warwickshire Bears (A 7) *	8	4	3	0	1	9.00	0.343
4	Durham (B 4) *	8	4	3	0	1	9.00	0.212
5	Glamorgan (C 2)	8	4	4	0	0	8.00	0.230
6	Somerset (C 1)......................	8	3	4	1	0	7.00	0.067
7	Middlesex Panthers (C 3)	8	3	4	0	1	7.00	-0.280
8	Sussex Sharks (A 3)	8	3	5	0	0	6.00	-0.501
9	Surrey (B 5)	8	1	5	1	1	4.00	-0.643

* Qualified for Quarter-Finals

(2013 group positions in brackets)

YORKSHIRE AVERAGES 2014

ROYAL LONDON ONE-DAY CUP

Played 9   Won 6   Lost 3

BATTING AND FIELDING

(Qualification 4 completed innings)

Player	M.	I.	N.O.	Runs	H.S.	100s	50s	Avge	ct/st
J A Leaning	8	7	3	220	111*	1	1	55.00	4
A Z Lees	9	9	1	368	102	1	3	46.00	2
A Lyth	9	9	1	317	84	0	2	39.62	10
A U Rashid	9	7	3	142	71	0	1	35.50	1
K S Williamson	9	8	0	184	70	0	1	23.00	4
A W Gale	9	8	1	142	45	0	0	20.28	1
T T Bresnan	9	5	1	77	32	0	0	19.25	6

Also played

Player	M.	I.	N.O.	Runs	H.S.	100s	50s	Avge	ct/st
A J Hodd	5	2	1	111	69*	0	1	111.00	9/2
G S Ballance	1	1	0	61	61	0	1	61.00	2
R M Pyrah	9	4	3	57	29*	0	0	57.00	1
J M Bairstow	4	4	1	63	45*	0	0	21.00	8/0
S A Patterson	7	2	1	9	8	0	0	9.00	0
J A Brooks	8	2	0	0	0	0	0	0.00	2
M D Fisher	3	0	0	0	—	0	0	—	0

BOWLING

(Qualification 4 wickets)

Player	Overs	Mdns	Runs	Wkts	Avge	Best	4wI	RPO
A U Rashid	86.5	4	409	21	19.47	5-33	1	4.71
R M Pyrah	66.4	3	333	15	22.20	4-51	1	4.99
T T Bresnan	75.2	6	371	15	24.73	4-28	1	4.92
S A Patterson	56	3	238	9	26.44	3-39	0	4.25
J A Brooks	72	5	323	11	29.36	3-30	0	4.48

Also bowled

Player	Overs	Mdns	Runs	Wkts	Avge	Best	4wI	RPO
M D Fisher	24	1	101	2	50.50	1-29	0	4.20
A Lyth	11	1	72	1	72.00	1-24	0	6.54
J A Leaning	6	0	38	0	—	0-13	0	6.33

Tourist Match — List A
Yorkshire v. Sri Lanka A

Played at Headingley, Leeds, on July 31, 2014
Sri Lanka won by 26 runs

Toss won by Sri Lanka

SRI LANKA

M D Gunathilaka, c Hodgson b Leaning		65
M L Udawatte, c Hodd b Wainman		16
§ L D Chandimal, c Lyth b Rashid		100
* S M A Priyanjan, c and b Rashid		0
P C de Silva, c Hodgson b Rashid		29
D A S Gunaratne, lbw b Rashid		2
S Prasanna, lbw b Gibson		17
R L B Rambukwella, not out		23
P L M Jayaratne, c and b Wainman		4
P L S Gamage, c Lees b Wainman		2
P V D Chameera, not out		2
Extras lb 7, w 7, nb 1		15
Total (9 wkts, 50 overs)		275

FoW: 1-41 (Udawatte), 2-142 (Gunathilaka), 3-143 (Priyanjan), 4-201 (de Silva), 5-218 (Gunaratne), 6-237 (Chandimal), 7-242 (Prasanna), 8-257 (Jayaratne), 9-267 (Gamage)

	O	M	R	W
Coad	8	3	38	0
Wainman	8	0	51	3
Waite	8	0	52	0
Gibson	9	1	43	1
Leaning	7	0	27	1
Rashid	10	0	57	4

YORKSHIRE

A Lyth, c Chandimal b Rambukwella		29
* A Z Lees, st Chandimal b de Silva		54
D M Hodgson, c Priyanjan b de Silva		51
J A Leaning, c Udawatte b de Silva		8
A U Rashid, c Priyanjan b de Silva		11
E Callis, lbw b Prasanna		10
§ A J Hodd, b Gamage		19
R Gibson, lbw b Prasanna		9
J C Wainman, c Gunaratne b Prasanna		33
M E Waite, lbw b Prasanna		12
B O Coad, not out		2
Extras b 1, lb 2, w 7, nb 1		11
Total (47.2 overs)		249

FoW: 1-70 (Lyth), 2-113 (Lees), 3-140 (Leaning), 4-156 (Rashid), 5-158 (Hodgson), 6-170 (Callis), 7-182 (Gibson), 8-215 (Hodd), 9-238 (Wainman), 10-249 (Waite)

	O	M	R	W
Gamage	6	0	42	1
Chameera	4	0	37	0
Rambukwella	9	0	45	1
Jayaratne	4	0	20	0
Prasanna	9.2	0	42	4
Priyanjan	5	0	27	1
de Silva	10	0	33	3

Umpires: P J Hartley and B V Taylor   Scorers: J T Potter and H Clayton

YORKSHIRE AVERAGES 2014

ALL LIST A MATCHES

Played 10   Won 6   Lost 4

BATTING AND FIELDING

(Qualification 4 completed innings)

Player	M.	I.	N.O.	Runs	H.S.	100s	50s	Avge	ct/st
A Z Lees	10	10	1	422	102	1	4	46.88	3
J A Leaning	9	8	3	228	111*	1	1	45.60	4
A Lyth	10	10	1	346	84	0	2	38.44	11
A U Rashid	10	8	3	153	71	0	1	30.60	2
K S Williamson	9	8	0	184	70	0	1	23.00	4
A W Gale	9	8	1	142	45	0	0	20.28	1
T T Bresnan	9	5	1	77	32	0	0	19.25	6

Also played

Player	M.	I.	N.O.	Runs	H.S.	100s	50s	Avge	ct/st
A J Hodd	6	3	1	130	69*	0	1	65.00	10/2
G S Ballance	1	1	0	61	61	0	1	61.00	2
R M Pyrah	9	4	3	57	29*	0	0	57.00	1
D M Hodgson	1	1	0	51	51	0	1	51.00	2
J C Wainman	1	1	0	33	33	0	0	33.00	1
J M Bairstow	4	4	1	63	45*	0	0	21.00	8
M E Waite	1	1	0	12	12	0	0	12.00	0
E Callis	1	1	0	10	10	0	0	10.00	0
R Gibson	1	1	0	9	9	0	0	9.00	0
S A Patterson	7	2	1	9	8	0	0	9.00	0
J A Brooks	8	2	0	0	0	0	0	0.00	2
B O Coad	1	1	1	2	2*	0	0	—	0
M D Fisher	3	0	0	0	—	0	0	—	0

BOWLING

(Qualification 4 wickets)

Player	Overs	Mdns	Runs	Wkts	Avge	Best	4wI	RPO
A U Rashid	96.5	4	466	25	18.64	5-33	2	4.81
R M Pyrah	66.4	3	333	15	22.20	4-51	1	4.99
T T Bresnan	75.2	6	371	15	24.73	4-28	1	4.92
S A Patterson	56	3	238	9	26.44	3-39	0	4.25
J A Brooks	72	5	323	11	29.36	3-30	0	4.48

Also bowled

Player	Overs	Mdns	Runs	Wkts	Avge	Best	4wI	RPO
J C Wainman	8	0	51	3	17.00	3-51	0	6.37
R Gibson	9	1	43	1	43.00	1-43	0	4.77
M D Fisher	24	1	101	2	50.50	1-29	0	4.20
J A Leaning	13	0	65	1	65.00	1-27	0	5.00
A Lyth	11	1	72	1	72.00	1-24	0	6.54
B O Coad	8	3	38	0	—	0-38	0	4.75
M E Waite	8	0	52	0	—	0-52	0	6.50

Fifth Royal London One-Day International
England v. India

Played at Headingley, Leeds, on September 5, 2014
England won by 41 runs

Toss won by India

ENGLAND

* A N Cook, c Dhoni b Raina		46
A D Hales, c Rahane b Yadav		4
M M Ali, c Yadav b Kumar		9
J E Root, c Ashwin b Shami		113
E J G Morgan, st Dhoni b Ashwin		14
§ J C Buttler, run out (Dhoni)		49
B A Stokes, not out		33
C R Woakes, b Shami		9
J C Tredwell, not out		8
J M Anderson		
S T Finn	Did not bat	
Extras b 1, lb 3, w 5		9
Total (7 wkts, 50 overs)		294

FoW: 1-23 (Hales), 2-39 (Ali), 3-91 (Cook), 4-117 (Morgan), 5-225 (Buttler), 6-249 (Root), 7-265 (Woakes)

	O	M	R	W
Kumar	8	0	45	1
Yadav	6	0	46	1
Shami	10	0	52	2
Ashwin	10	2	49	1
Raina	7	0	32	1
Jadeja	9	0	66	0

INDIA

A M Rahane, c Morgan b Anderson		0
S Dhawan, b Ali		31
V Kohli, c Cook b Anderson		13
A T Rayudu, c Cook b Stokes		53
S K Raina, c Buttler b Ali		18
§ * M S Dhoni, c Stokes b Finn		29
R A Jadeja, b Finn		87
R Ashwin, c Finn b Stokes		16
B Kumar, run out (Finn/Stokes)		1
M Shami, c Hales b Stokes		0
U Yadav, not out		0
Extras w 5		5
Total (48.4 overs)		253

FoW: 1-0 (Rahane), 2-25 (Kohli), 3-49 (Dhawan), 4-91 (Raina), 5-132 (Rayudu), 6-173 (Dhoni), 7-203 (Ashwin), 8-208 (Kumar), 9-209 (Shami), 10-253 (Jadeja)

	O	M	R	W
Anderson	10	0	39	2
Woakes	10	1	61	0
Ali	8	0	34	2
Finn	8.4	1	37	2
Tredwell	5	0	35	0
Stokes	7	0	47	3

Man of the Match: J E Root

Umpires: R A Kettleborough and P R Reiffel   Scorers: J T Potter and H Clayton
Third Umpire: M A Gough   Fourth Umpire: R J Bailey   Match Referee: R S Madugalle

NATWEST T20 BLAST
HIGHLIGHTS OF 2014

WINNERS

Warwickshire, who beat Lancashire by 4 runs

Totals of 150 and over (7)

200-5	v. Nottinghamshire at Leeds (lost)
186-8	v. Durham at Chester-le-Street (won)
183-4	v. Derbyshire at Chesterfield (won)
181-3	v. Northamptonshire at Northampton (won)
180-5	v. Lancashire at Manchester (won)
168-5	v. Leicestershire at Leeds (won)
162-7	v. Northamptonshire at Leeds (lost)

Match aggregates of 350 and over (2)

401	Yorkshire (200-5) lost to Nottinghamshire (201-4) by 6 wickets at Leeds
359	Lancashire (179-6) lost to Yorkshire (180-5) by 5 wickets at Manchester

Centuries (1)

J M Bairstow (1)

102* v. Durham at Chester-le-Street

3 catches in an innings (2)

A J Finch (1)

4 v. Durham at Chester-le-Street

T T Bresnan (1)

3 v. Nottinghamshire at Nottingham

Debuts (3)

t20 cricket: O E Robinson
For Yorkshire: A J Finch and K S Williamson

Match-By-Match Reports   DAVE CALDWELL

NatWest T20 BLAST in 2014

NORTH GROUP

		P	W	L	T	NR/A	PTS	NRR
1	Lancashire Lightning (N 2) *	14	10	2	0	2	22.00	0.846
2	Nottinghamshire Outlaws (N 1) *	14	9	3	0	2	20.00	0.642
3	Worcestershire Rapids (M 5) *	14	8	4	0	2	18.00	0.480
4	Birmingham Bears (M 4) *	14	7	5	0	2	16.00	0.235
5	**Yorkshire Vikings (N6) ....**	**14**	**6**	**5**	**0**	**3**	**15.00**	**0.588**
6	Durham Jets (N 3)	14	5	7	0	2	12.00	0.106
7	Northamptonshire Steelbacks (M 1)	14	4	7	0	3	11.00	-0.899
8	Leicestershire Foxes (N 4).............	14	4	9	0	1	9.00	-0.552
9	Derbyshire Falcons (N 5)	14	1	12	0	1	3.00	-1.406

SOUTH GROUP

		P	W	L	T	NR/A	PTS	NRR
1	Essex Eagles (S 3) *	14	10	4	0	0	20.00	0.401
2	Surrey(S 2) *.......................	14	9	5	0	0	18.00	0.426
3	Hampshire Royals (S 1) *	14	9	5	0	0	18.00	0.136
4	Glamorgan (M 3) *	14	6	5	1	2	15.00	0.145
5	Somerset (M 2)	14	6	7	0	1	13.00	-0.107
6	Kent Spitfires (S 5)	14	6	7	1	0	13.00	-0.229
7	Sussex Sharks (S 6)	14	6	8	0	0	12.00	-0.022
8	Gloucestershire (M 6) + ...	14	5	7	0	2	10.00	-0.362
9	Middlesex Panthers (S 4)..............	14	2	11	0	1	5.00	-0.457

* Qualified for the Quarter-Finals

+ Deducted 2 points for a poor pitch in 2013

(2013 group positions in brackets)

NatWest T20 BLAST — North Group
Yorkshire v. Northamptonshire

Played at Headingley, Leeds, on May 16, 2014

Northamptonshire won by 3 wickets

Toss won by Yorkshire
Northamptonshire 2 points, Yorkshire 0 points

YORKSHIRE

* A W Gale, c Coetzer b Butler		3
K S Williamson, run out (Willey)		17
J E Root, lbw b Azharullah		13
G S Ballance, c Levi b White		12
§ J M Bairstow, lbw b Butler		24
A U Rashid, c Willey b Butler		12
T T Bresnan, not out		34
L E Plunkett, c Spriegel b Butler		36
R M Pyrah, not out		2
R J Sidebottom		
J A Brooks	Did not bat	
Extras lb 5, w 2, nb 2		9
Total (7 wkts, 20 overs)		162

FoW: 1-12 (Gale), 2-30 (Williamson), 3-37 (Root), 4-57 (Ballance), 5-87 (Rashid), 6-87 (Bairstow), 7-151 (Plunkett)

	O	M	R	W
Spriegel	3	0	26	0
Stone	4	0	33	0
Butler	4	0	25	4
Azharullah	4	0	31	1
White	3	0	25	1
Crook	2	0	17	0

NORTHAMPTONSHIRE

R E Levi, c Brooks b Plunkett		19
D J Willey, c Ballance b Pyrah		43
* K J Coetzer, run out (Brooks)		0
R I Newton, b Plunkett		12
S P Crook, lbw b Pyrah		29
§ B M Duckett, not out		39
I G Butler, b Sidebottom		1
M N W Spriegel, run out (Sidebottom)		9
G G White, not out		4
M Azharullah		
O P Stone	Did not bat	
Extras b 1, lb 5, w 3		9
Total (7 wkts, 19.5 overs)		165

FoW: 1-45 (Levi), 2-45 (Coetzer), 3-81 (Willey), 4-82 (Newton), 5-124 (Crook), 6-134 (Butler), 7-154 (Spriegel)

	O	M	R	W
Brooks	3	0	19	0
Root	1	0	6	0
Sidebottom	3.5	0	40	1
Bresnan	4	0	34	0
Plunkett	3	0	20	2
Rashid	1	0	19	0
Pyrah	4	0	21	2

Man of the Match: I G Butler

Umpires: N A Mallender and D J Millns   Scorers: J T Potter and A C Kingston

Vikings tripped at the wire

Yorkshire fell agonisingly short of an opening win as Duckett's unbeaten 39 guided the reigning t20 champions to victory by three wickets with one ball to spare.

Duckett arrived at the crease with his side in trouble at 82-4 chasing 163 with front-line batsmen in short supply. Despite losing Crook on 124 and Butler soon afterwards the England Under-19s wicket-keeper stood firm, taking the game into the last over when his side still needed 13 to win.

This was achieved in fine style despite the loss of Spriegel, run out to the second ball of Sidebottom's over. Duckett despatched the third ball for six, then scampered a single, and White sealed the win off the last-

LIAM PLUNKETT: Top of batting and bowling for Yorkshire

but-one ball by driving lavishly through point for a boundary.

It was closer than anticipated after Levi and Willey had opened with 45 in a shade over five overs before Brooks caught Levi smartly in the deep off Plunkett, and next ball Brooks ran out Coetzer with a fine piece of fielding from short-third-man. Willey, after some clean striking, was taken at long-off against Pyrah, who also trapped Crook in front to finish with the commendable figures of 2-21.

Earlier, Yorkshire's innings had threatened to grind to a halt after many batsmen gained starts, only to fall when looking set. The Vikings slipped to 87-6 with only Gale failing to reach double figures. Ballance was caught sweeping at short-fine-leg for 12, while Bairstow seemed set to grab a stranglehold on proceedings but was lbw for 24 aiming to leg. Bresnan and Plunkett plundered an impressive 64 from a shade over 10 overs, Bresnan ending unbeaten on 34 from 21 deliveries, while Plunkett hammered six boundaries in his 22-ball 36 before falling in the 20th over. Butler claimed career-best figures of 4-25.

Yorkshire's next fixture, the visit to Warwickshire, was abandoned without a ball bowled.

NatWest T20 BLAST — North Group
Warwickshire v. Yorkshire

At Edgbaston, Birmingham, on May 23, 2014
Match abandoned without a ball bowled
Yorkshire 1 point, Warwickshire 1 point

Umpires: P J Hartley and P Willey
Scorers: J T Potter and M D Smith
Third Umpire: P R Pollard

Yorkshire v. Derbyshire

Played at Headingley, Leeds, on May 30, 2014
Yorkshire won by 8 wickets

Toss won by Derbyshire
Yorkshire 2 points, Derbyshire 0 points

DERBYSHIRE

C F Hughes, c Robinson b Plunkett		11
S C Moore, run out (Robinson)		18
W J Durston, lbw b Rashid		7
M J North, b Rashid		5
* W L Madsen, not out		34
S L Elstone, c Lees b Plunkett		14
§ G D Cross, b Pyrah		20
A L Hughes, not out		9
M L Turner		
M H A Footitt	Did not bat	
T C Knight		
Extras b 1, lb 3, w 5		9
Total (6 wkts, 20 overs)		127

FoW: 1-33 (Moore), 2-41 (C F Hughes), 3-48 (North), 4-49 (Durston), 5-82 (Elstone), 6-109 (Cross)

	O	M	R	W
Leaning	1	0	12	0
Brooks	3	0	21	0
Plunkett	4	0	25	2
Pyrah	4	0	24	1
Robinson	4	0	22	0
Rashid	4	0	19	2

YORKSHIRE

A J Finch, c and b North		19
* A W Gale, c Elstone b Footitt		7
A Z Lees, not out		61
§ J M Bairstow, not out		29
A Lyth		
J A Leaning		
A U Rashid		
L E Plunkett	Did not bat	
O E Robinson		
R M Pyrah		
J A Brooks		
Extras lb 6, w 6		12
Total (2 wkts, 14 overs)		128

FoW: 1-22 (Gale), 2-86 (Finch)

	O	M	R	W
Durston	2	0	14	0
Footitt	2	0	16	1
Turner	2	0	29	0
Knight	2	0	17	0
A L Hughes	1	0	8	0
North	2	0	17	1
Elstone	1	0	9	0
C F Hughes	2	0	12	0

Man of the match: A Z Lees

Umpires: S C Gale and N A Mallender
Scorers: J T Potter and J M Brown

Dominant Lees steals the show

All the pre-match hype surrounded the "Finch Factor" as the world-ranked No. 1 *t20* player, Aaron Finch, made his Yorkshire debut in front of 5,628 expectant fans.

Yet it was Alex Lees who claimed the headlines with an unbeaten half century as Vikings romped home with six overs to spare.

ALEX LEES: A cracking half-century as Vikings go on victory rampage

Chasing a below-par 128, Finch opened his *White Rose* account as his third ball drive sailed clean over the top before Gale miscued Footitt to point. Lees went on to dominate, Turner's second over and Yorkshire's final power play over disappearing for 21 with five boundaries as the hosts showed that they were in no mood to delay. Finch fell for 19 from 17 balls, skying a return catch to North, while Lees compiled a lovely half-century in 30 balls.

Lees was joined by an effervescent Bairstow, who was soon in the action, and they took their side to victory without alarm. Bairstow finished on 29 from 16 balls and Lees 61 from 44 balls with nine fours.

The Falcons briefly threatened to catch fire with a breezy start from Chesney Hughes and Moore after winning the toss. They put on 28 in the first three overs before *t20* debutant Oliver Robinson dismissed the dangerous Moore with an arrow-like throw running in from cover. From that point the Vikings had full control, despite a plethora of dropped catches. Leaning, the main culprit, put down four relatively simple chances to blot an otherwise impressive Yorkshire display.

Rashid picked up two scalps in his first over with the prize wickets of North and Durston, North to an ill-advised reverse-sweep. This reduced the visitors to 49-4 and effectively put the brakes on. Derbyshire simply could not find the means to accelerate, and their score limped along at barely six runs per over. Only a workmanlike unbeaten run-a-ball 34 from Madsen ensured a semi-competitive total. Yorkshire bowled tightly, with Rashid, Pyrah and Robinson all impressing.

NatWest T20 BLAST — North Group
Lancashire v. Yorkshire

Played at Old Trafford, Manchester, on June 6, 2014
Yorkshire won by 5 wickets

Toss won by Lancashire

Yorkshire 2 points, Lancashire 0 points

LANCASHIRE

T C Smith, c Finch b Rashid		55
A L Davies, c Bresnan b Pyrah		5
K R Brown, c and b Rashid		11
* P J Horton, b Robinson		60
§ J C Buttler, c Lyth b Bresnan		19
S J Croft, not out		21
J Clark, b Robinson		1
A M Lilley		
Kabir Ali		
S D Parry	Did not bat	
Junaid Khan		
Extras lb 4, w 3		7
Total (6 wkts, 20 overs)		179

FoW: 1-58 (Davies), 2-68 (Smith), 3-80 (Brown), 4-132 (Buttler), 5-177 (Horton), 6-180 (Clark)

	O	M	R	W
Bresnan	4	0	33	1
Brooks	3	0	42	0
Lyth	1	0	7	0
Pyrah	2	0	24	1
Rashid	4	0	22	2
Azeem Rafiq	3	0	21	0
Robinson	3	0	26	2

YORKSHIRE

* A W Gale, b Kabir Ali		1
A J Finch, c Junaid Khan b Smith		88
A Z Lees, b Junaid Khan		36
A Lyth, b Kabir Ali		7
§ J M Bairstow, not out		19
T T Bresnan, run out (Croft/Buttler)		2
R M Pyrah, not out		10
Azeem Rafiq		
A U Rashid		
O E Robinson	Did not bat	
J A Brooks		
Extras lb 5, p 6, w 4, nb 2		17
Total (5 wkts, 19.3 overs)		180

FoW: 1-3 (Gale), 2-102 (Lees), 3-129 (Lyth), 4-144 (Finch), 5-163 (Bresnan)

	O	M	R	W
Kabir Ali	3.3	0	22	2
Junaid Khan	4	0	25	1
Clark	4	0	44	0
Smith	4	0	37	1
Parry	3	0	31	0
Lilley	1	0	10	0

Man of the Match: A J Finch

Umpires: J H Evans and D J Millns

Scorers: J T Potter and D M White

Third Umpire: B J Debenham

Finch batters the *Red Rose*

AARON FINCH: Smote the sixes of Hercules

A six-run penalty against Lancashire and a Herculean innings by Finch brought a pulsating encounter to a thrilling finish in front of a 16,000 crowd as Yorkshire chased down a formidable 180.

Yorkshire lost Gale in the first over, playing a fairly agricultural stroke at Ali, but they rebuilt under Finch and the end of the powerplay saw them 43-1.

Finch was ominously poised in the 30s after a sharp return chance to Ali was dropped, and the Australian cut loose as the run-rate rose beyond 10, his 50 coming in 35 balls. Lees played a mature hand, and the pair added 99 before Khan's yorker beat Lees as he aimed to leg side. His pleasing 36 came in 29 balls.

Finch earmarked Clark as the man to attack, and in the 15th over he struck 16 runs with two enormous sixes, one crashing into The Point building and one alongside. Yorkshire needed 52 from five overs, and the game turned as Lyth was bowled by Ali's slower ball.

Finch continued undeterred until he sliced Smith to deep gully, having lit up the night with a 55-ball 88 containing eight fours and five sixes. Bairstow carried on the fight, and 20 were needed from two overs before news came that the umpires had penalised Lancashire for their slow over rate, leaving Yorkshire to make only nine from the last over. Pyrah's drive over cover for six won the game with three balls to spare.

Earlier, Smith produced a scintillating display for Lancashire with a 22-ball 50 to stifle prematch talk of a possible return by Flintoff. Lightning crashed 65 runs in the powerplay for the sole wicket of Davies, caught by Bresnan off Pyrah at mid-off. The prize wicket came in the seventh over as Rashid lured Smith down the pitch...the ball seemed to be sailing for six until a leaping Lyth took it, released it in mid-air, and Finch completed the dismissal, a stunning piece of fielding. Lancashire stumbled against the spin of Rafiq and the excellent Rashid — who took 2-22 in four overs.

NatWest T20 BLAST — North Group
Northamptonshire v. Yorkshire

Played at Wantage Road, Northampton, on June 13, 2014
Yorkshire won by 16 runs

Toss won by Yorkshire

Yorkshire 2 points, Northamptonshire 0 points

YORKSHIRE

* A W Gale, c Duckett b Azharullah		17
A J Finch, c Keogh b Stone		5
A Z Lees, c Coetzer b Spriegel		35
§ J M Bairstow, not out		60
A Lyth, not out		46
T T Bresnan		
R M Pyrah		
A U Rashid	Did not bat	
Azeem Rafiq		
O E Robinson		
S A Patterson		
Extras lb 5, w 9, nb 4		18
Total (3 wkts, 20 overs)		181

FoW: 1-16 (Finch), 2-38 (Gale), 3-91 (Lees)

	O	M	R	W
Stone	3	1	25	1
Willey	4	0	45	0
Crook	3	0	16	0
Azharullah	4	0	43	1
White	4	0	31	0
Spriegel	2	0	16	1

NORTHAMPTONSHIRE

R E Levi, c Lyth b Azeem Rafiq	76
D J Willey, c Finch b Patterson	5
* K J Coetzer, c Robinson b Patterson	1
§ B M Duckett, st Bairstow b Azeem Rafiq	6
D J G Sales, b Pyrah	17
S P Crook, b Rashid	23
M N W Spriegel, c Azeem Rafiq b Pyrah	10
R J Keogh, c Azeem Rafiq b Robinson	16
G G White, c Pyrah b Robinson	2
O P Stone, not out	4
M Azharullah, not out	0
Extras lb 2, w 3	5
Total (9 wkts, 20 overs)	165

FoW: 1-30 (Willey), 2-33 (Coetzer), 3-70 (Duckett), 4-101 (Levi), 5-133 (Sales),
6-133 (Crook), 7-149 (Spriegel), 8-159 (White), 9-161 (Keogh)

	O	M	R	W
Bresnan	4	0	32	0
Patterson	3	0	16	2
Pyrah	4	0	41	2
Azeem Rafiq	4	0	19	2
Rashid	3	0	28	1
Robinson	2	0	27	2

Man of the Match: Azeem Rafiq

Umpires: S C Gale and N J Llong

Scorers: J T Potter and A C Kingston

Bairstow blunts the Steelbacks

JONATHAN BAIRSTOW
Hard hits, hard running

Medium-pacer Oliver Robinson kept his nerve to bowl the last six balls with Steelbacks needing 25 runs to win, even collecting two wickets as Vikings won again.

Gale opted to bat, and the initial exchanges were dominated by the new-ball pair of Stone and Willey, and frustration got the better of Finch as he skied a catch to Keogh, running from wide mid-on to give Stone a deserved wicket-maiden.

Gale was caught at the wicket in the sixth over, trying to leave a lifting ball, for a far from fluent 17, but a recovery from the increasingly impressive Lees and Bairstow followed, the 50 partnership coming in the 11th over.

Bairstow took over as the main aggressor after a typically industrious start before Lees departed, driving loosely at Spriegel, for a well constructed 35 in 28 balls.

Lyth's arrival signalled a change in tempo, the reliance on boundaries less apparent than at Old Trafford the previous week. Running between the wickets was of the highest order, 61 coming in the last six overs. Bairstow came in unbeaten on a 37-ball 60, containing four fours, two sixes and a lot of running, while Lyth compiled a 31-ball 46 not out.

Northamptonshire were in hot pursuit as the powerful South African Levi launched Bresnan for two sixes, but paceman Patterson struck a double blow in the fourth over, two catches in the deep accounting for Willey and Coetzer. Levi ploughed a lone furrow, his 50 coming in the ninth over from 30 balls with a straight six off Rashid. Rafiq beat the reverse-sweeping Duckett as Northamptonshire moved to 91 from 11, but Rafiq and Bresnan bowled with innovation and guile to stem the tide. Levi holed out for 76 to Lyth at long-on from Rafiq, and Pyrah plucked out Sales's middle stump. Rashid turned the screw with the next ball, bowling Crook for 23, and the Vikings were on the run-in.

Headingley's Roses fixture was abandoned without a ball bowled.

NatWest T20 BLAST — North Group

Yorkshire v. Lancashire

At Headingley, Leeds, on June 27, 2014
Match abandoned without a ball bowled
Yorkshire 1 point, Lancashire 1 point
Umpires: M R Benson and G D Lloyd   Scorers: J T Potter and D M White
Third Umpire: M A Gough

Nottinghamshire v. Yorkshire

Played at Trent Bridge, Nottingham, on June 28, 2014
Nottinghamshire won by 22 runs

Toss won by Nottinghamshire   Nottinghamshire 2 points, Yorkshire 0 points

NOTTINGHAMSHIRE

P A Jaques, c Bairstow b Sidebottom	0
A D Hales, c and b Bresnan	12
M H Wessels, c Finch b Pyrah	14
S R Patel, c Azeem Rafiq	20
* J W A Taylor, not out	52
J E C Franklin, c Azeem Rafiq b Bresnan	27
§ C M W Read, c Bresnan b Sidebottom	4
S J Mullaney, c Bresnan b Robinson	1
A Shahzad, c Robinson b Sidebottom	6
L J Fletcher, c Lyth b Robinson	3
H F Gurney, not out	1
Extras lb 1, w 2	3
Total (9 wkts, 20 overs)	143

FoW: 1-0 (Jaques), 2-22 (Hales), 3-26 (Wessels), 4-55 (Patel), 5-103 (Franklin), 6-115 (Read), 7-117 (Mullaney), 8-129 (Shahzad), 9-133 (Fletcher)

	O	M	R	W
Sidebottom	4	0	24	3
Bresnan	4	0	31	2
Pyrah	2	0	19	1
Robinson	3	0	25	2
Rashid	4	0	25	0
Azeem Rafiq	3	0	18	1

YORKSHIRE

* A W Gale, c Gurney b Shahzad	7
A J Finch, c Gurney b Fletcher	10
A Z Lees, c Taylor b Patel	37
§ J M Bairstow, c Hales b Patel	3
A Lyth, run out (Mullaney)	2
T T Bresnan, c Franklin b Gurney	28
A U Rashid, b Fletcher	21
R M Pyrah, c Franklin b Gurney	3
O E Robinson, b Fletcher	2
Azeem Rafiq, not out	1
R J Sidebottom, not out	0
Extras lb 5, w 2	7
Total (9 wkts, 20 overs)	121

FoW: 1-15 (Finch), 2-38 (Gale), 3-54 (Bairstow), 4-60 (Lyth), 5-69 (Lees), 6-112 (Rashid), 7-117 (Pyrah), 8-117 (Bresnan), 9-121 (Robinson)

	O	M	R	W
Gurney	4	0	25	2
Fletcher	4	0	21	3
Shahzad	3	0	20	1
Patel	4	0	19	2
Mullaney	4	0	17	0
Franklin	1	0	14	0

Man of the Match: J W A Taylor

Umpires: M G Saggers and A G Wharf   Scorers: J T Potter and R Marshall
Third Umpire: R J Evans

Batsmen let down bowlers

Vikings were left to rue some indeterminate batting after a good performance with the ball had restricted a powerful line-up to 143.

Outstanding bowling at the death by Fletcher and Gurney and a sublime spell from Patel, gave the Outlaws a comfortable win.

Yorkshire began the chase positively, and there were two sumptuous cover-drives from Finch before he flicked a wayward leg-side delivery from Fletcher into the hands of Gurney at short-fine-leg.

Gale continued his struggle to impose himself at the top of the order, but he was caught flaying Shahzad

OLIVER ROBINSON: Two wickets and superb outfielding

towards the cover boundary. Lees maintained his excellent form in all formats, his drives over extra-cover very profitable and easy on the eye.

Bairstow fell for three, taken by Hales on the long-on boundary, and almost immediately Lyth was run out, having being turned down a run, with the score on 60. The onus was very much on Lees as the Outlaws turned the screw. The rate required was well over nine, and wickets tumbled. Lees fell for a run-a-ball 37, leaving Bresnan and Rashid to rebuild, and while they were together faint hope remained. The pair added 43 for the sixth wicket before Rashid was bowled for 21, and Bresnan crashed a four and a six off the 16th over before he was caught in the deep. Needing 32 from three overs, Yorkshire's innings subsided.

Yorkshire had bowled with excellent control, backed up by livewire out-cricket and superb catching in the deep. Jaques was taken in Sidebottom's first over by a diving Bairstow, and the Outlaws struggled to make any impression. Bresnan took a sharp return catch off the dangerous Hales, but Patel and Taylor repaired the damage until Rafiq bowled Patel. It was Taylor's undefeated half-century that effectively won the game as he saw his side to a competitive total. Sidebottom, Rashid and Rafiq impressed with the ball, as did the reliable Robinson who backed up his medium-pace with some superb outfielding.

NatWest T20 BLAST — North Group
Yorkshire v. Leicestershire

Played at Headingley, Leeds, on July 1, 2014
Yorkshire won by 14 runs

Toss won by Leicestershire · · · · · · · · · · · · · · Yorkshire 2 points, Leicestershire 0 points

YORKSHIRE

* A W Gale, st Eckersley b Cobb	....	55
A J Finch, b Raine	....	5
A Z Lees, lbw b Raine	....	0
§ J M Bairstow, c Smith b Naik	....	29
A Lyth, c Shreck b Raine	....	10
T T Bresnan, not out	....	29
R M Pyrah, not out	....	16
A U Rashid		
O E Robinson		
Azeem Rafiq	Did not bat	
R J Sidebottom		
Extras b 12, lb 4, w 1, nb 7	....	24
Total (5 wkts, 20 overs)	....	168

FoW: 1-41 (Finch), 2-41 (Lees), 3-100 (Bairstow), 4-111 (Gale), 5-123 (Lyth).

	O	M	R	W
Shreck	4	0	32	0
Buck	2.2	0	21	0
Raine	4	0	25	3
Naik	4	0	33	1
Cobb	4	0	21	1
Taylor	1.4	0	20	0

Buck was not allowed to complete his third over, which was finished by Taylor

LEICESTERSHIRE

* J J Cobb, c Finch b Rashid	....	27
G P Smith, c Rashid b Bresnan	....	56
§ E J H Eckersley, st Bairstow b Rashid	....	8
M A G Boyce, run out (Bresnan/Bairstow)	....	12
S B Styris, c Bairstow b Azeem Rafiq	....	6
T J Wells, c Finch b Sidebottom	....	16
R M L Taylor, b Sidebottom	....	2
B A Raine, run out (Azeem Rafiq)	....	0
J K H Naik, not out	....	10
N L Buck, not out	....	3
C E Shreck	Did not bat	
Extras b 5, lb 1, w 8	....	14
Total (8 wkts, 20 overs)	....	154

FoW: 1-61 (Cobb), 2-74 (Eckersley), 3-95 (Boyce), 4-105 (Styris), 5-125 (Smith),
6-128 (Taylor), 7-128 (Raine), 8-142 (Wells)

	O	M	R	W
Sidebottom	4	0	32	2
Bresnan	4	0	34	1
Pyrah	2	0	16	0
Rashid	4	0	24	2
Azeem Rafiq	4	0	26	1
Robinson	2	0	16	0

Men of the Match: A J Finch and A Lyth

Umpires: S J O'Shaughnessy and P Willey   Scorers: J T Potter and P J Rogers
Third Umpire: N G C Cowley

Victory on the boundary

RISE AND FALL: Adam Lyth, left, leaps to flick back a big hit by Josh Cobb, and Aaron Finch holds on as Adam falls over the rope

The Finch-and-Lyth fielding show was even more spectacular than their effort at Old Trafford a few weeks before. It was to prove a key wicket as it despatched Josh Cobb, who had threatened to take the game away with some uncompromising play.

The outcricket and fielding was to be the deciding factor in this tight game, with Yorkshire very much up to the task. Leicestershire chose to field first, and were helpless in the powerplay overs as Gale rediscovered much-needed form, while Finch was starved of the strike. With 41 on the board in the sixth over Finch was bowled by Raine for five, and Raine accounted for Lees first ball to a marginal lbw decision. Gale found his timing deserting him, but he battled on admirably. Bairstow was just finding his range when he fell short of the long-on boundary for 29, and then Gale was stumped by Eckersley for 55 from 51 balls. The Vikings 111-4 in the 16th. Lyth was taken in the deep, but an excellent unbroken sixth-wicket partnership of 45 between Bresnan, 29, and Pyrah, 16, took them to a challenging 168 on a pitch which made timing uncomfortable

Cobb and Smith initially made light work of the run chase — 61 coming by the seventh over before Cobb was taken in such fantastic fashion by the Lyth and Finch combination. Eckersley went cheaply after smart work by Bairstow behind the stumps to complete a wretched day for the *Foxes* wicket-keeper — 12 byes and two dropped catches to place alongside his eight runs. As so often, Rashid and Rafiq combined to bring the run rate down, the key wicket of Styris off Rafiq proving vital.

The Foxes were 105-4 in the 14th, and the run rate climbed as wickets fell. Smith completed an eccentric half-century before Bresnan claimed his scalp for a 49-ball 56, and Sidebottom returned to bowl two sublime overs in the dying stages as Foxes fell away 14 runs adrift.

NatWest T20 BLAST — North Group
Yorkshire v. Durham

Played at Headingley, Leeds, on July 2, 2014
Durham won by 28 runs

Toss won by Durham   Durham 2 points, Yorkshire 0 points

DURHAM

* M D Stoneman, c Rafiq b Sidebottom	....	0
§ P Mustard, st Bairstow b Rashid	....	40
P D Collingwood, c Lyth b Pyrah	....	9
M J Richardson, c Finch b Bresnan	....	2
G J Muchall, c Gale b Azeem Rafiq	....	4
S G Borthwick, c Lyth b Azeem Rafiq	....	0
R D Pringle, c Finch b Azeem Rafiq	....	17
G R Breese, not out	....	30
U Arshad, lbw b Rashid	....	0
J W Hasting, c Pyrah b Rashid	....	6
C Rushworth, not out	....	4
Extras b 6, lb 4, w 1	....	11
Total (9 wkts, 20 overs)	....	123

FoW: 1-5 (Stoneman), 2-29 (Collingwood), 3-33 (Richardson), 4-49 (Muchall), 5-49 (Borthwick), 6-73 (Pringle), 7-76 (Mustard), 8-80 (Arshad), 9-94 (Hastings)

	O	M	R	W
Sidebottom	3	0	22	1
Bresnan	4	0	21	1
Pyrah	4	0	24	1
Azeem Rafiq	4	0	20	3
Rashid	4	1	14	3
Robinson	1	0	12	0

YORKSHIRE

* A W Gale, c Richardson b Hastings	....	6
A J Finch, lbw b Borthwick	....	17
A Z Lees, b Hastings	....	19
§ J M Bairstow, c Breese b Collingwood	....	9
A Lyth, c and b Borthwick	....	0
O E Robinson, run out (Borthwick)	....	3
A U Rashid, c Borthwick b Breese	....	7
T T Bresnan, run out (Stoneman/Mustard)	....	1
R M Pyrah, lbw b Hastings	....	16
Azeem Rafiq, not out	....	7
R J Sidebottom, run out (Muchall/Mustard)	....	2
Extras lb 1, w 5, nb 2	....	8
Total (17.2 overs)	....	95

FoW: 1-7 (Gale), 2-47 (Lees), 3-49 (Finch), 4-49 (Lyth), 5-58 (Robinson), 6-64 (Bairstow), 7-66 (Bresnan), 8-73 (Rashid), 9-91 (Pyrah), 10-95 (Sidebottom)

	O	M	R	W
Rushworth	2	0	14	0
Hastings	4	0	22	3
Arshad	1	0	17	0
Borthwick	4	0	11	2
Collingwood	4	0	15	1
Breese	1.2	0	5	1
Pringle	1	0	10	0

Man of the Match: P Mustard

Umpires: N G C Cowley and P Willey   Scorers: J T Potter and B Hunt

Qualification hope in balance

Durham produced a stunning bowling performance backed by typically livewire fielding to beat apathetic Vikings and open up possibilities in the North Division.

The Jets elected to bat, but lost a wicket to Sidebottom in the first over as Stoneman miscued to Rafiq at point.

Runs were hard to come by for Mustard and Collingwood, and as Collingwood's patience finally wilted he skied a

Star is fallen: Stoneman's throw to Mustard runs out Tim Bresnan

drive to be taken superbly by Lyth running back from deep mid-off. 29-2 in the fifth over. Bresnan dismissed Richardson in the next over, courtesy of a sharp catch by Finch at slip, and pressure continued to build on Durham as spinners Rashid and Rafiq claimed six wickets between them for only 34 runs from their eight overs. Rafiq picked up two in successive balls in the 10th over as the Jets gave their wickets away.

Catches were taken frequently, often within the ring, as the batting looked careless and at times aimless. Had Rashid taken a sharp return chance at 94-9 he would have had career-best figures and Yorkshire would have been as good as home, yet a typically robust Breese finished unbeaten on 30 from 19 balls to propel his side to an unlikely 123-9.

Yorkshire seemed to be cruising after the loss of Gale to a poorly timed leg-side stroke, taken in the deep off Hastings's first ball. Lees and Finch looked in little trouble, adding 40 for the second wicket before the game turned on its head. Lees was bowled by Hastings as the ball jagged back at him, and in the next over Borthwick trapped Finch sweeping at the wrong length. Next ball Lyth fell to a breathtaking catch by Borthwick off his own bowling: 49-4. The promoted Robinson was run out by the irrepressible Borthwick for six, while the key wicket of Bairstow fell in the 12th over: 64-6. Next over Rashid ran out Bresnan.

Borthwick and Collingwood bowled beautifully in tandem, and the rate rocketed to nearly 10 an over. Pyrah and Rafiq attempted a recovery, but at 91 Pyrah was lbw and in the next over a calamitous run-out left Yorkshire's qualification hopes back in the balance.

The match at Worcester was abandoned without a ball bowled.

Worcestershire v. Yorkshire

At New Road, Worcester, on July 4, 2014
Match abandoned without a ball bowled
Yorkshire 1 point, Worcestershire 1 point
Umpires: J H Evans and R K Illingworth   Scorers: J T Potter and D E Pugh

Durham v. Yorkshire

Played at Durham ICG, Chester-le-Street on July 11, 2014
Yorkshire won by 49 runs

Toss won by Durham   Yorkshire 2 points, Durham 0 points

YORKSHIRE

K S Williamson, c Stoneman b Hastings		5
* A J Finch, c Collingwood b Hastings		0
A Z Lees, c Muchall b Collingwood		29
§ J M Bairstow, not out		102
A Lyth, b Breese		1
T T Bresnan, c Rushworth b Hastings		1
A U Rashid, b Rushworth		29
R M Pyrah, c Arshad b Breese		1
O E Robinson, run out (Breese)		0
Azeem Rafiq, not out		5
R J Sidebottom	Did not bat	
Extras b 1, w 6, nb 6		13
Total (8 wkts, 20 overs)		186

FoW:- 1-3 (Finch), 2-12 (Williamson), 3-55 (Lees), 4-69 (Lyth), 5-83 (Bresnan), 6-147 (Rashid), 7-168 (Pyrah), 8-168 (Robinson).

	O	M	R	W
Hastings	4	0	20	3
Rushworth	4	0	30	1
Arshad	4	0	51	0
Borthwick	1	0	13	0
Breese	3	0	40	2
Collingwood	4	0	31	1

DURHAM

§ P Mustard, c Bairstow b Pyrah		35
* M D Stoneman, c Finch b Williamson		0
C S MacLeod, b Sidebottom		0
P D Collingwood, b Rashid		14
G J Muchall, c Finch b Pyrah		1
R D Pringle, c Bairstow b Pyrah		0
J W Hastings, b Sidebottom		62
S G Borthwick, c Finch b Bresnan		7
U Arshad, c Lyth b Azeem Rafiq		10
G R Breese, not out		1
C Rushworth, c Finch b Azeem Rafiq		0
Extras lb 3, w 4		7
Total (19.4 overs)		137

FoW:- 1-3 (Stoneman), 2-4 (MacLeod), 3-40 (Collingwood), 4-43 (Muchall), 5-43 (Pringle), 6-63 (Mustard), 7-97 (Borthwick), 8-132 (Hastings), 9-136 (Arshad), 10-137 (Rushworth)

	O	M	R	W
Williamson	1	0	3	1
Sidebottom	4	1	27	2
Bresnan	4	0	22	1
Pyrah	4	0	19	3
Rashid	4	0	24	1
Robinson	2	0	34	0
Azeem Rafiq	0.4	0	5	2

Man of the Match: J M Bairstow

Umpires: S A Garratt and M A Gough   Scorers: J T Potter and B Hunt

Bairstow's century carnage

Bairstow produced an innings of precision, power and breathtaking ability to guide the Vikings to an emphatic victory and re-energise their quarter-final bid.

He compiled his first *t20* century — and the first by a non-overseas Yorkshire player — off only 58 balls, his second 50 spanning 18 deliveries as the last eight overs yielded 102 runs.

Finch was handed the captaincy because Gale was absent for paternal reasons. Both Finch and Williamson fell early, reducing the visitors to 12-2, as paceman Hastings induced leading edges.

Lees arrived in positive mood and his partnership with Bairstow was about to ignite when his 24-ball innings of 29 was ended by Collingwood. Wickets continued to blight Yorkshire's progress, Lyth and Bresnan falling cheaply,

JONATHAN BAIRSTOW
Power and precision

and the Vikings were 83-5 from 12 overs before Bairstow found an able ally in Rashid and carnage ensued. With two overs of the innings remaining Bairstow was on 71. He now struck Breese for three consecutive sixes over long-on. With four balls remaining and on 90, he edged a boundary, scampered two and reached his landmark with a maximum over mid-wicket. Yorkshire had posted a challenging total of 186, which would have seemed wishful thinking eight overs earlier.

Durham's reply was in tatters after two overs. Stoneman was taken by Finch off Williamson for a duck, and MacLeod also departed without troubling the scorers when Sidebottom clean bowled him. A brief response from Collingwood was halted by Rashid, and the Jets were 40-in the ninth over. This became 43-5 when Muchall provided a first wicket for Pyrah, who then had Pringle caught behind.

The Jets fell away meekly, despite a late onslaught from Hastings, the burly Aussie smashing 62 in 32 balls with five fours and four sixes before perishing to Sidebottom at the death. Hastings had propelled his side to 132-8 before the final two wickets were grabbed by Rafiq in the last over. Pyrah was the stand-out performer with 3-19 in his four overs.

NatWest T20 BLAST — North Group
Derbyshire v. Yorkshire

Played at Queen's Park, Chesterfield, on July 13, 2014
Yorkshire won by 59 runs

Toss won by Derbyshire   Yorkshire 2 points, Derbyshire 0 points

YORKSHIRE

A J Finch, c Godleman b Turner		10
K S Williamson, b North		41
A Z Lees, not out		67
§ J M Bairstow, st Cross b North		8
* A W Gale, c Turner b Cork		34
T T Bresnan, not out		16
A Lyth		
A U Rashid		
R M Pyrah	Did not bat	
Azeem Rafiq		
R J Sidebottom		
Extras lb 3, w 2, nb 2		7
Total (4 wkts, 20 overs)		183

FoW: 1-43 (Finch), 2-79 (Williamson), 3-99 (Bairstow), 4-164 (Gale)

	O	M	R	W
Durston	3	0	31	0
Turner	4	0	41	1
Cork	4	0	35	1
A L Hughes	2	0	17	0
C F Hughes	2	0	15	0
Wainwright	1	0	14	0
North	4	0	27	2

DERBYSHIRE

W J Durston, b Williamson	0
M J North, c and b Rashid	20
§ G D Cross, c Williamson b Pyrah	37
* W L Madsen, c Finch b Azeem Rafiq	6
B A Godleman, st Bairstow b Azeem Rafiq	3
A L Hughes, c Bresnan b Azeem Rafiq	2
C F Hughes, c Azeem Rafiq b Williamson	6
T C Knight, c Sidebottom b Lyth	27
D J Wainwright, not out	20
G T G Cork, c Azeem Rafiq b Rashid	1
M L Turner, c Pyrah b Lyth	1
Extras lb 1	1
Total (17.3 overs)	124

FoW: 1-0 (Durston), 2-46 (Cross), 3-60 (Madsen), 4-65 (Godleman), 5-69 (North), 6-73 (A L Hughes), 7-78 (C F Hughes), 8-107 (Knight), 9-122 (Cork), 10-124 (Turner)

	O	M	R	W
Williamson	4	0	26	2
Bresnan	1	0	15	0
Sidebottom	2	0	11	0
Pyrah	2	0	12	1
Azeem Rafiq	4	0	26	3
Rashid	3	0	28	2
Lyth	1.3	0	5	2

Man of the Match: A Z Lees

Umpires: M J D Bodenham and J W Lloyds   Scorers: J T Potter and J M Brown

Super craftsman Lees goes big

ALEX LEES: Calculated run-scoring at its best

The Vikings ruthlessly overran the lacklustre Falcons after an excellent unbeaten 67 from Lees.

Yorkshire lost the toss and batted first in glorious weather before a packed Queen's Park. Williamson showed his intent with three boundaries in Durston's first over, but Finch's timing again eluded him as he watched his Kiwi partner race into the 30s.

The powerplay overs brought 44 runs for the loss of Finch, whose leading edge landed in the hands of Godleman off Turner.

Lees had a stroke of luck on one, lofting high to wide long-off where the chance was palmed over the ropes for six. This did not stop Lees going big — no fielders were needed as his second maximum soared over the pavilion roof.

Williamson on 41 was bowled by an excellent one from North as he was forced back on his crease, the score having advanced to 79 from nine overs. Bairstow was stumped at 99 a long way from safety off North, who produced stand-out figures 2-27, and Lees was joined by Gale. The left-handed pair batted with sense and power in a display of calculated run-scoring at its best. They added 65 before Bresnan came to launch Turner's last over for some significant blows, 18 coming off it. Lees finished unbeaten on a superbly crafted 67, Vikings closing on an excellent 183 from their 20 overs.

Williamson's opening over conceded a single while he bowled Durston aiming across the line, but the game became a contest as former Lancashire wicket-keeper Cross produced some scintillating strokeplay. Bresnan's first over went for 15, and the score raced to 33 from three overs, all the runs to Cross. Pyrah scalped Cross in his first over as he failed to clear the ropes on the long-leg boundary, and Rashid, Rafiq and Williamson bowled with skill and discipline to keep the Falcons to seven runs per over from the next nine bowled. Wickets went down frequently, and the chase fell away when North was superbly caught and bowled. Knight and Wainwright took Derbyshire to a modicum of respectability.

NatWest T20 BLAST — North Group
Yorkshire v. Warwickshire

Played at Headingley, Leeds, on July 18, 2014
Warwickshire won by 5 wickets

Toss won by Yorkshire

Warwickshire 2 points, Yorkshire 0 points

YORKSHIRE

A J Finch, c Javid b Clarke	....	13
K S Williamson, lbw b Patel	....	24
A Z Lees, st Ambrose b Patel	....	15
§ J M Bairstow, c Best b Javid	....	12
* A W Gale, b Patel	....	0
A Lyth, b Patel	....	0
T T Bresnan, not out	....	45
A U Rashid, not out	....	29
R M Pyrah		
Azeem Rafiq	Did not bat	
R J Sidebottom		
Extras lb 7, w 2	....	9
Total (6 wkts, 20 overs)		147

FoW: 1-16 (Finch), 2-47 (Lees), 3-62 (Williamson), 4-62 (Gale), 5-62 (Lyth)
6-79 (Bairstow)

	O	M	R	W
Clarke	3	0	16	1
Hannon - Dalby	4	0	35	0
Gordon	2	0	23	0
Patel	4	0	19	4
Best	4	0	29	0
Javid	3	0	18	1

WARWICKSHIRE

W T S Porterfield, c Gale b Bresnan	....	4
J P Webb, c Finch b Sidebottom	....	15
* V Chopra, c Pyrah b Azeem Rafiq	....	9
§ T R Ambrose, c Lees b Sidebottom	....	6
R Clarke, c Azeem Rafiq b Rashid	....	23
L J Evans, not out	....	69
A Javid, not out	....	18
P M Best		
J S Patel		
R O Gordon	Did not bat	
O J Hannon-Dalby		
Extras lb 1, lb 1, w 2	....	4
Total (5 wkts, 19.4 overs)	....	148

FoW: 1-10 (Porterfield), 2-22 (Webb), 3-29 (Ambrose), 4-40 (Chopra), 5-83 (Clarke)

	O	M	R	W
Williamson	1	0	8	0
Bresnan	3.4	0	18	1
Sidebottom	4	0	38	2
Rashid	4	0	28	1
Azeem Rafiq	3	0	24	1
Pyrah	4	0	30	0

Man of the Match: L J Evans

Umpires: N A Mallender and M J Saggers   Scorers: J T Potter and M D Smith

Yorkshire v. Warwickshire

Hat-trick and agonising wait

Hopes of an automatic quarter-final berth were put on hold.

A Jeetan Patel hat-trick and an unbeaten half-century by Evans proved too much for a Vikings side who failed to grab the initiative in key phases of this low-scoring contest.

Patel's triple blow left Yorkshire 62-5 before 10 overs had been completed as Williamson, Gale and Lyth all perished to some fine bowling.

Most notably in this form of the game, all

Late rally: Tim Bresnan and Adil Rashid run up an undefeated 68

three wickets were what could be termed proper dismissals, Williamson trapped on the crease while the other two were undone with perfect deliveries clipping the top of off-stump.

A late rally from Rashid and, not for the first time, Bresnan, ensured that the hosts had a total of some substance to defend. The middle-order pair contributed an unbroken 68 from 44 balls, Bresnan in particular impressing with 45 from 36 balls. Rashid finished undefeated on 29. Yorkshire's total of 147-6 was still a little below par. They were kept in check after Patel's career-best 4-19, and managed only 16 fours and no sixes. Finch again missed out at the top of the order.

The Vikings wrestled back control with the ball, Bresnan and Sidebottom grabbing early wickets to reduce the Bears to 29-3. By the time Chopra was neatly taken by Pyrah off Rafiq for nine the score was 40-4 in the eighth over. A partnership of 43 between Clarke and Evans put Yorkshire on the back foot before Rashid had Clarke caught by Rafiq for 23. The game was in the balance.

Evans saw this as the signal to throw caution to the wind and it was his innings that made the difference. Pyrah and Sidebottom came in for some rough treatment as Evans and Javed found the rope with a regularity that had been absent for much of the evening. The winning runs came with two balls and four wickets remaining, Evans finishing with a career-best 69 from 43 balls to scoop the man-of-the-match award.

NatWest T20 BLAST — North Group
Yorkshire v. Nottinghamshire

Played at Headingley, Leeds, on July 25, 2014
Nottinghamshire won by 4 wickets

Toss won by Yorkshire   Nottinghamshire 2 points, Yorkshire 0 points

YORKSHIRE

K S Williamson, lbw b Ball		6
A J Finch, c Read b Franklin		89
A Z Lees, lbw b Ball		16
§ J M Bairstow, c Mullaney b Ball		60
* A W Gale, c Read b Mullaney		5
T T Bresnan, not out		19
A Lyth		
A U Rashid		
R M Pyrah	Did not bat	
Azeem Rafiq		
R J Sidebottom		
Extras lb 1, w 4		5
Total (5 wkts, 20 overs)		200

FoW: 1-33 (Williamson), 2-51 (Lees), 3-132 (Finch), 4-158 (Gale), 5-200 (Bairstow)

	O	M	R	W
Fletcher	4	0	38	0
Shahzad	4	0	39	0
Ball	4	0	38	3
Patel	4	0	48	0
Mullaney	3	0	28	1
Franklin	1	0	8	1

NOTTINGHAMSHIRE

S J Mullaney, c Lees b Bresnan		22
A D Hales, c Azeem Rafiq b Bresnan		67
M H Wessels, c Lees b Azeem Rafiq		29
S R Patel, c Finch b Pyrah		26
* J W A Taylor, not out		35
J E C Franklin, not out		19
§ C M W Read		
S K W Wood		
A Shahzad	Did not bat	
L J Fletcher		
J T Ball		
Extras b 1, lb 1, w 1		3
Total (4 wkts, 19.2 overs)		201

FoW: 1-32 (Mullaney), 2-102 (Wessels), 3-131 (Hales), 4-162 (Patel)

	O	M	R	W
Sidebottom	4	0	53	0
Bresnan	3.2	0	22	2
Pyrah	4	0	44	1
Lyth	1	0	14	0
Rashid	4	0	41	0
Azeem Rafiq	3	0	25	1

Man of the Match: A D Hales

Umpires: N L Bainton and R K Illingworth   Scorers: J T Potter and R Marshall

Third Umpire: D J Millns

Outlaw arrows hit the Vikings

The Vikings' campaign came to a sad end against the Outlaws as they failed to reach the knockout stages.

Requiring an imposing 201, the visitors timed their run chase to perfection, winning by six wickets with four balls remaining.

The first exchanges were dominated by Finch, playing in his last game before returning to Australia.

He made a circum-

AARON FINCH: Seven sixes and four fours in his blistering 89

spect start, only two coming from the opening over by Fletcher. The bustling Aussie then launched Shahzad over extra-cover for six and straight down the ground for a boundary to show his intent. The score was 33 in the fourth over when Williamson was trapped in front for six off Ball, and Lees went the same way at 51 for a breezy 16.

Unperturbed Finch and a patient Bairstow set about the Outlaws with precision, adding 81 in eight overs. Finch dealt almost exclusively in maximums, some of which threatened to leave the arena, and his blistering display of 89 from 46 balls with four fours and seven sixes was ended only by a fine leg-side catch from wicket-keeper Read. Bairstow duly took the reins and was last man out for a 54-ball 60.

The Outlaws were straight on target, quickly running up the required 10 per over as Hales and Mullaney combined to thrash their way to 32 before Mullaney was taken in the deep for 22 by Lees off Bresnan. The strike rate showed no signs of letting up as Hales and Wessels sailed into the hapless Vikings, helped by the baffling introduction in the powerplay overs of Lyth, whose six balls were promptly despatched for 14.

The score advanced to 102 before Lees pouched Wessels off Rafiq for 29, and the required rate was climbing towards 12 when what seemed like the decisive wicket fell, Hales holing out in the deep for 67. Patel, too, was caught in the deep, and the Outlaws needed 39 from 17 balls. Taylor and Franklin had few problems as Pyrah went for two successive sixes, and Taylor destroyed Sidebottom's figures with three fours and a huge six. Nottinghamshire needed a run a ball from the last over, but Franklin hit Bresnan back over his head for the 20th six of the match.

YORKSHIRE AVERAGES 2014

NATWEST T20 BLAST

Played 14   Won 6   Lost 5   Abandoned 3

BATTING AND FIELDING

(Qualification 4 completed innings)

Player	M.	I.	N.O.	Runs	H.S.	100s	50s	Avge	ct/st
J M Bairstow	11	11	4	355	102*	1	2	50.71	4/4
T T Bresnan	10	9	5	175	45*	0	0	43.75	5
A Z Lees	10	10	2	315	67*	0	2	39.37	4
A J Finch	10	10	0	256	89	0	2	25.60	14
A U Rashid	11	5	1	98	29*	0	0	24.50	3
K S Williamson	5	5	0	93	41	0	0	18.60	1
A W Gale	10	10	0	135	55	0	1	13.50	2
A Lyth	10	7	1	66	46*	0	0	11.00	6
Also played									
L E Plunkett	2	1	0	36	36	0	0	36.00	0
R M Pyrah	11	6	3	48	16*	0	0	16.00	4
J E Root	1	1	0	13	13	0	0	13.00	0
G S Ballance	1	1	0	12	12	0	0	12.00	1
R J Sidebottom	8	2	1	2	2	0	0	2.00	1
O E Robinson	7	3	0	5	3	0	0	1.66	3
Azeem Rafiq	9	3	3	13	7*	0	0	—	8
J A Brooks	3	0	0	0	—	0	0	—	1
S A Patterson	1	0	0	0	—	0	0	—	0
J A Leaning	1	0	0	0	—	0	0	—	0

BOWLING

(Qualification 4 wickets)

Player	Overs	Mdns	Runs	Wkts	Avge	Best	4wI	RPO
L E Plunkett	7	0	45	4	11.25	2-20	0	6.42
Azeem Rafiq	28.4	0	184	14	13.14	3-20	0	6.41
A U Rashid	39	1	272	14	19.42	3-14	0	6.97
R M Pyrah	36	0	274	13	21.07	3-19	0	7.61
R J Sidebottom	28.5	1	247	11	22.45	3-24	0	8.56
O E Robinson	17	0	162	6	27.00	2-25	0	9.52
T T Bresnan	36	0	262	9	29.11	2-22	0	7.27
Also bowled								
S A Patterson	3	0	16	2	8.00	2-16	0	5.33
K S Williamson	6	0	37	3	12.33	2-26	0	6.16
A Lyth	3.3	0	26	2	13.00	2- 5	0	8.66
J A Brooks	9	0	82	0	—	0-19	0	9.11
J E Root	1	0	6	0	—	0-6	0	6.00
J A Leaning	1	0	12	0	—	0-12	0	12.00

Second Eleven 2014

PLAYERS WHO APPEARED FOR YORKSHIRE SECOND ELEVEN IN 2014
(excluding First Eleven capped players)

Player	Date of Birth	Birthplace	Type
M A Ashraf *	January 5, 1992	Bradford	RHB/RF
K Carver *	March 26, 1996	Northallerton	LHB/SLA
B O Coad *	January 10, 1994	Harrogate	RHB/RM
M D Fisher*	November 9, 1997	York	RHB/RMF
D M Hodgson *	February 26, 1990	Northallerton	RHB/WK
A J Hodd *	January 12, 1984	Chichester	RHB/WK
J A Leaning *	October 18, 1993	Bristol	RHB/RMF
Azeem Rafiq *	February 27, 1991	Karachi, Pakistan	RHB/OB
W M H Rhodes *	March 2, 1995	Nottingham	LHB/RM
J Shaw *	January 3, 1996	Wakefield	RHB/RMF
J A Tattersall *	December 15, 1994	Knaresborough	RHB/LB
B L Ainsley	November 19, 1997	Middlesbrough	RHB /OB
J W P Brown	March 27, 1998	Sheffield	LHB/LM
E Callis	November 8, 1994	Doncaster	RHB
N J Firn	October 9, 1995	York	RHB /RM
B P Gibson	March 31, 1996	Leeds	RHB/WK
R Gibson	January 22, 1996	Middlesbrough	RHB/RM
M Hussain	March 27, 1997	Leeds	RHB/RM
J E G Logan	October 12, 1997	Wakefield	LHB/SLA
O E Robinson	December 1, 1993	Margate	RHB/RM
J A Thompson	October 9, 1996	Leeds	LHB/ RMF
J C Wainman	January 25, 1993	Harrogate	RHB/LM
M J Waite	December 24, 1995	Leeds	RHB/RMF
J Warner	November 14, 1996	Wakefield	RHB /RFM

* Second Eleven cap

SECOND ELEVEN HIGHLIGHTS OF 2014

CHAMPIONSHIP

Century partnerships (5)

For the 3rd wicket (2)

136	D M Hodgson and J A Tattersall	v. Durham at Harrogate
105	J A Leaning and D M Hodgson	v. Worcestershire at York

For the 4th wicket (1)

194	J A Leaning and W M H Rhodes	v. Nottinghamshire at Notts Sports Ground

For the 5th wicket (1)

120	J A Leaning and A J Hodd	v. Glamorgan at the SWALEC Stadium

For the 8th wicket (1)

158	M J Waite and N J Firn	v. MCC Young Cricketers at Shenley

This was the highest eighth-wicket stand in the Second Eleven Championship of 2014

Centuries (2)

D M Hodgson (1)

   113   v. Durham at Harrogate

M J Waite (1)

   112   v. MCC Young Cricketers at Shenley

10 wickets in a match (1)

J Shaw (1)

   10-71   (5-43 and 5-28)   v. Durham at Harrogate

Five wickets in an innings (3)

R M Pyrah (1)

   5-29 v Glamorgan at the SWALEC Stadium

M D Fisher (1)

   5-31 v. Worcestershire at York

J C Wainman (1)

   5-58 v. Leicestershire at York

Four victims in an innings (3)

A J Hodd (2)

   4 (4ct)   v. Glamorgan at the SWALEC Stadium

   4 (4ct)   v. Worcestershire at York

D M Hodgson (1)

   4 (4ct)   v. Durham at Harrogate

CHAMPIONSHIP MILESTONES IN 2014

Dan Hodgson achieved 1.000 runs. Matthew Waite achieved his maiden century for Yorkshire (112) in his maiden Championship innings. Josh Shaw (5-28); Richard Pyrah (5-29), Matthew Fisher (5-31) and James Wainman (5-58) achieved their best bowling figures

TROPHY

Century Partnerships (6)

For the 1st wicket (2)

146	E Callis and J A Tattersall	v. Nottinghamshire at Notts Sports Ground
115	A J Hodd and W M H Rhodes	v. Durham at Marske-by-the-Sea

For the 3rd wicket (2)

126	D M Hodgson and J A Leaning	v. Derbyshire at Swarkestone
105	A J Hodd and J A Tattersall	v. Warwickshire at Pudsey Congs

Century Partnerships *(continued)*

For the 4th wicket (1)

196   D M Hodgson and R M Pyrah v. Durham at Marske-by-the-Sea

This was the highest fourth-wicket partnership ever recorded for Yorkshire in the Trophy, passing the 149 by Neil Nicholson and Neil Hartley v. Lancashire at Old Trafford in 1989. It was the highest fourth-wicket stand in the 2014 competition.

For the 5th wicket (1)

112   W M H Rhodes and R Gibson v. Worcestershire at Stamford Bridge

Partnership Record 10th wicket

56   N J Firn and J E G Logan   v. Leicestershire at Barnsley

This was the highest last-wicket Trophy partnership recorded for Yorkshire, beating the previous best of 50 by John Blain and Dan Conway v. Durham at Sunderland in 2004. It was the highest last-wicket stand in the 2014 competition.

Centuries (3)

R M Pyrah (1)

    128   v. Durham at Marske-by-the-Sea

W M H Rhodes (1)

    124   v. Worcestershire at Stamford Bridge

A J Hodd (1)

    112   v. Warwickshire at Pudsey Congs

4 wickets in an innings

No instances. Best figures: 3-2 by James Wainman v. Warwickshire at Pudsey Congs

Five victims in an innings (1)

D M Hodgson (1)

    5 (5ct)   v. Warwickshire at Pudsey Congs

TROPHY MILESTONES IN 2014

Richard Pyrah (128), Will Rhodes (124) and Andrew Hodd (112) made their highest scores.

T20 COMPETITION

Century Partnerships (1)

For the 4th wicket (1)

110   J A Leaning and W M H Rhodes v Durham at York (1st match)

This was Yorkshire's record fourth-wicket stand in the competition, beating the 77 by Azeem Rafiq and J A Leaning v. Nottinghamshire at Headingley in 2013 (first match).

4 wickets in an innings (3)

R M Pyrah (1)

    4-13 v. Nottinghamshire at Notts Sports Ground (1st match).

K Carver (1)

    4-14 v. Derbyshire at Derby (2nd match)

M A Ashraf (1)

    4-19 v Nottinghamshire at Nottinghamshire Sports Ground (1st match)

Three victims in an innings (1)

W M H Rhodes (1)

    3 (3ct)   v. Nottinghamshire at Notts Sports Ground (1st match).

Debuts (5)

B L Ainsley, N J Firn, J E G Logan, M J Waite and J Warner

T20 MILESTONES IN 2014

Jack Leaning (102) hit Yorkshire's first century in this format in 54 deliveries, including five fours and seven sixes, and is the leading *T20* Second Eleven run-scorer with 474. Will Rhodes did the hat-trick v. Durham at York in the first game of the season.

Second Eleven Championship
Glamorgan v. Yorkshire

Played at the SWALEC Stadium on April 9,10 and 11, 2014
Match drawn at 6.14pm on the Third Day

Toss won by Glamorgan

Glamorgan 11 points, Yorkshire 11 points

Close of play: First Day, Glamorgan 48-1 (Mellor 21, Wright 6) Second Day, Yorkshire 103-4 (Hodd 37, Leaning 42}

First Innings	YORKSHIRE		Second Innings	
E Callis, b Owen	1		c Penrhyn-Jones b Glover	13
J A Tattersall, c Rouse b Waters	22		c Mellor b Glover	5
D M Hodgson, c Mellor b Penrhyn-Jones	47		c Rouse b Glover	0
J A Leaning, lbw b Owen	9		not out	80
W M H Rhodes, c Wright b Salter	49		b Owen	0
§ A J Hodd, lbw b Miller	27		b Owen	67
*Azeem Rafiq, lbw b Miller	0			
R M Pyrah, not out	30		(7) lbw b Miller	26
R Gibson, c Knight b Salter	2		(8) not out	32
J Shaw, lbw b Owen	0			
B O Coad, run out (Knight)	7			
M D Fisher	Did not bat			
Extras b 7, lb 2, nb 8	17		Extras b 5, lb 8, nb 4	17
Total (78.2 overs)	211		Total (6 wkts dec, 67 overs)	240

FoW: 1-2 (Callis), 2-38 (Tattersall), 3-85 (Leaning), 4-98 (Hodgson), 5-142 (Hodd), 1st 6-154 (Azeem Rafiq), 7-180 (Rhodes), 8-190 (Gibson), 9-161 (Shaw), 10-211 (Coad)

FoW: 1-17 (Tattersall), 2-17 (Hodgson), 3-18 (Callis), 4-34 (Rhodes), 5-154 (Hodd), 2nd 6-196 (Pyrah)

	O	M	R	W		O	M	R	W
Owen	13.2	4	32	3	Glover	7	5	12	3
Glover	14	5	27	0	Waters	3	1	10	0
Miller	15	3	30	2	Miller	19	3	52	1
Waters	13	4	21	1	Salter	15	2	74	0
Penrhyn-Jones	8	0	47	1	Owen	12	3	34	2
Salter	15	2	45	2	Lloyd	5	1	21	0
					Penrhyn-Jones	6	0	24	0

First Innings	GLAMORGAN		Second Innings	
A J Mellor, lbw b Pyrah	39		c Hodgson b Coad	15
J L Lawlor, c Hodd b Pyrah	15		c Tattersall b Coad	28
* B J Wright, c Leaning b Shaw	7		c and b Pyrah	67
D L Lloyd, c Tattersall b Coad	12		c Hodgson b Fisher	185
A P Rouse, c Hodd b Pyrah	0		c Hodgson b Fisher	19
§ G Knight, lbw b Gibson	0		c Hodd b Pyrah	19
A G Salter, c Hodd b Pyrah	28		lbw b Leaning	17
J C Glover, c Hodd b Coad	25			
W T Owen, c Hodgson b Pyrah	60		(8) c Tattersall b Leaning	0
H T Waters, c Pyrah b Leaning	7		(9) not out	5
A S Miller, not out	2		(10) not out	5
D Penrhyn-Jones	Did Not Bat			
Extras lb 15	15		Extras b 4, lb 6	10
Total (77.2 overs)	210		Total (8 wkts, 65 overs)	185

FoW: 1-32 (Lawlor), 2-55 (Wright), 3-79 (Lloyd), 4-80 (Rouse), 5-81 (Mellor), 1st 6-81 (Knight), 7-123 (Glover), 8-163 (Salter), 9-202 (Waters), 10-210 (Owen)

FoW: 1-24 (Mellor), 2-68 (Lawlor), 3-117 (Lloyd), 4-117 (Rouse), 5-153 (Knight), 2nd 6-168 (Wright), 7-175 (Owen), 8-175 (Salter)

	O	M	R	W		O	M	R	W
Coad	18	5	42	2	Coad	12	5	26	2
Fisher	10	4	22	0	Fisher	12	3	29	2
Pyrah	18.2	7	29	5	Shaw	11	2	24	0
Shaw	10	1	37	1	Pyrah	13	5	27	2
Azeem Rafiq	10	3	28	0	Gibson	4	0	11	0
Gibson	8	2	33	1	Leaning	14	1	58	2
Leaning	2	1	2	1					
Tattersall	1	0	2	0					

Umpires: P K Baldwin and L Hall

Scorers: G Watkins and H Clayton

Second Eleven Championship
Nottinghamshire v Yorkshire

Played at Nottinghamshire Sports Ground on April 15, 16 and 17, 2014

Match drawn at 5pm on the Third Day

Toss won by Yorkshire   Nottinghamshire 13 points, Yorkshire 12 points

Close of play: First Day, Nottinghamshire 85-3 (Root 18, Tillcock 12); Second Day, Yorkshire 63-3 (Leaning 6, Rhodes 3)

First Innings	YORKSHIRE		Second Innings	
E Callis, c Cross b Shazad		0	b Franks	32
J A Tattersall, c Cross b Kitt		40	c Hutton b Shahzad	3
§ D M Hodgson, c Cross b Hutton		19	lbw b L Wood	2
J A Leaning, b L Wood		1	lbw b S K W Wood	80
W M H Rhodes, b Franks		71	c L Wood b S K W Wood	89
O E Robinson, b Shahzad		14	lbw b S K W Wood	11
*Azeem Rafiq, c Kelsall b L Wood		28	not out	87
R M Pyrah, b L Wood		11	lbw b Kitt	1
J Shaw, lbw b L Wood		2	lbw b Hasan Azad	8
B O Coad, c Hasan Azad b Hutton		23		
M D Fisher, not out		21	(9) not out	5
M A Ashraf	Did not bat			
Extras b 11, lb 6, nb 6, w 2		25	Extras b 13, lb 18, nb 18, w 1	50
Total (77.2 overs)		255	Total (8 wkts dec, 97.3 overs)	368

FoW: 1-0 (Callis), 2-33 (Hodgson), 3-57 (Leaning), 4-79 (Tattersall), 5-115 (Robinson),
1st 6-190 (Azeem Rafiq), 7-192 (Rhodes), 8-199 (Shaw), 9-206 (Pyrah), 10-255 (Coad)

FoW: 1-29 (Tattersall), 2-50 (Hodgson), 3-50 (Callis), 4-244 (Rhodes), 5-245 (Leaning),
2nd 6-270 (Robinson), 7-296 (Pyrah), 8-363 (Shaw)

	O	M	R	W		O	M	R	W
Shahzad	15	5	44	2	Shahzad	15	5	42	1
Hutton	18.2	5	38	2	Hutton	16.3	5	71	0
L Wood	16	2	53	4	L Wood	16	6	45	1
Kitt	13	1	44	1	Franks	13	5	32	1
Tillcock	2	0	14	0	Tillcock	7	0	46	0
Franks	7	1	29	1	S K W Wood	17	5	55	3
S K W Wood	6	2	16	0	Kitt	12	2	44	1
					Hasan Azad	1	0	2	1

NOTTINGHAMSHIRE

S Kelsall, lbw b Pyrah		17
Hasan Azad, lbw b Ashraf		25
S K W Wood, c Leaning b Ashraf		0
W T Root, c Leaning b Pyrah		33
A D Tillcock, lbw b Shaw		115
§ M H Cross, c Hodgson b Coad		12
A Shahzad, c Coad b Azeem Rafiq		8
B A Hutton, c Hodgson b Pyrah		75
S Webster, c Azeem Rafiq b Shaw		0
*P J Franks, c Tattersall b Leaning		36
L Wood, not out		31
B M Kitt	Did not bat	
Extras lb 14, nb 10		24
Total (106.3 overs)		376

FoW: 1-50 (Hasan Azad), 2-50 (S K W Wood), 3-54 (Kelsall), 4-108 (Root), 5-125 (Cross),
6-134 (Shahzad), 7-298 (Tillcock), 8-298 (Webster), 9-324 (Hutton), 10-376 (Franks)

	O	M	R	W
Ashraf	17	8	46	2
Fisher	15	6	45	0
Pyrah	19	6	54	3
Shaw	14	2	66	2
Coad	13	3	29	1
Azeem Rafiq	15	2	55	1
Robinson	10	1	36	0
Leaning	3.3	0	31	1

Umpires: D J Millns and W B Jones   Scorers: Mrs A Cusworth and H Clayton

Second Eleven Championship
Yorkshire v. Warwickshire

Played at Stamford Bridge on June 2, 3 and 4, 2014
Match abandoned as a draw at 2.13pm on the Second Day

Toss won by Warwickshire   Yorkshire 9 points, Warwickshire 9 points
Close of play: First Day, Warwickshire 81-1 (Evans 50, Trott 12); Second and Third Day, no play.

YORKSHIRE

E Callis, lbw b Thomasson	33
* J A Tattersall, lbw b Thomasson	32
§ A J Hodd, c McKay b Trott	58
W M H Rhodes, c McKay b Trott	28
D M Hodgson, lbw b Poysden	39
O E Robinson, c Best b Trott	17
R M Pyrah, c Poysden b Thomasson	1
Azeem Rafiq, b Gordon	0
R Gibson, c Lewis b Best	33
J Shaw, c McKay b Poysden	8
B O Coad, not out	3
J C Wainman	Did not bat
Extras b 6, lb 11, nb 32	49
Total (77.2 overs)	301

FoW: 1-69 (Callis), 2-115 (Tattersall), 3-183 (Hodd), 4-192 (Rhodes), 5-224 (Robinson), 6-227 (Pyrah), 7-228 (Azeem Rafiq), 8-279 (Hodgson), 9-293 (Gibson), 10-301 (Shaw)

	O	M	R	W
Jones	12	1	48	0
Gordon	15	2	63	1
Trott	14	4	39	3
Thomasson	16	3	58	3
Best	14	2	43	1
Poysden	6	1	33	2

WARWICKSHIRE

F R J Coleman, c Hodd b Pyrah	17
L J Evans, not out	50
I J L Trott, not out	12
S R Hain	
T P Lewis	
J O Troughton	
* P M Best	
R A Jones	Did not bat
§ P J McKay	
A D Thomasson	
R O Gordon	
J E Poysden	
Extras nb 2	2
Total (1 wkt; 24 overs)	81

FoW: 1-52 (Coleman)

	O	M	R	W
Coad	6	3	9	0
Wainman	4	1	9	0
Shaw	5	0	31	0
Pyrah	6	1	20	1
Rhodes	3	1	12	0

Umpires: B J Debenham and T Lungley   Scorers: H Clayton and S Smith

Second Eleven Championship
Lancashire v. Yorkshire

Played at Northern CC, Crosby, on June 10, 11 and 12, 2014
Match drawn at 4.52pm on the Third Day

Toss won by Lancashire   Lancashire 13 points, Yorkshire 10 points
Close of play: First Day, Yorkshire 149-6 (Azeem Rafiq 17, Gibson 6); Second Day, Lancashire 54-1 (Reece 20)

YORKSHIRE

E Callis, b Griffiths		1
* J A Tattersall, b Jarvis		0
A J Hodd, c Lilley b Jarvis		2
W M H Rhodes, c Gowers b Jarvis		15
§ D M Hodgson, c Gowers b Clark		22
O E Robinson, lbw b Jarvis		62
Azeem Rafiq, c Clark b Newby		43
R Gibson, b Newby		9
J Shaw, b Griffiths		12
B O Coad, c Brown b Griffiths		27
J C Wainman, not out		4
M Hussain	Did not bat	
Extras lb 13, nb 14, w 1		28
Total (87.1 overs)		225

FoW: 1-1 (Tattersall), 2-3 (Hodd), 3-3 (Callis), 4-21 (Rhodes), 5-96 (Hodgson), 6-130 (Robinson), 7-180 (Gibson), 8-181 (Azeem Rafiq), 9-218 (Coad), 10-225 (Shaw)

	O	M	R	W
Jarvis	24	4	63	4
Griffiths	18.1	8	39	3
White	9	2	14	0
Newby	11	2	34	2
Clark	12	4	37	1
Procter	3	0	12	0
Parry	7	2	5	0
Lilley	3	0	8	0

LANCASHIRE

L M Reece, c Hodgson b Shaw		20
K R Brown, b Shaw		32
L A Procter, b Wainman		10
J Clark, c Gibson b Coad		8
W A White, c Shaw b Gibson		16
L S Livingstone, c Tattersall b Coad		75
* S D Parry, b Shaw		0
A M Lilley, c Hodgson b Wainman		93
O J Newby, c Azeem Rafiq b Shaw		50
K M Jarvis, not out		1
G T Griffiths, not out		7
§ A M Gowers	Did not bat	
Extras lb 6		6
Total (9 wkts dec; 106 overs)		318

FoW: 1-54 (Brown), 2-57 (Reece), 3-72 (Procter), 4-74 (Clark), 5-95 (White), 6-95 (Parry), 7-237 (Lilley), 8-290 (Livingstone), 9-311 (Newby)

	O	M	R	W
Coad	26	9	73	2
Shaw	24	7	85	4
Gibson	12	6	20	1
Rhodes	10	4	28	0
Wainman	21	8	43	2
Azeem Rafiq	12	1	60	0
Callis	1	0	3	0

Umpires: J H Evans and K Fergusson   Scorers: C Rimmer and H Clayton

Second Eleven Championship
Yorkshire v. Worcestershire

Played at York on July 15, 16 and 17, 2014

Yorkshire won by an innings and 10 runs at 2.12 pm on the Third Day

Toss won by Yorkshire   Yorkshire 23 points, Worcestershire 5 points
Close of play: First Day, Yorkshire 135-2 (Leaning 50, Hodgson 29); Second Day, Worcestershire 37-0 (Pardoe 26, Rhodes 7)

WORCESTERSHIRE

	First Innings		Second Innings	
M G Pardoe	c Leaning b Wainman	18	c Hodd b Shaw	28
§ J M Clarke	c Hodgson b Coad	47	(6) c Leaning b Fisher	2
R A Whiteley	b Shaw	30	(5) c Gibson b Fisher	0
B L D'Oliveira	c Leaning b Shaw	2	lbw b Wainman	37
E G Barnard	c Hodgson b Wainman	5	(3) c Hodd b Fisher	16
* G M Andrew	run out (Thompson)	4	(7) c Hodgson b Gibson	17
A Hepburn	b Wainman	5	(8) c Hodd b Fisher	5
G H Rhodes	c Hodgson b Fisher	9	(2) c Hodd b Wainman	9
B J Twoigh	c Gibson b Coad	13	c Leaning b Wainman	9
N L Harrison	b Fisher	0	c Hodgson b Fisher	0
G Cessford	not out	4	not out	0
G P Whiles	Did not bat		Did not bat	
Extras	b 5, lb 4, nb 2, w 5	16	b 5, lb 5, nb 2	12
Total	(49.3 overs)	153	(51.2 overs)	135

FoW: 1-38 (Pardoe), 2-101 (Whiteley), 3-103 (D'Oliveira), 4-107 (Clarke), 5-116 (Barnard),
1st   6-117 (Andrew), 7-131 (Hepburn), 8-137 (Rhodes), 9-137 (Harrison), 10-153 (Twoigh)
FoW: 1-39 (Pardoe), 2-51 (Rhodes), 3-65 (Barnard), 4-81 (Whiteley), 5-83 (Clarke), 6-121
2nd   (Andrew), 7-121 (D'Oliveira), 8-135 (Hepburn), 9-135 (Twoigh), 10-135 (Harrison)

	O	M	R	W		O	M	R	W
Coad	12.3	3	25	2	Coad	11	4	29	0
Wainman	11	2	45	3	Fisher	14.2	5	31	5
Fisher	13	6	26	2	Shaw	8	2	21	1
Rhodes	4	0	21	0	Wainman	13	5	35	3
Gibson	3	1	12	0	Rhodes	4	1	7	0
Shaw	6	0	15	2	Gibson	1	0	2	1

YORKSHIRE

A J Hodd	b Cessford	24
M Hussain	lbw b Whiteley	14
J A Leaning	c Rhodes b Harrison	74
§ D M Hodgson	c Clarke b Whiles	33
* W M H Rhodes	b Harrison	22
R Gibson	c Whiteley b Whiles	54
J A Thompson	c Rhodes b Cessford	10
J Shaw	c Barnard b Whiteley	18
J C Wainman	c Andrew b Whiteley	5
M D Fisher	run out (Barnard)	0
B O Coad	not out	16
K Carver	Did not bat	
Extras	b 9, lb 5, nb 6, w 8	28
Total	(104.4 overs)	298

FoW: 1-32 (Hodd), 2-48 (Hussain), 3-153 (Hodgson), 4-182 (Leaning), 5-196 (Rhodes),
6-216 (Thompson), 7-255 (Shaw), 8-273 (Wainman), 9-273 (Fisher), 10-298 (Gibson)

	O	M	R	W
Cessford	25	4	81	2
Whiles	19.4	6	60	2
Whiteley	13	3	30	3
Harrison	17	6	32	2
Twoigh	6	0	16	0
Barnard	9	2	16	0
D'Oliveira	5	1	27	0
Rhodes	10	1	22	0

Umpires: I Dawood and S J Malone   Scorers: H Clayton and Mrs S M Drinkwater

Second Eleven Championship
Yorkshire v. Durham

Played at Harrogate on July 23, 24 and 25, 2014

Yorkshire won by an innings and 62 runs at 12.31pm on the Third Day

Toss won by Yorkshire   Yorkshire 24 points, Durham 5 points

Close of play: First Day, Yorkshire 67-2 (Hodgson 23, Tattersall 15); Second Day, Durham 7-5 (Budge 6, Buckley 0)

DURHAM

	First Innings		Second Innings	
R Carr, c Hodd b Shaw	18	b Shaw	7
G Clark, c Hodgson b Shaw	57	(8) c Hussain b Shaw	19
A J Hickey, c Hussain b Shaw	10	(2) c Gibson b Coad	9
R Singh, c Hodd b Fisher	30	(3) c Hodgson b Coad	20
A A Shafique, lbw b Shaw	4	(4) c Hodgson b Fisher	4
M Arshad, lbw b Carver	10	(5) b Fisher	3
R S Buckley, not out	60	lbw b Rhodes	18
P Bousfield, c Hussain b Shaw	9	(9) c Hodgson b Shaw	6
M E Milnes, run out (Hodd)	11	(10) not out	1
M G Morley, c Gibson b Carver	8	(11) b Shaw	1
G T Main, c Hodd b Coad	1	Did not bat	
D E Budge	Did not bat	(6) c Hodgson b Shaw	34
Extras b 5, lb 1	6	Extras b 6, lb 2	8
Total (78 overs)	224	Total (45.1 overs)	135

FoW: 1-36 (Carr), 2-50 (Hickey), 3-101 (Clark), 4-107 (Shafique), 5-131 (Singh), 1st 6-131 (Arshad), 7-168 (Bousfield), 8-208 (Milnes), 9-221 (Morley), 10-224 (Main).

FoW: 1-7 (Carr), 2-26 (Hickey), 3-31 (Shafique), 4-39 (Arshad), 5-52 (Singh), 2nd 6-96 (Budge), 7-112 (Buckley), 8-128 (Clark), 9-128 (Bousfield), 10-130 (Morley).

	O	M	R	W		O	M	R	W
Fisher	12	5	29	1	Fisher	7	3	18	2
Wainman	8	2	25	0	Shaw	10.1	2	28	5
Shaw	15	6	43	5	Coad	12	3	36	2
Coad	13	2	38	1	Wainman	9	1	26	0
Rhodes	9	3	33	0	Rhodes	7	3	14	1
Carver	18	7	44	2					
Tattersall	3	1	6	0					

YORKSHIRE

§ A J Hodd, b Arshad		17
M Hussain, b Arshad		0
D M Hodgson, c Shafique b Milnes		113
J A Tattersall, c Shafique b Morley		64
* W M H Rhodes, c Shafique b Hickey		17
R Gibson, c Carr b Main		79
J A Thompson, lbw b Milnes		0
J Shaw, c Singh b Carr		30
J C Wainman, c Arshad b Carr		56
B O Coad, lbw b Hickey		4
K Carver, not out		7
M D Fisher	Did not bat	
Extras b 4, lb 12, nb 10, w 3		29
Total (104.2 overs)		416

FoW: 1-2 (Hussain), 2-29 (Hodd), 3-165 (Tattersall), 4-226 (Rhodes), 5-296 (Hodgson), 6-296 (Thompson), 7-326 (Gibson), 8-386 (Shaw), 9-396 (Coad), 10-416 (Wainman).

	O	M	R	W
Milnes	25	8	64	2
Arshad	6	1	25	2
Main	22	4	83	1
Bousfield	15	5	51	0
Morley	16	2	54	1
Budge	3	0	20	0
Buckley	5	1	25	0
Hickey	8	0	43	2
Carr	4.1	0	35	2

Umpires: I Dawood and S J Malone   Scorers: H Clayton and R V Hilton

Second Eleven Championship
Yorkshire v. Leicestershire

Played at York on August 5, 6 and 7, 2014

Leicestershire won by 8 wickets at 2.33pm on the Third Day

Toss won by Leicestershire   Yorkshire 5 points, Leicestershire 22 points

Close of play: First Day, Leicestershire 131-4 (Raine 26); Second Day, Yorkshire 145- (Firn 6, Logan 0)

First Innings	YORKSHIRE		Second Innings	
E Callis, c Pinner b Freckingham	0		c Taylor b Sheikh	15
§ D M Hodgson, c Sheikh b Taylor	28		b Raine	16
M Hussain, c Lowen b Sheikh	13		c Taylor b Sheikh	16
* R Gibson, c Lowen b Freckingham	6		c Lowen b Raine	10
J A Thompson, lbw b Taylor	31		lbw b Usman Mufazzar	22
B P Gibson, b Raine	16		lbw b Freckingham	20
J C Wainman, run out (Sheikh)	0		lbw b Raine	11
R J Sidebottom, c Pinner b Wyatt	34		b Raine	7
B O Coad, b Freckingham	9			
N J Firn, not out	35		(9) c Lowen b Raine	7
J E G Logan, c Eckersley b Raine	9		(10) not out	2
M A Ashraf	Did Not Bat		(11) c Lowen b Freckingham	2
Extras b 8, lb 6, nb 4	18		Extras b 8, lb 5, nb 10	23
Total (65.1 overs)	199		Total (58.2 overs)	151

FoW: 1-2 (Callis), 2-40 (Hussain), 3-43 (Hodgson), 4-70 (R Gibson), 5-101 (Thompson), 1st 6-102 (Wainman), 7-102 (B P Gibson), 8-130 (Coad), 9-175 (Sidebottom), 10-199 (Logan

FoW: 1-30 (Hodgson), 2-38 (Callis), 3-63 (Hussain), 4-77 (R Gibson), 5-111 (B P Gibson), 6-117 (Thompson), 7-134 (Sidebottom), 8-145 (Wainman), 9-148 (Firn), 10-150 (Ashraf

	O	M	R	W		O	M	R	W
Freckingham	16	5	53	3	Freckingham	14.2	3	36	2
Wyatt	14	5	40	1	Wyatt	4	2	13	0
Raine	12.1	2	32	2	Sheikh	12	4	25	2
Sheikh	12	5	27	1	Raine	18	7	31	5
Taylor	10	3	30	2	Taylor	4	0	27	0
Pinner	1	0	3	0	Usman Mufaffar	5	3	6	1

First Innings	LEICESTERSHIRE		Second Innings	
A K Patel, c Hodgson b Sidebottom	14		not out	57
M A Thornely, b Firn	33		c Firn b Wainman	52
E J H Eckersley, b Wainman	43		c Wainman b Logan	24
B A Raine, run out (Wainman)	34		not out	10
N D Pinner, c Hodgson b Logan	15			
* R M L Taylor, c Hussain b Wainman	0			
Aadil Ali, c R Gibson b Wainman	9			
§ C T Lowen, not out	20			
O H Freckingham, c Hodgson b Wainman	0			
A C F Wyatt, lbw b Wainman	10			
A Sheikh, b Sidebottom	13			
Usman Muzaffar	Did not bat			
Extras b 4, lb 2, nb 4	10		Extras b 4, lb 3	7
Total (62.3 overs)	201		Total (2 wkts, 35.2 overs)	150

FoW: 1-20 (Patel), 2-86 (Thornely), 3-94 (Eckersley), 4-131 (Pinner), 5-142 (Raine), 1st 6-142 (Taylor), 7-157 (Aadil Ali), 8-157 (Freckingham), 9-177 (Wyatt), 10-201 (Sheikh)

2nd 1-97 (Thornely), 2-136 (Eckersley)

	O	M	R	W		O	M	R	W
Sidebottom	8.3	2	25	2	Sidebottom	9	2	27	0
Coad	7.5	2	25	0	Ashraf	11	2	40	0
Wainman	20	5	58	5	Firn	3	1	3	0
Ashraf	11	1	41	0	Wainman	5	0	24	1
Firn	13.1	1	43	1	Logan	7.2	0	49	1
Logan	2	0	3	1					

Umpires: M Burns and I J Dixon   Scorers: H Clayton and P N Johnson

Second Eleven Championship
MCC Young Cricketers v. Yorkshire

Played at Shenley on August 12, 13 and 14, 2014

Match abandoned as a draw at 3.49pm on the Third Day

Toss won by Yorkshire   MCC Young Cricketers 10 points, Yorkshire 13 points

Close of play: First Day, MCC Young Cricketers 13-1 (Piesley 9, Gough 1); Second Day, Yorkshire 58-3 (Hodgson 10, Thompson 20)

YORKSHIRE

First Innings		Second Innings	
C Callis, lbw b Zain Shahzad	61	c Shafique b Hampton	10
S L Ainsley, c Shafique b Hampton	8	c Shafique b Joshi	12
D M Hodgson, b Zain Shahzad	34	c Davies b Joshi	15
R Gibson, c Gough b Piesley	1	b Joshi	6
A Thompson, b Graham b Piesley	9	c Mohammed Abid b Piesley	80
B P Gibson, c Joshi b Piesley	17	b Mohammed Abid	18
C Wainman, lbw b Piesley	14	lbw b Hampton	13
M J Waite, not out	112	c Graham b Piesley	13
N J Firn, b Mohammed Abid	64	not out	4
E G Logan, not out	12	b Renshaw	2
M A Ashraf			
R K J Dawson Did not bat			
Extras b 6, lb 4, nb 6	16	Extras b 5	5
Total (8 wkts dec, 97 overs)	348	Total (9 wkts dec, 53.5 overs)	174

FoW: 1-23 (Ainsley), 2-100 (Hodgson), 3-101 (R Gibson), 4-107 (Callis), 5-115 (Thompson),
1st   6-144 (B P Gibson), 7-149 (Wainman), 8-307 (Firn).

FoW: 1-22 (Ainsley), 2-22 (Callis), 3-31 (R Gibson), 4-63 (Hodgson), 5-96 (B P Gibson),
2nd   6-123 (Wainman), 7-167 (Waite), 8-168 (Thompson), 9-174 (Logan)

	O	M	R	W		O	M	R	W
Joshi	21	3	83	0	Zain Shahzad	13	2	39	0
Zain Shahzad	19	4	38	2	Joshi	16	2	36	3
Hampton	16	3	57	1	Hampton	9	2	50	2
Dobb	2.5	0	12	0	Piesley	6	0	9	2
Piesley	24.1	6	85	4	Mohammed Abid	8	0	32	1
Mohammed Abid	14	0	63	1	Renshaw	1.5	0	3	1

MCC YOUNG CRICKETERS

First Innings		Second Innings	
M T Renshaw, c Callis b Wainman	3	(2) not out	11
* C D Piesley, lbw b Gibson	71	(1) not out	10
L J Gough, b Firn b Logan	14		
S S Arthurton, c Hodgson b Wainman	35		
O J G Graham, c Hodgson b R Gibson	4		
§ A A Shafique, c Ainsley b R Gibson	24		
Mohammed Abid, lbw b Firn	26		
R W Davies, c R Gibson b Wainman	24		
P Joshi, c Firn b Logan	9		
D O D Hampton, c Callis b Wainman	18		
A M Dobb, not out	4		
Zain Shahzad Did not bat			
Extras b 2, nb 10, w 3	15	Extras lb 1, nb 2	3
Total (81.5 overs)	247	Total (0 wkts, 11.2 overs)	24

FoW: 1-4 (Renshaw), 2-48 (Gough), 3-121 (Arthurton), 4-126 (Graham), 5-135 (Piesley), 6-175
1st   (Shafique); 7-192 (Mohammed Abid); 8-207 (Joshi); 9-236 (Hampton); 10-247 (Davies)

	O	M	R	W		O	M	R	W
Wainman	19.5	6	55	4	Waite	6	2	7	0
Logan	23	5	60	2	Wainman	5	1	16	0
Waite	12	2	48	0	Firn	0.2	0	0	0
Firn	11	2	32	1					
R Gibson	14	1	39	3					
Ainsley	2	0	11	0					

R W Davies kept wicket for MCC Young Cricketers in Yorkshire's second innings

Umpires: P R Pollard and S J Ross   Scorers: A P Scarlett and H Clayton

Second Eleven Championship
Derbyshire v. Yorkshire

Played at Denby on August 27, 28 and 29, 2014

Match abandoned as a draw at 4.31pm on the Third Day

Toss won by Yorkshire

Derbyshire 11 points, Yorkshire 10 points

Close of play: First Day, Yorkshire 62-3 (Hodgson 19, Rhodes 8); Second Day, Derbyshire 75-0 (Slater 28, Evans 47)

First Innings	DERBYSHIRE		Second Innings	
B T Slater, c Callis b Rhodes	9		not out	112
H Evans, c Callis b Ashraf	2		b Ashraf	47
C F Hughes, lbw b Ashraf	0		run out (Hodd)	6
S L Elstone, c Hodgson b Ashraf	1		c Gibson b Waite	5
* T C Knight, c Rhodes b Waite	36		b Waite	1
G T G Cork, b Carver	15		c Rhodes b Wainman	55
§ H R Hosein, b Shaw	64		c Callis b Wainman	4
W A White, c Rhodes b Carver	24		c Rhodes b Wainman	7
M Higginbottom, b Waite	31		c Rhodes b Carver	6
M Critchley, not out	18		not out	4
J Marsden, lbw b Carver	1			
W S Davies	Did not bat			
Extras lb 2, w 6	8		Extras lb 1 w 1	2
Total (79.2 overs)	209		Total (8 wkts dec, 62 overs)	249

FoW: 1-3 (Evans), 2-3 (Hughes), 3-5 (Elstone), 4-24 (Slater), 5-53 (Cork)
1st 6-65 (Knight), 7-129 (White), 8-179 (Higginbottom), 9-200 (Hosein), 10-209 (Marsden)

FoW: 1-75 (Evans), 2-94 (Hughes), 3-100 (Elstone), 4-103 (Knight), 5-194 (Cork),
2nd 6-207 (Hosein), 7-226 (White), 8-236 (Higginbottom)

	O	M	R	W		O	M	R	W
Ashraf	14	3	39	3	Ashraf	14	4	35	1
Wainman	9	3	24	0	Wainman	11	2	44	3
Rhodes	10	3	28	1	Waite	15	4	36	2
Shaw	14	0	49	1	Shaw	6	1	42	0
Waite	14	6	35	2	Carver	15	1	78	1
Carver	17.2	8	29	3	Rhodes	1	0	13	0
Tattersall	1	0	3	0					

First Innings	YORKSHIRE		Second Innings	
A J Hodd, c Hosein b Higginbottom	25		b Marsden	1
E Callis, c Elstone b Higginbottom	1		not out	13
§ D M Hodgson, b Davis	35		not out	11
J A Tattersall, c and b Higginbottom	0			
* W M H Rhodes, lbw b Cork	32			
M Hussain, c Knight b Cork	6			
R Gibson, b Davis	16			
M J Waite, c Hughes b Crichley	37			
J Shaw, lbw b White	0			
J C Wainman, not out	20			
K Carver, b Crichley	0			
M A Ashraf	Did not bat			
Extras b 9, lb 4	13		Extras	0
Total (72.4 overs)	185		Total (1 wkt, 15 overs)	25

FoW: 1-9 (Callis), 2-36 (Hodd), 3-36 (Tattersall), 4-98 (Rhodes), 5-108 (Hussain),
1st 6-108 (Hodgson), 7-145 (Gibson), 8-151 (Shaw), 9-185 (Waite), 10-185 (Carver)
2nd: 1-1 (Hodd)

	O	M	R	W		O	M	R	W
Higginbottom	17	4	45	3	Higginbottom	8	5	11	0
Marsden	12	5	35	0	Marsden	5	2	12	1
White	15	6	22	1	Davis	2	1	2	0
Davis	10	1	39	2					
Crichley	7.4	1	15	2					
Elstone	1	1	0	0					
Cork	9	4	13	2					
Knight	1	0	3	0					

Umpires: R J Evans and H Fidler

Scorers: T M Cottam and H Clayton

SECOND ELEVEN CHAMPIONSHIP 2014

FINAL

Leicestershire (676) drew with **Essex** (374 and 107-3)
Leicestershire were deemed Champions by virtue of their first-innings lead

NORTHERN GROUP FINAL TABLE

		P	W	L	D	Tied	Aban.	Bonus Points Bat	Bowl	Pen.	Points
1	Leicestershire (9)	9	4	0	5	0	0	28	33	0	150
2	Nottinghamshire (6)	9	3	0	6	0	0	29	30	0	137
3	Lancashire (1)	9	2	0	7	0	0	25	31	0	123
4	**Yorkshire (4)**	**9**	**2**	**1**	**6**	**0**	**0**	**24**	**31**	**0**	**117**
5	Derbyshire (2)	9	2	2	5	0	0	24	31	0	112
6	Warwickshire (8)	9	2	2	5	0	0	22	27	0	106
7	MCC YC (7)	9	1	1	7	0	0	21	33	0	105
8	Durham (10)	9	1	4	4	0	0	27	32	0	95
9	Glamorgan (5)	9	1	4	4	0	0	22	33	0	91
10	Worcestershire (3)	9	1	5	3	0	0	17	26	0	74

SOUTHERN GROUP FINAL TABLE

		P	W	L	D	Tied	Aban.	Bonus Points Bat	Bowl	Pen.	Points
1	Essex (2)	9	3	0	6	0	0	34	30	0	142
2	Somerset (5)	9	4	1	4	0	0	23	30	0.5	136.5
3	Middlesex (1)	9	4	1	3	0	1	21	22	0	127
4	Surrey (7)	9	3	1	5	0	0	18	29	4	116.5
5	Sussex (9)	9	2	2	5	0	0	27	27	0	111
6	Kent (4)	9	2	3	4	0	0	18	31	0	101
7	Gloucestershire (3)	9	1	2	6	0	0	17	31	0	94
8	Northamptonshire (6) ...	9	1	3	3	0	2	23	25	0	89
9	Hampshire (8)	9	1	4	3	0	1	25	24	0	85
10	MCC Universities (10) ..	9	0	4	5	0	0	17	32	0	74

(2013 group positions in brackets)

SECOND ELEVEN CHAMPIONS

In the seasons in which Yorkshire have competed. The Championship has been split into two groups since 2009, the group winners playing off for the Championship. These groups were deemed North and South from the 2012 season.

Season	Champions	Yorkshire's Position	Season	Champions	Yorkshire's Position
1959	Gloucestershire	7th	1994	Somerset	2nd
1960	Northamptonshire	14th	1995	Hampshire	5th
1961	Kent	11th	1996	Warwickshire	4th
1975	Surrey	4th	1997	Lancashire	2nd
1976	Kent	5th	1998	Northamptonshire	9th
1977	**Yorkshire**	**1st**	1999	Middlesex	14th
1978	Sussex	5th	2000	Middlesex	5th
1979	Warwickshire	3rd	2001	Hampshire	2nd
1980	Glamorgan	5th	2002	Kent	3rd
1981	Hampshire	11th	**2003**	**Yorkshire**	**1st**
1982	Worcestershire	14th	2004	Somerset	8th
1983	Leicestershire	2nd	2005	Kent	10th
1984	**Yorkshire**	**1st**	2006	Kent	3rd
1985	Nottinghamshire	12th	2007	Sussex	10th
1986	Lancashire	5th	2008	Durham	5th
1987	**Yorkshire** and Kent	**1st**	2009	Surrey	A 2nd
1988	Surrey	9th	2010	Surrey	A 8th
1989	Middlesex	9th	2011	Warwickshire	A 10th
1990	Sussex	17th	2012	Kent	North 9th
1991	**Yorkshire**	**1st**	2013	Lancashire & Middlesex	
1992	Surrey	5th			(North) 4th
1993	Middlesex	3rd	2014	Leicestershire	(North) 4th

SECOND ELEVEN CHAMPIONSHIP
AVERAGES 2014

	Played 9	Won 2	Lost 1	Drawn 6

BATTING AND FIELDING
(Qualification 5 innings)

Player	M.	I.	N.O.	Runs	H.S.	Avge	100s	50s	ct/st
A Leaning	3	5	1	244	80*	61.00	0	3	7
Azeem Rafiq	4	5	1	158	87*	39.50	0	1	2
W M H Rhodes	7	9	0	323	89	35.88	0	2	0
D M Hodgson	9	14	1	414	113	31.84	1	0	23
A J Hodd	6	8	0	221	67	27.62	0	2	13
R Gibson	7	10	1	232	79	25.77	0	2	7
A Thompson	4	6	0	152	80	25.33	0	1	0
A Tattersall	6	8	0	166	64	20.75	0	1	5
J C Wainman	7	8	2	119	56	19.83	0	1	1
B O Coad	7	7	2	89	27	17.80	0	0	1
R M Pyrah	3	5	1	69	30*	17.25	0	0	2
E Callis	7	12	1	180	61	16.36	0	1	2
M Hussain	5	5	0	49	16	9.80	0	0	4
J Shaw	4	8	0	78	30	9.75	0	0	1

Also played

Player	M.	I.	N.O.	Runs	H.S.	Avge	100s	50s	ct/st
M J Waite	2	3	1	162	112*	81.00	1	0	0
N J Firn	2	4	0	110	64	55.00	0	1	3
O E Robinson	3	4	0	104	62	26.00	0	1	0
M D Fisher	4	3	2	26	21*	26.00	0	0	0
R J Sidebottom	1	2	0	41	34	20.50	0	0	0
B P Gibson	2	4	0	71	20	17.75	0	0	0
J G E Logan	2	4	2	25	12*	12.50	0	0	0
B L Ainsley	1	2	0	20	12	10.00	0	0	1
K Carver	3	2	1	7	7*	7.00	0	0	0
M A Ashraf	4	1	0	2	2	2.00	0	0	0
R K J Dawson	1	0	0	0	0	—	0	0	0

BOWLING
(Qualification 10 wickets)

Player	Overs	Mdns	Runs	Wkts	Avge	Best	5wI	10wM
R M Pyrah	56.2	19	130	11	11.81	5-29	1	0
M D Fisher	83.2	32	200	12	16.66	5-31	1	0
J C Wainman	135.5	36	404	21	19.24	5-58	1	0
J Shaw	123.1	23	441	21	21.00	5-28	1	1
B O Coad	131.2	39	332	12	27.66	2-25	0	0

Also bowled

Player	Overs	Mdns	Runs	Wkts	Avge	Best	5wI	10wM
R Gibson	41	10	117	6	19.50	3-39	0	0
J A Leaning	19.3	2	91	4	22.75	2-58	0	0
K Carver	50.2	16	151	6	25.16	2-44	0	0
R J Sidebottom	17.5	4	52	2	26.00	2-25	0	0
J G E Logan	32.2	39	112	4	28.00	2-60	0	0
M J Waite	47	5	126	4	31.50	2-35	0	0
N J Firn	27.3	14	78	2	39.00	1-32	0	0
M A Ashraf	67	4	201	4	50.25	3-39	0	0
W M H Rhodes	48	15	156	2	78.00	1-14	0	0
Azeem Rafiq	37	6	143	1	143.00	1-55	0	0
B L Ainsley	2	0	11	0	—	—	0	0
E Callis	1	0	3	0	—	—	0	0
O E Robinson	10	1	36	0	—	—	0	0
J A Tattersall	5	1	11	0	—	—	0	0

Glamorgan v. Yorkshire

Played at the SWALEC Stadium, Cardiff, on April 8, 2014

Glamorgan won by 4 wickets (D/L method) at 6.29pm

Toss won by Glamorgan   Glamorgan 2 points, Yorkshire 0 points

YORKSHIRE

E Callis, run out (Wright)	....	46
J A Tattersall, c Rouse b Owen	....	0
D M Hodgson, c Lloyd b Glover	....	11
J A Leaning, c Knight b Carey	....	2
* W M H Rhodes, b Carey	....	37
§ A J Hodd, run out (Owen)	....	5
Azeem Rafiq, st Knight b Salter	....	4
R M Pyrah, c and b Salter	....	4
J Shaw, b Glover	....	19
B O Coad, not out	....	17
M D Fisher, lbw b Glover	....	2
Extras lb 2, nb 2, w 13	....	17
Total (44.1 overs)	....	164

FoW: 1-2 (Tattersall), 2-26 (Hodgson), 3-28 (Leaning), 4-102 (Rhodes), 5-108 (Hodd), 6-117 (Azeem Rafiq), 7-123 (Callis), 8-128 (Pyrah), 9-160 (Shaw), 10-164 (Fisher)

	O	M	R	W
Owen	9	1	21	1
Glover	8.1	0	30	3
Waters	6	0	23	0
Carey	8.4	1	34	2
Lloyd	5	0	29	0
Lawlor	0.2	0	6	0
Salter	7	0	22	2

GLAMORGAN

(D/L target 164 in 45 overs

* B J Wright, lbw b Pyrah	....	23
A G Salter, c Fisher b Coad	....	0
A P Rouse, c and b Coad	....	0
D L Lloyd, b Pyrah	....	12
A J Mellor, lbw b Leaning	....	47
J L Lawlor, c Hodd b Fisher	....	40
§ G Knight, not out	....	36
J C Glover, not out	....	0
W T Owen		
H T Waters	Did not bat	
L J Carey		
Extras lb 2, w 4	....	6
Total (6 wkts, 41.5 overs)	....	164

FoW: 1-1 (Salter), 2-2 (Rouse), 3-33 (Lloyd), 4-38 (Wright), 5-95 (Mellor), 6-159 (Lawlor)

	O	M	R	W
Coad	7.5	0	34	2
Fisher	8	2	20	1
Shaw	4	1	8	0
Pyrah	7	1	43	2
Azeem rafiq	8	0	33	0
Leaning	7	0	24	1

Umpires: P K Baldwin and D Price   Scorers: B Jones and H Clayton

Second Eleven Trophy
Nottinghamshire v. Yorkshire

Played at Nottinghamshire Sports Ground, Nottingham, on April 14, 2014

Yorkshire won by 4 wickets at 6.04pm

Toss won by Yorkshire

Nottinghamshire 0 points, Yorkshire 2 points

NOTTINGHAMSHIRE

§ M H Cross, c Hodgson b Ashraf		13
S Kelsall, c Rhodes b Azem Rafiq		58
Hasan Azad, b Azem Rafiq		57
S K W Wood, lbw b Ashraf		45
A D Tillcock, lbw b Fisher		1
A Dal, run out (Ashraf)		24
B A Hutton, b Leaning		7
* P J Franks, c Pyrah b Shaw		3
S Webster, not out		12
L Wood, not out		12
B M Kitt	Did not bat	
Extras lb 4, nb 2, w 9		15
Total (8 wkts, 50 overs)		247

FoW: 1-13 (Cross), 2-120 (Kelsall), 3-153 (Hasan Azad), 4-154 (Tillcock), 5-194 (S K W Wood), 6-211 (Hutton), 7-218 (Franks), 8-219 (Dal)

	O	M	R	W
Coad	4	0	22	0
Ashraf	7	0	38	2
Fisher	8	0	42	1
Pyrah	10	1	36	0
Shaw	7	1	30	1
Azeem Rafiq	10	0	48	2
Leaning	4	0	27	1

YORKSHIRE

E Callis, lbw b Tillcock		78
J A Tattersall, lbw b Tillcock		72
§ D M Hodgson, b Kitt		42
J A Leaning, b Tillcock		2
* W M H Rhodes, b S K W Wood		28
Azeem Rafiq, c Dal b Kitt		0
R M Pyrah, not out		6
J Shaw, not out		3
B O Coad		
M D Fisher	Did not bat	
M A Ashraf		
Extras lb 10, nb 2, w 5		17
Total (6 wkts, 49 overs)		248

FoW: 1-146 (Tattersall), 2-165 (Callis), 3-171 (Leaning), 4-234 (Rhodes), 5-235 (Azeem Rafiq), 6-243 (Hodgson)

	O	M	R	W
Hutton	9	0	41	0
L Wood	8	0	52	0
Kitt	9	0	49	2
S K W Wood	7	0	27	1
Tillcock	10	0	46	3
Franks	6	0	23	0

Umpires: D J Millns and I Rich

Scorers: Mrs A Cusworth and H Clayton

Second Eleven Trophy
Lancashire v. Yorkshire

At Todmorden CC on June 9, 2014
Match abandoned without a ball bowled

No toss made

Lancashire 1 point, Yorkshire 1 point

Yorkshire v. Warwickshire

Played at Pudsey Congs CC on June 16, 2014
Yorkshire won by 136 runs at 5.22pm

Toss won by Warwickshire

Yorkshire 2 points, Warwickshire 0 points

YORKSHIRE

A J Hodd, c Milnes b Hannon-Dalby	112
W M H Rhodes, c Atkinson b Hannon-Dalby	11
§ D M Hodgson, b Thomasson	24
* J A Tattersall, c Lewis b Hannon-Dalby	65
M Hussain, c Lewis b Thomasson	9
O E Robinson, not out	34
R Gibson, not out	22
M D Fisher	
J C Wainman	
K Carver	Did not bat
B O Coad	
Extras lb 12, nb 2, w 11	25
Total (5 wkts, 50 overs)	302

FoW: 1-26; (Rhodes), 2-90 (Hodgson), 3-195 (Hodd), 4-220 (Hussain), 5-266 (Tattersall)

	O	M	R	W
Hannon-Dalby	10	0	63	3
Gordon	10	0	50	0
Milnes	7	0	40	0
Thomasson	10	1	52	2
Best	9	0	57	0
Poysden	4	0	28	0

WARWICKSHIRE

J P Webb, c Hodgson b Fisher	0
T P Lewis, c Hodgson b Carver	28
I J L Trott, c Hodgson b Fisher	70
F R J Coleman, c Gibson b Robinson	2
§ J J Atkinson, c Hodgson b Rhodes	11
T P Milnes, lbw b Carver	0
* P M Best, c Hodd b Wainman	23
A D Thomasson, c Hussain b Coad	17
R O Gordon, not out	6
O J Hannon-Dalby, c Robinson b Wainman	0
J E Poysden, c Hodgson b Wainman	0
Extras lb 1; nb 2, w 6	9
Total (35.5 overs)	166

FoW: 1-0 (Webb), 2-58 (Lewis), 3-61 (Coleman), 4-90 (Atkinson), 5-91 (Milnes), 6-133 (Trott), 7-155 (Best), 8-164 (Thomasson), 9-166 (Hannon-Dalby), 10-166 (Poysden)

	O	M	R	W
Fisher	7	1	41	2
Coad	7	0	31	1
Robinson	6	1	22	1
Carver	10	0	48	2
Rhodes	4	0	21	1
Wainman	1.5	1	2	3

Umpires: D M Warburton and P Willey

Scorers: H Clayton and S Smith

Second Eleven Trophy
Derbyshire v. Yorkshire

Played at Swarkestone CC on July 3, 2014
Derbyshire won by 29 runs at 5.55pm

Toss won by Derbyshire   Derbyshire 2 points, Yorkshire 0 points

DERBYSHIRE

A S T West, c Shaw b Rhodes		19
T C Knight, run out (Leaning)		125
* S L Elstone, b Gibson		19
§ G D Cross, c Thompson b Carver		12
T A Wood, c Shaw b Rhodes		6
A P Palladino, c Leaning b Shaw		22
R Hassan, c Hodd b Shaw		2
Rahib Ali, not out		10
T A I Taylor		
W S Davis	Did not bat	
M H A Footitt		
Extras lb 4, w 16		20
Total (7 wkts, 50 overs)		235

FoW: 1-53 (West), 2-84 (Elstone), 3-110 (Cross), 4-162 (Wood), 5-209 (Palladino), 6-216 (Hassan), 7-235 (Knight)

	O	M	R	W
Fisher	7	4	31	0
Ashraf	10	0	63	0
Rhodes	7	0	39	2
Shaw	8	1	35	2
Gibson	8	0	22	1
Carver	10	0	41	1

YORKSHIRE

* W M H Rhodes, lbw b Footitt		16
§ A J Hodd, c Rahib Ali b Taylor		14
D M Hodgson, lbw b Palladino		83
J A Leaning, b Taylor		54
M Hussain, run out (Cross)		2
R Gibson, c Wood b Taylor		4
J A Thompson, c Wood b Taylor		2
J Shaw, b Footitt		8
M A Ashraf, c Knight b Palladino		6
K Carver, not out		7
M D Fisher, not out		1
Extras lb 3, w 6		9
Total (9 wkts, 50 overs)		206

FoW: 1-21 (Rhodes), 2-45 (Hodd), 3-171 (Hodgson), 4-175 (Leaning), 5-179 (Gibson), 6-183 (Thompson), 7-183 (Hussain), 8-194 (Ashraf), 9-204 (Shaw)

	O	M	R	W
Palladino	10	0	39	2
Footitt	10	0	35	2
Taylor	10	2	33	4
Knight	7	0	33	0
Davis	7	0	31	0
Hassan	2	0	16	0
Elstone	4	0	16	0

Umpires: H Fidler and R J Warren   Scorers: T M Cottam and H Clayton

Second Eleven Trophy
Yorkshire v. Worcestershire

Played at Stamford Bridge CC on July 14, 2014
Yorkshire won by 43 runs at 6.13pm

Toss won by Yorkshire   Yorkshire 2 points, Worcestershire 0 points

YORKSHIRE

* W M H Rhodes, c Andrew b Harrison		124
§ A J Hodd, c Andrew b Whiles		0
D M Hodgson, c Clarke b Harrison		22
J A Leaning, st Clarke b Rhodes		32
O E Robinson, lbw b D'Oliveira		55
R Gibson, c Andrew b Harrison		66
J Shaw, not out		10
J C Wainman		
M A Ashraf		
M D Fisher	Did not bat	
K Carver		
Extras lb 3, nb 2, w 18		23
Total (6 wkts, 50 overs)		332

FoW: 1-3 (Hodd), 2-51 (Hodgson), 3-107 (Leaning), 4-191 (Robinson), 5-303 (Rhodes), 6-332 (Gibson)

	O	M	R	W
Cessford	8	0	60	0
Whiles	8	0	60	1
Harrison	9	0	57	3
Whiteley	5	0	28	0
Rhodes	8	0	51	1
D'Oliveira	10	0	64	1
Hepburn	2	0	19	0

WORCESTERSHIRE

M G Pardoe, c Leaning b Wainman		29
§ J M Clarke, lbw b Ashraf		30
R A Whiteley, c Fisher b Shaw		101
B L D'Oliveira, c Hodd b Rhodes		62
* G M Andrew, c Hodd b Shaw		12
E G Barnard, c Hodd b Fisher		32
A Hepburn, c Gibson b Wainman		3
G H Rhodes, c Leaning b Fisher		6
G Cessford, b Wainman		0
N L Harrison, c Hodd b Fisher		2
G P Whiles, not out		2
Extras lb 2, w 8		10
Total (48.1 overs)		289

FoW: 1-56 (Pardoe), 2-72 (Clarke), 3-194 (D'Oliveira), 4-240 (Andrew), 5-249 (Whiteley), 6-269 (Hepburn), 7-281 (Rhodes), 8-285 (Barnard), 9-285 (Cessford), 10-289 (Harrison)

	O	M	R	W
Ashraf	7	0	56	1
Fisher	9.1	2	27	3
Shaw	5	0	37	2
Rhodes	8	0	46	1
Wainman	9	1	46	3
Carver	5	0	41	0
Leaning	5	0	34	0

Umpires: N G B Cook and I J Dixon   Scorers: H Clayton and Mrs S M Drinkwater

Second Eleven Trophy
Yorkshire v. Durham

Played at Marske-by-the-Sea CC on July 22, 2014
Yorkshire won by 185 runs at 5.17pm

Toss won by Yorkshire   Yorkshire 2 points, Durham 0 points

YORKSHIRE

A J Hodd, c Singh b Morley		54
* W M H Rhodes, c Bousfield b Hickey		63
§ D M Hodgson, c Singh b Arshad		77
R Gibson, c Shafique b Hickey		1
R M Pyrah, b Arshad		128
Azeem Rafiq, not out		23
J A Thompson, not out		1
M A Ashraf		
K Carver		
B O Coad	Did not bat	
J C Wainman		
Extras lb 9, nb 12, w 15		36
Total (5 wkts, 50 overs)		383

FoW: 1-115 (Hodd), 2-136 (Rhodes), 3-138 (Gibson), 4-334 (Pyrah), 5-381 (Hodgson)

	O	M	R	W
Milnes	10	0	97	0
Weighell	8	1	84	0
Arshad	10	0	60	2
Main	7	0	67	0
Morley	10	0	32	1
Hickey	5	0	34	2

DURHAM

R Carr, c Rhodes b Wainman	11
* G Clark, c Thompson b Ashraf	9
A J Hickey, c Gibson b Pyrah	13
R Singh, c Azeem Rafiq b Coad	19
§ A A Shafique, c Pyrah b Coad	8
U Arshad, c Wainman b Azeem Rafiq	53
W J Weighell, c and b Pyrah	7
J P Bousfield, b Pyrah	5
M E Milnes, c Hodd b Azeem Rafiq	49
M G Morley, c Coad b Azeem Rafiq	21
G T Main, not out	0
Extras lb 2, w 1	3
Total (36 overs)	198

FoW: 1-13 (Clark), 2-21 (Carr), 3-51 (Singh), 4-61 (Shafique), 5-65 (Hickey), 6-89 (Weighell), 7-105 (Bousfield), 8-173 (Milnes), 9-196 (Arshad), 10-198 (Morley)

	O	M	R	W
Ashraf	8	3	28	1
Wainman	5	0	28	1
Pyrah	7	0	30	3
Coad	5	1	35	2
Azeem Rafiq	6	0	29	3
Carver	5	0	46	0

Umpires: A Clark and N A Mallender   Scorers: H Clayton and R V Hilton

Second Eleven Trophy
Yorkshire v. Leicestershire

Played at Barnsley CC on August 4, 2014
Leicestershire won by 102 runs at 5.29pm

Toss won by Leicestershire   Yorkshire 0 points, Leicestershire 2 points

LEICESTERSHIRE

B A Raine, c Hussain b Coad		17
M A Thornely, lbw b Wainman		1
E J H Eckersley, c Thompson b Firn		11
N D Pinner, st Hodgson b Carver		48
* R M L Taylor, c Wainman b Carver		90
Aadil Ali, c Logan b Firn		51
§ C T Lowen, c Hodgson b Coad		20
A K Patel, c Hodgson b Gibson		3
J C Pearson, b Wainman		7
O H Freckingham, b Coad		3
A C F Wyatt, not out		1
Extras lb 2, w 4		6
Total (48.4 overs)		258

FoW: 1-4 (Thornely), 2-19 (Raine), 3-44 (Eckersley), 4-108 (Pinner), 5-204 (Taylor), 6-241 (Aadil Ali), 7-244 (Patel), 8-248 (Lowen), 9-256 Pearson), 10-258 (Freckingham)

	O	M	R	W
Coad	7.4	0	32	3
Wainman	9	1	29	2
Firn	6	0	39	2
R Gibson	6	0	43	1
Logan	10	0	41	0
Carver	10	0	72	2

YORKSHIRE

E Callis, b Wyatt		2
§ D M Hodgson, b Pearson		20
J C Wainman, c Wyatt b Freckingham		16
M Hussain, b Taylor		16
* R Gibson, c Pinner b Wyatt		23
J A Thompson, b Taylor		1
B P Gibson, lbw b Taylor		0
B O Coad, b Wyatt		10
K Carver, c Lowen b Freckingham		0
N J Firn, not out		23
J E G Logan, c Aadil Ali b Pinner		28
Extras lb 3, nb 4, w 10		17
Total (41.5 overs)		156

FoW: 1-8 (Callis), 2-30 (Wainman), 3-50 (Hodgson), 4-64 (Hussain), 5-73 (Thompson), 6-73 (B P Gibson), 7-96 (R Gibson), 8-97 (Carver), 9-100 (Coad), 10-156 (Logan)

	O	M	R	W
Freckingham	10	3	22	2
Wyatt	9	0	49	3
Taylor	9	1	38	3
Pearson	8	2	21	1
Aadil Ali	5	1	22	0
Pinner	0.5	0	1	1

Umpires: N G C Cowley and I L Herbert   Scorers: H Clayton and P N Johnson

Second Eleven Trophy
MCC Young Cricketers v. Yorkshire

Played at Shenley on August 11, 2014

MCC Young Cricketers won by 9 wickets at 4.33pm

Toss won by MCC Young Cricketers   MCC Young Cricketers 2 points, Yorkshire 0 points

YORKSHIRE

E Callis, b Valand	17
§ D M Hodgson, c Davies b Babar	14
J C Wainman, b Babar	0
* R Gibson, b Valand	14
J A Thompson, lbw b Valand	2
B P Gibson, c Piesley b Babar	22
M J Waite, c and b Dobb	10
N J Firn, c Davies b Dobb	1
M A Ashraf, not out	24
K Carver, c Price b Piesley	2
J E G Logan, c Dobb b Hampton	1
Extras b 8, w 16	24
Total (38 overs)	131

FoW: 1-31 (Hodgson), 2-37 (Wainman), 3-52 (Callis), 4-58 (Thompson), 5-62 (R Gibson), 6-84 (Waite), 7-100 (Firn), 8-109 (B P Gibson), 9-112 (Carver), 10-131 (Logan).

	O	M	R	W
Hampton	6	1	22	1
Babar	9	1	19	3
Valand	10	0	29	3
Price	3	0	19	0
Dobb	6	0	14	2
Piesley	4	0	20	1

MCC YOUNG CRICKETERS

L J Gough, not out		55
* C D Piesley, run out (Thompson)		52
S S Arthurton, not out		15
M T Renshaw		
O J G Graham		
A M Dobb		
§ R W Davies	Did not bat	
J A Valand		
D O D Hampton		
A Babar		
J Price		
Extras lb 2, nb 2, w 6		10
Total (1 wkt, 29.4 overs)		132

FoW: 1-87 (Piesley)

	O	M	R	W
Ashraf	6	0	20	0
Wainman	3	0	12	0
Waite	5	1	19	0
Carver	6	1	33	0
Firn	4	0	23	0
Logan	5.4	1	23	0

Umpires: P R Pollard and P D Nicholls   Scorers: A P Scarlett and H Clayton

SECOND ELEVEN TROPHY 2014

NORTHERN GROUP – FINAL TABLE *(2013 in brackets)*

		P	W	L	Aban.	Points	Net run rate
1	Leicestershire (9)	9	7	1	1	15	0.640
2	Lancashire (1)	9	5	3	1	11	0.335
3	**Yorkshire (4)**	**9**	**4**	**4**	**1**	**9**	**0.327**
4	Warwickshire (8)	9	4	4	1	9	0.111
5	Nottinghamshire (2)	9	4	4	1	9	0.093
6	Worcestershire (10)	9	4	4	1	9	0.037
7	Glamorgan (3)	9	4	4	1	9	-0.147
8	Durham (6)	9	3	5	1	7	-0.612
9	Derbyshire (7)	9	3	6	0	6	-0.014
10	MCC Young Cricketers (5)	9	3	6	0	6	-0.714

SOUTHERN GROUP – FINAL TABLE *(2013 in brackets)*

		P	W	L	Aban.	Points	Net run rate
1	Sussex (6)	9	7	2	0	0	14
2	Middlesex (1)	9	5	2	1	1	12
3	Essex (8)	9	5	4	0	0	10
4	Somerset (9)	9	4	3	1	1	10
5	Surrey (3)	9	4	4	0	1	9
6	Kent (7)	9	3	3	1	2	8
7	Unicorns (2)	9	4	5	0	0	8
8	Northamptonshire (5)	9	3	4	0	2	8
9	Hampshire (10)	9	3	4	1	1	8
10	Gloucestershire (4)	9	1	8	0	0	2

SEMI-FINALS

Middlesex (202-5) lost to Leicestershire (203-5) by 5 wickets
Sussex (120-7) lost to Lancashire (121-3) by 7 wickets
(Match reduced to 17 overs per side before the start)

FINAL

Leicestershire (295-6) beat Lancashire (127) by 168 runs

SECOND ELEVEN TROPHY

PREVIOUS WINNERS

1986	**Northamptonshire**, who beat Essex by 14 runs
1987	**Derbyshire**, who beat Hampshire by 7 wickets
1988	**Yorkshire**, who beat Kent by 7 wickets
1989	**Middlesex**, who beat Kent by 6 wickets
1990	**Lancashire**, who beat Somerset by 8 wickets
1991	**Nottinghamshire**, who beat Surrey by 8 wickets
1992	**Surrey**, who beat Northamptonshire by 8 wickets
1993	**Leicestershire**, who beat Sussex by 142 runs
1994	**Yorkshire**, who beat Leicestershire by 6 wickets
1995	**Leicestershire**, who beat Gloucestershire by 3 runs
1996	**Leicestershire**, who beat Durham by 46 runs
1997	**Surrey**, who beat Gloucestershire by 3 wickets
1998	**Northamptonshire**, who beat Derbyshire by 5 wickets
1999	**Kent**, who beat Hampshire by 106 runs.
2000	**Leicestershire,** who beat Hampshire by 25 runs.
2001	**Surrey**, who beat Somerset by 6 wickets
2002	**Kent**, who beat Hampshire by 5 wickets
2003	**Hampshire**, who beat Warwickshire by 8 wickets
2004	**Worcestershire**, who beat Essex by 8 wickets
2005	**Sussex**, who beat Nottinghamshire by 6 wickets
2006	**Warwickshire**, who beat Yorkshire by 93 runs
2007	**Middlesex**, who beat Somerset by 1 run
2008	**Hampshire**, who beat Essex by 7 runs
2009	**Yorkshire,** who beat Lancashire by 2 wickets
2010	**Essex**, who beat Lancashire by 14 runs
2011	**Nottinghamshire**, who beat Lancashire by 4 wickets
2012	**Lancashire**, who beat Durham by 76 runs
2013	**Lancashire**, who beat Nottinghamshire by 76 runs

SECOND ELEVEN TROPHY
AVERAGES 2014

Played 9   Won 4   Lost 4   Abandoned 1

BATTING AND FIELDING

(Qualification 3 innings)

Player	M.	I.	N.O.	Runs	H.S.	Avge	100s	50s	ct/s
R M Pyrah	3	3	1	138	128	69.00	1	0	3
W M H Rhodes	6	6	0	279	124	46.50	1	1	2
J A Tattersall	3	3	0	137	72	45.66	0	2	0
A J Hodd	5	5	0	185	112	37.00	1	1	8
D M Hodgson	8	8	0	293	83	36.62	0	2	8/1
E Callis	4	4	0	143	78	35.75	0	1	0
R Gibson	6	6	1	130	66	26.00	0	1	3
J A Leaning	4	4	0	90	54	22.50	0	1	3
J Shaw	4	4	2	40	19	20.00	0	0	2
Azeem Rafiq	3	3	1	27	23*	13.50	0	0	1
M Hussain	3	3	0	27	16	9.00	0	0	3
K Carver	6	3	1	9	7*	4.50	0	0	0
J A Thompson	4	4	1	6	2	2.00	0	0	3
Also batted									
O E Robinson	2	2	1	89	55	89.00	0	1	1
M A Ashraf	5	2	1	30	24*	30.00	0	0	0
B O Coad	5	2	1	27	17*	27.00	0	0	2
N J Firn	2	2	1	24	23*	24.00	0	0	0
J E G Logan	2	2	0	29	28	14.50	0	0	1
B P Gibson	2	2	0	22	22	11.00	0	0	0
M J Waite	1	1	0	10	10	10.00	0	0	0
J C Wainman	5	2	0	16	16	8.00	0	0	2
M D Fisher	5	2	1	3	2	3.00	0	0	2

BOWLING

(Qualification 5 wickets)

Player	Overs	Mdns	Runs	Wkts	Avge	Best	4wI
J C Wainman	27.5	3	117	9	13.00	3-2	0
B O Coad	31.3	1	154	8	19.25	3-32	0
R M Pyrah	24	2	109	5	21.80	3-30	0
J Shaw	24	3	110	5	22.00	3-29	0
Azeem Rafiq	24	0	110	5	22.00	3-29	0
M D Fisher	39	9	161	7	23.00	3-27	0
K Carver	19	1	281	5	56.20	—	0
Also bowled							
O E Robinson	6	1	22	1	22.00	1-22	0
W M H Rhodes	19	0	106	4	26.50	2-39	0
N J Firn	1	0	62	2	31.00	2-39	0
R Gibson	14	0	65	2	32.50	1-22	0
J A Leaning	16	0	85	2	42.50	1-24	0
M A Ashraf	38	3	205	4	51.25	2-38	0
J E G Logan	15	1	64	0	—	—	0
M J Waite	5	1	19	0	—	—	0

Second Eleven Twenty20
Yorkshire v. Durham

Played at Clifton Park, York, on May 6, 2014
Durham won by 7 wickets at 2.12pm

Toss won by Durham   Yorkshire 0 points, Durham 2 points

YORKSHIRE

J A Tattersall, c Buckley b Ireland	16
§ D M Hodgson, b Arshad	22
* Azeem Rafiq, run out (MacLeod)	4
J A Leaning, st Poynter b Ireland	52
W M H Rhodes, c Breese b Ireland	39
O E Robinson, b Arshad	4
R M Pyrah, not out	2
R Gibson, c Breese b Arshad	0
J Shaw, not out	4
B O Coad	
M A Ashraf Did not bat	
Extras b 1, lb 11, nb 2, w 8	22
Total (7 wkts, 20 overs)	165

FoW: 1-39 (Tattersall), 2-43 (Hodgson), 3-45 (Azeem Rafiq), 4-155 (Rhodes), 5-155 (Leaning), 6-161 (Robinson), 7-161 (Gibson)

	O	M	R	W
Breese	3	0	16	0
Main	4	0	34	0
Ireland	4	0	23	3
Buckley	3	0	29	0
Arshad	4	0	32	3
Burnham	2	0	19	0

DURHAM

R Singh, c Gibson b Shaw	3
C S MacLeod, not out	103
U Arshad, c Azeem Rafiq b Pyrah	14
G Clark, b Pyrah	11
* G J Muchall, not out	32
G R Breese	
§ S W Poynter	
J T A Burnham Did not bat	
A W Ireland	
R S Buckley	
G T Main	
Extras b 4, w 1	5
Total (3 wkts, 18.2 overs)	168

FoW: 1-12 (Singh), 2-37 (Arshad), 3-54 (Clark)

	O	M	R	W
Ashraf	3	0	28	0
Coad	2.2	0	21	0
Shaw	1	0	9	1
Pyrah	4	0	36	2
Robinson	3	0	31	0
Azeem Rafiq	4	0	26	0
Leaning	1	0	13	0

Umpires: S J Malone and R T Robinson   Scorers: H Clayton and R V Hilton

Second Eleven Twenty20
Yorkshire v. Durham

Played at Clifton Park, York, on May 6, 2014
Durham won by 6 wickets at 5.26pm

Toss won by Durham

Yorkshire 0 points, Durham 2 points

YORKSHIRE

J A Tattersall, c Clark b Arshad	17
§ D M Hodgson, b Main	5
O E Robinson, c Poynter b Main	0
J A Leaning, c Main b Burnham	28
W M H Rhodes, c MacLeod b Breese	8
* Azeem Rafiq, c Main b Burnham	21
R Gibson, c Burnham b Ireland	16
§ B P Gibson, c Main b Ireland	7
J Shaw, not out	10
B O Coad, b Arshad	2
K Carver, c Singh b Arshad	1
Extras lb 2, w 6	8
Total (19.2 overs)	123

FoW: 1-8 (Hodgson), 2-8 (Robinson), 3-46 (Tattersall), 4-55 (Rhodes), 5-86 (Leaning), 6-86 (Azeem Rafiq), 7-110 (R Gibson), 8-110 (B P Gibson), 9-115 (Coad), 10-123 (Carver)

	O	M	R	W
Breese	4	0	19	1
Main	3	0	19	2
Ireland	4	0	26	2
Arshad	3	0	19	3
Buckley	3	0	27	0
Burnham	2	0	11	2

DURHAM

R Singh, c Coad b Rhodes	2
C S MacLeod, c B P Gibson b Rhodes	33
U Arshad, c Sub (Ashraf) b Rhodes	2
G Clark, not out	47
* G J Muchall, c R Gibson b Carver	23
G R Breese, not out	16
§ S W Poynter	
J T A Burnham	
A W Ireland	Did not bat
R S Buckley	
G T Main	
Extras w 5	5
Total (4 wkts, 15.4 overs)	128

* *Will Rhodes performed the hat-trick by removing R Singh, C S MacLeod and U Arshad*

FoW: 1-40 (Singh), 2-40 (MacLeod), 3-43 (Arshad), 4-95 (Muchall)

	O	M	R	W
Tattersall	3	0	34	0
Coad	1	0	11	0
Shaw	1	0	8	0
Rhodes	4	1	21	3
Carver	4	0	27	1
Azeem Rafiq	2	0	20	0
Robinson	0.4	0	7	0

Umpires: S J Malone and R T Robinson

Scorers: H Clayton and R V Hilton

Second Eleven Twenty20

Yorkshire v. Lancashire

At Abbeydale Park, Sheffield, on May 9, 2014
Match abandoned without a ball bowled

No toss made   Yorkshire 1 point, Lancashire 1 point

Yorkshire v. Lancashire

At Abbeydale Park, Sheffield, on May 9, 2014
Match abandoned without a ball bowled

No toss made   Yorkshire 1 point, Lancashire 1 point

Nottinghamshire v. Yorkshire

Played at Trent College, Little Eaton, on May 14, 2014
Yorkshire won by 43 runs at 2.17pm

Toss won by Nottinghamshire   Nottinghamshire 0 points, Yorkshire 2 points

YORKSHIRE

A Z Lees, c Hutton b L Wood		10
* J A Tattersall, c Kelsall b Gurney		6
§ D M Hodgson, b Kelsall b Hutton		7
J A Leaning, st Cross b S K W Wood		19
W M H Rhodes, lbw b Tillcock		6
R M Pyrah, c Hutton b Fletcher		44
Azeem Rafiq, b Gurney		15
J Shaw, run out (Fletcher)		3
B O Coad, not out		6
M A Ashraf, not out		3
K Carver	Did not bat	
Extras lb 3; nb 4; w 10		17
Total (8 wkts, 20 overs)		136

FoW: 1-11 (Tattersall), 2-25 (Lees), 3-32 (Hodgson), 4-41 (Rhodes), 5-63 (Leaning), 6-99 (Azeem Rafiq), 7-124 (Pyrah), 8-127 (Shaw)

	O	M	R	W
Gurney	4	0	38	2
Fletcher	4	0	20	1
L Wood	2	0	13	1
Hutton	2	0	9	1
Tillcock	4	0	26	1
S K W Wood	4	0	27	1

NOTTINGHAMSHIRE

* S Kelsall, c Rhodes b Pyrah		6
§ M H Cross, lbw b Ashraf		7
B M Shafayat, c Rhodes b Carver		10
S K W Wood, c Azeem Rafiq b Pyrah		4
A D Tillcock, c Rhodes b Pyrah		1
B A Hutton, b Azeem Rafiq		8
Hasan Azad, c Hodgson b Ashraf		21
L J Fletcher, c Leaning b Ashraf		13
S P Seymour, c Lees b Ashraf		10
L Wood, not out		1
H F Gurney, c Lees b Pyrah		0
Extras lb 3; w 9		12
Total (18.2 overs)		93

FoW: 1-12 (Cross), 2-18 (Kelsall), 3-24 (S K W Wood), 4-30 (Tillcock), 5-40 (Shafayat), 6-54 (Hutton), 7-77 (Hasan Azad), 8-89 (Fletcher), 9-92 (Seymour), 10-93 (Gurney)

	O	M	R	W
Ashraf	4	0	19	4
Coad	3	0	6	0
Pyrah	3.2	0	13	4
Carver	4	0	22	1
Azeem Rafiq	4	0	30	1

Umpires: R J Evans and T Lungley   Scorers: Mrs A Cusworth and H Clayton

Second Eleven Twenty20
Nottinghamshire v. Yorkshire

Played at Trent College, Little Eaton, on May 14, 2014

Yorkshire won by 1 wicket at 5.59pm

Toss won by Nottinghamshire   Nottinghamshire 0 points, Yorkshire 2 points

NOTTINGHAMSHIRE

S Kelsall, lbw b Azeem Rafiq		28
§ M H Cross, b Carver		21
S J Mullaney, not out		103
B M Shafayat, st Hodd b Carver		8
S K W Wood, c Robinson b Ashraf		24
A D Tillcock, c Carver b Pyrah		5
B A Hutton, not out		0
Hasan Azad		
L J Fletcher		
S P Seymour	Did not bat	
L Wood		
Extras lb 2; nb 2; w 2		6
Total (5 wkts, 20 overs)		195

FoW: 1-45 (Kelsall), 2-57 (Cross), 3-67 (Shafayat), 4-163 (S K W Wood), 5-175 (Tillcock)

	O	M	R	W
Ashraf	4	0	39	1
Shaw	3	0	27	0
Robinson	3	0	45	0
Azeem Rafiq	4	0	25	1
Carver	4	0	23	2
Pyrah	2	0	34	1

YORKSHIRE

A Z Lees, c Fletcher b L Wood		4
* J A Tattersall, b S K W Wood		27
§ D M Hodgson, lbw b Fletcher		0
J A Leaning, c Tillcock b Hutton		102
R M Pyrah, st Cross b Tillcock		11
Azeem Rafiq, run out (Kelsall)		4
§ A J Hodd, b Tillcock		3
O E Robinson, c Cross b Fletcher		14
J Shaw, c Hasan Azad b Fletcher		4
M A Ashraf, not out		7
K Carver, not out		3
Extras b 1; lb 2; nb 10; w 4		17
Total (9 wkts, 20 overs)		196

FoW: 1-7 (Lees), 2-16 (Hodgson), 3-47 (Tattersall), 4-83 (Pyrah), 5-87 (Azeem Rafiq), 6-97 (Hodd), 7-136 (Robinson), 8-173 (Shaw), 9-184 (Leaning)

	O	M	R	W
S K W Wood	4	0	27	1
L Wood	3	0	51	1
Hutton	4	0	38	1
Fletcher	4	0	33	3
Tillcock	4	0	30	2
Seymour	1	0	14	0

Umpires: R J Evans and T Lungley   Scorers: Mrs A Cusworth and H Clayton

Second Eleven Twenty20
Derbyshire v. Yorkshire

Played at Derby on May 15, 2014
Derbyshire won by 26 runs at 2.18pm

Toss won by Yorkshire   Derbyshire 2 points, Yorkshire 0 points

DERBYSHIRE

C F Hughes, b Tattersall	....	10
* P M Borrington, c Coad b Shaw	....	18
B T Slater, c Rhodes b Shaw	....	21
Rahat Ali, c Tattersall b Azeem Rafiq	....	1
G T G Cork, c Hodd b Shaw	....	0
T C Knight, not out	....	32
A P Palladino, c Leaning b Azeem Rafiq	....	9
§ H R Hosein, lbw b Carver	....	1
R Hassan, c Hodgson b Rhodes	....	19
M L Turner, not out	....	2
M Higginbottom	Did not bat	
Extras w4	....	4
Total (8 wkts, 20 overs)	....	117

FoW: 1-10 (Hughes), 2-44 (Borrington), 3-47 (Rahat Ali), 4-52 (Slater), 5-53 (Cork), 6-63 (Palladino), 7-71 (Hosein), 8-106 (Hassan)

	O	M	R	W
Tattersall	2	0	16	1
Coad	2	0	15	0
Rhodes	4	0	22	1
Shaw	4	0	25	3
Azeem Rafiq	4	1	7	2
Carver	4	0	32	1

YORKSHIRE

A Z Lees, c Hosein b Turner	....	4
* J A Tattersall, c Higginbottom b Turner	....	0
D M Hodgson, c Hosein b Higginbottom	....	0
J A Leaning, b Higginbottom	....	0
W M H Rhodes, c Hughes b Higginbottom	....	5
§ A J Hodd, lbw b Knight	....	36
Azeem Rafiq, run out (Hassan)	....	0
O E Robinson, b Palladino	....	11
J Shaw, b Hassan	....	0
B O Coad, c Hassan b Palladino	....	7
K Carver, not out	....	8
Extras lb 2, nb 2, w 5	....	9
Total (19.3 overs)	....	91

FoW: 1-5 (Tattersall), 2-5 (Hodgson), 3-5 (Leaning), 4-9 (Lees), 5-19 (Rhodes), 6-20 (Azeem Rafiq), 7-49 (Robinson), 8-73 (Shaw), 9-75 (Hodd), 10-91 (Coad)

	O	M	R	W
Turner	4	1	16	2
Higginbottom	4	0	11	3
Cork	2	0	12	0
Palladino	3.3	0	19	2
Hughes	2	0	11	0
Knight	2	0	12	1
Hassan	2	0	8	1

Umpires: N L Bainton and A Payne   Scorers: T M Cottam and H Clayton

Second Eleven Twenty20
Derbyshire v. Yorkshire

Played at Derby on May 15, 2014
Derbyshire won by 4 wickets at 5.33pm

Toss won by Yorkshire

Derbyshire 2 points, Yorkshire 0 points

YORKSHIRE

A Z Lees, c Durston b Clare		25
* J A Tattersall, c Wainwright b Durston		2
§ D M Hodgson, b Footitt		0
J A Leaning, c Cross b Groenewald		1
W M H Rhodes, c Slater b C F Hughes		27
A J Hodd, c Madsen b Clare		3
Azeem Rafiq, c and b Elstone		8
O E Robinson, not out		34
J Shaw, run out (Groenewald)		4
B O Coad, not out		0
K Carver	Did not bat	
Extras lb 2, nb 6, w 9		17
Total (8 wkts, 20 overs)		121

FoW: 1-3 (Tattersall), 2-5 (Hodgson), 3-12 (Leaning), 4-46 (Lees), 5-52 (Hodd), 6-75 (Azeem Rafiq), 7-99 (Rhodes), 8-111 (Shaw)

	O	M	R	W
Durston	3	0	11	1
Footitt	3	0	25	1
Groenewald	3	0	28	1
Clare	2	0	7	2
Wainwright	2	0	7	0
Elstone	2	0	16	1
A L Hughes	3	0	17	0
C F Hughes	2	0	8	1

DERBYSHIRE

C F Hughes, c Tattersall b Carver		30
B T Slater, c Tattersall b Coad		3
W J Durston, c Azeem Rafiq b Robinson		3
* W L Madsen, c Lees b Carver		18
S L Elstone, not out		26
A L Hughes, lbw b Carver		1
J L Clare, c Lees b Carver		5
§ G D Cross, not out		29
T D Groenewald		
D J Wainwright	Did not bat	
M H A Footitt		
Extras lb 4, w 4		8
Total (6 wkts, 18.4 overs)		123

FoW: 1-6 (Slater), 2-28 (Durston), 3-60 (C F Hughes), 4-61 (Madsen), 5-73 (A L Hughes), 6-81 (Clare)

	O	M	R	W
Leaning	4	1	11	0
Coad	3	0	21	1
Robinson	2.4	0	17	1
Azeem Rafiq	4	0	43	0
Carver	4	0	14	4
Rhodes	1	0	13	0

Umpires: N L Bainton and A Payne

Scorers: T M Cottam and H Clayton

SECOND ELEVEN
TWENTY20 2014

(Two matches played against the same opponents
at the same venue on the same day)

GROUP A – FINAL TABLE

	P	W	L	Tie	No result	Aban.	Points	Net run rate
1 Lancashire (2)	8	4	0	0	1	3	12	2.048
2 Derbyshire (4)	8	3	2	0	2	1	9	0.170
3 Durham (1)	8	4	4	0	0	0	8	0.318
4 Yorkshire (3)	**8**	**2**	**4**	**0**	**0**	**2**	**6**	**-0.380**
5 Nottinghamshire (6)	8	2	5	0	1	0	5	-1.306

England Under-19s did not take part in the 2014 competition

GROUP B – FINAL TABLE

	P	W	L	Tie	No result	Aban.	Points	Net run rate
1 Somerset (2)	8	5	1	1	1	0	12	1.099
2 Worcestershire (3)	8	3	2	0	1	2	9	-0.859
3 Warwickshire (5)	8	2	3	1	0	2	7	0.866
4 Glamorgan (4)	8	2	4	0	0	2	6	-0.380
5 Gloucestershire (1)	8	2	4	0	0	2	6	-1.161

GROUP C – FINAL TABLE

	P	W	L	Tie	No result	Aban.	Points	Net run rate
1 Leicestershire (5)	8	3	0	0	2	3	11	2.26
2 Middlesex (1)	8	3	1	0	2	2	10	0.608
3 Essex (3)	8	3	3	0	1	1	8	-0.377
4 Unicorns (2)	8	1	3	0	1	3	6	-0.594
5 Northamptonshire (4) ...	8	1	4	0	2	1	5	-0.909

GROUP D – FINAL TABLE

	P	W	L	Tie	No result	Aban.	Points	Net run rate
1 Hampshire (5)	8	4	2	1	0	1	10	-0.071
2 MCC YC (4)	8	4	3	0	1	0	9	0.571
3 Kent (2)	8	2	2	0	0	4	8	-0.594
4 Sussex (3)	8	2	3	0	0	3	7	0.443
5 Surrey (1)	8	1	3	1	1	2	6	-0.823

(2013 positions in brackets)

SEMI-FINALS

Leicestershire (185-5) beat Lancashire (156-6) by 29 runs
Hampshire (158-5) lost to Somerset (159-2) by eight wickets

FINAL

Leicestershire (159-7) beat Somerset (148) by 11 runs

PREVIOUS WINNERS

2011	**Sussex**, who beat Durham by 24 runs
2012	**England Under-19s**, who beat Sussex by eight wickets
2013	**Surrey**, who beat Middlesex by six runs

SECOND ELEVEN TWENTY20
AVERAGES 2014

Played 8   Won 2   Lost 4   Abandoned 2

BATTING AND FIELDING

(Qualification 3 innings)

Player	M.	I.	N.O.	Runs	H.S.	Avge	100s	50s	ct/st
J A Leaning	6	6	0	202	102	33.66	1	1	2
R M Pyrah	3	3	1	57	44	28.50	0	0	0
W M H Rhodes	5	5	0	85	39	17.00	0	0	4
O E Robinson	5	5	1	63	34*	15.75	0	0	1
A J Hodd	3	3	0	42	36	14.00	0	1	1/1
K Carver	5	3	2	12	8*	12.00	0	0	1
J A Tattersall	6	6	0	68	27	11.33	0	0	3
A Z Lees	4	4	0	43	25	10.75	0	0	4
J Shaw	6	6	2	36	11	9.00	0	0	0
Azeem Rafiq	6	6	0	52	21	8.66	0	0	3
B O Coad	5	4	2	15	7	7.50	0	0	2
D M Hodgson	6	6	0	34	22	5.66	0	0	2
Also batted									
R Gibson	2	2	0	16	16	8.00	0	0	2
B P Gibson	1	1	0	7	7	7.00	0	0	1
M A Ashraf	3	2	2	10	7*	—	0	0	0

BOWLING

(Qualification 5 wickets)

Player	Overs	Mdns	Runs	Wkts	Avge	Best	4wI
R M Pyrah	9	0	83	7	11.85	4-13	1
K Carver	20	0	118	9	13.11	4-14	1
M A Ashraf	11	0	86	5	17.20	4-19	1
Also bowled							
W M H Rhodes	9	1	56	4	14.00	3-21	0
J Shaw	9	0	69	4	17.25	3-25	0
Azeem Rafiq	22	1	151	4	37.75	2-7	0
J A Tattersall	5	0	50	1	50.00	1-16	0
B O Coad	11.2	0	74	1	74.00	1-21	0
O E Robinson	9.2	0	100	1	100.00	1-17	0
J A Leaning	5	1	24	0	—	—	0

Other Second Eleven Match
Lancashire v. Yorkshire

Played at Northop Hall CC, Flintshire, on April 22, 23 and 24, 2014
Match drawn at 6.17pm on the Third Day

Toss won by Yorkshire

Close of play: First Day, Lancashire 201-2 (Croft 80, Clark 8); Second Day, Yorkshire 99-9 (Pyrah 13, Carver 0)

LANCASHIRE

§ A L Davies, c Shaw b Azeem Rafiq		34
K R Brown, c Hodgson b Shaw		78
S J Croft, c Leaning b Pyrah		197
J Clark, c Hodgson b Shaw		12
L S Livingstone, c Tattersall b Shaw		14
* S D Parry, b Carver		17
O J Newby, b Carver		42
K Ali, not out		28
A M Lilley		
T E Bailey		
K M Jarvis	Did not bat	
Adnan Ghaus		
Extras b2, lb3		5
Total (7 wkts dec, 93.3 overs)		427

FoW: 1-70 (Davies), 2-179 (Brown), 3-205 (Clark), 4-245 (Livingstone), 5-282 (Parry), 6-372 (Newby), 7-427 (Croft).

	O	M	R	W
Ashraf	16	1	68	0
Pyrah	16.3	5	45	1
Shaw	13	3	44	3
Robinson	14	1	65	0
Azeem Rafiq	9	0	67	1
Carver	15	0	87	2
Root	7	0	24	0
Tattersall	3	0	22	0

YORKSHIRE

First Innings		Second Innings	
E Callis, b Jarvis	0	c Livingstone b Jarvis	45
J A Tattersall, lbw b Jarvis	20	c Davies b Jarvis	10
J E Root, b Crown b Jarvis	8	c Davies b Bailey	61
J A Leaning, b Jarvis	8	b Parry	16
W M H Rhodes, b Ali	0	c Newby b Lilley	16
§ D M Hodgson, lbw b Jarvis	7	st Davies b Parry	9
* Azeem Rafiq, lbw b Newby	21	b Lilley	9
O E Robinson, b Jarvis	11	b Lilley	60
R M Pyrah, not out	40	not out	22
J Shaw, c Croft b Newby	0	not out	11
K Carver, c Davies b Adnan Ghaus	13		
M A Ashraf	Did not bat		
Extras (b 4, lb 9, w 1, nb 4)	18	Extras b 1, lb 3, w 6, nb 14	24
Total (35.3 overs)	146	Total (8 wkts, 82.1 overs)	283

FoW: 1-1 (Callis), 2-9 (Root), 3-33 (Leaning), 4-36 (Rhodes), 5-43 (Hodgson),
1st 6-52 (Tattersall), 7-66 (Robinson), 8-95 (Azeem Rafiq), 9-95 (Shaw), 10-146 (Carver).
FoW: 1-25 (Tattersall), 2-122 (Callis), 3-144 (Root), 4-167 (Rhodes), 5-167 (Leaning),
2nd 6-182 (Azeem Rafiq), 7-194 (Hodgson), 8-266 (Robinson).

	O	M	R	W		O	M	R	W
Jarvis	11	3	47	6	Jarvis	14.1	2	58	2
Ali	9	2	27	1	Ali	9	0	50	0
Parry	1	0	5	0	Parry	17	6	41	2
Lilley	2	1	8	0	Lilley	11	2	36	3
Bailey	2	0	5	0	Bailey	15	3	36	1
Newby	5	0	17	2	Newby	7	3	17	0
Adnan Ghaus	5.3	1	24	1	Adnan Ghaus	5	0	33	0
					Clark	4	0	8	0

Umpires: M Burns and I Laurrence   Scorers: D M White and H Clayton

Other Second Eleven Match
Yorkshire v. Lancashire

Played at Headingley, Leeds, on April 28, 29 and 30, 2014
Yorkshire won by 6 wickets at 3.34pm on the Third Day
Toss won by Lancashire

Close of play: First Day, Yorkshire 81-2 (Tattersall 24); Second Day, Lancashire 77-4 (Clark 27, Parry 12)

LANCASHIRE

	First Innings		Second Innings	
§ A L Davies, c Callis b Robinson	9	c Robinson b Bresnan	6
K R Brown, c Rhodes b Ashraf	28	c Tattersall b Coad	19
S J Croft, c Robinbson b Bresnan	54	c Gibson b Bresnan	8
J Clark, c Gibson b Ashraf	49	c Robinson b Bresnan	33
L S Livingstone, c Bresnan b Ashraf	10	c Gibson b Robinson	5
* S D Parry, c Gale b Robinson	7	c Leaning b Ashraf	46
O J Newby, lbw b Bresnan	15	c Bresnan b Ashraf	15
A M Lilley, c Robinson b Ashraf	2	c Callis b Robinson	10
T E Bailey, lbw b Carver	0	c Callis b Coad	19
G T Griffiths, run out (Tattersall)	21	c Bresnan b Ashraf	1
Adnan Ghaus, not out	11	(11), not out	0
L J Hurt	Did not bat		
Extras b 1, lb 9, nb 6	16	Extras lb 1	1
Total (78.2 overs)	222	Total (53.1 overs)	163

FoW: 1-27 (Davies), 2-47 (Brown), 3-147 (Croft), 4-158 (Clark), 5-167 (Parry),
1st 6-173 (Livingstone), 7-187 (Lilley), 8-188 (Bailey), 9-188 (Newby), 10-222 (Griffiths),

FoW: 1-12 (Davies), 2-22 (Croft), 3-51 (Brown), 4-65 (Livingstone), 5-93 (Clark),
2nd 6-129 (Newby), 7-138 (Parry), 8-146 (Lilley), 9-163 (Griffiths), 10-163 (Bailey)

	O	M	R	W		O	M	R	W
Bresnan	13	7	17	2	Bresnan	15	5	31	3
Coad	15.2	8	19	0	Coad	13.1	3	26	2
Robinson	18	3	68	2	Robinson	12	1	60	2
Ashraf	14	5	25	4	Ashraf	13	1	45	3
Carver	14	2	52	1					
Azeem Rafiq	3	0	28	0					
Tattersall	1	0	3	0					

YORKSHIRE

	First Innings		Second Innings	
E Callis, c Clark b Newby	1	lbw b Bailey	2
* J A Tattersall, c Clark b Bailey	41	not out	54
A W Gale, c Davies b Griffiths	40	c Croft b Clark	16
J A Leaning, c Davies b Bailey	60	c Davies b Clark	0
W M H Rhodes, c Davies b Newby	6	c Davies b Bailey	21
T T Bresnan, b Bailey	1		
Azeem Rafiq, c Livingstone b Newby	3		
O E Robinson, lbw b Clark	78	(6) not out	8
§ B P Gibson, b Clark	0		
B O Coad, lbw b Bailey	1		
K Carver, not out	0		
M A Ashraf	Did not bat		
Extras b 10, lb 11, nb 16, w 5	42	Extras b 13, lb 1	14
Total (81.4 overs)	273	Total (4 wkts, 27.5 overs)	115

FoW: 1-2 (Callis), 2-81 (Gale), 3-121 (Tattersall), 4-128 (Rhodes), 5-131 (Bresnan),
1st 6-140 (Azeem Rafiq), 7-264 (Robinson), 8-264 (Gibson), 9-272 (Leaning), 10-273 (Coad)

2nd: 1-13 (Callis), 2-42 (Gale), 3-42 (Leaning), 4-107 (Rhodes)

	O	M	R	W		O	M	R	W
Newby	21	2	63	3	Griffiths	7	2	15	0
Bailey	21.4	2	71	4	Bailey	8.5	3	32	2
Griffiths	18	2	52	1	Clark	7	1	31	2
Adnan Ghaus	7	1	27	0	Hurt	5	0	23	0
Clark	6	1	26	2					
Parry	8	1	13	0					

Umpires: M A Gough and R J Warren

Scorers: H Clayton and D M White

Other Second Eleven Match
Yorkshire v. Lancashire

Played at Headingley, Leeds, on May 2, 2014
Lancashire won by 27 runs at 1.32pm (T20)
Toss won by Yorkshire

LANCASHIRE

W A White, c and b Ashraf		1
§ A L Davies, not out		101
R P Zelem, c Bairstow b Pyrah		9
J Clark, b Pyrah		3
L S Livingstone, c Robinson b Azeem Rafiq		34
R P Jones, not out		19
* S D Parry		
A M Lilley		
T E Bailey	Did not bat	
G T Griffiths		
L J Hurt		
Extras b 1, w 2, nb 2		5
Total (4 wkts, 20 overs)		172

FoW: 1-14 (White), 2-47 (Zelem), 3-51 (Clark), 4-111 (Livingstone)

	O	M	R	W
Ashraf	4	0	25	1
Shaw	1	0	12	0
Tattersall	1	0	12	0
Pyrah	4	0	26	2
Robinson	3	0	19	0
Azeem Rafiq	4	0	33	1
Gibson	1	0	22	0
Carver	2	0	22	0

YORKSHIRE

E Callis, c White b Griffiths	0
W M H Rhodes, c Zelem b Bailey	1
* Azeem Rafiq, b Bailey	10
§ J M Bairstow, c Parry b Clark	77
J A Tattersall, c White b Parry	8
O E Robinson, c Davies b Clark	9
R M Pyrah, c Davies b Clark	0
R Gibson, b Lilley	7
J Shaw, c Lilley b Clark	7
K Carver, not out	2
M A Ashraf, c Zelem b Griffiths	11
Extras b 4, lb 8, w 1	13
Total (18.5 overs)	145

FoW: 1-0 (Callis), 2-11 (Azeem Rafiq), 3-22 (Rhodes), 4-59 (Tattersall), 5-88 (Robinson), 6-88 (Pyrah), 7-116 (Gibson), 8-132 (Bairstow), 9-132 (Shaw), 10-145 (Ashraf)

	O	M	R	W
Griffiths	3.5	0	23	2
Bailey	2	0	14	2
White	3	0	18	0
Clark	4	0	28	4
Parry	2	0	24	1
Lilley	4	0	26	1

Umpires: M Burns and R J Warren   Scorers: H Clayton and D M White

Other Second Eleven Match
Yorkshire v. Lancashire

Played at Headingley, Leeds, on May 2, 2014
Yorkshire won by 3 wkts at 5.38pm (T20)
Toss won by Lancashire

LANCASHIRE

W A White, c Hodgson b Coad	6
§ A L Davies, c Hodgson b Shaw	1
* S D Parry, b Shaw	1
J Clark, c B P Gibson b Pyrah	3
L S Livingstone, c B P Gibson b R Gibson	2
R P Jones, b Azeem Rafiq	13
R P Zelem, not out	35
A M Lilley, c B P Gibson b Rhodes	24
T E Bailey, not out	28
S Mahmood	
L J Hurt Did not bat	
Extras lb 6, w 13	19
Total (7 wkts, 20 overs)	132

FoW: 1-8 (White), 2-8 (Davies), 3-9 (Parry), 4-18 (Livingstone), 5-23 (Clark), 6-44 (Jones), 7-71 (Lilley)

	O	M	R	W
Coad	4	0	28	1
Shaw	3	0	23	2
R Gibson	3	0	10	1
Pyrah	4	0	10	1
Azeem Rafiq	4	0	34	1
Rhodes	2	0	21	1

YORKSHIRE

A Z Lees, c Jones b Hurt	58
J A Tattersall, c Davies b Bailey	0
* Azeem Rafiq, c Jones b Hurt	9
J A Leaning, run out (Lilley)	7
W M H Rhodes, c Livingstone b Mahmood	42
D M Hodgson, lbw b Bailey	7
R M Pyrah, run out (Jones)	0
R Gibson, not out	2
§ B P Gibson, not out	0
J Shaw	
B O Coad Did not bat	
Extras b 1, lb 1, w 2, nb 4	8
Total (7 wkts, 20 overs)	133

FoW: 1-6 (Tattersall), 2-40 (Azeem Rafiq), 3-52 (Leaning), 4-110 (Lees), 5-131 (Rhodes), 6-131 (Hodgson), 7-132 (Pyrah)

	O	M	R	W
Mahmood	3	0	21	1
Bailey	4	0	24	2
Clark	4	0	25	0
Hurt	4	0	26	2
Jones	1	0	10	0
White	2	0	10	0
Livingstone	2	0	15	0

Umpires: D M Warburton and R J Warren   Scorers: H Clayton and D M White

Other Second Eleven Match
Yorkshire v. Kent

Played at Scarborough on May 27, 28 and 29, 2014
Match drawn. No play was possible after 10.53am on the First Day
Toss won by Yorkshire

YORKSHIRE

E Callis, c Davies b Griffiths	1
* J A Tattersall, lbw b Hartley	1
J A Leaning, not out	8
W M H Rhodes, not out	9
§ D M Hodgson	
Azeem Rafiq	
O E Robinson	
R M Pyrah	Did not bat
J Shaw	
B O Coad	
K Carver	
Extras	0
Total (2 wkts, 9 overs)	19

FoW: 1-2 (Callis), 2-2 (Tattersall)

	O	M	R	W
Griffiths	5	2	9	1
Hartley	4	1	10	1

KENT

F K Cowdrey	
C D Piesley	
* A J Blake	
G J Harte	
S S Arthurton	
§ R C Davies	Did not bat
Z Crawley	
C F Hartley	
P F B Richardson	
D A Griffiths	
Imran Qayyum	

Umpires: R J Evans and S J Malone   Scorers: H Clayton and A L Bateup

Other Second Eleven Match
Yorkshire v. Scotland A

Played at Scarborough on June 24, 25 and 26, 2014
Match drawn at 4.50pm on the Third Day
Toss won by Scotland A

Close of play: First Day, Yorkshire 46-2 (Hodgson 10, Rhodes 13); Second Day, Scotland A 50-3 (Mommsen 31, Evans 0)

SCOTLAND A	First Innings		Second Innings	
M D Parker, run out (Coad)	0		c Hodgson b Fisher	7
H J W Gardiner, b Shaw	84		c Hussain b Fisher	7
* P L Mommsen, c Tattersall b Fisher	64		c Rafiq b Fisher	38
M M Iqbal, b Shaw	5		c Hodgson b Rhodes	0
R D Berrington, c Hodgson b Rhodes	18		(6) c Robinson b Rhodes	24
M A Leask, b Coad	54		(7) not out	122
S M Sharif, c Rafiq b Rhodes	2		(8) not out	173
G Goudie, b Rhodes	0			
I Wardlaw, b Rhodes	2			
A C Evans, not out	2		(5) lbw b Rafiq	0
H Tahir, c Fisher b Coad	1			
§ S W S Whait	Did not bat			
Extras lb 5, nb 2	7		Extras b 5, lb 13, w 1, nb 10	29
Total (71.5 overs)	239		Total (6 wkts dec, 87 overs)	400

FoW: 1-10 (Parker), 2-147 (Mommsen), 3-160 (Iqbal), 4-163 (Gardiner), 5-232 (Berrington),
1st 6-234 (Sharif), 7-234 (Goudie), 8-234 (Leask), 9-236 (Wardlaw), 10-239 (Tahir)
FoW: 1-8 (Parker), 2-31 (Gardiner), 3-39 (Iqbal), 4-60 (Mommsen), 5-123 (Evans),
2nd 6-358 (Berrington)

	O	M	R	W		O	M	R	W
Ashraf	11	3	39	0	Ashraf	15	1	51	0
Coad	8.5	4	17	2	Coad	11	1	64	0
Fisher	9	2	41	1	Fisher	18	3	87	3
Robinson	12	3	49	0	Robinson	5	1	26	0
Shaw	13	2	35	2	Shaw	14	5	53	0
Rhodes	11	3	36	4	Rhodes	13	4	51	2
Rafiq	6	0	15	0	Rafiq	11	2	50	1
Tattersall	1	0	2	0					

YORKSHIRE

E Callis, lbw b Wardlaw	5
J A Tattersall, lbw b Evans	5
§ D M Hodgson, c Whait b Wardlaw	118
* W M H Rhodes, c Parker b Sharif	32
M Hussain, run out (Gardiner)	91
O E Robinson, lbw b Sharif	85
Azeem Rafiq, c Iqbal b Wardlaw	10
J A Thompson, c Gardiner b Sharif	9
J Shaw, c Leask b Sharif	20
M D Fisher, not out	13
B O Coad	
M A Ashraf	Did not bat
Extras b 10, lb 5, nb 14. pen5)	34
Total (9 wkts dec, 101.3 overs)	422

Five penalty points awarded for the ball hitting the helmet, stationed behind the wicket-keeper
FoW: 1-14 (Tattersall), 2-16 (Callis), 3-85 (Rhodes), 4-244 (Hodgson), 5-341 (Hussain),
6-355 (Rafiq), 7-380 (Thompson), 8-399 (Robinson), 9-422 (Shaw)

	O	M	R	W
Wardlaw	24	1	114	3
Evans	21	5	63	1
Sharif	20.3	2	78	4
Tahir	19	2	59	0
Goudie	8	1	41	0
Iqbal	5	0	26	0
Leask	4	0	21	0

Umpires: I Dawood abd I J Dixon   Scorers: H Clayton and C N Rawson

Other Second Eleven Match
Gloucestershire v. Yorkshire

Played at Bristol on July 7, 2014
Gloucestershire won by 5 wickets (D/L Method) at 7.09pm
Toss won by Yorkshire

YORKSHIRE

A J Hodd, b Sharif	32
* W M H Rhodes, c Smith b Sharif	68
§ D M Hodgson, c and b Miles	1
J A Tattersall, not out	102
M Hussain, c and b Shrewsbury	28
O E Robinson, b Shrewsbury	10
R Gibson, run out (Montgomery)	37
J Shaw, not out	7
M D Fisher	
B O Coad	
M A Ashraf Did not bat	
K Carver	
Extras b 1, lb 2, w 11, nb 6	20
Total (6 wkts, 50 overs)	305

FoW: 1-63 (Hodd), 2-67 (Hodgson), 3-143 (Rhodes), 4-199 (Hussain), 5-217 (Robinson), 6-293 (Gibson)

	O	M	R	W
McCarter	10	0	63	0
Montgomery	10	0	77	0
Sharif	10	0	47	2
Miles	5	1	16	1
Housego	4	0	24	0
Shrewsbury	8	0	52	2
Smithson	3	0	23	0

GLOUCESTERSHIRE

* D M Housego, c Gibson b Carver	74
M D Lezar, b Robinson	40
R J Montgomery, c Hodgson b Fisher	39
J H Barrett, not out	38
K C B Smith, b Carver	4
C N Miles, b Shaw	16
S M Sharif, not out	8
§ P J Grieshaber	
G L McCarter	
T W Shrewsbury Did not bat	
O W Smithson	
Extras b 4, lb 4, w 5, nb 4	17
Total (5 wkts, 31.4 overs)	236

Gloucestershire's target was adjusted after rain to 235 from 32 overs

FoW: 1-78 (Lezar), 2-152 (Montgomery), 3-171 (Housego), 4-182 (Smith), 5-209 (Miles)

	O	M	R	W
Coad	3	0	17	0
Fisher	6	0	35	1
Rhodes	5	0	47	0
Shaw	3	0	26	1
Gibson	3	0	28	0
Carver	5	0	30	2
Robinson	6.4	0	45	1

Umpires: I D Blackwell and R C Hampshire   Scorers: S P Cashbury and H Clayton

Other Second Eleven Match
Gloucestershire v. Yorkshire

Played at Bristol on July 8, 9 and 10, 2014
Match drawn at 4.50pm on the Third Day

Toss won by Gloucestershire

Close of play: First Day, Yorkshire 65-3 (Rhodes 18, Robinson 12); Second Day, Gloucestershire 19-0 (Roderick 19; Housego 4)

GLOUCESTERSHIRE

	First Innings			Second Innings	
* D M Housego, b Shaw		12	(2) c Shaw b Carver		114
G H Roderick, c Hood b Robinson		30	(1) not out		152
K C B Smith, c Hood b Robinson		1	(5) not out		0
J M R Taylor, lbw b Shaw		5	(3) b Carver		10
J L N Garrett, c Hussain b Rhodes		4			
J H Barrett, lbw b Rhodes		9			
M A H Hammond, c Hodgson b Fisher		0			
C N Miles, not out		71			
S M Sharif, c Hodd b Robinson		16			
§ P J Grieshaber, b Shaw		6			
G J McCarter, lbw b Fisher		24	(4) c Shaw b Carver		0
C J Skidmore	Did not bat				
Extras b 4, lb 6		10	Extras b 3, lb 2, nb 6		11
Total (62.3 overs)		188	Total (3 wkts, 84 overs)		287

FoW: 1-42 (Roderick), 2-42 (Housego), 3-48 (Smith), 4-52 (Taylor), 5-65 (Garrett), 6-69
1st (Hammond), 7-69 (Barrett), 8-111 (Sharif), 9-140 (Grieshaber), 10-188 (McCarter)
2nd 1-256 (Housego), 2-283 (Taylor), 3-283 (McCarter)

	O	M	R	W		O	M	R	W
Coad	10	2	31	0	Coad	11	4	32	0
Fisher	12.3	5	39	2	Fisher	11	2	29	0
Shaw	9	3	41	3	Shaw	9	3	26	0
Robinson	14	5	35	3	Robinson	15	3	44	0
Rhodes	13	6	25	2	Rhodes	6	1	27	0
Carver	4	1	7	0	Carver	23	7	71	3
					Gibson	8	2	42	0
					Hussain	1	0	11	0

YORKSHIRE

§ A J Hodd, b McCarter		19
M Hussain, lbw b McCarter		5
D M Hodgson, b McCarter		8
* W M H Rhodes, c Tay6lor b Skidmore		25
O E Robinson, lbw b Taylor		119
J A Tattersall, c Taylor b Skidmore		137
R Gibson, c Grieshaber b McCarter		43
J Shaw, c and b Hammond		30
M D Fisher, not out		36
B O Coad, not out		10
K Carver		
M A Ashraf	Did not bat	
Extras b 15, lb 17, nb 4		36
Total (8 wkts dec, 118 overs)		468

FoW: 1-19 (Hussain), 2-27 (Hodgson), 3-38 (Hodd), 4-98 (Rhodes), 5-243 (Robinson),
6-312 (Gibson), 7-387 (Shaw), 8-437 (Tattersall)

	O	M	R	W
McCarter	28	3	119	4
Skidmore	22	5	71	2
Miles	4	0	16	0
Sharif	19	1	69	0
Taylor	30	6	96	1
Hammond	15	0	65	1

Umpires: I D Blackwell and A J Wheeler   Scorers: S P Cashbury and H Clayton

Other Second Eleven Match
Malton and Old Malton CC v. Yorkshire

Played at Malton and Old Malton CC on July 28, 2014
Yorkshire won by 58 runs at 7.09pm (T20)
Toss won by Yorkshire

YORKSHIRE

E Callis, c Turnbull b Gaughan	75
A J Hodd, c Foxton b W Dawson	13
D M Hodgson, c Gill b Whatmore	27
*R Gibson, c Fraser b Gillbank	8
§ B P Gibson, run out(Hudson)	9
J C Wainman, not out	61
M J Waite, not out	1
Did not bat: B O Coad, J W P Brown, N J Firn, M A Ashraf and J E G Logan	
Extras	0
Total (5 wkts, 20 overs)	194

FoW: 1-26 (Hodd), 2-100 (Hodgson), 3-120 (R Gibson), 4-124 (Callis), 5-159 (B P Gibson)

	O	M	R	W
Hudson	2	0	11	0
W Dawson	3	0	31	1
Gaughan	3	0	29	1
Whatmore	3	0	25	1
Spencer	2	0	22	0
Gillbank	3	0	34	1
M Linsley	2	0	23	0
Turnbull	2	0	19	0

MALTON AND OLD MALTON CC

S Harland, lbw b Logan	26
N Johnson, c R Gibson b Brown	24
W Dawson, b Waite	0
M Dawson, c B P Gibson b Logan	16
M Turnbull, b R Gibson	31
M Linsley, not out	16
S Baxter, b Waite	4
*S Linsley, c Hodgson b R Gibson	4
T Audsley, c Ashraf b Hodgson	3
D Foxton, not out	1
Did not bat: S Whatmore, M Fraser, O Gillbank, W Spencer § B Gill, R Gaughan and C Hudson	
Extras b 5, w 5, nb 1	11
Total (8 wkts, 20 overs)	136

FoW: 1-50 (Johnson), 2-56 (W Dawson), 3-60 (Harland), 4-90 (M Dawson), 5-110 (Turnbull), 6-115 (Baxter), 7-129 (S Linsley), 8-128 (Audsley)

	O	M	R	W
Logan	4	0	13	2
Ashraf	2	0	22	0
Coad	2	0	10	0
Brown	3	0	28	1
Waite	4	0	22	2
Firn	2	0	19	0
R Gibson	2	0	7	2
Hodgson	1	0	10	1

Umpires: J Foxton and S Oldfield   Scorers: Mrs S Harland and H Clayton

This game came about as the result of a promise made by Yorkshire County Cricket Club Chief Executive Mark Arthur when he attended a club dinner in 2013. The Old Malton section of the club had lost their pavilion to fire, and a Yorkshire Eleven visit was planned to raise funds. The game lasted three hours, and £5,000 was raised for the new pavilion.
By mutual agreement no-balls attracted only one penalty run for this fixture.

Other Second Eleven Match
England Under-19s v. Yorkshire

Played at Sleaford CC on July 29 and 30, 2014 (first innings restricted to 60 overs)
Match drawn at 6.30pm on the Second Day
Toss won by England Under-19s
Close of play: First Day, Yorkshire 191-1 (Callis 92; Hodgson 36)

First Innings	ENGLAND UNDER-19s	Second Innings	
J A Tattersall, c Gibson b Firn	59		
D P Sibley, c Hodd b Ashraf	33	(5) not out	26
E G Barnard, c Callis b Coad	19	(2) c Hussain b Firn	76
* W M H Rhodes, not out	116		
T P Alsop, not out	38	(1) c Ashraf b |Logan	52
§ J M Clarke			
J Shaw			
T E Barber			
M A H Hammond	Did not bat	(4) c Wainman b Logan	17
R P Jones		(3) not out	75
L Wood			
B J Taylor			
Extras lb 5, nb 2	7	Extras lb 1, w 1, nb 10	12
Total (3 wkts, 60 overs, inns closed)	272	Total (3 wkts dec, 62 overs)	258

FoW: 1-62 (Sibley), 103 (Tattersall), 3-119 (Barnard)
2nd: 1-90 (Clarke), 2-175 (Barnard), 3-212 (Hammond)

	O	M	R	W		O	M	R	W
Coad	10	5	15	1	Coad	5	0	22	0
Wainman	10	1	37	0	Wainman	5	1	20	0
Ashraf	10	1	33	1	Ashraf	7	0	26	0
Waite	11	2	73	1	Warner	6	2	14	0
Warner	7	1	46	1	Firn	4	0	21	1
Firn	5	0	23	1	Logan	19	0	94	2
Logan	7	1	40	0	Fisher	8	0	35	0
					Callis	7	2	24	0
					Hodgson	1	0	1	0

First Innings	YORKSHIRE	Second Innings	
§ A J Hodd, b Taylor	56	(5) c Rhodes b Sibley	34
E Callis, not out	124	(1) b Sibley	13
D M Hodgson, st Clarke b Hammond	41	(2) c Tattersall b Jones	76
M Hussain, c Barnard b Barber	24	c Barnard b Rhodes	0
* R Gibson, not out	2	(4) b Sibley	26
M A Ashraf			
B O Coad		(9) b Barnard	0
N J Firn		(10) not out	0
J E G Logan	Did not bat		
J C Wainman		(6) c Jones b Tattersall	15
M J Waite		(8) not out	35
J Warner		(7) c Clarke b Barnard	23
M D Fisher			
Extras b 5, lb 2, nb 2	9	Extras b 13, lb1	14
Total (3 wkts dec, 50 overs)	256	Total (8 wkts, 37 overs)	232

FoW: 1-115 (Hodd); 2-217 (Hodgson); 3-250 (Hussain)
2nd: 1-49 (Callis), 2-57 (Hussain), 3-110 (Hodgson), 4-136 (Gibson), 5-161 (Hodd), 6-185 (Wainman), 7-214 (Warner), 8-228 (Coad)

	O	M	R	W		O	M	R	W
Wood	10	3	34	0	Wood	7	2	29	0
Shaw	8	0	39	0	Shaw	6	1	49	0
Barnard	3	2	5	0	Barnard	3	0	13	2
Hammond	9	1	82	1	Rhodes	7	2	27	2
Barber	7	0	36	1	Sibley	7	0	34	2
Rhodes	4	1	13	0	Jones	4	0	42	1
Taylor	7	0	35	1	Tattersall	3	0	29	1
Sibley	2	0	5	0					

Umpires: T Lungley and N R Roper
Scorers: R Dickinson and H Clayton

Other Second Eleven Match
Yorkshire v. Nottinghamshire

Played at Harrogate on September 1, 2 and 3, 2014
Yorkshire won by 2 runs at 5.47pm on the Third Day
Toss won by Yorkshire

Close of play: First Day, Nottinghamshire 63-1 (Wood 30, W T Root 0); Second Day, Yorkshire 3-3 (Rhodes 16, Gibson 25)

First Innings		YORKSHIRE	Second Innings	
J Hodd, c Franks b Tillcock	166		lbw b Hutton	15
Callis, c Wood b Hutton	48		lbw b Franks	1
D M Hodgson, c Wood b Hutton	0		(3) b Hutton	0
A Tattersall, c Hutton b Franks	0		(4) b Carter	32
W M H Rhodes, b Carter	8		(5) lbw b Tillcock	127
Gibson, c and b Franks	37		(6) c Freeman b Carter	16
J Waite, lbw b Franks	0		(7) st Cross b Carter	16
Shaw, c Cross b Dal	58		(8) c Kitt b Carter	6
C Wainman, c Carter b Wood	16		(9) st Cross b Tillcock	9
Warner, c Freeman b Wood	16		(10) c Dal b Tillcock	11
Carver, not out	2		(11) not out	0
A Ashraf		Did not bat		
Extras b 8, lb 3, w 9	20		Extras b 4, lb 6, nb 4	14
Total (83 overs)	371		Total (55.3 overs)	249

FoW: 1-87 (Callis), 2-87 (Hodgson), 3-88 (Tattersall), 4-125 (Rhodes), 5-208 (Gibson), 6-208 (Waite), 7-318 (Shaw), 8-344 (Hodd), 9-358 (Wainman), 10-371 (Warner)
FoW: 1-16 (Hodd), 2-16 (Callis), 3-18 (Tattersall), 4-113 (Rhodes), 5-175 (Waite), 6-203 (Shaw), 7-229 (Wainman), 8-229 (Gibson), 9-249 (Carver), 10-249 (Warner)

	O	M	R	W		O	M	R	W
Hutton	19	3	75	2	Hutton	11	0	61	2
Kitt	9	0	71	0	Kitt	5	0	28	0
Wood	14	4	52	2	Wood	8	0	32	0
Franks	12	4	30	3	Franks	5	2	16	1
Carter	11	0	56	1	Carter	19	5	71	4
Tillcock	14	1	53	1	Tillcock	7.3	0	31	3
Dal	6	0	23	1					

First Innings		NOTTINGHAMSHIRE	Second Innings	
K W Wood, c Callis b Carver	114		c Warner b Ashraf	18
D Libby, b Hodgson b Shaw	29		c Rhodes b Shaw	112
W T Root, c Warner b Wainman	49		c Shaw b Wainman	24
Dal, c Callis b Tattersall	56		run out (Hodd)	7
Freeman, c Callis b Ashraf	3		c Callis b Shaw	26
M H Cross, not out	12		c and b Rhodes	5
D Tillcock			b Shaw	34
P J Franks		Did not bat	lbw b Carver	10
M Carter			b Shaw	22
M Kitt			run out (Rhodes)	18
			not out	0
Extras b 13, lb 8	21		Extras lb 4, nb 2	6
Total (5 wkts dec, 104.2 overs)	336		Total (53.5 overs)	282

FoW: 1-57 (Libby), 2-162 (Root), 3-230 (Wood), 4-274 (Dal), 5-291 (Freeman),
FoW: 1-26 (Wood), 2-85 (Root), 3-97 (Dal), 4-173 (Hutton), 5-186 (Freeman), 6-228 (Cross), 7-233 (Libby), 8-247 (Tillcock), 9-278 (Carter), 10-282 (Franks)

	O	M	R	W		O	M	R	W
Ashraf	15	5	47	1	Ashraf	7	1	35	1
Waite	15	3	56	0	Waite	1	0	4	0
Shaw	9.2	2	29	1	Shaw	12.5	0	59	4
Wainman	14	2	48	1	Wainman	9	2	32	1
Warner	8	1	27	0	Warner	7	0	41	0
Carver	27	6	63	1	Carver	10	0	62	1
Gibson	2	0	9	0	Rhodes	5	0	33	1
Tattersall	14	1	36	1	Tattersall	2	0	12	0

Umpires: I J Dixon and R J Warren   Scorers: H Clayton and Mrs A Cusworth

Yorkshire v. Lancashire

Played at Headingley, Leeds, on September 10, 11 and 12, 2014

Lancashire won by 11 runs at 5.31pm on the Third Day

Toss won by Lancashire

Close of play, First Day: Yorkshire 40-0 (Hodd 26, Callis 7); Second Day: Lancashire 175 (Agathangelou 107, Hameed 65)

LANCASHIRE

First Innings				Second Innings	
L M Reece, b Tattersall			93		
H Hameed, c R Gibson b Ashraf			4	not out	65
A P Agathangelou, c Hodd b Shaw			9	(1) not out	107
L S Livingstone, b Rhodes b Shaw			204		
§ A L Davies, b Ashraf			85		
J Clark, not out			12		
R P Jones					
M H McKiernan					
S Mahmood	Did not bat				
L J Hurt					
D J Lamb					
A M Lilley					
Extras lb 5, w 1, nb 4			10	Extras lb 3	3
Total (5 wkts dec, 89.1 overs)			417	Total (0 wkts dec, 41 overs)	175

FoW: 1-17 (Hameed), 2-32 (Agathangelou), 3-222 (Reece), 4-397 (Davies), 5-417 (Livingstone

	O	M	R	W		O	M	R	W
Ashraf	15	3	55	2	Ashraf	5	1	15	0
Shaw	16.1	1	78	2	Shaw	4	1	22	0
R Gibson	3.3	0	29	0	Wainman	6	2	12	0
Wainman	10	2	28	0	Warner	5	0	19	0
Warner	8.3	0	42	0	Carver	12	1	58	0
Carver	10	0	56	0	Rhodes	6	0	26	0
Rhoders	8	1	31	0	Tattersall	3	0	20	0
Tattersall	17	0	85	1					
Callis	1	0	8	0					

YORKSHIRE

First Innings				Second Innings	
§ A J Hodd, b Lilley			61	c McKiernan b Hurt	11
E Callis, lbw b Reece			31	st Davies b McKiernan	72
D M Hodgson, b Reece			5	c Davies b Jones	124
J A Tattersall, c Jones b Mahmood			6	b Mahmood	19
* W M H Rhodes, c Davies b Lilley			6	c Davies b Mahmood	9
R Gibson, lbw b Reece			10	c Agathangelou b Jones	21
J Shaw, c Hameed b Lilley			6	c Hameed b Jones	3
J C Wainman, c Davies b Hurt			12	c Jones b Reece	25
J Warner, c Agathangelou b Lilley			1	c Reece b Lilley	20
K Carver, not out			36	b Reece	2
M A Ashraf, c Livingstone b McKiernan			16	not out	2
B R Gibson	Did not bat				
Extras b 16, lb 11, w 1, nb 12			40	Extras b 21, lb 14, 8 nb	43
Total (74.1 overs)			230	Total (93.2 overs)	351

FoW: 1-87 (Callis), 2-95 (Hodgson), 3-111 (Tattersall), 4-128 (Rhodes), 5-137 (Hodd
1st 6-147 (R Gibson), 7-151 (Shaw), 8-157 (Warner), 9-169 (Wainman), 10-230 (Ashra
FoW: 1-15 (Hodd), 2-163 (Callis), 3-195 (Tattersall), 4-219 (Rhodes), 5-256 (R Gibson
2nd 6-280 (Shaw), 7-289 (Hodgson), 8-341 (Wainman), 9-345 (Carver), 10-351 (Warne

	O	M	R	W		O	M	R	W
Mahmood	15	3	39	1	Mahmood	11	2	45	2
Hurt	15	1	66	1	Hurt	10	0	45	1
Lilley	16	3	61	4	Lilley	27.2	3	68	1
Reece	19	6	17	3	Reece	9	1	28	2
McKiernan	11.1	3	20	1	McKiernan	10	2	36	1
					Livingstone	1	0	4	0
					Jones	12	5	43	3

Umpires: I J Dixon and P Willey — Scorers: H Clayton and C Rimmer

Other Second Eleven Match
Somerset v. Yorkshire

Played at Taunton Vale on September 16, 17 and 18, 2014
Somerset won by 10 wickets at 1.01pm on the Second Day
Toss won by Somerset

Close of play, First Day: Yorkshire (2) 36-1 (Hodd 24, Hodgson 3)

First Innings	YORKSHIRE		Second Innings	
A J Hodd, run out (Stewart)	4		c Regan b Davey	56
E Callis, c Regan b Davey	9		c Davey b Dibble	0
§ D M Hodgson, c Peatman b Dibble	0		c Waller b Meschede	4
J A Tattersall, lbw b Dibble	1		c Overton b Meschede	10
W M H Rhodes, c Regan b Meschede	9		c Regan b Dibble	5
R Gibson, c Davey b Stewart	33		c Dibble b Popplewell	14
J Shaw, lbw b Stewart	1		c Regan b Overton	17
J C Wainman, c Dibble b Peatman	17		c and b Overton	0
J Warner, b Overton	0		b Waller	4
K Carver, not out	0		lbw b Stewart	5
M A Ashraf, retired hurt	0		not out	39
* R K J Dawson	Did not bat			
Extras lb 1, nb 2	3		Extras b 6, lb 9, w 2	17
Total (24.4 overs)	77		Total (44.2 overs)	171

FoW: 1-6 (Hodd), 2-13 (Hodgson), 3-15 (Callis), 4-15 (Tattersall), 5-39 (Rhodes),
1st   6-40 (Shaw), 7-61 (Gibson), 8-65 (Warner), 9-77 (Wainman)

FoW: 1-1 (Callis), 2-49 (Hodgson), 3-75 (Hodd), 4-86 (Tattersall), 5-86 (Rhodes),
2nd   6-109 (Gibson), 7-117 (Shaw), 8-118 (Wainman), 9-123 (Warner), 10-171 (Carver)

	O	M	R	W		O	M	R	W
Dibble	6	1	8	2	Dibble	8	1	26	2
Davey	5	2	7	1	Davey	8	2	35	1
Meschede	5	1	17	1	Meschede	5	1	20	2
Stewart	5	1	32	2	Stewart	0.2	0	1	1
Overton	2	2	0	1	Overton	10	3	31	2
Peatman	1.4	0	12	1	Peatman	4	2	3	0
					Waller	6	1	33	1
					Popplewell	3	1	7	1

First Innings	SOMERSET		Second Innings	
* M T C Waller, c Rhodes b Warner	61		not out	10
S J D Underdown, c Hodgson b Wainman	2		not out	0
A W R Barrow, lbw b Shaw	20			
J H Davey, c Hodgson b Gibson	11			
C A J Meschede, b Gibson	4			
§ J A Regan, c Hodgson b Wainman	30			
A J Mellor, lbw b Carver	66			
A J Dibble, c Warner b Carver	8			
J Overton, b Carver	13			
C M Stewart, not out	2			
H G Popplewell, lbw b Carver	5			
J J Peatman	Did not bat			
Extras lb 2, nb 11	13		Extras lb 2, nb 2	4
Total (65 overs)	235		Total (0 wkts, 2.5 overs)	10

FoW: 1-36 (Underdown), 2-78 (Waller), 3-96 (Barrow), 4-105 (Meschede), 5-110 (Davey),
6-196 (Mellor), 7-206 (Dibble), 8-228 (Overton), 9-228 (Regan), 10-235 (Popplewell)

	O	M	R	W		O	M	R	W
Shaw	14	3	50	1	Ashraf	1.5	0	12	0
Wainman	16	7	26	2	Warner	1	1	0	0
Warner	7	0	53	1					
Gibson	5	0	20	2					
Rhodes	7	2	18	0					
Carver	16	3	66	4					

Umpires: I D Blackwell and N J Llong   Scorers: Mrs L M (Polly) Rhodes and H Clayton

239

YORKSHIRE ECB COUNTY PREMIER LEAGUE 2014

*	P	CW	CL	IW1	IL1	IW2	IL2	IW3	IL3	C	A	T	Points
Yorkshire Acad. (2)	24	13	0	0	0	0	0	3	2	5	1	0	140
York (1)	24	12	5	0	0	0	0	2	3	3	0	0	126
Barnsley (8)	24	8	4	0	1	1	0	1	1	5	3	0	102
Harrogate (3)	24	9	6	0	0	1	1	0	1	4	2	0	97
Cleethorpes (9)	24	8	4	0	1	0	0	0	1	7	3	0	96
Sheffield Coll. (7)	24	5	4	0	1	0	1	3	1	6	3	0	88
Driffield Town (6)	24	3	6	2	0	1	0	3	1	3	5	0	84
Doncaster Town ((5)	24	6	8	0	0	0	1	2	0	4	3	0	82
Rotherham Town ((11)	24	5	4	0	0	1	1	1	1	4	6	2	0	77
Appleby Frod. (10)	24	5	8	1	0	0	0	2	2	2	4	0	76
Castleford (13)	24	2	6	0	0	2	1	2	4	4	3	0	62
Scarborough (4)	24	1	11	0	0	0	0	3	2	5	2	0	47
Sheffield United (14)	24	1	15	0	0	0	1	0	1	4	2	0	27

* P = Played; CW = Complete win (8 points); CL = Complete loss (0 points); IW1 = Incomplete win (6 points); IL1 = Incomplete loss (2 points); IW2 = Incomplete win (6 points); IL2 = Incomplete loss 1 (1 point); IW3 = Incomplete win (6 points); IL3 = Incomplete loss (0 points); C = Cancelled no play (3 points); A = Abandoned incomplete (3 points); T = Tied (4 points)

(2013 positions in brackets. Hull return to the League in 2015, having not competed in 2014)

Yorkshire League Cup: Winners: Yorkshire Academy. Runners-up: Barnsley

YORKSHIRE ACADEMY BATTING IN ECB LEAGUE AND CUP

Player	M.	I.	N.O.	Runs	H.S.	Avge	100s	50s	Run Rate	ct/st
R Gibson	22	20	4	883	160	55.18	3	4	89.25	5
W M H Rhodes	19	17	2	783	128*	52.20	3	4	86.14	6
E Callis	23	22	1	890	139	42.38	3	2	73.45	7
J Shaw	13	8	3	143	75	28.60	0	1	101.47	—
Azeem Rafiq	6	6	1	136	79	27.20	0	1	80.47	—
M Hussain	18	17	5	316	50	26.33	0	1	47.59	5
J A Thompson	22	19	4	378	60	25.20	0	2	81.16	7
J Warner	19	9	5	94	23	23.50	0	0	69.11	4
B P Gibson	24	18	2	353	49	22.06	0	0	69.70	35/4
B L Ainsley	7	5	0	104	49	20.80	0	0	45.81	—
Y Imtiaz	7	4	0	81	47	20.25	0	0	75.00	—
K Carver	18	6	4	35	10*	17.50	0	0	166.66	2
E Barnes	9	5	3	34	17*	17.00	0	0	75.55	—
M J Waite	24	14	4	170	49	17.00	0	0	125.92	5
M D Fisher	14	6	3	49	21	16.33	0	0	132.43	7
L Stabler	4	3	1	18	11*	9.00	0	0	163.63	—
J G E Logan	11	4	1	9	5	3.00	0	0	33.33	—

YORKSHIRE ACADEMY BOWLING IN ECB LEAGUE AND CUP

Player	Overs	Mdns	Runs	Wkts	Avge	Best	5wI	Econ.	Strike Rate
B P Gibson	2	1	1	3	0.33	3-1	0	0.50	4.00
A U Rashid	11	5	21	6	3.50	6-21	1	1.90	11.00
J C Wainman	8	2	12	3	4.00	3-7	0	1.50	16.00
J Warner	87.2	8	321	39	8.23	5-21	1	3.67	13.43
J G E Logan	101.1	27	266	23	11.56	6-39	1	2.62	26.39
E Barnes	44.3	7	135	11	12.27	4-34	0	3.08	23.36
M D Fisher	99.2	21	280	21	13.33	4-30	0	2.81	28.40
K Carver	128.5	22	404	27	14.96	5-32	2	3.13	28.62
J Shaw	76.4	8	315	20	15.75	4-16	0	4.10	23.00

RECORDS SECTION

(All records in this section relate to First-Class Yorkshire matches only — except where otherwise stated)

HONOURS

County Champions (33)

1867, 1870, 1893, 1896, 1898, 1900, 1901, 1902, 1905, 1908, 1912,
1919, 1922, 1923, 1924, 1925, 1931, 1932, 1933, 1935, 1937, 1938,
1939, 1946, 1959, 1960, 1962, 1963, 1966, 1967, 1968, 2001, 2014

Joint Champions (2)
1869, 1949

Promoted to Division 1
2005
2012

Gillette Cup Winners (2)
1965, 1969

Cheltenham & Gloucester Trophy (1)
2002

Benson & Hedges Cup Winners (1)
1987

John Player Special League Winners (1)
1983

Fenner Trophy Winners (3)
1972, 1974, 1981

Asda Challenge Winners (1)
1987

Ward Knockout Cup (1)
1989

Joshua Tetley Festival Trophy (7)
1991, 1992 (Joint), 1993, 1994, 1996, 1997 and 1998

Tilcon Trophy Winners (2)
1978 and 1988

Pro-Arch Trophy (1)
2007-08

Second Eleven Champions (4)
1977, 1984, 1991, 2003

Joint Champions (1)
1987

Minor Counties Champions (5)
1947, 1957, 1958, 1968, 1971

Under-25 Competition Winners (3)
1976, 1978, 1987

Bain Clarkson Trophy Winners (2)
1988 and 1994

Second Eleven Trophy (1)
2009

YORKSHIRE'S CHAMPIONSHIP CAPTAINS

1867 to 2014

R Iddison (2)	1867, 1870
Lord Hawke (8)	1893, 1896, 1898, 1900, 1901, 1902, 1905, 1908
Sir Archibald White (1)	1912
D C F Burton (1)	1919
G Wilson (3)	1922, 1923, 1924
A W Lupton (1)	1925
F E Greenwood (2)	1931, 1932
A B Sellers (6)	1933, 1935, 1937, 1938, 1939, 1946
J R Burnet (1)	1959
J V Wilson (2)	1960, 1962
D B Close (4)	1963, 1966, 1967, 1968
D Byas (1)	2001
A W Gale (1)	2014

Joint Champions

R Iddison (1)	1869
N W D Yardley (1)	1949

RECORDS SECTION INDEX

CHAMPION COUNTIES SINCE 1873

The County Championship

The County Championship was officially constituted in 1890, and before that Yorkshire were generally considered Champions by the Press in 1867 and 1870, and equal top in 1869. From 1873 the list was generally accepted in the form as it is today.

		Yorkshire's Position
1873	{ Gloucestershire / Nottinghamshire	.......7th
1874	Gloucestershire	.4th
1875	Nottinghamshire	.4th
1876	Gloucestershire	.3rd
1877	Gloucestershire	.7th
1878	Middlesex	.6th
1879	Nottinghamshire/Lancashire	..6th
1880	Nottinghamshire	.5th
1881	Lancashire	.3rd
1882	Nottinghamshire/Lancashire	..3rd
1883	Nottinghamshire	.2nd
1884	Nottinghamshire	.3rd
1885	Nottinghamshire	.2nd
1886	Nottinghamshire	.4th
1887	Surrey	.3rd
1888	Surrey	.2nd
1889	{ Surrey/Lancashire / Nottinghamshire	.......7th
1890	Surrey	.3rd
1891	Surrey	.8th
1892	Surrey	.6th
1893	**Yorkshire**	**1st**
1894	Surrey	.2nd
1895	Surrey	.3rd
1896	**Yorkshire**	**1st**
1897	Lancashire	.4th
1898	**Yorkshire**	**1st**
1899	Surrey	.3rd
1900	**Yorkshire**	**1st**
1901	**Yorkshire**	**1st**
1902	**Yorkshire**	**1st**
1903	Middlesex	.3rd
1904	Lancashire	.2nd
1905	**Yorkshire**	**1st**
1906	Kent	.2nd
1907	Nottinghamshire	.2nd
1908	**Yorkshire**	**1st**

		Yorkshire's Position
1909	Kent	.3rd
1910	Kent	.8th
1911	Warwickshire	.7th
1912	**Yorkshire**	**1st**
1913	Kent	.2nd
1914	Surrey	.4th
1919	**Yorkshire**	**1st**
1920	Middlesex	.4th
1921	Middlesex	.3rd
1922	**Yorkshire**	**1st**
1923	**Yorkshire**	**1st**
1924	**Yorkshire**	**1st**
1925	**Yorkshire**	**1st**
1926	Lancashire	.2nd
1927	Lancashire	.3rd
1928	Lancashire	.4th
1929	Nottinghamshire	.2nd
1930	Lancashire	.3rd
1931	**Yorkshire**	**1st**
1932	**Yorkshire**	**1st**
1933	**Yorkshire**	**1st**
1934	Lancashire	.5th
1935	**Yorkshire**	**1st**
1936	Derbyshire	.3rd
1937	**Yorkshire**	**1st**
1938	**Yorkshire**	**1st**
1939	**Yorkshire**	**1st**
1946	**Yorkshire**	**1st**
1947	Middlesex	.7th
1948	Glamorgan	.4th
1949	**Yorkshire/Middlesex**	**1st**
1950	Lancashire/Surrey	.3rd
1951	Warwickshire	.2nd
1952	Surrey	.2nd
1953	Surrey	.12th
1954	Surrey	.2nd
1955	Surrey	.2nd
1956	Surrey	.7th
1957	Surrey	.3rd

		Yorkshire's Position			*Yorkshire's Position*
1958	Surrey	11th	1987	Nottinghamshire	8th
1959	**Yorkshire**	**1st**	1988	Worcestershire	13th
1960	**Yorkshire**	**1st**	1989	Worcestershire	16th
1961	Hampshire	2nd	1990	Middlesex	10th
1962	**Yorkshire**	**1st**	1991	Essex	14th
1963	**Yorkshire**	**1st**	1992	Essex	16th
1964	Worcestershire	5th	1993	Middlesex	12th
1965	Worcestershire	4th	1994	Warwickshire	13th
1966	**Yorkshire**	**1st**	1995	Warwickshire	8th
1967	**Yorkshire**	**1st**	1996	Leicestershire	6th
1968	**Yorkshire**	**1st**	1997	Glamorgan	6th
1969	Glamorgan	13th	1998	Leicestershire	3rd
1970	Kent	4th	1999	Surrey	6th
1971	Surrey	13th	2000	Surrey	3rd
1972	Warwickshire	10th	**2001**	**Yorkshire**	**1st**
1973	Hampshire	14th	2002	Surrey	9th
1974	Worcestershire	11th	2003	Sussex	Div 2, 4th
1975	Leicestershire	2nd	2004	Warwickshire	Div 2, 7th
1976	Middlesex	8th	2005	Nottinghamshire	Div 2, 3rd
1977	Kent/Middlesex	12th	2006	Sussex	Div 1, 6th
1978	Kent	4th	2007	Sussex	Div 1, 6th
1979	Essex	7th	2008	Durham	Div 1, 7th
1980	Middlesex	6th	2009	Durham	Div 1, 7th
1981	Nottinghamshire	10th	2010	Nottinghamshire	Div 1, 3rd
1982	Middlesex	10th	2011	Lancashire	Div 1, 8th
1983	Essex	17th	2012	Warwickshire	Div 2, 2nd
1984	Essex	14th	2013	Durham	Div 1, 2nd
1985	Middlesex	11th	**2014**	**Yorkshire**	**Div 1, 1st**
1986	Essex	10th			

SEASON-BY-SEASON RECORD OF ALL FIRST-CLASS MATCHES PLAYED BY YORKSHIRE 1863-2014

Season	Played	Won	Lost	Drawn	Abd§	Season	Played	Won	Lost	Drawn	Abd§
1863	4	2	1	1	0	1921	30	17	5	8	0
1864	7	2	4	1	0	1922	33	20	2	11	0
1865	9	0	7	2	0	1923	35	26	1	8	0
1866	3	0	2	1	0	1924	35	18	4	13	0
1867	7	7	0	0	0	1925	36	22	0	14	0
1868	7	4	3	0	0	1926	35	14	0	21	1
1869	5	4	1	0	0	1927	34	11	3	20	1
1870	7	6	0	1	0	1928	32	9	0	23	0
1871	7	3	3	1	0	1929	35	11	2	22	0
1872	10	2	7	1	0	1930	34	13	3	18	2
1873	13	7	5	1	0	1931	33	17	1	15	1
1874	14	10	3	1	0	1932	32	21	2	9	2
1875	12	6	4	2	0	1933	36	21	5	10	0
1876	12	5	3	4	0	1934	35	14	7	14	0
1877	14	2	7	5	0	1935	36	24	2	10	0
1878	20	10	7	3	0	1935-6	3	1	0	2	0
1879	17	7	5	5	0	1936	35	14	2	19	0
1880	20	6	8	6	0	1937	34	22	3	9	1
1881	20	11	6	3	0	1938	36	22	2	12	0
1882	24	11	9	4	0	1939	34	23	4	7	1
1883	19	10	2	7	0	1945	2	0	0	2	0
1884	20	10	6	4	0	1946	31	20	1	10	0
1885	21	8	3	10	0	1947	32	10	9	13	0
1886	21	5	8	8	0	1948	31	11	6	14	0
1887	20	6	5	9	0	1949	33	16	3	14	0
1888	20	7	7	6	0	1950	34	16	6	12	1
1889	16	3	11	2	1	1951	35	14	3	18	0
1890	20	10	4	6	0	1952	34	17	3	14	0
1891	17	5	11	1	2	1953	35	7	7	21	0
1892	19	6	6	7	0	1954	35	16	3	16*	0
1893	23	15	5	3	0	1955	33	23	6	4	0
1894	28	18	6	4	1	1956	35	11	7	17	0
1895	31	15	10	6	0	1957	34	16	5	13	1
1896	32	17	6	9	0	1958	33	10	8	15	2
1897	30	14	7	9	0	1959	35	18	8	9	0
1898	30	18	3	9	0	1960	38	19	7	12	0
1899	34	17	4	13	0	1961	39	19	5	15	0
1900	32	19	1	12	0	1962	37	16	5	16	0
1901	35	23	2	10	1	1963	33	14	4	15	0
1902	31	15	3	13	1	1964	33	12	4	17	0
1903	31	16	5	10	0	1965	33	12	4	17	0
1904	32	10	2	20	1	1966	32	16	6	10	1
1905	33	21	4	8	0	1967	31	16	5	10	2
1906	33	19	6	8	0	1968	32	13	4	15	0
1907	31	14	5	12	2	1969	29	4	7	18	0
1908	33	19	0	14	0	1970	26	10	5	11	0
1909	30	12	5	13	0	1971	27	5	8	14	0
1910	31	11	8	12	0	1972	21	4	5	12	1
1911	32	16	9	7	0	1973	22	3	5	14*	0
1912	35	14	3	18	1	1974	22	6	7	9	1
1913	32	16	5	11	0	1975	21	11	1	9	0
1914	31	16	4	11	2	1976	22	7	7	8	0
1919	31	12	5	14	0	1977	23	7	5	11	1
1920	30	17	6	7	0	1978	24	10	3	11	1

Season	Played	Won	Lost	Drawn	Abd§	Season	Played	Won	Lost	Drawn	Abd§
1979	22	6	3	13	1	1997	20	7	4	9	0
1980	24	5	4	15	0	1998	19	9	3	7	0
1981	24	5	9	10	0	1999	17	8	6	3	0
1982	22	5	1	16	1	2000	18	7	4	7	0
1983	23	1	5	17	1	2001	16	9	3	4	0
1984	24	5	4	15	0	2002	16	2	8	6	0
1985	25	3	4	18	1	2003	17	4	5	8	0
1986	25	4	6	15	0	2004	16	3	4	9	0
1986-7	1	0	0	1	0	2005	17	6	1	10	0
1987	24	7	4	13	1	2006	16	3	6	7	0
1988	24	5	6	13	0	2007	17	5	4	8	0
1989	22	3	9	10	0	2008	16	2	5	9	0
1990	24	5	9	10	0	2009	17	2	2	13	0
1991	24	4	6	14	0	2010	18	6	2	10	0
1991-2	1	0	1	0	0	2011	17	4	6	7	0
1992	22	4	6	12	1	2012	17	5	0	12	0
1992-3	1	0	0	1	0	2013	17	8	2	7	0
1993	19	6	4	9	0	2014	17	8	1	8	0
1994	20	7	6	7	0						
1995	20	8	8	4	0		3566	1499	648	1419	38
1995-6	2	2	0	0	0						
1996	19	8	5	6	0	*Includes one tie in each season.					

§ All these matches were abandoned without a ball being bowled, except Yorkshire v Kent at Harrogate, 1904, which was abandoned under Law 9. The two in 1914 and the one in 1939 were abandoned because of war. All these matches are excluded from the total played.

Of the 1,499 matches won, 515 have been by an innings margin, 85 by 200 runs or more, and 132 by 10 wickets. Of the 648 matches lost, 109 have been by an innings margin, 12 by 200 runs or more and 34 by 10 wickets.

ANALYSIS OF RESULTS VERSUS ALL FIRST-CLASS
TEAMS 1863-2014

COUNTY CHAMPIONSHIP

Opponents	Played	Won	Lost	Drawn	Tied
Derbyshire	205	103	19	83	0
Durham	32	13	8	11	0
Essex	160	84	25	51	0
Glamorgan	111	53	13	45	0
Gloucestershire	200	102	43	55	0
Hampshire	165	72	19	74	0
Kent	200	84	39	77	0
Lancashire	255	75	52	128	0
Leicestershire	166	84	15	66	1
Middlesex	229	81	55	92	1
Northamptonshire	142	67	26	49	0
Nottinghamshire	250	89	47	114	0
Somerset	169	89	22	58	0
Surrey	240	85	67	88	0
Sussex	197	84	33	80	0
Warwickshire	186	83	31	72	0
Worcestershire	138	68	21	49	0
Cambridgeshire	8	3	4	1	0
Total	3053	1319	539	1193	2

OTHER FIRST-CLASS MATCHES

Opponents	Played	Won	Lost	Drawn	Tied
Derbyshire	2	1	1	0	0
Essex	2	2	0	0	0
Hampshire	1	0	0	1	0
Lancashire	12	5	3	4	0
Leicestershire	2	1	1	0	0
Middlesex	1	1	0	0	0
Nottinghamshire	2	1	1	0	0
Surrey	1	0	0	1	0
Sussex	2	0	0	2	0
Warwickshire	2	0	0	2	0
Totals	27	11	6	10	0
Australians	55	6	19	30	0
Indians	14	5	1	8	0
New Zealanders	10	2	0	8	0
Pakistanis	4	1	0	3	0
South Africans	17	1	3	13	0
Sri Lankans	3	0	0	3	0
West Indians	17	3	7	7	0
Zimbabweans	2	0	1	1	0
Bangladesh A	1	1	0	0	0
India A	2	0	0	2	0
Pakistan A	1	1	0	0	0
South Africa A	1	0	0	1	0
Totals	127	20	31	76	0
Cambridge University/U C C E	88	42	17	29	0
Canadians	1	1	0	0	0
Combined Services	1	0	0	1	0
Durham MCCU	1	1	0	0	0
England XI's	6	1	2	3	0
Hon. M.B. Hawke's XI	1	0	1	0	0
International XI	1	1	0	0	0
Ireland	3	3	0	0	0
Jamaica	3	1	0	2	0
Leeds/Bradford MCCU	3	1	0	2	0
Liverpool and District*	3	2	1	0	0
Loughborough UCCE	2	1	0	1	0
MCC	153	54	39	60	0
Mashonaland	1	1	0	0	0
Matebeleland	1	1	0	0	0
Minor Counties	1	1	0	0	0
Oxford University	44	21	3	20	0
Philadelphians	1	0	0	1	0
Rest of England	16	4	5	7	0
Royal Air Force	1	0	0	1	0
Scotland**	11	7	0	4	0
South of England	2	1	0	1	0
C. I. Thornton's XI	5	2	0	3	0
United South of England	1	1	0	0	0
Western Province	2	0	1	1	0
Windward Islands	1	0	0	1	0
I Zingari	6	2	3	1	0
Totals	359	149	72	138	0
Grand Totals	3566	1499	648	1417	2

*Matches played in 1889, 1891, 1892 and 1893 are excluded. **Match played in 1878 is included

ABANDONED MATCHES (38)

1889	v. MCC at Lord's
1891 (2)	v. MCC at Lord's
	v. MCC at Scarborough
1894	v. Kent at Bradford
1901	v. Surrey at The Oval
1902	v. Leicestershire at Leicester (AR)
1904	v. Kent at Harrogate (Law 9 — now Law 10)
1907 (2)	v. Derbyshire at Sheffield
	v. Nottinghamshire at Huddersfield
1912	v. Surrey at Sheffield
1914 (2)	v. England at Harrogate (due to war)
	v. MCC at Scarborough (due to war)
1926	v. Nottinghamshire at Leeds
1927	v. Kent at Bradford
1930 (2)	v. Derbyshire at Chesterfield*
	v. Northamptonshire at Harrogate*
1931	v. Sussex at Hull
1932 (2)	v. Derbyshire at Chesterfield
	v. Kent at Sheffield
1937	v. Cambridge University at Bradford
1939	v. MCC at Scarborough (due to war)
1950	v. Cambridge University at Cambridge
1957	v. West Indians at Bradford
1958 (2)	v. Nottinghamshire at Hull
	v. Worcestershire at Bradford
1966	v. Oxford University at Oxford
1967 (2)	v. Leicestershire at Leeds
	v. Lancashire at Manchester
1972	v. Australians at Bradford
1974	v. Hampshire at Bournemouth
1977	v. Gloucestershire at Bristol
1978	v. Pakistan at Bradford
1979	v. Nottinghamshire at Sheffield (AP)
1982	v. Nottinghamshire at Harrogate
1983	v. Middlesex at Lord's
1985	v. Essex at Sheffield (AP)
1987	v. Sussex at Hastings
1992	v. Oxford University at Oxford

*Consecutive matches

ANALYSIS OF RESULTS ON GROUNDS IN YORKSHIRE USED IN 2014

FIRST-CLASS MATCHES

Ground	Played	Won	Lost	Drawn	Tied
Leeds Headingley 1891-2014	438	162 (36.98%)	78 (17.81%)	198 (45.21%)	0 (0.00%)
Scarborough North Marine Road 1874-2014	249	100 (40.16%)	35 (14.06%)	114 (45.78%)	0 (0.00%)

HIGHEST MATCH AGGREGATES – OVER 1350 RUNS

Runs	Wkts	
1665	33	Yorkshire (351 and 481) lost to Warwickshire (601:9 dec and 232:4) by 6 wkts at Birmingham, 2002
1606	31	Yorkshire (438 and 363:5 dec) lost to Somerset (326 and 479:6) by 4 wkts at Taunton, 2009
1479	28	Yorkshire (405 and 333:4 dec) lost to Somerset (377 and 364:4) by 6 wkts at Taunton , 2010
1473	17	Yorkshire (600:4 dec. and 231:3 dec.) drew with Worcestershire (453:5 dec. and 189:5) at Scarborough, 1995.
1442	29	Yorkshire (501:6 dec. and 244:6 dec.) beat Lancashire (403:7 dec. and 294) by 48 runs at Scarborough, 1991.
1439	32	Yorkshire (536:8 dec. and 205:7 dec.) beat Glamorgan (482: 7 dec. and 216) by 43 runs at Cardiff, 1996.
1431	32	Yorkshire (388 and 312:6) drew with Sussex (398 and 333:6 dec) at Scarborough, 2011
1417	33	Yorkshire (422 and 193:7) drew with Glamorgan (466 and 336:6 dec) at Colwyn Bay, 2003
1406	37	Yorkshire (354 and 341:8) drew with Derbyshire (406 and 305:9 dec) at Derby, 2004
1400	32	Yorkshire (299 and 439: 4 dec.) drew with Hampshire (296 and 366:8) at Southampton, 2007
1393	35	Yorkshire (331 and 278) lost to Kent (377 and 407:5 dec) by 175 runs at Maidstone, 1994.
1390	34	Yorkshire (431:8 dec and 265:7) beat Hampshire (429 and 265) by 3 wkts at Southampton, 1995.
1390	33	Durham (573 and 124:3) beat Yorkahire (274 and 419) by 7 wkts at Scarborough, 2013.
1376	33	Yorkshire (531 and 158:3) beat Lancashire (373 and 314) by 7 wkts at Leeds, 2001
1376	20	Yorkshire (677: 7 dec.) drew with Durham (518 and 181:3 dec.) at Leeds, 2006
1374	36	Yorkshire (594: 9 dec. and 266:7 dec.) beat Surrey (344 and 170) by 346 runs at The Oval, 2007
1373	36	Yorkshire (520 and 114:6) drew with Derbyshire (216 and 523) at Derby, 2005
1364	35	Yorkshire (216 and 433) lost to Warwickshire (316 and 399:5 dec.) by 66 runs at Birmingham, 2006
1359	25	Yorkshire (561 and 138:3 dec.) drew with Derbyshire (412:4 dec. and 248:8) at Sheffield, 1996.
1359	30	Yorkshire (358 and 321) lost to Somerset (452 and 228:0) by 10 wkts at Taunton, 2011
1353	18	Yorkshire (377:2 dec. and 300:6) beat Derbyshire (475:7 dec. and 201:3 dec.) by 4 wkts at Scarborough, 1990.

LOWEST MATCH AGGREGATES – UNDER 225 RUNS IN A COMPLETED MATCH

Runs	Wkts	
165	30	Yorkshire (46 and 37:0) beat Nottinghamshire (24 and 58 by 10 wkts at Sheffield, 1888.
175	29	Yorkshire (104) beat Essex (30 and 41) by an innings and 33 runs at Leyton, 1901.
182	15	Yorkshire (4:0 dec. and 88.5) beat Northamptonshire (4:0 dec. and 86) by 5 wkts at Bradford, 1931.
193	29	Yorkshire (99) beat Worcestershire (43 and 51) by an innings and 5 runs at Bradford, 1900.
219	30	Yorkshire (113) beat Nottinghamshire (71 and 35) by an innings and 7 runs at Nottingham, 1881.
222	32	Yorkshire (98 and 14:2) beat Gloucestershire (68 and 42) by 8 wkts at Gloucester, 1924.
223	40	Yorkshire (58 and 51) lost to Lancashire (64 and 50) by 5 runs at Manchester, 1893.

LOWEST MATCH AGGREGATES – UNDER 325 RUNS IN A MATCH IN WHICH ALL 40 WICKETS FELL

Runs	Wkts	
223	40	Yorkshire (58 and 51) lost to Lancashire (64 and 50) by 5 runs at Manchester, 1893.
288	40	Yorkshire (55 and 68) lost to Lancashire (89 and 76) by 42 runs at Sheffield, 1872.
295	40	Yorkshire (71 and 63) lost to Surrey (56 and 105) by 27 runs at The Oval, 1886.
303	40	Yorkshire (109 and 77) beat Middlesex (63 and 54) by 69 runs at Lord's, 1891.
318	40	Yorkshire (96 and 96) beat Lancashire (39 and 87) by 66 runs at Manchester, 1874.
318	40	Yorkshire (94 and 104) beat Northamptonshire (61 and 59) by 78 runs at Bradford, 1955.
319	40	Yorkshire (84 and 72) lost to Derbyshire (106 and 57) by 7 runs at Derby, 1878.
320	40	Yorkshire (98 and 91) beat Surrey (72 and 59) by 58 runs at Sheffield, 1893.
321	40	Yorkshire (88 and 37) lost to I Zingari (103 and 93) by 71 runs at Scarborough, 1877.
321	40	Yorkshire (80 and 67) lost to Derbyshire (129 and 45) by 27 runs at Sheffield, 1879.

LARGE MARGINS OF VICTORY – BY AN INNINGS AND OVER 250 RUNS

Inns and 397 runs	Yorkshire (548:4 dec.) beat Northamptonshire (58 and 93) at Harrogate, 1921.
Inns and 387 runs	Yorkshire (662) beat Derbyshire (118 and 157) at Chesterfield, 1898.
Inns and 343 runs	Yorkshire (673:8 dec) beat Northamptonshire (184 and 146) at Leeds, 2003
Inns and 321 runs	Yorkshire (437) beat Leicestershire (58 and 58) at Leicester, 1908.
Inns and 314 runs	Yorkshire (356:8 dec) beat Northamptonshire (27 and 15) at Northampton, 1908. (Yorkshire's first match v. Northamptonshire).
Inns and 313 runs	Yorkshire (555:1 dec) beat Essex (78 and 164) at Leyton, 1932.
Inns and 307 runs	Yorkshire (681:5 dec.) beat Sussex (164 and 210) at Sheffield, 1897.
Inns and 302 runs	Yorkshire (660) beat Leicestershire (165 and 193) at Leicester, 1896.
Inns and 301 runs	Yorkshire (499) beat Somerset (125 and 73) at Bath, 1899.
Inns and 294 runs	Yorkshire (425:7 dec.) beat Gloucestershire (47 and 84) at Bristol, 1964.

LARGE MARGINS OF VICTORY – BY AN INNINGS
AND OVER 250 RUNS *(Continued)*

Inns and 284 runs	Yorkshire (467:7 dec) beat Leicestershire (111 and 72) at Bradford, 1932.
Inns and 282 runs	Yorkshire (481:8 dec) beat Derbyshire (106 and 93) at Huddersfield, 1901.
Inns and 280 runs	Yorkshire (562) beat Leicestershire (164 and 118) at Dewsbury, 1903.
Inns and 271 runs	Yorkshire (460) beat Hampshire (128 and 61) at Hull, 1900.
Inns and 271 runs	Yorkshire (495:5 dec) beat Warwickshire (99 and 125) at Huddersfield, 1922.
Inns and 266 runs	Yorkshire (352) beat Cambridgeshire (40 and 46) at Hunslet, 1869.
Inns and 260 runs	Yorkshire (521: 7dec.) beat Worcestershire (129 and 132) at Leeds, 2007.
Inns and 258 runs	Yorkshire (404:2 dec) beat Glamorgan (78 and 68) at Cardiff, 1922. (Yorkshire's first match v. Glamorgan).
Inns and 256 runs	Yorkshire (486) beat Leicestershire (137 and 93) at Sheffield, 1895.
Inns and 251 runs	Yorkshire (550) beat Leicestershire (154 and 145) at Leicester, 1933.

LARGE MARGINS OF VICTORY – BY OVER 300 RUNS

389 runs	Yorkshire (368 and 280:1 dec) beat Somerset (125 and 134) at Bath, 1906.
370 runs	Yorkshire (194 and 274) beat Hampshire (62 and 36) at Leeds, 1904.
351 runs	Yorkshire (280 and 331) beat Northamptonshire (146 and 114) at Northampton, 1947.
346 runs	Yorkshire (594: 9 dec. and 266: 7 dec.) beat Surrey (344 and 179) at The Oval, 2007.
328 runs	Yorkshire (186 and 318:1 dec) beat Somerset (43 and 133) at Bradford, 1930.
328 runs	Yorkshire (280 and 277:7 dec) beat Glamorgan (104 and 105) at Swansea, 2001
320 runs	Yorkshire (331 and 353:9 dec) beat Durham (150 and 214) at Chester-le-Street, 2004
308 runs	Yorkshire (89 and 420) beat Warwickshire (72 and 129) at Birmingham, 1921.

LARGE MARGINS OF VICTORY – BY 10 WICKETS
(WITH OVER 100 RUNS SCORED IN THE 4th INNINGS)

4th Innings

167:0 wkt	Yorkshire (247 and 167:0) beat Northamptonshire 233 and 180) at Huddersfield, 1948.
147:0 wkt	Yorkshire (381 and 147:0) beat Middlesex (384 and 142) at Lord's, 1896.
142:0 wkt	Yorkshire (304 and 142:0) beat Sussex (254 and 188) at Bradford, 1887.
139:0 wkt	Yorkshire (163:9 dec and 139:0) beat Nottinghamshire (234 and 67) at Leeds, 1932.
138:0 wkt	Yorkshire (293 and 138:0) beat Hampshire (251 and 179) at Southampton, 1897.
132:0 wkt	Yorkshire (328 and 132:0) beat Northamptonshire (281 and 175) at Leeds, 2005
129:0 wkt	Yorkshire (355 and 129:0) beat Durham MCCU (196 and 287) at Durham, 2011
127:0 wkt	Yorkshire (258 and 127:0) beat Cambridge University (127 and 257) at Cambridge, 1930.
119:0 wkt	Yorkshire (109 and 119:0) beat Essex (108 and 119) at Leeds, 1931.
118:0 wkt	Yorkshire (121 and 118:0) beat MCC (125 and 113) at Lord's, 1883.
116:0 wkt	Yorkshire (147 and 116:0) beat Hampshire (141 and 120) at Bournemouth, 1930.
114:0 wkt	Yorkshire (135 and 114:0) beat Hampshire (71 and 176) at Bournemouth, 1948.

HEAVY DEFEATS – BY AN INNINGS
AND OVER 250 RUNS

Inns and 272 runs	Yorkshire (78 and 186) lost to Surrey (536) at The Oval, 1898.
Inns and 261 runs	Yorkshire (247 and 89) lost to Sussex (597: 8 dec.) at Hove, 2007.
Inns and 255 runs	Yorkshire (125 and 144) lost to All England XI (524) at Sheffield, 1865.

HEAVY DEFEATS – BY OVER 300 RUNS

324 runs	Yorkshire (247 and 204) lost to Gloucestershire (291 and 484) at Cheltenham, 1994.
305 runs	Yorkshire (119 and 51) lost to Cambridge University (312 and 163) at Cambridge, 1906.

HEAVY DEFEATS – BY 10 WICKETS
(WITH OVER 100 RUNS SCORED IN THE 4th INNINGS)

4th Innings

228:0 wkt   Yorkshire (358 and 321) lost to Somerset (452 and 228:0)
          at Taunton, 2011

148:0 wkt   Yorkshire (83 and 216) lost to Lancashire (154 and 148:0)
          at Manchester, 1875.

119:0 wkt   Yorkshire (92 and 109) lost to Nottinghamshire (86 and 119:0 wkt)
          at Leeds, 1989.

108:0 wkt   Yorkshire (236 and 107) lost to Hampshire (236 and 108:0 wkt)
          at Southampton, 2008

100:0 wkt   Yorkshire (95 and 91) lost to Gloucestershire (88 and 100:0)
          at Bristol, 1956.

NARROW VICTORIES – BY 1 WICKET

Yorkshire (70 and 91:9) beat Cambridgeshire (86 and 74) at Wisbech, 1867.
Yorkshire (91 and 145:9) beat MCC (73 and 161) at Lord's, 1870.
Yorkshire (265 and 154:9) beat Derbyshire (234 and 184) at Derby, 1897.
Yorkshire (177 and 197:9) beat MCC (188 and 185) at Lord's, 1899.
Yorkshire (391 and 241:9) beat Somerset (349 and 281) at Taunton, 1901.
Yorkshire (239 and 168:9) beat MCC (179 and 226) at Scarborough, 1935.
Yorkshire (152 and 90:9) beat Worcestershire (119 and 121) at Leeds, 1946.
Yorkshire (229 and 175:9) beat Glamorgan (194 and 207) at Bradford, 1960.
Yorkshire (265.9 dec and 191:9) beat Worcestershire (227 and 227) at Worcester, 1961.
Yorkshire (329:6 dec and 167:9) beat Essex (339.9 dec and 154) at Scarborough, 1979.
Yorkshire (Innings forfeited and 251:9 beat Sussex (195 and 55.1 dec) at Leeds, 1986.
Yorkshire (314 and 150:9) beat Essex (200 and 261) at Scarborough, 1998.

NARROW VICTORIES – BY 5 RUNS OR LESS

By 1 run   Yorkshire (228 and 214) beat Middlesex (206 and 235) at Bradford, 1976.
By 1 run   Yorkshire (383 and inns forfeited) beat Loughborough UCCE (93: 3 dec.
        and 289) at Leeds, 2007.
By 2 runs   Yorkshire (108 and 122) beat Nottinghamshire (56 and 172)
        at Nottingham, 1870.
By 2 runs   Yorkshire (304:9 dec and 135) beat Middlesex (225:2 dec and 212)
        at Leeds, 1985.
By 3 runs   Yorkshire (446:9 dec and 172:4 dec) beat Essex (300:3 dec and 315)
        at Colchester, 1991.
By 5 runs   Yorkshire (271 and 147:6 dec) beat Surrey (198 and 215) at Sheffield, 1950.
By 5 runs   Yorkshire (151 and 176) beat Hampshire (165 and 157) at Bradford, 1962.
By 5 runs   Yorkshire (376:4 and 106) beat Middlesex (325:8 and 152) at Lord's, 1975.
By 5 runs   Yorkshire (323:5 dec and inns forfeited) beat Somerset (inns forfeited
        and 318) at Taunton, 1986.

NARROW DEFEATS – BY 1 WICKET

Yorkshire (224 and 210) lost to Australian Imperial Forces XI (265 and 170:9)
    at Leeds, 1985.
Yorkshire (101 and 159) lost to Warwickshire (45 and 216:9) at Scarborough, 1934.
Yorkshire (239 and 184:9 dec.) lost to Warwickshire (125 and 302:9)
    at Birmingham, 1983.
Yorkshire (289 and 153) lost to Surrey (250:2 dec and 193:9) at Guildford, 1991.
Yorkshire (341 and Inns forfeited) lost to Surrey (39:1 dec and 306:9) at Bradford, 1992.

NARROW DEFEATS – BY 5 RUNS OR LESS

By 1 run   Yorkshire (135 and 297) lost to Essex (139 and 294) at Huddersfield, 1897.
By 1 run   Yorkshire (159 and 232) lost to Gloucestershire (164 and 228) at Bristol, 1906.
By 1 run   Yorkshire (126 and 137) lost to Worcestershire (101 and 163)
        at Worcester, 1968.
By 1 run   Yorkshire (366 and 217) lost to Surrey (409 and 175) at The Oval, 1995.
By 2 runs   Yorkshire (172 and 107) lost to Gloucestershire (157 and 124)
        at Sheffield, 1913.
By 2 runs   Yorkshire (179:9 dec and 144) lost to MCC (109 and 216) at Lord's, 1957.
By 3 runs   Yorkshire (126 and 181) lost to Sussex (182 and 128) at Sheffield, 1883.
By 3 runs   Yorkshire (160 and 71) lost to Lancashire (81 and 153) at Huddersfield, 1889.
By 3 runs   Yorkshire (134 and 158) lost to Nottinghamshire (200 and 95) at Leeds, 1923.
By 4 runs   Yorkshire (169 and 193) lost to Middlesex (105 and 261) at Bradford, 1920.
By 5 runs   Yorkshire (58 and 51) lost to Lancashire (64 and 50) at Manchester, 1893.
By 5 runs   Yorkshire (119 and 115) lost to Warwickshire (167 and 72) at Bradford, 1969.

HIGH FOURTH INNINGS SCORES – 300 AND OVER

By Yorkshire

To Win:	406:4	beat Leicestershire by 6 wkts at Leicester, 2005
	402:6	beat Gloucestershire by 4 wkts at Bristol, 2012
	400:4	beat Leicestershire by 6 wkts at Scarborough, 2005
	339:6	beat Durham by 4 wkts at Chester-le-Street, 2013
	331:8	beat Middlesex by 2 wkts at Lord's, 1910.
	327:6	beat Nottinghamshire by 4 wkts at Nottingham, 1990.*
	323:5	beat Nottinghamshire by 5 wkts at Nottingham, 1977.
	318:3	beat Glamorgan by 7 wkts at Middlesbrough, 1976.
	316:8	beat Gloucestershire by 2 wkts at Scarborough, 2012
	309:7	beat Somerset by 3 wkts at Taunton, 1984.
	305:8	beat Nottinghamshire by 2 wkts at Worksop, 1982.
	305:3	beat Lancashire by 7 wkts at Manchester, 1994.
	304:4	beat Derbyshire by 6 wkts at Chesterfield, 1959.
	300:4	beat Derbyshire by 6 wkts at Chesterfield, 1981.
	300:6	beat Derbyshire by 4 wkts at Scarborough, 1990.*
To Draw:	341:8	(set 358) drew with Derbyshire at Derby, 2004.
	333:7	(set 369) drew with Essex at Chelmsford, 2010
	316:6	(set 326) drew with Oxford University at Oxford, 1948.
	312:6	(set 344) drew with Sussex at Scarborough 2011
	316:7	(set 320) drew with Somerset at Scarborough, 1990.
	300:5	(set 392) drew with Kent at Canterbury, 2010
To Lose:	433	(set 500) lost to Warwickshire by 66 runs at Birmingham, 2006
	380	(set 406) lost to MCC. by 25 runs at Lord's, 1937.
	343	(set 490) lost to Durham by 146 runs at Leeds 2011
	324	(set 485) lost to Northamptonshire by 160 runs at Luton, 1994.
	322	(set 344) lost to Middlesex by 21 runs at Lord's, 1996.
	309	(set 400) lost to Middlesex by 90 runs at Lord's 1878.

*Consecutive matches

By Opponents:

To Win:	479:6	Somerset won by 4 wkts at Taunton, 2009
	472:3	Middlesex won by 7 wkts at Lord's, 2014
	404:5	Hampshire won by 5 wkts at Leeds, 2006
	392:4	Gloucestershire won by 6 wkts at Bristol, 1948.
	364:4	Somerset won by 6 wkts at Taunton, 2010
	354:5	Nottinghamshire won by 5 wkts at Scarborough, 1990.
	337:4	Worcestershire won by 6 wkts at Kidderminster, 2007.
	334:6	Glamorgan won by 4 wkts at Harrogate, 1955.
	329:5	Worcestershire won by 5 wkts at Worcester, 1979.
	306:9	Surrey won by 1 wkt at Bradford, 1992.
	305:7	Lancashire won by 3 wkts at Manchester, 1980.
	302:9	Warwickshire won by 1 wkt at Birmingham, 1983

By Opponents:

To Draw:
366:8	(set 443) Hampshire drew at Southampton, 2007.
334:7	(set 339) MCC. drew at Scarborough, 1911.
322:9	(set 334) Middlesex drew at Leeds, 1988.
317:6	(set 355) Nottinghamshire drew at Nottingham, 1910.
300:9	(set 314) Northamptonshire drew at Northampton, 1990.

To Lose:
370	(set 539) Leicestershire lost by 168 runs at Leicester, 2001
319	(set 364) Gloucestershire lost by 44 runs at Leeds, 1987.
318	(set 324) Somerset lost by 5 runs at Taunton, 1986.
315	(set 319) Essex lost by 3 runs at Colchester, 1991.
314	(set 334) Lancashire lost by 19 runs at Manchester, 1993.
310	(set 417) Warwickshire lost by 106 runs at Scarborough, 1939.
306	(set 413) Kent lost by 106 runs at Leeds, 1952.
300	(set 330) Middlesex lost by 29 runs at Sheffield, 1930.

TIE MATCHES

Yorkshire (351:4 dec and 113) tied with Leicestershire (328 and 136) at Huddersfield, 1954.
Yorkshire (106:9 dec and 207) tied with Middlesex (102 and 211) at Bradford, 1973.

HIGHEST SCORES BY AND AGAINST YORKSHIRE

Yorkshire versus: —

Yorkshire versus:	By Yorkshire:	Against Yorkshire:
Derbyshire:		
In Yorkshire:	677:7 dec at Leeds 2013	491 at Bradford, 1949
Away:	662 at Chesterfield, 1898	523 at Derby, 2005
Durham:		
In Yorkshire:	677:7 dec. at Leeds, 2006	573 at Scarborough, 2013
Away:	589-8 dec at Chester-le-Street, 2014	481 at Chester-le-Street, 2007
Essex:		
In Yorkshire:	516 at Scarborough, 2010	622:8 dec. at Leeds, 2005
Away:	555:1 dec. at Leyton, 1932	521 at Leyton, 1905
Glamorgan:		
In Yorkshire:	580:9 dec at Scarborough, 2001	498 at Leeds, 1999
Away:	536:8 dec. at Cardiff, 1996	482:7 dec. at Cardiff, 1996
Gloucestershire:		
In Yorkshire:	504:7 dec. at Bradford, 1905	411 at Leeds, 1992
Away:	494 at Bristol, 1897	574 at Cheltenham, 1990
Hampshire:		
In Yorkshire:	493:1 dec. at Sheffield, 1939	498:6 dec at Scarborough, 2010
Away:	585:3 dec at Portsmouth 1920	599:3 at Southampton, 2011
Kent:		
In Yorkshire:	550:9 at Scarborough, 1995	537:9 dec at Leeds, 2012
Away:	559 at Canterbury, 1887	580: 9 dec. at Maidstone, 1998
Lancashire:		
In Yorkshire:	590 at Bradford, 1887	517 at Leeds, 2007.
Away:	616:6 dec at Manchester, 2014	537 at Manchester, 2005
Leicestershire:		
In Yorkshire	562 { at Scarborough, 1901 / at Dewsbury, 1903	681:7 dec. at Bradford, 1996
Away:	660 at Leicester, 1896	425 at Leicester, 1906

SMASH AND GRAB: Joe Root, who was in dazzling form for England in their one-day international against India at Headingley in September. His superb 113 earned him the man-of-the-match award, and led England to victory by 41 runs.

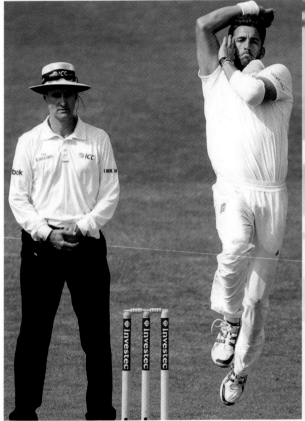

YORKSHIRE'S 2014 ENGLAND HEROES

LAST-OVER NIGHTMARE: England lost a pulsating Headingley Test against Sri Lanka by 100 runs when James Anderson was dismissed in the final over. Yet nothing could take away from Yorkshire paceman Liam Plunkett, above, his best Test figures of 5-64 in the first innings and a match return of 9-176.

HERE TO STAY: Gary Ballance, who scored 74 and 0 in the Headingley Test against Sri Lanka — but by the end of 2014 he had hit three centuries and three half-centuries in a career of only eight Tests.

THE SHAPE OF THINGS TO COME

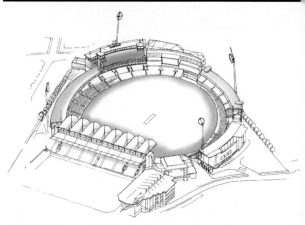

HEADINGLEY MASTERPLAN: An aerial sketch of the proposed redevelopment of the cricket ground which will increase capacity from 17,000 to 20,000 and make it one of the finest venues in the world. Below: an impression of the proposed North/South Stand overlooking the ground. Opposite Page: A drawing of the new pavilion to be built next to the Carnegie Pavilion. *David Warner — Page 51.*

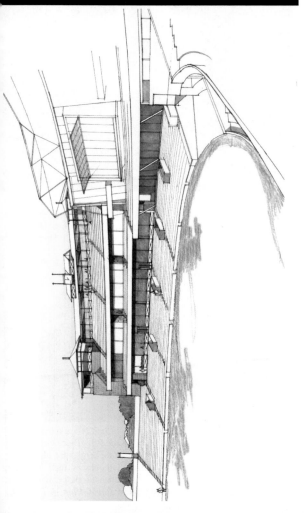

HAT-TRICK AWARDS: Adam Lyth scooped three Club awards in 2014 — Players' Player of the Year, Members' Player of the Year and Fielder of the Year. Here he catches Durham's Paul Collingwood in their *NatWest T20 Blast* clash at Headingley.

HAT-TRICK EGG: David Allan, left, chairman of Yorkshire Cricket Foundation Archives Committee, receives the Billy Bates Ostrich Egg from Trevor Bates, great-great nephew of the Yorkshire all-rounder who took England's first Test hat-trick at Melbourne in 1883. The Egg, which was presented to Bates by the Australians, is on permanent display in the Cricket Museum at Headingley. *David Allan — Page 49.*

DOUBLE FIRST: Yorkshire Academy won both the ECB Yorkshire County Premier League and Cup titles in 2014, the first "double" in the Academy's 20-year history, and Yorkshire President Harold "Dickie" Bird is the most enthusiastic supporter at Weetwood, Leeds, above, as he presents the League trophy to captain Will Rhodes. Below: the squad who made Yorkshire history. Back row, left to right: Mosun Hussain, James Logan, Jared Warner, Jordan Thompson, Eddie Barnes and Barney Gibson. Front row: Matthew Waite, Josh Shaw, Ryan Gibson, Will Rhodes (captain), Eliot Callis, Matthew Fisher and Karl Carver. *(Photos: Richard Damms)*

COLTS CAPPED: Players' mentor Anthony McGrath, back row extreme left, and coach Richard Dawson present Second Eleven headgear to five hopefuls. Back row, left to right: Karl Carver, Josh Shaw and Ben Coad. Front row: Will Rhodes and Jonathan Tattersall. *(Photo: Richard Damms)*

TOP OF THE FORM: Yorkshire Schools' Cricket Association's 11a team which triumphed in all of their 18 matches last season and were winners of the Taunton Festival for the third consecutive year. They received their awards from three of the younger members of Yorkshire's playing staff at the association's junior presentation evening in the Long Room at Headingley. Back row, left to right: Dick Whaley (manager), Owen Davey, Leo Johnson, Ben Cliff, Cooper Smith, Matthew Bird, Louis Adlard, Will Holmes and Linda Whaley. Front row: James Wainman, Cain Robb, Romir Singh, Karl Carver, Sam Elstone (captain), Dan Ford, Tom Senior and Ben Coad.

HIGHEST SCORES BY AND AGAINST YORKSHIRE *(Continued)*

Yorkshire versus: —

Middlesex:	**By Yorkshire:**	**Against Yorkshire:**
In Yorkshire:	575:7 dec. at Bradford, 1899	527 at Huddersfield, 1887
Away:	538:6 dec. at Lord's, 1925	488 at Lord's, 1899
Northamptonshire:		
In Yorkshire:	673:8 dec at Leeds, 2003	517:7 dec at Scarborough, 1999
Away	546:3 dec at Northampton, 2014	531:4 dec at Northampton, 1996
Nottinghamshire:		
In Yorkshire:	572:8 dec at Scarborough, 2013	545:7 dec at Leeds, 2010
Away	534:9 dec at Nottingham, 2011	490 at Nottingham, 1897
Somerset:		
In Yorkshire:	525:4 dec. at Leeds, 1953	630 at Leeds, 1901
Away:	589:5 dec at Bath, 2001	592 at Taunton, 1892
Surrey:		
In Yorkshire:	582:7 dec. at Sheffield, 1935	510 at Leeds, 2002
Away:	704 at The Oval, 1899	634:5 dec at The Oval, 2013
Sussex:		
In Yorkshire:	681:5 dec. at Sheffield, 1897	566 at Sheffield, 1937
Away:	522:7 dec. at Hastings, 1911	597:8 dec. at Hove, 2007
Warwickshire:		
In Yorkshire	561:7 dec at Scarborough 2007	482 at Leeds, 2011
Away:	887 at Birmingham, 1896	601:9 dec. at Birmingham, 2002
	(Highest score by a First-Class county)	
Worcestershire:		
In Yorkshire:	600: 4 dec. at Scarborough, 1995	453:5 dec. at Scarborough, 1995
Away:	560:6 dec. at Worcester, 1928	456:8 at Worcester, 1904
Australians:		
In Yorkshire:	377 at Sheffield, 1953	470 at Bradford, 1893
Indians:		
In Yorkshire:	385 at Hull, 1911	490:5 dec at Sheffield, 1946
New Zealanders:		
In Yorkshire:	419 at Bradford, 1965	370:7 dec. at Bradford, 1949
Pakistanis:		
In Yorkshire:	433:9 dec. at Sheffield, 1954	356 at Sheffield, 1954
South Africans:		
In Yorkshire:	579 at Sheffield, 1951	454:8 dec at Sheffield, 1951
Sri Lankans:		
In Yorkshire:	314:8 dec. at Leeds, 1991	422:8 dec. at Leeds, 1991
West Indians:		
In Yorkshire:	312:5 dec. at Scarborough, 1973	426 at Scarborough, 1995
Zimbabweans:		
In Yorkshire:	298:9 dec at Leeds, 1990	235 at Leeds, 2000
Cambridge University:		
In Yorkshire:	359 at Scarborough, 1967	366 at Leeds, 1998
Away:	540 at Cambridge, 1938	425:7 at Cambridge, 1929
Durham MCCU:		
Away:	355 at Durham, 2011	287 at Durham, 2011
Leeds/Bradford MCCU:		
In Yorkshire	454 at Leeds, 2014	211 at Leeds, 2012
Loughborough MCCU:		
In Yorkshire:	383:6 dec at Leeds, 2007	289 at Leeds, 2007

Yorkshire versus: —

MCC:	**By Yorkshire:**	**Against Yorkshire:**
In Yorkshire:	557:8 dec. at Scarborough, 1933	478:8 at Scarborough, 1904
Away:	528:8 dec. at Lord's, 1919	488 at Lord's, 1919
Oxford University:		
In Yorkshire:	173 at Harrogate, 1972	190:6 dec at Harrogate, 1972
Away:	468:6 dec. at Oxford, 1978	422:9 dec. at Oxford, 1953

LOWEST SCORES BY AND AGAINST YORKSHIRE

Yorkshire versus:

	By Yorkshire:	**Against Yorkshire:**
Derbyshire:		
In Yorkshire:	50 at Sheffield, 1894	20 at Sheffield, 1939
Away:	44 at Chesterfield, 1948	26 at Derby, 1880
Durham:		
In Yorkshire:	93 at Leeds, 2003	125 at Harrogate, 1995
Away:	108 at Durham, 1992	74 at Chester-le-Street, 1998
Essex:		
In Yorkshire:	31 at Huddersfield, 1935	52 at Harrogate, 1900
Away:	98 at Leyton, 1905	30 at Leyton, 1901
Glamorgan:		
In Yorkshire:	83 at Sheffield, 1946	52 at Hull, 1926
Away:	92 at Swansea, 1956	48 at Cardiff, 1924
Gloucestershire:		
In Yorkshire:	61 at Leeds, 1894	36 at Sheffield, 1903
Away:	35 at Bristol, 1959	42 at Gloucester, 1924
Hampshire:		
In Yorkshire:	23 at Middlesbrough, 1965	36 at Leeds, 1904
Away:	96 at Bournemouth, 1971	36 at Southampton, 1898
Kent:		
In Yorkshire:	30 at Sheffield, 1865	39 { at Sheffield, 1882
		{ at Sheffield, 1936
Away:	62 at Maidstone, 1889	63 at Canterbury, 1901
Lancashire:		
In Yorkshire:	33 at Leeds, 1924	30 at Holbeck, 1868
Away:	51 { at Manchester, 1888	
	{ at Manchester, 1893	39 at Manchester, 1874
Leicestershire:	By Yorkshire:	Against Yorkshire:
In Yorkshire:	93 at Leeds, 1935	34 at Leeds, 1906
Away:	47 at Leicester, 1911	57 at Leicester, 1898
Middlesex:		
In Yorkshire:	45 at Leeds, 1898	45 at Huddersfield, 1879
Away:	43 at Lord's, 1888	49 at Lord's in 1890
Northamptonshire:		
In Yorkshire:	85 at Sheffield, 1919	51 at Bradford, 1920
Away	64 at Northampton, 1959	15 at Northampton, 1908 (and 27 in first innings)
Nottinghamshire:		
In Yorkshire:	32 at Sheffield, 1876	24 at Sheffield, 1888
Away:	43 at Nottingham, 1869	13 at Nottingham, 1901 (second smallest total by a First-Class county)

Yorkshire versus:

	By Yorkshire:	**Against Yorkshire:**
Somerset:		
In Yorkshire:	73 at Leeds, 1895	43 at Bradford, 1930
Away:	83 at Wells, 1949	35 at Bath, 1898
Surrey:		
In Yorkshire:	54 at Sheffield, 1873	31 at Holbeck, 1883
Away:	26 at The Oval, 1909	44 at The Oval, 1935
Sussex:		
In Yorkshire:	61 at Dewsbury, 1891	20 at Hull, 1922
Away:	42 at Hove, 1922	24 at Hove, 1878
Warwickshire:		
In Yorkshire:	49 at Huddersfield, 1951	35 at Sheffield, 1979
Away:	54 at Birmingham, 1964	35 at Birmingham, 1963
Worcestershire:		
In Yorkshire:	62 at Bradford, 1907	24 at Huddersfield, 1903
Away:	72 at Worcester, 1977	65 at Worcester, 1925
Australians:		
In Yorkshire:	48 at Leeds, 1893	23 at Leeds, 1902
Indians:		
In Yorkshire:	146 at Bradford, 1959	66 at Harrogate, 1932
New Zealanders:		
In Yorkshire:	189 at Harrogate, 1931	134 at Bradford, 1965
Pakistanis:		
In Yorkshire:	137 at Bradford, 1962	150 at Leeds, 1967
South Africans:		
In Yorkshire:	113 at Bradford, 1907	76 at Bradford, 1951
Sri Lankans:		
In Yorkshire:	Have not been dismissed. Lowest is 184:1 dec at Leeds, 1991	287:5 dec at Leeds, 1988
West Indians:		
In Yorkshire:	50 at Harrogate, 1906	58 at Leeds, 1928
Zimbabweans:		
In Yorkshire:	124 at Leeds, 2000	68 at Leeds, 2000
Cambridge University:		
In Yorkshire:	110 at Sheffield, 1903	39 at Sheffield, 1903
Away:	51 at Cambridge, 1906	30 at Cambridge, 1928
Durham MCCU:		
Away	355 at Durham, 2011	196 at Durham, 2011
Leeds/Bradford MCCU:		
In Yorkshire	135 at Leeds, 2012	118 at Leeds, 2013
Loughborough MCCU:		
In Yorkshire	348:5 dec at Leeds, 2010	289 at Leeds, 2007
MCC:		
In Yorkshire:	46 { at Scarborough, 1876 / at Scarborough, 1877	31 at Scarborough, 1877
Away:	44 at Lord's, 1880	27 at Lord's, 1902
Oxford University:		
In Yorkshire:	Have not been dismissed. Lowest is 115:8 at Harrogate, 1972	133 at Harrogate, 1972
Away:	141 at Oxford, 1949	46 at Oxford, 1956

INDIVIDUAL INNINGS OF 150 AND OVER

A complete list of all First-class Centuries up to and including 2007 is to be found in the 2008 edition

J M BAIRSTOW (4)

205	v. Nottinghamshire	Nottingham	2011
182	v. Leicestershire	Scarborough	2012
186	v. Derbyshire	Leeds	2013
161*	v. Sussex	Arundel	2014

G S BALLANCE (1)

174	v. Northamptonshire	Leeds	2014

W BARBER (7)

162	v. Middlesex	Sheffield	1932
168	v. MCC	Lord's	1934
248	v. Kent	Leeds	1934
191	v. Sussex	Leeds	1935
255	v. Surrey	Sheffield	1935
158	v. Kent	Sheffield	1936
157	v. Surrey	Sheffield	1938

M G BEVAN (2)

153*	v. Surrey	The Oval	1995
160*	v. Surrey	Middlesbrough	1996

H D BIRD (1)

181*	v. Glamorgan	Bradford	1959

R J BLAKEY (3)

204*	v. Gloucestershire	Leeds	1987
196	v. Oxford University	Oxford	1991
223*	v. Northamptonshire	Leeds	2003

G BLEWETT (1)

190	v. Northamptonshire	Scarborough	1999

M W BOOTH (1)

210	v. Worcestershire	Worcester	1911

G BOYCOTT (32)

165*	v. Leicestershire	Scarborough	1963
151	v. Middlesex	Leeds	1964
151*	v. Leicestershire	Leicester	1964
177	v. Gloucestershire	Bristol	1964
164	v. Sussex	Hove	1966
220*	v. Northamptonshire	Sheffield	1967
180*	v. Warwickshire	Middlesbrough	1968
260*	v. Essex	Colchester (Garrison Ground)	1970
169	v. Nottinghamshire	Leeds	1971
233	v. Essex	Colchester (Garrison Ground)	1971
182*	v. Middlesex	Lord's	1971
169	v. Lancashire	Sheffield	1971
151	v. Leicestershire	Bradford	1971
204*	v. Leicestershire	Leicester	1972
152*	v. Worcestershire	Worcester	1975
175*	v. Middlesex	Scarborough	1975
201*	v. Middlesex	Lord's	1975
161*	v. Gloucestershire	Leeds	1976

INDIVIDUAL INNINGS OF 150 AND OVER *(Continued)*

G BOYCOTT (Continued)

207*	v. Cambridge University	Cambridge	1976
156*	v. Glamorgan	Middlesbrough	1976
154	v Nottinghamshire	Nottingham	1977
151*	v Derbyshire	Leeds	1979
167	v Derbyshire	Chesterfield	1979
175*	v Nottinghamshire	Worksop	1979
154*	v Derbyshire	Scarborough	1980
159	v Worcestershire	Sheffield (Abbeydale Park)	1982
152*	v Warwickshire	Leeds	1982
214*	v Nottinghamshire	Worksop	1983
163	v Nottinghamshire	Bradford	1983
169*	v Derbyshire	Chesterfield	1983
153*	v Derbyshire	Harrogate	1984
184	v Worcestershire	Worcester	1985

G L BROPHY (1)

177*	v Worcestershire	Worcester	2011

J T BROWN (8)

168*	v Sussex	Huddersfield	1895
203	v Middlesex	Lord's	1896
311	v Sussex	Sheffield	1897
300	v Derbyshire	Chesterfield	1898
150	v Sussex	Hove	1898
168	v Cambridge University	Cambridge	1899
167	v Australians	Bradford	1899
192	v Derbyshire	Derby	1899

D BYAS (5)

153	v Nottinghamshire	Worksop	1991
156	v Essex	Chelmsford	1993
181	v Cambridge University	Cambridge	1995
193	v Lancashire	Leeds	1995
213	v Worcestershire	Scarborough	1995

D B CLOSE (5)

164	v Combined Services	Harrogate	1954
154	v Nottinghamshire	Nottingham	1959
198	v Surrey	The Oval	1960
184	v Nottinghamshire	Scarborough	1960
161	v Northamptonshire	Northampton	1963

D DENTON (11)

153*	v Australians	Bradford	1905
165	v Hampshire	Bournemouth	1905
172	v Gloucestershire	Bradford	1905
184	v Nottinghamshire	Nottingham	1909
182	v Derbyshire	Chesterfield	1910
200*	v Warwickshire	Birmingham	1912
182	v Gloucestershire	Bristol	1912
221	v Kent	Tunbridge Wells	1912
191	v Hampshire	Southampton	1912
168*	v Hampshire	Southampton	1914
209*	v Worcestershire	Worcester	1920

INDIVIDUAL INNINGS OF 150 AND OVER *(Continued)*

A W GALE (3)

150	v. Surrey	The Oval	2008
151*	v. Nottinghamshire	Nottingham	2010
272	v. Nottinghamshire	Scarborough	2013

P A GIBB (1)

157*	v. Nottinghamshire	Sheffield	1935

S HAIGH (1)

159	v. Nottinghamshire	Sheffield	1901

L HALL (1)

160	v. Lancashire	Bradford	1887

J H HAMPSHIRE (5)

150	v. Leicestershire	Bradford	1964
183*	v. Sussex	Hove	1971
157*	v. Nottinghamshire	Worksop	1974
158	v. Gloucestershire	Harrogate	1974
155*	v. Gloucestershire	Leeds	1976

I J HARVEY (1)

209*	v. Somerset	Leeds	2005

LORD HAWKE (1)

166	v. Warwickshire	Birmingham	1896

G H HIRST (15)

186	v. Surrey	The Oval	1899
155	v. Nottinghamshire	Scarborough	1900
214	v. Worcestershire	Worcester	1901
153	v. Leicestershire	Dewsbury	1903
153	v. Oxford University	Oxford	1904
152	v. Hampshire	Portsmouth	1904
157	v. Kent	Tunbridge Wells	1904
341	v. Leicestershire	Leicester (Aylestone Road)	1905
232*	v. Surrey	The Oval	1905
169	v. Oxford University	Oxford	1906
158	v. Cambridge University	Cambridge	1910
156	v. Lancashire	Manchester	1911
218	v. Sussex	Hastings	1911
166*	v. Sussex	Hastings	1913
180*	v. MCC	Lord's	1919

P HOLMES (16)

302*	v. Hampshire	Portsmouth	1920
150	v. Derbyshire	Chesterfield	1921
277*	v. Northamptonshire	Harrogate	1921
209	v. Warwickshire	Birmingham	1922
220*	v. Warwickshire	Huddersfield	1922
199	v. Somerset	Hull	1923
315*	v. Middlesex	Lord's	1925
194	v. Leicestershire	Hull	1925
159	v. Hampshire	Southampton	1925
180	v. Gloucestershire	Gloucester	1927
175*	v. New Zealanders	Bradford	1927
179*	v. Middlesex	Leeds	1928

P HOLMES *(Continued)*

275	v. Warwickshire	Bradford	1928
285	v. Nottinghamshire	Nottingham	1929
250	v. Warwickshire	Birmingham	1931
224*	v. Essex	Leyton	1932

L HUTTON *(31)*

196	v. Worcestershire	Worcester	1934
163	v. Surrey	Leeds	1936
161	v. MCC	Lord's	1937
271*	v. Derbyshire	Sheffield	1937
153	v. Leicestershire	Hull	1937
180	v. Cambridge University	Cambridge	1938
158	v. Warwickshire	Birmingham	1939
280*	v. Hampshire	Sheffield	1939
151	v. Surrey	Leeds	1939
177	v. Sussex	Scarborough	1939
183*	v. Indians	Bradford	1946
171*	v. Northamptonshire	Hull	1946
197	v. Glamorgan	Swansea	1947
197	v. Essex	Southend-on-Sea	1947
270*	v. Hampshire	Bournemouth	1947
176*	v. Sussex	Sheffield	1948
155	v. Sussex	Hove	1948
167	v. New Zealanders	Bradford	1949
201	v. Lancashire	Manchester	1949
165	v. Sussex	Hove	1949
269*	v. Northamptonshire	Wellingborough	1949
156	v. Essex	Colchester (Castle Park)	1950
153	v. Nottinghamshire	Nottingham	1950
156	v. South Africans	Sheffield	1951
151	v. Surrey	The Oval	1951
194*	v. Nottinghamshire	Nottingham	1951
152	v. Lancashire	Leeds	1952
189	v. Kent	Leeds	1952
178	v. Somerset	Leeds	1953
163	v. Combined Services	Harrogate	1954
194	v. Nottinghamshire	Nottingham	1955

R A HUTTON *(1)*

189	v. Pakistanis	Bradford	1971

R ILLINGWORTH *(2)*

150	v. Essex	Colchester (Castle Park)	1959
162	v. Indians	Sheffield	1959

Hon F S JACKSON *(3)*

160	v. Gloucestershire	Sheffield	1898
155	v. Middlesex	Bradford	1899
158	v. Surrey	Bradford	1904

P A JAQUES *(7)*

243	v. Hampshire	Southampton (Rose Bowl)	2004
173	v. Glamorgan	Leeds	2004
176	v. Northamptonshire	Leeds	2005
219	v. Derbyshire	Leeds	2005
172	v. Durham	Scarborough	2005
160	v. Gloucestershire	Bristol	2012
152	v. Durham	Scarborough	2013

INDIVIDUAL INNINGS OF 150 AND OVER *(Continued)*

R KILNER (5)

169	v. Gloucestershire	Bristol	1914
206*	v. Derbyshire	Sheffield	1920
166	v. Northamptonshire	Northampton	1921
150	v. Northamptonshire	Harrogate	1921
150	v. Middlesex	Lord's	1926

F LEE (1)

165	v. Lancashire	Bradford	1887

A Z LEES (1)

275*	v. Derbyshire	Chesterfield	2013

D S LEHMANN (13)

177	v. Somerset	Taunton	1997
163*	v. Leicestershire	Leicester	1997
182	v. Hampshire	Portsmouth	1997
200	v. Worcestershire	Worcester	1998
187*	v. Somerset	Bath	2001
252	v. Lancashire	Leeds	2001
193	v. Leicestershire	Leicester	2001
216	v. Sussex	Arundel	2002
187	v. Lancashire	Leeds	2002
150	v. Warwickshire	Birmingham	2006
193	v. Kent	Canterbury	2006
172	v. Kent	Leeds	2006
339	v. Durham	Leeds	2006

E I LESTER (5)

186	v. Warwickshire	Scarborough	1949
178	v. Nottinghamshire	Nottingham	1952
157	v. Cambridge University	Hull	1953
150	v. Oxford University	Oxford	1954
163	v. Essex	Romford	1954

M LEYLAND (17)

191	v. Glamorgan	Swansea	1926
204*	v. Middlesex	Sheffield	1927
247	v. Worcestershire	Worcester	1928
189*	v. Glamorgan	Huddersfield	1928
211*	v. Lancashire	Leeds	1930
172	v. Middlesex	Sheffield	1930
186	v. Derbyshire	Leeds	1930
189	v. Middlesex	Sheffield	1932
153	v. Leicestershire	Leicester (Aylestone Road)	1932
166	v. Leicestershire	Bradford	1932
153*	v. Hampshire	Bournemouth	1932
192	v. Northamptonshire	Leeds	1933
210*	v. Kent	Dover	1933
263	v. Essex	Hull	1936
163*	v. Surrey	Leeds	1936
167	v. Worcestershire	Stourbridge	1937
180*	v. Middlesex	Lord's	1939

E LOCKWOOD (1)

208	v. Kent	Gravesend	1883

INDIVIDUAL INNINGS OF 150 AND OVER *(Continued)*

J D LOVE (4)

163	v. Nottinghamshire	Bradford	1976
170*	v. Worcestershire	Worcester	1979
161	v. Warwickshire	Birmingham	1981
154	v. Lancashire	Manchester	1981

F A LOWSON (10)

155	v. Kent	Maidstone	1951
155	v. Worcestershire	Bradford	1952
166	v. Scotland	Glasgow	1953
259*	v. Worcestershire	Worcester	1953
165	v. Sussex	Hove	1954
164	v. Essex	Scarborough	1954
150*	v. Kent	Dover	1954
183*	v. Oxford University	Oxford	1956
154	v. Somerset	Taunton	1956
154	v. Cambridge University	Cambridge	1957

R G LUMB (2)

159	v. Somerset	Harrogate	1979
165*	v. Gloucestershire	Bradford	1984

A LYTH (3)

248 *	v. Leicestershire	Leicester	2012
230	v. Northamptonshire	Northampton	2014
251	v. Lancashire	Manchester	2014

A McGRATH (7)

165	v. Lancashire	Leeds	2002
174	v. Derbyshire	Derby	2004
165*	v. Leicestershire	Leicester	2005
173*	v. Worcestershire	Leeds	2005
158	v. Derbyshire	Derby	2005
188*	v. Warwickshire	Birmingham	2007
211	v. Warwickshire	Birmingham	2009

D R MARTYN (1)

238	v. Gloucestershire	Leeds	2003

A A METCALFE (7)

151	v. Northamptonshire	Luton	1986
151	v. Lancashire	Manchester	1986
152	v. MCC	Scarborough	1987
216*	v. Middlesex	Leeds	1988
162	v. Gloucestershire	Cheltenham	1990
150*	v. Derbyshire	Scarborough	1990
194*	v. Nottinghamshire	Nottingham	1990

A MITCHELL (7)

189	v. Northamptonshire	Northampton	1926
176	v. Nottinghamshire	Bradford	1930
177*	v. Gloucestershire	Bradford	1932
150*	v. Worcestershire	Worcester	1933
158	v. MCC	Scarborough	1933
152	v. Hampshire	Bradford	1934
181	v. Surrey	Bradford	1934

INDIVIDUAL INNINGS OF 150 AND OVER *(Continued)*

F MITCHELL (2)

194	v. Leicestershire	Leicester	1899
162*	v. Warwickshire	Birmingham	1901

M D MOXON (14)

153	v. Lancashire	Leeds	1983
153	v. Somerset	Leeds	1985
168	v. Worcestershire	Worcester	1985
191	v. Northamptonshire	Scarborough	1989
162*	v. Surrey	The Oval	1989
218*	v. Sussex	Eastbourne	1990
200	v. Essex	Colchester (Castle Park)	1991
183	v. Gloucestershire	Cheltenham	1992
171*	v. Kent	Leeds	1993
161*	v. Lancashire	Manchester	1994
274*	v. Worcestershire	Worcester	1994
203*	v. Kent	Leeds	1995
213	v. Glamorgan	Cardiff (Sophia Gardens)	1996
155	v. Pakistan 'A'	Leeds	1997

E OLDROYD (5)

151*	v. Glamorgan	Cardiff	1922
194	v. Worcestershire	Worcester	1923
162*	v. Glamorgan	Swansea	1928
168	v. Glamorgan	Hull	1929
164*	v. Somerset	Bath	1930

D E V PADGETT (1)

161*	v. Oxford University	Oxford	1959

R PEEL (2)

158	v. Middlesex	Lord's	1889
210*	v. Warwickshire	Birmingham	1896

A U RASHID (3)

157*	v. Lancashire	Leeds	2009
180	v. Somerset	Leeds	2013
159*	v. Lancashire	Manchester	2014

W RHODES (8)

196	v. Worcestershire	Worcester	1904
201	v. Somerset	Taunton	1905
199	v. Sussex	Hove	1909
176	v. Nottinghamshire	Harrogate	1912
152	v. Leicestershire	Leicester (Aylestone Road)	1913
167*	v. Nottinghamshire	Leeds	1920
267*	v. Leicestershire	Leeds	1921
157	v. Derbyshire	Leeds	1925

P E ROBINSON (2)

150*	v. Derbyshire	Scarborough	1990
189	v. Lancashire	Scarborough	1991

J E ROOT (4)

160	v. Sussex	Scarborough	2011
222*	v. Hampshire	Southampton (West End)	2012
182	v. Durham	Chester-le-Street	2013
236	v. Derbyshire	Leeds	2013

2013 innings consecutive

INDIVIDUAL INNINGS OF 150 AND OVER *(Continued)*

J W ROTHERY (1)

161	v. Kent	Dover	1908

J A RUDOLPH (5)

220	v. Warwickshire	Scarborough	2007
155	v. Somerset	Taunton	2008
198	v. Worcestershire	Leeds	2009
191	v. Somerset	Taunton	2009
228*	v. Durham	Leeds	2010

H RUDSTON (1)

164	v. Leicestershire	Leicester (Aylestone Rd)	1904

J J SAYERS (3)

187	v. Kent	Tunbridge Wells	2007
173	v. Warwickshire	Birmingham	2009
152	v. Somerset	Taunton	2009

A B SELLERS (1)

204	v. Cambridge University	Cambridge	1936

K SHARP (2)

173	v. Derbyshire	Chesterfield	1984
181	v. Gloucestershire	Harrogate	1986

P J SHARPE (4)

203*	v. Cambridge University	Cambridge	1960
152	v. Kent	Sheffield	1960
197	v. Pakistanis	Leeds	1967
172*	v. Glamorgan	Swansea	1971

G A SMITHSON (1)

169	v. Leicestershire	Leicester	1947

W B STOTT (2)

181	v. Essex	Sheffield	1957
186	v. Warwickshire	Birmingham	1960

H SUTCLIFFE (39)

174	v. Kent	Dover	1919
232	v. Surrey	The Oval	1922
213	v. Somerset	Dewsbury	1924
160	v. Sussex	Sheffield	1924
255*	v. Essex	Southend-on-Sea	1924
235	v. Middlesex	Leeds	1925
206	v. Warwickshire	Dewsbury	1925
171	v. MCC	Scarborough	1925
200	v. Leicestershire	Leicester (Aylestone Road)	1926
176	v. Surrey	Leeds	1927
169	v. Nottinghamshire	Bradford	1927
228	v. Sussex	Eastbourne	1928
150	v. Northamptonshire	Northampton	1929
150*	v. Essex	Dewsbury	1930
173	v. Sussex	Hove	1930
173*	v. Cambridge University	Cambridge	1931
230	v. Kent	Folkestone	1931
183	v. Somerset	Dewsbury	1931
195	v. Lancashire	Sheffield	1931

267

INDIVIDUAL INNINGS OF 150 AND OVER (Continued)

H SUTCLIFFE (Continued)

187	v. Leicestershire	Leicester (Aylestone Road)	1931
153*	v. Warwickshire	Hull	1932
313	v. Essex	Leyton	1932
270	v. Sussex	Leeds	1932
182	v. Derbyshire	Leeds	1932
194	v. Essex	Scarborough	1932
205	v. Warwickshire	Birmingham	1933
177	v. Middlesex	Bradford	1933
174	v. Leicestershire	Leicester (Aylestone Road)	1933
152	v. Cambridge University	Cambridge	1934
166	v. Essex	Hull	1934
203	v. Surrey	The Oval	1934
187*	v. Worcestershire	Bradford	1934
200*	v. Worcestershire	Sheffield	1935
212	v. Leicestershire	Leicester (Aylestone Road)	1935
202	v. Middlesex	Scarborough	1936
189	v. Leicestershire	Hull	1937
165	v. Lancashire	Manchester	1939
234*	v. Leicestershire	Hull	1939
175	v. Middlesex	Lord's	1939

W H H SUTCLIFFE (3)

171*	v. Worcestershire	Worcester	1952
181	v. Kent	Canterbury	1952
161*	v. Glamorgan	Harrogate	1955

K TAYLOR (8)

168*	v. Nottinghamshire	Nottingham	1956
159	v. Leicestershire	Sheffield	1961
203*	v. Warwickshire	Birmingham	1961
178*	v. Oxford University	Oxford	1962
163	v. Nottinghamshire	Leeds	1962
153	v. Lancashire	Manchester	1964
160	v. Australians	Sheffield	1964
162	v. Worcestershire	Kidderminster	1967

T L TAYLOR (1)

156	v. Hampshire	Harrogate	1901

J TUNNICLIFFE (2)

243	v. Derbyshire	Chesterfield	1898
158	v. Worcestershire	Worcester	1900

G ULYETT (1)

199*	v. Derbyshire	Sheffield	1887

M P VAUGHAN (7)

183	v. Glamorgan	Cardiff (Sophia Gardens)	1996
183	v. Northamptonshire	Northampton	1996
161	v. Essex	Ilford	1997
177	v. Durham	Chester-le-Street	1998
151	v. Essex	Chelmsford	1999
153	v. Kent	Scarborough	1999
155*	v. Derbyshire	Leeds	2000

INDIVIDUAL INNINGS OF 150 AND OVER *(Continued)*

E WAINWRIGHT (3)

171	v. Middlesex	Lord's	1897
153	v. Leicestershire	Leicester	1899
228	v. Surrey	The Oval	1899

W WATSON (7)

153*	v. Surrey	The Oval	1947
172	v. Derbyshire	Scarborough	1948
162*	v. Somerset	Leeds	1953
163	v. Sussex	Sheffield	1955
174	v. Lancashire	Sheffield	1955
214*	v. Worcestershire	Worcester	1955
162	v. Northamptonshire	Harrogate	1957

C WHITE (6)

181	v. Lancashire	Leeds	1996
172*	v. Worcestershire	Leeds	1997
186	v. Lancashire	Manchester	2001
183	v. Glamorgan	Scarborough	2001
161	v. Leicestershire	Scarborough	2002
173*	v. Derbyshire	Derby	2003

K S WILLIAMSON (1)

189	v. Sussex	Scarborough	2014

B B WILSON (2)

150	v. Warwickshire	Birmingham	1912
208	v. Sussex	Bradford	1914

J V WILSON (7)

157*	v. Sussex	Leeds	1949
157	v. Essex	Sheffield	1950
166*	v. Sussex	Hull	1951
223*	v. Scotland	Scarborough	1951
154	v. Oxford University	Oxford	1952
230	v. Derbyshire	Sheffield	1952
165	v. Oxford University	Oxford	1956

M J WOOD (5)

200*	v. Warwickshire	Leeds	1998
157	v. Northamptonshire	Leeds	2003
207	v. Somerset	Taunton	2003
155	v. Hampshire	Scarborough	2003
202*	v. Bangladesh 'A'	Leeds	2005

N W D YARDLEY (2)

177	v. Derbyshire	Scarborough	1947
183*	v. Hampshire	Leeds	1951

YOUNUS KHAN (2)

202*	v. Hampshire	Southampton (Rose Bowl)	2007
217*	v. Kent	Scarborough	2007

CENTURIES BY CURRENT PLAYERS

**A complete list of all First-class Centuries up to and including 2007
is to be found in the 2008 edition**

AZEEM RAFIQ (1)

100	v Worcestershire	Worcester	2009

J M BAIRSTOW (8)

205	v. Nottinghamshire	Nottingham	2011
136	v. Somerset	Taunton	2011
182	v. Leicestershire	Scarborough	2012
118	v. Leicestershire	Leicester	2012
107	v. Kent	Leeds	2012
186	v. Derbyshire	Leeds	2013
123	v. Leeds/Bradford	Leeds	2014
161*	v. Sussex	Arundel	2014

G S BALLANCE (11)

111	v. Warwickshire	Birmingham	2011
121*	v. Gloucestershire	Bristol	2012
112	v. Leeds/Bradford MCCU	Leeds	2013
107	v. Somerset	Leeds	2013
141	v. Nottinghamshire	Scarborough	2013
112	v. Warwickshire	Leeds	2013
148	v. Surrey 1st inns	The Oval **	2013
108*	v. Surrey 2nd inns	The Oval **	2013
101	v. Leeds/Bradford MCCU	Leeds **	2014

*(** consecutive innings)*

174	v. Northamptonshire	Leeds	2014
130	v. Middlesex	Lord's	2014

T T BRESNAN (2)

116	v. Surrey	The Oval	2007
101*	v. Warwickshire	Scarborough	2007

A J FINCH (1)

110	v. Warwickshire	Birmingham	2014

A W GALE (16)

149	v. Warwickshire	Scarborough	2006
138	v. Hampshire	Leeds	2008
150	v. Surrey	The Oval	2008
136	v. Lancashire	Manchester	2008
101	v. Worcestershire	Worcester	2009
121	v. Lancashire	Manchester	2009
101	v. Somerset	Leeds	2010
135	v. Essex	Scarborough	2010
151*	v. Nottinghamshire	Nottingham	2010
145*	v. Nottinghamshire	Leeds	2011
101*	v. Durham	Chester-le-Street	2011
272	v. Nottinghamshire	Scarborough	2013
103	v. Middlesex	Lord's	2013
148	v. Surrey	Leeds	2013

(2013 consecutive innings)

124	v. Durham	Chester-le-Street	2014
126*	v. Middlesex	Scarborough	2014

CENTURIES BY CURRENT PLAYERS *(Continued)*

A Z LEES (5)

121	v. Leeds/Bradford MCCU	Leeds	2013
100	v. Middlesex	Lord's	2013
275*	v. Derbyshire	Chesterfield	2013
138	v. Northamptonshire	Northampton	2014
108	v. Durham	Leeds	2014

A LYTH (14)

132	v. Nottinghamshire	Nottingham	2008
142	v. Somerset	Taunton	2010
133	v. Hampshire	Southampton	2010
100	v. Lancashire	Manchester	2010
248*	v. Leicestershire	Leicester	2012
111	v. Leeds/Bradford	Leeds	2013
105	v. Somerset	Taunton	2013
130	v. Leeds/Bradford MCCU	Leeds	2014
104	v. Durham	Chester-le-Street	2014
230	v. Northamptonshire	Northampton	2014
143	v. Durham	Leeds	2014
117	v. Middlesex	Scarborough	2014
251	v. Lancashire	Manchester	2014
122	v. Nottinghamshire	Nottingham	2014

R M PYRAH (3)

106	v. Loughborough UCCE	Leeds	2007
134*	v. Loughborough MCCU	Leeds	2010
117	v. Lancashire	Leeds	2011

A U RASHID (9)

108	v. Worcestershire	Kidderminster	2007
111	v. Sussex	Hove	2008
117*	v. Hampshire	Basingstoke	2009
157*	v. Lancashire	Leeds	2009
180	v. Somerset	Leeds	2013
110*	v. Warwickshire	Birmingham	2013
103	v. Somerset	Taunton	2013

(2013 consecutive innings)

108	v. Somerset	Taunton	2014
159*	v. Lancashire	Manchester	2014

J E ROOT (5)

160	v. Sussex	Scarborough	2011
222*	v. Hampshire	Southampton (West End)	2012
125	v. Northamptonshire	Leeds	2012
182	v. Durham	Chester-le-Street	2013
236	v. Derbyshire	Leeds	2013

K S WILLIAMSON (1)

189	v. Sussex	Scarborough	2014

CENTURIES
(Including highest score)

112	H Sutcliffe	313	v Essex	at Leyton	1932
103	G Boycott	260*	v Essex	at Colchester (Garrison Gd)	1970
85	L Hutton	280*	v Hampshire	at Sheffield	1939
62	M Leyland	263	v Essex	at Hull	1936
61	D Denton	221	v Kent	at Tunbridge Wells	1912

60	P Holmes	315*	v Middlesex	at Lord's	1925
56	G H Hirst	341	v Leicestershire	at Leicester (Aylestone Rd)	1905
46	W Rhodes	267*	v Leicestershire	at Leeds	1921
41	M D Moxon	274*	v Worcestershire	at Worcester	1994
39	A Mitchell	189	v Northamptonshire	at Northampton	1926
37	E Oldroyd	194	v Worcestershire	at Worcester	1923
34	J H Hampshire	183*	v Sussex	at Hove	1971
34	A McGrath	211	v Warwickshire	at Birmingham	2009
33	D B Close	198	v Surrey	at The Oval	1960
30	F A Lowson	259*	v Worcestershire	at Worcester	1953
29	D E V Padgett	161*	v Oxford University	at Oxford	1959
29	J V Wilson	230	v Derbyshire	at Sheffield	1952
28	D Byas	213	v Worcestershire	at Scarborough	1995
27	W Barber	255	v Surrey	at Sheffield	1935
26	D S Lehmann	339	v Durham	at Leeds	2006
26	W Watson	214*	v Worcestershire	at Worcester	1955
25	A A Metcalfe	216*	v Middlesex	at Leeds	1988
24	E I Lester	186	v Warwickshire	at Scarborough	1949
23	J T Brown	311	v Sussex	at Sheffield	1897
23	P J Sharpe	203*	v Cambridge University	at Cambridge	1960
22	R G Lumb	165*	v Gloucestershire	at Bradford	1984
22	J Tunnicliffe	243	v Derbyshire	at Chesterfield	1898
21	Hon F S Jackson	160	v Gloucestershire	at Sheffield	1898
20	M P Vaughan	183	v Glamorgan	at Cardiff (Sophia Gardens)	1996
	and	183	v Northamptonshire	at Northampton	1996
19	C White	186	v Lancashire	at Manchester	2001
18	J A Rudolph	228*	v Durham	at Leeds	2010
18	E Wainwright	228	v Surrey	at The Oval	1899
17	W B Stott	186	v Warwickshire	at Birmingham	1960
17	N W D Yardley	183*	v Hampshire	at Leeds	1951
16	A W Gale	272	v. Nottinghamshire	at Scarborough	2013
16	K Taylor	203*	v Warwickshire	at Birmingham	1961
16	M J Wood	207	v Somerset	at Taunton	2003
15	R Kilner	206*	v Derbyshire	at Sheffield	1920
15	G Ulyett	199*	v Derbyshire	at Sheffield	1887
15	B B Wilson	208	v Sussex	at Bradford	1914
14	R Illingworth	162	v Indians	at Sheffield	1959
14	A Lyth	251	v. Lancashire	at Manchester	2014
13	J D Love	170*	v Worcestershire	at Worcester	1979
12	R J Blakey	223*	v Northamptonshire	at Leeds	2003
12	H Halliday	144	v Derbyshire	at Chesterfield	1950
11	G S Ballance	174	v. Northamptonshire	at Leeds	2014
11	P A Jaques	243	v. Hampshire	at Southampton (Rose Bowl)	2004
11	K Sharp	181	v Gloucestershire	at Harrogate	1986
10	C W J Athey	134	v Derbyshire	at Derby	1982
10	Lord Hawke	166	v Warwickshire	at Birmingham	1896
10	F Mitchell	194	v Leicestershire	at Leicester	1899
9	D L Bairstow	145	v Middlesex	at Scarborough	1980
9	M G Bevan	160*	v Surrey	at Middlesbrough	1996
9	L Hall	160	v Lancashire	at Bradford	1887
9	A U Rashid	180	v. Somerset	at Leeds	2013
9	J J Sayers	187	v Kent	at Tunbridge Wells	2007
8	J M Bairstow	205	v. Nottinghamshire	at Nottingham	2011
8	W Bates	136	v Sussex	at Hove	1886
8	M J Lumb	144	v Middlesex	at Southgate	2006
8	T L Taylor	156	v Hampshire	at Harrogate	1901

7	J B Bolus	146*	v Hampshire	at Portsmouth	1960
7	E Robinson	135*	v Leicestershire	at Leicester (Aylestone Rd)	1921
7	P E Robinson	189	v Lancashire	at Scarborough	1991
6	E Lockwood	208	v Kent	at Gravesend	1883
6	R Peel	210*	v Warwickshire	at Birmingham	1896
6	W H H Sutcliffe	181	v Kent	at Canterbury	1952
5	A Z Lees	275*	v. Derbyshire	at Chesterfield	2013
5	C M Old	116	v Indians	at Bradford	1974
5	J E Root	236	v. Derbyshire	at Leeds	2013
4	I Grimshaw	129*	v Cambridge University	at Sheffield	1885
4	S Haigh	159	v Nottinghamshire	at Sheffield	1901
4	S N Hartley	114	v Gloucestershire	at Bradford	1982
4	R A Hutton	189	v Pakistanis	at Bradford	1971
4	A B Sellers	204	v Cambridge University	at Cambridge	1936
3	G L Brophy	177*	v Worcestershire	at Worcester	2011
3	P Carrick	131*	v Northamptonshire	at Northampton	1980
3	A J Dalton	128	v Middlesex	at Leeds	1972
3	A Drake	147*	v Derbyshire	at Chesterfield	1911
3	F Lee	165	v Lancashire	at Bradford	1887
3	G G Macaulay	125*	v Nottinghamshire	at Nottingham	1921
3	R Moorhouse	113	v Somerset	at Taunton	1896
3	R M Pyrah	134*	v Loughborough MCCU	at Leeds	2010
3	J W Rothery	161	v Kent	at Dover	1908
3	J Rowbotham	113	v Surrey	at The Oval	1873
3	T F Smailes	117	v Glamorgan	at Cardiff	1938
3	Younus Khan	217*	v Kent	at Scarborough	2007
2	M W Booth	210	v Worcestershire	at Worcester	1911
2	T T Bresnan	116	v Surrey	at The Oval	2007
2	D C F Burton	142*	v Hampshire	at Dewsbury	1919
2	K R Davidson	128	v Kent	at Maidstone	1934
2	P A Gibb	157*	v Nottinghamshire	at Sheffield	1935
2	P J Hartley	127*	v Lancashire	at Manchester	1988
2	I J Harvey	209*	v Somerset	at Leeds	2005
2	C Johnson	107	v Somerset	at Sheffield	1973
2	S A Kellett	125*	v Derbyshire	at Chesterfield	1991
2	N Kilner	112	v Leicestershire	at Leeds	1921
2	B Parker	138*	v Oxford University	at Oxford	1997
2	A Sellers	105	v Middlesex	at Lord's	1893
2	E Smith (Morley)	129	v Hampshire	at Bradford	1899
2	G A Smithson	169	v Leicestershire	at Leicester	1947
2	G B Stevenson	115*	v Warwickshire	at Birmingham	1982
2	F S Trueman	104	v Northamptonshire	at Northampton	1963
2	C Turner	130	v Somerset	at Sheffield	1936
2	D J Wainwright	104*	v Sussex	at Hove	2008
2	T A Wardall	106	v Gloucestershire	at Gloucester (Spa Ground)	1892
1	Azeem Rafiq	100	v Worcestershire	at Worcester	2009
1	A T Barber	100	v England XI	at Sheffield	1929
1	H D Bird	181*	v Glamorgan	at Bradford	1959
1	T J D Birtles	104	v Lancashire	at Sheffield	1914
1	G S Blewett	190	v Northamptonshire	at Scarborough	1999
1	M T G Elliott	127	v Warwickshire	at Birmingham	2002
1	T Emmett	104	v Gloucestershire	at Clifton	1873
1	G M Fellows	109	v Lancashire	at Manchester	2002
1	A J Finch	110	v. Warwickshire	at Birmingham	2014
1	J N Gillespie	123*	v Surrey	at The Oval	2007
1	D Gough	121	v Warwickshire	at Leeds	1996

1	A K D Gray	104	v Somerset	at Taunton	2003
1	A P Grayson	100	v Worcestershire	at Worcester	1994
1	F E Greenwood	104*	v Glamorgan	at Hull	1929
1	G M Hamilton	125	v Hampshire	at Leeds	2000
1	W E Harbord	109	v Oxford University	at Oxford	1930
1	R Iddison	112	v Cambridgeshire	at Hunslet	1869
1	W G Keighley	110	v Surrey	at Leeds	1951
1	R A Kettleborough				
		108	v Essex	at Leeds	1996
1	B Leadbeater	140*	v Hampshire	at Portsmouth	1976
1	D R Martyn	238	v Gloucestershire	at Leeds	2003
1	J T Newstead	100*	v Nottinghamshire	at Nottingham	1908
1	R B Richardson	112	v Warwickshire	at Birmingham	1993
1	H Rudston	164	v Leicestershire	at Leicester (Aylestone Road)	1904
1	A Sidebottom	124	v Glamorgan	at Cardiff (Sophia Gardens)	1977
1	I G Swallow	114	v MCC	at Scarborough	1987
1	S R Tendulkar	100	v Durham	at Durham	1992
1	J Thewlis	108	v Surrey	at The Oval	1868
1	C T Tyson	100*	v Hampshire	at Southampton	1921
1	H Verity	101	v Jamaica	at Kingston (Sabina Park)	1935/36
1	A Waddington	114	v Worcestershire	at Leeds	1927
1	W A I Washington				
		100*	v Surrey	at Leeds	1902
1	H Wilkinson	113	v MCC	at Scarborough	1904
1	W H Wilkinson	103	v Sussex	at Sheffield	1909
1	K S Williamson	189	v. Sussex	at Scarborough	2014
1	E R Wilson	104*	v Essex	at Bradford	1913
1	A Wood	123*	v Worcestershire	at Sheffield	1935
1	J D Woodford	101	v Warwickshire	at Middlesbrough	1971

SUMMARY OF CENTURIES
FOR AND AGAINST YORKSHIRE 1863-2014

FOR YORKSHIRE				AGAINST YORKSHIRE		
Total	In Yorkshire	Away		Total	In Yorkshire	Away
110	65	45	Derbyshire	57	27	30
26	12	14	Durham	22	13	9
75	34	41	Essex	46	21	25
68	38	30	Glamorgan	23	13	10
87	41	46	Gloucestershire	53	27	26
88	36	52	Hampshire	56	25	31
81	37	44	Kent	60	29	31
111	56	55	Lancashire	113	58	55
97	52	45	Leicestershire	46	23	23
94	47	47	Middlesex	86	37	49
81	35	46	Northamptonshire	53	25	28
121	57	64	Nottinghamshire	82	33	49
98	49	49	Somerset	58	21	37
114	48	66	Surrey	107	38	69
89	42	47	Sussex	74	33	41
104	36	68	Warwickshire	71	27	44
72	30	42	Worcestershire	40	14	26
1	1	0	Cambridgeshire	0	0	0
1517	716	801	Totals	1047	464	583
9	9	0	Australians	16	16	0
9	9	0	Indians	7	7	0
8	8	0	New Zealanders	3	3	0
5	5	0	Pakistanis	1	1	0
9	9	0	South Africans	7	7	0
5	5	0	Sri Lankans	1	1	0
5	5	0	West Indians	6	6	0
1	1	0	Zimbabweans	0	0	0
3	3	0	Bangladesh 'A'	1	1	0
0	0	0	India 'A'	1	1	0
1	1	0	Pakistan 'A'	1	1	0
45	1	44	Cambridge University	20	2	18
2	2	0	Combined Services	0	0	0
1	0	1	Durham MCCU	1	0	1
4	3	1	England XI's	3	2	1
0	0	0	International XI	1	1	0
1	0	1	Ireland	0	0	0
3	0	3	Jamaica	3	0	3
6	6	0	Leeds/Bradford MCCU	0	0	0
1	0	1	Liverpool & District	0	0	0
2	2	0	Loughborough MCCU	1	1	0
1	0	1	Mashonaland	0	0	0
2	0	2	Matebeleland	1	0	1
52	38	14	MCC	52	34	18
39	0	39	Oxford University	11	0	11
6	0	6	Rest of England	15	0	15
9	5	4	Scotland	1	0	1
3	3	0	C I Thornton's XI	4	4	0
0	0	0	Western Province	1	0	1
1	1	0	I Zingari	1	1	0
233	116	117	Totals	161	91	70
1750	832	918	Grand Totals	1208	555	653

FOUR CENTURIES IN ONE INNINGS

			F S Jackson	117
			E Wainwright	126
1896	v.	Warwickshire	Lord Hawke	166
		at Birmingham	R Peel	*210

(First instance in First-Class cricket)

THREE CENTURIES IN ONE INNINGS

			L Hall	116
1884	v.	Cambridge University	W Bates	133
		at Cambridge	I Grimshaw	115
			G Ulyett	124
1887	v.	Kent	L Hall	110
		at Canterbury	F Lee	119
			J T Brown	311
1897	v.	Sussex	J Tunnicliffe	147
		at Sheffield	E Wainwright	*104
			F S Jackson	155
1899	v.	Middlesex	D Denton	113
		at Bradford	F Mitchell	121
			D Denton	105
1904	v.	Surrey	G H Hirst	104
		at The Oval	J Tunnicliffe	*139
			H Sutcliffe	118
1919	v.	Gloucestershire	D Denton	122
		at Leeds	R Kilner	*115
			P Holmes	130
1925	v.	Glamorgan	H Sutcliffe	121
		at Huddersfield	E Robinson	*108
			P Holmes	105
1928	v.	Middlesex	E Oldroyd	108
		at Lord's	A Mitchell	105
			H Sutcliffe	129
1928	v.	Essex	P Holmes	136
		at Leyton	M Leyland	*133
			E Oldroyd	168
1929	v.	Glamorgan	W Barber	114
		at Hull	F E Greenwood	*104
			H Sutcliffe	107
1933	v.	MCC	A Mitchell	158
		at Scarborough	M Leyland	133
			H Sutcliffe	129
1936	v.	Surrey	L Hutton	163
		at Leeds	M Leyland	*163
			H Sutcliffe	189
1937	v.	Leicestershire	L Hutton	153
		at Hull	M Leyland	*118
			L Hutton	137
1947	v.	Leicestershire	N W D Yardley	100
		at Leicester	G.A Smithson	169
			J H Hampshire	*116
1971	v.	Oxford University	R A Hutton	101
		at Oxford	A J Dalton	111

THREE CENTURIES IN ONE INNINGS *(Continued)*

		G Boycott	141
1975	v. Gloucestershire	R G Lumb	101
	at Bristol	J H Hampshire	*106
		M D Moxon	130
1995	v. Cambridge University	D Byas	181
	at Cambridge	M G Bevan	*113
		M J Wood	102
2001	v. Leicestershire	M J Lumb	122
	at Leeds	D S Lehmann	104
		C White	183
2001	v. Glamorgan	M J Wood	124
	at Scarborough	D Byas	104
		J A Rudolph	122
2007	v. Surrey	T T Bresnan	116
	at The Oval	J N Gillespie	*123
		A Lyth	130
2014	v. Leeds/Bradford MCCU	G S Ballance	101
	At Leeds	J M Bairstow	123

CENTURY IN EACH INNINGS

D Denton	107 and 109*	v. Nottinghamshire at Nottingham, 1906
G H Hirst	111 and 117*	v. Somerset at Bath, 1906
D Denton	133 and 121	v. MCC at Scarborough, 1908
W Rhodes	128 and 115	v. MCC at Scarborough, 1911
P Holmes	126 and 111*	v. Lancashire at Manchester, 1920
H Sutcliffe	107 and109*	v. MCC at Scarborough, 1926
H Sutcliffe	111 and 100*	v. Nottinghamshire at Nottingham, 1928
E I Lester	126 and 142	v. Northamptonshire at Northampton, 1947
L Hutton	197 and 104	v. Essex at Southend, 1947
E I Lester	125* and 132	v. Lancashire at Manchester, 1948
L Hutton	165 and 100	v. Sussex at Hove, 1949
L Hutton	103 and 137	v. MCC at Scarborough, 1952
G Boycott	103 and 105	v. Nottinghamshire at Sheffield, 1966
G Boycott	163 and 141*	v. Nottinghamshire at Bradford, 1983
M D Moxon	123 and 112*	v. Indians at Scarborough, 1986
A A Metcalfe	194* and 107	v. Nottinghamshire at Nottingham, 1990
M P Vaughan	100 and 151	v. Essex at Chelmsford, 1999
Younus Khan	106 and 202*	v. Hampshire at Southampton, 2007
G S Ballance	148 and 108*	v. Surrey at The Oval, 2013

HIGHEST INDIVIDUAL SCORES
FOR AND AGAINST YORKSHIRE

Highest For Yorkshire:
341 G H Hirst v. Leicestershire at Leicester, 1905

Highest Against Yorkshire:
318* W G Grace for Gloucestershire at Cheltenham, 1876

Yorkshire versus:

Derbyshire	For Yorkshire:	300 — J T Brown at Chesterfield, 1898
	Against:	270* — C F Hughes at Leeds, 2013
Most Centuries	For Yorkshire:	G Boycott 9
	Against:	K J Barnett and W Storer 4 each
Durham	For Yorkshire:	339 — D S Lehmann at Leeds, 2006
	Against:	184 — M J di Venuto at Chester-le-Street, 2008
Most Centuries	For Yorkshire:	A McGrath 5
	Against:	M J Di Venuto 4

Yorkshire versus

Essex

	For Yorkshire:	313 — H Sutcliffe at Leyton, 1932
	Against:	219* — D J Insole at Colchester, 1949
Most Centuries	*For Yorkshire:*	H Sutcliffe 9
	Against:	F L Fane, K W R Fletcher, G A Gooch and D J Insole 3 each

Glamorgan

	For Yorkshire:	213 — M D Moxon at Cardiff, 1996
	Against:	202* — H Morris at Cardiff, 1996
Most Centuries	*For Yorkshire:*	G Boycott, P Holmes and H Sutcliffe 5 each
	Against:	H Morris 5

Gloucestershire

	For Yorkshire:	238 — D R Martyn at Leeds, 2003
	Against:	318*— W G Grace at Cheltenham, 1876
Most Centuries	*For Yorkshire:*	G Boycott 6
	Against:	W G Grace 9

Hampshire

	For Yorkshire:	302* — P Holmes at Portsmouth, 1920
	Against:	300* — M A Carberry at Southampton, 2011
Most Centuries	*For Yorkshire:*	H Sutcliffe 6
	Against:	C P Mead 10

Kent

	For Yorkshire:	248 — W Barber at Leeds, 1934.
	Against:	207 — D P Fulton at Maidstone, 1998
Most Centuries	*For Yorkshire:*	A McGrath 6
	Against:	F E Woolley 5

Lancashire

	For Yorkshire:	252 — D S Lehmann at Leeds, 2001
	Against:	225 — G D Lloyd at Leeds, 1997 (Non-Championship)
		206 — S G Law at Leeds, 2007
Most Centuries	*For Yorkshire:*	G Boycott and H Sutcliffe 9 each
	Against:	M A Atherton and C H Lloyd 6 each.

Leicestershire

	For Yorkshire:	341— G H Hirst at Leicester, 1905
	Against:	218— J J Whitaker at Bradford, 1996
Most Centuries	*For Yorkshire:*	H Sutcliffe 10
	Against:	J J Whitaker and C J B Wood 5 each

Middlesex

	For Yorkshire:	315*— P Holmes at Lord's, 1925
	Against:	243*— A J Webbe at Huddersfield, 1887
Most Centuries	*For Yorkshire:*	P Holmes and H Sutcliffe 7 each
	Against:	M W Gatting 8

Northamptonshire

	For Yorkshire:	277* — P Holmes at Harrogate, 1921
	Against:	235 — A J Lamb at Leeds, 1990
Most Centuries	*For Yorkshire:*	H Sutcliffe 5
	Against:	W Larkins 5

Nottinghamshire

	For Yorkshire:	285 — P Holmes at Nottingham, 1929
	Against:	251* — D J Hussey at Leeds, 2010
Most Centuries	*For Yorkshire:*	G Boycott 15
	Against:	R T Robinson 6

Somerset

	For Yorkshire:	213 — H Sutcliffe at Dewsbury, 1924
	Against:	297 — M J Wood at Taunton, 2005
Most Centuries	*For Yorkshire:*	G Boycott 6
	Against:	L C H Palairet, IVA. Richards, M E Trescothick 5 each

Surrey

	For Yorkshire:	255 — W Barber at Sheffield, 1935
	Against:	273 — T W Hayward at The Oval, 1899
Most Centuries	*For Yorkshire:*	H Sutcliffe 9
	Against:	J B Hobbs 8

HIGHEST INDIVIDUAL SCORES FOR AND AGAINST
YORKSHIRE *(continued)*

Yorkshire versus

Sussex	*For Yorkshire:*	311 — J T Brown at Sheffield, 1897
	Against:	274* — M W Goodwin at Hove, 2011
Most Centuries	*For Yorkshire:*	L Hutton 8
	Against:	C B Fry 7
Warwickshire	*For Yorkshire:*	275 — P Holmes at Bradford, 1928
	Against:	225 — D P Ostler at Birmingham, 2002
Most Centuries	*For Yorkshire:*	G Boycott and H Sutcliffe 8 each
	Against:	D L Amiss, H E Dollery, R B Khanhai and W G Quaife 4 each.
Worcestershire	*For Yorkshire:*	274* — M D Moxon at Worcester, 1994
	Against:	259 — D Kenyon at Kidderminster, 1956
Most Centuries	*For Yorkshire:*	M Leyland 6
	Against:	D Kenyon and G M Turner 5 each
Australians	*For Yorkshire:*	167 — J T Brown at Bradford, 1899
	Against:	193* — B C Booth at Bradford, 1964
Most Centuries	*For Yorkshire:*	G Boycott and D Denton 2 each
	Against:	N C O'Neill 2
Indians	*For Yorkshire:*	183* — L Hutton at Bradford, 1946
	Against:	244* — V S Hazare at Sheffield, 1946
Most Centuries	*For Yorkshire:*	M D Moxon 2
	Against:	V S Hazare, V Mankad, P R Umrigar D K Gaekwad, G A Parkar and R Lamba 1 each
New Zealanders	*For Yorkshire:*	175 — P Holmes at Bradford, 1927
	Against:	126 — W M Wallace at Bradford, 1949
Most Centuries	*For Yorkshire:*	L Hutton and D B Close 2 each
	Against:	H G Vivian, W M Wallace and J G Wright 1 each
Pakistanis	*For Yorkshire:*	197 — P J Sharpe at Leeds, 1967
	Against:	139 — A H Kardar at Sheffield, 1954
Most Centuries	*For Yorkshire:*	P J Sharpe 2
	Against:	A H Kardar 1
South Africans	*For Yorkshire:*	156 — L Hutton at Sheffield, 1951
	Against:	168 — I J Seidle at Sheffield, 1929
Most Centuries	*For Yorkshire:*	L Hutton 2
	Against:	H B Cameron, J D Lindsay, B Mitchell, D P B Morkel, I J Seidle, L J Tancred, C B van Ryneveld 1 each
Sri Lankans	*For Yorkshire:*	132 — M D Moxon at Leeds, 1988
	Against:	112 — S A R Silva at Leeds, 1988
Most Centuries	*For Yorkshire:*	K Sharp 2
	Against:	S A R Silva 1
West Indians	*For Yorkshire:*	112* — D Denton at Harrogate, 1906
	Against:	164 — S F A Bacchus at Leeds, 1980
Most Centuries	*For Yorkshire:*	M G Bevan, D Denton, L Hutton, R G Lumb and A A Metcalfe 1 each
	Against:	S F A Bacchus, C O Browne, S Chanderpaul P A Goodman, C L Hooper and G St A Sobers 1 each

Yorkshire versus

Zimbabweans	*For Yorkshire:*	113 — M D Moxon at Leeds, 1990
	Against:	89 — G J Whittall at Leeds, 2000
Most Centuries	*For Yorkshire:*	M D Moxon 1
	Against:	None
Cambridge	*For Yorkshire:*	207* — G Boycott at Cambridge, 1976
University	*Against:*	171* — G L Jessop at Cambridge, 1899
		171 — P B H May at Cambridge, 1952
Most Centuries	*For Yorkshire:*	H Sutcliffe 4
	Against:	G M Kemp 2
Durham MCCU	*For Yorkshire:*	139 — J J Sayers at Durham, 2011
	Against:	127 — T Westley at Durham, 2011
Most Centuries	*For Yorkshire:*	J J Sayers 1
	Against:	T Westley 1
Leeds Bradford MCCU	*For Yorkshire:*	130 — A Lyth at Leeds, 2014
	Against:	69 — A MacQueen at Leeds, 2012
Most Centuries	*For Yorkshire:*	J M Bairstow and A Lyth, 2 each
Loughborough MCCU	*For Yorkshire:*	134* — R M Pyrah at Leeds, 2010
	Against:	107 — C P Murtagh at Leeds, 2007
Most Centuries	*For Yorkshire:*	R M Pyrah 2
	Against:	C P Murtagh 1
MCC	*For Yorkshire:*	180* — G H Hirst at Lord's, 1919
	Against:	214 — E H Hendren at Lord's, 1919
Most Centuries	*For Yorkshire:*	L Hutton 8
	Against:	R E S Wyatt 5
Oxford University	*For Yorkshire:*	196 — R J Blakey at Oxford, 1991
	Against:	201 — J E Raphael at Oxford, 1904
Most Centuries	*For Yorkshire:*	M Leyland 4
	Against:	A A Baig and Nawab of Pataudi (Jun.) 2 each

J B Hobbs scored 11 centuries against Yorkshire – the highest by any individual (8 for Surrey and 3 for the Rest of England).

Three players have scored 10 centuries against Yorkshire – W G Grace (9 for Gloucestershire and 1 for MCC). E H Hendren (6 for Middlesex, 3 for MCC and 1 for the Rest of England) and C P Mead (all 10 for Hampshire).

CARRYING BAT THROUGH A COMPLETED INNINGS

Batsman	Score	Total	Against	Season
G R Atkinson	30*	73	Nottinghamshire at Bradford	1865
L Hall	31*	94	Sussex at Hove	1878
L Hall	124*	331	Sussex at Hove	1883
L Hall	128*	285	Sussex at Huddersfield	1884
L Hall	32*	81	Kent at Sheffield	1885
L Hall	79*	285	Surrey at Sheffield	1885
L Hall	37*	96	Derbyshire at Derby	1885
L Hall	50*	173	Sussex at Huddersfield	1886
L Hall	74*	172	Kent at Canterbury	1886
G Ulyett	199*	399	Derbyshire at Sheffield	1887
L Hall	119*	334	Gloucestershire at Dewsbury	1887
L Hall	82*	218	Sussex at Hove	1887
L Hall	34*	104	Surrey at The Oval	1888
L Hall	129*	461	Gloucestershire at Clifton	1888
L Hall	85*	259	Middlesex at Lord's	1889
L Hall	41*	106	Nottinghamshire at Sheffield	1891
W Rhodes	98*	184	MCC at Lord's	1903
W Rhodes	85*	152	Essex at Leyton	1910
P Holmes	145*	270	Northamptonshire at Northampton	1920
H Sutcliffe	125*	307	Essex at Southend	1920
P Holmes	175*	377	New Zealanders at Bradford	1927
P Holmes	110*	219	Northamptonshire at Bradford	1929
H Sutcliffe	104*	170	Hampshire at Leeds	1932
H Sutcliffe	114*	202	Rest of England at The Oval	1933
H Sutcliffe	187*	401	Worcestershire at Bradford	1934
H Sutcliffe	135*	262	Glamorgan at Neath	1935
H Sutcliffe	125*	322	Oxford University at Oxford	1939
L Hutton	99*	200	Leicestershire at Sheffield	1948
L Hutton	78*	153	Worcestershire at Sheffield	1949
F A Lowson	76*	218	MCC at Lord's	1951
W B Stott	144*	262	Worcestershire at Worcester	1959
D E V Padgett	115*	230	Gloucestershire at Bristol	1962
G Boycott	114*	297	Leicestershire at Sheffield	1968
G Boycott	53*	119	Warwickshire at Bradford	1969
G Boycott	182*	320	Middlesex at Lord's	1971
G Boycott	138*	232	Warwickshire at Birmingham	1971
G Boycott	175*	360	Nottinghamshire at Worksop	1979
G Boycott	112*	233	Derbyshire at Sheffield	1983
G Boycott	55*	183	Warwickshire at Leeds	1984
G Boycott	55*	131	Surrey at Sheffield	1985
M J Wood	60*	160	Somerset at Scarborough	2004
J J Sayers	122*	326	Middlesex at Scarborough	2006
J J Sayers	149*	414	Durham at Leeds	2007
A Lyth	248*	486	Leicestershire at Leicester	2012

44 instances, of which L Hall (14 times), G Boycott (8) and H Sutcliffe (6) account for 28 between them.

The highest percentage of an innings total is 61.17 by H. Sutcliffe (104* v. Hampshire at Leeds in 1932) but P Holmes was absent ill, so only nine wickets fell.

Other contributions exceeding 55% are:

59.48%	G Boycott	(138*	v. Warwickshire at Birmingham, 1971)
56.87%	G Boycott	(182*	v. Middlesex at Lord's, 1971)
56.43%	H Sutcliffe	(114*	v. Rest of England at The Oval, 1933)
55.92%	W Rhodes	(85*	v. Essex at Leyton, 1910)

2,000 RUNS IN A SEASON

Batsman	Season	M	I	NO	Runs	HS	Avge	100s
G H Hirst	1904	32	44	3	2257	157	55.04	8
D Denton	1905	33	52	2	2258	172	45.16	8
G H Hirst	1906	32	53	6	2164	169	46.04	6
D Denton	1911	32	55	4	2161	137*	42.37	6
D Denton	1912	36	51	4	2088	221	44.23	6
P Holmes	1920	30	45	6	2144	302*	54.97	7
P Holmes	1925	35	49	9	2351	315*	58.77	6
H Sutcliffe	1925	34	48	8	2236	235	55.90	7
H Sutcliffe	1928	27	35	5	2418	228	80.60	11
P Holmes	1928	31	40	4	2093	275	58.13	6
H Sutcliffe	1931	28	33	8	2351	230	94.04	9
H Sutcliffe	1932	29	41	5	2883	313	80.08	12
M Leyland	1933	31	44	4	2196	210*	54.90	7
A Mitchell	1933	34	49	10	2100	158	53.84	6
H Sutcliffe	1935	32	47	3	2183	212	49.61	8
L Hutton	1937	28	45	6	2448	271*	62.76	8
H Sutcliffe	1937	32	52	5	2054	189	43.70	4
L Hutton	1939	29	44	5	2316	280*	59.38	10
L Hutton	1947	19	31	2	2068	270*	71.31	10
L Hutton	1949	26	44	6	2640	269*	69.47	9
F A Lowson	1950	31	54	5	2067	141*	42.18	5
D E V Padgett	1959	35	60	8	2158	161*	41.50	4
W B Stott	1959	32	56	2	2034	144*	37.66	3
P J Sharpe	1962	36	62	8	2201	138	40.75	7
G Boycott	1971	18	25	4	2221	233	105.76	11
A A Metcalfe	1990	23	44	4	2047	194*	51.17	6

1,000 RUNS IN A SEASON

Batsman		Runs scored	Runs scored	Runs scored
C W J Athey	(2)	1113 in 1980	1339 in 1982	—
D L Bairstow	(3)	1083 in 1981	1102 in 1983	1163 in 1985
J M Bairstow	(1)	1015 in 2011	—	—
G S Ballance	(1)	1363 in 2013	—	—
W Barber	(8)	1000 in 1932	1595 in 1933	1930 in 1934
		1958 in 1935	1466 in 1937	1455 in 1938
		1501 in 1939	1170 in 1946	—
M G Bevan	(2)	1598 in 1995	1225 in 1996	—
R J Blakey	(5)	1361 in 1987	1159 in 1989	1065 in 1992
		1236 in 1994	1041 in 2002	—
J B Bolus	(2)	1245 in 1960	1970 in 1961	—
M W Booth	(2)	1189 in 1911	1076 in 1913	—
G Boycott	(19)	1628 in 1963	1639 in 1964	1215 in 1965
		1388 in 1966	1530 in 1967	1004 in 1968
		1558 in 1970	2221 in 1971	1156 in 1972
		1478 in 1974	1915 in 1975	1288 in 1976
		1259 in 1977	1074 in 1978	1160 in 1979
		1913 in 1982	1941 in 1983	1567 in 1984
		1657 in 1985	—	—
J T Brown	(9)	1196 in 1894	1260 in 1895	1755 in 1896
		1634 in 1897	1641 in 1898	1375 in 1899
		1181 in 1900	1627 in 1901	1291 in 1903
D Byas	(5)	1557 in 1991	1073 in 1993	1297 in 1994
		1913 in 1995	1319 in 1997	—

Batsman		Runs scored	Runs scored	Runs scored
D B Close	(13)	1192 in 1952	1287 in 1954	1131 in 1955
		1315 in 1957	1335 in 1958	1740 in 1959
		1699 in 1960	1821 in 1961	1438 in 1962
		1145 in 1963	1281 in 1964	1127 in 1965
		1259 in 1966	—	—
K R Davidson	(1)	1241 in 1934	—	—
D Denton	(20)	1028 in 1896	1357 in 1897	1595 in 1899
		1378 in 1900	1400 in 1901	1191 in 1902
		1562 in 1903	1919 in 1904	2258 in 1905
		1905 in 1906	1128 in 1907	1852 in 1908
		1765 in 1909	1106 in 1910	2161 in 1911
		2088 in 1912	1364 in 1913	1799 in 1914
		1213 in 1919	1324 in 1920	—
A Drake	(2)	1487 in 1911	1029 in 1913	—
A W Gale	(1)	1076 in 2013	—	—
A P Grayson	(1)	1046 in 1994	—	—
S Haigh	(1)	1031 in 1904	—	—
L Hall	(1)	1120 in 1887	—	—
H Halliday	(4)	1357 in 1948	1484 in 1950	1351 in 1952
		1461 in 1953	—	—
J H Hampshire	(12)	1236 in 1963	1280 in 1964	1424 in 1965
		1105 in 1966	1244 in 1967	1133 in 1968
		1079 in 1970	1259 in 1971	1124 in 1975
		1303 in 1976	1596 in 1978	1425 in 1981
Lord Hawke	(1)	1005 in 1895	—	—
G H Hirst	(19)	1110 in 1896	1248 in 1897	1546 in 1899
		1752 in 1900	1669 in 1901	1113 in 1902
		1535 in 1903	2257 in 1904	1972 in 1905
		2164 in 1906	1167 in 1907	1513 in 1908
		1151 in 1909	1679 in 1910	1639 in 1911
		1119 in 1912	1431 in 1913	1655 in 1914
		1312 in 1919	—	—
P Holmes	(14)	1876 in 1919	2144 in 1920	1458 in 1921
		1614 in 1922	1884 in 1923	1610 in 1924
		2351 in 1925	1792 in 1926	1774 in 1927
		2093 in 1928	1724 in 1929	1957 in 1930
		1431 in 1931	1191 in 1932	—
L Hutton	(12)	1282 in 1936	2448 in 1937	1171 in 1938
		2316 in 1939	1322 in 1946	2068 in 1947
		1792 in 1948	2640 in 1949	1581 in 1950
		1554 in 1951	1956 in 1952	1532 in 1953
R Illingworth	(5)	1193 in 1957	1490 in 1959	1029 in 1961
		1610 in 1962	1301 in 1964	—
F S Jackson	(4)	1211 in 1896	1300 in 1897	1442 in 1898
		1468 in 1899	—	—
P A Jaques	(2)	1118 in 2004	1359 in 2005	—
S A Kellett	(2)	1266 in 1991	1326 in 1992	—
R Kilner	(10)	1586 in 1913	1329 in 1914	1135 in 1919
		1240 in 1920	1137 in 1921	1132 in 1922
		1265 in 1923	1002 in 1925	1021 in 1926
		1004 in 1927	—	—
A Z Lees	(1)	1018 in 2014	—	—
D S Lehmann	(5)	1575 in 1997	1477 in 2000	1416 in 2001
		1136 in 2002	1706 in 2006	—

1,000 RUNS IN A SEASON *(Continued)*

Batsman		Runs scored	Runs scored	Runs scored
E I Lester	(6)	1256 in 1948	1774 in 1949	1015 in 1950
		1786 in 1952	1380 in 1953	1330 in 1954
M Leyland	(17)	1088 in 1923	1203 in 1924	1560 in 1925
		1561 in 1926	1478 in 1927	1554 in 1928
		1407 in 1929	1814 in 1930	1127 in 1931
		1821 in 1932	2196 in 1933	1228 in 1934
		1366 in 1935	1621 in 1936	1120 in 1937
		1640 in 1938	1238 in 1939	—
J D Love	(2)	1161 in 1981	1020 in 1983	
F A Lowson	(8)	1678 in 1949	2067 in 1950	1607 in 1951
		1562 in 1952	1586 in 1953	1719 in 1954
		1082 in 1955	1428 in 1956	
M J Lumb	(1)	1038 in 2003	—	—
R G Lumb	(5)	1002 in 1973	1437 in 1975	1070 in 1978
		1465 in 1979	1223 in 1980	
A Lyth	(2)	1509 in 2010	1619 in 2014	—
A McGrath	(3)	1425 in 2005	1293 in 2006	1219 in 2010
A A Metcalfe	(6)	1674 in 1986	1162 in 1987	1320 in 1988
		1230 in 1989	2047 in 1990	1210 in 1991
A Mitchell	(10)	1320 in 1928	1633 in 1930	1351 in 1932
		2100 in 1933	1854 in 1934	1530 in 1935
		1095 in 1936	1602 in 1937	1305 in 1938
		1219 in 1939	—	—
F Mitchell	(2)	1678 in 1899	1801 in 1901	—
R Moorhouse	(1)	1096 in 1895	—	—
M D Moxon	(11)	1016 in 1984	1256 in 1985	1298 in 1987
		1430 in 1988	1156 in 1989	1621 in 1990
		1669 in 1991	1314 in 1992	1251 in 1993
		1458 in 1994	1145 in 1995	—
E Oldroyd	(10)	1473 in 1921	1690 in 1922	1349 in 1923
		1607 in 1924	1262 in 1925	1197 in 1926
		1390 in 1927	1304 in 1928	1474 in 1929
		1285 in 1930	—	—
D E V Padgett	(12)	1046 in 1956	2158 in 1959	1574 in 1960
		1856 in 1961	1750 in 1962	1380 in 1964
		1220 in 1965	1194 in 1966	1284 in 1967
		1163 in 1968	1078 in 1969	1042 in 1970
R Peel	(1)	1193 in 1896	—	—
W Rhodes	(17)	1251 in 1904	1353 in 1905	1618 in 1906
		1574 in 1908	1663 in 1909	1355 in 1910
		1961 in 1911	1030 in 1912	1805 in 1913
		1325 in 1914	1138 in 1919	1329 in 1921
		1368 in 1922	1168 in 1923	1030 in 1924
		1256 in 1925	1071 in 1926	—
E Robinson	(2)	1104 in 1921	1097 in 1929	—
P E Robinson	(3)	1173 in 1988	1402 in 1990	1293 in 1991
J A Rudolph	(4)	1078 in 2007	1292 in 2008	1366 in 2009
		1375 in 2010	—	—
J J Sayers	(1)	1150 in 2009	—	—
A B Sellers	(1)	1109 in 1938	—	—
K Sharp	(1)	1445 in 1984	—	—

Batsman		Runs scored	Runs scored	Runs scored
J Sharpe	(10)	1039 in 1960	1240 in 1961	2201 in 1962
		1273 in 1964	1091 in 1965	1352 in 1967
		1256 in 1968	1012 in 1969	1149 in 1970
		1320 in 1973	—	—
W B Stott	(5)	1362 in 1957	1036 in 1958	2034 in 1959
		1790 in 1960	1409 in 1961	—
H Sutcliffe	(21)	†1839 in 1919	1393 in 1920	1235 in 1921
		1909 in 1922	1773 in 1923	1720 in 1924
		2236 in 1925	1672 in 1926	1814 in 1927
		2418 in 1928	1485 in 1929	1636 in 1930
		2351 in 1931	2883 in 1932	1986 in 1933
		1511 in 1934	2183 in 1935	1295 in 1936
		2054 in 1937	1660 in 1938	1416 in 1939

† First season in First-Class cricket – The record for a debut season.

Batsman		Runs scored	Runs scored	Runs scored
W H H Sutcliffe	(1)	1193 in 1955	—	—
K Taylor	(6)	1306 in 1959	1107 in 1960	1494 in 1961
		1372 in 1962	1149 in 1964	1044 in 1966
T L Taylor	(2)	1236 in 1901	1373 in 1902	—
S R Tendulkar	(1)	1070 in 1992	—	—
J Tunnicliffe	(12)	1333 in 1895	1368 in 1896	1208 in 1897
		1713 in 1898	1434 in 1899	1496 in 1900
		1295 in 1901	1274 in 1902	1650 in 1904
		1096 in 1905	1232 in 1906	1195 in 1907
C Turner	(1)	1153 in 1934	—	—
G Ulyett	(4)	1083 in 1878	1158 in 1882	1024 in 1885
		1285 in 1887	—	—
M P Vaughan	(4)	1066 in 1994	1235 in 1995	1161 in 1996
		1161 in 1998	—	—
E Wainwright	(3)	1492 in 1897	1479 in 1899	1044 in 1901
W A I Washington	(1)	1022 in 1902	—	—
W Watson	(8)	1331 in 1947	1352 in 1948	1586 in 1952
		1350 in 1953	1347 in 1954	1564 in 1955
		1378 in 1956	1455 in 1957	—
W H Wilkinson	(1)	1282 in 1908	—	—
B B Wilson	(5)	1054 in 1909	1455 in 1911	1453 in 1912
		1533 in 1913	1632 in 1914	—
J V Wilson	(12)	1460 in 1949	1548 in 1950	1985 in 1951
		1349 in 1952	1531 in 1953	1713 in 1954
		1799 in 1955	1602 in 1956	1287 in 1957
		1064 in 1960	1018 in 1961	1226 in 1962
A Wood	(1)	1237 in 1935	—	—
M J Wood	(4)	1080 in 1998	1060 in 2001	1432 in 2003
		1005 in 2005	—	—
N W D Yardley	(4)	1028 in 1939	1299 in 1947	1413 in 1949
		1031 in 1950	—	—

PLAYERS WHO HAVE SCORED CENTURIES
FOR AND AGAINST YORKSHIRE

Player		For	Venue	Season
C W J Athey (5)	114*	Gloucestershire	Bradford	1984
(10 for Yorkshire)	101	Gloucestershire	Gloucester	1985
	101*	Gloucestershire	Leeds	1987
	112	Sussex	Scarborough	1993
	100	Sussex	Eastbourne	1996
M G Bevan (1)	142	Leicestershire	Leicester	2002
(9 for Yorkshire)				
J B Bolus (2)	114	Nottinghamshire	Bradford	1963
(7 for Yorkshire)	138	Derbyshire	Sheffield	1973
D B Close (1)	102	Somerset	Taunton	1971
(33 for Yorkshire)				
M T G Elliott (1)	125	Glamorgan	Leeds	2004
(1 for Yorkshire)				
P A Gibb (1)	107	Essex	Brentwood	1951
(2 for Yorkshire)				
P A Jaques (1)	222	Northamptonshire	Northampton	2003
(7 for Yorkshire)				
N Kilner (2)	119	Warwickshire	Hull	1932
(2 for Yorkshire)	197	Warwickshire	Birmingham	1933
M J Lumb (1)	135	Nottinghamshire	Scarborough	2013
(8 for Yorkshire)				
P J Sharpe (1)	126	Derbyshire	Chesterfield	1976
(23 for Yorkshire)				

BATSMEN WHO HAVE SCORED OVER 10,000 RUNS

Player	M	I	NO	Runs	HS	Av'ge	100s
H Sutcliffe	602	864	96	38558	313	50.20	112
D Denton	676	1058	61	33282	221	33.38	61
G Boycott	414	674	111	32570	260*	57.85	103
G H Hirst	717	1050	128	32024	341	34.73	56
W Rhodes	883	1195	162	31075	267*	30.08	46
P Holmes	485	699	74	26220	315*	41.95	60
M Leyland	548	720	82	26180	263	41.03	62
L Hutton	341	527	62	24807	280*	53.34	85
D B Close	536	811	102	22650	198	31.94	33
J H Hampshire	456	724	89	21979	183*	34.61	34
J V Wilson	477	724	75	20548	230	31.66	29
D E V Padgett	487	774	63	20306	161*	28.55	29
J Tunnicliffe	472	768	57	19435	243	27.33	22
M D Moxon	277	476	42	18973	274*	43.71	41
A Mitchell	401	550	49	18189	189	37.81	39
P J Sharpe	411	666	71	17685	203*	29.72	23
E Oldroyd	383	509	58	15891	194	35.23	37
J T Brown	345	567	41	15694	311	29.83	23
W Barber	354	495	48	15315	255	34.26	27
R Illingworth	496	668	131	14986	162	27.90	14
D Byas	268	449	42	14398	213	35.37	28
G Ulyett	355	618	53	14157	199*	24.11	15
R J Blakey	339	541	84	14150	223*	30.96	12
A McGrath	242	405	29	14091	211	37.47	34
W Watson	283	430	65	13953	214*	38.22	26
F A Lowson	252	404	31	13897	259*	37.25	30
Lord Hawke	510	739	91	13133	166	20.26	10
R Kilner	365	478	46	13018	206*	30.13	15
D L Bairstow	429	601	113	12985	145	26.60	9
K Taylor	303	505	35	12864	203*	27.37	16
N W D Yardley	302	420	56	11632	183*	31.95	17
R G Lumb	239	395	30	11525	165*	31.57	22
E Wainwright	352	545	30	11092	228	21.53	18
S Haigh	513	687	110	10993	159	19.05	4
E I Lester	228	339	27	10616	186	34.02	24
A A Metcalfe	184	317	19	10465	216*	35.11	25
C White	221	350	45	10376	186	34.01	19
Hon F S Jackson	207	328	22	10371	160	33.89	21
J D Love	247	388	58	10263	170*	31.10	13

RECORD PARTNERSHIPS FOR YORKSHIRE

1st wkt	555	P Holmes (224*) and H Sutcliffe (313) v. Essex at Leyton, 1932
2nd wkt	346	W Barber (162) and M Leyland (189) v. Middlesex at Sheffield, 1932
3rd wkt	346	J J Sayers (173) and A McGrath (211) v. Warwickshire at Birmingham, 2009
4th wkt	358	D S Lehmann (339) and M J Lumb (98) v. Durham at Leeds, 2006
5th wkt	340	E Wainwright (228) and G H Hirst (186) v. Surrey at The Oval, 1899
6th wkt	276	M Leyland (191) and E Robinson (124*) v. Glamorgan at Swansea, 1926
7th wkt	254	W Rhodes (135) and D C F Burton (142*) v. Hampshire at Dewsbury, 1919
8th wkt	292	R Peel (210*) and Lord Hawke (166) v. Warwickshire at Birmingham, 1896
9th wkt	246	T T Bresnan (116) and J N Gillespie (123*) v. Surrey at The Oval, 2007
10th wkt	149	G Boycott (79) and G B Stevenson (115*) v. Warwickshire at Birmingham, 1982

RECORD PARTNERSHIPS AGAINST YORKSHIRE

1st wkt	372	R R Montgomerie (127) and M B Loye (205) for Northamptonshire at Northampton, 1996
2nd wkt	417	K J Barnett (210*) and TA Tweats (189) for Derbyshire at Derby, 1997
3rd wkt	523	M A Carberry (300*) and N D McKenzie (237) for Hampshire at Southampton, 2011
4th wkt	447	R Abel (193) and T Hayward (273) for Surrey at The Oval, 1899
5th wkt	261	W G Grace (318*) and W O Moberley (103) for Gloucestershire at Cheltenham, 1876
6th wkt	294	D R Jardine (157) and P G H Fender (177) for Surrey at Bradford, 1928
7th wkt	315	D M Benkenstein (151) and O D Gibson (155) for Durham at Leeds, 2006
8th wkt	178	A P Wells (253*) and B T P Donelan (59) for Sussex at Middlesbrough, 1991
9th wkt	233	I J L Trott (161*) and J S Patel (120) for Warwickshire at Birmingham, 2009
10th wkt	132	A Hill (172*) and M Jean-Jacques (73) for Derbyshire at Sheffield, 1986

CENTURY PARTNERSHIPS FOR THE FIRST WICKET IN BOTH INNINGS

128	108	G Ulyett (82 and 91) and L Hall (87 and 37) v. Sussex at Hove, 1885
		(First instance in First-Class cricket)
138	147*	J T Brown (203 and 81*) and J Tunnicliffe (62 and 63*) v. Middlesex at Lord's, 1896
		(Second instance in First-Class cricket)
105	265*	P Holmes (51 and 127*) and H Sutcliffe (71 and 131*) v. Surrey at The Oval, 1926
184	210*	P Holmes (83 and 101*) and H Sutcliffe (111 and 100*) v. Nottinghamshire at Nottingham, 1928
110	117	L Hutton (95 and 86) and W Watson (34 and 57) v. Lancashire at Manchester, 1947
122	230	W B Stott (50 and 114) and K Taylor (79 and 140) v. Nottinghamshire at Nottingham, 1957
136	138	J B Bolus (108 and 71) and K Taylor (89 and 75) v. Cambridge University at Cambridge, 1962
105	105	G Boycott (38 and 64) and K Taylor (85 and 49) v. Leicestershire at Leicester, 1963
116	112*	K Taylor (45 and 68) and J H Hampshire (68 and 67*) v. Oxford University at Oxford, 1964
104	104	G Boycott (117 and 49*) and R G Lumb (47 and 57) v. Sussex at Leeds, 1974
134	185*	M D Moxon (57 and 89*) and A A Metcalfe (216* and 78*) v. Middlesex at Leeds, 1988
118	129*	G S Ballance (72 and 73*) and J J Sayers (139 and 53*) v. Durham MCCU at Durham, 2011

CENTURY PARTNERSHIPS FOR THE FIRST WICKET IN BOTH INNINGS BUT WITH CHANGE OF PARTNER

109		W H H Sutcliffe (82) and F A Lowson (46)
	143	W H H Sutcliffe (88) and W Watson (52) v. Canadians at Scarborough, 1954
109		G Boycott (70) and R G Lumb (44)
	135	G Boycott (74) and JH Hampshire (58) v. Northamptonshire at Bradford, 1977

CENTURY PARTNERSHIPS

FIRST WICKET (Qualification 200 runs)

555	P Holmes (224*) and H Sutcliffe (313) v. Essex at Leyton, 1932
554	J T Brown (300) and J Tunnicliffe (243) v. Derbyshire at Chesterfield, 1898
378	J T Brown (311) and J Tunnicliffe (147) v. Sussex at Sheffield, 1897
375	A Lyth (230) and (A Z Lees (138) v. Northamptonshire at Northampton, 2014
362	M D Moxon (213) and M P Vaughan (183) v. Glamorgan at Cardiff, 1996
351	G Boycott (184) and M D Moxon (168) v. Worcestershire at Worcester, 1985
347	P Holmes (302*) and H Sutcliffe (131) v. Hampshire at Portsmouth, 1920
323	P Holmes (125) and H Sutcliffe (195) v. Lancashire at Sheffield, 1931
315	H Sutcliffe (189) and L Hutton (153) v. Leicestershire at Hull, 1937
315	H Sutcliffe (116) and L Hutton (280*) v. Hampshire at Sheffield, 1939
309	P Holmes (250) and H Sutcliffe (129) v. Warwickshire at Birmingham, 1931
309	C White (186) and M J Wood (115) v. Lancashire at Manchester, 2001
290	P Holmes (179*) and H Sutcliffe (104) v. Middlesex at Leeds, 1928
288	G Boycott (130*) and R G Lumb (159) v. Somerset at Harrogate, 1979
286	L Hutton (156) and F A Lowson (115) v. South Africans at Sheffield, 1951
282	M D Moxon (147) and A A Metcalfe (151) v. Lancashire at Manchester, 1986
281*	W B Stott (138*) and K Taylor (130*) v. Sussex at Hove, 1960
279	P Holmes (133) and H Sutcliffe (145) v. Northamptonshire at Northampton, 1919
274	P.Holmes (199) and H Sutcliffe (139) v. Somerset at Hull, 1923
274	P Holmes (180) and H Sutcliffe (134) v. Gloucestershire at Gloucester, 1927
272	P Holmes (194) and H Sutcliffe (129) v. Leicestershire at Hull, 1925
272	M J Wood (202*) and J J Sayers (115) v. Bangladesh 'A' at Leeds, 2005
270	A Lyth (143) and A Z Lees (108) v. Durham at Leeds, 2014
268	P Holmes (136) and H Sutcliffe (129) v. Essex at Leyton, 1928
267	W Barber (248) and L Hutton (70) v. Kent at Leeds, 1934
265*	P Holmes (127*) and H Sutcliffe (131*) v. Surrey at The Oval, 1926
264	G Boycott (161*) and R G Lumb (132) v. Gloucestershire at Leeds, 1976
253	P Holmes (123) and H Sutcliffe (132) v. Lancashire at Sheffield, 1919
248	G Boycott (163) and A A Metcalfe (122) v. Nottinghamshire at Bradford, 1983
245	L Hutton (152) and F A Lowson (120) v. Lancashire at Leeds, 1952
244	J A Rudolph (149) and J J Sayers (86) v Nottinghamshire at Nottingham, 2009
241	P Holmes (142) and H Sutcliffe (123*) v. Surrey at The Oval, 1929
240	G Boycott (233) and P J Sharpe (92) v. Essex at Colchester, 1971
238*	P Holmes (126*) and H Sutcliffe (105*) v. Cambridge University at Cambridge, 1923
236	G Boycott (131) and K Taylor (91) v. Lancashire at Manchester, 1964
235	P Holmes (130) and H Sutcliffe (132*) v. Glamorgan at Sheffield, 1930
233	G Boycott (141*) and R G Lumb (90) v. Cambridge University at Cambridge, 1973
233	H Halliday (116) and W Watson (108) v. Northamptonshire at Northampton, 1948
231	M P Vaughan (151) and D Byas (90) v. Essex at Chelmsford, 1999
230	H Sutcliffe (129) and L Hutton (163) v. Surrey at Leeds, 1936
230	W B Stott (114) and K Taylor (140*) v. Nottinghamshire at Nottingham, 1957
228	H Halliday (90) and J V Wilson (223*) v. Scotland at Scarborough, 1951
228	G Boycott (141) and R G Lumb (101) v. Gloucestershire at Bristol, 1975
227	P Holmes (110) and H Sutcliffe (119) v. Leicestershire at Leicester, 1928
225	R G Lumb (101) and C W J Athey (125*) v. Gloucestershire at Sheffield, 1980
224	C W J Athey (114) and J D Love (104) v. Warwickshire at Birmingham, 1980

222	W B Stott (141) and K Taylor (90) v. Sussex at Bradford, 1958
221	P Holmes (130) and H Sutcliffe (121) v. Glamorgan at Huddersfield, 1925
221	M D Moxon (141) and A A Metcalfe (73) v. Surrey at The Oval, 1992
221	A Lyth (111) and A Z Lees (121) v. Leeds/Bradford MCCU at Leeds, 2013
219	P Holmes (102) and A Mitchell (130*) v. Somerset at Bradford, 1930
218	M Leyland (110) and H Sutcliffe (235) v. Middlesex at Leeds, 1925
218	R G Lumb (145) and M D Moxon (111) v. Derbyshire at Sheffield, 1981
210*	P Holmes (101*) and H Sutcliffe (100*) v. Nottinghamshire at Nottingham, 1928
210	G Boycott (128) and P J Sharpe (197) v. Pakistanis at Leeds, 1967
209	F A Lowson (115) and D E V Padgett (107) v. Scotland at Hull, 1956
208	A Mitchell (85) and E Oldroyd (111) v. Cambridge University at Cambridge, 1929
207	A Mitchell (90) and W Barber (107) v. Middlesex at Lord's, 1935
206	G Boycott (118) and R G Lumb (87) v. Glamorgan at Sheffield, 1978
204	M D Moxon (66) and A A Metcalfe (162) v. Gloucestershire at Cheltenham, 1990
203	L Hutton (119) and F A Lowson (83) v. Somerset at Huddersfield, 1952
203	M D Moxon (117) and S A Kellett (87) v. Somerset at Middlesbrough, 1992
203	M D Moxon (134) and M P Vaughan (106) v. Matebeleland at Bulawayo, 1996
200*	P Holmes (107*) and H Sutcliffe (80*) v. Oxford University at Oxford, 1930

Note: P Holmes and H Sutcliffe shared 69 century opening partnerships for Yorkshire; G Boycott and R G Lumb 29; L Hutton and F A Lowson 22; M D Moxon and A A Metcalfe 21; J T Brown and J Tunnicliffe 19; H Sutcliffe and L Hutton 15, and L Hall and G Ulyett 12.

SECOND WICKET (Qualification 200 runs)

346	W Barber (162) and M Leyland (189) v. Middlesex at Sheffield, 1932
343	F A Lowson (183*) and J V Wilson (165) v. Oxford University at Oxford, 1956
333	P Holmes (209) and E Oldroyd (138*) v. Warwickshire at Birmingham, 1922
314	H Sutcliffe (255*) and E Oldroyd (138) v. Essex at Southend-on-Sea, 1924
311	A Z Lees (275*) and P A Jaques (139) v. Derbyshire at Chesterfield, 2013
305	J W.Rothery (134) and D Denton (182) v. Derbyshire at Chesterfield, 1910
302	W Watson (172) and J V Wilson (140) v. Derbyshire at Scarborough, 1948
301	P J Sharpe (172*) and D E V Padgett (133) v. Glamorgan at Swansea, 1971
288	H Sutcliffe (165) and A Mitchell (136) v. Lancashire at Manchester, 1939
280	L Hall (160) and F Lee (165) v. Lancashire at Bradford, 1887
266*	K Taylor (178*) and D E V Padgett (107*) v. Oxford University at Oxford, 1962
264	P A Jaques (152) and K S Williamson (97) v. Durham at Scarborough, 2013
261*	L Hutton (146*) and J V Wilson (110*) v. Scotland at Hull, 1949
260	R G Lumb (144) and K Sharp (132) v. Glamorgan at Cardiff, 1984
258	H Sutcliffe (230) and E Oldroyd (93) v. Kent at Folkestone, 1931
253	B B Wilson (150) and D Denton (200*) v. Warwickshire at Birmingham, 1912
248	H Sutcliffe (200) and M. Leyland (116) v. Leicestershire at Leicester, 1926
244	P. Holmes (138) and E Oldroyd (151*) v. Glamorgan at Cardiff, 1922
243	G Boycott (141) and J D Love (163) v. Nottinghamshire at Bradford, 1976
243	C White (183) and M J Wood (124) v. Glamorgan at Scarborough, 2001
237	H Sutcliffe (118) and D Denton (122) v. Gloucestershire at Leeds, 1919
237	M D Moxon (132) and K Sharp (128) v. Sri Lankans at Leeds, 1988
236	F A Lowson (112) and J V Wilson (157) v. Essex at Leeds, 1950
235	M D Moxon (130) and D Byas (181) v. Cambridge University at Cambridge, 1995
230	L Hutton (180) and A Mitchell (100) v. Cambridge University at Cambridge, 1938
230	M P Vaughan (109) and B Parker (138*) v. Oxford University at Oxford, 1997.
227	M J Wood (102) and M J Lumb (122) v. Leicestershire at Leeds, 2001
225	H Sutcliffe (138) and E Oldroyd (97) v. Derbyshire at Dewsbury, 1928
223	M D Moxon (153) and R J Blakey (90) v. Somerset at Leeds, 1985
222	H Sutcliffe (174) and D Denton (114) v. Kent at Dover, 1919
219	F S Jackson (155) and D Denton (113) v. Middlesex at Bradford, 1899
217	R G Lumb (107) and J D Love (107) v. Oxford University at Oxford, 1978
216	M P Vaughan (105) and D Byas (102) v. Somerset at Bradford, 1994

CENTURY PARTNERSHIPS *(Continued)*

215	A W Gale (136) and A McGrath (99) v. Lancashire at Manchester, 2008
211	J A Rudolph (141) and A McGrath (80) v Nottinghamshire at Leeds, 2010
207	P A Jaques (115) and A McGrath (93) v. Essex at Chelmsford, 2004
206	J Tunnicliffe (102) and F S Jackson (134*) v. Lancashire at Sheffield, 1898
206	H Sutcliffe (187) and M Leyland (90) v. Leicestershire at Leicester, 1931
205	H Sutcliffe (174) and A Mitchell (95) v. Leicestershire at Leicester, 1933
205	G Boycott (148) and P J Sharpe (108) v. Kent at Sheffield, 1970
203	A T Barber (100) and E Oldroyd (143) v. An England XI at Sheffield, 1929
203	J J Sayers (187) and A McGrath (100) v. Kent at Tunbridge Wells, 2007
202*	W Rhodes (115*) and G H Hirst (117*) v. Somerset at Bath, 1906
202	G Boycott (113) and C W J Athey (114) v. Northamptonshire at Northampton, 1978

THIRD WICKET (Qualification 200 runs)

346	J J Sayers (173) and A McGrath (211) v. Warwickshire at Birmingham, 2009
323*	H Sutcliffe (147*) and M Leyland (189*) v. Glamorgan at Huddersfield, 1928
317	A McGrath (165) and D S Lehmann (187) v. Lancashire at Leeds, 2002
310	A McGrath (134) and P A Jaques (219) v. Derbyshire at Leeds, 2005
301	H Sutcliffe (175) and M Leyland (180*) v. Middlesex at Lord's, 1939
293*	A A Metcalfe (150*) and P E Robinson (150*) v. Derbyshire at Scarborough, 1990
269	D Byas (101) and R J Blakey (196) v. Oxford University at Oxford, 1991
258*	J T Brown (134*) and F Mitchell (116*) v. Warwickshire at Bradford, 1901
252	D E V Padgett (139*) and D B Close (154) v. Nottinghamshire at Nottingham, 1959
249	D E V Padgett (95) and D B Close (184) v. Nottinghamshire at Scarborough, 1960
248	C Johnson (102) and J H Hampshire (155*) v. Gloucestershire at Leeds, 1976
247	P Holmes (175*) and M Leyland (118) v. New Zealanders at Bradford, 1927
244	D E V Padgett (161*) and D B Close (144) v. Oxford University at Oxford, 1959
240	L Hutton (151) and M Leyland (95) v. Surrey at Leeds, 1939
237	J A Rudolph (198) and A McGrath (120) v. Worcestershire at Leeds, 2009
236	H Sutcliffe (107) and R Kilner (137) v. Nottinghamshire at Nottingham, 1920
236	M J Wood (94) and D S Lehmann (200) v. Worcestershire at Worcester, 1998
234*	D Byas (126*) and A McGrath (105*) v. Oxford University at Oxford, 1997.
233	L Hutton (101) and M Leyland (167) v. Worcestershire at Stourbridge, 1937
230	D Byas (103) and M J Wood (103) v. Derbyshire at Leeds, 1998
229	L Hall (86) and R Peel (158) v. Middlesex at Lord's, 1889
228	A Mitchell (142) and M Leyland (133) v. Worcestershire at Sheffield, 1933
228	W Barber (141) and M Leyland (114) v. Surrey at The Oval, 1939
228	J V Wilson (132*) and D E V Padgett (115) v. Warwickshire at Birmingham, 1955
226	D E V Padgett (117) and D B Close (198) v. Surrey at The Oval, 1960
224	J V Wilson (110) and D B Close (114) v. Cambridge University at Cambridge, 1955
224	G Boycott (140*) and K Sharp (121) v. Gloucestershire at Cheltenham, 1983
221	A Mitchell (138) and M Leyland (134) v. Nottinghamshire at Bradford, 1933
219	L Hall (116) and W Bates (133) v. Cambridge University at Cambridge, 1884
218	J A Rudolph (127) and A W Gale (121) v. Lancashire at Manchester, 2009
217	A McGrath (144) and J A Rudolph (129) v. Kent at Canterbury, 2008
216	R G Lumb (118) and J H Hampshire (127) v. Surrey at The Oval, 1975
215	A Mitchell (73) and M Leyland (139) v. Surrey at Bradford, 1928
213	E Oldroyd (168) and W Barber (114) v. Glamorgan at Hull, 1929
208	J V Wilson (157*) and E I Lester (112) v. Sussex at Leeds, 1949
206	A McGrath (105) and J A Rudolph (228*) v Durham at Leeds, 2010
205*	E Oldroyd (122*) and M Leyland (100*) v. Hampshire at Harrogate, 1924
205	F S Jackson (124) and D Denton (112) v. Somerset at Taunton, 1897
205	D E V Padgett (83) and D B Close (128) v. Somerset at Bath, 1959
204	M P Vaughan (113) and A McGrath (70) v. Essex at Scarborough, 2001
203	D Denton (132) and J Tunnicliffe (102) v. Warwickshire at Birmingham, 1905
203	A A Metcalfe (216*) and P E Robinson (88) v. Middlesex at Leeds, 1988
201	J Tunnicliffe (101) and T L Taylor (147) v. Surrey at The Oval, 1900

THIRD WICKET (Qualification 200 runs) *(Continued)*

201	H Sutcliffe (87) and W Barber (130) v. Leicestershire at Leicester, 1938
200	M D Moxon (274*) and A P Grayson (100) v. Worcestershire at Worcester, 1994

FOURTH WICKET (Qualification 175 runs)

358	D S Lehmann (339) and M J Lumb (98) v. Durham at Leeds, 2006
330	M J Wood (116) and D R Martyn (238) v. Gloucestershire at Leeds, 2003
312	D Denton (168*) and G H Hirst (146) v. Hampshire at Southampton, 1914
299	P Holmes (277*) and R Kilner (150) v. Northamptonshire at Harrogate, 1921
272	D Byas (138) and A McGrath (137) v. Hampshire at Harrogate, 1996
271	B B Wilson (208) and W Rhodes (113) v. Sussex at Bradford, 1914
259	A Drake (115) and G H Hirst (218) v. Sussex at Hastings, 1911
258	J Tunnicliffe (128) and G H Hirst (152) v. Hampshire at Portsmouth, 1904
258	P E Robinson (147) and D Byas (117) v. Kent at Scarborough, 1989
249	W B Stott (143) and G Boycott (145) v. Lancashire at Sheffield, 1963
247*	R G Lumb (165*) and S N Hartley (104*) v. Gloucestershire at Bradford, 1984
247	M Leyland (263) and L Hutton (83) v. Essex at Hull, 1936
238	D S Lehmann (216) and M J Lumb (92) v. Sussex at Arundel, 2002
233	D Byas (120) and P E Robinson (189) v. Lancashire at Scarborough, 1991
231	J E Root (236) and J M Bairstow (186) v. Derbyshire at Leeds, 2013
226	W H Wilkinson (89) and G H Hirst (140) v. Northamptonshire at Hull, 1909
225	C H Grimshaw (85) and G H Hirst (169) v. Oxford University at Oxford, 1906
212	B B Wilson (108) and G H Hirst (166*) v. Sussex at Hastings, 1913
212	G Boycott (260*) and J H Hampshire (80) v. Essex at Colchester, 1970
211	J V Wilson (120) and W Watson (108) v. Derbyshire at Harrogate, 1951
210*	A Mitchell (150*) and M Leyland (117*) v. Worcestershire at Worcester, 1933
210	E I Lester (178) and W Watson (97) v. Nottinghamshire at Nottingham, 1952
207	D Byas (213) and C White (107*) v. Worcestershire at Scarborough, 1995
206	J A Rudolph (121) and A W Gale (150) v. Surrey at The Oval, 2008
205*	G Boycott (151*) and P J Sharpe (79*) v. Leicestershire at Leicester, 1964
205	E Oldroyd (121) and R Kilner (117) v. Worcestershire at Dudley, 1922
205	W Watson (162*) and E I Lester (98) v. Somerset at Leeds, 1953
204	A W Gale (148) and G S Ballance (90) v. Surrey at Leeds, 2013
201*	J H Hampshire (105*) and D B Close (101*) v. Surrey at Bradford, 1965
203	P A Jaques (160) and G S Ballance (121*) v. Gloucestershire at Bristol, 2012
201	W H H Sutcliffe (181) and L Hutton (120) v. Kent at Canterbury, 1952
200	J V Wilson (92) and W Watson (122) v. Somerset at Taunton, 1950
198	A A Metcalfe (138) and D Byas (95) v. Warwickshire at Leeds, 1989
198	A W Gale (124) and J M Bairstow (95) v. Durham at Chester-le-Street, 2014
197	N W D Yardley (177) and A Coxon (58) v. Derbyshire at Scarborough, 1947
197	A Lyth (248*) and J M Bairstow (118) v. Leicestershire at Leicester, 2012
196	M D Moxon (130) and D L Bairstow (104) v. Derbyshire at Harrogate, 1987
193	A Drake (85) and G H Hirst (156) v. Lancashire at Manchester, 1911
192	J V Wilson (132) and W Watson (105) v. Essex at Bradford, 1955
191	M Leyland (114) and C Turner (63) v. Essex at Ilford, 1938
188	H Myers (60) and G H Hirst (158) v. Cambridge University at Cambridge, 1910
187	E Oldroyd (168) and F E Greenwood (104*) v. Glamorgan at Hull, 1929
187	K Taylor (203*) and W B Stott (57) v. Warwickshire at Birmingham, 1961
186	D S Lehmann (193) and D Byas (100) v. Leicestershire at Leicester, 2001
184	J H Hampshire (96) and R Illingworth (100*) v. Leicestershire at Sheffield, 1968
182*	E I Lester (101*) and W Watson (103*) v. Nottinghamshire at Bradford, 1952
180*	G Boycott (207*) and B Leadbeater (50*) v. Cambridge University at Cambridge, 1976
180	J Tunnicliffe (139*) and G H Hirst (108) v. Surrey at The Oval, 1904
179	J H Hampshire (179) and S N Hartley (63) v. Surrey at Harrogate, 1981
179	M D Moxon (171*) and R J Blakey (71) v. Kent at Leeds, 1993
178	E I Lester (186) and J V Wilson (71) v. Warwickshire at Scarborough, 1949
177	J D Love (105*) and J H Hampshire (89) v. Lancashire at Manchester, 1980
175	L Hutton (177) and W Barber (84) v. Sussex at Scarborough, 1939
175	A McGrath (188*) and J A Rudolph (82) v. Warwickshire at Birmingham, 2007

CENTURY PARTNERSHIPS *(Continued)*

FIFTH WICKET (Qualification 150 runs)

340	E Wainwright (228) and G H Hirst (186) v. Surrey at The Oval, 1899	
329	F Mitchell (194) and E Wainwright (153) v. Leicestershire at Leicester, 1899	
297	A W Gale (272) and G S Ballance (141) v. Nottinghamshire at Scarborough, 2013	
276	W Rhodes (104*) and R Kilner (166) v. Northamptonshire at Northampton, 1921	
273	L Hutton (270*) and N W D Yardley (136) v. Hampshire at Bournemouth, 1947	
245*	H Sutcliffe (107*) and W Barber (128*) v. Northamptonshire at Northampton, 1939	
229	D S Lehmann (193) and C White (79) v. Kent at Canterbury, 2006	
217	D B Close (140*) and R Illingworth (107) v. Warwickshire at Sheffield, 1962	
207	G S Ballance (107) and A U Rashid (180) v. Somerset at Leeds, 2013	
198	E Wainwright (145) and R Peel (111) v. Sussex at Bradford, 1896	
198	W Barber (168) and K R Davidson (101*) v. MCC at Lord's, 1934	
196*	R Kilner (115*) and G H Hirst (82*) v. Gloucestershire at Leeds, 1919	
195	M J Lumb (93) and C White (173*) v. Derbyshire at Derby, 2003	
194*	Younus Khan (202*) and G L Brophy (100*) v. Hampshire at Southampton, 2007	
193	A Mitchell (189) and W Rhodes (88) v. Northamptonshire at Northampton, 1926	
193	J D Love (106) and S N Hartley (108) v. Oxford University at Oxford, 1985	
192	C W J Athey (114*) and J D Love (123) v. Surrey at The Oval, 1982	
191*	L Hutton (271*) and C Turner (81*) v. Derbyshire at Sheffield, 1937	
191	M G Bevan (105) and A A Metcalfe (100) v. West Indians at Scarborough, 1995	
190*	R J Blakey (204*) and J D Love (79*) v. Gloucestershire at Leeds, 1987	
189	J E Root (160) and G S Ballance (87) v. Sussex at Scarborough 2011	
188	D E V Padgett (146) and J V Wilson (72) v. Sussex at Middlesbrough, 1960	
187	J V Wilson (230) and H Halliday (74) v. Derbyshire at Sheffield, 1952	
185	G Boycott (104*) and K Sharp (99) v. Kent at Tunbridge Wells, 1984	
182	E Lockwood (208) and E Lumb (40) v. Kent at Gravesend, 1882	
182	B B Wilson (109) and W Rhodes (111) v. Sussex at Hove, 1910	
182	D B Close (164) and J V Wilson (55) v. Combined Services at Harrogate, 1954	
182	A W Gale (126*) and J A Leaning (76) v. Middlesex at Scarborough, 2014	
181	A A Metcalfe (149) and J D Love (88) v. Glamorgan at Leeds, 1986	
177	Hon F S Jackson (87) and G H Hirst (232*) v. Surrey at The Oval, 1905	
176	L Hutton (176*) and A Coxon (72) v. Sussex at Sheffield, 1948	
175	A Drake (108) and R Kilner (77) v. Cambridge University at Cambridge, 1913	
173	H Sutcliffe (206) and R Kilner (124) v. Warwickshire at Dewsbury, 1925	
170	W Rhodes (157) and R Kilner (87) v. Derbyshire at Leeds, 1925	
170	J V Wilson (130*) and N W D Yardley (67) v. Lancashire at Manchester, 1954	
169	W Watson (147) and A B Sellers (92) v. Worcestershire at Worcester, 1947	
168	A T Barber (63) and A Mitchell (122*) v. Worcestershire at Worcester, 1929	
167	J M Bairstow (136) and G S Ballance (61) v. Somerset at Taunton 2011	
165	E Oldroyd (143) and W Rhodes (110) v. Glamorgan at Leeds, 1922	
165	K Sharp (100*) and P Carrick (73) v. Middlesex at Lord's, 1980	
164	A A Metcalfe (151) and D L Bairstow (88) v. Northamptonshire at Luton, 1986	
159*	J D Love (170*) and D L Bairstow (52*) v. Worcestershire at Worcester, 1979	
159	D B Close (128) and R Illingworth (74) v. Lancashire at Sheffield, 1959	
159	J H Hampshire (183*) and C Johnson (53) v. Sussex at Hove, 1971	
158*	G Boycott (153*) and P E Robinson (74*) v. Derbyshire at Harrogate, 1984	
157	T L Taylor (135*) and G H Hirst (72) v. An England XI at Hastings, 1901	
157	G H Hirst (142) and F Smith (51) v. Somerset at Bradford, 1903	
157	W Barber (87) and N W D Yardley (101) v. Surrey at The Oval, 1937	
156	A McGrath (158) and I J Harvey (103) v. Derbyshire at Derby, 2005	
153	S N Hartley (87) and M D Moxon (112*) v. Indians at Scarborough, 1986	
152	J H Hampshire (83) and S N Hartley (106) v. Nottinghamshire at Nottingham, 1981	
151*	G H Hirst (102*) and R Kilner (50*) v. Kent at Bradford, 1913	
151	G H Hirst (120) and F Smith (55) v. Kent at Leeds, 1903	
151	W Rhodes (57) and R Kilner (90) v. Nottinghamshire at Nottingham, 1925	

CENTURY PARTNERSHIPS *(Continued)*

SIXTH WICKET (Qualification 150 runs)

296	A Lyth (251) and A U Rashid (159*) v. Lancashire at Manchester, 2014	
276	M Leyland (191) and E Robinson (124*) v. Glamorgan at Swansea, 1926	
252	C White (181) and R J Blakey (109*) v. Lancashire at Leeds, 1996	
233	M W Booth (210) and G H Hirst (100) v. Worcestershire at Worcester, 1911	
229	W Rhodes (267*) and N Kilner (112) v. Leicestershire at Leeds, 1921	
225	E Wainwright (91) and Lord Hawke (127) v. Hampshire at Southampton, 1899	
217*	H Sutcliffe (200*) and A Wood (123*) v. Worcestershire at Sheffield, 1935	
214	W Watson (214*) and N W D Yardley (76) v. Worcestershire at Worcester, 1955	
205	G H Hirst (125) and S Haigh (159) v. Nottinghamshire at Sheffield, 1901	
200	D Denton (127) and G H Hirst (134) v. Essex at Bradford, 1902	
198	M Leyland (247) and W Rhodes (100*) v. Worcestershire at Worcester, 1928	
190	W Rhodes (126) and M Leyland (79) v. Middlesex at Bradford, 1923	
190	J A Rudolph (122) and A U Rashid (86) v. Surrey at The Oval, 2007	
188	W Watson (174) and R Illingworth (53) v. Lancashire at Sheffield, 1955	
188	M P Vaughan (161) and R J Blakey (92) v. Essex at Ilford, 1997.	
188	G S Ballance (111) and A U Rashid (82) v. Warwickshire at Birmingham 2011	
184	R Kilner (104) and M W Booth (79) v. Leicestershire at Leeds, 1913	
183	G H Hirst (131) and E Smith (129) v. Hampshire at Bradford, 1899	
183	W Watson (139*) and R Illingworth (78) v. Somerset at Harrogate, 1956	
178*	D Denton (108*) and G H Hirst (112*) v. Lancashire at Manchester, 1902	
178*	N W D Yardley (100*) and R Illingworth (71*) v. Gloucestershire at Bristol, 1955	
178	E Robinson (100) and D C F Burton (83) v. Derbyshire at Hull, 1921	
178	H Sutcliffe (135) and P A Gibb (157*) v. Nottinghamshire at Sheffield, 1935	
175	G M Fellows (88) and R J Blakey (103) v. Warwickshire at Birmingham, 2002	
174	D S Lehmann (136) and G M Hamilton (73) v. Kent at Maidstone, 1998	
172	A J Dalton (119*) and D L Bairstow (62) v. Worcestershire at Dudley, 1971	
170*	A U Rashid 103*) and A J Hodd (68*) v. Somerset at Taunton, 2013	
170	A W Gale (101) and T T Bresnan (97) v. Worcestershire at Worcester, 2009	
169	W Barber (124) and H Verity (78*) v. Warwickshire at Birmingham, 1933	
169	R Illingworth (162) and J Birkenshaw (37) v. Indians at Sheffield, 1959	
166	E Wainwright (116) and E Smith (61) v. Kent at Catford, 1900	
166	D B Close (161) and F S Trueman (104) v. Northamptonshire at Northampton, 1963	
162*	G Boycott (220*) and J G Binks (70*) v. Northamptonshire at Sheffield, 1967	
161*	D L Bairstow (100*) and P Carrick (59*) v. Middlesex at Leeds, 1983	
159*	D S Lehmann (187*) and R J Blakey (78*) v. Somerset at Bath, 2001	
159	J M Bairstow (182) and A McGrath (90) v. Leicestershire at Scarborough, 2012	
156	W Rhodes (82*) and E Robinson (94) v. Derbyshire at Chesterfield, 1919	
154	C Turner (84) and A Wood (79) v. Glamorgan at Swansea, 1936	
153*	J A Rudolph (92*) and A U Rashid (73*) v. Worcestershire at Kidderminster, 2007	
153	J A Rudolph (69*) and J M Bairstow (81) v. Warwickshire at Birmingham, 2010	
151	D Denton (91) and W Rhodes (76) v. Middlesex at Sheffield, 1904	
151	G Boycott (152*) and P Carrick (75) v. Warwickshire at Leeds, 1982	
150	G Ulyett (199*) and J M Preston (93) v. Derbyshire at Sheffield, 1887	

SEVENTH WICKET (Qualification 125 runs)

254	W Rhodes (135) and D C F Burton (142*) v. Hampshire at Dewsbury, 1919	
247	P Holmes (285) and W Rhodes (79) v. Nottinghamshire at Nottingham, 1929	
215	E Robinson (135*) and D C F Burton (110) v. Leicestershire at Leicester, 1921	
185	E Wainwright (100) and G H Hirst (134) v. Gloucestershire at Bristol, 1897	
183	G H Hirst (341) and H Myers (57) v. Leicestershire at Leicester, 1905	
183	J A Rudolph (220) and T T Bresnan (101*) v. Warwickshire at Scarborough, 2007	
180	C Turner (130) and A Wood (97) v. Somerset at Sheffield, 1936	
168	G L Brophy (99) and A U Rashid (157*) v. Lancashire at Leeds, 2009	
170	G S Blewett (190) and G M Hamilton (84*) v. Northamptonshire at Scarborough, 1999	
166	R Peel (55) and I Grimshaw (122*) v. Derbyshire at Holbeck, 1886 .	
162	E Wainwright (109) and S Haigh (73) v. Somerset at Taunton, 1900	
162	R J Blakey (90) and R K J Dawson (87) v. Kent at Canterbury, 2002	
162	A W Gale (149) and G L Brophy (97) v. Warwickshire at Scarborough, 2006	

161 R G Lumb (118) and C M Old (89) v. Worcestershire at Bradford, 1980
160 J Tunnicliffe (158) and D Hunter (58*) v. Worcestershire at Worcester, 1900
157* F A Lowson (259*) and R Booth (53*) v. Leicestershire at Worcester, 1953
157 K S Wiiliamson (189) and T T Bresnan (61) v. Sussex at Scarborough, 2014
155 D Byas (122*) and P Carrick (61) v. Leicestershire at Leicester.1991.
154* G H Hirst (76*) and J T Newstead (100*) v. Nottinghamshire at Nottingham, 1908
148 J Rowbotham (113) and J Thewlis (50) v. Surrey at The Oval, 1873
147 E Wainwright (78) and G Ulyett (73) v. Somerset at Taunton, 1893
147 M P Vaughan (153) and R J Harden (64) v. Kent at Scarborough, 1999
143 C White (135*) and A K D Gray (60) v. Durham at Chester-le-Street, 2003
141 G H Hirst (108*) and S Haigh (48) v. Worcestershire at Worcester, 1905
141 J H Hampshire (149*) and J G Binks (72) v. MCC at Scarborough, 1965
140 E Wainwright (117) and S Haigh (54) v. CI Thornton's XI at Scarborough, 1900
140 D Byas (67) and P J Hartley (75) v. Derbyshire at Chesterfield, 1990
138 D Denton (78) and G H Hirst (103*) v. Sussex at Leeds, 1905
136 GH Hirst (93) and S Haigh (138) v. Warwickshire at Birmingham, 1904
136 E Robinson (77*) and A Wood (65) v. Glamorgan at Scarborough, 1931
133* W Rhodes (267*) and M Leyland (52*) v. Leicestershire at Leeds, 1921
133* E I Lester (86*) and A B Sellers (73*) v. Northamptonshire at Northampton, 1948
133 D Byas (100) and P W Jarvis (80) v. Northamptonshire at Scarborough, 1992
132 W Rhodes (196) and S Haigh (59*) v. Worcestershire at Worcester, 1904
131* D L Bairstow (79*) and A Sidebottom (52*) v. Oxford University at Oxford, 1981
130 P J Sharpe (64) and J V Wilson (134) v. Warwickshire at Birmingham, 1962
128 W Barber (66) and T F Smailes (86) v. Cambridge University at Cambridge, 1938
128 D B Close (88*) and A Coxon (59) v. Essex at Leeds, 1949
126 E Wainwright (171) and R Peel (46) v. Middlesex at Lord's, 1897
126 W Rhodes (91) and G G Macaulay (63) v. Hampshire at Hull, 1925
126 J C Balderstone (58) and J G Binks (57) v. Middlesex at Lord's, 1964
126 J M Bairstow (70) and A U Rashid (59) v. Kent at Canterbury, 2010
125 A B Sellers (109) and T F Smailes (65) v. Kent at Bradford, 1937

EIGHTH WICKET (Qualification 125 runs)

292 R Peel (210*) and Lord Hawke (166) v. Warwickshire at Birmingham, 1896
238 I J Harvey (209*) and T T Bresnan (74) v. Somerset at Leeds, 2005
192* W Rhodes (108*) and G G Macaulay (101*) v. Essex at Harrogate, 1922
192 A U Rashid (117*) and A Shahzad (78) v. Hampshire at Basingstoke, 2009
180 W Barber (191) and T F Smailes (89) v. Sussex at Leeds, 1935
165 S Haigh (62) and Lord Hawke (126) v. Surrey at The Oval, 1902
163 G G Macaulay (67) and A Waddington (114) v. Worcestershire at Leeds, 1927
159 E Smith (95) and W Rhodes (105) v. MCC at Scarborough, 1901
157 A Shahzad (88) and D J Wainwright (85*) v. Sussex at Hove, 2009
156 G S Ballance (112) and R J Sidebottom (40) v. Leeds/Bradford MCCU at Leeds, 2013
152 W Rhodes (98) and J W Rothery (70) v. Hampshire at Portsmouth, 1904
151 W Rhodes (201) and Lord Hawke (51) v. Somerset at Taunton, 1905
151 R J Blakey (80*) and P J Hartley (89) v. Sussex at Eastbourne, 1996
149 G L Brophy (177*) and R J Sidebottom (61) v. Worcestershire at Worcester 2011
147 J P G Chadwick (59) and F S Trueman (101) v. Middlesex at Scarborough, 1965
146 S Haigh (159) and Lord Hawke (89) v. Nottinghamshire at Sheffield, 1901
144 G L Brophy (85) and D J Wainwright (102*) v. Warwickshire at Scarborough, 2009
138 E Wainwright (100) and Lord Hawke (81) v. Kent at Tonbridge, 1899
137 E Wainwright (171) and Lord Hawke (75) v. Middlesex at Lord's, 1897
135 P W Jarvis (55) and P J Hartley (69) v. Nottinghamshire at Scarborough, 1992
133 R Illingworth (61) and F S Trueman (74) v. Leicestershire at Leicester, 1955
132 G H Hirst (103) and E Smith (59) v. Middlesex at Sheffield, 1904
132 W Watson (119) and J H Wardle (65) v. Leicestershire at Leicester, 1949
131 P E Robinson (85) and P Carrick (64) v. Surrey at Harrogate, 1990
130 E Smith (98) and Lord Hawke (54) v. Lancashire at Leeds, 1904
128 H Verity (96*) and T F Smailes (77) v. Indians at Bradford, 1936
128 D L Bairstow (145) and G B Stevenson (11) v. Middlesex at Scarborough, 1980

127	E Robinson (70*) and A Wood (62) v. Middlesex at Leeds, 1928
126	R Peel (74) and E Peate (61) v. Gloucestershire at Bradford, 1883
126	M W Booth (56) and E R Wilson (104*) v. Essex at Bradford, 1913
126	J D Middlebrook (84) and C E W Silverwood (70) v. Essex at Chelmsford, 2001
126	M J Lumb (115*) and D Gough (72) v. Hampshire at Southampton, 2003

NINTH WICKET (Qualification 100 runs)

246	T T Bresnan (116) and J N Gillespie (123*) v. Surrey at The Oval, 2007
192	G H Hirst (130*) and S Haigh (85) v. Surrey at Bradford, 1898
179	R A Hutton (189) and G A Cope (30*) v. Pakistanis at Bradford, 1971
176*	R Moorhouse (59*) and G H Hirst (115*) v. Gloucestershire at Bristol, 1894
173	S Haigh (85) and W Rhodes (92*) v. Sussex at Hove, 1902
167	H Verity (89) and T F Smailes (80) v. Somerset at Bath, 1936
162	W Rhodes (94*) and S Haigh (84) v. Lancashire at Manchester, 1904
161	E Smith (116*) and W Rhodes (79) v. Sussex at Sheffield, 1900
154	R M Pyrah (117) and R J Sidebottom (52) v.Lancashire at Leeds 2011
151	J M Bairstow (205) and R J Sidebottom (45*) v. Nottinghamshire at Nottingham 2011
150	Azeem Rafiq (100) and M J Hoggard (56*) v. Worcestershire at Worcester, 2009
149*	R J Blakey (63*) and A K D Gray (74*) v. Leicestershire at Scarborough, 2002
149	G H Hirst (232*) and D Hunter (40) v. Surrey at The Oval, 1905
146	G H Hirst (214) and W Rhodes (53) v. Worcestershire at Worcester, 1901
144	T T Bresnan (91) and J N Gillespie (44) v. Hampshire at Leeds, 2006
140	A U Rashid (111) and D J Wainwright (104) v. Sussex at Hove, 2008
136	R Peel (210*) and G H Hirst (85) v. Warwickshire at Birmingham, 1896
125*	L Hutton (269*) and A Coxon (65*) v. Northamptonshire at Wellingborough, 1949
124	P J Hartley (87*) and P W Jarvis (47) v. Essex at Chelmsford, 1986
120	G H Hirst (138) and W Rhodes (38) v. Nottinghamshire at Nottingham, 1899
119	A B Sellers (80*) and E P Robinson (66) v. Warwickshire at Birmingham, 1938
118	S Haigh (96) and W Rhodes (44) v. Somerset at Leeds, 1901
114	E Oldroyd (194) and A Dolphin (47) v. Worcestershire at Worcester, 1923
114	N Kilner (102*) and G G Macaulay (60) v. Gloucestershire at Bristol, 1923
113	G G Macaulay (125*) and A Waddington (44) v. Nottinghamshire at Nottingham, 1921
113	A Wood (69) and H.Verity (45*) v. MCC at Lord's, 1938
112	G H Hirst (78) and Lord Hawke (61*) v. Essex at Leyton, 1907
109	Lees Whitehead (60) and W Rhodes (81*) v. Sussex at Harrogate, 1899
108	A McGrath (133*) and C E W Silverwood (80) v. Durham at Chester-le-Street, 2005
106	L E Plunkett (86) and S A Patterson (43) v. Warwickshire at Leeds, 2014
105	J V Wilson (134) and A G Nicholson (20*) v. Nottinghamshire at Leeds, 1962
105	C M Old (100*) and H P Cooper (30) v. Lancashire at Manchester, 1978
105	C White (74*) and J D Batty (50) v. Gloucestershire at Sheffield, 1993
104	L Hall (129*) and R Moorhouse (86) v. Gloucestershire at Clifton, 1888
100	G Pollitt (51) and Lees Whitehead (54) v. Hampshire at Bradford, 1899

TENTH WICKET (Qualification 100 runs)

149	G Boycott (79) and G B Stevenson (115*) v. Warwickshire at Birmingham, 1982
148	Lord Hawke (107*) and D Hunter (47) v. Kent at Sheffield, 1898
144	A Sidebottom (124) and A L Robinson (30*) v. Glamorgan at Cardiff, 1977
121	J T Brown (141) and D Hunter (25*) v. Liverpool & District at Liverpool, 1894
118	Lord Hawke (110*) and D Hunter (41) v. Kent at Leeds, 1896
113	P J Hartley (88*) and R D Stemp (22) v. Middlesex at Lord's, 1996
110	C E W. Silverwood (45*) and R D Stemp (65) v. Durham at Chester-le-Street, 1996
109	A Shahzad (70) and R J Sidebottom (28*) v. Worcestershire at Scarborough, 2011
108	Lord Hawke (79) and Lees Whitehead (45*) v. Lancashire at Manchester, 1903
108	G Boycott (129) and M K Bore (37*) v. Nottinghamshire at Bradford, 1973
106	A B Sellers (79) and D V Brennan (30) v. Worcestershire at Worcester, 1948
103	A Dolphin (62*) and E Smith (49) v. Essex at Leyton, 1919
102	D Denton (77*) and D Hunter (45) v. Cambridge University at Cambridge, 1895

FIFTEEN WICKETS OR MORE IN A MATCH

A complete list of 12, 13 and 14 wickets in a match up to and including 2007 is to be found in the 2008 edition

W E BOWES (1)

16 for 35 (8 for 18 and 8 for 17) v. Northamptonshire at Kettering, 1935

A DRAKE (1)

15 for 51 (5 for 16 and 10 for 35) v. Somerset at Weston-super-Mare, 1914

T EMMETT (1)

16 for 38 (7 for 15 and 9 for 23) v. Cambridgeshire at Hunslet, 1869

G H HIRST (1)

15 for 63 (8 for 25 and 7 for 38) v. Leicestershire at Hull, 1907

R ILLINGWORTH (1)

15 for 123 (8 for 70 and 7 for 53) v. Glamorgan at Swansea, 1960

R PEEL (1)

15 for 50 (9 for 22 and 6 for 28) v. Somerset at Leeds, 1895

W RHODES (1)

15 for 56 (9 for 28 and 6 for 28) v. Essex at Leyton, 1899

H VERITY (4)

17 for 91 (8 for 47 and 9 for 44) v. Essex at Leyton, 1933
15 for 129 (8 for 56 and 7 for 73) v. Oxford University at Oxford, 1936
15 for 38 (6 for 26 and 9 for 12) v. Kent at Sheffield, 1936
15 for 100 (6 for 52 and 9 for 48) v. Essex at Westcliffe-on-Sea, 1936

J H WARDLE (1)

16 for 112 (9 for 48 and 7 for 64) v. Sussex at Hull, 1954

TEN WICKETS IN A MATCH

(including best analysis)

61	W Rhodes	15 for	56	v Essex	at Leyton	1899
48	H Verity	17 for	91	v Essex	at Leyton	1933
40	G H Hirst	15 for	63	v Leicestershire	at Hull	1907
31	G G Macaulay	14 for	92	v Gloucestershire	at Bristol	1926
28	S Haigh	14 for	43	v Hampshire	at Southampton	1898
27	R Peel	14 for	33	v Nottinghamshire	at Sheffield	1888
25	W E Bowes	16 for	35	v Northamptonshire	at Kettering	1935
25	J H Wardle	16 for	112	v Sussex	at Hull	1954
22	E Peate	14 for	77	v Surrey	at Huddersfield	1881
20	F S Trueman	14 for	123	v Surrey	at The Oval	1960
19	T Emmett	16 for	38	v Cambridgeshire	at Hunslet	1869
17	R Appleyard	12 for	43	v Essex	at Bradford	1951
15	E Wainwright	14 for	77	v Essex	at Bradford	1896
11	R Illingworth	15 for	123	v Glamorgan	at Swansea	1960
10	A Waddington	13 for	48	v Northamptonshire	at Northampton	1920
9	M W Booth	14 for	160	v Essex	at Leyton	1914
9	R Kilner	12 for	55	v Sussex	at Hove	1924
8	W Bates	11 for	47	v Nottinghamshire	at Nottingham	1881
8	G Freeman	13 for	60	v Surrey	at Sheffield	1869
7	E P Robinson	13 for	115	v Lancashire	at Leeds	1939
7	D Wilson	13 for	52	v Warwickshire	at Middlesbrough	1967

6 G A Cope	12 for 116	v Glamorgan	at Cardiff (Sophia Gardens)	1968
6 A Hill	12 for 59	v Surrey	at The Oval	1871
6 T F Smailes	14 for 58	v Derbyshire	at Sheffield	1939
5 P Carrick	12 for 89	v Derbyshire	at Sheffield (Abbeydale Pk)	1983
5 J M Preston	13 for 63	v MCC	at Scarborough	1888
5 E Robinson	12 for 95	v Northamptonshire	at Huddersfield	1927
4 J T Newstead	11 for 72	v Worcestershire	at Bradford	1907
3 T W Foster	11 for 93	v Liverpool & District	at Liverpool	1894
3 G P Harrison	11 for 76	v Kent	at Dewsbury	1883
3 F S Jackson	12 for 80	v Hampshire	at Southampton	1897
3 P W Jarvis	11 for 92	v Middlesex	at Lord's	1986
3 S P Kirby	13 for 154	v Somerset	at Taunton	2003
3 A G Nicholson	12 for 73	v Glamorgan	at Leeds	1964
3 R K Platt	10 for 87	v Surrey	at The Oval	1959
3 A Sidebottom	11 for 64	v Kent	at Sheffield (Abbeydale Pk)	1980
3 G Ulyett	12 for 102	v Lancashire	at Huddersfield	1889
2 T Armitage	13 for 46	v Surrey	at Sheffield	1876
2 R Aspinall	14 for 65	v Northamptonshire	at Northampton	1947
2 J T Brown (Darfield)	12 for 109	v Gloucestershire	at Huddersfield	1899
2 R O Clayton	12 for 104	v Lancashire	at Manchester	1877
2 D B Close	11 for 116	v Kent	at Gillingham	1965
2 M J Cowan	12 for 87	v Warwickshire	at Birmingham	1960
2 A Coxon	10 for 57	v Derbyshire	at Chesterfield	1949
2 D Gough	10 for 80	v Lancashire	at Leeds	1995
2 G M Hamilton	11 for 72	v Surrey	at Leeds	1998
2 P J Hartley	11 for 68	v Derbyshire	at Chesterfield	1995
2 R A Hutton	11 for 62	v Lancashire	at Manchester	1971
2 E Leadbeater	11 for 162	v Nottinghamshire	at Nottingham	1950
2 M A Robinson	12 for 124	v Northamptonshire	at Harrogate	1993
2 M Ryan	10 for 77	v Leicestershire	at Bradford	1962
2 E Smith (Morley)	10 for 97	v MCC	at Scarborough	1893
2 R J Sidebottom	11 for 43	v Kent	at Leeds	2000
2 G B Stevenson	11 for 74	v Nottinghamshire	at Nottingham	1980
2 S Wade	11 for 56	v Gloucestershire	at Cheltenham	1886
2 E R Wilson	11 for 109	v Sussex	at Hove	1921
1 A B Bainbridge	12 for 111	v Essex	at Harrogate	1961
1 J Birkenshaw	11 for 134	v Middlesex	at Leeds	1960
1 A Booth	10 for 91	v Indians	at Bradford	1946
1 H P Cooper	11 for 96	v Northamptonshire	at Northampton	1976
1 A Drake	15 for 51	v Somerset	at Weston-Super-Mare	1914
1 L Greenwood	11 for 71	v Surrey	at The Oval	1867
1 P M Hutchison	11 for 102	v Pakistan 'A'	at Leeds	1997
1 L Hutton	10 for 101	v Leicestershire	at Leicester (Aylestone Rd)	1937
1 R Iddison	10 for 68	v Surrey	at Sheffield	1864
1 M Leyland	10 for 94	v Leicestershire	at Leicester (Aylestone Rd)	1933
1 J D Middlebrook	10 for 170	v Hampshire	at Southampton	2000
1 F W Milligan	12 for 110	v Sussex	at Sheffield	1897
1 H Myers	12 for 192	v Gloucestershire	at Dewsbury	1904
1 C M Old	11 for 46	v Gloucestershire	at Middlesbrough	1969
1 D Pickles	12 for 133	v Somerset	at Taunton	1957
1 A U Rashid	11 for 114	v Worcestershire	at Worcester	2011
1 W Ringrose	11 for 135	v Australians	at Bradford	1905
1 C E W Silverwood	12 for 148	v Kent	at Leeds	1997
1 W Slinn	12 for 53	v Nottinghamshire	at Nottingham	1864
1 J Waring	10 for 63	v Lancashire	at Leeds	1966
1 F Wilkinson	10 for 129	v Hampshire	at Bournemouth	1938
1 A C Williams	10 for 66	v Hampshire	at Dewsbury	1919

TEN WICKETS IN AN INNINGS

Bowler				Year
A Drake	10 for 35	v.	Somerset at Weston-super-Mare	1914
H Verity	10 for 36	v.	Warwickshire at Leeds	1931
*H Verity	10 for 10	v.	Nottinghamshire at Leeds	1932
T F Smailes	10 for 47	v.	Derbyshire at Sheffield	1939

*Includes the hat trick.

EIGHT WICKETS OR MORE IN AN INNINGS

(Ten wickets in an innings also listed above)
A complete list of seven wickets in an innings up to and including 2007 is to be found in the 2008 edition

R APPLEYARD (1)

8 for 76 v. MCC at Scarborough, 1951

R ASPINALL (1)

8 for 42 v. Northamptonshire at Northampton, 1947

W BATES (2)

8 for 45 v. Lancashire at Huddersfield, 1878
8 for 21 v. Surrey at The Oval, 1879

M W BOOTH (4)

8 for 52 v. Leicestershire at Sheffield, 1912
8 for 47 v. Middlesex at Leeds, 1912
8 for 86 v. Middlesex at Sheffield, 1913
8 for 64 v. Essex at Leyton, 1914

W E BOWES (9)

8 for 77 v. Leicestershire at Dewsbury, 1929
8 for 69 v. Middlesex at Bradford, 1930
9 for 121 v. Essex at Scarborough, 1932
8 for 62 v. Sussex at Hove, 1932
8 for 69 v. Gloucestershire at Gloucester, 1933
8 for 40 v. Worcestershire at Sheffield, 1935
8 for 18 v. Northamptonshire at Kettering, 1935
8 for 17 v. Northamptonshire at Kettering, 1935
8 for 56 v. Leicestershire at Scarborough, 1936

J T BROWN (Darfield) (1)

8 for 40 v. Gloucestershire at Huddersfield, 1899

P CARRICK (2)

8 for 33 v. Cambridge University at Cambridge, 1973
8 for 72 v. Derbyshire at Scarborough, 1975

R O CLAYTON (1)

8 for 66 v. Lancashire at Manchester, 1877

D B CLOSE (2)

8 for 41 v. Kent at Leeds, 1959
8 for 43 v. Essex at Leeds, 1960

H P COOPER (1)

8 for 62 v. Glamorgan at Cardiff, 1975

G A COPE (1)

8 for 73 v. Gloucestershire at Bristol, 1975

M J COWAN (1)

9 for 43 v. Warwickshire at Birmingham, 1960

A COXON (1)

8 for 31 v. Worcestershire at Leeds, 1946

A DRAKE (2)

8 for 59 v. Gloucestershire at Sheffield, 1913
10 for 35 v. Somerset at Weston-super-Mare, 1914

T EMMETT (8)

9 for 34 v. Nottinghamshire at Dewsbury, 1868
9 for 23 v. Cambridgeshire at Hunslet, 1869
8 for 31 v. Nottinghamshire at Sheffield, 1871
8 for 46 v. Gloucestershire at Clifton, 1877
8 for 16 v. MCC at Scarborough, 1877
8 for 22 v. Surrey at The Oval, 1881
8 for 52 v. MCC at Scarborough, 1882
8 for 32 v. Sussex at Huddersfield, 1884

S D FLETCHER (1)

8 for 58 v. Essex at Sheffield, 1988

T W FOSTER (1)

9 for 59 v. MCC at Lord's, 1894

G FREEMAN (2)

8 for 11 v. Lancashire at Holbeck, 1868
8 for 29 v. Surrey at Sheffield, 1869

L GREENWOOD (1)

8 for 35 v. Cambridgeshire at Dewsbury, 1867

S HAIGH (5)

8 for 78 v. Australians at Bradford, 1896
8 for 35 v. Hampshire at Harrogate, 1896
8 for 21 v. Hampshire at Southampton, 1898
8 for 33 v. Warwickshire at Scarborough, 1899
9 for 25 v. Gloucestershire at Leeds, 1912

P J HARTLEY (2)

8 for 111 v. Sussex at Hove, 1992
9 for 41 v. Derbyshire at Chesterfield, 1995

G H HIRST (8)

8 for 59 v. Warwickshire at Birmingham, 1896
8 for 48 v. Australians at Bradford, 1899
8 for 25 v. Leicestershire at Hull, 1907
9 for 45 v. Middlesex at Sheffield, 1907
9 for 23 v. Lancashire at Leeds, 1910
8 for 80 v. Somerset at Sheffield, 1910
9 for 41 v. Worcestershire at Worcester, 1911
9 for 69 v. MCC at Lord's, 1912

EIGHT WICKETS OR MORE IN AN INNINGS *(Continued)*

R ILLINGWORTH (5)

8 for 69 v. Surrey at The Oval, 1954
9 for 42 v. Worcestershire at Worcester, 1957
8 for 70 v. Glamorgan at Swansea, 1960
8 for 50 v. Lancashire at Manchester, 1961
8 for 20 v. Worcestershire at Leeds, 1965

R KILNER (2)

8 for 26 v. Glamorgan at Cardiff, 1923
8 for 40 v. Middlesex at Bradford, 1926

S P KIRBY (1)

8 for 80 v. Somerset at Taunton, 2003

E LEADBEATER (1)

8 for 83 v. Worcestershire at Worcester, 1950

M LEYLAND (1)

8 for 63 v. Hampshire at Huddersfield, 1938

G G MACAULAY (3)

8 for 43 v. Gloucestershire at Bristol, 1926
8 for 37 v. Derbyshire at Hull, 1927
8 for 21 v. Indians at Harrogate, 1932

H MYERS (1)

8 for 81 v. Gloucestershire at Dewsbury, 1904

A G NICHOLSON (2)

9 for 62 v. Sussex at Eastbourne, 1967
8 for 22 v. Kent at Canterbury, 1968

E PEATE (6)

8 for 24 v. Lancashire at Manchester, 1880
8 for 30 v. Surrey at Huddersfield, 1881
8 for 69 v. Sussex at Hove, 1881
8 for 32 v. Middlesex at Sheffield, 1882
8 for 5 v. Surrey at Holbeck, 1883
8 for 63 v. Kent at Gravesend, 1884

R PEEL (6)

8 for 12 v. Nottinghamshire at Sheffield, 1888
8 for 60 v. Surrey at Sheffield, 1890
8 for 54 v. Cambridge University at Cambridge, 1893
9 for 22 v. Somerset at Leeds, 1895
8 for 27 v. South of England XI at Scarborough, 1896
8 for 53 v. Kent at Halifax, 1897

J M PRESTON (2)

8 for 27 v. Sussex at Hove, 1888
9 for 28 v. MCC at Scarborough, 1888

W RHODES (18)

9 for 28 v. Essex at Leyton, 1899
8 for 38 v. Nottinghamshire at Nottingham, 1899
8 for 68 v. Cambridge University at Cambridge, 1900
8 for 43 v. Lancashire at Bradford, 1900
8 for 23 v. Hampshire at Hull, 1900
8 for 72 v. Gloucestershire at Bradford, 1900
8 for 28 v. Essex at Harrogate, 1900
8 for 53 v. Middlesex at Lord's, 1901
8 for 55 v. Kent at Canterbury, 1901
8 for 26 v. Kent at Catford, 1902
8 for 87 v. Worcestershire at Worcester, 1903
8 for 61 v. Lancashire at Bradford, 1903
8 for 90 v. Warwickshire at Birmingham, 1905
8 for 92 v. Northamptonshire at Northampton, 1911
8 for 44 v. Warwickshire at Bradford, 1919
8 for 39 v. Sussex at Leeds, 1920
8 for 48 v. Somerset at Huddersfield, 1926
9 for 39 v. Essex at Leyton, 1929

W RINGROSE (1)

9 for 76 v. Australians at Bradford, 1905

E ROBINSON (3)

9 for 36 v. Lancashire at Bradford, 1920
8 for 32 v. Northamptonshire at Huddersfield, 1927
8 for 13 v. Cambridge University at Cambridge, 1928

E P ROBINSON (2)

8 for 35 v. Lancashire at Leeds, 1939
8 for 76 v. Surrey at The Oval, 1946

M A ROBINSON (1)

9 for 37 v. Northamptonshire at Harrogate, 1993

A SIDEBOTTOM (1)

8 for 72 v. Leicestershire at Middlesbrough, 1986

T F SMAILES (2)

8 for 68 v. Glamorgan at Hull, 1938
10 for 47 v. Derbyshire at Sheffield, 1939

G B STEVENSON (2)

8 for 65 v. Lancashire at Leeds, 1978
8 for 57 v. Northamptonshire at Leeds, 1980

F S TRUEMAN (8)

8 for 70 v. Minor Counties at Lord's, 1949
8 for 68 v. Nottinghamshire at Sheffield, 1951
8 for 53 v. Nottinghamshire at Nottingham, 1951
8 for 28 v. Kent at Dover, 1954
8 for 84 v. Nottinghamshire at Worksop, 1962
8 for 45 v. Gloucestershire at Bradford, 1963
8 for 36 v. Sussex at Hove, 1965
8 for 37 v. Essex at Bradford, 1966

EIGHT WICKETS OR MORE IN AN INNINGS *(Continued)*

H VERITY (20)

9 for 60 v. Glamorgan at Swansea, 1930
10 for 36 v. Warwickshire at Leeds, 1931
8 for 33 v. Glamorgan at Swansea, 1931
8 for 107 v. Lancashire at Bradford, 1932
8 for 39 v. Northamptonshire at Northampton, 1932
10 for 10 v. Nottinghamshire at Leeds, 1932
8 for 47 v. Essex at Leyton, 1933
9 for 44 v. Essex at Leyton, 1933
9 for 59 v. Kent at Dover, 1933
8 for 28 v. Leicestershire at Leeds, 1935
8 for 56 v. Oxford University at Oxford, 1936
8 for 40 v. Worcestershire at Stourbridge, 1936
9 for 12 v. Kent at Sheffield, 1936
9 for 48 v. Essex at Westcliff-on-Sea, 1936
8 for 42 v. Nottinghamshire at Bradford, 1936
9 for 43 v. Warwickshire at Leeds, 1937
8 for 80 v. Sussex at Eastbourne, 1937
8 for 43 v. Middlesex at The Oval, 1937
9 for 62 v. MCC at Lord's, 1939
8 for 38 v. Leicestershire at Hull, 1939

A WADDINGTON (3)

8 for 34 v. Northamptonshire at Leeds, 1922
8 for 39 v. Kent at Leeds, 1922
8 for 35 v. Hampshire at Bradford, 1922

E WAINWRIGHT (3)

8 for 49 v. Middlesex at Sheffield, 1891
9 for 66 v. Middlesex at Sheffield, 1894
8 for 34 v. Essex at Bradford, 1896

J H WARDLE (4)

8 for 87 v. Derbyshire at Chesterfield, 1948
8 for 26 v. Middlesex at Lord's, 1950
9 for 48 v. Sussex at Hull, 1954
9 for 25 v. Lancashire at Manchester, 1954

C WHITE (1)

8 for 55 v. Gloucestershire at Gloucester, 1998

A C WILLIAMS (1)

9 for 29 v. Hampshire at Dewsbury, 1919

R WOOD (1)

8 for 45 v. Scotland at Glasgow, 1952

SIX WICKETS IN AN INNINGS AT LESS THAN FOUR RUNS EACH

A complete list of 5 wickets at less than 4 runs each up to and including 2007 is to be found in the 2008 edition

R APPLEYARD (2)

6 for 17 v. Essex at Bradford, 1951
6 for 12 v. Hampshire at Bournemouth, 1954

T ARMITAGE (1)

6 for 20 v. Surrey at Sheffield, 1876

R ASPINALL (1)

6 for 23 v. Northamptonshire at Northampton, 1947

W BATES (5)

6 for 11 v. Middlesex at Huddersfield, 1879
6 for 22 v. Kent at Bradford, 1881
6 for 17 v. Nottinghamshire at Nottingham, 1881
6 for 12 v. Kent at Sheffield, 1882
6 for 19 v. Lancashire at Dewsbury, 1886

A BOOTH (1)

6 for 21 v. Warwickshire at Birmingham, 1946

W E BOWES (4)

6 for 17 v. Middlesex at Lord's, 1934
6 for 16 v. Lancashire at Bradford, 1935
6 for 20 v. Gloucestershire at Sheffield, 1936
6 for 23 v. Warwickshire at Birmingham, 1947

J T BROWN (Darfield) (1)

6 for 19 v. Worcestershire at Worcester, 1899

R.O CLAYTON (1)

6 for 20 v. Nottinghamshire at Sheffield, 1876

A COXON (1)

6 for 17 v. Surrey at Sheffield, 1948

T EMMETT (6)

6 for 7 v. Surrey at Sheffield, 1867
6 for 13 v. Lancashire at Holbeck, 1868
6 for 21 v. Middlesex at Scarborough, 1874
6 for 12 v. Derbyshire at Sheffield, 1878
6 for 19 v. Derbyshire at Bradford, 1881
6 for 22 v. Australians at Bradford, 1882

H FISHER (1)

6 for 11 v. Leicestershire at Bradford, 1932

SIX WICKETS IN AN INNINGS AT LESS THAN FOUR
RUNS EACH *(Continued)*

S HAIGH (10)

6 for 18 v. Derbyshire at Bradford, 1897
6 for 22 v. Hampshire at Southampton, 1898
6 for 21 v. Surrey at The Oval, 1900
6 for 23 v. Cambridge University at Cambridge, 1902
6 for 19 v. Somerset at Sheffield, 1902
6 for 22 v. Cambridge University at Sheffield, 1903
6 for 21 v. Hampshire at Leeds, 1904
6 for 21 v. Nottinghamshire at Sheffield, 1905
6 for 13 v. Surrey at Leeds, 1908
6 for 14 v. Australians at Bradford, 1912

A HILL (2)

6 for 9 v. United South of England XI at Bradford, 1874
6 for 18 v. MCC at Lord's, 1881

G H HIRST (7)

6 for 23 v. MCC at Lord's, 1893
6 for 20 v. Lancashire at Bradford, 1906
6 for 12 v. Northamptonshire at Northampton, 1908
6 for 7 v. Northamptonshire at Northampton, 1908
6 for 23 v. Surrey at Leeds, 1908
6 for 23 v. Lancashire at Manchester, 1909
6 for 20 v. Surrey at Sheffield, 1909

R ILLINGWORTH (2)

6 for 15 v. Scotland at Hull, 1956
6 for 13 v. Leicestershire at Leicester, 1963

F S JACKSON (1)

6 for 19 v. Hampshire at Southampton, 1897

R KILNER (5)

6 for 22 v. Essex at Harrogate, 1922
6 for 13 v. Hampshire at Bournemouth, 1922
6 for 14 v. Middlesex at Bradford, 1923
6 for 22 v. Surrey at Sheffield, 1923
6 for 15 v. Hampshire at Portsmouth, 1924

G G MACAULAY (10)

6 for 10 v. Warwickshire at Birmingham, 1921
6 for 3 v. Derbyshire at Hull, 1921
6 for 8 v. Northamptonshire at Northampton, 1922
6 for 12 v. Glamorgan at Cardiff, 1922
6 for 18 v. Northamptonshire at Bradford, 1923
6 for 19 v. Northamptonshire at Northampton, 1925
6 for 22 v. Leicestershire at Leeds, 1926
6 for 11 v. Leicestershire at Hull, 1930
6 for 22 v. Leicestershire at Bradford, 1933
6 for 22 v. Middlesex at Leeds, 1934

SIX WICKETS IN AN INNINGS AT LESS THAN FOUR
RUNS EACH *(Continued)*

E PEATE (5)

6 for 14 v. Middlesex at Huddersfield, 1879
6 for 12 v. Derbyshire at Derby, 1882
6 for 13 v. Gloucestershire at Moreton-in-Marsh, 1884
6 for 16 v. Sussex at Huddersfield, 1886
6 for 16 v. Cambridge University at Sheffield, 1886

R PEEL (4)

6 for 21 v. Nottinghamshire at Sheffield, 1888
6 for 19 v. Australians at Huddersfield, 1888
6 for 22 v. Gloucestershire at Bristol, 1891
6 for 19 v. Leicestershire at Scarborough, 1896

A C RHODES (1)

6 for 19 v. Cambridge University at Cambridge, 1932

W RHODES (12)

6 for 21 v. Somerset at Bath, 1898
6 for 16 v. Gloucestershire at Bristol, 1899
6 for 4 v. Nottinghamshire at Nottingham, 1901
6 for 15 v. MCC at Lord's, 1902
6 for 16 v. Cambridge University at Cambridge, 1905
6 for 9 v. Essex at Huddersfield, 1905
6 for 22 v. Derbyshire at Glossop, 1907
6 for 17 v. Leicestershire at Leicester, 1908
6 for 13 v. Sussex at Hove, 1922
6 for 23 v. Nottinghamshire at Leeds, 1923
6 for 22 v. Cambridge University at Cambridge, 1924
6 for 20 v. Gloucestershire at Dewsbury, 1927

W RINGROSE (1)

6 for 20 v. Leicestershire at Dewsbury, 1903

R J SIDEBOTTOM (1)

6 for 16 v. Kent at Leeds, 2000

W SLINN (1)

6 for 19 v. Nottinghamshire at Nottingham, 1864

G B STEVENSON(1)

6 for 14 v. Warwickshire at Sheffield, 1979

F S TRUEMAN (4)

6 for 23 v. Oxford University at Oxford, 1955
6 for 23 v. Oxford University at Oxford, 1958
6 for 18 v. Warwickshire at Birmingham, 1963
6 for 20 v. Leicestershire at Sheffield, 1968

H VERITY (5)

6 for 11 v. Surrey at Bradford, 1931
6 for 21 v. Glamorgan at Swansea, 1931
6 for 12 v. Derbyshire at Hull, 1933
6 for 10 v. Essex at Ilford, 1937
6 for 22 v. Hampshire at Bournemouth, 1939

SIX WICKETS IN AN INNINGS AT LESS THAN FOUR
RUNS EACH *(Continued)*

A WADDINGTON (2)

6 for 21 v. Northamptonshire at Harrogate, 1921
6 for 21 v. Northamptonshire at Northampton, 1923

S WADE (1)

6 for 18 v. Gloucestershire at Dewsbury, 1887

E WAINWRIGHT (4)

6 for 16 v. Sussex at Leeds, 1893
6 for 23 v. Sussex at Hove, 1893
6 for 18 v. Sussex at Dewsbury, 1894
6 for 22 v. MCC at Scarborough, 1894

J H WARDLE (8)

6 for 17 v. Sussex at Sheffield, 1948
6 for 10 v. Scotland at Edinburgh, 1950
6 for 12 v. Gloucestershire at Hull, 1950
6 for 20 v. Kent at Scarborough, 1950
6 for 23 v. Somerset at Sheffield, 1951
6 for 21 v. Glamorgan at Leeds, 1951
6 for 18 v. Gloucestershire at Bristol, 1951
6 for 6 v. Gloucestershire at Bristol, 1955

D WILSON (3)

6 for 22 v. Sussex at Bradford, 1963
6 for 15 v. Gloucestershire at Middlesbrough, 1966
6 for 22 v. Middlesex at Sheffield, 1966

FOUR WICKETS IN FOUR BALLS

A Drake v. Derbyshire at Chesterfield, 1914

FOUR WICKETS IN FIVE BALLS

F S Jackson v. Australians at Leeds, 1902
A Waddington v. Northamptonshire at Northampton, 1920
G G Macaulay v. Lancashire at Manchester, 1933
P J Hartley v. Derbyshire at Chesterfield, 1995
D Gough v. Kent at Leeds, 1995
J D Middlebrook v. Hampshire at Southampton, 2000

BEST BOWLING ANALYSES IN A MATCH
FOR AND AGAINST YORKSHIRE

Best For Yorkshire:
17 for 91 (8 for 47 and 9 for 44) H Verity v Essex at Leyton, 1933

Against Yorkshire:
17 for 91 (9 for 62 and 8 for 29) H Dean for Lancashire at Liverpool, 1913
(non-championship)

County Championship
16 for 114 (8 for 48 and 8 for 66) G Burton for Middlesex at Sheffield, 1888

Yorkshire versus:

Derbyshire	*For Yorkshire:*	14 for 58 (4 for 11 and 10 for 47) T F Smailes at Sheffield, 1939
	Against:	13 for 65 (7 for 33 and 6 for 32) W Mycroft at Sheffield, 1879
Most 10 wickets in a match	*For Yorkshire:*	P Carrick and E Peate 4 each
	Against:	W Mycroft 3
Durham	*For Yorkshire:*	10 for 101 (6 for 57 and 4 for 44) M A Robinson at Durham, 1992
	Against:	10 for 144 (7 for 81 and 3 for 63) O D Gibson at Chester-le-Street, 2007
Most 10 wickets in a match	*For Yorkshire:*	M A Robinson 1
	Against:	G R Breese and O D Gibson 1 each
Essex	*For Yorkshire:*	17 for 91 (8 for 47 and 9 for 44) H Verity at Leyton, 1933
	Against:	14 for 127 (7 for 37 and 7 for 90) W Mead at Leyton, 1899
Most 10 wickets in a match	*For Yorkshire:*	W Rhodes 7
	Against:	J K Lever, W Mead 2 each
Glamorgan	*For Yorkshire:*	15 for 123 (8 for 70 and 7 for 53) R Illingworth at Swansea. 1960
	Against:	12 for 76 (7 for 30 and 5 for 46) D J Shepherd at Cardiff, 1957
Most 10 wickets in a match	*For Yorkshire:*	H Verity 5
	Against:	D J Shepherd, J S Pressdee 1 each
Gloucestershire	*For Yorkshire:*	14 for 64 (7 for 58 and 7 for 6) R Illingworth at Harrogate, 1967
	Against:	15 for 79 (8 for 33 and 7 for 46) W G Grace at Sheffield, 1872
Most 10 wickets in a match	*For Yorkshire:*	W Rhodes 8
	Against:	E G Dennett 5
Hampshire	*For Yorkshire:*	14 for 43 (8 for 21 and 6 for 22) S Haigh at Southampton, 1898
	Against:	12 for 145 (7 for 78 and 5 for 67) D Shackleton at Bradford, 1962
Most 10 wickets in a match	*For Yorkshire:*	W Rhodes, E Robinson, H Verity 3 each
	Against:	A S Kennedy 3

Yorkshire versus

Kent	*For Yorkshire:*	15 for 38 (6 for 26 and 9 for 12) H Verity at Sheffield, 1936
	Against:	13 for 48 (5 for 13 and 8 for 35) A Hearne at Sheffield, 1885
Most 10 wickets *in a match*	*For Yorkshire:*	E Peate and J H Wardle 4 each
	Against:	C Blythe 6
Lancashire	*For Yorkshire:*	14 for 80 (6 for 56 and 8 for 24) E Peate at Manchester, 1880
	Against:	17 for 91 (9 for 62 and 8 for 29) H Dean at Liverpool, 1913 (non-championship) 14 for 90 (6 for 47 and 8 for 43) R Tattersall at Leeds, 1956 (championship)
Most 10 wickets *in a match*	*For Yorkshire:*	T Emmett 5
	Against:	J Briggs 8
Leicestershire	*For Yorkshire:*	15 for 63 (8 for 25 and 7 for 38) G H Hirst at Hull, 1907
	Against:	12 for 139 (8 for 85 and 4 for 54) A D Pougher at Leicester, 1895
Most 10 wickets *in a match*	*For Yorkshire:*	G H Hirst 5
	Against:	A D Pougher 2
Middlesex	*For Yorkshire:*	13 for 94 (6 for 61 and 7 for 33) S Haigh at Leeds, 1900
	Against:	16 for 114 (8 for 48 and 8 for 66) G Burton at Sheffield, 1888
Most 10 wickets *in a match*	*For Yorkshire:*	W Rhodes 5
	Against:	J T Hearne 7
Northamptonshire	*For Yorkshire:*	16 for 35 (8 for 18 and 8 for 17) W E Bowes at Kettering, 1935
	Against:	15 for 31 (7 for 22 and 8 for 9) G E Tribe at Northampton, 1958
Most 10 wickets *in a match*	*For Yorkshire:*	W E Bowes, G G Macaulay, H Verity, A Waddington 3 each
	Against:	G E Tribe 3
Nottinghamshire	*For Yorkshire:*	14 for 33 (8 for 12 and 6 for 21) R Peel at Sheffield, 1888
	Against:	14 for 94 (8 for 38 and 6 for 56) F Morley at Nottingham, 1878
Most 10 wickets *in a match*	*For Yorkshire:*	G H Hirst 5
	Against:	F Morley, J C Shaw 4 each
Somerset	*For Yorkshire:*	15 for 50 (9 for 22 and 6 for 28) R Peel at Leeds, 1895
	Against:	15 for 71 (6 for 30 and 9 for 41) L C Braund at Sheffield, 1902
Most 10 wickets *in a match*	*For Yorkshire:*	G H Hirst 7
	Against:	L C Braund 3

Yorkshire versus

Surrey	*For Yorkshire:*	14 for 77 (6 for 47 and 8 for 30)
		E Peate at Huddersfield, 1881
	Against:	15 for 154 (7 for 55 and 8 for 99)
		T Richardson at Leeds, 1897
Most 10 wickets	*For Yorkshire:*	W Rhodes 7
in a match	*Against:*	G A Lohmann, T Richardson 6 each
Sussex	*For Yorkshire:*	16 for 112 (9 for 48 and 7 for 64)
		J H Wardle at Hull, 1954
	Against:	12 for 110 (6 for 71 and 6 for 39)
		G R Cox at Sheffield, 1907
Most 10 wickets	*For Yorkshire:*	R Peel, E Wainwright 3 each
in a match	*Against:*	Twelve players 1 each
Warwickshire	*For Yorkshire:*	14 for 92 (9 for 43 and 5 for 49)
		H Verity at Leeds, 1937
	Against:	12 for 55 (5 for 21 and 7 for 34)
		T W Cartwright at Bradford, 1969
Most 10 wickets	*For Yorkshire:*	S Haigh 4
in a match	*Against:*	E F Field 4
Worcestershire	*For Yorkshire:*	14 for 211 (8 for 87 and 6 for 124)
		W Rhodes at Worcester, 1903
	Against:	13 for 76 (4 for 38 and 9 for 38)
		J A Cuffe at Bradford, 1907
Most 10 wickets	*For Yorkshire:*	S Haigh, G G Macaulay 4 each
in a match	*Against:*	N Gifford 2
Australians	*For Yorkshire:*	13 for 149 (8 for 48 and 5 for 101)
		G H Hirst at Bradford, 1899
	Against:	13 for 170 (6 for 91 and 7 for 79)
		J M Gregory at Sheffield, 1919
Most 10 wickets	*For Yorkshire:*	S Haigh 2
in a match	*Against:*	C V Grimmett, F R Spofforth, C T B Turner, H Trumble 2 each

BEST BOWLING ANALYSES IN AN INNINGS
FOR AND AGAINST YORKSHIRE

Best For Yorkshire:
10 for 10 H Verity v Nottinghamshire at Leeds, 1932

Against Yorkshire:
10 for 37 C V Grimmett for Australians at Sheffield, 1930
(non-championship)

County Championship
10 for 51 H Howell for Warwickshire at Birmingham, 1923

Yorkshire versus:

Derbyshire	*For Yorkshire:*	10 for 47	T F Smailes at Sheffield, 1939
	Against:	9 for 27	J J Hulme at Sheffield, 1894
Most 5 wickets	*For Yorkshire:*	S Haigh, E Peat, W Rhodes 11 each	
in an innings	*Against:*	W Mycroft 10	

Yorkshire versus

Durham

	For Yorkshire:	6 for 37	R D Stemp at Durham, 1994
		6 for 37	J N Gillespie at Chester-le-Street, 2006
	Against:	7 for 58	J Wood at Leeds, 1999
Most 5 wickets	For Yorkshire:	D Gough and M J Hoggard 2 each	
in an innings	Against:	G R Breese, S J E Brown, S J Harmison	
		and G Onions 2 each	

Essex

	For Yorkshire:	9 for 28	W Rhodes at Leyton, 1899
	Against:	8 for 44	F G Bull at Bradford, 1896
Most 5 wickets	For Yorkshire:	W Rhodes 18	
in an innings	Against:	W Mead 14	

Glamorgan

	For Yorkshire:	9 for 60	H Verity at Swansea, 1930
	Against:	9 for 43	J S Pressdee at Swansea, 1965
Most 5 wickets	For Yorkshire:	H Verity 12	
in an innings	Against:	D J Shepherd 6	

Gloucestershire

	For Yorkshire:	9 for 25	S Haigh at Leeds, 1912
	Against:	9 for 36	C W L Parker at Bristol, 1922
Most 5 wickets	For Yorkshire:	W Rhodes 22	
in an innings	Against:	T W J Goddard 17	

Hampshire

	For Yorkshire:	9 for 29	A C Williams at Dewsbury, 1919
	Against:	8 for 49	O W Herman at Bournemouth, 1930
Most 5 wickets	For Yorkshire:	G H Hirst 10	
in an innings	Against:	A S Kennedy 10	

Kent

	For Yorkshire:	9 for 12	H Verity at Sheffield, 1936
	Against:	8 for 35	A Hearne at Sheffield, 1885
Most 5 wickets	For Yorkshire:	W Rhodes 12	
in an innings	Against:	A P Freeman 14	

Lancashire

	For Yorkshire:	9 for 23	G H Hirst at Leeds, 1910
	Against:	9 for 41	A Mold at Huddersfield, 1890
Most 5 wickets	For Yorkshire:	T Emmett 16	
in an innings	Against:	J Briggs 19	

Leicestershire

	For Yorkshire:	8 for 25	G H Hirst at Hull, 1907
	Against:	9 for 63	C T Spencer at Huddersfield, 1954
Most 5 wickets	For Yorkshire:	G H Hirst 15	
in an innings	Against:	H A Smith 7	

Middlesex

	For Yorkshire:	9 for 45	G H Hirst at Sheffield 1907
	Against:	9 for 57	F A Tarrant at Leeds, 1906
Most 5 wickets	For Yorkshire:	W Rhodes 18	
in an innings	Against:	J T Hearne 21	

Northamptonshire

	For Yorkshire:	9 for 37	M A Robinson at Harrogate, 1993
	Against:	9 for 30	A E Thomas at Bradford, 1920
Most 5 wickets	For Yorkshire:	G G Macaulay 14	
in an innings	Against:	G E Tribe, W Wells 7 each	

Nottinghamshire

	For Yorkshire:	10 for 10	H Verity at Leeds, 1932
	Against:	8 for 32	J C Shaw at Nottingham, 1865
Most 5 wickets	For Yorkshire:	W Rhodes 17	
in an innings	Against:	F Morley 17	

BEST BOWLING ANALYSES IN AN INNINGS
FOR AND AGAINST YORKSHIRE *(continued)*

Yorkshire versus

Somerset	*For Yorkshire:*	10 for 35	A Drake at Weston-super-Mare, 1914
	Against:	9 for 41	L C Braund at Sheffield, 1902
Most 5 wickets	*For Yorkshire:*	G H Hirst 16	
in an innings	*Against:*	E J Tyler 8	
Surrey	*For Yorkshire:*	8 for 5	E Peate at Holbeck, 1883
	Against:	9 for 47	T Richardson at Sheffield, 1893
Most 5 wickets	*For Yorkshire:*	W Rhodes 17	
in an innings	*Against:*	W Southerton 19	
Sussex	*For Yorkshire:*	9 for 48	J H Wardle at Hull, 1954
	Against:	9 for 34	James Langridge at Sheffield, 1934
Most 5 wickets	*For Yorkshire:*	W Rhodes 14	
in an innings	*Against:*	G R Cox, J A Snow 6 each	
Warwickshire	*For Yorkshire:*	10 for 36	H Verity at Leeds, 1930
	Against:	10 for 51	H Howell at Birmingham, 1923
Most 5 wickets	*For Yorkshire:*	W Rhodes 18	
in an innings	*Against:*	E F Field, W E Hollies 7 each	
Worcestershire	*For Yorkshire:*	9 for 41	G H Hirst at Worcester, 1911
	Against:	9 for 38	J A Cuffe at Bradford, 1907
Most 5 wickets	*For Yorkshire:*	S Haigh, W Rhodes 11 each	
in an innings	*Against:*	R T D Perks 7	
Australians	*For Yorkshire:*	9 for 76	W Ringrose at Bradford, 1905
	Against:	10 for 37	C V Grimmett at Sheffield, 1930
Most 5 wickets	*For Yorkshire:*	R Peel 7	
in an innings	*Against:*	F R Spofforth 7	

HAT-TRICKS

G Freeman v. Lancashire at Holbeck, 1868
G Freeman v. Middlesex at Sheffield, 1868
A Hill v. United South of England XI at Bradford, 1874
A Hill v. Surrey at The Oval, 1880
E Peate v. Kent at Sheffield, 1882
G Ulyett v. Lancashire at Sheffield, 1883
E Peate v. Gloucestershire at Moreton-in-Marsh, 1884
W Fletcher v. MCC at Lord's, 1892
E Wainwright v. Sussex at Dewsbury, 1894
G H Hirst v. Leicestershire at Leicester, 1895
J T Brown v. Derbyshire at Derby, 1896
R Peel v. Kent at Halifax, 1897
S Haigh v. Derbyshire at Bradford, 1897
W Rhodes v. Kent at Canterbury, 1901
S Haigh v. Somerset at Sheffield, 1902
H A Sedgwick v. Worcestershire at Hull, 1906
G Deyes v. Gentlemen of Ireland at Bray, 1907
G H Hirst v. Leicestershire at Hull, 1907
J T Newstead v. Worcestershire at Bradford, 1907
S Haigh v. Lancashire at Manchester, 1909
M W Booth v. Worcestershire at Bradford, 1911
A Drake v. Essex at Huddersfield, 1912

HAT-TRICKS (Continued)

M W Booth v. Essex at Leyton, 1912
A Drake v. Derbyshire at Chesterfield, 1914 (4 in 4)
W Rhodes v. Derbyshire at Derby, 1920
A Waddington v. Northamptonshire at Northampton, 1920 (4 in 5)
G G Macaulay v. Warwickshire at Birmingham, 1923
E Robinson v. Sussex at Hull, 1928
G G Macaulay v. Leicestershire at Hull, 1930
E Robinson v. Kent at Gravesend, 1930
H Verity v. Nottinghamshire at Leeds, 1932
H Fisher v. Somerset at Sheffield, 1932 (all lbw)
G G Macaulay v. Glamorgan at Cardiff, 1933
G G Macaulay v. Lancashire at Manchester, 1933 (4 in 5)
M.Leyland v. Surrey at Sheffield, 1935
E Robinson v. Kent at Leeds, 1939
A Coxon v. Worcestershire at Leeds, 1946
F S Trueman v. Nottinghamshire at Nottingham, 1951
F S Trueman v. Nottinghamshire at Scarborough, 1955
R Appleyard v. Gloucestershire at Sheffield, 1956
F S.Trueman v. MCC at Lord's, 1958
D Wilson v. Nottinghamshire at Middlesbrough, 1959
F S Trueman v. Nottinghamshire at Bradford, 1963
D Wilson v. Nottinghamshire at Worksop, 1966
D Wilson v. Kent at Harrogate, 1966
G A Cope v. Essex at Colchester, 1970
A L Robinson v. Nottinghamshire at Worksop, 1974
P W Jarvis v. Derbyshire at Chesterfield, 1985
P J Hartley v. Derbyshire at Chesterfield, 1995 (4 in 5)
D Gough v. Kent at Leeds, 1995 (4 in 5)
C White v. Gloucestershire at Gloucester, 1998
M J Hoggard v. Sussex at Hove, 2009

52 Hat-Tricks: G G Macaulay and F S Trueman took four each, S Haigh and D Wilson three each. There have been seven hat-tricks versus Kent and Nottinghamshire, and six versus Derbyshire.

200 WICKETS IN A SEASON

Bowler	Season	Overs	Maidens	Runs	Wickets	Average
W Rhodes	1900	1366.4	411	3054	240	12.72
W Rhodes	1901	1455.3	474	3497	233	15.00
G H Hirst	1906	1111.1	262	3089	201	15.36
G G Macaulay	1925	1241.2	291	2986	200	14.93
R Appleyard†	1951	1323.2	394	2829	200	14.14

† First full season in First-Class cricket.

100 WICKETS IN A SEASON

Bowler		Wickets taken	Wickets taken	Wickets taken
R Appleyard	(3)	200 in 1951	141 in 1954	110 in 1956
A Booth	(1)	111 in 1946	—	—
M W Booth	(3)	104 in 1912	167 in 1913	155 in 1914
W E Bowes	(8)	117 in 1931	168 in 1932	130 in 1933
		109 in 1934	154 in 1935	113 in 1936
		106 in 1938	107 in 1939	—

313

100 WICKETS IN A SEASON *(Continued)*

Bowler		Wickets taken	Wickets taken	Wickets taken
D B Close	(2)	105 in 1949	114 in 1952	—
A Coxon	(2)	101 in 1949	129 in 1950	—
A Drake	(2)	115 in 1913	158 in 1914	—
T Emmett	(1)	112 in 1886	—	—
S Haigh	(10)	100 in 1898	160 in 1900	154 in 1902
		102 in 1903	118 in 1904	118 in 1905
		161 in 1906	120 in 1909	100 in 1911
		125 in 1912	—	—
G H Hirst	(12)	150 in 1895	171 in 1901	121 in 1903
		114 in 1904	100 in 1905	201 in 1906
		169 in 1907	164 in 1908	138 in 1910
		130 in 1911	113 in 1912	100 in 1913
R Illingworth	(5)	103 in 1956	120 in 1961	116 in 1962
		122 in 1964	105 in 1968	—
R Kilner	(4)	107 in 1922	143 in 1923	134 in 1924
		123 in 1925	—	—
G G Macaulay	(10)	101 in 1921	130 in 1922	163 in 1923
		184 in 1924	200 in 1925	133 in 1926
		130 in 1927	117 in 1928	102 in 1929
		141 in 1933	—	—
J T Newstead	(1)	131 in 1908	—	—
A G Nicholson	(2)	113 in 1966	101 in 1967	—
E Peate	(3)	131 in 1880	133 in 1881	165 in 1882
R Peel	(6)	118 in 1888	132 in 1890	106 in 1892
		134 in 1894	155 in 1895	108 in 1896
W Rhodes	(22)	141 in 1898	153 in 1899	240 in 1900
		233 in 1901	174 in 1902	169 in 1903
		118 in 1904	158 in 1905	113 in 1906
		164 in 1907	100 in 1908	115 in 1909
		105 in 1911	117 in 1914	155 in 1919
		156 in 1920	128 in 1921	100 in 1922
		127 in 1923	102 in 1926	111 in 1928
		100 in 1929	—	—
E Robinson	(1)	111 in 1928	—	—
E P Robinson	(4)	104 in 1938	120 in 1939	149 in 1946
		108 in 1947	—	—
T F Smailes	(4)	105 in 1934	125 in 1936	120 in 1937
		104 in 1938	—	—
F S Trueman	(8)	129 in 1954	140 in 1955	104 in 1959
		150 in 1960	124 in 1961	122 in 1962
		121 in 1965	107 in 1966	—
H Verity	(9)	169 in 1931	146 in 1932	168 in 1933
		100 in 1934	199 in 1935	185 in 1936
		185 in 1937	137 in 1938	189 in 1939
A Waddington	(5)	100 in 1919	140 in 1920	105 in 1921
		132 in 1922	105 in 1925	—
E Wainwright	(3)	114 in 1893	157 in 1894	102 in 1896
J H Wardle	(10)	148 in 1948	100 in 1949	172 in 1950
		122 in 1951	169 in 1952	126 in 1953
		122 in 1954	159 in 1955	146 in 1956
		106 in 1957	—	—
D Wilson	(3)	100 in 1966	107 in 1968	101 in 1969

BOWLERS WHO HAVE TAKEN OVER 500 WICKETS

Player	M	Runs	Wkts	Av'ge	Best
W Rhodes	883	57634	3598	16.01	9 for 28
G H Hirst	717	44716	2481	18.02	9 for 23
S Haigh	513	29289	1876	15.61	9 for 25
G G Macaulay	445	30554	1774	17.22	8 for 21
F S Trueman	459	29890	1745	17.12	8 for 28
H Verity	278	21353	1558	13.70	10 for 10
J H Wardle	330	27917	1539	18.13	9 for 25
R Illingworth	496	26806	1431	18.73	9 for 42
W E Bowes	301	21227	1351	15.71	9 for 121
R Peel	318	20638	1311	15.74	9 for 22
T Emmett	299	15465	1216	12.71	9 for 23
D Wilson	392	22626	1104	20.49	7 for 19
P Carrick	425	30530	1018	29.99	8 for 33
E Wainwright	352	17744	998	17.77	9 for 66
D B Close	536	23489	967	24.29	8 for 41
Emmott Robinson	413	19645	893	21.99	9 for 36
A G Nicholson	.282	17296	876	19.74	9 for 62
R Kilner	365	14855	857	17.33	8 for 26
A Waddington	255	16203	835	19.40	8 for 34
T F Smailes	262	16593	802	20.68	10 for 47
E Peate	154	9986	794	12.57	8 for 5
Ellis P Robinson	208	15141	735	20.60	8 for 35
C M Old	222	13409	647	20.72	7 for 20
R Appleyard	133	9903	642	15.42	8 for 76
W Bates	202	10692	637	16.78	8 for 21
G A Cope	230	15627	630	24.80	8 for 73
P J Hartley	195	17438	579	30.11	9 for 41
A Sidebottom	216	13852	558	24.82	8 for 72
M W Booth	144	11017	557	19.17	8 for 47
A Hill	140	7002	542	12.91	7 for 14
Hon F S Jackson	207	9690	506	19.15	7 for 42

BOWLERS UNCHANGED IN A MATCH
(IN WHICH THE OPPONENTS WERE DISMISSED TWICE)

There have been 31 instances. The first and most recent are listed below.
A complete list is to be found in the 2008 edition.

First: L Greenwood (11 for 71) and G Freeman (8 for 73) v. Surrey
at The Oval, 1867
Yorkshire won by an innings and 111 runs

Most Recent: E Robinson (8 for 65) and G G Macaulay (12 for 50) v. Worcestershire
at Leeds, 1927
Yorkshire won by an innings and 106 runs

FIELDERS (IN MATCHES FOR YORKSHIRE)

MOST CATCHES IN AN INNINGS

6	E P Robinson	v. Leicestershire	at Bradford, 1938
5	J Tunnicliffe	v. Leicestershire	at Leeds, 1897
5	J Tunnicliffe	v. Leicestershire	at Leicester, 1900
5	J Tunnicliffe	v. Leicestershire	at Scarborough, 1901
5	A B Sellers	v. Essex	at Leyton, 1933
5	D Wilson	v. Surrey	at The Oval, 1969
5	R G Lumb	v. Gloucestershire	at Middlesbrough, 1972

MOST CATCHES IN A MATCH

7	J Tunnicliffe	v. Leicestershire	at Leeds, 1897
7	J Tunnicliffe	v. Leicestershire	at Leicester, 1900
7	A B Sellers	v Essex	at Leyton, 1933
7	E P Robinson	v. Leicestershire	at Bradford, 1938
7	A Lyth	v. Middlesex	at Scarborough, 2014

MOST CATCHES IN A SEASON

70	J Tunnicliffe	in 1901
70	P J Sharpe	in 1962
61	J Tunnicliffe	in 1895
60	J Tunnicliffe	in 1904
59	J Tunnicliffe	in 1896
57	J V Wilson	in 1955
54	J V Wilson	in 1961
53	J V Wilson	in 1957
51	J V Wilson	in 1951

MOST CATCHES IN A CAREER

665	J Tunnicliffe	(1.40 per match)
586	W Rhodes	(0.66 per match)
564	D B Close	(1.05 per match)
525	P J Sharpe	(1.27 per match)
520	J V Wilson	(1.09 per match)
518	G H Hirst	(0.72 per match)

WICKET-KEEPERS IN MATCHES FOR YORKSHIRE

MOST DISMISSALS IN AN INNINGS

7	(7ct)	D L Bairstow	v. Derbyshire	at Scarborough	1982
6	(6ct)	J Hunter	v. Gloucestershire	at Gloucester	1887
6	(5ct,1st)	D Hunter	v. Surrey	at Sheffield	1891
6	(6ct)	D Hunter	v. Middlesex	at Leeds	1909
6	(2ct,4st)	W R Allen	v. Sussex	at Hove	1921
6	(5ct,1st)	J G Binks	v. Lancashire	at Leeds	1962
6	(6ct)	D L Bairstow	v. Lancashire	at Manchester	1971
6	(6ct)	D L Bairstow	v. Warwickshire	at Bradford	1978
6	(5ct,1st)	D L Bairstow	v. Lancashire	at Leeds	1980
6	(6ct)	D L Bairstow	v. Derbyshire	at Chesterfield	1984
6	(6ct)	R J Blakey	v. Sussex	at Eastbourne	1990
6	(5ct,1st)	R J Blakey	v. Gloucestershire	at Cheltenham	1992
6	(5ct,1st)	R J Blakey	v. Glamorgan	at Cardiff	1994
6	(6ct)	R J Blakey	v. Glamorgan	at Leeds	2003
6	(6ct)	G L Brophy	v. Durham	at Chester-le-Street	2009
6	(6ct)	J M Bairstow	v. Middlesex	at Leeds	2013
6	(6ct)	J M Bairstow	v. Sussex	at Arundel	2014

MOST DISMISSALS IN A MATCH

11	(11ct)	D L Bairstow	v. Derbyshire	at Scarborough	1982
		(Equalled World Record)			
9	(9ct)	J.Hunter	v. Gloucestershire	at Gloucester	1887
9	(8ct,1st)	A Dolphin	v. Derbyshire	at Bradford	1919
9	(9ct)	D L Bairstow	v. Lancashire	at Manchester	1971
9	(9ct)	R J Blakey	v. Sussex	at Eastbourne	1990
8	(2ct,6st)	G Pinder	v. Lancashire	at Sheffield	1872
8	(2ct,6st)	D Hunter	v. Surrey	at Bradford	1898
8	(8ct)	A Bairstow	v. Cambridge University	at Cambridge	1899
8	(8ct)	A Wood	v. Northamptonshire	at Huddersfield	1932
8	(8ct)	D L Bairstow	v. Lancashire	at Leeds	1978
8	(7ct,1st)	D L Bairstow	v. Derbyshire	at Chesterfield	1984
8	(6ct,2st)	D L Bairstow	v. Derbyshire	at Chesterfield	1985
8	(8ct)	R J Blakey	v. Hampshire	at Southampton	1989
8	(8ct)	R J Blakey	v. Northamptonshire	at Harrogate	1993
8	(8ct)	A J Hodd	v. Glamorgan	at Leeds	2012
8	(8ct)	J M Bairstow	v. Middlesex	at Leed	2013

MOST DISMISSALS IN A SEASON

107	(96ct,11st)	J G Binks, 1960
94	(81ct,13st)	JG Binks, 1961
89	(75ct,14st)	A Wood, 1934
88	(80ct,8st)	J G Binks, 1963
86	(70ct,16st)	J G Binks, 1962
82	(52ct,30st)	A Dolphin, 1919
80	(57ct,23st)	A. Wood, 1935

MOST DISMISSALS IN A CAREER

1186	(863ct,323st)	D Hunter (2.29 per match)
1044	(872ct,172st)	J G Binks (2.12 per match)
1038	(907ct,131st)	D L Bairstow (2.41 per match)
855	(612ct,243st)	A Wood (2.09 per match)
829	(569ct,260st)	A Dolphin (1.94 per match)
824	(768ct, 56st)	R J Blakey (2.43 per match)

YORKSHIRE PLAYERS WHO HAVE COMPLETED THE "DOUBLE"

(all First-Class matches)

Player	Year	Runs	Average	Wickets	Average
M W Booth (1)	1913	1,228	27.28	181	18.46
D B Close (2)	†1949	1,098	27.45	113	27.87
	1952	1,192	33.11	114	24.08
A Drake (1)	1913	1,056	23.46	116	16.93
S Haigh (1)	1904	1,055	26.37	121	19.85
G H Hirst (14)	1896	1,122	28.20	104	21.64
	1897	1,535	35.69	101	23.22
	1901	1,950	42.39	183	16.38
	1903	1,844	47.28	128	14.94
	1904	2,501	54.36	132	21.09
	1905	2,266	53.95	110	19.94
	††1906	2,385	45.86	208	16.50
	1907	1,344	28.38	188	15.20
	1908	1,598	38.97	114	14.05
	1909	1,256	27.30	115	20.05
	1910	1,840	32.85	164	14.79
	1911	1,789	33.12	137	20.40
	1912	1,133	25.75	118	17.37
	1913	1,540	35.81	101	20.13
R Illingworth (6)	1957	1,213	28.20	106	18.40
	1959	1,726	46.64	110	21.46
	1960	1,006	25.79	109	17.55
	1961	1,153	24.53	128	17.90
	1962	1,612	34.29	117	19.45
	1964	1,301	37.17	122	17.45
F S Jackson (1)	1898	1,566	41.21	104	15.67
R Kilner (4)	1922	1,198	27.22	122	14.73
	1923	1,404	32.24	158	12.91
	1925	1,068	30.51	131	17.92
	1926	1,187	37.09	107	22.52
R Peel (1)	1896	1,206	30.15	128	17.50
W Rhodes (16)	1903	1,137	27.07	193	14.57
	1904	1,537	35.74	131	21.59
	1905	1,581	35.93	182	16.95
	1906	1,721	29.16	128	23.57
	1907	1,055	22.93	177	15.57
	1908	1,673	31.56	115	16.13
	1909	2,094	40.26	141	15.89
	1911	2,261	38.32	117	24.07
	1914	1,377	29.29	118	18.27
	1919	1,237	34.36	164	14.42
	1920	1,123	28.07	161	13.18
	1921	1,474	39.83	141	13.27
	1922	1,511	39.76	119	12.19
	1923	1,321	33.02	134	11.54
	1924	1,126	26.18	109	14.46
	1926	1,132	34.30	115	14.86
T F Smailes (1)	1938	1,002	25.05	113	20.84
E Wainwright (1)	1897	1,612	35.82	101	23.06

† First season in First-Class cricket.

†† The only instance in First-Class cricket of 2,000 runs and 200 wickets in a season.

H Sutcliffe (194) and M Leyland (45) hit 102 off six consecutive overs for Yorkshire v. Essex at Scarborough in 1932.

From 1898 to 1930 inclusive, Wilfred Rhodes took no less than 4,187 wickets, and scored 39,969 runs in First-Class cricket at home and abroad, a remarkable record. He also took 100 wickets and scored 1,000 in a season 16 times, and G H Hirst 14 times.

Of players with a qualification of not less than 50 wickets, Wilfred Rhodes was first in bowling in First-Class cricket in 1900, 1901, 1919, 1920, 1922, 1923 and 1926; Schofield Haigh in 1902, 1905, 1908 and 1909; Mr E R Wilson in 1921; G G Macaulay in 1924; H Verity in 1930, 1933, 1935, 1937 and 1939; W E Bowes in 1938; A Booth in 1946; R Appleyard in 1951 and 1955, and F S Trueman in 1952 and 1963.

The highest aggregate of runs made in one season in First-Class cricket by a Yorkshire player is 3,429 by L Hutton in 1949. This total has been exceeded three times, viz: D C S Compton 3,816 and W J Edrich 3,539 in 1947, and 3,518 by T Hayward in 1906. H Sutcliffe scored 3,336 in 1932.

Three players have taken all 10 Yorkshire wickets in an innings. G Wootton, playing for All England XI at Sheffield in 1865, took all 10 wickets for 54 runs. H Howell performed the feat for Warwickshire at Edgbaston in 1923 at a cost of 51 runs; and C V Grimmett, Australia, took all 10 wickets for 37 runs at Sheffield in 1930.

The match against Sussex at Dewsbury on June 7th and 8th, 1894, was brought to a summary conclusion by a remarkable bowling performance on the part of Edward Wainwright. In the second innings of Sussex, he took the last five wickets in seven balls, including the "hat trick". In the whole match he obtained 13 wickets for only 38 runs.

M D Moxon has the unique distinction of scoring a century in each of his first two First-Class matches in Yorkshire — 116 (2nd inns.) v. Essex at Leeds and 111 (1st inns.) v. Derbyshire at Sheffield, June 1981).

In the Yorkshire v. Norfolk match — played on the Hyde Park Ground, Sheffield, on July 14th to 18th, 1834 — 851 runs were scored in the four innings, of which no fewer than 128 were extras: 75 byes and 53 wides. At that time wides were not run out, so that every wide included in the above total represents a wide actually bowled. This particular achievement has never been surpassed in the annals of county cricket.

L Hutton reached his 1,000 runs in First-Class cricket in 1949 as early as June 9th.

W Barber reached his 1,000 runs in 1934 on June 13th. P Holmes reached his 1,000 in 1925 on June 16th, as also did H Sutcliffe in 1932. J T Brown reached his 1,000 in 1899 on June 22nd. In 1905, D Denton reached his 1,000 on June 26th; and in 1906 G H Hirst gained the same total on June 27th.

In 1912, D Denton scored over 1,000 runs during July, while M Leyland and H Sutcliffe both scored over 1,000 runs in August 1932.

L Hutton scored over 1,000 in June and over 1,000 runs in August in 1949.

H Verity took his 100th wicket in First-Class cricket as early as June 19th in 1936 and on June 27th in 1935. In 1900, W Rhodes obtained his 100th wicket on June 21st, and again on the same date in 1901, while G H Hirst obtained his 100th wicket on June 28th, 1906.

In 1930, Yorkshiremen (H Sutcliffe and H Verity) occupied the first places by English players in the batting and the bowling averages of First-Class cricket, which is a record without precedent. H Sutcliffe was also first in the batting averages in 1931 and 1932.

G Boycott was the first player to have achieved an average of over 100 in each of two English seasons. In 1971, he scored 2,503 runs for an average of 100.12, and in 1979 he scored 1,538 runs for an average of 102.53.

FIRST-CLASS MATCHES BEGUN AND FINISHED IN ONE DAY

Yorkshire v. Somerset, at Huddersfield, July 9th, 1894.

Yorkshire v. Hampshire, at Southampton, May 27th, 1898.

Yorkshire v. Worcestershire, at Bradford, May 7th, 1900

For England

YORKSHIRE TEST CRICKETERS 1877-2014 (Correct to August 17, 2014)

Player	M.	I	NO	Runs	HS.	Av'ge.	100s	50s	Balls	R	W	Av'ge	Best	5wI	10wM	c/st
APPLEYARD, R ...1954-56	9	9	6	51	19*	17.00	—	—	1,596	554	31	17.87	5-51	1	—	4
ARMITAGE, T ...1877	2	3	0	33	21	11.00	—	—	12	15	0	—	—	—	—	0
ATHEY, C W J ...1980-88	23	41	1	919	123	22.97	1	4	—	—	—	—	—	—	—	13
BAIRSTOW, D L ...1979-81	4	7	1	125	59	20.83	—	1	—	—	—	—	—	—	—	12/1
BAIRSTOW, J M .2012/13-14	14	24	2	593	95	26.95	—	4	—	—	—	—	—	—	—	16
BALLANCE, G S 2013/14-14	8	13	1	729	156	60.75	3	3	—	—	—	—	—	—	—	7
BARBER, W ...1935	2	4	0	83	44	20.75	—	—	12	5	0	0.00	1-0	—	—	1
BATES, W ...1881-87	15	26	2	656	64	27.33	—	5	2,364	821	50	16.42	7-28	4	1	9
BINKS, J G ...1964	2	4	0	91	55	22.75	—	1	—	—	—	—	—	—	—	8/0
BLAKEY, R J ...1993	2	4	0	7	6	1.75	—	—	—	—	—	—	—	—	—	2/0
BOOTH, M W ...1913-14	2	2	0	46	32	23.00	—	—	312	130	7	18.57	4-49	—	—	0
BOWES, W E ...1932-46	15	11	5	28	10*	4.66	—	—	3,655	1,519	68	22.33	6-33	6	—	2
†BOYCOTT, G ...1964-82	108	193	23	8,114	246*	47.72	22	42	944	382	7	54.57	3-47	—	—	33
BRENNAN, D V ...1951	2	2	0	16	16	8.00	—	—	—	—	—	—	—	—	—	0/1
BRESNAN, T T .2009-13/14	23	26	4	575	91	26.13	—	3	4,674	2,357	72	32.73	5-48	1	—	8
BROWN, J T ...1894-99	8	16	3	470	140	36.15	1	1	35	22	0	—	—	—	—	7
†CLOSE, D B ...1949-76	22	37	2	887	70	25.34	—	4	1,212	532	18	29.55	4-35	—	—	24
COPE, G A ...1977-78	3	3	0	40	22	13.33	—	—	864	277	8	34.62	3-102	—	—	1
COXON, A ...1948	1	2	0	19	19*	9.50	—	—	378	172	3	57.33	2-90	—	—	0
DAWSON, R K J ...2002-03	7	13	3	114	104	11.40	1	—	1,116	677	11	61.54	4-134	—	—	3
DENTON, D ...1905-10	11	22	1	424	104	20.19	1	—	—	—	—	—	—	—	—	8
DOLPHIN, A ...1921	1	2	0	1	1	0.50	—	—	—	—	—	—	—	—	—	1/0
EMMETT, T ...1877-82	7	13	1	160	48	13.33	—	1	728	284	9	31.55	7-68	1	—	9
GIBB, P A ...1938-46	8	13	0	581	120	44.69	2	3	—	—	—	—	—	—	—	3/1
GOUGH, D ...1994-2003	58	86	18	855	65	12.57	—	2	11,821	6,503	229	28.39	6-42	9	—	13

YORKSHIRE TEST CRICKETERS 1877-2014 (Continued)

Player	M.	I	NO	Runs	HS.	Av'ge	100s	50s	Balls	R	W	Av'ge	Best	5wI	10wM	c/st
GREENWOOD, A 1877	2	4	0	77	49	19.25	—	—								2
HAIGH, S 1899-1912	11	18	3	113	25	7.53	—	—	1,294	622	24	25.91	6-11	1	—	8
HAMILTON, G.M. 1999	1	2	0	0	0	0.00	—	—	90	63	0	—	—	—	—	0
HAMPSHIRE, J H ...1969-75	8	16	1	403	107	26.86	1	2	—	—	—	—	—	—	—	9
†HAWKE, LORD 1896-99	5	8	1	55	30	7.85	—	—	—							3
HILL, A 1877	2	4	2	101	49	50.50	—	—	340	130	7	18.57	4-27	—	—	1
HIRST, G H 1897-1909	24	38	3	790	85	22.57	—	5	3,967	1,770	59	30.00	5-48	3	—	18
HOGGARD, M J ..2000-2008	67	92	27	473	38	7.27	—	—	13,909	7,564	248	30.50	7-61	7	1	24
HOLMES, P 1921-32	7	14	1	357	88	27.46	—	4	—							3
HUNTER, J 1884-85	5	7	2	93	39*	18.60	—	—	—							8/3
†HUTTON, L 1937-55	79	138	15	6,971	364	56.67	19	33	260	232	3	77.33	1-2	—	—	57
HUTTON, R A 1971	5	8	2	219	81	36.50	—	2	738	257	9	28.55	3-72	—	—	9
†ILLINGWORTH, R .1958-73	61	90	11	1,836	113	23.24	2	5	11,934	3,807	122	31.20	6-29	3	—	45
†JACKSON, Hon F S1893-1905	20	33	4	1,415	144*	48.79	5	6	1,587	799	24	33.29	5-52	1	—	10
JARVIS, P W 1988-93	9	15	2	132	29*	10.15	—	—	1,912	965	21	45.95	4-107	—	—	2
KILNER, R 1924-26	9	8	1	233	74	33.28	—	2	2,368	734	24	30.58	4-51	—	—	6
LEADBEATER, E ..1951-52	2	2	0	40	38	20.00	—	—	289	218	2	109.00	1-38	—	—	3
LEYLAND, M 1928-38	41	65	5	2,764	187	46.06	9	10	1,103	585	6	97.50	3-91	—	—	13
LOWSON, F A ...1951-55	7	13	0	245	68	18.84	—	2	—							5
McGRATH, A 2003	4	5	0	201	81	40.20	—	2	102	56	4	14.00	3-16	—	—	3
MACAULAY, G G ..1923-33	8	10	4	112	76	18.66	—	1	1,701	662	24	27.58	5-64	1	—	5
MILLIGAN, F W 1899	2	4	0	58	38	14.50	—	—	45	29	0	—	—	—	—	1
MITCHELL, A 1933-36	6	10	0	298	72	29.80	—	2	6	4	0	—	—	—	—	9
*MITCHELL, F 1899	2	4	0	88	41	22.00	—	—	—							2
MOXON, M D 1986-89	10	17	1	455	99	28.43	—	3	48	30	0	—	—	—	—	10

For England

YORKSHIRE TEST CRICKETERS 1877-2014 (Continued)

Player	M.	I	NO	Runs	HS.	Av'ge	100s	50s	Balls	R	W	Av'ge	Best	5wI	10wM	c/st
OLD, CM 1972-81	46	66	9	845	65	14.82	—	2	8,858	4,020	143	28.11	7-50	4	—	22
PADGETT, D E V 1960	2	4	0	51	31	12.75	—	—	12	8	0	—	—	—	—	0
PEATE, E 1881-86	9	14	8	70	13	11.66	—	—	2,096	682	31	22.00	6-85	2	—	2
PEEL, R 1884-96	20	33	4	427	83	14.72	—	3	5,216	1,715	101	16.98	7-31	5	1	17
PLUNKET, L E .2005/6-2014	13	20	5	238	55*	15.86	—	—	2659	1536	41	37.46	5-64	1	—	3
RHODES, W ...1899-1930	58	98	21	2,325	179	30.19	2	11	8,231	3,425	127	26.96	8-68	6	1	60
ROOT, J E 2012/13-14	22	40	6	1732	200*	50.94	5	7	510	225	4	56.25	2- 9	—	—	15
SHARPE, P J 1963-69	12	21	4	786	111	46.23	1	4	—	—	—	—	—	—	—	17
SHAHZAD, A 2010	1	1	1	5	5	5.00	—	—	102	63	4	15.75	3-45	—	—	2
SIDEBOTTOM, A 1985	1	1	0	2	2	2.00	—	—	112	65	1	65.00	1-65	—	—	0
SIDEBOTTOM, R J .2001-10	22	31	11	313	31	15.65	—	—	4,812	2,231	79	28.24	7-47	5	1	5
SILVERWOOD, CEW 1997-2003	6	7	3	29	10	7.25	—	—	828	444	11	40.36	5-91	1	—	2
SMAILES, T F 1946	1	1	0	25	25	25.00	—	—	120	62	3	20.66	3-44	—	—	0
SMITHSON, G A 1948	2	3	0	70	35	23.33	—	—	—	—	—	—	—	—	—	0
†STANYFORTH, R T 1927-28	4	6	1	13	6*	2.60	—	—	—	—	—	—	—	—	—	7/2
STEVENSON, G B .1980-81	2	2	1	28	27*	28.00	—	—	312	183	5	36.60	3-111	—	—	0
SUTCLIFFE, H ...1924-35	54	84	9	4,555	194	60.73	16	23	—	—	—	—	—	—	—	23
TAYLOR, K 1959-64	3	5	0	57	24	11.40	—	—	12	6	0	—	—	—	—	1
TRUEMAN, F S ..1952-65	67	85	14	981	39*	13.81	—	—	15,178	6,625	307	21.57	8-31	17	3	64
ULYETT, G 1877-90	25	39	0	949	149	24.33	1	7	2,627	1,020	50	20.40	7-36	1	—	19
†VAUGHAN M P .1999-2008	82	147	9	5,719	197	41.44	18	18	978	561	6	93.50	2-71	—	—	44
VERITY, H 1931-39	40	44	12	669	66*	20.90	—	3	11,173	3,510	144	24.37	8-43	5	2	30
WADDINGTON, A .1920-21	2	4	0	16	7	4.00	—	—	276	119	1	119.00	1-35	—	—	1
WAINWRIGHT, E ..1893-98	5	9	0	132	49	14.66	—	—	127	73	0	—	—	—	—	2
WARDLE, J H ...1948-57	28	41	8	653	66	19.78	—	2	6,597	2,080	102	20.39	7-36	5	1	12
WATSON, W 1951-59	23	37	3	879	116	25.85	2	3	—	—	—	—	—	—	—	8

For England

Player	M.	I	NO	Runs	HS	Av'ge	100s	50s	Balls	R	W	Av'ge	Best	5wI	10wM	c/st
WHITE, C 1994-2002	30	50	7	1,052	121	24.46	1	5	3,959	2,220	59	37.62	5-32	3	—	14
WILSON, C E M 1899	2	4	1	42	18	14.00	—	—	—	—	—	—	—	—	—	0
WILSON, D 1964-71	6	7	1	75	42	12.50	—	—	1,472	466	11	42.36	2-17	—	—	1
WILSON, E R 1921	1	2	0	10	5	5.00	—	—	123	36	3	12.00	2-28	—	—	0
WOOD, A 1938-39	4	5	1	80	53	20.00	—	1	—	—	—	—	—	—	—	10/1
†YARDLEY, N W D ...1938-50	20	34	2	812	99	25.37	—	4	1,662	707	21	33.66	3-67	—	—	14

†Captained England
*Also represented and captained South Africa

For South Africa

Player	M.	I	NO	Runs	HS	Av'ge	100s	50s	Balls	R	W	Av'ge	Best	5wI	10wM	c/st
†MITCHELL, F 1912	3	6	0	28	12	4.66	—	—	—	—	—	—	—	—	—	0

†Captained South Africa

Overseas Players
(Qualification: 20 first-class matches for Yorkshire)

For Australia

Player	M.	I	NO	Runs	HS	Av'ge	100s	50s	Balls	R	W	Av'ge	Best	5wI	10wM	c/st
BEVAN, M G 1994-98	18	30	3	785	91	29.07	—	6	1,285	703	29	24.24	6-82	1	1	8
GILLESPIE, J N ...1996-2006	71	93	28	1,218	201*	18.73	1	2	14,234	6,770	259	26.13	7-37	8	—	27
JAQUES, P A 2005-2008	11	19	0	902	150	47.47	3	6	—	—	—	—	—	—	—	7
LEHMANN, D S ...1999-2004	27	42	2	1,798	177	44.95	5	10	974	412	15	27.46	3-42	—	—	11

For South Africa

Player	M.	I	NO	Runs	HS	Av'ge	100s	50s	Balls	R	W	Av'ge	Best	5wI	10wM	c/st
RUDOLPH, J A ...2003-12/13	48	83	9	2,622	222*	35.43	6	11	664	432	4	108.00	1-1	—	—	29

For West Indies

Player	M.	I	NO	Runs	HS	Av'ge	100s	50s	Balls	R	W	Av'ge	Best	5wI	10wM	c/st
RICHARDSON, R B 1983-84/95	86	146	12	5,949	194	44.39	16	27	66	18	0	—	—	—	—	90

CENTURIES FOR ENGLAND

C W J ATHEY (1)
123 v. Pakistan at Lord's, 1987

G S BALLANCE (3)
104* v. Sri Lanka at Lord's, 2014   256 v. India at Southampton, 2014
110 v. India at Lord's, 2014

G BOYCOTT (22)

113	v. Australia at The Oval, 1964	112	v West Indies at Port-of-Spain, 1974
117	v. South Africa at Port Elizabeth, 1965	107	v. Australia at Nottingham, 1977
246*	v. India at Leeds, 1967	191	v. Australia at Leeds, 1977
116	v. West Indies at Georgetown, 1968	100*	v. Pakistan at Hyderabad, 1978
128	v. West Indies at Manchester, 1969	131	v. New Zealand at Nottingham, 1978
106	v. West Indies at Lord's, 1969	155	v. India at Birmingham, 1979
142*	v. Australia at Sydney, 1971	125	v. India at The Oval, 1979
119*	v. Australia at Adelaide, 1971	128*	v. Australia at Lord's, 1980
121*	v. Pakistan at Lord's, 1971	104*	v. West Indies at St John's, 1981
112	v. Pakistan at Leeds, 1971	137	v. Australia at The Oval, 1981
115	v. New Zealand at Leeds, 1973	105	v. India at Delhi, 1981

J T BROWN (1)
140 v. Australia at Melbourne, 1895

D DENTON (1)
104 v. South Africa at Old Wanderers, Johannesburg, 1910

P A GIBB (2)
106 v. South Africa at Old Wanderers, Johannesburg, 1938
120 v. South Africa at Kingsmead, Durban, 1939

J H HAMPSHIRE (1)
107 v. West Indies at Lord's, 1969

L HUTTON (19)

100	v. New Zealand at Manchester, 1937	206	v. New Zealand at The Oval, 1949
100	v. Australia at Nottingham, 1938	202*	v. West Indies at The Oval, 1950
364	v. Australia at The Oval, 1938	156*	v. Australia at Adelaide, 1951
196	v. West Indies at Lord's, 1939	100	v. South Africa at Leeds, 1951
165*	v. West Indies at The Oval, 1939	150	v. India at Lord's, 1952
122*	v. Australia at Sydney, 1947	104	v. India at Manchester, 1952
100	v. South Africa at Leeds, 1947	145	v. Australia at Lord's, 1953
158	v. South Africa at Ellis Park, J'b'rg, 1948	169	v. West Indies at Georgetown, 1954
123	v. South Africa at Ellis Park, J'b'rg, 1949	205	v. West Indies at Kingston, 1954
101	v. New Zealand at Leeds, 1949		

R ILLINGWORTH (2)
113 v. West Indies at Lord's, 1969
107 v. India at Manchester, 1971

Hon. F S JACKSON (5)

103	v. Australia at The Oval, 1893	144*	v. Australia at Leeds, 1905
118	v. Australia at The Oval, 1899	113	v. Australia at Manchester, 1905
128	v. Australia at Manchester, 1902		

M LEYLAND (9)

137	v. Australia at Melbourne, 1929	161	v. South Africa at The Oval, 1935
102	v. South Africa at Lord's, 1929	126	v. Australia at Woolloongabba, Brisbane, 1936
109	v. Australia at Lord's, 1934		
153	v. Australia at Manchester, 1934	111*	v. Australia at Melbourne, 1937
110	v. Australia at The Oval, 1934	187	v. Australia at The Oval, 1938

W RHODES (2)
179 v. Australia at Melbourne, 1912
152 v. South Africa at Old Wanderers, Johannesburg, 1913

CENTURIES FOR ENGLAND

J E ROOT (5)

104	v. New Zealand at Leeds, 2013	154*	v. India at Nottingham, 2014
180	v. Australia at Lord's, 2013	149*	v. India at The Oval, 2014
200*	v. Sri Lanka at Lord's, 2014		

P J SHARPE (1)

111 v. New Zealand at Nottingham, 1969

H SUTCLIFFE (16)

122	v. South Africa at Lord's, 1924	114	v. South Africa at Birmingham, 1929
115	v. Australia at Sydney, 1924	100	v. South Africa at Lord's, 1929
176	v. Australia at Melbourne, 1925 (1st Inns)	104	v. South Africa at The Oval, 1929 (1st inns)
127	v. Australia at Melbourne, 1925 (2nd Inns)	109*	v. South Africa at The Oval, 1929 (2nd inns)
143	v. Australia at Melbourne, 1925	161	v. Australia at The Oval, 1930
161	v. Australia at The Oval, 1926	117	v. New Zealand at The Oval, 1931
102	v. South Africa at Old Wanderers, Jbg.1927	109*	v. New Zealand at Manchester, 1931
135	v. Australia at Melbourne, 1929	194	v. Australia at Sydney, 1932

G ULYETT (1)

149 v. Australia at Melbourne, 1882

M P VAUGHAN (18)

120	v. Pakistan at Manchester, 2001	105	v. Sri Lanka at Kandy, 2003
115	v. Sri Lanka at Lord's, 2002	140	v. West Indies at Antigua, 2004
100	v. India at Lord's, 2002	103	v. West Indies at Lord's (1st inns) 2004
197	v. India at Nottingham, 2002	101*	v. West Indies at Lord's (2nd inns) 2004
195	v. India at The Oval, 2002	120	v. Bangladesh at Lord's, 2005
177	v. Australia at Adelaide, 2002	166	v. Australia at Manchester,2005
145	v. Australia at Melbourne, 2002	103	v. West Indies at Leeds, 2007
183	v. Australia at Sydney, 2003	124	v. India at Nottingham, 2007
156	v. South Africa at Birmingham, 2003	106	v. New Zealand at Lord's, 2008

W WATSON (2)

109	v. Australia at Lord's, 1953	116	v. West Indies at Kingston, 1954

C WHITE (1)

121 v. India at Ahmedabad, 2001

Summary of the Centuries

versus	Total	In England	Away
Australia	41	22	19
Bangladesh	1	1	0
India	16	14	2
New Zealand	10	10	—
Pakistan	5	4	1
South Africa	18	10	8
Sri Lanka	4	3	1
West Indies	17	10	7
Totals	112	74	38

For Australia

J N GILLESPIE (1)

201* v. Bangladesh at Chittagong, 2006

P A JAQUES (3)

100	v. Sri Lanka at Brisbane, 2007	108	v. West Indies at Bridgetown, 2008
150	v. Sri Lanka at Hobart, 2007		

D S LEHMANN (5)

160	v. West Indies at Port of Spain, 2003	129	v. Sri Lanka at Galle, 2004
110	v. Bangladesh at Darwin, 2003	153	v. Sri Lanka at Columbo, 2004
177	v. Bangladesh at Cairns, 2003		

10 WICKETS IN A MATCH FOR ENGLAND

W BATES (1)
14 for 102 (7 for 28 and 7 for 74) v. Australia at Melbourne, 1882

M J HOGGARD (1)
12 for 205 (5 for 144 and 7 for 61) v. South Africa at Johannesburg, 2005

R PEEL (1)
11 for 68 (7 for 31 and 4 for 37) v. Australia at Mancester, 1888
Note: The scorebook for the Australia v. England Test match at Sydney in February 1888
shows that the final wicket to fall was taken by W Attewell, and not by Peel
Peel therefore took 9, and not 10 wickets, in the match
His career totals have been amended to take account of this alteration

W RHODES (1)
15 for 124 (7 for 56 and 8 for 68) v. Australia at Melbourne, 1904

R J SIDEBOTTOM (1)
10 for 139 (4 for 90 and 6 for 49) v. New Zealand at Hamilton, 2008

F S TRUEMAN (3)
11 for 88 (5 for 58 and 6 for 30) v. Australia at Leeds, 1961
11 for 152 (6 for 100 and 5 for 52) v. West Indies at Lord's, 1963*
12 for 119 (5 for 75 and 7 for 44) v. West Indies at Birmingham, 1963*
consecutive Tests

H VERITY (2)
11 for 153 (7 for 49 and 4 for 104) v. India at Chepauk, Madras, 1934
15 for 104 (7 for 61 and 8 for 43) v. Australia at Lord's, 1934

J H WARDLE (1)
12 for 89 (5 for 53 and 7 for 36) v. South Africa at Cape Town, 1957

Summary of Ten Wickets in a Match

versus	Total	In England	Away
Australia	5	3	2
India	1	—	1
New Zealand	1	—	1
Pakistan	—	—	—
South Africa	2	—	2
Sri Lanka	—	—	—
West Indies	2	2	—
Totals	11	5	6

For Australia

M G BEVAN (1)
10 for 113 (4 for 31and 6 for 82) v. West Indies at Adelaide, 1997

5 WICKETS IN AN INNINGS FOR ENGLAND

R APPLEYARD (1)
5 for 51 v. Pakistan at Nottingham, 1954

W BATES (4)
7 for 28 v. Australia at Melbourne, 1882   5 for 31 v. Australia at Adelaide, 1884
7 for 74 v. Australia at Melbourne, 1882   5 for 24 v. Australia at Sydney, 1885

5 WICKETS IN AN INNINGS FOR ENGLAND *(Continued)*

W E BOWES (6)

6-34	v. New Zealand	at Auckland	1933	5-100	v. South Africa	at Manchester	1935
6-142	v. Australia	at Leeds	1934*	5-49	v. Australia	at The Oval	1938
5-55	v. Australia	at The Oval	1934*	6-33	v. West Indies	at Manchester	1939

consecutive Test matches

T T BRESNAN (1)

5-48   v. India   at Nottingham   2011

T EMMETT (1)

7-68   v. Australia   at Melbourne   1879

D GOUGH (9)

6-49	v. Australia	at Sydney	1995	5-70	v. South Africa	at Johannesburg	1999
5-40	v.New Zealand	at Wellington	1997	5-109	v. West Indies	at Birmingham	2000
5-149	v. Australia	at Leeds	1997	5-61	v. Pakistan	at Lord's	2001
6-42	v.South Africa	at Leeds	1998	5-103	v. Australia	at Leeds	2001
5-96	v. Australia	at Melbourne	1998				

S HAIGH (1)

6-11   v. South Africa   at Cape Town   1909

G H HIRST (3)

5-77	v. Australia	at The Oval	1902	5-58	v. Australia	at Birmingham	1909
5-48	v. Australia	at Melbourne	1904				

M J HOGGARD (7)

7-63	v. New Zealand	at Christchurch	2002	5-73	v. Bangladesh	at Chester-le-Street	
5-92	v. Sri Lanka	at Birmingham	2002				2005
5-144	v. South Africa	at Johannesburg	2005*	6-57	v. India	at Nagpur	2006
7-61	v. South Africa	at Johannesburg	2005*	7-109	v. Australia	at Adelaide	2006

Consecutive Test innings

R ILLINGWORTH (3)

6-29	v. India	at Lord's	1967	5-70	v. India	at The Oval	1971
6-87	v. Australia	at Leeds	1968				

Hon F S JACKSON (1)

5-52   v. Australia   at Nottingham   1905

G G MACAULAY (1)

5-64   v. South Africa   at Cape Town   1923

C M OLD (4)

5-113	v. New Zealand	at Lord's	1973	6-54	v. New Zealand	at Wellington	1978
5-21	v. India	at Lord's	1974	7-50	v. Pakistan	at Birmingham	1978

E PEATE (2)

5-43   v. Australia   at Sydney   1882   6-85   v. Australia   at Lord's   1884

R PEEL (5)

5-51	v. Australia	at Adelaide	1884	6-67	v. Australia	at Sydney	1894
5-18	v. Australia	at Sydney	1888	6-23	v. Australia	at The Oval	1896
7-31	v. Australia	at Manchester	1888				

L E PLUNKETT (1)

5-64   v. Sri Lanka   at Leeds   2014

5 WICKETS IN AN INNINGS FOR ENGLAND (Continued)

W RHODES (6)

7-17	v. Australia	at Birmingham	1902	7-56	v. Australia	at Melbourne	1904*
5-63	v. Australia	at Sheffield	1902	8-68	v. Australia	at Melbourne	1904*
5-94	v. Australia	at Sydney	1903*	5-83	v. Australia	at Manchester	1909

consecutive Test innings

C E W SILVERWOOD (1)

5-91   v. South Africa   at Cape Town   2000

R J SIDEBOTTOM (5)

5-88	v. West Indies	at Chester-le-Street		5-105	v. New Zealand	at Wellington	2008
			2007	7-47	v. New Zealand	at Napier	2008
6-49	v. New Zealand	at Hamilton	2008	6-47	v. New Zealand	at Nottingham	2008

F S TRUEMAN (17)

8-31	v. India	at Manchester	1952	6-31	v. Pakistan	at Lord's	1962
5-48	v. India	at The Oval	1952	5-62	v. Australia	at Melbourne	1963
5-90	v. Australia	at Lord's	1956	7-75	v. New Zealand	at Christchurch	1963
5-63	v. West Indies	at Nottingham	1957	6-100	v. West Indies	at Lord's	1963*
5-31	v. New Zealand	at Birmingham	1958	5-52	v. West Indies	at Lord's	1963*
5-35	v. West Indies	at Port-of-Spain	1960	5-75	v. West Indies	at Birmingham	1963*
5-27	v. South Africa	at Nottingham	1960	7-44	v. West Indies	at Birmingham	1963*
5-58	v. Australia	at Leeds	1961*	5-48	v. Australia	at Lord's	1964
6-30	v. Australia	at Leeds	1961*				

G ULYETT (1)

7-36   v. Australia   at Lord's   1884

H VERITY (5)

5-33	v. Australia	at Sydney	1933	8-43	v. Australia	at Lord's	1934*
7-49	v. India	at Chepauk, Madras	1934	5-70	v. South Africa	at Cape Town	1939
7-61	v. Australia	at Lord's	1934*				

J H WARDLE (5)

7-56	v. Pakistan	at The Oval	1954	7-36	v. South Africa	at Cape Town	1957*
5-79	v. Australia	at Sydney	1955	5-61	v. South Africa	at Kingsmead	
						Durban	1957*
5-53	v. South Africa	at Cape Town	1957*				

C WHITE (3)

5-57	v. West Indies	at Leeds	2000	5-32	v. West Indies	at The Oval	2000
	5-127	v. Australia	at Perth	2002			

consecutive Test innings

Summary of Five Wickets in an Innings

versus	Total	In England	Away
Australia	42	22	20
Bangladesh	1	1	0
India	7	5	2
India	8	6	2
New Zealand	11	3	8
Pakistan	5	5	0
South Africa	13	3	10
Sri Lanka	2	2	0
West Indies	11	10	1
Totals	93	52	41

5 WICKETS IN AN INNINGS

M G BEVAN (1)

6-82	v. West Indies	at Adelaide	1997

J N GILLESPIE (8)

5-54	v. South Africa	at Port Elizabeth	1997
7-37	v. England	at Leeds	1997
5-88	v. England	at Perth	1998
5-89	v. West Indies	at Adelaide	2000
6-40	v. West Indies	at Melbourne	2000
5-53	v. England	at Lord's	2001
5-39	v. West Indies	at Georgetown	2003
5-56	v. India	at Nagpur	2004

HAT-TRICKS

W Bates	v. Australia	at Melbourne	1882
D Gough	v. Australia	at Sydney	1998
M J Hoggard	v. West Indies	at Bridgetown	2004
R J Sidebottom	v. New Zealand	at Hamilton	2008

FOUR WICKETS IN FIVE BALLS

C M Old	v. Pakistan	at Birmingham	1978

THREE WICKETS IN FOUR BALLS

R Appleyard	v. New Zealand	at Auckland	1955
D Gough	v. Pakistan	at Lord's	2001

YORKSHIRE PLAYERS WHO PLAYED ALL THEIR TEST CRICKET AFTER LEAVING YORKSHIRE

For England

Player	M.	I	NO	Runs	HS.	Av'ge.	100s	50s	Balls	R	W	Av'ge	Best	5wI	10wM	c/st
BALDERSTONE, J C ...1976	2	4	0	39	35	9.75	—	—	96	80	1	80.00	1:80	—	—	1
BATTY, G J ...2003	4	7	1	136	38	22.66	—	1	992	504	8	63.00	3:55	—	—	0
BIRKENSHAW, J ...1973-74	5	7	0	148	64	21.14	—	1	1,017	469	13	36.07	5:57	1	—	3
BOLUS, J B ...1963-64	7	12	0	496	88	41.33	—	4	18	16	0	—	—	—	—	2
†PARKIN, C H ...1920-24	10	16	3	160	36	12.30	—	—	2,095	1,128	32	35.25	5:38	2	—	3
RHODES, S J ...1994-95	11	17	5	294	65*	24.50	—	1	—	—	—	—	—	—	—	46/3
†SUGG, F H ...1888	2	2	0	55	31	27.50	—	—	—	—	—	—	—	—	—	0
WARD, A ...1893-95	7	13	0	487	117	37.46	1	3	—	—	—	—	—	—	—	1
WOOD, B ...1972-78	12	21	0	454	90	21.61	—	2	98	50	0	—	—	—	—	6

For South Africa

Player	M.	I	NO	Runs	HS.	Av'ge.	100s	50s	Balls	R	W	Av'ge	Best	5wI	10wM	c/st
THORNTON, P G ...1902	1	1	1	1	1*	—	—	—	24	20	1	20.00	1:20	—	—	1

†Born outside Yorkshire

CENTURIES FOR ENGLAND

A WARD (1)
117 v. Australia at Sydney, 1894

5 WICKETS IN AN INNINGS FOR ENGLAND

J BIRKENSHAW (1)
5 : 57 v. Pakistan at Karachi, 1973

C H PARKIN (2)
5 : 60 v. Australia at Adelaide, 1921
5 : 38 v. Australia at Manchester, 1921

YORKSHIRE'S TEST CRICKET RECORDS

R APPLEYARD

Auckland 1954-55: took 3 wickets in 4 balls as New Zealand were dismissed for the lowest total in Test history (26).

C W J ATHEY

Perth 1986-87: shared an opening stand of 223 with B C Broad – England's highest for any wicket at the WACA Ground.

W BATES

Melbourne 1882-83 (Second Test): achieved the first hat-trick for England when he dismissed P S McDonnell, G Giffen and G J Bonnor in Australia's first innings. Later in the match, he became the first player to score a fifty (55) and take 10 or more wickets (14 for 102) in the same Test.

W E BOWES

Melbourne 1932-33: enjoyed the unique satisfaction of bowling D G Bradman first ball in a Test match (his first ball to him in Test cricket).

G BOYCOTT

Leeds 1967: scored 246 not out off 555 balls in 573 minutes to establish the record England score against India. His first 100 took 341 minutes (316 balls) and he was excluded from the next Test as a disciplinary measure; shared in hundred partnerships for three successive wickets.

Adelaide 1970-71: with J H Edrich, became the third opening pair to share hundred partnerships in both innings of a Test against Australia.

Port-of-Spain 1973-74: first to score 99 and a hundred in the same Test.

Nottingham 1977: with A P E Knott, equalled England v. Australia sixth-wicket partnership record of 215 – the only England v. Australia stand to be equalled or broken since 1938. Batted on each day of the five-day Test (second after M L Jaisimha to achieve this feat).

Leeds 1977: first to score his 100th First Class hundred in a Test; became the fourth England player to be on the field for an entire Test.

Perth: 1978-79: eighth to score 2,000 runs for England against Australia.

Birmingham 1979: emulated K F Barrington by scoring hundreds on each of England's six current home grounds.

Perth: 1979-80: fourth to carry his bat through a completed England.

innings (third v. Australia) and the first to do so without scoring 100; first to score 99 not out in a Test.

Lord's 1981: 100th Test for England – second after M C Cowdrey (1968).

The Oval, 1981: second after Hon F S Jackson to score five hundreds v. Australia in England.

Gained three Test records from M C Cowdrey: exceeded England aggregate of 7,624 runs in 11 fewer Tests (Manchester 1981); 61st fifty – world record (The Oval 1981); 189th innings – world record (Bangalore 1981-82).

Delhi, 4.23p.m. on 23 December 1981: passed G St.A Sobers's world Test record of 8,032 runs, having played 30 more innings and batted over 451 hours (cf. 15 complete five-day Tests); his 22nd hundred equalled the England record.

J T BROWN

Melbourne 1894-95: his 28-minute fifty remains the fastest in Test cricket, and his 95-minute hundred was a record until 1897-98; his third-wicket stand of 210 with A Ward set a Test record for any wicket.

D B CLOSE

Manchester 1949: at 18 years 149 days he became – and remains – the youngest to represent England.

Melbourne 1950-51: became the youngest (19 years 301 days) to represent England against Australia.

T EMMETT

Melbourne 1878-79: first England bowler to take seven wickets in a Test innings.

P A GIBB

Johannesburg 1938-39: enjoyed a record England debut, scoring 93 and 106 as well as sharing second-wicket stands of 184 and 168 with E Paynter.

Durban 1938-39: shared record England v. South Africa second-wicket stand of 280 with W J Edrich, his 120 in 451 minutes including only two boundaries.

D GOUGH

Sydney 1998-99: achieved the 23rd hat-trick in Test cricket (ninth for England and first for England v. Australia since 1899).

Lord's 2001: took 3 wickets in 4 balls v. Pakistan.

S HAIGH

Cape Town 1898-99: bowled unchanged through the second innings with A E Trott, taking 6 for 11 as South Africa were dismissed for 35 in the space of 114 balls.

J H HAMPSHIRE

Lord's 1969: became the first England player to score 100 at Lord's on his debut in Tests.

A HILL

Melbourne 1876-77: took the first wicket to fall in Test cricket when he bowled N Thompson, and held the first catch when he dismissed T P Horan.

G H HIRST

The Oval 1902: helped to score the last 15 runs in a match-winning tenth-wicket partnership with W Rhodes.

Birmingham 1909: shared all 20 Australian wickets with fellow left-arm spinner C Blythe (11 for 102).

M J HOGGARD

Bridgetown 2004: became the third Yorkshire player to take a hat-trick in Test cricket (see W Bates and D Gough). It was the 10th hat-trick for England and the third for England versus West Indies.

L HUTTON

Nottingham 1938: scored 100 in his first Test against Australia.

The Oval 1938: his score (364) and batting time (13 hours 17 minutes – the longest innings in English First-Class cricket) remain England records, and were world Test records until 1958. It remains the highest Test score at The Oval. His stand of 382 with M Leyland is the England second-wicket record in all Tests and the highest for any wicket against Australia. He also shared a record England v. Australia sixth-wicket stand of 216 with J Hardstaff Jr. – the first instance of a batsman sharing in two stands of 200 in the same Test innings. 770 runs were scored during his innings (Test record) which was England's 100th century against Australia, and contained 35 fours. England's total of 903 for 7 declared remains the Ashes Test record.

Lord's 1939: added 248 for the fourth wicket with D C S Compton in 140 minutes.

L HUTTON *(Continued)*

The Oval 1939: shared (then) world-record third-wicket stand of 264 with W R Hammond, which remains the record for England v. West Indies. Hutton's last eight Tests had brought him 1,109 runs.

The Oval 1948: last out in the first innings, he was on the field for all but the final 57 minutes of the match.

Johannesburg 1948-49: shared (then) world-record first-wicket stand of 359 in 310 minutes with C Washbrook on the opening day of Test cricket at Ellis Park; it remains England's highest opening stand in all Tests.

The Oval 1950: scored England's first 200 in a home Test v. West Indies, and remains alone in carrying his bat for England against them; his 202 not out (in 470 minutes) is the highest score by an England batsman achieving this feat.

Adelaide 1950-51: only England batsman to carry his bat throughout a complete Test innings twice, and second after R Abel (1891-92) to do so for any country against Australia.

Manchester 1951: scored 98 not out, just failing to become the first to score his 100th First Class hundred in a Test match.

The Oval 1951: became the only batsman to be out 'obstructing the field' in Test cricket.

1952: first professional to be appointed captain of England in the 20th Century.

The Oval 1953: first captain to win a rubber after losing the toss in all five Tests.

Kingston 1953-54: scored the first 200 by an England captain in a Test overseas.

R ILLINGWORTH

Manchester 1971: shared record England v. India eighth-wicket stand of 168 with P. Lever.

Hon. F S JACKSON

The Oval 1893: his 100 took 135 minutes, and was the first in a Test in England to be completed with a hit over the boundary (then worth only four runs).

The Oval 1899: his stand of 185 with T W Hayward was then England's highest for any wicket in England, and the record opening partnership by either side in England v. Australia Tests.

Nottingham 1905: dismissed M A Noble, C Hill and J Darling in one over (W01W0W).

Leeds 1905: batted 268 minutes for 144 not out – the first hundred in a Headingley Test.

Manchester 1905: first to score five Test hundreds in England.

The Oval 1905: first captain to win every toss in a five-match rubber.

M LEYLAND

Melbourne 1928-29: scored 137 in his first innings against Australia.

1934: first to score three hundreds in a rubber against Australia in England.

Brisbane 1936-37: scored England's only 100 at 'The Gabba' before 1974-75.

The Oval 1938: contributed 187 in 381 minutes to the record Test total of 903 for 7 declared, sharing in England's highest stand against Australia (all wickets) and record second-wicket stand in all Tests: 382 with L Hutton. First to score hundreds in his first and last innings against Australia.

G G MACAULAY

Cape Town 1922-23: fourth bowler (third for England) to take a wicket (G A L Hearne) with his first ball in Test cricket. Made the winning hit in the fourth of only six Tests to be decided by a one-wicket margin.

Leeds 1926: shared a match-saving ninth-wicket stand of 108 with G Geary.

C M OLD

Birmingham 1978: took 4 wickets in 5 balls in his 19th over (0WW no-ball WW1) to emulate the feat of M J C Allom.

R PEEL

Took his 50th wicket in his ninth Test and his 100th in his 20th Test – all against Australia.

W RHODES

Birmingham 1902: his first-innings analysis of 7 for 17 remains the record for all Tests at Edgbaston.

The Oval 1902: helped to score the last 15 runs in a match-winning tenth-wicket partnership with G H Hirst.

Sydney 1903-04: shared record England v. Australia tenth-wicket stand of 130 in 66 minutes with R E Foster.

Melbourne 1903-04: first to take 15 wickets in England v. Australia Tests; his match analysis of 15 for 124 remains the record for all Tests at Melbourne.

Melbourne 1911-12: shared record England v. Australia first-wicket stand of 323 in 268 minutes with J B Hobbs.

Johannesburg 1913-14: took his 100th wicket and completed the first 'double' for England (in 44 matches).

Sydney 1920-21: first to score 2,000 runs and take 100 wickets in Test cricket.

Adelaide 1920-21: third bowler to take 100 wickets against Australia.

The Oval 1926: set (then) record of 109 wickets against Australia.

Kingston 1929-30: ended the world's longest Test career (30 years 315 days) as the oldest Test cricketer (52 years 165 days).

H SUTCLIFFE

Birmingham 1924: shared the first of 15 three-figure partnerships with J B Hobbs at the first attempt.

Lord's 1924: shared stand of 268 with J B Hobbs, which remains the first-wicket record for all Lord's Tests, and was then the England v. South Africa record.

Sydney 1924-25: his first opening stands against Australia with J B Hobbs realised 157 and 110.

Melbourne 1924-25 (Second Test): with J B Hobbs achieved the first instance of a batting partnership enduring throughout a full day's Test match play; they remain the only England pair to achieve this feat, and their stand of 283 in 289 minutes remains the longest for the first wicket in this series. Became the first to score 100 in each innings of a Test against Australia, and the first Englishman to score three successive hundreds in Test cricket.

Melbourne 1924-25 (Fourth Test): first to score four hundreds in one rubber of Test matches; it was his third 100 in successive Test innings at Melbourne. Completed 1,000 runs in fewest Test innings (12) – since equalled.

Sydney 1924-25: his aggregate of 734 runs was the record for any rubber until 1928-29.

The Oval 1926: shared first-wicket stand of 172 with J B Hobbs on a rain-affected pitch.

The Oval 1929: first to score hundreds in each innings of a Test twice; only England batsman to score four hundreds in a rubber twice.

Sydney 1932-33: his highest England innings of 194 overtook J B Hobbs's world record of 15 Test hundreds.

F S TRUEMAN

Leeds 1952: reduced India to 0 for 4 in their second innings by taking 3 wickets in 8 balls on his debut.

Manchester 1952: achieved record England v. India innings analysis of 8 for 31.

The Oval 1952: set England v. India series record with 29 wickets.

YORKSHIRE'S TEST CRICKET RECORDS *(Continued)*

F S TRUEMAN *(Continued)*

Leeds 1961: took 5 for 0 with 24 off-cutters at a reduced pace v. Australia.

Lord's 1962: shared record England v. Pakistan ninth-wicket stand of 76 with T W Graveney.

Christchurch 1962-63: passed J B Statham's world Test record of 242 wickets; his analysis of 7 for 75 remains the record for Lancaster Park Tests and for England in New Zealand.

Birmingham 1963: returned record match analysis (12 for 119) against West Indies in England and for any Birmingham Test, ending with a 6 for 4 spell from 24 balls.

The Oval 1963: set England v. West Indies series record with 34 wickets.

The Oval 1964: first to take 300 wickets in Tests.

G ULYETT

Sydney 1881-82: with R G Barlow shared the first century opening partnership in Test cricket (122).

Melbourne 1881-82: his 149 was the first Test hundred for England in Australia, and the highest score for England on the first day of a Test in Australia until 1965-66.

M P VAUGHAN

Scored 1481 runs in 2002 – more than any other England player in a calendar year, surpassing the 1379 scored by D L Amiss in 1979. It was the fourth highest in a calendar year.

Scored 633 runs in the 2002-3 series versus Australia – surpassed for England in a five Test series versus Australia only by W R Hammond, who scored 905 runs in 1928-29, H Sutcliffe (734 in 1924-25), J B Hobbs (662 in 1911-12) and G Boycott (657 in 1970-71), when he played in five of the six Tests.

Scored six Test Match centuries in 2002 to equal the record set for England by D C S Compton in 1947.

Lord's 2004: scored a century in each innings (103 and 101*) versus West Indies and so became the third player (after G A Headley and G A Gooch) to score a century in each innings of a Test match at Lord's.

Lord's 2005: only the second player (J B Hobbs is the other) to have scored centuries in three consecutive Test match innings at Lord's. Scored the 100th century for England by a Yorkshire player.

H VERITY

Lord's 1934: took 14 for 80 on the third day (six of them in the final hour) to secure England's first win against Australia at Lord's since 1896. It remains the most wickets to fall to one bowler in a day of Test cricket in England. His match analysis of 15 for 104 was then the England v. Australia record, and has been surpassed only by J C Laker.

W WATSON

Lord's 1953: scored 109 in 346 minutes in his first Test against Australia.

N W D YARDLEY

Melbourne 1946-47: dismissed D G Bradman for the third consecutive innings without assistance from the field. Became the first to score a fifty in each innings for England and take five wickets in the same match.

Nottingham 1947: shared record England v. South Africa fifth-wicket stand of 237 with D C S Compton.

* * *

Facts adapted by Bill Frindall from his *England Test Cricketers – The Complete Record from 1877* (Collins Willow, 1989). With later additions.

TEST MATCHES AT HEADINGLEY, LEEDS 1899-2014

1899 **Australia 172** (J Worrall 76) and **224** (H Trumble 56, J T Hearne hat-trick). **England 220** (A F A Lilley 55, H Trumble 5 for 60) and **19 for 0 wkt.**
Match drawn
Toss: Australia

1905 **England 301** (Hon F S Jackson 144*) and **295 for 5 wkts dec** (J T Tyldesley 100, T W Hayward 60, W W. Armstrong 5 for 122). **Australia 195** (W W Armstrong 66, A R Warren 5 for 57) and **224 for 7 wkts** (M A Noble 62).
Match drawn
Toss: England

1907 **England 76** (G A Faulkner 6 for 17) and **162** (C B Fry 54). **South Africa 110** (C Blythe 8 for 59) and **75** (C Blythe 7 for 40).
England won by 53 runs
Toss: England

1909 **Australia 188** and **207** (S F Barnes 6 for 63). **England 182** (J Sharp 61, J T Tyldesley 55, C G Macartney 7 for 58) and **87** (A Cotter 5 for 38).
Australia won by 126 runs
Toss: Australia

1912 **England 242** (F E Woolley 57) and **238** (R H Spooner 82, J B Hobbs 55). **South Africa 147** (S F Barnes 6 for 52) and **159**.
England won by 174 runs
Toss: England

1921 **Australia 407** (C G Macartney 115, W W Armstrong 77, C E Pellew 52, J M Taylor 50) and **273 for 7 wkts dec** (T J E Andrew 92). **England 259** (J W H T Douglas 75, Hon L H Tennyson 63, G Brown 57) and **202.**
Australia won by 219 runs
Toss: Australia

1924 **England 396** (E H Hendren 132, H Sutcliffe 83) and **60 for 1 wkt.** **South Africa 132** (H W Taylor 59*, M W Tate 6 for 42) and **323** (H W Taylor 56, R H Catterall 56).
England won by 9 wickets
Toss: England

1926 **Australia 494** (C G Macartney 151, W M Woodfull 141, A J Richardson 100). **England 294** (G G Macaulay 76, C V Grimmett 5 for 88) and **254 for 3 wkts** (H Sutcliffe 94, J B Hobbs 88).
Match drawn
Toss: England

1929 **South Africa 236** (R H Catterall 74, C L Vincent 60, A P Freeman 7 for 115) and **275** (H G Owen-Smith 129). **England 328** (F E Woolley 83, W R Hammond 65, N A Quinn 6 for 92) and **186 for 5 wkts** (F E Woolley 95*).
England won by 5 wickets
Toss: South Africa

1930 **Australia 566** (D G Bradman 334, A F Kippax 77, W M Woodfull 50, M W Tate 5 for 124). **England 391** (W R Hammond 113, C V Grimmett 5 for 135) and **95 for 3 wkts.**
Match drawn
Toss: Australia

1934 **England 200** and **229 for 6 wkts.** **Australia 584** (D G Bradman 304, W H Ponsford 181, W E Bowes 6 for 142).
Match drawn
Toss: England

1935 **England 216** (W R Hammond 63, A Mitchell 58) and **294 for 7 wkts dec** (W R Hammond 87*, A Mitchell 72, D Smith 57). **South Africa 171** (E A B Rowan 62) and **194 for 5 wkts** (B Mitchell 58).
Match drawn
Toss: England

1938 **England 223** (W R Hammond 76, W .J O'Reilly 5 for 66) and **123** (.W J O'Reilly 5 for 56). **Australia 242** (D G Bradman 103, B A Barnett 57) and **107 for 5 wkts.**
Australia won by 5 wickets
Toss: England

1947 **South Africa 175** (B Mitchell 53, A Nourse 51) and **184** (A D Nourse 57). **England 317 for 7 wkts dec** (L Hutton 100, C Washbrook 75) and **47 for 0 wkt.**
England won by 10 wickets
Toss: South Africa

1948 **England 496** (C Washbrook 143, W .J Edrich 111, L Hutton 81, A V Bedser 79) and **365 for 8 wkts dec** (D C S. Compton 66, C Washbrook 65, L Hutton 57, W J Edrich 54). **Australia 458** (R N Harvey 112, S J E Loxton 93, R R Lindwall 77, K R Miller 58) and **404 for 3 wkts** (A R Morris 182, D G Bradman 173*).
Australia won by 7 wickets
Toss: England

1949 **England 372** (D C S Compton 114, L Hutton 101, T B Burtt 5 for 97, J Cowie 5 for 127) and **267 for 4 wkts dec** (C Washbrook 103*, W J Edrich 70). **New Zealand 341** (F B Smith 96, M P Donnelly 64, T E Bailey 6 for 118) and **195 for 2 wkts** (B Sutcliffe 82, F Smith 54*).
Match drawn   Toss: England

1951 **South Africa 538** (E A B Rowan 236, P N F Mansell 90, C B. van Ryneveld 83, R A McLean 67) and **87 for 0 wkt** (E A B Rowan 60*). **England 505** (P B H May 138, L Hutton 100, T E Bailey 95, F A Lowson 58, A M B Rowan 5 for 174).
Match drawn   Toss: South Africa

1952 **India 293** (V L Manjrekar 133, V S Hazare 89) and 165 (D G Phadkar 64, V S Hazare 56). **England 334** (T W Graveney 71, T G Evans 66, Ghulam Ahmed 5 for 100) and **128 for 3 wkts** (R T Simpson 51).
England won by 7 wickets   Toss: India

1953 **England 167** (T W Graveney 55, R R Lindwall 5 for 54) and **275** (W J Edrich 64, D C S Compton 61). **Australia 266** (R N Harvey 71, G B Hole 53, A V Bedser 6 for 95) and **147 for 4 wkts.**
Match drawn   Toss: Australia

1955 **South Africa 171** and **500** (D J McGlew 133, W R Endean 116*, T L Goddard 74, H J Keith 73). **England 191** (D C S Compton 61) and **256** (P B H May 97, T L Goddard 5 for 69, H J Tayfield 5 for 94).
South Africa won by 224 runs   Toss: South Africa

1956 **England 325** (P B H May 101, C Washbrook 98). **Australia 143** (J C Laker 5 for 58) and **140** (R N Harvey 69, J C Laker 6 for 55).
England won by an innings and 42 runs   Toss: England

1957 **West Indies 142** (P J Loader 6 for 36, including hat-trick) and **132. England 279** (P B H May 69, M C Cowdrey 68, Rev D S Sheppard 68, F M M Worrell 7 for 70).
England won by an innings and 5 runs   Toss: West Indies

1958 **New Zealand 67** (J C Laker 5 for 17) and **129** (G A R Lock 7 for 51). **England 267 for 2 wkts dec** (P B H May 113*, C A Milton 104*).
England won by an innings and 71 runs   Toss: New Zealand

1959 **India 161** and **149. England 483 for 8 wkts dec** (M C Cowdrey 160, K F Barrington 80, W G A Parkhouse 78, G Pullar 75).
England won by an innings and 173 runs   Toss: India

1961 **Australia 237** (R N Harvey 73, C C McDonald 54, F S Trueman 5 for 58) and **120** (R N Harvey 53, F S Trueman 6 for 30); **England 299** (M C Cowdrey 93, G Pullar 53, A K Davidson 5 for 63) and **62 for 2 wkts.**
England won by 8 wickets   Toss: Australia

1962 **England 428** (P H Parfitt 119, M J Stewart 86, D A Allen 62, Munir Malik 5 for 128). **Pakistan 131** (Alimuddin 50) and **180** (Alimuddin 60, Saeed Ahmed 54).
England won by an innings and 117 runs   Toss: Pakistan

1963 **West Indies 397** (G St.A Sobers 102, R B Kanhai 92, J S Solomon 62) and **229** (B F Butcher 78, G St.A Sobers 52). **England 174** (G A R Lock 53, C C Griffith 6 for 36) and **231** (J M Parks 57, D B Close 56).
West Indies won by 221 runs   Toss: West Indies

1964 **England 268** (J M Parks 68, E R Dexter 66, N J N Hawke 5 for 75) and 229 (K F Barrington 85). **Australia 389** (P J P Burge 160, W M Lawry 78) and **111 for 3 wkts** (I R Redpath 58*).
Australia won by 7 wickets   Toss: England

1965 **England 546 for 4 wkts dec** (J H Edrich 310*, K F Barrington 163). **New Zealand 193** (J R Reid 54) and **166** (V Pollard 53, F J Titmus 5 for 19).
England won by an innings and 187 runs   Toss: England

1966 **West Indies 500 for 9 wkts dec** (G.St.A Sobers 174, S M Nurse 137). **England 240** (B L D'Oliveira 88, G.St.A Sobers 5 for 41) and **205** (R W Barber 55, L R Gibbs 6 for 39).
West Indies won by an innings and 55 runs   Toss: West Indies

1967 **England 550 for 4 wkts dec** (G Boycott 246*, B L D'Oliveira 109, K F Barrington 93, T W Graveney 59) and **126 for 4 wkts.** **India 164** (Nawab of Pataudi jnr 64) and **510** (Nawab of Pataudi jnr 148, A L Wadekar 91, F M Engineer 87, Hanumant Singh 73).
England won by 6 wickets Toss: England

1968 **Australia 315** (I R Redpath 92, I M Chappell 65) and **312** (I M Chappell 81, K D Walters 56, R Illingworth 6 for 87). **England 302** (R M Prideaux 64, J H Edrich 62, A N Connolly 5 for 72) and **230 for 4 wkts** (J H Edrich 65).
Match drawn Toss: Australia

1969 **England 223** (J H Edrich 79) and **240** (G.St A Sobers 5 for 42). **West Indies 161** and **272** (B F Butcher 91, G S Camacho 71).
England won by 30 runs Toss: England

1971 **England 316** (G Boycott 112, B L D'Oliveira 74) and **264** (B L D'Oliveira 72, D L Amiss 56) **Pakistan 350** (Zaheer Abbas 72, Wasim Bari 63, Mushtaq Mohammad 57) and **205** (Sadiq Mohammad 91).
England won by 25 runs Toss: England

1972 **Australia 146** (K R Stackpole 52) and **136** (D L Underwood 6 for 45). **England 263** (R Illingworth 57, A A Mallett 5 for 114) and **21 for 1 wkt.**
England won by 9 wickets Toss: Australia

1973 **New Zealand 276** (M G Burgess 87, V Pollard 62) and **142** (G M Turner 81, G G Arnold 5 for 27). **England 419** (G Boycott 115, K W R Fletcher 81, R Illingworth 65, RO Collinge 5 for 74).
England won by an innings and 1 run Toss: New Zealand

1974 **Pakistan 285** (Majid Khan 75, Safraz Nawaz 53) and **179**. **England 183** and **238 for 6 wkts** (J H Edrich 70, K W R Fletcher 67*).
Match drawn Toss: Pakistan

1975 **England 288** (D S Steele 73, J H Edrich 62, A W Greig 51, G J Gilmour 6 for 85) and **291** (D S Steele 92). **Australia 135** (P H Edmonds 5 for 28) and **220 for 3 wkts** (R B McCosker 95*, I M Chappell 62).
Match drawn Toss: England

1976 **West Indies 450** (C G Greenidge 115, R C Fredericks 109, I V A Richards 66, L G Rowe 50) and **196** (C L King 58, R G D Willis 5 for 42). **England 387** (A W Greig 116, A P E Knott 116) and **204** (A W Greig 76*).
West Indies won by 55 runs Toss: West Indies

1977 **England 436** (G Boycott 191, A P E Knott 57). **Australia 103** (I T Botham 5 for 21) and **248** (R W Marsh 63).
England won by an innings and 85 runs Toss: England

1978 **Pakistan 201** (Sadiq Mohammad 97). **England 119 for 7 wkts** (Safraz Nawaz 5 for 39).
Match drawn Toss: Pakistan

1979 **England 270** (I T Botham 137). **India 223 for 6 wkts** (S M Gavaskar 78, D B Vengsarkar 65*).
Match drawn Toss: England

1980 **England 143 and 227 for 6 wkts dec** (G A Gooch 55). **West Indies 245.**
Match drawn Toss: West Indies

1981 **Australia 401 for 9 wkts dec** (J Dyson 102, K J Hughes 89, G N Yallop 58, I T Botham 6 for 95) and **111** (R G D Willis 8 for 43). **England 174** (I T Botham 50) and **356** (I T Botham 149*, G R Dilley 56, T M Alderman 6 for 135).
England won by 18 runs Toss: Australia

1982 **Pakistan 275** (Imran Khan 67*, Mudassar Nazar 65, Javed Miandad 54) and **199** (Javed Miandad 52, I T Botham 5 for 74). **England 256** (D I Gower 74, I T Botham 57, Imran Khan 5 for 49) and **219 for 7 wkts** (G Fowler 86).
England won by 3 wickets Toss: Pakistan

1983 **England 225** (C J Tavaré 69, A J Lamb 58, B L Cairns 7 for 74) and **252** (D I Gower 112*, E J Chatfield 5 for 95). **New Zealand 377** (J G Wright 93, B A Edgar 84, R J Hadlee 75) and **103 for 5 wkts** (R G D Willis 5 for 35).
New Zealand won by 5 wickets Toss: New Zealand

1984 **England 270** (A J Lamb 100) and **159** (G Fowler 50, M D Marshall 7 for 53). **West Indies 302** (H A Gomes 104*, M A Holding 59, P J W Allott 6 for 61) and **131 for 2 wkts.**
West Indies won by 8 wickets   Toss: England

1985 **Australia 331** (A M J Hilditch 119) and **324** (W B Phillips 91, A M J Hilditch 80, K C Wessels 64, J E Emburey 5 for 82). **England 533** (R T Robinson 175, I T Botham 60, P R Downton 54, M W Gatting 53) and **123 for 5 wkts.**
England won by 5 wickets   Toss: Australia

1986 **India 272** (D B Vengsarkar 61) and **237** (D B Vengsarkar 102*, R M H Binny 5 for 40) and **128.**
India won by 279 runs   Toss: India

1987 **England 136** (D J Capel 53) and **199** (D I Gower 55, Imran Khan 7 for 40). **Pakistan 353** (Salim Malik 99, Ijaz Ahmed 50, N A Foster 8 for 107).
Pakistan won by an innings and 18 runs   Toss: England

1988 **England 201** (A J Lamb 64*) and **138** (G A Gooch 50). **West Indies 275** (R A Harper 56, D L Haynes 54, D R Pringle 5 for 95) and **67 for 0 wkt.**
West Indies won by 10 wickets   Toss: West Indies

1989 **Australia 601 for 7 wkts dec** (S R Waugh 177*, M A Taylor 136, D M Jones 79, M G Hughes 71, A R Border 66) and **230 for 3 wkts dec** (M A Taylor 60, A R Border 60*). **England 435** (A J Lamb 125, K J Barnett 80, R A Smith 66, T M Alderman 5 for 107) and **191.** (G A Gooch 68, T M Alderman 5 for 44).
Australia won by 210 runs   Toss: England

1991 **England 198** (R A Smith 54) and **252** (G A Gooch 154*, C E L Ambrose 6 for 52). **West Indies 173** (I V A Richards 73) and **162** (R B Richardson 68).
England won by 115 runs   Toss: West Indies

1992 **Pakistan 197** (Salim Malik 82*) and **221** (Salim Malik 84*, Ramiz Raja 63, N A Mallinder 5 for 50). **England 320** (G A Gooch 135, M A Atherton 76, Waqar Younis 5 for 117) and **99 for 4 wkts.**
England won by 6 wickets   Toss: Pakistan

1993 **Australia 653 for 4 wkts dec** (A R Border 200*, S R Waugh 157*, D C Boon 107, M J Slater 67, M E Waugh 52). **England 200** (G A Gooch 59, M A Atherton 55, P R Reiffel 5 for 65) and **305** (A J Stewart 78, M A Atherton 63).
Australia won by an innings and 148 runs   Toss: Australia

1994 **England 477 for 9 wkts dec** (M A Atherton 99, A J Stewart 89, G P Thorpe 72, S J Rhodes 65*) and **267 for 5 wkts dec** (G A Hick 110, G P Thorpe 73). **South Africa 447** (P N Kirsten 104, B M McMillan 78, C R Matthews 62*) and **116 for 3 wkts** (G Kirsten 65).
Match drawn   Toss: England

1995 **England 199** (M A Atherton 81, I R Bishop 5 for 32) and **208** (G P Thorpe 61). **West Indies 282** (S L Campbell 69, J C Adams 58, B C Lara 53) and **129 for 1 wkt** (C L Hooper 73*).
West Indies won by 9 wickets   Toss: West Indies

1996 **Pakistan 448** (Ijaz Ahmed 141, Mohin Khan 105, Salim Malik 55, Asif Mujtaba 51, D G Cork 5 for 113) and **242 for 7 wkts dec** (Inzamam-ul-Haq 65, Ijaz Ahmed sen 52) **England 501** (A J Stewart 170, N V Knight 113, J P Crawley 53).
Match drawn   Toss: England

1997 **England 172** (J N. Gillespie 7 for 37) and **268** (N Hussain 105, J P Crawley 72, P R Reiffel 5 for 49). **Australia 501 for 9 wkts dec** (M T G Elliott 199, R T Ponting 127, P R Reiffel 54*, D Gough 5 for 149).
Australia won by an innings and 61 runs   Toss: Australia

1998 **England 230** (M A Butcher 116) and **240** (N Hussain 94, S M Pollock 5 for 53, A A Donald 5 for 71). **South Africa 252** (W J. Cronje 57, A R C Fraser 5 for 42) and **195** (J N Rhodes 85, B M McMillan 54, D Gough 6 for 42).
England won by 23 runs   Toss: England

2000 **West Indies 172** (R R Sarwan 59*, C White 5 for 57) and **61** (A R Caddick 5 for 14). **England 272** (M P Vaughan 76, G A Hick 59).
England won by an innings and 39 runs   Toss: West Indies

2001 **Australia 447** (R T Ponting 144, D R Martyn 118, M E Waugh 72, D Gough 5 for 103) and **176 for 4 wkts dec** (R T Ponting 72). **England 309** (A J Stewart 76*, G D McGrath 7 for 76) and **315 for 4 wkts** (M A Butcher 173*, N Hussain 55).
England won by 6 wickets Toss: Australia

2002 **India 628 for 8 wkts dec** (S R Tendulkar 193, R S Dravid 148, S C Ganguly 128, S B Bangar 68). **England 273** (A J Stewart 78*, M P Vaughan 61) and **309** (N Hussain 110.)
India won by an innings and 46 runs Toss: India

2003 **South Africa 342** (G Kirsten 130, M Zondeki 59, J A Rudolph 55) and **365** (A J Hall 99*, G Kirsten 60). **England 307** (M A Butcher 77, M E Trescothick 59, A Flintoff 55) and **209** (M A Butcher 61, A Flintoff 50, J H Kallis 6 for 54.)
South Africa won by 191 runs Toss: South Africa

2004 **New Zealand 409** (S P Fleming 97, M H W Papps 86, B B McCullum 54) and **161. England 526** (M E Trescothick 132, G O Jones 100, A Flintoff 94, A J Strauss 62) and **45 for 1 wkt**
England won by 9 wickets Toss: England

2006 **England 515** (K P Pietersen 135, I R Bell 119, Umar Gul 5 for 123) and **345** (A J Strauss 116, M E Trescothick 58, C M W Reid 55). **Pakistan 538** (Mohammad Yousuf 192, Younis Khan 173) and **155**.
England won by 167 runs Toss: England

2007 **England 570 for 7 wkts dec** (K P Pietersen 226, M P Vaughan 103, M J Prior 75). **West Indies 146** and **141** (D J Bravo 52).
England won by an innings and 283 runs Toss: England

2008 **England 203** and **327** (S C J Broad 67*, A N Cook 60). **South Africa 522** (A B de Villiers 174, A G Prince 149) and **9 for 0 wkt**.
South Africa won by 10 wickets Toss: South Africa

2009 **England 102** (P M Siddle 5 for 21) and **263** (G P Swann 62, S C J Broad 61, M G Johnson 5 for 69). **Australia 445** (M J North 110, M J Clarke 93, R T Ponting 78, S R Watson 51, S C J Broad 6 for 91).
Australia won by an innings and 80 runs Toss: England

2010 **Australia 88** and **349** (R T Ponting 66, M J Clarke 77, S P D Smith 77). **Pakistan 258** (S R Watson 6-33) and **180-7** (Imran Farhat 67, Azhar Ali 51).
Pakistan won by 3 wickets Toss: Australia
(This was a Home Test Match for Pakistan)

2012 **South Africa 419** (A N Petersen 182, G C Smith 52) and **258-9 dec** (J A Rudolph 69, GC Smith 52, S C J Broad 5-69). **England 425** (K P Pietersen 149, M J Prior 68) and **130-4.**
Match drawn Toss: England

2013 **England 354** (J E Root 104, J M Bairstow 64, T M Boult 5-57) and **287-5 dec** (A N Cook 130, I J L Trott 76). **New Zealand 174** and **220** (L R P L Taylor 70, G P Swann 6-90)
England won by 247 runs Toss: England

2014 **Sri Lanka 257** (K C Sangakkara 79, L E Plunkett 5-64) and **457** (K C Sangakkara 55, DPMD Jayawardene 79, A D Mathews 160). **England 365** (S D Robson 127, G S Ballance 74, I R Bell 64) and **249** (M M Ali 108*, K T G D Prasad 5-50)
Sri Lanka won by 100 runs Toss: England

SUMMARY OF RESULTS

ENGLAND	First played	Last played	Played	Won	Lost	Drawn
v. Australia	1899	2009	24	7	9	8
v. India	1952	2002	6	3	2	1
v. New Zealand	1949	2013	7	5	1	1
v. Pakistan	1962	2006	9	5	1	3
v. South Africa	1907	2012	13	6	3	4
v. Sri Lanka	2014	2014	1	0	1	0
v. West Indies	1957	2007	12	5	6	1
Totals	1899	2014	72	31	23	18

SIX HIGHEST AGGREGATES

Runs	Wkts	
Runs	*Wkts*	
1723	31	in 1948 (England 496 and 365 for 8 wkts dec; Australia 458 and 404 for 3 wkts)
1553	40	in 2006 (England 515 and 345; Pakistan 538 and 155)
1452	30	in 1989 (Australia 601 for 7 wkts dec and 230 for 3 wkts dec; England 430 and 191)
1350	28	in 1967 (England 550 for 4 wkts dec and 126 for 4 wkts; India 164 and 510)
1311	35	in 1985 (Australia 331 and 324; England 533 and 123 for 5 wkts)
1307	28	in 1994 (England 477 and 267 for 5 wkts dec; South Africa 447 and 116 for 3 wkts)

Note: The highest aggregate prior to the Second World War

1141	37	in 1921 (Australia 407 and 272 for 7 wkts dec; England 259 and 202)

SIX LOWEST AGGREGATES

Runs	Wkts	
423	40	in 1907 (England 76 and 162; South Africa 110 and 75)
463	22	in 1958 (New Zealand 67 and 129; England 267 for 2 wkts)
505	30	in 2000 (West Indies 172 and 61; England 272)
553	30	in 1957 (West Indies 142 and 132; England 279)
566	31	in 1972 (Australia 146 and 136; England 263 and 21 for 1 wkt)
608	30	in 1956 (England 325; Australia 143 and 140)

SIX HIGHEST TOTALS

653 for 4 wkts dec	Australia v. England, 1993
608 for 8 wkts dec	India v. England, 2002
601 for 7 wkts dec	Australia v. England, 1989
584	Australia v. England, 1934
570 for 7 wkts dec	England v. West Indies, 2007
566	Australia v. England, 1930

SIX LOWEST TOTALS

61	West Indies v. England, 2000
67	New Zealand v. England, 1958
75	South Africa v. England, 1907
76	England v. South Africa, 1907
87	England v Australia, 1909
88	Australia v. Pakistan, 2010

SIX HIGHEST INDIVIDUAL SCORES

For England

310*	J H Edrich versus New Zealand, 1965
246*	G Boycott versus India, 1967
226	K P Pietersen versus West Indies, 2007
191	G Boycott versus Australia, 1977
175	R T Robinson versus Australia, 1985
173*	M A Butcher versus Australia, 2001

For Australia

334	D G Bradman, 1930
304	D G Bradman, 1934
200*	A R Border, 1993
199	M T G Elliott, 1997
182	A R Morris, 1948
181	W H Ponsford, 1934

For Pakistan

192	Mohammad Yousuf, 2006
173	Younis Khan, 2006
141	Ijaz Ahmed, 1996
105	Moin Khan, 1996
99	Salim Malik, 1987
97	Sadiq Mohammad, 1978

SIX HIGHEST INDIVIDUAL SCORES *(Continued)*

	For India		For South Africa
193	S R Tendulkar, 2002	236	E A B Rowan, 1951
148	Nawab of Pataudi jnr, 1967	182	A N Petersen, 2012
148	R S Dravid, 2002	174	A B de Villiers, 2008
133	V L Manjrekar, 1952	149	A G Prince, 2008
128	S C Ganguly, 2002	133	D J McGlew, 1955
102*	D B Vengsarkar, 1986	130	G Kirsten, 2003

	For New Zealand		For West Indies
97	S P Fleming, 2004	174	G St.A Sobers, 1966
96	F B Smith, 1949	137	S M Nurse, 1966
93	J G Wright, 1983	115	C G. Greenidge, 1976
87	M G Burgess, 1973	109	R C Fredericks, 1976
86	M H W Papps, 2004	104*	H A Gomes, 1984
84	B A Edgar, 1983	102	G St A Sobers, 1963

HUNDRED BEFORE LUNCH

First day

112*	C G Macartney for Australia, 1926
105*	D G Bradman for Australia, 1930

Third day

102	(from 27* to 129) H G Owen-Smith for South Africa, 1929

CARRYING BAT THROUGH A COMPLETED INNINGS

154* out of 252 G A Gooch, England v. West Indies, 1991

MOST CENTURIES IN AN INNINGS

3	1926	C G Macartney (151), W M Woodfull (141) and A J Richardson for Australia
3	1993	A R Border (200*), S R Waugh (157*) and D C Boon (107) for Australia
3	2002	S R Tendulkar (193), R S Dravid (148) and S C Ganguly (128) for India

MOST CENTURIES IN A MATCH

5	1948	C Washbrook (143) and W J Edrich (111) for England; R N Harvey (112), A R Morris (182) and D G Bradman (173*) for Australia
5	2006	K P Pietersen (135), I R Bell (119) and A J Strauss (116) for England: Younis Khan (173) and Mohammad Yousuf (192) for Pakistan
4	1976	C G Greenidge (115) and R C Fredericks (109) for West Indies; A W Greig (116) and A P E Knott (116) for England
4	1996	Ijaz Ahmed (141) and Moin Khan (105) for Pakistan; A J Stewart (170) and N V Knight (113) for England
4	2002	S R Tendulkar (193), R S Dravid (148) and S C Ganguly (128) for India; N Hussain (110) for England

CENTURY PARTNERSHIPS

For England
(six highest)
For the 1st wicket

168	L Hutton (81) and C Washbrook (143) v. Australia, 1948 (1st inns)	
168	G A Gooch (135) and M A Atherton (76) v. Pakistan, 1992	
158	M E Trescothick (58) and A J Strauss (116) v. Pakistan, 2006	
156	J B Hobbs (88) and H Sutcliffe (94) v. Australia, 1926	
153	M E Trescothick (132) and A J Strauss (62) v. New Zealand, 2004	
146	W G A Parkhouse (78) and G Pullar (75) v. India, 1959	

For all other wickets

369	(2nd wkt) J H Edrich (310*) and K F Barrington (163) v. New Zealand, 1965
252	(4th wkt) G Boycott (246*) and B L D'Oliveira (109) v. India, 1967
194*	(3rd wkt) C A Milton (104*) and P B H May (113*) v. New Zealand, 1958
193	(4th wkt) M C Cowdrey (160) and K F Barrington (80) v. India, 1959
187	(4th wkt) P B H May (101) and C Washbrook (98) v. Australia, 1956
181	(3rd wkt) M A Butcher (173*) and N Hussain (55) v. Australia, 2001

For Australia
(six highest)
For the 1st wkt – none

For all other wickets

388	(4th wkt) W H Ponsford (181) and D G Bradman (304), 1934
332*	(5th wkt) A R Border (200*) and S R Waugh (157*), 1993
301	(2nd wkt) A R Morris (182) and D G Bradman (173*), 1948
268	(5th wkt) M T G Elliott (199) and R T Ponting (127), 1997
235	(2nd wkt) W M Woodfull (141) and C G Macartney (151), 1926
229	(3rd wkt) D G Bradman (334) and A F Kippax (77), 1930

For other countries in total

India

249	(4th wkt) S R Tendulkar (193) and S C Ganguly (128), 2002
222	(4th wkt) V S Hazare (89) and V L Manjrekar (133), 1952
170	(2nd wkt) S B Bangar (68) and R S Dravid (148), 2002
168	(2nd wkt) F M Engineer (87) and A L Wadekar (91), 1967
150	(3rd wkt) R S Dravid (148) and S R Tendulkar (193), 2002
134	(5th wkt) Hanumant Singh (73) and Nawab of Pataudi jnr (148), 1967
105	(6th wkt) V S Hazare (56) and D G Phadkar (64), 1952

New Zealand

169	(2nd wkt) M H W Papps (86) and S P Fleming (97), 2004
120	(5th wkt) M P Donnelly (64) and F B Smith (96), 1949
116	(2nd wkt) J G Wright (93) and M D Crowe (37), 1983
112	(1st wkt) B Sutcliffe (82) and V J Scott (43), 1949
106	(5th wkt) M G Burgess (87) and V Pollard (62), 1973

Pakistan

363	(3rd wkt) Younis Khan (173) and Mohammad Yousuf (192), 2006
130	(4th wkt) Ijaz Ahmed (141) and Salim Malik (55), 1996
129	(3rd wkt) Zaheer Abbas (72) and Mushtaq Mohammed (57), 1971
112	(7th wkt) Asif Mujtaba (51) and Moin Khan (105), 1996
110	(2nd wkt) Imran Farhat (67) and Azhar Ali (51), 2010 v. Australia
100	(3rd wkt) Mudassar Nazar (65) and Javed Miandad (54), 1982
100	(4th wkt) Majid Khan (75) and Zaheer Abbas (48), 1974

CENTURY PARTNERSHIPS *(Continued)*

South Africa

212	(5th wkt)	A G Prince (149)	and A B de Villiers (174)	2008
198	(2nd wkt)	E A B Rowan (236)	and C B van Ryneveld (83)	1951
176	(1st wkt)	D J McGlew (133)	and T L Goddard (74)	1955
150	(8th wkt)	G Kirsten (130)	and M Zondeki (59)	2003
120	(1st wkt)	A N Petersen (182)	and G C Smith (52)	2012
120	(1st wkt)	J A Rudolph (69)	and G C Smith (52)	2012
117	(6th wkt)	J N Rhodes (85)	and B M McMillan (54)	1998
115	(7th wkt)	P N Kirsten (104)	and B M McMillan (78)	1994
108	(5th wkt)	E A B Rowan (236)	and R A McLean (67)	1951
103	(10th wkt)	H G Owen-Smith (129)	and A J Bell (26*)	1929

Sri Lanka

149	(8th wkt)	A D Mathews (160)	and H M R K B Herath (48)	2014

West Indies

265	(5th wkt)	S M Nurse (137)	and G St A Sobers (174)	1966
192	(1st wkt)	R C Fredericks (109)	and C G Greenidge (115)	1976
118*	(2nd wkt)	C L Hooper (73*)	and B C Lara (48*)	1995
143	(4th wkt)	R B Kanhai (92)	and G St A Sobers (102)	1963
108	(3rd wkt)	G S Camacho (71)	and B F Butcher (91)	1969
106	(1st wkt)	C G Greenidge (49)	and D L Haynes (43)	1984

6 BEST INNINGS ANALYSES

For England

8-43	R G D Willis	v. Australia	1981
8-59	C Blythe	v. South Africa	1907 (1st inns)
8-107	N A Foster	v. Pakistan	1987
7-40	C Blythe	v. South Africa,	1907 (2nd inns)
7-51	G A R Lock	v. New Zealand	1958
7-115	A P Freeman	v. South Africa	1929

For Australia

7-37	J N Gilliespie	1997	
7-58	C G Macartney	1909	
7-76	G D McGrath	2001	
6-33	S R Watson	2010	v. Pakistan
6-85	G J Gilmour	1975	
6-135	T M Alderman	1981	

5 WICKETS IN AN INNINGS

For India (2)
5-40	R M H Binny	1986
5-100	Ghulam Ahmed	1952

For New Zealand (6)
7-74	B L Cairns	1983
5-57	T A Boult	2013
5-74	R O Collinge	1973
5-95	E J Chatfield	1983
5-97	T B Burtt	1949
5-127	J Cowie	1949

For Pakistan (6)
7-40	Imran Khan	1987
5-39	Sarfraz Nawaz	1978
5-49	Imran Khan	1982
5-117	Waqar Younis	1992
5-123	Umar Gul	2006
5-128	Munir Malik	1962

For South Africa (8)
6-17	G A Faulkner	1907
6-92	N A Quinn	1929
6-54	J H Kallis	2003
5-53	S M Pollock	1998
5-69	T L Goddard	1955
5-71	A A Donald	1998
5-94	H J Tayfield	1955
5-174	A M B Rowan	1951

For Sri Lanka
5-50	K T G D Prasad	2014

For West Indies (8)
7-53	M D Marshall	1984
7-70	F M Worrell	1957
6-36	C C Griffith	1963
6-39	L R Gibbs	1996
6-52	C E L Ambrose	1991
5-32	I R Bishop	1995
5-41	G.St.A Sobers	1966
5-42	G.St A Sobers	1969

10 WICKETS IN A MATCH

For England (8)
15-99	(8-59 and 7-40)	C Blythe	v. South Africa	1907
11-65	(4-14 and 7-51)	G A R Lock	v. New Zeland	1958
11-88	(5-58 and 6-30)	F S Trueman	v. Australia	1961
11-113	(5-58 and 6-55)	J C Laker	v. Australia	1956
10-82	(4-37 and 6-45)	D L Underwood	v. Australia	1972
10-115	(6-52 and 4-63)	S F Barnes	v. South Africa	1912
10-132	(4-42 and 6-90)	G P Swann	v. New Zealand	2013
10-207	(7-115 and 3-92)	A P Freeman	v. South Africa	1929

For Australia (3)
11-85	(7-58 and 4-27)	C G Macartney	1909
10-122	(5-66 and 5-56)	W J O'Reilly	1938
10-151	(5-107 and 5-44)	T M Alderman	1989

For New Zealand (1)
10-144	(7-74 and 3-70)	B L Cairns	1983

For Pakistan (1)
10-77	(3-37 and 7-40)	Imran Khan	1987

Note: Best bowling in a match for:
India	7-58	(5-40 and 2-18)	R M H Binney	1986
Sri Lanka	6-125	(1-75 and 5-50)	K T G D Prasad	2014
South Africa	9-75	(6-17 and 3-58)	G A Faulkner	1907
West Indies	9-81	(6 -36 and 3-45)	C C Griffith	1963

HAT-TRICKS

J T Hearne	v. Australia	1899
P J Loader	v. West Indies	1957

TEST MATCH AT BRAMALL LANE, SHEFFIELD 1902

1902 **Australia 194** (S F Barnes 6 for 49) and **289** (C Hill 119, V T Trumper 62, W Rhodes 5 for 63) **England 145** (J V Saunders 5 for 50, M A Noble 5 for 51) and **195** (A C MacLaren 63, G L Jessop 55, M A Noble 6 for 52).
Australia won by 143 runs   Toss: Australia

YORKSHIRE ONE-DAY INTERNATIONAL CRICKETERS 1971-2014/15 (Correct to December 16, 2014)

For England

Player	M	I	NO	Runs	HS	Av'ge	100s	50s	Balls	Runs	W	Av'ge	Best	4wI	Ct/St
ATHEY, C W J ...1980-88	31	30	3	848	142*	31.40	2	4	—	—	—	—	—	—	16
BAIRSTOW, D L ...1979-84	21	20	6	206	23*	14.71	0	0	—	—	—	—	—	—	17/4
BAIRSTOW, J M ...2011-12	7	6	1	119	41*	23.80	0	0	—	—	—	—	—	—	3
BALLANCE, G S ...2013-14	12	11	1	261	79	26.10	0	2	—	—	—	—	—	—	7
BLAKEY, R J ...1992-93	3	2	0	25	25	12.50	0	0	—	—	—	—	—	—	2/1
BOYCOTT, G ...1971-81	36	34	4	1,082	105	36.06	1	9	168	105	5	21.00	2-14	—	5
BRESNAN, T T ...2006-13/14	84	64	20	871	80	19.79	0	1	4,185	3,802	108	35.20	5-48	4	20
COPE, G A ...1977-78	2	1	1	1	1*	—	0	0	112	35	2	17.50	1-16	—	0
GOUGH, D ...1994-2006	158	87	38	609	46*	12.42	0	0	8,422	6,154	234	26.29	5-44	10	24
HAMPSHIRE, J H ...1971-72	3	3	1	48	25*	24.00	0	0	—	—	—	—	—	—	0
HOGGARD, M J ...2001-06	26	6	3	17	7	4.25	0	0	1,306	1,152	32	36.00	5-49	1	5
JARVIS, P W ...1988-93	16	8	2	31	16*	5.16	0	0	879	672	24	28.00	5-35	2	1
LOVE, J D ...1981	3	3	2	61	43	20.33	0	0	—	—	—	—	—	—	1
McGRATH, A ...2003-04	14	12	2	166	52	16.60	0	1	228	175	4	43.75	1-13	—	4
MOXON, M D ...1985-88	8	8	0	174	70	21.75	0	1	—	—	—	—	—	—	5
OLD, C M ...1973-81	32	25	7	338	51*	18.77	0	1	1,755	999	45	22.20	4-8	2	8
RASHID, A U ...2009	5	4	1	60	31*	20.00	0	0	204	191	3	63.66	1-16	—	2
ROOT, J E ...2012/13-14/15	43	41	5	1,498	113	41.61	3	7	726	695	11	63.18	2-15	—	15
SHAHZAD, A ...2010-11	11	8	5	39	9	13.00	0	0	588	490	17	28.82	3-41	—	4
SIDEBOTTOM, R J ...2001-10	25	18	8	133	24	6.50	0	0	1,277	1,039	29	35.82	3-19	—	6
SILVERWOOD, C E W ...1996-2001	7	4	0	17	12	4.25	0	0	306	244	6	40.66	3-43	—	0
STEVENSON, G B ...1980-81	4	4	3	43	28*	43.00	0	0	192	125	7	17.85	4-33	1	2
VAUGHAN, M P ...2001-07	86	83	10	1,982	90*	27.15	0	16	796	649	16	40.56	4-22	1	25
WHITE, C ...1994-2003	51	41	5	568	57*	15.77	0	1	2,364	1,726	65	26.55	5-21	2	12

For Scotland

Player	M	I	NO	Runs	HS	Av'ge	100s	50s	Balls	Runs	W	Av'ge	Best	4wI	Ct/St
BLAIN, J A R ...1999-2009	33	25	6	284	41	14.94	0	0	1,329	1,173	41	28.60	5-22	4	8
HAMILTON, G M ...1999-2010	38	38	3	1,231	119	35.17	2	7	220	160	3	53.33	2-36	—	6/1
WARDLAW, I ...2012/13-14	14	9	5	15	7*	3.75	0	0	751	655	23	28.47	4-43	1	0

YORKSHIRE PLAYERS WHO PLAYED ALL THEIR ONE-DAY INTERNATIONAL CRICKET AFTER LEAVING YORKSHIRE

For England

Player	M	I	NO	Runs	HS	Av'ge	100s	50s	Balls	Runs	W	Av'ge	Best	4wI	Ct/St
BATTY, G J 2002-09	10	8	2	30	17	5.00	0	0	440	366	5	73.20	2-40	—	4
CLOSE, D B 1972	3	3	0	49	43	16.33	0	0	18	21	0	—	—	—	1
GRAYSON, A P ...2000-01	2	2	0	6	6	3.00	0	0	90	60	3	20.00	3-40	—	1
ILLINGWORTH, R .1971-72	3	2	0	5	4	2.50	0	0	130	84	4	21.00	3-50	—	1
LUMB, M J 2013/14	3	3	0	165	106	55.00	1	0	—	—	—	—	—	—	1
PLUNKETT, L E ** 2005/6-2010/11	29	25	10	315	56	21.00	0	1	1,363	1,321	39	33.87	3-24	—	7
RHODES, S J ..1989-95	9	8	3	107	56	17.83	0	1				—	—	—	9/2
WHARF, A G ...2004-05	13	5	3	19	9	9.50	0	0	584	428	18	23.77	4-24	1	1
WOOD, B ...1972-82	13	12	2	314	78*	31.40	0	2	420	224	9	24.88	2-14	—	6

** before joining Yorkshire

Overseas Players

(Qualification: 24 List A matches for Yorkshire)

For Australia

Player	M	I	NO	Runs	HS	Av'ge	100s	50s	Balls	Runs	W	Av'ge	Best	4wI	Ct/St
BEVAN, M G ...1994-2004	232	196	67	6,912	108*	53.58	6	46	1,966	1,655	36	45.97	3-36	—	128
HARVEY, I J .1997/98-2004	73	51	11	715	48*	17.87	0	0	3,279	2,577	85	30.31	4-16	4	17
JAQUES, P A ...2006-2007	6	6	0	125	94	20.83	0	1	—	—	—	—	—	—	3
LEHMANN, D S .1996-2005	117	101	22	3,078	119	38.96	4	17	1,793	1,445	52	27.78	4-7	1	26

For South Africa

Player	M	I	NO	Runs	HS	Av'ge	100s	50s	Balls	Runs	W	Av'ge	Best	4wI	Ct/St
RUDOLPH, J A 2003-06	43	37	6	1,157	81	37.32	0	7	24	26	0	—	—	—	11

For West Indies

Player	M	I	NO	Runs	HS	Av'ge	100s	50s	Balls	Runs	W	Av'ge	Best	4wI	Ct/St
RICHARDSON, R B 1983-96	224	217	30	6,248	122	33.41	5	44	58	46	1	46.00	1-4	—	75

LIMITED-OVERS INTERNATIONAL MATCHES
AT HEADINGLEY, LEEDS 1973-2014

1973 **West Indies 181** (54 overs) (R B Kanhai 55). **England 182 for 9 wkts** (54.3 overs)
(M H Denness 66).
England won by 1 wicket   **Award: M H Denness**

1974 **India 265** (53.5 overs) (B P Patel 82, A L Wadekar 67). **England 266 for 6 wkts** (51.1
overs) (J H Edrich 90).
England won by 4 wickets   **Award: J H Edrich**

1975 **Australia 278 for 7 wkts** (60 overs) (R Edwards 80*). **Pakistan 205** (53 overs) (Majid
Khan 65, Asif Iqbal 53, D K Lillee 5 for 34).
Australia won by 73 runs   **Award: D K Lillee**

1975 **East Africa 120** (55.3 overs). **India 123 for 0 wkt** (29.5 overs) (S M Gavaskar 65*
F M Engineer 54*).
India won by 10 wickets   **Award: F M Engineer**

1975 **England 93** (36.2 overs) (G J Gilmour 6 for 14). **Australia 94 for 6 wkts** (28.4 overs).
Australia won by 4 wickets   **Award: G J Gilmour**

1979 **Canada 139 for 9 wkts** (60 overs). **Pakistan 140 for 2 wkts** (40.1 overs) (Sadiq
Mohammed 57*).
Pakistan won by 8 wickets   **Award: Sadiq Mohammed**

1979 **India 182 (55.5 overs)** (S M Gavaskar 55). **New Zealand 183 for 2 wkts** (57 overs)
(B A Edgar 84*).
New Zealand won by 8 wickets   **Award: B A Edgar**

1979 **England 165 for 9 wkts** (60 overs). **Pakistan 151** (56 overs) (Asif Iqbal 51, M
Hendrick 4 for 15)
England won by 14 runs   **Award: M Hendrick**

1980 **West Indies 198** (55 overs) (C G Greenidge 78). **England 174** (51.2 overs) (C J Tavaré
82*).
West Indies won by 24 runs   **Award: C J Tavaré**

1981 **Australia 236 for 8 wkts** (55 overs) (G M Wood 108). **England 165** (46.5 overs) (R M
Hogg 4 for 29).
Australia won by 71 runs   **Award: G M Wood**

1982 **India 193** (55 overs) (Kapil Dev 60, I T Botham 4 for 56). **England 194 for 1 wkt**
(50.1 overs) (B Wood 78*, C J Tavaré 66).
England won by 9 wickets   **Award: B Wood**

1983 **West Indies 252 for 9 wkts** (60 overs) (H A Gomes 78). **Australia 151** (30.3 overs)
(W W Davis 7 for 51).
West Indies won by 101 runs   **Award: W W Davis**

1983 **Pakistan 235 for 7 wkts** (60 overs) (Imran Khan 102*, Shahid Mahboob 77, A L F de
Mel 5 for 39). **Sri Lanka 224** (58.3 overs) (S Wettimuny 50, Abdul Qadir 5 for 44).
Pakistan won by 11 runs   **Award: Abdul Qadir**

1983 **Sri Lanka 136** (50.4 overs). **England 137 for 1 wkt** (24.1 overs) (G Fowler 81*).
England won by 9 wickets   **Award: R G D Willis**

1986 **New Zealand 217 for 8 wkts** (55 overs) (J J Crowe 66). **England 170** (48.2 overs).
New Zealand won by 47 runs   **Award: J J Crowe**

1988 **England 186 for 8 wkts** (55 overs). **West Indies 139** (46.3 overs).
England won by 47 runs   **Award: D R Pringle**

1990 **England 295 for 6 wkts** (55 overs) (R A Smith 128, G A Gooch 55). **New Zealand
298 for 6 wkts** (54.5 overs) (M J Greatbatch 102*, J G Wright 52, A H Jones 51).
New Zealand won by 4 wickets   **Award: M J Greatbatch**

1990 **England 229** (54.3 overs) (A J Lamb 56, D I Gower 50). **India 233 for 4 wkts** (53
overs) (S V Manjrekar 82, M Azharuddin 55*)
India won by 6 wickets   **Award: A Kumble**

1996 **India 158** (40.2 overs). **England 162 for 4 wkts** (39.3 overs) (G P Thorpe 79*).
England won by 6 wickets   **Award: G P Thorpe**

1997 **Australia 170 for 8 wkts** (50 overs).**England 175 for 4 wkts** (40.1 overs) (G P Thorpe 75*, A J Hollioake 66*).
England won by 6 wickets   **Award: G P Thorpe**

1998 **South Africa 205 for 8 wkts** (50 overs) (S M Pollock 56). **England 206 for 3 wkts** (35 overs) (A D Brown 59, N V Knight 51).
England won by 7 wickets   **Award: A D Brown**

1999 **Pakistan 275 for 8 wkts** (50 overs) (Inzamam-ul-Haq 81, Abdur Razzaq 60). **Australia 265** (49.5 overs) (M G Bevan 61, Wasim Akram 4-40).
Pakistan won by 10 runs   **Award: Inazmam-ul-Haq**

1999 **Zimbabwe 175** (49.3 overs) (M A Goodwin 57). **New Zealand 70 for 3 wkts** (15 overs).
No result   **No Award**

1999 **South Africa 271 for 7 wkts** (50 overs) (H H Gibbs 101, D J Cullinan 50). **Australia 275 for 5 wkts** (49.4 overs) (S R. Waugh 120*, R T Ponting 69).
Australia won by 5 wickets   **Award: S R Waugh**

2001 **England 156 (45.2 overs)** (B C Hollioake 53, Waqar Younis 7 for 36). **Pakistan 153 for 4 wkts** (39.5 overs) (Abdur Razzaq 75).
Pakistan won — England conceding the match following a pitch invasion.
       Award: Waqar Younis

2002 **Sri Lanka 240 for 7 wkts** (32 overs) (S T Jayasuriya 112). **England 241 for 7 wkts** (31.2 overs) (M E Trescothick 82).
England won by 3 wkts   **Award: S T Jayasuriya**

2003 **England 81 for 4 wkts. Zimbabwe** did not bat.
No result   **No Award**

2004 **West Indies 159** (40.1 overs). **England 160 for 3 wkts** (22 overs) (M E Trescothick 55).
England won by 7 wickets   **Award: S J Harmison**

2005 **Bangladesh 208 for 7 wkts** (50 overs) (Belim 81, A Flintoff 4-29). **England 209 for 5 wkts** (38.5 overs) (A J Strauss 98)
England won by 5 wickets   **Award: A J Strauss**

     Australia 219 for 7 wkts (50 overs) (P D Collingwood 4-34). **England 221 for 1 wkt** (46 overs) (M E Trescothick 104*, M P Vaughan 59*).
England won by 9 wickets   **Award: M E Trescothick**

2006 **England 321 for 7 wkts** (50 overs) (M E Trescothick 121, S L Malinga 4-44). **Sri Lanka 324 for 2 wkts** (37.3 overs) (S T Jayasuriya 152, W U Tharanga 109).
Sri Lanka won by 8 wickets   **Award: S T Jayasuriya**

2007 **India 324 for 6 wkts** (50 overs) (Yuvraj Singh 72, S R Tendulkar 71, S C Ganguly 59, G Gambhir 51). **England 242 for 8 wkts** (39 overs) (P D Collingwood 91*)
India won by 38 runs *(D/L Method)*   **Award: S C Ganguly**

2008 **England 275 for 4 wkts** (50 overs) (K P Pietersen 90*, A Flintoff 78). **South Africa 255** (J H Kallis 52).
England won by 20 runs   **Award: K P Pietersen**

2009 **England v. West Indies**   **Match abandoned without a ball bowled**

2010 **Pakistan 294 for 8 wkts** (50 overs) (Kamran Akmal 74, Asad Shafiq 50, S C J Broad 4-81). **England 295 for 6 wkts** (A J Strauss 126, I J L Trott 53)
England won by 4 wickets   **Award: A J Strauss**

2011 **Sri Lanka 309 for 5 wkts** (50 overs) (D P M D Jayawardene 144, K C Sangakkara 69) **England 240 all out** (E J G Morgan 52)
Sri Lanka won by 69 runs   **Award: D P M D Jayawardene**

2012 **England v. West Indies**   **Match abandoned without a ball bowled**

2013 **England v. Australia**   **Match abandoned without a ball bowled**

2014 **England 294 for 7 wkts** (50 overs) (J E Root 113). **India** 253 all out (48.4 overs) (R A Jadeja 87)

England won by 41 runs   Award: **J E Root**

SUMMARY OF RESULTS

ENGLAND	Played	Won	Lost
v. Australia	4	2	2
v. Bangladesh	1	1	0
v. India	6	4	2
v. New Zealand	2	0	2
v. Pakistan	3	2	1
v. South Africa	2	2	0
v. Sri Lanka	4	2	2
v. West Indies	4	3	1
v. Zimbabwe	1*	0	0
Totals	27	16	10

*No result. In addition to two matches v. West Indies abandoned and one match v. Australia abandoned

AUSTRALIA	Played	Won	Lost
v. England	4	2	2
v. Pakistan	2	1	1
v. South Africa	1	1	0
v. West Indies	1	0	1
Totals	8	4	4

In addition to one match abandoned

BANGLADESH	Played	Won	Lost
v. England	1	0	1

INDIA	Played	Won	Lost
v. England	6	2	4
v. East Africa	1	1	0
v. New Zealand	1	0	1
Totals	8	3	5

NEW ZEALAND	Played	Won	Lost
v. England	2	2	0
v. India	1	1	0
v. Zimbabwe	1*	0	0
Totals	4	3	0

*No result

PAKISTAN	Played	Won	Lost
v. Australia	2	1	1
v. Canada	1	1	0
v. England	3	1	2
v. Sri Lanka	1	1	0
Totals	7	4	3

SOUTH AFRICA	Played	Won	Lost
v. Australia	1	0	1
v. England	2	0	2
Totals	3	0	3

SRI LANKA	Played	Won	Lost
v. England	4	2	2
v. Pakistan	1	0	1
Totals	5	2	3

WEST INDIES	Played	Won	Lost
v. Australia	1	1	0
v. England	4	1	3
Totals	5	2	3

In addition to two matches abandoned

ZIMBABWE	Played	Won	Lost
v. England	1*	0	0
v. New Zealand	1*	0	0
Totals	2*	0	0

*No result

CANADA	Played	Won	Lost
v. Pakistan	1	0	1
EAST AFRICA	Played	Won	Lost
v. India	1	0	1

CENTURIES

152	S J Jayasuriya	for Sri Lanka	v. England	2006
144	D P M D Jayawardene	for Sri Lanka	v. England	2011
128	R A Smith	for England	v. New Zealand	1990
126	A J Strauss	for England	v. Pakistan	2010
121	M E Trescothick	for England	v. Sri Lanka	2006
120*	S R Waugh	for Australia	v. South Africa	1999
113	J E Root	for England	v. India	2014
112	S J Jayasuriya	for Sri Lanka	v. England	2002
109	W U Tharanga	for Sri Lanka	v. England	2006
108	G M Wood	for Australia	v. England	1981
104*	M E Trescothick	for England	v. Australia	2005
102*	Imran Khan	for Pakistan	v. Sri Lanka	1983
102*	M J Greatbatch	for New Zealand	v. England	1990
101	H H Gibbs	for South Africa	v. Australia	1999

4 WICKETS IN AN INNINGS

7-36	Waqar Younis	for Pakistan	v. England	2001
7-51	W W Davis	for West Indies	v. Australia	1983
6-14	G J Gilmour	for Australia	v. England	1975
5-34	D K Lillee	for Australia	v. Pakistan	1975
5-39	A L F de Mel	for Sri Lanka	v. Pakistan	1983
5-44	Abdul Qadir	for Pakistan	v. Sri Lanka	1983
4-15	M Hendrick	for England	v. Pakistan	1979
4-29	R M Hogg	for Australia	v England	1981
4-29	A Flintoff	for England	v. Bangladesh	2005
4-34	P D Collingwood	for England	v. Australia	2005
4-40	Wasim Akram	for Pakistan	v. Australia	1999
4-44	S L Malinga	for Sri Lanka	v. England	2006
4-56	I T Botham	for England	v. India	1982
4-81	S J C Broad	for England	v. Pakistan	2010

LIMITED-OVERS INTERNATIONAL MATCHES
AT NORTH MARINE ROAD, SCARBOROUGH 1976-1978

1976 **England 202 for 8 wkts** (55 overs) (G D Barlow 80*, A M E Roberts 4 for 32).
West Indies 207 for 4 wkts (41 overs) (I V A Richards 119*).
West Indies won by 6 wickets   **Award: I V A Richards**

1978 **England 206 for 8 wkts** (55 overs) (G A Gooch 94, B L Cairns 5 for 28).
New Zealand 187 for 8 wkts (55 overs) (B E Congdon 52*).
England won by 19 runs   **Award: G A Gooch**

LIST OF PLAYERS AND CAREER AVERAGES IN ALL FIRST-CLASS MATCHES FOR YORKSHIRE 1863-2014

Based on research by John T Potter, Roy D Wilkinson and the late Anthony Woodhouse

The Editor and Statistics Editor welcome any information which will help in keeping this list up to date. The present compilers do not believe that we should alter the status of matches from that determined at the time they were played. Therefore, these averages include the match versus Gentlemen of Scotland in 1878, and exclude the matches versus Liverpool and District played in 1889, 1891, 1892 and 1893 in line with what appear to be the decisions of the Club at the time.

* Played as an amateur   © Awarded County Cap   § Born outside Yorkshire

Player	Date of Birth	Date of Death (if known)	First Played	Last Played	M	Inns	NO	Runs	HS	Av'ge	100s	Runs	Wkts	Av'ge	Ct/St
Ackroyd, A *	Aug. 29, 1858	Oct. 3, 1927	1879	1879	1	1	1	2	2*	—	0	7	0	—	0
Allen, S *	Dec. 20, 1893	Oct. 9, 1978	1924	1924		2	0	8	6	4.00	0	116	2	58.00	0
Allen, W R	Apr 14, 1893	Oct 14, 1950	1921	1925	30	32	10	475	95*	21.59	0	—	—	—	45/21
Ambler, J	Feb 12, 1860	Feb 10 1899	1886	1886	4	7	0	68	25	9.71	0	22	0	—	2
Anderson, G	Jan 20, 1826	Nov 27, 1892	1851	1869	19	31	6	520	99*	20.80	0	—	—	—	19
Anderson, P N	Apr. 28, 1966		1988	1988	1	1	0	0	0	0.00	0	—	—	—	1
Anson, C E *	Oct 14, 1889	Mar 26, 1969	1924	1924	3	2	0	27	14	13.50	0	47	1	47.00	0
Appleton, C *	May15, 1844	Feb 26, 1925	1865	1865	3	6	1	56	18	11.20	0	—	—	—	0
Appleyard, R	© June 27, 1924		1950	1958	133	122	43	679	63	8.59	0	9,903	642	15.42	70
Armitage, C I *	Apr 24, 1849	Apr 24, 1917	1873	1878	3	5	0	26	12	5.20	0	29	0	—	0
Armitage, T *	Apr 25, 1848	Sept 21, 1922	1872	1878	52	85	8	1,053	95	13.67	0	1,614	107	15.08	20
Ash, D L	Feb 18, 1944		1965	1965	3	3	0	22	12	7.33	0	—	—	—	0
Ashman, J R	May 20, 1926		1951	1951	1	1	1	0	0*	—	0	116	4	29.00	0
Ashraf, Moin A	**Jan 5, 1992**		**2010**	**2013**	**21**	**19**	**5**	**56**	**10**	**4.00**	**0**	**1,268**	**43**	**29.48**	**2**
Aspinall, R	© Oct 26, 1918	Aug 16, 1999	1946	1950	36	48	8	763	75*	19.07	0	2,670	131	20.38	18
Aspinall, W	Mar 24, 1858	Jan 27, 1910	1880	1880	2	3	0	16	14	5.33	0	—	—	—	0
Asquith, F T	Feb 5, 1870	Jan 11, 1916	1903	1903	1	1	0	0	0	0.00	0	—	—	—	0
Athey, C W J	© Sept 27, 1957		1976	1983	151	246	21	6,320	134	28.08	10	1,003	21	47.76	144/2
Atkinson, G R	Sept 21, 1830	May 3, 1906	1861	1870	27	38	8	399	44	13.30	0	1,146	54	21.22	14
Atkinson, H	Feb 1, 1881	Dec 22, 1959	1907	1907	1	2	0	0	0	0.00	0	17	0	—	0
Azeem Rafiq	Feb 27, 1991		2009	2014	22	25	2	511	100	22.21	1	1,717	47	36.53	9
Backhouse, E N	May 13, 1901	Nov 1, 1936	1931	1931	1	1	0	2	2	2.00	0	4	2	2.00	0
Badger, H D *	Mar 7, 1900	Aug 10, 1975	1921	1922	2	4	2	6	6*	3.00	0	145	6	24.16	1

LIST OF PLAYERS AND CAREER AVERAGES IN ALL FIRST-CLASS MATCHES FOR YORKSHIRE (Continued)

Player	Date of Birth	Date of Death (if known)	First Played	Last Played	M	Inns	NO	Runs	HS	Av'ge	100s	Runs	Wkts	Av'ge	Ct/St
Bainbridge, A B	Oct 15, 1932		1961	1963	5	10	0	93	24	9.30	0	358	20	17.90	3
Baines, F E *	June 18, 1864	Nov 17, 1948	1888	1888	1	1	0	0	0	0.00	0	—	—	—	—
Bairstow, A	Aug 14, 1868	Dec 7, 1945	1896	1900	24	24	1	69	12	4.92	0	—	—	—	41/18
Bairstow, D L	© Sept 1, 1951	Jan 5, 1998	1970	1990	429	601	113	12,985	145	26.60	9	192	6	32.00	907/131
Bairstow, J M	© **Sept 26, 1989**		**2009**	**2014**	**73**	**116**	**19**	**4,431**	**205**	**45.68**	**8**	**1**	**0**	—	**181/9**
Baker, G R	Apr 18, 1862	Feb 6, 1938	1884	1884	7	11	1	42	13	4.20	0	43	0	—	5
Baker, R *	July 13, 1849	June 21, 1896	1874	1875	3	5	1	45	22	11.25	0	—	—	—	3
Balderstone, J C	Nov 16, 1940	Mar 6, 2000	1961	1969	68	81	6	1,332	82	17.76	0	790	37	21.35	24
§**Ballance, G S**	© **Nov 22, 1989**		**2008**	**2014**	**55**	**82**	**12**	**3,618**	**174**	**51.68**	**11**	**132**	**0**	—	**40**
Barber, A T *	© June 17, 1905	Mar 10, 1985	1929	1930	42	54	3	1,050	100	20.58	1	0	0	—	40
Barber, W	Apr 18, 1901	Sept 10, 1968	1926	1947	354	495	48	15,315	255	34.26	27	404	14	28.85	169
Barraclough, E S	Mar 30, 1923	May 21, 1999	1949	1950	2	4	2	43	24*	21.50	0	136	4	34.00	4
Bates, W	Nov 19, 1855	Jan 8, 1900	1877	1887	202	331	15	6,499	136	20.37	8	10,692	637	16.78	163
Bates, W E	© Mar 5, 1884	Jan 17, 1957	1907	1913	113	167	11	2,634	81	17.32	0	57	2	28.50	64
Batty G J	Oct 13, 1977		1997	1997	1	2	0	18	18	9.00	0	70	2	35.00	0
Batty, J D	May 15, 1971		1989	1994	64	67	20	703	51	14.95	0	5,286	140	37.75	25
Bayes, G W	Feb 27, 1884	Dec 6, 1960	1910	1921	18	24	11	165	36	12.69	0	1,534	48	31.95	7
Beaumont, H	Oct 14, 1916	Nov. 15, 2003	1946	1947	28	46	3	716	60	17.90	0	236	9	26.22	11
Beaumont, J	Sept 16, 1855	May 1, 1920	1877	1878	5	9	3	60	24	10.00	0	50	2	25.00	0
Bedford, H	July 17, 1907	July 5, 1968	1928	1928	5	5	1	57	24	14.25	0	179	8	22.37	0
Bedford, W	Feb 24, 1879	July, 28 1939	1903	1903	2	2	1	38	30*	38.00	0	117	2	58.50	1
Bell, J T	June 16, 1895	Aug 8, 1974	1921	1923	7	8	1	125	54	17.85	0	—	—	—	0
Berry, John	Jan 10, 1823	Feb 26, 1895	1849	1867	18	32	2	492	78	16.40	0	149	8	18.62	12
Berry, Joseph	Nov 29, 1829	Apr 20, 1894	1861	1874	3	4	0	68	30	17.00	0	—	—	—	1
Berry, P J	Dec 28, 1966		1986	1990	7	7	6	76	31*	76.00	0	401	7	57.28	2
§ Best T L	Aug 26, 1981		2010	2010	9	9	0	86	40	9.55	0	793	18	44.05	4
Betts, G	Sept 19, 1843	Sept. 26, 1902	1873	1874	2	4	1	56	44*	18.66	0	—	—	—	1
§ Bevan, M G	© May 8, 1970		1995	1996	32	56	8	2,823	160*	58.81	9	720	10	72.00	24
Binks, J G	Oct 5, 1935		1955	1969	491	587	128	6,745	95	14.69	0	66	0	—	872/172
Binns, J	Mar 31, 1870	Dec 8, 1934	1898	1898	1	1	0	4	4	4.00	0	—	—	—	0/3
Bird, H D	Apr 19, 1933		1956	1959	14	25	2	613	181*	26.65	1	—	—	—	3

LIST OF PLAYERS AND CAREER AVERAGES IN ALL FIRST-CLASS MATCHES FOR YORKSHIRE (Continued)

Player	Date of Birth	Date of Death (if known)	First Played	Last Played	M	Inns	NO	Runs	HS	Av'ge	100s	Runs	Wkts	Av'ge	Ct/St
Birkenshaw, J	Nov 13, 1940	Jan 13, 1971	1958	1960	30	42	7	588	42	16.80	0	1,819	69	26.36	21
Birtles, T J D	Oct 26, 1886	Feb 19, 1987	1913	1924	37	57	11	876	104	19.04	1	20	0	—	19
Blackburn, J D H *	Oct 27, 1924	July 8, 1922	1956	1956	1	2	—	18	15	9.00	0	—	—	—	0
Blackburn, J S	Sept 24, 1852	June 3, 1941	1876	1877	6	11	1	102	28	10.20	0	173	7	24.71	4
§ Blackburn, W E *	Nov 24, 1888		1919	1920	10	13	6	26	6*	3.71	0	1,113	45	24.73	9
§ Blain J A R	Jan 4, 1979		2004	2010	15	17	7	137	28*	13.70	0	1,312	38	34.52	4
Blake, W	Nov 29, 1854	Not known	1880	1880	2	3	0	44	21	14.66	0	17	1	17.00	0
Blakey, R J	© Jan 15, 1967		1985	2003	339	541	84	14,150	223*	30.96	12	68	1	68.00	768/56
Blamires, E	July 31, 1850	Mar 22, 1886	1877	1877	1	2	0	23	17	11.50	0	82	5	16.40	0
§ Blewett, G S	© Oct 29, 1971		1999	1999	12	23	2	655	190	31.19	1	212	5	42.40	5
Bloom, G R	Sept 13, 1941		1964	1964	1	1	0	2	2	2.00	0	—	—	—	0
Bocking, H	Dec 10, 1835	Feb 22, 1907	1865	1865	2	2	0	14	11	7.00	0	252	13	19.38	5
Boden, J G *	Dec 27, 1848	Jan 3, 1928	1878	1878	1	1	0	6	6	6.00	0	407	13	31.30	0
Bolton, B C *	Sept 23, 1862	Nov 18, 1910	1890	1891	4	6	0	25	11	4.16	0	—	—	—	1
Bolus, J B	© Jan 31, 1934		1956	1962	107	179	18	4,712	146*	29.26	7	—	—	—	45
Booth, A	© Nov 3, 1902	Aug 17, 1974	1931	1947	23	36	16	114	29	5.70	0	1,684	122	13.80	10
Booth, M W	© Dec 10, 1886	July 1, 1916	1908	1914	144	218	31	4,244	210	22.69	2	11,017	557	19.17	114
Booth, P A	Sept 5, 1965		1982	1989	40	29	9	193	33*	9.65	0	1,517	35	43.34	7
Booth, R	Oct 1, 1926		1951	1955	74	76	28	730	53*	15.20	0	—	—	—	79/29
Bore, M K	June 2, 1947		1969	1977	65	78	21	481	37*	8.43	0	4,866	162	30.03	27
Borrill, P D	July 4, 1951		1971	1971	2	4	1	20	7	—	0	—	—	—	—
Bosomworth W E	Mar 8, 1847	June 7, 1891	1872	1880	4	7	1	20	7	3.33	0	140	9	15.55	2
Bottomley, I H *	Apr 9, 1855	Apr 23, 1922	1878	1880	9	12	0	166	32	13.83	0	75	1	75.00	0
Bottomley, T	Dec 26, 1910	Feb 19, 1977	1934	1935	6	7	0	142	51	20.28	0	188	1	188.00	5
Bower, W H	Oct 17, 1857	Jan 31, 1943	1883	1883	1	2	0	10	10	5.00	0	—	—	—	0
Bowes, W E	July 25, 1908	Sept 4, 1987	1929	1947	301	257	117	1,251	43*	8.93	0	21,227	1,351	15.71	118
Boycott, G	© Oct 21, 1940		1962	1986	414	674	111	32,570	260*	57.85	103	665	28	23.75	200
Brackin, T	Jan 5, 1859	Oct 7, 1924	1882	1882	3	6	0	12	7	2.00	0	—	—	—	0
Brayshay P B *	Oct 14, 1916	July 6, 2004	1952	1952	2	3	0	20	13	6.66	0	104	3	34.66	0
Brearley, H *	June 26, 1913	Aug 14, 2007	1937	1937	1	2	0	17	9	8.50	0	—	—	—	0
Brennan, D V *	© Feb 10, 1920	Jan 9, 1985	1947	1953	204	221	66	1,653	47	10.66	0	—	—	—	280/100

LIST OF PLAYERS AND CAREER AVERAGES IN ALL FIRST-CLASS MATCHES FOR YORKSHIRE (Continued)

Player	Date of Birth	Date of Death (if known)	First Played	Last Played	M	Inns	NO	Runs	HS	Av'ge	100s	Runs	Wkts	Av'ge	Ct/St
Bresnan, T T ....©	**Feb 28, 1985**		**2003**	**2014**	105	140	23	3,098	116	26.47	2	9,019	291	30.99	43
Britton, G	Feb 7, 1843	Jan 3, 1910	1867	1867	3	2	0	3	3	1.50	0	252	5	50.40	0
Broadbent, A	June 7, 1879	July 19, 1958	1909	1910	3	5	0	66	29	13.20	0				1
Broadhead, W B	May 31, 1903	Apr 2, 1986	1929	1929	1	2	0	5	5	2.50	0				0
Broadhurst, M	June 20, 1974		1991	1994	5	3	0	7	6	2.33	0	231	7	33.00	0
§ Brophy, G L ....©	Nov 26, 1975		2006	2012	73	112	12	3,012	177*	30.12	3	6	0	—	176/15
Brooke, J W	Feb 1, 1897		1923	1923	1	1	0	0	0	0.00	0				0
Brooke, B	Mar 3, 1930	Mar.3 1989	1950	1950	2	4	0	16	14	4.00	0				0
§ Brooks, J A ....©	**June 4, 1984**		**2013**	**2014**	29	29	15	248	37*	17.71	0	2,849	108	26.37	10
Broughton, P N	Oct 22, 1935		1956	1956	6	3	0	19	12	6.33	0	365	16	22.81	4
Brown, A	June 10, 1854	Nov 2, 1900	1872	1872	1	2	0	6	5	3.00	0				0
Brown, J T (Driffield) ©	Aug 20, 1869	Nov 4, 1904	1889	1904	345	567	41	15,694	311	29.83	23	5,183	177	29.28	188
Brown, J T (Darfield) ©	Nov 24, 1874	Apr 12, 1950	1897	1903	30	32	3	333	37*	11.48	0	2,071	97	21.35	18
Brown, W	Nov 19, 1876	July 27, 1945	1902	1908	14	20	3	185	25	10.88	0				7
Brownhill, T	Oct 10, 1838	Jan 6, 1915	1861	1871	1	1	0	2	2	2.00	0	84	4	21.00	2
Brumfitt, J *	Feb. 18, 1917	Mar 16, 1987	1938	1938	1	1	0	9	9	9.00	0				7
Buller, J S	Aug 23, 1909	Aug 7, 1970	1930	1930	1	2	1	5	5	2.50	0				2
Bulmer, J R L	Dec 28, 1867	Jan 20, 1917	1891	1891	1	2	1	0	0*	0.00	0				0
Burgess, T	Oct 1, 1859	Feb 22, 1922	1895	1895	1	2	1	0	0	0.00	0				2
Burgin, E	Jan 4, 1924		1952	1953	12	10	3	92	32	13.14	0	79	1	79.00	7
Burman, J	Oct 5, 1838	May 14, 1900	1867	1867	6	10	6	4	1*	1.00	0	795	31	25.64	2
Burnet, J R * ....©	Oct 11, 1918	Mar 7, 1999	1958	1959	54	75	6	889	54	12.88	0	26	1	26.00	44
§ Burrows, M	Aug 18, 1855	May 29, 1893	1880	1880	6	10	0	82	23	8.20	0				2
Burton, D C F * ....©	Sept 13, 1887	Sept 24, 1971	1907	1921	104	130	15	2,273	142*	19.76	2				44
Burton, R C *	Apr 11, 1891	Apr 30, 1971	1914	1914	2	2	0	47	47	23.50	0	73	6	12.16	2
Butterfield, E B * ....©	Oct 22, 1848	May 6, 1899	1870	1870	1	2	0	18	9	9.00	0				0
Byas, D ....©	Aug 26, 1963		1986	2001	268	449	42	14,398	213	35.37	28	727	12	60.58	351
Byrom, J L *	July, 20, 1851	Aug 24, 1931	1874	1874	2	4	0	19	11	4.75	0				1
Cammish, J W *	May 21, 1921	July 16, 1974	1954	1954	2	1	0	0	0	0.00	0	155	3	51.66	0
Carrick, P ....©	July, 16 1952	Jan 11, 2000	1970	1993	425	543	102	9,994	131*	22.66	3	30,530	1,018	29.99	183

LIST OF PLAYERS AND CAREER AVERAGES IN ALL FIRST-CLASS MATCHES FOR YORKSHIRE *(Continued)*

Player	Date of Birth	Date of Death (if known)	First Played	Last Played	M	Inns	NO	Runs	HS	Av'ge	100s	Runs	Wkts	Av'ge	Ct/St
Carter, Rev E V S *	Feb 3, 1845	May 23, 1923	1876	1881	14	21	2	210	39*	11.05	0	104	8	13.00	4
Cartman, W H	June 20, 1861	Jan 16, 1935	1891	1891	3	6	1	57		9.50	0	—	—	—	0
Carver, K	**March 26, 1996**		**2014**	**2014**	**1**	**1**	**0**	**2**	**2***	**—**	**0**	**65**	**3**	**21.66**	**1**
Cawthray, G	Sept 28, 1913	Jan 5, 2000	1939	1952	4	6	0	114	30	19.00	0	304	4	76.00	1
Chadwick, J P G	Nov 8, 1934		1960	1965	6	9	3	106	59	17.66	0	67	2	33.50	7
Champion, A	Dec 27, 1851	June 26, 1909	1876	1879	14	23	4	148	29	7.78	0	17	1	17.00	7
Chapman, C A	June 8, 1971		1990	1998	8	13	2	238	80	21.63	0	—	—	—	13/3
Charlesworth, A P	Feb 19, 1865	May 11, 1926	1894	1895	7	12	1	241	63	21.90	0	—	—	—	2
§ Chichester-Constable, R C J *	Dec 21, 1890	May 26, 1963	1919	1919	1	1	0	0	0	0.00	0	6	0	—	0
Clarkson, A	Sept 5, 1939		1963	1963	6	8	1	80	30	11.42	0	92	5	18.40	5
§ Claughton, H M	Dec 24, 1891	Oct 17, 1980	1914	1919	4	6	0	39	15	6.50	0	176	3	58.66	0
§ Claydon, M E	Nov 25, 1982		2005	2006	3	2	0	38	38	19.00	0	263	3	87.66	0
§ Clayton, R O	Jan 1, 1844	Nov 26, 1901	1870	1879	70	115	23	992	62	10.78	0	2,478	153	16.19	26
§ Cleary, M F	July 19, 1980		2005	2005	2	2	0	23	12	11.50	0	250	8	31.25	2
Clegg, H	Dec 8, 1850	Dec 30, 1920	1881	1881	6	8	1	63	25*	9.00	0	—	—	—	2
Clifford, C C	July 5, 1942		1972	1972	11	12	4	39	12*	4.87	0	666	26	25.61	5
Close, D B	Feb 24, 1931	©	1949	1970	536	811	102	22,650	198	31.94	33	23,489	967	24.29	564
Clough, G D	May 23, 1978		1998	1998	1	2	0	34	33	17.00	0	11	0	—	1
Collinson, R W *	Nov 6, 1875	Dec 26, 1963	1897	1897	2	3	0	58	34	19.33	0	—	—	—	0
Cooper, H P	Apr 17, 1949		1971	1980	98	107	29	1,159	56	14.85	0	6,327	227	27.87	60
Cooper, P E *	Feb 19, 1885	May 21, 1950	1910	1910	1	2	0	0	0	0.00	0	—	—	—	0
Cope, G A	Feb 23, 1947	©	1966	1980	230	249	89	2,241	78	14.00	0	15,627	630	24.80	64
Corbett, A M	Nov 25, 1855	Oct 7, 1934	1881	1881	1	2	0	0	0	0.00	0	—	—	—	0
Coverdale, S P	Nov 20, 1954		1973	1980	6	4	0	31	18	7.75	0	—	—	—	11/4
Coverdale, W *	July 8, 1862	Sept 23, 1934	1888	1888	2	2	0	2	1	1.00	0	—	—	—	2
Cowan, M J	June 10, 1933	©	1953	1962	91	84	48	170	19*	4.72	0	6,389	266	24.01	37
Cownley, J M	Feb 24, 1929	Nov 7, 1998	1952	1952	2	1	0	19	19	19.00	0	119	1	119.00	0
Coxon, A	Jan 18, 1916	Jan 22, 2006	1945	1950	142	182	33	2,747	83	18.43	0	9,528	464	20.53	124
Craven, V J	July 31, 1980		2000	2004	33	55	6	1,206	81*	24.61	0	584	15	38.93	18
Crawford, G H	Dec 15, 1890	June 28, 1975	1914	1926	9	8	0	46	21	5.75	0	541	21	25.76	3

LIST OF PLAYERS AND CAREER AVERAGES IN ALL FIRST-CLASS MATCHES FOR YORKSHIRE (Continued)

Player	Date of Birth	Date of Death (if known)	First Played	Last Played	M	Inns	NO	Runs	HS	Av'ge	100s	Runs	Wkts	Av'ge	Ct/St
Crawford, M G *	July 30, 1920	Dec 2, 2012	1951	1951	1	2	0	22	13	11.00	0	181	10	18.10	1
Creighton, E	July 9, 1859	Feb 17, 1931	1888	1888	4	8	2	33	10	5.50	0	—	0	—	0
Crick, H	Jan 29, 1910	Feb 10, 1960	1937	1947	8	10	2	88	20	8.80	0	—	—	—	18/4
Crookes, R	Oct 9, 1846	Feb 15, 1897	1879	1879	1	2	1	2	2*	2.00	0	14	0	—	0
Crossland, S M	Aug 16, 1851	April 11, 1906	1883	1886	4	6	2	32	20	8.00	0	—	—	—	3/5
Crowther, A	Aug 1, 1878	June 4, 1946	1905	1905	1	2	2	0	0	0.00	0	—	—	—	1
Cuttell, W	Jan 28, 1835	June 10, 1896	1862	1871	15	27	6	271	56	12.90	0	596	36	16.55	4
Dalton, A J	Mar 14, 1947		1969	1972	21	31	2	710	128	24.48	3	—	—	—	6
§ Darnton, T	Feb 12, 1836	Oct 11, 1874	1864	1868	13	22	1	314	81*	14.95	0	349	12	29.08	3
Davidson, K R	Dec 24, 1905	Dec 25, 1954	1933	1935	30	46	5	1,331	128	32.46	2	—	—	—	18
© Dawes, J	Feb 14, 1836	Not known	1865	1865	5	9	2	93	28*	13.28	0	196	5	39.20	3
Dawood, I	July 23, 1976		2004	2005	20	31	7	636	75	26.50	0	—	—	—	46/3
Dawson, E	May 1, 1835	Dec 1, 1888	1863	1874	16	25	1	224	20	9.33	0	—	—	—	5
Dawson, R K J	Aug 4, 1980		2001	2006	72	106	9	2,179	87	22.46	0	6,444	157	41.04	39
Dawson, W A *	Dec 3, 1850	Mar 6, 1916	1870	1870	1	2	0	0	0	0.00	0	—	—	—	1
Day, A G *	Sept 20, 1865	Oct 16, 1908	1885	1888	6	10	0	78	25	7.80	0	—	—	—	3
© Dennis, F	June 11, 1907	Nov 21, 2000	1928	1933	89	100	28	1,332	67	18.50	0	4,517	156	28.95	58
© Dennis, S J	Oct 18, 1960		1980	1988	67	62	24	338	53*	8.89	0	5,548	173	32.06	19
Denton, D	July 4, 1874	Feb 16, 1950	1894	1920	676	1,058	61	33,282	221	33.38	61	957	34	28.14	360/1
Denton, J	Feb 3, 1865	June 15, 1946	1887	1888	15	24	1	222	59	9.65	0	—	—	—	6
Dewse, H	Feb 23, 1836	July 8, 1910	1873	1873	1	2	0	14	12	7.00	0	15	0	—	1
Deyes, G	Feb 11, 1879	Jan 11, 1963	1905	1907	17	24	4	44	12	2.20	0	944	41	23.02	6
Dick, R D *	Apr 16, 1889	Dec 14, 1983	1911	1911	1	1	0	2	2	2.00	0	37	2	18.50	1
Dobson, M J	Feb 22, 1854	Sept 17, 1932	1879	1879	2	3	0	1	1	0.33	0	—	—	—	1
Doidge, M J	July 2, 1970		1990	1990	1						0	106	0	—	0
© Dolphin, A	Dec 24, 1885	Oct 23, 1942	1905	1927	427	446	157	3,325	66	11.50	0	28	1	28.00	569/260
Douglas, J S	Apr 4, 1903	Dec 27, 1971	1925	1934	23	26	8	125	19	6.94	0	1,310	49	26.73	14
© Drake, A	Apr 16, 1884	Feb 14, 1919	1909	1914	156	244	24	4,789	147*	21.76	3	8,623	479	18.00	93
Drake, A	Sept 1, 1893	May 22, 1967	1923	1924	3	4	1	21	10	7.00	0	117	1	117.00	2
Driver, J	May 16, 1861	Dec 10, 1946	1889	1889	2	4	1	24	8	8.00	0	—	—	—	2

Player	Date of Birth	Date of Death (if known)	First Played	Last Played	M	Inns	NO	Runs	HS	Av'ge	100s	Runs	Wkts	Av'ge	Ct/St
Dury, T S *	June 12, 1854	Mar 20, 1932	1878	1881	13	24	1	329	46	14.30	0	21	0	—	3
Dyson, W L	Dec 11, 1857	May 1, 1936	1887	1887	2	4	0	8	6	2.00	0	—	—	—	2
Earnshaw, W	Sept 20, 1867	Nov 24, 1941	1893	1896	6	7	3	44	23	11.00	0	—	—	—	6/2
Eastwood, T D	Mar 30, 1848	May 17, 1903	1870	1877	29	51	2	591	68	12.06	0	349	11	31.72	16
Eckersley, R	Sept 4, 1925	May 30, 2009	1945	1945	2	1	1	9	9*	—	0	62	0	—	0
Elam, F W *	Sept 13, 1871	Mar 19, 1943	1900	1902	1	3	1	48	28	24.00	0	—	—	—	0
§ Elliott, M T G	Sept 28, 1971		2002	2002	5	10	1	487	127	54.11	1	77	1	77.00	7
Ellis, J E	Nov 10, 1864	Dec 1, 1927	1888	1892	11	15	6	14	4*	1.55	0	—	—	—	11/10
Ellis, S *	Nov 23, 1851	Oct 28, 1930	1880	1880	2	3	0	12	9	4.00	0	—	—	—	2
Elms, J E	Dec 24, 1874	Nov 1, 1951	1905	1905	2	2	0	20	20	10.00	0	28	1	28.00	1
Elstub, C J	Feb 3, 1981		2000	2002	1	2	1	20	18*	20.00	0	356	9	39.55	2
Emmett, T ...©	Sept 3, 1841	June 29, 1904	1866	1888	299	484	65	6,315	104	15.07	1	15,465	1,216	12.71	179
Farrar, A	Apr 29, 1884	Dec 25, 1954	1906	1906	1	1	0	2	2	2.00	0	—	—	—	1
Fearnley, M C	Aug 21, 1936	July 7, 1979	1962	1964	3	4	2	19	11*	9.50	0	133	6	22.16	—
Featherby, W D	Aug 18, 1888	Nov 20, 1958	1920	1920	2	1	1	—	—	—	—	12	0	—	—
Fellows, G M	July 30, 1978		1998	2003	46	71	6	1,526	109	23.47	1	1,202	32	37.56	23
Fiddling, K	Oct 13, 1917	June 19, 1992	1938	1946	18	24	6	182	25	10.11	0	—	—	—	24/13
§ Finch, A J ...©	Nov 27, 1986		2014	2014	5	6	0	291	110	48.50	1	39	1	39.00	8
Firth, A *	Sept 3, 1847	Jan 16, 1927	1869	1869	1	1	0	4	4	4.00	0	—	—	—	0
Firth, Rev E B *	Apr 11, 1863	July 25, 1905	1894	1894	1	1	0	1	1	1.00	0	—	—	—	0
Firth, J D	June 27, 1918	Sept 7, 1981	1949	1950	8	8	5	134	67*	44.66	0	—	—	—	14/2
Fisher, H ...©	Aug 3, 1903	Apr 16, 1974	1928	1936	52	58	14	681	76*	15.47	0	2,621	93	28.18	22
Fisher, I D	Mar 31, 1976		1996	2001	24	32	9	545	76*	23.69	0	1,382	43	32.13	1
Flaxington, S	Oct 14, 1860	Mar 10, 1895	1882	1882	4	8	0	121	57	15.12	0	—	—	—	1
§ Fleming, S P ...©	Apr 1, 1973		2003	2003	7	14	2	469	98	39.08	0	—	—	—	13
Fletcher, S D	June 8, 1964		1983	1991	107	91	31	414	28*	6.90	0	7,966	234	34.04	25
Fletcher, W	Feb 16, 1866	June 1, 1935	1892	1892	5	8	1	80	31	11.42	0	157	7	22.42	4
Foord, C W	June 11, 1924		1947	1953	51	34	16	114	35	6.33	0	3,412	126	27.07	19
Foster, E	Nov 23, 1873	April 16, 1956	1901	1901	1	1	0	2	2	2.00	0	27	0	—	0
Foster, M J	Sept 17, 1972		1993	1994	5	7	1	165	63*	27.50	0	156	6	25.00	6
§ Foster, T W	Nov 12, 1871	Jan 31, 1947	1894	1895	14	20	5	138	25	9.20	0	952	58	16.41	6

LIST OF PLAYERS AND CAREER AVERAGES IN ALL FIRST-CLASS MATCHES FOR YORKSHIRE (Continued)

Player	Date of Birth	Date of Death (if known)	First Played	Last Played	M	Inns	NO	Runs	HS	Av'ge	100s	Runs	Wkts	Av'ge	Ct/St
Frank, J *	Dec 17, 1857	Oct 22, 1940	1881	1881	1	2	0	10	7	5.00	0	17	1	17.00	3
Frank R W *	May 29, 1864	Sept 9, 1950	1889	1903	18	28	4	298	58	12.41	0	9	0	—	8
Freeman, G	July 27, 1843	Nov 18, 1895	1865	1880	32	54	2	752	53	14.46	0	2,079	209	9.94	16
Gale, A W	©Nov 28, 1983		2004	2014	117	180	16	6,110	272	37.25	16	238	1	238.00	40
Geldart, C J	©Dec 17, 1991		2010	2011	2	2	0	51	34	25.50	0	—	—	—	1
Gibb, P A *	©July 11, 1913	Dec 7, 1977	1935	1946	36	54	7	1,545	157*	32.87	2	82	3	27.33	25/8
Gibson, B P P **	Mar 31, 1996		2011	2011	1	1	0	1	1*	1.00	0	—	—	—	6/0
§ Gitkins, C J *	Feb 19, 1856	Jan 31, 1897	1880	1880	2	3	0	30	23	10.00	0	—	—	—	1
Gilbert, C R	Apr 16, 1984		2007	2007	1	1	0	64	64	64.00	0	—	—	—	1
Gill, F	Sept 3, 1883	Nov 1, 1917	1906	1906	2	4	0	18	11	4.50	0	—	—	—	0
§ Gillespie, J N	©April 19, 1975		2006	2007	26	34	11	640	123*	27.82	1	2,013	59	34.11	4
Gillhouley, K	Aug 8, 1934		1961	1961	24	31	8	323	56*	13.45	0	1,702	77	22.10	16
Gough, D	©Sept 18, 1970		1989	2008	146	188	29	2,922	121	18.37	0	12,487	453	27.56	30
Goulder, A	Aug 16, 1907		1929	1929	3	2	0	6	3	3.00	0	90	3	30.00	0
§ Gray, A K D	May 19, 1974		2001	2004	18	26	3	649	104	28.21	1	1,357	30	45.23	16
Grayson, A P	Mar 31, 1971		1990	1995	52	80	12	1,958	100	27.97	1	846	13	65.07	36
Greenwood, A	Aug 20, 1847	Feb 12, 1889	1869	1880	95	166	12	2,762	91	17.93	0	9	0	—	33
Greenwood, F E *	Sept 28, 1905	July 30, 1963	1929	1932	57	66	8	1,458	104*	25.13	1	36	2	18.00	37
Greenwood, L	July 13, 1834	Nov 1, 1909	1861	1874	50	84	12	885	83	12.29	0	1,615	85	19.00	24
Grimshaw, C H	May 12, 1880	Sept 25, 1947	1904	1908	54	75	7	1,219	85	17.92	1	221	7	31.57	42
Grimshaw, I	May 4, 1857	Jan 18, 1911	1880	1887	125	194	14	3,354	129*	18.63	4	8	0	—	76/3
Guy, S M	Nov 17, 1978		2000	2011	37	52	6	742	52	16.13	0				98/12
Haggas, S	Apr 18, 1856	Mar 14, 1926	1878	1882	31	47	3	478	43	10.86	0	—	—	—	10
Haigh, S	Mar 19, 1871	Feb 27, 1921	1895	1913	513	687	110	10,993	159	19.05	4	29,289	1,876	15.61	276
Hall, C H	Sept 16, 1929	Feb 27, 1989	1952	1952	1	2	0	14	10	7.00	0	55	1	55.00	1
Hall, L H	Apr 5, 1906	Dec 11, 1976	1928	1934	23	22	9	67	15*	5.15	0	1,226	45	27.24	11
§ Hall, L	Nov 11, 1815	Apr 17, 1888	1844	1863	1	2	0	4	4	2.00	0	—	—	—	2
Hall, L	©Nov 1, 1852	Nov 19, 1915	1873	1894	275	477	58	9,757	160	23.28	9	781	15	52.06	173

** At 15 years and 27 days on April 27, 2011, First Day of Yorkshire's match v. Durham MCCU, he became the youngest ever English First Class cricketer.

LIST OF PLAYERS AND CAREER AVERAGES IN ALL FIRST-CLASS MATCHES FOR YORKSHIRE (Continued)

Player	Date of Birth	Date of Death (if known)	First Played	Last Played	M	Inns	NO	Runs	HS	Av'ge	100s	Runs	Wkts	Av'ge	Ct/St
Halliday, H	© Feb 9, 1920	Aug 27, 1967	1938	1953	182	279	18	8,361	144	32.03	12	3,119	101	30.88	140
Halliley, C	Dec 5, 1852	Mar 23, 1929	1872	1872	3	5	0	27	17	5.40	0	—	—	—	2
Hamer, A	Dec 8, 1916	Nov 3, 1993	1938	1938	2	2	0	3	3	1.50	0	64	1	64.00	2
§ Hamilton, G M	Sept 16, 1974		1994	2003	73	108	18	2,228	125	24.75	1	5,479	222	24.68	25
Hampshire, A W	Oct 18, 1950		1975	1975	2	2	0	18	17	9.00	0	—	—	—	1
Hampshire, J	Oct 5, 1913	May 23, 1997	1937	1937	1	2	0	5	5	2.50	0	109	5	21.80	—
Hampshire, J H	© Feb 10, 1941		1961	1981	456	724	89	21,979	183*	34.61	34	1,108	24	46.16	368
Hannon-Dalby, O J	Jun 20, 1989		2008	2012	24	25	10	45	11*	3.00	0	1,938	43	45.06	2
§ Harbord, W E *	Dec 15, 1908	July 28, 1992	1929	1935	16	21	1	411	109	20.55	0	—	—	—	7
§ Harden, R J	Aug 16, 1965		1999	2000	12	22	3	439	69	23.10	0	—	—	—	2
Hardisty, C H	© Dec 10, 1885	Mar 2, 1968	1906	1909	38	55	5	991	84	19.82	0	—	—	—	18
Hargreaves, H S	Mar 22, 1913	Sept 29, 1990	1934	1938	18	20	6	51	9	3.64	0	1,145	55	20.81	3
§ Harmison, S J	Oct 23, 1978		2012	2012	3	3	0	25	23	8.33	0	195	8	24.37	1
Harris, W	Nov 21, 1861	May 23, 1923	1884	1887	4	8	2	45	25	7.50	0	18	0	—	—
Harrison, G P	© Feb 11, 1862	Sept 14, 1940	1883	1892	59	87	26	407	28	6.67	0	3,276	226	14.49	36
Harrison, H	Jan 26, 1885	Feb 11, 1962	1907	1907	2	6	1	12	4*	2.40	0	39	2	19.50	1
Harrison, W H	May 27, 1863	July 15, 1939	1888	1888	1	2	0	6	4	3.00	0	32	2	16.00	—
Hart, H W *	Sept 21, 1859	Nov 2, 1895	1888	1888	3	2	0	6	3	3.00	0	—	—	—	—
Hart, P R	Jan 12, 1947		1981	1981	1	5	0	23	11	4.60	0	140	2	70.00	2
Hartington, H E	Sept 18, 1881	Feb 16, 1950	1910	1911	10	10	4	51	16	8.50	0	764	23	33.21	60
Hartley, P J	© Apr 18, 1960		1985	1997	195	237	51	3,844	127*	20.66	2	17,438	579	30.11	47
Hartley, S N	© Mar 18, 1956		1978	1988	133	199	27	4,193	114	24.37	4	2,052	42	48.85	12
§ Harvey, I J	Apr 10, 1972		2004	2005	20	31	2	1,045	209*	36.03	2	831	37	22.45	—
Hatton, A	Mar 25, 1937		1960	1961	3	1	1	4	4*	—	0	202	6	33.66	3
§ Hawke, Lord *	© Aug 16, 1860	Oct 10, 1938	1881	1911	510	739	91	13,133	166	20.26	10	16	0	—	159
Hayley, H	Feb 22, 1860	June 3, 1922	1884	1898	7	12	1	122	24	11.09	0	48	0	—	3
Haywood, W J	Feb 25, 1841	Jan 7, 1912	1878	1878	1	2	0	7	7	3.50	0	14	1	14.00	—
Hicks, J	Dec 10, 1850	June 10, 1912	1872	1876	15	25	3	313	66	14.22	0	17	0	—	12
Higgins, J	Mar 13, 1877	July 19, 1954	1901	1905	9	14	5	93	28*	10.33	0	—	—	—	10/3
Hill, A	Nov 14, 1843	Aug 29, 1910	1871	1882	140	223	25	1,705	49	8.61	0	7,002	542	12.91	91
Hill, H *	Nov 29, 1858	Aug 14, 1935	1888	1891	14	27	2	337	34	13.48	0	—	—	—	10

Player	Date of Birth	Date of Death (if known)	First Played	Last Played	M	Inns	NO	Runs	HS	Av'ge	100s	Runs	Wkts	Av'ge	Ct/St
Hill, L G *	Nov 2, 1860	Aug 27, 1940	1882	1882	1	2	0	13	8	6.50	0	—	—	—	1
Hirst, E T *	May 6, 1857	Oct 26, 1914	1877	1888	21	33	2	328	87*	10.58	0	—	—	—	7
Hirst, E W *	Feb 27, 1855	Oct 24, 1933	1881	1881	2	3	0	33	28	11.00	0	3	0	—	0
Hirst, G H	©Sept 7, 1871	May 10, 1954	1891	1921*	717	1,050	128	32,024	341	34.73	56	44,716	2,481	18.02	518
Hirst, T H	May 21, 1865		1899	1899	1	1	1	5	5*		0	27	0	—	—
Hodd, A J	**Jan 12, 1984**		**2012**	**2014**	**18**	**20**	**3**	**452**	**68***	**26.58**	**0**	—	—	—	**53/2**
Hodgson D M	**Feb 26, 1990**		**2014**	**2014**	**1**	**1**	**0**	**18**	**18**	**18.00**	**0**	—	—	—	**1**
Hodgson, G	July 24, 1938		1964	1964	1	1	0	4	4	4.00	0	—	—	—	0/2
Hodgson, I	Nov 15, 1828	Nov 24, 1867	1855	1866	21	35	14	164	21*	7.80	0	1,537	88	17.46	11
Hodgson, L J	Jun 29, 1986		2009	2010	3	3	0	99	34	33.00	0	158	2	79.00	1
Hodgson, P	Sept 21, 1935		1954	1956	13	6	3	33	8*	8.25	0	648	22	29.45	6
Hoggard, M J	©Dec 31, 1976		1996	2009	102	120	34	956	89*	11.11	0	8,956	331	27.05	23
Holdsworth, W E N	Sept 17, 1928		1952	1953	27	26	12	111	22*	7.92	0	1,598	53	30.15	7
Holgate, G	June 23, 1839	July 11, 1895	1865	1867	12	19	0	174	38	9.15	0	—	—	—	17/1
Holmes, P	©Nov 25, 1886	Sept 3, 1971	1913	1933	485	699	74	26,220	315*	41.95	60	124	1	124.00	319
Horner, N F	May 10, 1926	Dec 24, 2003	1950	1950	2	4	1	114	43	28.50	0	—	—	—	2
Houseman I J	Oct 12, 1969		1989	1991	5	2	1	18	18	18.00	0	311	3	103.66	0/1
Hoyle, T H	Mar 19, 1884	June 2, 1953	1919	1919	1	2	1	7	5	3.50	0	—	—	—	0
Hudson, B	June 29, 1852	Nov 11, 1901	1880	1880	3	4	0	13	5	3.25	0	—	—	—	2
Hunter, D	©Feb 23, 1860	Jan 11, 1927	1888	1909	517	681	323	4,177	58*	11.66	0	43	0	—	863/323
Hunter, J	Aug 3, 1855	Jan 4, 1891	1878	1888	143	213	61	1,183	30	7.78	0	—	—	—	207/102
Hutchinson, P M	June 9, 1977		1996	2001	39	39	23	187	30	11.68	0	3,244	143	22.68	8
Hutton, L	©June 23, 1916	Sept, 6, 1990	1934	1955	341	527	62	24,807	280*	53.34	85	4,221	154	27.40	278
Hutton, R A	©Sept 6, 1942		1962	1974	208	292	45	4,986	189	20.18	4	10,254	468	21.91	160
Iddison, R	Sept 15, 1834	Mar 19, 1890	1855	1876	72	108	15	1,916	112	20.60	0	1,540	102	15.09	70
Illingworth, R	©June 8, 1932		1951	1983	496	668	131	14,986	162	27.90	14	26,806	1,431	18.73	286
§ Imran Tahir	Mar 27, 1979		2007	2007	1	1	0	5	5	2.50	0	141	0	—	0
Ingham, P G	Sept 28, 1956		1979	1981	8	14	0	290	64	20.71	0	—	—	—	0
Inglis, J W	Oct 19, 1979		2000	2000	1	2	0	4	2*	2.00	0	—	—	—	0
§ Inzamam-ul-Haq	Mar 1, 1970		2007	2007	3	4	0	89	51	22.25	0	—	—	—	5

LIST OF PLAYERS AND CAREER AVERAGES IN ALL FIRST-CLASS MATCHES FOR YORKSHIRE *(Continued)*

Player	Date of Birth	Date of Death (if known)	First Played	Last Played	M	Inns	NO	Runs	HS	Av'ge	100s	Runs	Wkts	Av'ge	Ct/St
Jackson, Hon F S * ...©	Nov 21, 1870	Mar 9, 1947	1890	1907	207	328	22	10,371	160	33.89	21	9,690	506	19.15	129
Jackson, S R * ...	July 15, 1859	July 19, 1941	1891	1891	1	2	0	9	9	4.50	0	—	—	—	0
Jacques, T A ...	Feb 19, 1905	Feb 23, 1995	1927	1936	28	20	7	162	35*	12.46	0	1,786	57	31.33	12
Jakeman, F ...	Jan 10, 1920	May 18, 1986	1946	1947	10	16	2	262	51	18.71	0	—	—	—	3
James, B ...	Apr 23, 1934		1954	1954	4	5	2	22	11*	11.00	0	228	8	28.50	1
§ Jaques, P A ...©	May 3, 1979		2004	2013	53	82	3	4,039	243	51.12	11	112	1	112.00	46
Jarvis, P W ...	June 29, 1965		1981	1993	138	160	46	1,898	80	16.64	0	11,990	449	26.70	36
Johnson, C ...	Sept 5, 1947		1969	1979	100	152	14	2,960	107	21.44	2	265	4	66.25	50
Johnson, J ...	May 16, 1916	Jan 16, 2011	1936	1939	3	3	2	5	4*	5.00	0	27	5	5.40	1
Johnson, M ...	Apr 23, 1958		1981	1981	4	4	2	2	2	1.00	0	301	7	43.00	1
Joy, J ...	Sept 29, 1826	Sept 27, 1889	1849	1867	3	5	0	107	74	21.40	0	5	0	—	3
Judson, A ...	July 10, 1885	Apr 8, 1975	1920	1920	1	—	—	—	—	—	—	5	0	—	0
§ Katich, S M ...	Aug 21, 1975		2002	2002	1	2	0	37	21	18.50	0	25	0	—	1
Kaye, Harold S * ...	May 9, 1882	Nov 6, 1953	1907	1908	18	25	1	243	37	10.12	0	—	—	—	9
Kaye, Haven ...	June 11, 1846	Jan 24, 1892	1872	1873	8	14	0	117	33	8.35	0	—	—	—	3
Keedy, G ...	Nov 27, 1974		1994	1994	1	1	0	1	1	1.00	0	—	—	—	0
§ Keighley, W G * ...©	Jan 10, 1925	June 14, 2005	1947	1951	35	51	5	1,227	110	26.67	1	18	0	—	12
Kellett, S A ...	Oct 16, 1967		1989	1995	86	147	10	4,204	125*	30.68	6	7	0	—	74
Kennie, G ...	May 17, 1904	Apr 11, 1994	1927	1927	1	2	0	6	6	3.00	0	—	—	—	0
Kettleborough, R A ...	Mar 15, 1973		1994	1997	13	19	2	446	80	26.23	0	153	3	51.00	9
Kilburn, J S ...	Oct 16, 1868	Sept 25, 1940	1896	1896	1	1	0	8	8	8.00	0	—	—	—	0
Kilner, N ...	July 21, 1895	Apr 28, 1979	1919	1923	69	73	7	1,253	112	18.98	2	8	0	—	34
Kilner, R ...©	Oct 17, 1890	Apr 5, 1928	1911	1927	365	478	46	13,018	206*	30.13	15	14,855	857	17.33	231
King, A M ...	Oct 8, 1932		1955	1955	1	1	0	12	12	12.00	0	—	—	—	0
Kippax, P J ...	Oct 15, 1940		1961	1962	4	7	2	37	9	7.40	0	279	8	34.87	0
§ Kirby, S P ...©	Oct 4, 1977		2001	2004	47	61	14	342	57	7.27	0	5,143	182	28.25	11
§ Kruis, G J ...©	May 9, 1974		2005	2009	54	64	31	617	50*	18.69	0	5,431	154	35.26	11
§ Lambert, G A ...	Jan 4, 1980		2000	2000	2	3	2	6	3*	6.00	0	133	4	33.25	0
Lancaster, W W ...	Feb 4, 1873	Dec 30, 1938	1895	1895	2	10	0	163	51	16.30	0	29	0	—	0
§ Landon, C W * ...	May 30, 1850	Mar 5, 1903	1878	1882	9	13	0	51	18	3.92	0	74	0	—	7

LIST OF PLAYERS AND CAREER AVERAGES IN ALL FIRST-CLASS MATCHES FOR YORKSHIRE (Continued)

Player	Date of Birth	Date of Death (if known)	First Played	Last Played	M	Inns	NO	Runs	HS	Av'ge	100s	Runs	Wkts	Av'ge	Ct/St
§ Law, W *	Apr 9, 1851	Dec 20, 1892	1871	1873	4	7	1	51	22	7.28	0	1,699	42	40.45	3
Lawson, M A K	Oct 24, 1985		2004	2007	15	21	5	197	44	12.31	0	5	1	5.00	7
Leadbeater, B ©	Aug 14, 1943		1966	1979	144	236	27	5,247	140*	25.10	1	5,657	201	28.14	80
Leadbeater, E	Aug 15, 1927	Apr 17, 2011	1949	1956	81	94	29	898	91	13.81	0	—	—	—	49
Leadbeater, H *	Dec 31, 1863	Oct 9, 1928	1884	1890	6	10	2	141	65	17.62	0	11	0	—	4
§ **Leaning, J A**	Oct 18, 1993		2013	2014	12	16	2	478	99	34.14	0	35	0	—	4
Leatham, G A B *	Apr 30, 1851	June 19, 1932	1874	1886	12	18	5	61	14	4.69	0	—	—	—	21/7
Leather, R S *	Aug 17, 1880	Jan 31, 1913	1906	1906	1	2	0	19	14	9.50	0	—	—	—	0
Lee, C	Mar 17, 1924	Sept 4, 1999	1952	1952	2	4	0	98	74	24.50	0	—	—	—	1
Lee, F ©	Nov 18, 1856	Sept 13, 1896	1882	1890	105	182	10	3,622	165	21.05	3	—	—	—	53/1
Lee, G H	Aug 24, 1854	Oct 4, 1919	1879	1879	1	2	0	13	12	6.50	0	—	—	—	0
Lee, Herbert	July 2, 1856	Feb 4, 1908	1885	1885	5	6	0	20	9	3.33	0	—	—	—	2
Lee, J E *	Mar 23, 1838	Apr 2, 1880	1867	1867	2	3	0	9	9	3.00	0	—	—	—	0
Lee, J E	Dec 23, 1988		2006	2009	2	3	1	24	21*	12.00	0	149	2	74.50	0
Lees, A Z ©	Apr 14, 1993		2010	2014	27	41	3	1,677	275*	44.13	5	14	0	—	12
Legard, A D *	June 19, 1878	Aug 15, 1939	1910	1910	4	5	0	50	15	10.00	0	26	2	13.00	0
§ Lehmann, D S ©	Feb 5, 1970		1997	2006	88	137	8	8,871	339	68.76	26	1,952	61	32.00	35
Lester, E I ©	Feb 18, 1923	Jan 1, 1967	1945	1956	228	339	27	10,616	186	34.02	24	160	3	53.33	106
Leyland, M ©	July 20, 1900	Jan 1, 1967	1920	1946	548	720	82	26,180	263	41.03	62	11,079	409	27.08	204
Lilley, A E	Apr 17, 1992		2011	2011	1	1	0	0	0	0.00	0	—	—	—	0
Linaker, L	Apr 8, 1885	Nov 17, 1961	1909	1909	7	11	1	36	10	3.60	0	—	—	—	0
Lister, B	Dec 9, 1850	Dec 3, 1919	1874	1878	2	2	1	13	7*	13.00	0	—	—	—	2
Lister-Kaye, K A *	Mar 27, 1892	Feb 28, 1955	1928	1928	2	4	0	35	16	8.75	0	64	1	64.00	2
Lister, J *	Jan 28, 1930	Jan 28, 1991	1954	1954	2	4	0	35	16	8.75	0	—	—	—	2
Lockwood, E	Apr 4, 1845	Dec 19, 1921	1868	1884	214	364	29	7,789	208	23.25	6	2,265	141	16.06	164/2
Lockwood, H	Oct 20, 1855	Feb 18, 1930	1877	1882	16	27	2	408	90	16.32	0	37	0	—	8
Lodge, J T	July 16, 1921	July 9, 2002	1948	1948	2	3	0	48	16	16.00	0	17	0	—	0
Love, J D ©	Apr 22, 1955		1975	1989	247	388	58	10,263	170*	31.10	13	835	12	69.58	123
Love, G E *	Jan 12, 1878	Aug 15, 1932	1902	1902	1	1	1	5	5*	—	0	—	—	—	1
Lowe, J R	Oct 19, 1991		2010	2010	1	1	0	5	5	5.00	0	—	—	—	0

LIST OF PLAYERS AND CAREER AVERAGES IN ALL FIRST-CLASS MATCHES FOR YORKSHIRE (Continued)

Player	Date of Birth	Date of Death (if known)	First Played	Last Played	M	Inns	NO	Runs	HS	Av'ge	100s	Runs	Wkts	Av'ge	Ct/St
Lowson, F A ... ◎	July 1, 1925	Sept 8, 1984	1949	1958	252	404	31	13,897	259*	37.25	30	15		—	180
§ Loxley-Firth, E *	Mar 7, 1886	Jan 8, 1949	1912	1912	2	4	0	43	37	10.75	0	84	8	10.50	1
§ Lucas, D S	Aug 19, 1978		2005	2005	1	—	—	—	—	—	—	—	—	—	1
Lumb, E * ... ◎	Sept 12, 1852	Apr 5, 1891	1872	1886	14	23	4	311	70*	16.36	0	—	—	—	5
§ Lumb, M J ... ◎	Feb 12, 1980		2000	2006	78	135	12	4,194	144	34.09	8	199	5	39.80	43
Lumb, R G ... ◎	Feb 27, 1950		1970	1984	239	395	30	11,525	165*	31.57	22	5	0	—	129
Lupton, A W * ... ◎	Feb 23, 1879	Apr 14, 1944	1908	1927	104	79	15	668	43*	10.43	0	88	0	—	25
Lynas, G G	Sept 7, 1832	Dec 8, 1896	1867	1867	2	3	1	4	4*	2.00	0	—	—	—	2
Lyth, A ... ◎	**Sept 25, 1987**		**2007**	**2014**	**94**	**150**	**7**	**6,198**	**251**	**43.34**	**14**	**612**	**12**	**51.00**	**117**
Macaulay, G G ... ◎	Dec 7, 1897	Dec 13, 1940	1920	1935	445	430	112	5,717	125*	17.97	3	30,554	1,774	17.22	361
McGrath, A ... ◎	Oct 6, 1975		1995	2012	242	405	29	14,091	211	37.47	34	4,652	128	36.34	168
McHugh, F P	Nov 15, 1925		1949	1949	3	1	0	2	2	2.00	0	147	4	36.75	—
Marshall, A	July 10, 1849		1874	1874	1	2	1	1	1	1.00	0	11	0	—	2
§ Martyn, D R	Oct 21, 1971		2003	2003	2	3	1	342	238	171.00	1	—	—	—	2
Mason, A	May 2, 1921	Mar, 2006.	1947	1950	18	19	3	105	22	6.56	0	1,473	51	28.88	6
Maude, E *	Dec 31, 1839	July 2, 1876	1866	1866	2	2	0	17	16	8.50	0	—	—	—	—
Metcalfe, A A ... ◎	Dec 25, 1963		1983	1995	184	317	19	10,465	216*	35.11	25	344	3	114.66	72
Micklethwait, W H *	Dec 13, 1885	Oct 7, 1947	1911	1911	1	1	0	44	44	44.00	0	—	—	—	—
Middlebrook, J D	May 13, 1977		1998	2001	23	31	3	485	84	17.32	0	1,458	49	29.75	14
Middlebrook, W	May 23, 1858	Apr 26, 1919	1888	1889	17	27	2	88	19*	4.40	0	895	50	17.90	17
Midgley, C A *	Nov 11, 1877	June 24, 1942	1906	1906	4	6	2	115	59*	28.75	0	149	8	18.62	3
Milburn, S M	Sept 29, 1972		1992	1995	6	8	2	22	7	3.66	0	431	14	30.78	4
Milligan, F W * ... ◎	Mar 19, 1870	Mar 31, 1900	1894	1898	81	113	10	1,879	74	18.24	0	2,736	112	24.42	40
Mitchell, A ... ◎	Sept 13, 1902	Dec 25, 1976	1922	1945	401	550	69	18,189	189	37.81	39	291	5	58.20	406
Mitchell, F * ... ◎	Aug 13, 1872	Oct 11, 1935	1894	1904	83	125	5	4,104	194	34.20	10	16	1	16.00	52
Monks, G D	Sept 3, 1929		1952	1952	1	1	0	3	3	3.00	0	—	—	—	1
Moorhouse, R ... ◎	Sept 7, 1866	Jan 7, 1921	1888	1899	206	315	45	5,217	113	19.32	3	1,232	43	28.65	92
§ Morkel, M	Oct 6, 1984		2008	2008	1	2	0	8	8	4.00	0	33	1	33.00	—
Morris, A C ... ◎	Oct 4, 1976		1995	1997	16	23	2	362	60	17.23	0	508	9	56.44	12
Mosley, H	Mar 8, 1852	Nov 29, 1933	1881	1881	2	4	0	1	1	0.25	0	34	3	11.33	1

LIST OF PLAYERS AND CAREER AVERAGES IN ALL FIRST-CLASS MATCHES FOR YORKSHIRE (Continued)

Player	Date of Birth	Date of Death (if known)	First Played	Last Played	M	Inns	NO	Runs	HS	Av'ge	100s	Runs	Wkts	Av'ge	Ct/St
Motley, A *	Feb 5, 1858	Sept 28, 1897	1879	1879	2	2		10	8*	10.00	0	135	7	19.28	1
Mounsey, J T	Aug 30, 1871	Apr 6, 1949	1891	1897	92	145	21	1,939	64	15.63	0	444	10	44.40	45
Moxon, M D ...©©	May 4, 1960		1981	1997	277	476	42	18,973	274*	43.71	41	1,213	22	55.13	190
Myers, H ...©	Jan 2, 1875	June 12, 1944	1901	1910	201	289	46	4,450	91	18.31	0	7,095	282	25.15	106
Myers, M	Apr 12, 1847	Dec 8, 1919	1876	1878	22	40	4	537	49	14.91	0	20	0		11
§ Naved-ul-Hasan, Rana	Feb 28, 1978		2008	2009	11	16	3	207	32	15.92	0	1,018	26	39.15	3
Naylor, J E	Dec 11, 1930	June 26, 1996	1953	1953	1							88	0		1
Newstead, J T ...©©	Sept 8, 1877	Mar 25, 1952	1903	1913	96	128	17	1,791	100*	16.13	1	5,555	297	18.70	75
Nicholson, A G ...©©	June 25, 1938	Nov 3, 1985	1962	1975	282	267	125	1,667	50	11.73	0	17,296	876	19.74	85
Nicholson, N G	Oct 17, 1963		1988	1989	5	8	3	134	56*	26.80	0	25	0		5
Oates, William	Jan 1, 1852	Dec 9, 1940	1874	1875	7	13	7	34	14*	5.66	0				5/1
Oates, W F	June 11, 1929	May 15, 2001	1956	1956	3	3	0	20	9	6.66	0				
Old, C M ...©	Dec 22, 1948		1966	1982	222	262	56	4,785	116	23.22	5	13,409	647	20.72	131
Oldham, S ...©	July 26, 1948		1974	1985	59	39	18	212	50	10.09	0	3,849	130	29.60	18
Oldroyd, E ...©	Oct 1, 1888	Dec 29, 1964	1910	1931	383	509	58	15,891	194	35.23	37	1,658	42	39.47	203
Oyston, C	May 12, 1869	July 15, 1942	1900	1909	15	21	8	96	22	7.38	0	872	31	28.12	3
Padgett, D E V ...©	July 20, 1934		1951	1971	487	774	63	20,306	161*	28.55	29	208	6	34.66	250
Padgett, G H	Oct 9, 1931		1952	1952	6	9	4	56	32*	18.66	0	336	4	84.00	5
Padgett, J H	Nov 21, 1860	Aug 2, 1943	1882	1889	6	9	0	92	22	10.22	0				2
Parker, B	June 23, 1970		1992	1998	44	71	10	1,839	138*	30.14	2	3	0		19
§ Parkin, C H	Feb 18, 1886	June 15, 1943	1906	1906	1	1	0	0	0	0.00	0	25	2	12.50	0
Parratt, J	Mar 24, 1859	May 6, 1905	1888	1890	1	2	0	11	11	5.50	0	75	1	75.00	4
§ Parton, J W	Jan 31, 1863	Jan. 30, 1906	1889	1889	1	2	0	16	14	8.00	0	4	1	4.00	0
Patterson, S A ...©©...	Oct 3, 1983		2005	2014	89	97	30	990	53	14.77	0	6,510	231	28.18	14
Pearson, H E	Aug 7, 1851	July 8, 1903	1878	1880	4	5	0	31	10*	15.50	0	90	5	18.00	0
Pearson, J H	May 14, 1915	May 13, 2007	1934	1936	3	3	0	54	44	18.00	0				0
Peate, E ...©	Mar 2, 1855	Mar 11, 1900	1879	1887	154	226	61	1,793	95	10.86	0	9,986	794	12.57	97
Peel, R ...©	Feb 12, 1857	Aug 12, 1941	1882	1897	318	510	42	9,322	210*	19.91	6	20,638	1,311	15.74	141
Penny, J H	Sept 29, 1856	July 29, 1902	1891	1891	1	1	1	8	8*		0	31	2	15.50	1
Pickles, C S	Jan 30, 1966		1985	1992	58	76	21	1,336	66	24.29	0	3,638	83	43.83	24

LIST OF PLAYERS AND CAREER AVERAGES IN ALL FIRST-CLASS MATCHES FOR YORKSHIRE (Continued)

Player	Date of Birth	Date of Death (if known)	First Played	Last Played	M	Inns	NO	Runs	HS	Av'ge	100s	Runs	Wkts	Av'ge	Ct/St
Pickles D	Nov 16, 1935		1957	1960	41	40	20	74	12	3.70	0	2,062	96	21.47	10
Pinder, G	July 15, 1841	Jan 15, 1903	1867	1880	125	199	44	1,639	57	10.57	0	325	19	17.10	145/102
Platt, R K	© Dec 26, 1932		1955	1963	96	103	47	405	57*	7.23	0	6,389	282	22.65	35
Plunkett, L E ©	Apr 6, 1985		2013	2014	21	27	4	604	86	26.26	0	1,728	68	25.41	13
Pollard, D	Aug 7, 1835	Mar 26, 1909	1865	1865	2	2	0	3	3	1.50	0	19	0	—	1
Pollitt, G	June 3, 1874	Not known	1899	1899	1	1	0	3	3	3.00	0	—	—	—	1
Prest, C H *	Dec 9, 1841	Mar 4, 1875	1864	1864	2	1	0	51	51	51.00	0	51	1	51.00	—
Preston, J M ©	Aug 23, 1864	Nov 26, 1890	1885	1889	79	134	11	1,935	93	15.73	0	3,232	178	18.15	36
Pride, T	July 23, 1864	Feb 16, 1919	1887	1887	1	2	1	57	57*	57.00	0	—	—	—	4/3
Priestley, I M	Sept 25, 1967		1989	1989	1	2	0	25	23	12.50	0	119	4	29.75	—
Pullan, P ©	Mar 29, 1857	Mar 3, 1901	1884	1884	2	4	2	28	14	14.00	0	5	—	—	1
Pyrah, R M ©	Nov 1, 1982		2004	2014	48	57	8	1,417	134*	28.91	3	2,454	55	44.61	22
§ Radcliffe, E J R H * ©	Jan 27, 1884	Nov 23, 1969	1909	1911	64	89	13	826	54	10.86	0	134	2	67.00	21
Ramage, A	Nov 29, 1957		1979	1983	23	22	9	219	52	16.84	0	1,649	44	37.47	1
Ramsden, G	Mar 2, 1983		2000	2000	1	1	1	0	0*	—	0	68	1	68.00	0
Randhawa, G S	Jan 25, 1992		2011	2011	1	1	0	5	5	5.00	0	62	2	31.00	0
Raper, J R S *	Aug 9, 1909	Mar 9, 1997	1936	1947	3	4	0	24	15	6.00	0	62	2	31.00	0
Rashid, A U © *	Feb 17, 1988		2006	2014	115	159	30	4,627	180	35.86	9	11,617	343	33.86	59
Rawlin, E R	Oct 4, 1897	Jan 11, 1943	1927	1936	8	10	1	72	35	8.00	0	498	21	23.71	2
Rawlin, J T	Nov 10, 1856	Jan 19, 1916	1880	1885	27	36	2	274	31	8.05	0	258	11	23.45	13
Rawlinson, E B	Apr 10, 1837	Feb 17, 1892	1867	1875	37	68	5	991	55	15.73	0	62	5	12.40	16
Redfearn, J	May 13, 1862	Jan 14, 1931	1890	1890	1	1	0	5	5	5.00	0	—	—	—	0
Render, G W A	Jan 5, 1887	Sept 17, 1922	1919	1919	1	1	0	5	5	5.00	0	—	—	—	0
Rhodes, A C ©	Oct 14, 1906	May 21, 1957	1932	1934	61	70	19	917	64*	17.98	0	3,026	107	28.28	45
§ Rhodes, H E *	Jan 11, 1852	Sept 10, 1889	1878	1883	10	16	1	269	64	17.93	0	—	—	—	1
Rhodes, S J	June 17, 1964		1981	1984	3	2	1	41	35	41.00	0	—	—	—	—
§ Rhodes, Wilfred ©	Oct 29, 1877	July 8, 1973	1898	1930	883	1,195	162	31,075	267*	30.08	46	57,634	3,598	16.01	586
Rhodes, William	Mar 4, 1883	Aug 5, 1941	1911	1911	1	1	1	1	1*	—	0	40	—	—	0
Richardson, J A *	Aug 4, 1908	Apr 2, 1985	1936	1947	7	12	2	308	61	30.80	0	—	—	—	0
§ Richardson, R B	Jan 12, 1962		1993	1994	23	39	1	1,310	112	34.47	1	90	2	45.00	18
§ Richardson, S A	Sept 5, 1977		2000	2003	13	23	2	377	69	17.95	0	23	1	23.00	11

LIST OF PLAYERS AND CAREER AVERAGES IN ALL FIRST-CLASS MATCHES FOR YORKSHIRE (Continued)

Player	Date of Birth	Date of Death (if known)	First Played	Last Played	M	Inns	NO	Runs	HS	Av'ge	100s	Runs	Wkts	Av'ge	Ct/St
Riley, H	Aug 17, 1875	Nov 6, 1922	1895	1900	4	5	1	36	25*	9.00	0	54	1	54.00	1
Riley, M *	Apr 5, 1851	June 1, 1899	1878	1882	17	28	1	361	92	13.37	0	10	0	—	3
Ringrose, W	Sept 2, 1871	Sept 14, 1943	1901	1906	57	66	9	353	23	6.19	0	3,224	155	20.80	25
Robinson, A L	© Aug 17, 1946		1971	1977	84	69	31	365	30*	9.60	0	4,927	196	25.13	48
Robinson, Edward *	Dec 27, 1862	Sept 3, 1942	1887	1887	1	2	1	23	23*	23.00	0	—	—	—	0
Robinson, Emmott	© Nov 16, 1883	Nov 17, 1969	1919	1931	413	455	77	9,651	135*	25.53	7	19,645	893	21.99	318
Robinson, E P	© Aug 10, 1911	Nov 10, 1998	1934	1949	208	253	46	2,596	75*	12.54	0	15,141	735	20.60	189
Robinson, H	May 12, 1858	Dec 14, 1909	1879	1879	1	2	0	5	4	2.50	0	20	1	20.00	0
Robinson, M A	© Nov 23, 1966		1991	1995	90	93	36	240	23	4.21	0	6,866	218	31.49	17
Robinson, P E	© Aug 3, 1963		1984	1991	132	217	31	6,668	189	35.84	7	238	1	238.00	96
Robinson, W	Nov 29, 1851	Aug 14, 1919	1876	1877	7	14	1	151	68	11.61	0	—	—	—	3
Roebuck C G	© Aug 14, 1851		1877	1877	1	1	0	23	23	23.00	0	—	—	—	0
Root, J E	© Dec 30, 1990		2010	2014	38	63	7	2,463	236	43.98	5	530	9	58.88	19
Roper, E *	Apr 8, 1851	Apr 27, 1921	1878	1880	5	7	1	85	68	14.16	0	—	—	—	3
Rothery, J W	© Sept 5, 1877	June 2, 1919	1903	1910	150	236	18	4,614	161	21.16	3	44	2	22.00	45
Rowbotham, J	July 8, 1831	Dec 22, 1899	1861	1876	94	162	9	2,624	113	17.15	3	37	3	12.33	52
§ Rudolph J A	May 4, 1981		2007	2011	68	112	8	5,429	228*	52.20	18	311	1	311.00	79
Rudston, H	Nov 22, 1879	April 14, 1962	1902	1907	21	30	0	609	164	20.30	1	—	—	—	3
Ryan, M	June 23, 1933		1954	1965	150	149	58	682	26*	7.49	0	9,466	413	22.92	59
Ryder, L	Aug 28, 1899	Jan 24, 1955	1924	1924	2	2	1	1	1	1.00	0	151	4	37.75	2
Sanderson B W	Jan 3, 1989		2008	2010	3	2	1	6	6	6.00	0	190	6	31.66	0
Savile, G *	Apr 26, 1847	Sept 4, 1904	1867	1874	5	7	0	140	65	20.00	0	—	—	—	2
Sayers, J J	© Nov 5, 1983		2004	2011	91	161	13	4,855	187	32.80	9	166	6	27.66	45
Schofield, C J	Mar 21, 1976		1996	1996	1	1	0	25	25	25.00	0	—	—	—	0
Schofield, D	Oct 9, 1947		1970	1974	3	2	0	16	8	8.00	0	112	5	22.40	1
Scott, E	July 6, 1834	Dec 3, 1898	1864	1864	1	2	1	6	6*	6.00	0	—	—	—	0
Sedgwick, H A	Apr 8, 1883	Dec 28, 1957	1906	1906	2	3	0	53	34	17.66	0	27	2	13.50	0
Sellers, Arthur *	© May 31, 1870	Sept 25, 1941	1890	1899	49	88	1	1,643	105	18.88	1	84	2	42.00	40
Sellers, A B *	© Mar 5, 1907	Feb 20, 1981	1932	1948	334	437	51	8,949	204	23.18	4	653	8	81.62	264
Shackleton, W A	Mar 9, 1908	Nov 16, 1971	1928	1934	5	6	0	49	25	8.16	0	130	6	21.66	3

LIST OF PLAYERS AND CAREER AVERAGES IN ALL FIRST-CLASS MATCHES FOR YORKSHIRE (Continued)

Player	Date of Birth	Date of Death (if known)	First Played	Last Played	M	Inns	NO	Runs	HS	Av'ge	100s	Runs	Wkts	Av'ge	Ct/St
Shahzad, Ajmal ©	July 27, 1985		2006	2012	45	58	14	1,145	88	26.02	0	4,196	125	33.56	5
Sharp, K ©	Apr. 6, 1959		1976	1990	195	320	35	8,426	181	29.56	11	836	12	69.66	95
§ Sharpe, C M *	Sept 6, 1851	June 25, 1935	1875	1875	1	1	0	15	15	15.00	0	17	0	—	0
Sharpe, P J ©	Dec 27, 1936	May 19, 2014	1958	1974	411	666	71	17,685	203*	29.72	23	140	2	70.00	526
Shaw C	Feb 17, 1964		1984	1988	61	58	27	340	31	10.96	0	4,101	123	33.34	9
Shaw, J	Mar 12, 1865	Jan 22, 1921	1896	1897	3	3	0	8	7	2.66	0	181	7	25.85	2
Sheepshanks, E R *	Mar 22, 1910	Dec 31, 1937	1929	1929	1	1	0	26	26	26.00	0				0
Shepherd, D A *	Mar 10, 1916	May 29, 1998	1938	1938	1	1	0	0	0	0.00	0				0
Shotton, W	Dec 1, 1840	May 26, 1909	1865	1874	2	4	0	13	7	3.25	0				0
Sidebottom, A ©	Apr 1, 1954		1973	1991	216	249	50	4,243	124	21.32	1	13,852	558	24.82	60
Sidebottom, R J	**Jan 15, 1978**		**1997**	**2014**	**109**	**137**	**33**	**1,444**	**61**	**13.88**	**0**	**8,175**	**351**	**23.29**	**31**
Sidgwick, R *	Aug 7, 1851	1934	1882	1882	7	13	0	64	17	4.92	0				7
Silverwood, C E W * ©	Mar 5, 1975		1993	2005	131	179	33	2,369	80	16.22	0	11,413	427	26.73	30
Silvester, S	Mar 12, 1951		1976	1977	6	5	2	30	14	10.00	0	313	12	26.08	2
Simpson, E T B *	Mar 5, 1867	Mar 20, 1944	1889	1889	1	2	0	1	1	0.50	0				0
§ Sims, Rev H M *	Mar 15, 1853	Oct 5, 1885	1875	1877	5	10	1	109	35*	12.11	0				5
Slinn, W	Dec 13, 1826	June 19, 1888	1861	1864	9	14	3	22	11	2.00	0	742	48	15.45	2
Smailes, T F ©	Mar 27, 1910	Dec 1, 1970	1932	1948	262	339	42	5,686	117	19.14	3	16,593	802	20.68	153
Smales, K	Sept 15, 1927		1948	1950	13	19	3	165	45	10.31	0	766	22	34.81	4
Smith, A F	Mar 7, 1847	Jan 6, 1915	1868	1874	28	49	4	692	89	15.37	0				11
Smith, E (Barnsley)	July 11, 1888	Jan 2, 1972	1914	1926	16	21	5	169	49	10.56	0	1,090	46	23.69	5
Smith, Ernest (Morley)*	© Oct 19, 1869	Feb 9, 1945	1888	1907	154	234	18	4,453	129	20.61	2	6,278	248	25.31	112
Smith, Fred (Idle)	Dec 26, 1885	Not known	1911	1911	1	1	0	11	11	11.00	0				3
Smith, Fred (Yeadon)	Dec 18, 1879	Oct 20, 1905	1903	1906	13	19	1	292	55	16.22	0				3
Smith, G	Jan 13, 1876	Jan 16, 1929	1901	1906	2	2	1	7	7	7.00	0				0
Smith, J	Mar 23, 1833	Feb 12, 1909	1865	1865	2	3	0	28	16	9.33	0				3
Smith, N	Apr 1, 1949	Mar 4, 2003	1970	1971	8	11	5	82	20	13.66	0	45	0	—	14/3
Smith, R	Apr 6, 1944		1969	1970	5	8	3	99	37*	19.80	0	72	6	12.00	8
Smith, Walker	Aug 14, 1847	July 7, 1900	1874	1874	8	9	0	152	59	16.88	0				8
§ Smith, William	Nov 1, 1839	Apr 19, 1897	1865	1874	11	19	3	260	90	16.25	0				3
Smithson, G A ©	Nov 1, 1926	Sept 6, 1970	1946	1950	39	60	5	1,449	169	26.34	2	84	1	84.00	21

LIST OF PLAYERS AND CAREER AVERAGES IN ALL FIRST-CLASS MATCHES FOR YORKSHIRE (Continued)

Player	Date of Birth	Date of Death (if known)	First Played	Last Played	M	Inns	NO	Runs	HS	Av'ge	100s	Runs	Wkts	Av'ge	Ct/St
Smurthwaite, J	Oct 17, 1916	Oct 20, 1989	1938	1939	7	9	5	29	20*	7.25	0	237	12	19.75	4
Sowden, A	Dec 1, 1853	July 5, 1921	1878	1887	8	11	0	137	37	12.45	0	22	0	—	1
Squire, D	Dec 31, 1864	Apr 28, 1922	1893	1893	1	2	0	0	0	0.00	0	25	0	—	0
Squires, P J	Aug 4, 1951		1972	1976	49	84	8	1,271	70	16.72	0	32	0	—	14
Stanley, H C *	Feb 16, 1888	May 18, 1934	1911	1913	8	13	0	155	42	11.92	0				6
§ Stanyforth, R T *	May 30, 1892	Feb 20, 1964	1928	1928	3	3	1	26	10	8.66	0				2
§ Starc, M A	Jan 13, 1990		2012	2012	2	1	—	28	28*	—	0	153	7	21.85	6
Stead, B	June 21, 1939	Apr 15, 1980	1959	1959	2	3	0	28	8	2.66	0	115	7	16.42	0
§ Stemp, R D	Dec 11, 1967		1993	1998	104	135	36	1,267	65	12.79	0	8,557	241	35.50	49
Stephenson, E	June 5, 1832	July 5, 1898	1861	1873	36	61	5	803	67	14.33	0		0	—	30/27
Stephenson, J S *	Nov 10, 1903	Oct 7, 1975	1923	1926	16	19	2	182	60	10.70	0	65	0	—	6
© Stevenson, G B	Dec 16, 1955		1973	1986	177	217	32	3,856	115*	20.84	2	13,254	464	28.56	73
© Stott, W B	July 18, 1934		1952	1963	187	309	19	9,168	186	31.61	17	112	2	16.00	91
Stringer, P M	Feb 23, 1943		1967	1969	19	17	8	101	15*	11.22	0	696	32	21.75	7
Stuchbury, S	June 22, 1954		1978	1981	3	3	2	7	4*	7.00	0	236	8	29.50	0
§ Sugg, F H	Jan 11, 1862	May 29, 1933	1883	1883	8	12	4	80	13*	10.00	0				4/1
§ Sugg, W	May 21, 1860	May 21, 1933	1881	1881	1	1	0	9	9	9.00	0				0
§ Sullivan, J H B *	Sept 21, 1890	Feb 8, 1932	1912	1912	1	2	0	41	26	20.50	0	43	0	—	0
Sutcliffe, H	© Nov 24, 1894	Jan 22, 1978	1919	1945	602	864	96	38,558	313	50.20	112	381	8	47.62	402
§ Sutcliffe, W H H *	Oct 10, 1926	Sept 16, 1998	1948	1957	177	273	34	6,247	181	26.13	6	152	6	25.33	80
§ Swallow, I G	Dec 18, 1962		1983	1989	61	82	18	1,296	114	20.25	1	3,270	64	51.09	28
§ Swanepoel, P J	Mar 30, 1977		2003	2003	2	3	0	20	17	6.66	0	129	3	43.00	1
§ Tait, T	Oct 7, 1872	Sept 6, 1954	1898	1899	2	3	1	7	3	3.50	0				1
§ Tasker, J *	Feb 4, 1887	Aug 24, 1975	1912	1913	31	43	4	586	67	15.02	0				14
Tattersall, G *	Apr 21, 1882	June 29, 1917	1905	1905	1	2	0	26	26	13.00	0				0
Taylor, C R	Feb 21, 1981		2001	2005	16	27	3	416	52*	17.33	0				8
Taylor, H	Dec 18, 1900	Oct 28, 1987	1924	1925	9	13	0	153	36	11.76	0				1
Taylor, H S	Dec 11, 1856	Nov 16, 1896	1879	1879	3	5	0	36	22	7.20	0				0
Taylor, J	Apr 2, 1850	May 27, 1924	1880	1881	9	13	1	107	44	8.91	0				4
© Taylor, K	Aug 21, 1935		1953	1968	303	505	35	12,864	203*	27.37	16	3,680	129	28.52	146

LIST OF PLAYERS AND CAREER AVERAGES IN ALL FIRST-CLASS MATCHES FOR YORKSHIRE (Continued)

Player	Date of Birth	Date of Death (if known)	First Played	Last Played	M	Inns	NO	Runs	HS	Av'ge	100s	Runs	Wkts	Av'ge	Ct/St
Taylor, N S	June 2, 1963		1982	1983	8	6	1	10	4	2.00	0	720	22	32.72	2
Taylor, T L *	©May 25, 1878	Mar. 16, 1960	1899	1906	82	122	10	3,933	156	35.11	8	—	—	—	47/2
§ Tendulkar, S R	Apr 24, 1973		1992	1992	16	25	2	1,070	100	46.52	1	195	4	48.75	2
10thewlis, H	Aug 31, 1865	Nov 30, 1920	1888	1888	2	4	1	4	2*	1.33	0	—	—	—	2
Thewlis, John Jun.	Sept 21, 1850	Aug 9, 1901	1879	1879	3	4	0	21	10	5.25	0	—	—	—	0
Thewlis, John Sen.	Mar 11, 1828	Dec 29, 1899	1861	1875	44	80	3	1,280	108	16.62	1	—	—	—	21/1
Thornicroft, N D	Jan 23, 1985		2002	2007	7	10	4	50	30	8.33	0	545	16	34.06	2
Thornton, A	July 20, 1854	Apr 18, 1915	1881	1881	3	4	0	21	7	5.25	0	—	—	—	2
Thornton, G *	Dec 24, 1867	Jan 31, 1939	1891	1891	3	4	0	21	16	5.25	0	74	2	37.00	2
Thorpe, G.	Feb 20, 1834	Mar 2, 1899	1864	1864	1	2	1	14	9*	14.00	0	—	—	—	2
Threapleton, J W	July 20, 1857	July 30, 1918	1881	1881	1	2	1	8	8*	—	0	—	—	—	2/1
Tinsley, H J	Feb 20, 1865	Dec 10, 1938	1890	1891	9	13	0	56	15	4.30	0	57	4	14.25	1
Townsley, R A J	June 24, 1952		1974	1975	2	4	0	22	12	5.50	0	0	0	—	1
Towse, A D	Apr 22, 1968		1988	1988	1	1	0	1	1	1.00	0	50	3	16.66	—
Trueman, F S	©Feb 6, 1931	July 1, 2006	1949	1968	459	533	81	6,852	104	15.15	0	29,890	1,745	17.12	325
Tunnicliffe, J	©Aug 26, 1866	July 11, 1948	1891	1907	472	768	57	19,435	243	27.33	22	388	7	55.42	665
Turner, A	Sept 2, 1885	Aug 29, 1951	1910	1911	9	16	1	163	37	10.86	0	—	—	—	7
Turner, B	July 25, 1938		1960	1961	2	4	2	7	3*	3.50	0	47	4	11.75	4
Turner, C	©Jan 11, 1902	Nov 19, 1968	1925	1946	200	266	32	6,132	130	26.20	2	5,320	173	30.75	181
Turner, F I	Sept 3, 1894	Oct 18, 1954	1924	1924	5	7	3	33	12	4.71	0	—	—	—	2
Tyson, C T	Jan 24, 1889	Apr 3, 1940	1921	1921	5	5	2	232	100*	77.33	1	—	—	—	—
Ullathorne, C E	Apr 11, 1845	May 2, 1904	1868	1875	27	46	8	283	28	7.44	0	—	—	—	19
Ulyett, G	©Oct 21, 1851	June 18, 1898	1873	1893	355	618	31	14,157	199*	24.11	15	8,181	457	17.90	235
§ Usher, J	Feb 26, 1859	Aug 9, 1905	1888	1888	1	2	1	7	5	3.50	0	31	2	15.50	1
van Geloven, J	Jan 4, 1934	Aug 21, 2003	1955	1955	3	2	1	17	16	17.00	0	224	6	37.33	—
§ Vaughan, M P	Oct 29, 1974		1993	2009	151	267	14	9,160	183	36.20	20	4,268	92	46.39	55
§ Verelst, H W *	July 2, 1846	Apr 5, 1918	1868	1869	3	4	1	66	33*	22.00	0	—	—	—	2
Verity, H	©May 18, 1905	July 31, 1943	1930	1939	278	294	77	3,898	101	17.96	1	21,353	1,558	13.70	191
Waddington, A	©Feb 4, 1893	Oct 28, 1959	1919	1927	255	250	65	2,396	114	12.95	1	16,203	835	19.40	222

LIST OF PLAYERS AND CAREER AVERAGES IN ALL FIRST-CLASS MATCHES FOR YORKSHIRE (Continued)

Player	Date of Birth	Date of Death (if known)	First Played	Last Played	M	Inns	NO	Runs	HS	Av'ge	100s	Runs	Wkts	Av'ge	Ct/St
© Wade, S	Feb 8, 1858	Nov 5, 1931	1886	1890	65	111	20	1,438	74*	15.80	0	2,498	133	18.78	31
Wainwright, D J	Mar 21, 1985		2004	2011	29	36	11	914	104*	36.56	2	2,480	69	35.94	6
© Wainwright, E	Apr 8, 1865	Oct 28, 1919	1888	1902	352	545	30	11,092	228	21.53	18	17,744	998	17.77	327
Wainwright, W	Jan 21, 1882	Dec 31, 1961	1903	1905	24	36	3	648	62	19.63	0	582	19	30.63	21
Wake, W R *	May 21, 1852	Mar 14, 1896	1881	1881	3	3	0	13	11	4.33	0	—	—	—	2
Walker, A *	June 22, 1844	May 26, 1927	1863	1870	9	16	1	138	26	9.20	0	74	1	74.00	2
Walker, C	June 26, 1919	Dec 3, 1992	1947	1948	5	9	2	268	91	38.28	0	71	2	35.50	1
Walker, T	Apr 3, 1854	Aug 28, 1925	1879	1880	14	22	2	179	30	8.95	0	7	—	—	3
Wallgate, L *	Dec 3, 1864	Dec 11, 1937	1893	1894	3	4	0	17	13	4.25	0	70	4	17.50	1
Ward, A	Nov 12, 1849	May 9, 1887	1875	1878	3	3	0	9	6	3.00	0	17	1	17.00	3
Ward, A	Nov 21, 1865	Jan 6, 1939	1886	1886	4	7	1	41	22	6.83	0	16	0	—	1
© Ward, H P *	Aug 31, 1881	Feb 28, 1948	1903	1903	1	1	0	0	0	0.00	0	—	—	—	—
© Wardall, T A	Apr 19, 1862	Dec 16, 1946	1884	1894	43	73	2	1,003	106	14.12	2	489	23	21.26	25
Wardlaw, I	June 29, 1985		2011	2012	4	3	2	31	17*	31.00	0	368	4	92.00	2
© Wardle, J H	Jan 8, 1923	July 23, 1985	1946	1966	330	418	57	5,765	79	15.96	0	27,917	1,539	18.13	210
Waring, J S	Oct 1, 1942		1963	1966	28	27	15	137	26	11.41	0	1,122	53	21.16	17
Waring, S	Nov 4, 1838	Apr 17, 1919	1870	1870	1	1	0	9	9	9.00	0	—	—	—	—
© Washington, W A I	Dec 11, 1879	Oct 20, 1927	1900	1902	44	62	6	1,290	100*	23.03	1	—	—	—	18
Watson, H	Sept 26, 1880	Nov 24, 1951	1908	1914	29	35	11	141	41	5.87	0	75	0	—	46/10
Watson, W	Mar 7, 1920	Apr 24, 2004	1939	1957	283	430	65	13,953	214*	38.22	26	—	—	—	170
Waud, B W *	June 4, 1837	May 31, 1889	1862	1864	6	10	1	165	42	18.33	0	—	—	—	2
Webster, C	June 9, 1838	Jan 6, 1881	1861	1868	3	5	1	30	10	7.50	0	—	—	—	—
Webster, H H	May 8, 1844		1868	1868	2	3	0	10	10	3.33	0	—	—	—	1
§ Weekes, L C	July 19, 1971		1994	2000	2	3	1	20	10	10.00	0	—	—	—	1
West, J	Oct 16, 1844	Jan 27, 1890	1868	1876	38	64	13	461	41	9.03	0	191	10	19.10	—
Wharf, A G	June 4, 1975		1994	1997	7	9	1	186	62	23.25	0	853	53	16.09	14
Whatmough, F J	Dec 4, 1856	June 3, 1904	1878	1882	7	11	1	51	20	5.10	0	454	11	41.27	2
Wheater, C H *	Mar 4, 1860	May 11, 1885	1880	1880	2	4	1	45	27	15.00	0	111	5	22.20	4
© White, Sir A W *	Oct 14, 1877	Dec 16, 1945	1908	1920	97	128	28	1,457	55	14.57	0	7	0	—	50

LIST OF PLAYERS AND CAREER AVERAGES IN ALL FIRST-CLASS MATCHES FOR YORKSHIRE (Continued)

Player	Date of Birth	Date of Death (if known)	First Played	Last Played	M	Inns	NO	Runs	HS	Av'ge	100s	Runs	Wkts	Av'ge	Ct/St
White, C ...Ⓒ	Dec 16, 1969		1990	2007	221	350	45	10,376	186	34.01	19	7,649	276	27.71	140
Whitehead, J P	Sept 3, 1925	Aug 15, 2000	1946	1951	37	38	17	387	58*	18.42	0	2,610	96	27.47	11
Whitehead, Lees ...Ⓒ	Mar 14, 1864	Nov 22, 1913	1889	1904	119	172	38	2,073	67*	15.47	0	2,408	99	24.32	68
Whitehead, Luther	June 25, 1869	Jan 16, 1931	1893	1893	2	4	0	21	13	5.25	0	—	—	—	0
Whiteley, J P	Feb 28, 1955		1978	1982	45	38	17	231	20	11.00	0	2,410	70	34.42	21
Whiting, C P	Apr 18, 1888	Jan 14, 1959	1914	1920	6	10	2	92	26	11.50	0	416	15	27.73	2
Whitwell, J F *	Feb 22, 1869	Nov 6, 1932	1890	1890	1	2	0	8	4	4.00	0	11	1	11.00	2
§ Whitwell, W F *	Dec 12, 1867	Apr 12, 1942	1890	1890	10	14	2	67	26	5.58	0	518	25	20.72	2
Widdup, S	Nov 10, 1977		2000	2001	11	18	1	245	44	14.41	0	22	1	22.00	5
Wigley, D H	Oct 26, 1981		2002	2002	1	2	1	19	15	19.00	0	116	1	116.00	0
§ Wilkinson, A J A *	May 28, 1835	Dec 11, 1905	1865	1868	5	6	0	57	53	21.50	0	—	—	—	1
Wilkinson, F	May 23, 1914	Mar 26, 1984	1937	1939	14	14	1	73	18*	5.61	0	590	26	22.69	12
Wilkinson, H * ...Ⓒ	Dec 11, 1877	Apr 15, 1967	1903	1905	48	75	3	1,382	113	19.19	1	121	3	40.33	19
Wilkinson, R	Nov 11, 1977		1998	1998	1	1	0	9	9	9.00	0	35	1	35.00	0
Wilkinson, W H ...Ⓒ	Mar 12, 1881	June 4, 1961	1903	1910	126	192	14	3,812	103	21.41	0	971	31	31.32	93
Williams, A C	Mar 1, 1887	June 1, 1966	1911	1919	12	14	10	95	48*	23.75	0	678	30	22.60	6
§ Williamson, K S ...Ⓢ	Sept 8, 1990		2013	2014	14	22	3	1,032	189	54.31	1	407	9	45.22	14
Wilson, B B ...Ⓒ	Dec 11, 1879	Sept 14, 1957	1906	1914	185	308	12	8,053	208	27.50	15	278	2	139.00	53
Wilson, C E M * ...Ⓒ	May 15, 1875	Feb 8, 1944	1896	1899	8	13	3	256	91*	25.60	0	257	12	21.41	3
Wilson, D ...Ⓒ	Aug 7, 1937	July 21, 2012	1957	1974	392	502	85	5,788	83	13.88	0	22,626	1,104	20.49	235
Wilson, E R * ...Ⓒ	Mar 25, 1879	July 21, 1957	1899	1923	66	72	18	902	104*	16.70	0	3,106	197	15.76	30
Wilson, Geoffrey ...Ⓒ	Aug 21, 1895	Nov 29, 1960	1919	1924	92	94	14	983	70	12.28	0	11	—	—	33
Wilson, G A *	Feb 2, 1916	Sept 24, 2002	1936	1939	15	25	5	352	55*	17.60	0	138	1	138.00	7
Wilson, John *	June 30, 1857	Nov 11, 1931	1887	1888	4	5	1	17	13*	4.25	0	165	12	13.75	3
Wilson, J P *	Apr 3, 1889	Oct 3, 1959	1911	1912	9	14	1	81	36	6.23	0	24	1	24.00	2
Wilson, J V ...Ⓒ	Jan 17, 1921	June 5, 2008	1946	1962	477	724	75	20,548	230	31.66	29	313	3	104.33	520
Wood, A ...Ⓒ	Aug 25, 1898	Apr 1, 1973	1927	1946	408	481	80	8,579	123*	21.39	1	33	1	33.00	612/243
Wood, B	Dec 26, 1942		1964	1964	5	7	2	63	35	12.60	0	—	—	—	4

LIST OF PLAYERS AND CAREER AVERAGES IN ALL FIRST-CLASS MATCHES FOR YORKSHIRE (Continued)

Player	Date of Birth	Date of Death (if known)	First Played	Last Played	M	Inns	NO	Runs	HS	Av'ge	100s	Runs	Wkts	Av'ge	Ct/St
Wood, C H	July 26, 1934	June 26, 2006	1959	1959	4	4	1	22	10	7.33	0	319	11	29.00	1
Wood, G W	Nov 18, 1862	Dec 4, 1948	1895	1895	2	2	0	2	2	1.00	0	—	—	—	0/1
Wood, H *	Mar 22, 1855	July 31, 1941	1879	1880	10	16	1	156	36	10.40	0	212	10	21.20	8
Wood, J H *			1881	1881	2	1	0	14	14	14.00	0	—	—	—	0
Wood, M J ©	Apr 6, 1977		1997	2007	128	222	20	6,742	207	33.37	16	27	2	13.50	113
Wood, R	June 3, 1929	May 22, 1990	1952	1956	22	18	4	60	17	4.28	0	1,346	51	26.39	5
Woodford, J D	Sept 9, 1943		1968	1972	38	61	2	1,204	101	20.40	1	185	4	46.25	12
Woodhead, F E *	May 29, 1868	Aug 25, 1943	1893	1894	4	8	2	57	18	7.12	0	—	—	—	3
Woodhouse, W H *	Apr 16, 1856	Mar 4, 1938	1884	1885	9	13	0	218	63	16.76	0	—	—	—	6
Wormald, A	May 10, 1855	Feb 6, 1940	1885	1891	7	11	3	161	80	20.12	0	—	—	—	10/2
Worsley, W A * ©	Apr 5, 1890	Dec 4, 1973	1928	1929	60	50	4	722	60	15.69	0	—	—	—	32
Wrathmell, L F	Jan 22, 1855	Sept 16, 1928	1886	1886	1	2	0	18	9	9.00	0	—	—	—	0
Wright, R	July 19, 1852	May 25, 1891	1877	1877	2	4	1	28	22	9.33	0	—	—	—	0
Wright, T J *	Mar 5, 1900	Nov 7, 1962	1919	1919	1	1	0	12	12	12.00	0	—	—	—	0
Yardley, N W D * ©	Mar 19, 1915	Oct 4, 1989	1936	1955	302	420	56	11,632	183*	31.95	17	5,818	195	29.83	220
Yeadon, J	Dec 10, 1861	May 30, 1914	1888	1888	3	6	2	41	22	10.25	0	—	—	—	5/3
§ Younus Khan ©	Nov 29, 1977		2007	2007	13	19	2	824	217*	48.47	3	342	8	42.75	11
§ Yuvraj Singh	Dec 12, 1981		2003	2003	7	12	2	145	56	14.50	0	130	3	43.33	12

In the career averages it should be noted that the bowling analysis for the second Cambridgeshire innings at Ashton-under-Lyne in 1865 has not been found. G R Atkinson took 3 wickets, W Cuttell 2, G Freeman 4 and R Iddison 1. The respective bowling averages have been calculated excluding these wickets.

MOST FIRST-CLASS APPEARANCES FOR YORKSHIRE

Matches	Player	Matches	Player
883	W Rhodes (1898-1930)	477	J V Wilson (1946-1962)
717	G H Hirst (1891-1929)	472	J Tunnicliffe (1891-1907)
676	D Denton (1894-1920)	459	F S Trueman (1949-1968)
602	H Sutcliffe (1919-1945)	456	J H Hampshire (1961-1981)
548	M Leyland (1920-1947)	445	G G Macaulay (1920-1935)
536	D B Close (1949-1970)	429	D L Bairstow (1970-1990)
517	D Hunter (1888-1909)	427	A Dolphin (1905-1927)
513	S Haigh (1895-1913)	425	P Carrick (1970-1993)
510	Lord Hawke (1881-1911)	414	G Boycott (1962-1986)
496	R Illingworth (1951-1983)	413	E. Robinson (1919-1931)
491	† J G Binks (1955-1969)	411	P J Sharpe (1958-1974)
487	D E V Padgett (1951-1971)	408	A Wood (1927-1946)
485	P Holmes (1913-1933)	401	A Mitchell (1922-1945)

† Kept wicket in 412 consecutive Championship matches 1955-1969

MOST TOTAL APPEARANCES FOR YORKSHIRE
(First-Class, Domestic List A and t20)

Matches	Player	Matches	Player
883	W Rhodes (1898-1930)	513	S Haigh (1895-1913)
832	D L Bairstow (1970-1990)	510	Lord Hawke (1881-1911)
729	P Carrick (1970-1993)	502	P J Sharpe (1958-1974)
719	R J Blakey (1985-2004)	485	P Holmes (1913-1933)
717	G H Hirst (1891-1929)	477	J V Wilson (1946-1962)
690	J H Hampshire (1961-1981)	472	J Tunnicliffe (1891-1907)
678	G Boycott (1962-1986)	470	F S Trueman (1949-1968)
676	D Denton (1894-1920)	467	J D Love (1975-1989)
602	H Sutcliffe (1919-1945)	453	D Wilson (1957-1974)
583	A McGrath (1995-2012)	452	A Sidebottom (1973-1991)
581	D Byas (1986-2001)	445	G G Macaulay (1920-1935)
568	D B Close (1949-1970)	443	C M Old (1966-1982)
548	M Leyland (1920-1947)	427	A Dolphin (1905-1927)
546	C White (1990-2007)	414	P J Hartley (1985-1997)
544	D E V Padgett (1951-1971)	413	E Robinson (1919-1931)
537	R Illingworth (1951-1983)	408	A Wood (1927-1946)
521	J G Binks (1955-1969)	402	A G Nicholson (1962-1975)
517	D Hunter (1888-1909)	401	A Mitchell (1922-1945)
514	M D Moxon (1980-1997)		

Yorkshire County Cricket Club thanks Statistician JOHN T. POTTER, who in 2014 has revamped and streamlined Yorkshire's One-Day Records Section. John's symbols in the pages that follow are:

$ = Sunday and National Leagues, Pro 40, Clydesdale Bank 40 and Yorkshire Bank 40

= Benson & Hedges Cup

+ = Gillette Cup, NatWest Trophy, Cheltenham & Gloucester Trophy, Friends Provident Trophy and Royal London Cup

LIST A
WINNERS OF THE GILLETTE CUP, NATWEST TROPHY, CHELTENHAM & GLOUCESTER TROPHY FRIENDS PROVIDENT TROPHY AND ROYAL LONDON ONE-DAY CUP

GILLETTE CUP

Year	Winner	Yorkshire's Position
1963	Sussex	Quarter-Final
1964	Sussex	Round 2
1965	**Yorkshire**	**Winner**
1966	Warwickshire	Round 2
1967	Kent	Quarter-Final
1968	Warwickshire	Round 2
1969	**Yorkshire**	**Winner**
1970	Lancashire	Round 1
1971	Lancashire	Round 2
1972	Lancashire	Round 1
1973	Gloucestershire	Round 1
1974	Kent	Quarter-Final
1975	Lancashire	Round 2
1976	Northamptonshire	Round 1
1977	Middlesex	Round 2
1978	Sussex	Quarter-Final
1979	Somerset	Quarter-Final
1980	Middlesex	Semi-Final

NATWEST TROPHY

Year	Winner	Yorkshire's Position
1981	Derbyshire	Round 1
1982	Surrey	Semi-Final
1983	Somerset	Round 2
1984	Middlesex	Round 1
1985	Essex	Round 2
1986	Sussex	Quarter-Final
1987	Nottinghamshire	Quarter-Final
1988	Middlesex	Round 2
1989	Warwickshire	Round 2
1990	Lancashire	Quarter-Final
1991	Hampshire	Round 1
1992	Northamptonshire	Round 2
1993	Warwickshire	Quarter-Final
1994	Worcestershire	Round 2
1995	Warwickshire	Semi-Final
1996	Lancashire	Semi-Final
1997	Essex	Quarter-Final
1998	Lancashire	Round 2
1999	Gloucestershire	Semi-Final
2000	Gloucestershire	Round 4

CHELTENHAM & GLOUCESTER TROPHY

Year	Winner	Yorkshire's Position
2001	Somerset	Quarter-Final
2002	**Yorkshire**	**Winner**
2003	Gloucestershire	Round 4
2004	Gloucestershire	Semi-Final
2005	Hampshire	Semi-Final
2006	Sussex	North 7 (10)

FRIENDS PROVIDENT TROPHY

Year	Winner	Yorkshire's Position
2007	Durham	North 5 (10)
2008	Essex	Semi-Final
2009	Hampshire	Group C 3 (5)

ROYAL LONDON ONE-DAY CUP

Year	Winner	Yorkshire's Position
2104	Durham	Quarter-Final

WINNERS OF THE NATIONAL AND SUNDAY LEAGUES, PRO 40, CLYDESDALE BANK 40 AND YORKSHIRE BANK 40 1969-2014

		Yorkshire's Position			*Yorkshire's Position*
SUNDAY LEAGUE			1993	Glamorgan	9th
1969	Lancashire	8th	1994	Warwickshire	5th
1970	Lancashire	14th	1995	Kent	12th
1971	Worcestershire	15th	1996	Surrey	3rd
1972	Kent	4th	1997	Warwickshire	10th
1973	Kent	2nd	1998	Lancashire	9th
1974	Leicestershire	=6th	**NATIONAL LEAGUE**		
1975	Hampshire	=5th	1999	Lancashire	5th Div 1
1976	Kent	15th	2000	Gloucestershire	2nd Div 1
1977	Leicestershire	=13th	2001	Kent	6th Div 1
1978	Hampshire	7th	2002	Glamorgan	4th Div 1
1979	Somerset	=4th	2003	Surrey	8th Div 1
1980	Warwickshire	=14th	2004	Glamorgan	4th Div 2
1981	Essex	=7th	2005	Essex	8th Div 2
1982	Sussex	16th	2006	Essex	9th Div 2
1983	**Yorkshire**	**1st**	2007	Worcestershire	6th Div 2
1984	Essex	=14th	2008	Sussex	2nd Div 2
1985	Essex	6th	2009	Sussex	7th Div 1
1986	Hampshire	8th	**CLYDESDALE BANK 40**		
1987	Worcestershire	=13th	2010	Warwickshire	Group B 1 (7) (Semi-Final)
1988	Worcestershire	8th			
1989	Lancashire	11th	2011	Surrey	Group A 6 (7)
1990	Derbyshire	6th	2012	Hampshire	Group C 5 (7)
1991	Nottinghamshire	7th	2013	Nottinghamshire	Group C 6 (7)
1992	Middlesex	15th			

BENSON & HEDGES WINNERS 1972-2002

		Yorkshire's Position			*Yorkshire's Position*
1972	Leicestershire	Final	1988	Hampshire	Group B 4 (5)
1973	Kent	Group N 3 (5)	1989	Nottinghamshire	Group C 3 (5)
1974	Surrey	Quarter-Final	1990	Lancashire	Group C 3 (5)
1975	Leicestershire	Quarter-Final	1991	Worcestershire	Semi-Final
1976	Kent	Group D 3 (5)	1992	Hampshire	Group C 5 (5)
1977	Gloucestershire	Group D 3 (5)	1993	Derbyshire	Round One
1978	Kent	Group D 4 (5)	1994	Warwickshire	Round One
1979	Essex	Semi-Final	1995	Lancashire	Quarter-Final
1980	Northamptonshire	Group B 4 (5)	1996	Lancashire	Semi-Final
1981	Somerset	Quarter-Final	1997	Surrey	Quarter-Final
1982	Somerset	Group A 5 (5)	1998	Essex	Semi-Final
1983	Middlesex	Group B 5 (5)	1999	Gloucestershire	Final
1984	Lancashire	Semi-Final	2000	Gloucestershire	Quarter-Final
1985	Leicestershire	Group B 3 (5)	2001	Surrey	Semi-Final
1986	Middlesex	Group B 3 (5)	2002	Warwickshire	Quarter-Final
1987	**Yorkshire**	**Winner**			

SEASON-BY-SEASON RECORD OF ALL LIST A
MATCHES PLAYED BY YORKSHIRE 1963-2014

Season	Played	Won	Lost	Tie	N R	Abd	Season	Played	Won	Lost	Tie	N R	Abd
1963	2	1	1	0	0	0	1990	22	13	9	0	0	1
1964	1	0	1	0	0	0	1991	24	13	10	0	1	0
1965	4	4	0	0	0	1	1992	21	8	13	0	0	2
1966	1	0	1	0	0	0	1993	21	10	10	0	1	0
1967	2	1	1	0	0	0	1994	19	11	8	0	0	1
1968	1	0	1	0	0	0	1995	27	15	11	0	1	1
1969	19	12	7	0	0	2	1996	27	18	9	0	0	0
1970	17	5	10	0	2	0	1997	25	14	10	1	0	1
1971	15	5	10	0	0	2	1998	25	14	10	0	1	0
1972	25	15	8	0	2	1	1999	23	13	10	0	0	0
1973	21	14	7	0	0	0	2000	24	13	10	0	1	0
1974	22	12	9	0	1	1	2001	26	13	13	0	0	0
1975	22	12	10	0	0	0	2002	27	16	11	0	0	1
1976	22	9	13	0	0	0	2003	18	6	12	0	0	0
1977	19	5	10	0	4	2	2004	23	13	8	0	2	0
1978	22	10	11	0	1	2	2005	22	8	14	0	0	0
1979	21	12	6	0	3	3	2006	15	4	10	0	1	2
1980	23	9	14	0	0	0	2007	17	8	7	0	2	1
1981	19	9	8	0	2	3	2008	18	10	4	1	3	0
1982	23	7	14	1	1	1	2009	16	6	9	0	1	0
1983	19	11	7	0	1	3	2010	13	10	3	0	0	0
1984	23	10	13	0	0	0	2011	12	5	7	0	0	0
1985	19	9	9	0	1	3	2012	11	4	7	0	0	1
1986	22	11	9	1	1	1	2013	13	4	9	0	0	0
1987	24	14	9	0	1	2	2014	10	6	4	0	0	0
1988	21	9	9	0	3	1							
1989	23	10	13	0	0	0		951	471	439	4	37	39

Abandoned matches are not included in the list of matches played.

ABANDONED LIST A MATCHES (39)

1965	v. South Africa at Bradford
1969 (2)	v. Warwickshire at Harrogate $
	v. Lancashire at Manchester $
1971 (2)	v. Gloucestershire at Sheffield $
	v. Somerset at Weston-Super-Mare $
1972	v. Sussex at Leeds $
1974	v. Warwickshire at Leeds $
1977 (2)	v. Warwickshire at Birmingham $
	v. Surrey at Leeds $
1978 (2)	v. Essex at Bradford $
	v. Gloucestershire at Hull $
1979 (3)	v. Leicestershire at Middlesbrough $
	v. Kent at Huddersfield $
	v. Worcestershire at Worcester $
1981 (3)	v. Warwickshire at Birmingham $
	v. Lancashire at Leeds #
	v. Sussex at Hove $
1982	v. Glamorgan at Bradford $
1983 (3)	v. Derbyshire at Chesterfield #
	v. Surrey at Leeds $
	v. Essex at Chelmsford $

1985 (3)	v. Derbyshire at Scarborough $
	v. Warwickshire at Birmingham $
	v. Lancashire at Leeds $
1986	v. Kent at Canterbury $
1987 (2)	v. Sussex at Hull $
	v. Hampshire at Leeds $
1988	v. Northamptonshire at Northampton $
1990	v. Glamorgan at Newport $
1992 (2)	v. Sussex at Hove $
	v. Durham at Darlington $
1994	v. Essex at Leeds $
1995	v. Derbyshire at Chesterfield #
1997	v. Sussex at Scarborough $
2002	v. Nottinghamshire at Nottingham $
2006 (2)	v. Nottinghamshire at Leeds +
	v. Derbyshire at Derby $
2007	v. Warwickshire at Birmingham +
2012	v. Northamptonshire at Leeds $

378

ANALYSIS OF LIST A RESULTS V. ALL TEAMS 1963-2014
DOMESTIC MATCHES

		HOME				AWAY				
Opponents	Played	Won	Lost	Tied	N. R	Won	Lost	Tied	N. R	Abd
Derbyshire	60	19	9	0	1	18	9	1	3	4
Durham	26	9	5	0	0	5	6	0	1	1
Essex	45	12	12	0	0	9	12	0	0	3
Glamorgan	39	9	8	0	0	9	13	0	0	0
Gloucestershire	53	12	11	0	1	8	19	0	2	2
Hampshire	44	11	9	0	1	9	14	0	0	1
Kent	54	13	11	0	1	9	20	0	0	2
Lancashire	60	9	16	0	2	13	18	0	2	3
Leicestershire	63	17	16	0	0	11	16	1	2	1
Middlesex	48	14	4	0	3	9	16	0	2	-
Northamptonshire	55	16	11	0	2	18	7	0	1	2
Nottinghamshire	57	18	8	1	2	9	16	0	3	2
Somerset	53	13	13	0	1	11	15	0	0	1
Surrey	53	12	13	0	0	11	17	0	0	2
Sussex	46	11	11	0	1	11	12	0	0	5
Warwickshire	59	11	16	1	2	13	16	0	0	6
Worcestershire	60	13	18	0	2	16	11	0	0	1
Bedfordshire	1	0	0	0	0	1	0	0	0	0
Berkshire	2	0	0	0	0	2	0	0	0	0
Cambridgeshire	3	2	0	0	0	1	0	0	0	0
Cheshire	1	0	0	0	0	1	0	0	0	0
Combined Universities	3	0	2	0	0	1	0	0	0	0
Devon	4	0	0	0	0	4	0	0	0	0
Dorset	1	0	0	0	0	1	0	0	0	0
Durham (M C)	3	1	1	0	0	1	0	0	0	0
Herefordshire	1	0	0	0	0	1	0	0	0	0
Ireland	4	3	0	0	0	1	0	0	0	0
Minor Counties	11	6	0	0	0	5	0	0	0	0
Netherlands	4	1	1	0	0	1	1	0	0	0
Norfolk	2	1	0	0	0	1	0	0	0	0
Northumberland	1	1	0	0	0	0	0	0	0	0
Scotland	16	8	0	0	0	8	0	0	0	0
Shropshire	2	0	0	0	0	1	1	0	0	0
Unicorns	4	2	0	0	0	2	0	0	0	0
Wiltshire	1	0	0	0	0	1	0	0	0	0
Yorkshire Cricket Board	1	0	0	0	0	1	0	0	0	0
Total	**940**	**244**	**195**	**2**	**19**	**223**	**239**	**2**	**16**	**38**

OTHER MATCHES

Australia	3	0	1	0	2	0	0	0	0	0
Bangladesh A	1	1	0	0	0	0	0	0	0	0
South Africa	0	0	0	0	0	0	0	0	0	1
Sri Lanka A	3	0	3	0	0	0	0	0	0	0
West Indies	1	1	0	0	0	0	0	0	0	0
West Indies A	1	0	1	0	0	0	0	0	0	0
Young Australia	1	1	0	0	0	0	0	0	9	0
Zimbabwe	1	1	0	0	0	0	0	0	0	0
Total	**11**	**4**	**5**	**0**	**2**	**0**	**0**	**0**	**0**	**1**
Grand Total	**951**	**248**	**200**	**2**	**21**	**223**	**239**	**2**	**16**	**39**

Abandoned matches are not included in the list of matches played.

LIST A HIGHEST AND LOWEST SCORES BY AND AGAINST YORKSHIRE PLUS INDIVIDUAL BEST BATTING AND BOWLING

The lowest score is the lowest all-out total or the lowest score at completion of the allotted overs. 10-over matches not included

Yorkshire versus:

		By Yorkshire			Against Yorkshire		
Derbyshire							
Highest Score:	In Yorkshire	241:4		at Leeds 2006 +	251:6		at Leeds 2006 +
	Away	288:6		at Derby 2002 #	268:8		at Chesterfield 2010 $
Lowest Score:	In Yorkshire	117		at Huddersfield 1978 $	87		at Scarborough 1973 $
	Away	132		at Chesterfield 1986 $	127		at Chesterfield 1972 #
Best Batting:	In Yorkshire	118*	S A Kellett	at Leeds 1992 $	101	K J Barnett	at Leeds 1989 $
	Away	115*	M J Wood	at Derby 2002 $	109*	C J Adams	at Derby 1997 $
Best Bowling:	In Yorkshire	6-32	S A Patterson	at Leeds 2010 $	4-20	F E Rumsey	at Bradford 1973 #
	Away	5-35	C W J Athey	at Chesterfield 1981 $	5-24	C J Tunnicliffe	at Derby 1981 #
Durham							
Highest Score:	In Yorkshire	269:5		at Leeds 1998 $	266:8		at Leeds 1998 $
	Away	271:7		at Chester-le-Street 2002 #	256:4		at Chester-le-Street 2002 #
Lowest Score:	In Yorkshire	133		at Leeds 1995 $	121		at Scarborough 1997 $
	Away	122		at Chester-le-Street 2007 $	136		at Chester-le-Street 1996 $
Best Batting:	In Yorkshire	119	D S Lehmann	at Leeds 1998 #	114	W Larkins	at Leeds 1993 $
	Away	101*	C White	at Chester-le-Street 2006 +	124*	J P Maher	at Chester-le-Street 2006 +
Best Bowling	In Yorkshire	4-18	C White	at Scarborough 1997 $	4-20	S J E Brown	at Leeds 1995 $
	Away	4-26	C E W Silverwood	at Chester-le-Street 1996 $	4-31	P D Collingwood	at Chester-le-Street 2000 #
Essex							
Highest Score:	In Yorkshire	290:6		at Scarborough 2014 +	291:5		at Scarborough 2014 +
	Away	307:3		at Chelmsford 1995 +	285:8		at Chelmsford 2008 +
Lowest Score:	In Yorkshire	54		at Leeds 2003 $	108		at Leeds 1996 $
	Away	119:8		at Colchester 1987 $	123		at Colchester 1974 $
Best Batting:	In Yorkshire	111*	J A Leaning	at Scarborough 2014 +	119*	R N ten Doeschate	at Scarborough 2014 +
	Away	125*	A W Gale	at Chelmsford 2010 $	136*	N Hussain	at Chelmsford 2002 #
Best Bowling:	In Yorkshire	4-20	G B Stevenson	at Barnsley 1977 #	6-18	R E East	at Hull 1969 $
	Away	4-31	A L Robinson	at Leyton 1976 $	5-20	R E East	at Colchester 1979 $

Yorkshire versus:

Glamorgan

	By Yorkshire			Against Yorkshire		
Highest Score:	In Yorkshire	253:4		at Leeds 1991 $	216:6		at Leeds 2013 $

		By Yorkshire		Against Yorkshire		
Highest Score:	In Yorkshire	253:4	at Leeds 1991 $	216:6		at Leeds 2013 $
	Away	257	at Colwyn Bay 2013 $	285:7		at Colwyn Bay 2013 $
Lowest Score:	In Yorkshire	139	at Hull 1981 $	83		at Leeds 1987 +
	Away	93-8	at Swansea 1985 $	90		at Neath 1969 $
Best Batting:	In Yorkshire	96 A A Metcalfe	at Leeds 1991 $	97* G P Ellis	at Leeds 1976 $
	Away	141* M D Moxon	at Cardiff 1991 #	127 A R Butcher	at Cardiff 1991 #
Best Bowling:	In Yorkshire	5-22 P Carrick	at Leeds 1991 $	5-26 D S Harrison	at Leeds 2002 $
	Away	6-40 R J Sidebottom	at Cardiff 1998 $	5-16 G C Holmes	at Swansea 1985 $

Gloucestershire

		By Yorkshire		Against Yorkshire	
Highest Score:	In Yorkshire	247:5	at Leeds 2010 $	269	at Leeds 2009 +
	Away	262:7	at Bristol 1996 $	294:6	at Cheltenham 2010 $
Lowest Score:	In Yorkshire	115	at Leeds 1973 $	91	at Scarborough 2001 $
	Away	133	at Cheltenham 1999 $	90	at Tewkesbury 1972 $
Best Batting:	In Yorkshire	118 J A Rudolph	at Leeds 2009 +	146* S Young	at Leeds 1997 $
	Away	100* J D Love	at Gloucester in 1985 $	143* C M Spearman	at Bristol 2004 $
		100* R J Blakey	at Cheltenham 1990 $		
Best Bowling:	In Yorkshire	5-42 N D Thornicroft	at Leeds 2003 $	5-33 M C J Ball	at Leeds 2003 $
	Away	4-25 R D Stemp	at Bristol 1996 $	5-42 M C J Ball	at Cheltenham 1999 $

Hampshire

		By Yorkshire		Against Yorkshire	
Highest Score:	In Yorkshire	259:4	at Middlesbrough 1985 $	257:6	at Middlesbrough 1985 $
	Away	264:2	at Southampton 1995 $	261	at Bournemouth 1977 +
Lowest Score:	In Yorkshire	74:9	at Hull 1970 $	50	at Leeds 1991 #
	Away	118	at Southampton 1990 +	133	at Bournemouth 1976 $
Best Batting:	In Yorkshire	104* D Byas	at Leeds 1999 #	155* B A Richards	at Hull 1970 $
	Away	97* M G Bevan	at Southampton 1995 $	125* C G Greenidge	at Bournemouth 1986 $
Best Bowling:	In Yorkshire	5-16 G M Hamilton	at Leeds 1998 $	5-33 A J Murtagh	at Huddersfield 1977 $
	Away	5-33 A U Rashid	at Southampton 2014 +	5-31 D W White	at Southampton 1969 $

381

LIST A HIGHEST AND LOWEST SCORES BY AND AGAINST YORKSHIRE PLUS INDIVIDUAL BEST BATTING AND BOWLING *(Continued)*

Yorkshire versus:

Kent

		By Yorkshire	Against Yorkshire
Highest Score:	In Yorkshire	299:3 at Leeds 2002 $	232:8 at Leeds 2011 $
	Away	263:3 at Maidstone 1998 $	266:5 at Maidstone 1998 $
Lowest Score:	In Yorkshire	75 at Leeds 1995 $	133 at Leeds 1974 $
	In Yorkshire		133 at Leeds 1979 #
Best Batting:	Away	114 at Canterbury 1978 #	105 at Canterbury 1969 $
	In Yorkshire	130* R J Blakey at Scarborough 1991 $	118* M H Denness at Scarborough 1976 $
	Away	102 A McGrath at Canterbury 2001 $	118* C J Tavare at Canterbury 1981 +
Best Bowling:	In Yorkshire	4-15 A G Nicholson at Leeds 1974 $	6-32 M T Coles at Leeds 2012 $
	Away	6-18 D Wilson at Canterbury 1969 $	5-25 B D Julien at Canterbury 1971 +

Lancashire

		By Yorkshire	Against Yorkshire
Highest Score:	In Yorkshire	292:4 at Leeds 2006 +	287:9 at Leeds 2006 +
	Away	324:7 at Manchester 2014 +	293:9 at Manchester 1996 +
Lowest Score:	In Yorkshire	81 at Leeds 1998 $	68 at Leeds 2000 $
	In Yorkshire	81 at Leeds 2002 #	
	Away	125 at Manchester 1973 #	123:8 at Manchester 1976 $
Best Batting:	In Yorkshire	111* D Byas at Leeds 1996 $	102* N J Speak at Leeds 1992 $
	Away	135* A McGrath at Manchester 2007 +	141* B J Hodge at Manchester 2007 +
Best Bowling:	In Yorkshire	5-25 C White at Leeds 2000 #	6-25 G Chapple at Leeds 1998 $
	Away	4-18 G S Blewett at Manchester 1999 +	5-49 M Watkinson at Manchester 1991 #

Leicestershire

		By Yorkshire	Against Yorkshire
Highest Score:	In Yorkshire	303:4 at Leeds 2008 $	302:7 at Leeds 2008 $
	Away	318:7 at Leicester 1993 $	298:9 at Leicester 1997 $
Lowest Score:	In Yorkshire	93 at Leeds 1998 $	141 at Hull 1975 $
	Away	89:9 at Leicester 1989 $	53 at Leicester 2000 $
Best Batting:	In Yorkshire	120 J A Rudolph at Leeds 2008 $	108 N E Briers at Bradford 1984 $
	Away	148 C White at Leicester 1997 $	108 E J H Eckersley at Leicester 2013 $
Best Bowling:	In Yorkshire	4-18 H P Cooper at Leeds 1975 +	5-24 C W Henderson at Leeds 2004 $
	Away	5-16 S Stuchbury at Leicester 1982 $	4-25 J Ormond at Leicester 2001 #

LIST A HIGHEST AND LOWEST SCORES BY AND AGAINST YORKSHIRE PLUS INDIVIDUAL BEST BATTING AND BOWLING (Continued)

Yorkshire versus:

Middlesex

	By Yorkshire		Against Yorkshire	
Highest Score: In Yorkshire	271:7	at Scarborough 1990 $	245:8	at Scarborough 2010 $
Away	275:4	at Lord's 2011 $	273:6	at Southgate 2004 $
Lowest Score: In Yorkshire	148	at Leeds 1974 $	23	at Leeds 1974 $
Away	90	at Lord's 1964 #	107	at Lord's 1979 #
Best Batting: In Yorkshire	J A Rudolph 124*	at Scarborough 2010 $	P N Weekes 104	at Leeds 1996 +
Away	A A Metcalfe 116	at Lord's 1991	O A Shah 125*	at Southgate 2004 $
Best Bowling: In Yorkshire	R Illingworth 4-6	at Hull 1983 $	N G Cowans 4-24	at Leeds 1986 +
Away	H P Cooper 4-28	at Lord's 1979 #	T M Lamb 5-44	at Lord's 1975 #

Northamptonshire

	By Yorkshire		Against Yorkshire	
Highest Score: In Yorkshire	270	at Leeds 2005 +	314:4	at Leeds 2007 +
Away	341:3	at Northampton 2006 +	339:7	at Northampton 2006 +
Lowest Score: In Yorkshire	129	at Leeds 2000 $	127	at Huddersfield 1974 $
Away	112	at Northampton 1975 $	109	at Northampton 2000 $
Best Batting: In Yorkshire	J H Hampshire 114*	at Scarborough 1978 $	U Afzaal 132	at Leeds 2007 +
Away	D S Lehmann 118*	at Northampton 2006 +	D J G Sales 161	at Northampton 2006 +
Best Bowling: In Yorkshire	C M Old 5-38	at Sheffield 1972 $	B S Crump 5-16	at Bradford 1969 $
Away	P W Jarvis 5-29	at Northampton 1992 $	Sarfraz Nawaz 5-15	at Northampton 1975 $

Nottinghamshire

	By Yorkshire		Against Yorkshire	
Highest Score: In Yorkshire	352:6	at Scarborough 2001 $	251:5	at Scarborough 1996 $
Away	280:4	at Nottingham 2007 +	291:6	at Nottingham 2004 $
Lowest Score: In Yorkshire	120:9	at Scarborough 1998 $	66	at Bradford 1969 $
Away	147	at Nottingham 1975 $	134:8	at Nottingham 1973 $
Best Batting: In Yorkshire	D S Lehmann 191	at Scarborough 2001 $	M J Harris 101	at Hull 1973 #
Away	R B Richardson 103	at Nottingham 1993 $	D W Randall 123	at Nottingham 1987 $
Best Bowling: In Yorkshire	A G Nicholson 5-17	at Hull 1972 $	C L Cairns 5-41	at Scarborough 1996 $
Away	C M Old 4-12	at Nottingham 1977 $	F D Stephenson 5-30	at Nottingham 1991 #

Yorkshire versus:

Somerset

		By Yorkshire		Against Yorkshire	
Highest Score:	In Yorkshire	283:9	at Scarborough 2002 $	338:5	at Leeds 2013 $
	Away	343:9	at Taunton 2005 $	345:4	at Taunton 2005 $
Lowest Score:	In Yorkshire	110	at Scarborough 1977 $	103	at Sheffield 1972 $
	Away	120	at Taunton 1992 #	63	at Taunton 1965 +
Best Batting:	In Yorkshire	127 J A Rudolph	at Scarborough 2007 $	140* P D Trego	at Leeds 2013 $
	Away	148 A McGrath	at Taunton 2006 $	131 D B Close	at Bath 1974 $
Best Bowling:	In Yorkshire	6-36 A G Nicholson	at Sheffield 1972 $	4-10 I T Botham	at Scarborough 1979 $
	Away	6-15 F S Trueman	at Taunton 1965 +	5-27 J Garner	at Bath 1985 $

Surrey

		By Yorkshire		Against Yorkshire	
Highest Score:	In Yorkshire	263:8	at Bradford 1985 $	375:4	at Scarborough 1994 $
	Away	334:5	at The Oval 2005 $	329:8	at The Oval 2009 +
Lowest Score:	In Yorkshire	76	at Harrogate 1970 +	90	at Leeds 1996 $
	Away	128:8	at The Oval 1971 $	134	at The Oval 1969 +
Best Batting:	In Yorkshire	118* J D Love	at Leeds 1987 $	136 M A Lynch	at Bradford 1985 $
	Away	146 G Boycott	at Lord's 1965 +	177 S A Newman	at The Oval 2009 +
Best Bowling:	In Yorkshire	5-25 D Gough	at Leeds 1998 $	7-33 R D Jackman	at Harrogate 1970 +
	Away	5-29 R Illingworth	at Lord's 1965 +	5-22 R D Jackman	at The Oval 1978 $

Sussex

		By Yorkshire		Against Yorkshire	
Highest Score:	In Yorkshire	302:4	at Scarborough 2011 $	267	at Scarborough 2011 $
	Away	270	at Hove 1963 +	292	at Hove 1963 +
Lowest Score:	In Yorkshire	89:7	at Huddersfield 1969 $	85	at Bradford 1972 #
	Away	89	at Hove 1998 $	108	at Hove 1971 $
Best Batting:	In Yorkshire	132* J A Rudolph	at Scarborough 2011 $	129 A W Greig	at Scarborough 1976 $
	Away	111* J H Hampshire	at Hastings 1973 $	103 L J Wright	at Hove 2012 $
Best Bowling:	In Yorkshire	5-34 G M Hamilton	at Scarborough 2000 $	4-15 Imran Khan	at Sheffield 1985 $
	Away	5-13 D Gough	at Hove 1994 $	4-10 M H Yardy	at Hove 2011 $

LIST A HIGHEST AND LOWEST SCORES BY AND AGAINST YORKSHIRE PLUS INDIVIDUAL BEST BATTING AND BOWLING (Continued)

Yorkshire versus:

Warwickshire

		By Yorkshire			Against Yorkshire		
Highest Score:	In Yorkshire	274:3		at Leeds 2003 $	276:4		at Leeds 1984 #
	Away	247:8		at Birmingham 1984 $	309-3		at Birmingham 2005 $
Lowest Score:	In Yorkshire	158		at Scarborough 2012 $	59		at Leeds 2001 $
	Away	56		at Birmingham 1995 $	158:9		at Birmingham 2003 $
Best Batting:	In Yorkshire	139*	S P Fleming	at Leeds 2003 $	105	J D Ratcliffe	at Leeds 1993 +
	Away	100*	J H Hampshire	at Birmingham 1975 $	137	I R Bell	at Birmingham 2005 $
Best Bowling:	In Yorkshire	5-31	M D Moxon	at Leeds 1991 #	4-16	N M Carter	at Scarborough 2012 $
	Away	4-27	H P Cooper	at Birmingham 1973 $	7-32	R G D Willis	at Birmingham 1981 #

Worcestershire

		By Yorkshire			Against Yorkshire		
Highest Score:	In Yorkshire	290:7		at Leeds 1982 +	286:5		at Leeds 1982 +
	Away	292:4		at Worcester 1996 #	289:3		at Worcester 1996 #
Lowest Score:	In Yorkshire	88		at Leeds 1995 #	86		at Leeds 1969 $
	Away	90		at Worcester 1987 $	122		at Worcester 1975 $
Best Batting:	In Yorkshire	101	M G Bevan	at Scarborough 1995 $	113*	G A Hick	at Scarborough 1995 $
	Away	142	G Boycott	at Worcester 1980 #	115	Younis Ahmed	at Worcester 1980 #
Best Bowling:	In Yorkshire	7-15	R A Hutton	at Leeds 1969 $	5-36	Kabir Ali	at Leeds 2002 $
	Away	6-14	H P Cooper	at Worcester 1975 $	5-30	R J Chapman	at Worcester 1998 $

Bedfordshire +

		By Yorkshire			Against Yorkshire		
Highest Score:	Away	212:6		at Luton 2001	211:9		at Luton 2001
Best Batting:	Away	88	D S Lehmann	at Luton 2001	34	O J Clayton	at Luton 2001
Best Bowling:	Away	4-39	R J Sidebottom	at Luton 2001	4-54	S R Rashid	at Luton 2001

Berkshire +

		By Yorkshire			Against Yorkshire		
Highest Score:	Away	131:3		at Reading 1983	128:9		at Reading 1983
Lowest Score:	Away				105		at Finchampstead 1988
Best Batting:	Away	74*	A A Metcalfe	at Finchampstead 1988	29	G R J Roope	at Reading 1983
Best Bowling:	Away	5-27	G B Stevenson	at Reading 1983	1-15	M Lickley	at Reading 1983

385

LIST A HIGHEST AND LOWEST SCORES BY AND AGAINST YORKSHIRE PLUS INDIVIDUAL BEST BATTING AND BOWLING (Continued)

Yorkshire versus:

Cambridgeshire +

		By Yorkshire		Against Yorkshire	
Highest Score:	In Yorkshire	177:1	at Leeds 1986	176: 8	at Leeds 1986
	Away	299:5	at March 2003	214:8	at March 2003
Lowest Score:	In Yorkshire			176: 8	at Leeds 1986
	Away	299:5	at March 2003	214:8	at March 2003
Best Batting:	In Yorkshire	75 M D Moxon	at Leeds 1986	85 J D R Benson	at Leeds 1986
	Away	118* M J Wood	at March 2003	53 N T Gadsby	at March 2003
Best Bowling:	In Yorkshire	3-11 A G Nicholson	at Castleford 1967	2-8 D H Fairey	at Castleford 1967
	Away	3-37 A K D Gray	at March 2003	3-53 Ajaz Akhtar	at March 2003

Cheshire +

		By Yorkshire		Against Yorkshire	
Highest Score:	In Yorkshire	160:0	at Oxton 1985	159:7 S P James	at Oxton 1985
Best Batting:	Away	82* M D Moxon	at Oxton 1985	46 K Teasdale	at Oxton 1985
Best Bowling:	Away	2-17 G B Stevenson	at Oxton 1985		

Combined Universities

		By Yorkshire		Against Yorkshire	
Highest Score:	In Yorkshire	197:8	at Leeds 1990	200:8	at Leeds 1990
	Away	151:1	at Oxford 1980	150:7	at Oxford 1980
Lowest Score:	In Yorkshire	197:8	at Leeds 1990	200:8	at Leeds 1990
	Away	151:1	at Oxford 1980	150:7	at Oxford 1980
Best Batting:	Away	74* C W J Athey	at Oxford 1980	63 S P James	at Oxford 1980
	In Yorkshire			63 J O D Orders	at Leeds 1990
Best Bowling:	In Yorkshire	3-34 P J Hartley	at Leeds 1990	3-44 M E W Brooker	at Barnsley 1976
	Away	2-43 H P Cooper	at Oxford 1980	1-16 C J Ross	at Oxford 1980

Devon +

		By Yorkshire		Against Yorkshire	
Highest Score:	Away	411:6	at Exmouth 2004	279-8	at Exmouth 2004
Lowest Score:	Away	259:5	at Exmouth 2002	80	at Exmouth 1998
Best Batting:	Away	160 M J Wood	at Exmouth 2004	83 P M Roebuck	at Exmouth 1994
Best Bowling:	Away	4-26 D S Lehmann	at Exmouth 2002	2-42 A O F Le Fleming	at Exmouth 1994

Yorkshire versus:

Dorset +

	By Yorkshire			Against Yorkshire	
Highest Score:	101:2	Away	at Bournemouth 2004	97	at Bournemouth 2004
Best Batting:	71* M J Wood	Away	at Bournemouth 2004	23 C L Park	at Bournemouth 2004
Best Bowling:	4-18 C E W Silverwood	Away	at Bournemouth 2004	2-31 D J Worrad	at Bournemouth 2004

Durham M C +

	By Yorkshire			Against Yorkshire	
Highest Score:	249:6	In Yorkshire	at Middlesbrough 1978	138:5	at Middlesbrough 1978
	214:6	Away	at Chester-le-Street 1979	213:9	at Chester-le-Street 1979
Lowest Score:	135	In Yorkshire	at Harrogate 1973	136:7	at Middlesbrough 1978
		Away		213:9	at Chester-le-Street 1979
Best Batting:	110 J H Hampshire	In Yorkshire	at Middlesbrough 1978	52 N A Riddell	at Middlesbrough 1978
	92 G Boycott	Away	at Chester-le-Street 1979	52 Wasim Raja	at Chester-le-Street 1979
Best Bowling:	4-9 C M Old	In Yorkshire	at Middlesbrough 1978	5-15 B R Lander	at Harrogate 1973
	3-39 H P Cooper	Away	at Chester-le-Street 1979	2-35 B L Cairns	at Chester-le-Street 1979

Herefordshire +

	By Yorkshire			Against Yorkshire	
Highest Score:	275:8	Away	at Kington 1999	124:5	at Kington 1999
Best Batting:	77 G S Blewett	Away	at Kington 1999	39 R D Hughes	at Kington 1999
Best Bowling:	2-22 G M Hamilton	Away	at Kington 1999	2-41 C W Boroughs	at Kington 1999

Ireland +

	By Yorkshire			Against Yorkshire	
Highest Score:	299:6	In Yorkshire	at Leeds 1995	228:7	at Leeds 1995
	202:4	Away	at Belfast 2005	201:7	at Belfast 2005
Lowest Score:	249	In Yorkshire	at Leeds 1997	53	at Leeds 1997
		Away		201:7	at Belfast 2005
Best Batting:	113 C White	In Yorkshire	at Leeds 1995	82 S J S Warke	at Leeds 1995
	58 M P Vaughan	Away	at Belfast 2005	59 E J G Morgan	at Belfast 2005
Best Bowling:	7-27 D Gough	In Yorkshire	at Leeds 1997	3-26 P McCrum	at Leeds 1997
	4-43 C White	Away	at Belfast 2005	1-29 W K McCallan	at Belfast 2005

LIST A HIGHEST AND LOWEST SCORES BY AND AGAINST YORKSHIRE PLUS INDIVIDUAL BEST BATTING AND BOWLING *(Continued)*

Yorkshire versus:

Minor Counties

		By Yorkshire		Against Yorkshire	
Highest Score:	In Yorkshire	309:5	at Leeds 1997	206:6	at Leeds 1988
	Away	218:3	at Scunthorpe 1975	182	at Scunthorpe 1975
		218:9	at Jesmond 1979		
Lowest Score:	In Yorkshire	309:5	at Leeds 1997	109	at Leeds 1974
	Away	218:3	at Scunthorpe 1975	85	at Jesmond 1979
		218:9	at Jesmond 1979		
Best Batting:	In Yorkshire	109* A McGrath	at Leeds 1997	80* J D Love	at Leeds 1991
	Away	83* G Boycott	at Chester-le-Street 1973	61 N A Folland	at Jesmond 1989
Best Bowling:	In Yorkshire	6-27 A G Nicholson	at Middlesbrough 1972	3-37 S Oakes	at Leeds 1997
	Away	5-32 S Oldham	at Scunthorpe 1975	3-27 I E Conn	at Jesmond 1989

Netherlands $

		By Yorkshire		Against Yorkshire	
Highest Score:	In Yorkshire	204:6	at Leeds 2010	200:8	at Leeds 2010
	Away	158:5	at Rotterdam 2010	154:9	at Rotterdam 2010
	In Yorkshire	188:8	at Leeds 2011	190:8	at Leeds 2011
Lowest Score:	Away	123	at Amsterdam 2011	154:9	at Rotterdam 2010
Best Batting:	In Yorkshire	83* J A Rudolph	at Leeds 2010	62 M G Dighton	at Leeds 2010
	Away	46* J M Bairstow	at Rotterdam 2010	34 P W Borren	at Amsterdam 2011
Best Bowling:	In Yorkshire	3-34 S A Patterson	at Leeds 2010	3-26 Mudassar Bukhari	at Leeds 2011
	Away	4-24 R M Pyrah	at Rotterdam 2010	3-28 Mudassar Bukhari	at Amsterdam 2011

Norfolk +

		By Yorkshire		Against Yorkshire	
Highest Score:	In Yorkshire	106:0	at Leeds 1990	104	at Leeds 1990
	Away	167	at Lakenham 1969	78	at Lakenham 1969
Lowest Score:	In Yorkshire			104	at Leeds 1990
	Away	167	at Lakenham 1969	78	at Lakenham 1969
Best Batting:	In Yorkshire	56* M D Moxon	at Leeds 1990	25 R J Finney	at Leeds 1990
	Away	55 J H Hampshire	at Lakenham 1969	21 G J Donaldson	at Lakenham 1969
Best Bowling:	In Yorkshire	3-8 P Carrick	at Leeds 1990		
	Away	3-14 C M Old	at Lakenham 1969	6-48 T I Moore	at Lakenham 1969

LIST A HIGHEST AND LOWEST SCORES BY AND AGAINST YORKSHIRE
PLUS INDIVIDUAL BEST BATTING AND BOWLING (Continued)

Yorkshire versus:

Northumberland +

		By Yorkshire		Against Yorkshire	
Highest Score:		138: 2	at Leeds 1992	137 G R Morris	at Leeds 1992
Best Batting:		38 S A Kellett	at Leeds 1992	47 G R Morris	at Leeds 1992
Best Bowling:		3-18 M A Robinson	at Leeds 1992	2-22 S Greensword	at Leeds 1992

Scotland

		By Yorkshire		Against Yorkshire	
Highest Score:	In Yorkshire	317:5	at Leeds 1986 #	244	at Leeds 2008 +
	Away	259:8	at Edinburgh 2007 +	217	at Edinburgh 2007 +
Lowest Score:	In Yorkshire	228:6	at Bradford 1981 #	142	at Leeds 1996 #
	Away	199:8	at Edinburgh 2004 $	129	at Glasgow 1995 #
Best Batting:	In Yorkshire	118* J D Love	at Leeds 1986 #	73 I L Philip	at Leeds 1989 +
	Away	91 A A Metcalfe	at Glasgow 1987 #	78 J A Beukes	at Edinburgh 2005 $
Best Bowling:	In Yorkshire	5-28 C E W Silverwood	at Leeds 1996 #	2-22 P J C Hoffman	at Leeds 2006 +
	Away	4-20 R K J Dawson	at Edinburgh 2004 $	3-42 Asim Butt	at Linlithgow 1998 #

Shropshire +

		By Yorkshire		Against Yorkshire	
Highest Score:	Away	192	at Telford 1984	229:5	at Telford 1984
Lowest Score:	Away	192	at Telford 1984	185	at Wellington 1976
Best Batting:	Away	59 J H Hampshire	at Wellington 1976	80 Mushtaq Mohammad	at Telford 1984
Best Bowling:	Away	3-17 A L Robinson	at Wellington 1976	3-26 Mushtaq Mohammad	at Telford 1984

Unicorns $

		By Yorkshire		Against Yorkshire	
Highest Score:	In Yorkshire	266:6	at Leeds 2013	234	at Leeds 2013
	Away	191:5	at Chesterfield 2013	189:9	at Chesterfield 2013
Lowest Score:	In Yorkshire			150:6	at Leeds 2012
	Away			184	at Scarborough 2012
Best Batting:	In Yorkshire	139 G S Ballance	at Leeds 2013	107 M S Lineker	at Leeds 2013
	Away	103* G S Ballance	at Scarborough 2012	83* T J New	at Scarborough 2012
Best Bowling:	In Yorkshire	5-22 J A Leaning	at Leeds 2012	2-25 R J Woolley	at Leeds 2012
	Away	3-34 R M Pyrah	at Chesterfield 2013	2-31 W W Lee	at Chesterfield 2013

LIST A HIGHEST AND LOWEST SCORES BY AND AGAINST YORKSHIRE PLUS INDIVIDUAL BEST BATTING AND BOWLING (Continued)

Yorkshire versus:

Wiltshire +

	By Yorkshire			Against Yorkshire		
Highest Score:	Away	304:7	at Trowbridge 1987	175		at Trowbridge 1987
Best Batting:	Away	85	A A Metcalfe	at Trowbridge 1987	62	J J Newman	at Trowbridge 1987
Best Bowling:	Away	4-40	K Sharp	at Trowbridge 1987	2-38	R C Cooper	at Trowbridge 1987

Yorkshire Cricket Board +

	By Yorkshire			Against Yorkshire		
Highest Score:	Away	240:5	at Harrogate 2000	110		at Harrogate 2000
Best Batting:	Away	70	M P Vaughan	at Harrogate 2000	31	R A Kettleborough	at Harrogate 2000
Best Bowling:	Away	5-30	D Gough	at Harrogate 2000	1-25	A E McKenna	at Harrogate 2000

Australians

	By Yorkshire			Against Yorkshire		
Highest Score:	In Yorkshire	188	at Leeds 1989	297:3		at Leeds 1989
Lowest Score:	In Yorkshire	140	at Bradford 1972	297:3		at Leeds 1989
Best Batting:	In Yorkshire	105	G Boycott	at Bradford 1972	172	D C Boon	at Leeds 1989
Best Bowling:	In Yorkshire	2-23	D Wilson	at Bradford 1972	3-30	D J Colley	at Bradford 1972

Bangladesh A

	By Yorkshire			Against Yorkshire		
Highest Score:	In Yorkshire	198	at Leeds 2013	191		at Leeds 2013
Best Batting:	In Yorkshire	47*	L E Plunkett	at Leeds 2013	69	Anamul Haque	at Leeds 2013
Best Bowling:	In Yorkshire	5-30	Azeem Rafiq	at Leeds 2013	3-25	Elias Sunny	at Leeds 2013

Sri Lanka A

	By Yorkshire			Against Yorkshire		
Highest Score:	In Yorkshire	249	at Leeds 2014	275:9		at Leeds 2014
Lowest Score:	In Yorkshire	179:7	at Leeds 2004			
Best Batting:	In Yorkshire	81	A W Gale	at Leeds 2007	100	L D Chandimal	at Leeds 2014
Best Bowling:	In Yorkshire	5-51	A Shahzad	at Leeds 2007	4-42	S Prasanna	at Leeds 2014

West Indians

	By Yorkshire			Against Yorkshire		
Highest Score:	In Yorkshire	253:4	at Scarborough 1995	242		at Scarborough 1995
Best Batting:	In Yorkshire	106	A McGrath	at Scarborough 1995	54	R B Richardson	at Scarborough 1995
Best Bowling:	In Yorkshire	3-42	G M Hamilton	at Scarborough 1995	3-48	R Dhanraj	at Scarborough 1995

LIST A HIGHEST AND LOWEST SCORES BY AND AGAINST YORKSHIRE PLUS INDIVIDUAL BEST BATTING AND BOWLING (*Continued*)

Yorkshire versus:

	West Indians A		**By Yorkshire**		**Against Yorkshire**		
Highest Score:	In Yorkshire	139		at Leeds 2002	140:2		at Leeds 2002
Best Batting:	In Yorkshire	48	M J Wood	at Leeds 2002	57	D Ganga	at Leeds 2002
Best Bowling:	In Yorkshire	1-31	C J Elstub	at Leeds 2002	4-24	J J C Lawson	at Leeds 2002
	Young Australians						
Highest Score:	In Yorkshire	224:6		at Leeds 1995	156		at Leeds 1995
Best Batting:	In Yorkshire	76	M P Vaughan	at Leeds 1995	51	A C Gilchrist	at Leeds 1995
Best Bowling:	In Yorkshire	5-32	A C Morris	at Leeds 1995	2-21	S Young	at Leeds 1995
	Zimbabwe						
Highest Score:	In Yorkshire	203:7		at Sheffield 1982	202		at Sheffield 1982
Best Batting:	In Yorkshire	98*	G Boycott	at Sheffield 1982	53	D A G Fletcher	at Sheffield 1982
Best Bowling:	In Yorkshire	3-47	P W Jarvis	at Sheffield 1982	3-30	D A G Fletcher	at Sheffield 1982

LIST A HIGHEST TEAM TOTALS

BY YORKSHIRE

411:6	v.	Devon at Exmouth	2004 +
352:6	v.	Nottinghamshire at Scarborough	2001 $
345:5	v.	Nottinghamshire at Leeds	1996 +
343:9	v.	Somerset at Taunton	2005 $
341:3	v.	Northamptonshire at Northampton	2006 +
334:5	v.	Surrey at The Oval	2005 $
330:6	v.	Surrey at The Oval	2009 +
324:7	v.	Lancashire at Manchester	2014 +
318:7	v.	Leicestershire at Leicester	1993 $
317:4	v.	Surrey at Lord's	1965 +
317:5	v.	Scotland at Leeds	1986 #
310:5	v.	Leicestershire at Leicester	1997 #
309:5	v.	Minor Counties at Leeds	1997 #
307:3	v.	Essex at Chelmsford	1995 +
307:4	v.	Somerset at Taunton	2002 $
304:7	v.	Wiltshire at Trowbridge	1986 +
303:3	v.	Northamptonshire at Northampton	2002 +
303:4	v.	Leicestershire at Leeds	2008 $
302:4	v.	Sussex at Scarborough	2011 $
299:6	v.	Ireland at Leeds	1995 +
299:3	v	Kent at Leeds	2002 $
299:5	v.	Cambridgeshire at March	2003 +

AGAINST YORKSHIRE

375:4	for Surrey at Scarborough	1994 $
345:4	for Somerset at Taunton	2005 $
339:7	fo r Northamptonshire at Northampton	2006 +
338:5	for Somerset at Leeds	2013 $
329:8	for Surrey at The Oval	2009 +
325:7	for Northamptonshire at Northampton	1992 $
314:4	for Northamptonshire at Leeds	2007 +
309:3	for Warwickshire at Birmingham	2005
308:6	for Surrey at The Oval	1995 $
306:8	for Somerset at Taunton	2002 $
302:7	for Leicestershire at Leeds	2008 $
298:9	for Leicestershire at Leicester	1997 $
297:3	for Australians at Leeds	1989
294:6	for Gloucestershire at Cheltenham	2010 $
293:9	for Lancashire at Manchester	1996 +
292	for Sussex at Hove	1963 +
291:5	for Essex at Scarborough	2014 +
291:6	for Nottinghamshire at Nottingham	2004 $
291:9	for Gloucestershire at Lord's	1999 #
291	for Surrey at The Oval	2005 $
289:3	for Worcestershire at Worcester	1996 #
287:9	for Lancashire at Leeds	2006 $

LIST A HIGHEST INDIVIDUAL SCORES

BY YORKSHIRE

191	D S Lehmann	v.	Nottinghamshire at Scarborough	2001 $
160	M J Wood	v.	Devon at Exmouth	2004 +
148	C White	v.	Leicestershire at Leicester	1997 $
148	A McGrath	v.	Somerset at Taunton	2006 $
146	G Boycott	v.	Surrey at Lord's	1965 +
142	G Boycott	v.	Worcestershire at Worcester	1980 #
141*	M D Moxon	v	Glamorgan at Cardiff	1991 #
139*	S P Fleming	v.	Warwickshire at Leeds	2003 $
139	G S Ballance	v.	Unicorns at Leeds	2013 $
137	M D Moxon	v.	Nottinghamshire at Leeds	1996 +
135*	A McGrath	v.	Lancashire at Manchester	2007 +
132*	J A Rudolph	v.	Sussex at Scarborough	2011 $
130*	R J Blakey	v.	Kent at Scarborough	1991 $
129*	M D Moxon	v.	Surrey at The Oval	1991 $
128*	M T G Elliott	v.	Somerset at Lord's	2002 +

AGAINST YORKSHIRE

177	S A Newman for	Surrey at The Oval	2009 +
172	D C Boon for	Australia at Leeds	1989
161	D J G Sales for	Northamptonshire at Northampton	2006 +
155*	B A Richards for	Hampshire at Hull	1970 $
146*	S Young for	Gloucestershire at Leeds	1997 $
143*	C M Spearman for	Gloucestershire at Bristol	2004 $
141*	B J Hodge for	Lancashire at Manchester	2007 +
140*	P D Trego for	Somerset at Leeds	2013 $
137	I R Bell for	Warwickshire at Birmingham	2005 $
136*	N Hussain for	Essex at Chelmsford	2002 #
136	M A Lynch for	Surrey at Bradford	1985 $
135*	D J Bicknell for	Surrey at The Oval	1989 +
133	A D Brown for	Surrey at Scarborough	1994 $
132	U Afzaal for	Northamptonshire at Leeds	2007 +
131	D B Close for	Somerset at Bath	1974 $

MOST RUNS IN LIST A MATCHES

690	v.	Devon at Exmouth	2004 +	Y 411:6	D 279:8
688	v.	Somerset at Taunton	2005 $	S 345:4	Y 343:9
680	v.	Northamptonshire at Northampton	2006 +	Y 342:3	N 339:7
659	v.	Surrey at The Oval	2009 +	S 329:8	Y 330:6
625	v.	Surrey at The Oval	2005 $	Y 334:5	S 291
613	v.	Somerset at Taunton	2002 $	Y 307:4	S 306:8
605	v.	Leicestershire at Leeds	2008 $	Y 303:4	L 302:7
604	v.	Surrey at The Oval	1995 $	S 308:6	Y 296:6
601	v.	Lancashire at Manchester	2014 +	Y 324:7	L 277
596	v.	Leicestershire at Leicester	1997 $	L 298:9	Y 298:9
581	v.	Worcestershire at Worcester	1996 #	W 289:3	Y 292:3
581	v.	Essex at Scarborough	2014 +	Y 290:6	E 291:5

LIST A BEST BOWLING

BY YORKSHIRE

7-15	R A Hutton	v.	Worcestershire at Leeds	1969 $
7-27	D Gough	v.	Ireland at Leeds	1997 +
6-14	H P Cooper	v.	Worcestershire at Worcester	1975 $
6-15	F S Trueman	v.	Somerset at Taunton	1965 +
6-18	D Wilson	v.	Kent at Canterbury	1969 $
6-27	A G Nicholson	v.	Minor Counties at Middlesbrough	1972 #
6-27	P W Jarvis	v.	Somerset at Taunton	1989 $
6-32	S A Patterson	v.	Derbyshire at Leeds	2010 $
6-36	A G Nicholson	v	Somerset At Sheffield	1972 $
6-40	R J Sidebottom	v.	Glamorgan at Cardiff	1998 $
5-13	D Gough	v.	Sussex at Hove	1994 $
5-16	S Stuchbury	v.	Leicestershire at Leicester	1982 $
5-16	G M Hamilton	v.	Hampshire at Leeds	1998 $
5-17	A G Nicholson	v.	Nottinghamshire at Hull	1972 $
5-18	P W Jarvis	v.	Derbyshire at Leeds	1990 $

AGAINST YORKSHIRE

7-32	R G D Willis	for	Warwickshire at Birmingham	1981 #
7-33	R D Jackman	for	Surrey at Harrogate	1970 +
6-15	A A Donald	for	Warwickshire at Birmingham	1995 $
6-18	R E East	for	Essex at Hull	1969 $
6-25	G Chapple	for	Lancashire at Leeds	1998 $
6-32	M T Coles	for	Kent at Leeds	2012 $
6-48	T I Moore	for	Norfolk at Lakenham	1969 +
5-15	B R Lander	for	Durham M C at Harrogate	1973 +
5-15	Sarfraz Nawaz	for	Northamptonshire at Northampton	1975 $
5-16	B S Crump	for	Northamptonshire at Bradford	1969 $
5-16	G C Holmes	for	Glamorgan at Swansea	1985 $
5-20	R E East	for	Essex at Colchester	1979 $
5-22	R D Jackman	for	Surrey at The Oval	1978 $
5-24	C J Tunnicliffe	for	Derbyshire at Derby	1981 #
5-24	C W Henderson	for	Leicestershire at Leeds	2004 $

LIST A ECONOMICAL BOWLING

BY YORKSHIRE

11-9-3-1	C M Old	v.	Middlesex at Lord's	1979 #
8-5-3-3	A L Robinson	v.	Derbyshire at Scarborough	1973 $

AGAINST YORKSHIRE

8-4-6-2	P J Sainsbury	for	Hampshire at Hull	1970 $
8-5-6-3	M J Procter	for	Gloucestershire at Cheltenham	1979 $

LIST A MOST EXPENSIVE BOWLING

BY YORKSHIRE

9-0-87-1	T T Bresnan	v.	Somerset at Taunton	2005 $

AGAINST YORKSHIRE

12-1-96-0	M E Waugh	for	Essex at Chelmsford	1995 +

LIST A HAT-TRICKS FOR YORKSHIRE (4)

P W Jarvis	v. Derbyshire at Derby	1982 $	
D Gough	v. Lancashire at Leeds	1998 $	
D Gough	v. Ireland at Leeds	1997 +	
C White	v. Kent at Leeds	2000 $	

LIST A MAN-OF-THE-MATCH AWARDS (134)

M D Moxon	12	M P Vaughan	5	M J Wood	3
G Boycott	11	A Sidebottom	4	R J Blakey	2
D L Bairstow	8	C E W Silverwood	4	G L Brophy	2
C White	8	D Byas	3	P Carrick	2
A A Metcalfe	7	D Gough	3	R A Hutton	2
J H Hampshire	6	P J Hartley	3	P J Sharpe	2
D S Lehmann	6	J D Love	3	G B Stevenson	2
C W J Athey	5	A McGrath	3		
M G Bevan	5	C M Old	3		

One each: T T Bresnan, D B Close, M T G Elliott, G M Fellows, S D Fletcher, G M Hamilton, S N Hartley, P M Hutchinson, R Illingworth, C Johnson, S A Kellett, B Leadbeater, M J Lumb, A G Nicholson, S Oldham, R M Pyrah, P E Robinson, R D Stemp, F S Trueman and D Wilson.

ALL LIST A CENTURIES 1963-2014 (102)

C W J ATHEY (2)

118	v.	Leicestershire	at Leicester	1978 $
115	v.	Kent	at Leeds	1980 +

D L BAIRSTOW (1)

103 *	v	Derbyshire	at Derby	1981 #

J M BAIRSTOW (1)

114	v	Middlesex	at Lord's	2011 $

G S BALLANCE (2)

139	v	Unicorns	at Leeds	2013 $
103 *	v	Unicorns	at Scarborough	2012 $

M G BEVAN (2)

103 *	v	Gloucestershire	at Middlesbrough	1995 $
101	v	Worcestershire	at Scarborough	1995 $

G BOYCOTT (7)

146	v	Surrey	at Lord's	1965 +
142	v	Worcestershire	at Worcester	1980 #
108 *	v	Northamptonshire	at Huddersfield	1974 $
106	v	Northamptonshire	at Bradford	1984 #
105	v	Australians	at Bradford	1972
104 *	v	Glamorgan	at Colwyn Bay	1973 $
102	v	Northamptonshire	at Middlesbrough	1977 #

R J BLAKEY (3)

130	v	Kent	at Scarborough	1991 $
105 *	v	Warwickshire	at Scarborough	1992 $
100 *	v	Gloucestershire	at Cheltenham	1990 $

D BYAS (5)

116 *	v	Surrey	at The Oval	1996 #
111 *	v	Lancashire	at Leeds	1996 $
106 *	v	Derbyshire	at Chesterfield	1993 $
104 *	v	Hampshire	at Leeds	1999 #
101 *	v	Nottinghamshire	at Leeds	1994 $

M T G ELLIOTT (3)

128 *	v	Somerset	at Lord's	2002 +
115 *	v	Kent	at Leeds	2002 $
109	v	Leicestershire	at Leicester	2002 $

S P FLEMING (1)

139 *	v	Warwickshire	at Leeds	2003 $

M J FOSTER (1)

118	v	Leicestershire	at Leicester	1993 $

A W GALE (2)

125 *	v	Essex	at Chelmsford	2010 $
112	v	Kent	at Canterbury	2011 $

J H HAMPSHIRE (7)

119	v	Leicestershire	at Hull	1971 $
114 *	v	Northamptonshire	at Scarborough	1978 $
111 *	v	Sussex	at Hastings	1973 $
110	v	Durham M C	at Middlesbrough	1978 +
108	v	Nottinghamshire	at Sheffield	1970 $
106 *	v	Lancashire	at Manchester	1972 $
100 *	v	Warwickshire	at Birmingham	1975 $

P A JAQUES (1)

105	v	Sussex	at Leeds	2004 $

S A KELLETT (2)

118 *	v	Derbyshire	at Leeds	1992 $
107	v	Ireland	at Leeds	1995 +

J A LEANING (1)

111 *	v	Essex	at Scarborough	2014 +

A Z LEES (1)

102	v	Northamptonshire	at Northampton	2014 +

D S LEHMANN (8)

191	v	Nottinghamshire	at Scarborough	2001 $
119	v	Durham	at Leeds	1998 #
118 *	v	Northamptonshire	at Northampton	2006 +
105	v	Glamorgan	at Cardiff	1995 +
104	v	Somerset	at Taunton	2002 $
103	v	Derbyshire	at Leeds	2001 #
103	v	Leicestershire	at Scarborough	2001 $
102 *	v	Derbyshire	ar Derby	1998 #

J D LOVE (4)

118 *	v	Scotland	at Bradford	1981 #
118 *	v	Surrey	at Leeds	1987 $
104 *	v	Nottinghamshire	at Hull	1986 $
100 *	v	Gloucestershire	at Gloucester	1985 $

R G LUMB (1)

101	v	Nottinghamshire	at Scarborough	1976 $

A LYTH (1)

109 *	v	Sussex	at Scarborough	2009 $

A McGRATH (7)

148	v	Somerset	at Taunton	2006 $
135 *	v	Lancashire	at Manchester	2007 +
109 *	v	Minor Counties	at Leeds	1997 #
106	v	West Indies	at Scarborough	1995
105 *	v	Scotland	at Leeds	2008 +
102	v	Kent	at Canterbury	2001 $
100	v	Durham	at Leeds	2007 +

A A METCALFE (4)

127 *	v	Warwickshire	at Leeds	1990 +
116	v	Middlesex	at Lord's	1991 $
115 *	v	Gloucestershire	at Scarborough	1984 $
114	v	Lancashire	at Manchester	1991 #

M D MOXON (7)

141 *	v	Glamorgan	at Cardiff	1991 #
137	v	Nottinghamshire	at Leeds	1996+
129 *	v	Surrey	at The Oval	1991 $
112	v	Sussex	at Middlesbrough	1991 $
107 *	v	Warwickshire	at Leeds	1990 +
106 *	v	Lancashire	at Manchester	1986 #
105	v	Somerset	at Scarborough	1990 $

R B RICHARDSON (1)

103	v	Nottinghamshire	at Nottingham	1993 $

J A RUDOLPH (9)

132 *	v	Sussex	at Scarborough	2011 $
127	v	Somerset	at Scarborough	2007 $
124 *	v	Middlesex	at Scarborough	2010 $
120	v	Leicestershire	at Leeds	2008 $
118	v	Gloucestershire	at Leeds	2009 +
106	v	Warwickshire	at Scarborough	2010 $
105	v	Derbyshire	at Chesterfield	2010 $
101 *	v	Essex	at Chelmsford	2010 $
100	v	Leicestershire	at Leeds	2007 +

K SHARP (3)

114	v	Essex	at Chelmsford	1985 $
112 *	v	Worcestershire	at Worcester	1985 $
105 *	v	Scotland	at Leeds	1984 #

S R TENDULKAR (1)

107	v	Lancashire	at Leeds	1992 $

ALL LIST A CENTURIES 1963-2014 *(Continued)*

M P VAUGHAN (3)

125 *	v	Somerset	at Taunton	2001 #
116 *	v	Lancashire	at Manchester	2004 +
116 *	v	Kent	at Leeds	2005 $

C WHITE (5)

148	v	Leicestershire	at Leicester	1997 $
113	v	Ireland	at Leeds	1995 +
112	v	Northamptonshire	at Northampton	2006 +
101 *	v	Durham	at Chester-le-Street	2006 +
100 *	v	Surrey	at Leeds	2002 +

M J WOOD (5)

160	v	Devon	at Exmouth	2004 +
118 *	v	Cambridgeshire	at March	2003 +
115 *	v	Derbyshire	at Derby	2002 #
111	v	Surrey	at The Oval	2005 $
105 *	v	Somerset	at Taunton	2002$

YOUNUS KHAN (1)

100	v	Nottinghamshire	at Nottingham	2007 +

LIST A PARTNERSHIPS OF 150 AND OVER 1963-2014 (43)

242*	1st wkt	M D Moxon (107)	and A A Metcalfe (127*)	v. Warwickshire at Leeds	1990 +
233*	1st wkt	A W Gale (125*)	and J A Rudolph (101*)	v. Essex at Chelmsford	2010 $
213	1st wkt	M D Moxon (141*)	and A A Metcalfe (84)	v. Glamorgan at Cardiff	1991 #
211*	1st wkt	M D Moxon (93*)	and A A Metcalfe (94*)	v. Warwickshire at Birmingham	1987 #
207	4th wkt	S A Kellett (107)	and C White (113)	v. Ireland at Leeds	1995 +
202	2nd wkt	G Boycott (87)	and C W J Athey (115)	v. Kent at Leeds	1980 +
201	1st wkt	J H Hampshire (86)	and C W J Athey (118)	v. Leicestershire at Leicester	1978 $
198*	4th wkt	M T G Elliott (115*)	and A McGrath (85*)	v. Kent at Leeds	2002 $
195	1st wkt	A Lyth (84)	and A Z Lees (102)	v. Northamptonshire at Northampton	2014 +
192	2nd wkt	G Boycott (146)	and D B Close (79)	v. Surrey at Lord's	1965 +
190	1st wkt	G Boycott (89*)	and R G Lumb (101)	v. Nottinghamshire at Scarborough	1976 $
190	5th wkt	R J Blakey (96)	and M J Foster (118)	v. Leicestershire at Leicester	1993 $
186	1st wkt	G Boycott (99)	and J H Hampshire (92*)	v. Gloucestershire at Scarborough	1975 $
186	1st wkt	G S Blewett (71)	and D Byas (104*)	v. Hampshire at Leeds	1999 #
184	3rd wkt	M P Vaughan (70)	and D S Lehmann (119)	v. Durham at Leeds	1998 $
181	5th wkt	M T G Elliott (109)	and A McGrath (78)	v. Leicestershire at Leicester	2002 $
176	3rd wkt	R J Blakey (86)	and S R Tendulkar (107)	v. Lancashire at Leeds	1992 $
172	2nd wkt	D Byas (86)	and D S Lehmann (99)	v. Kent at Maidstone	1998 $
172	3rd wkt	A McGrath (38)	and D S Lehmann (191)	v. Nottinghamshire at Scarborough	2001 $
171	1st wkt	M D Moxon (112)	and A A Metcalfe (68)	v. Sussex at Middlesbrough	1991 $
170	4th wkt	M J Wood (105*)	and D S Lehmann (104)	v. Somerset at Taunton	2002 $
170	1st wkt	A W Gale (89)	and J A Rudolph (120)	v. Leicestershire at Leeds	2008 $
167*	6th wkt	M G Bevan (95*)	and R J Blakey ((80*)	v. Lancashire at Manchester	1996 #
167*	1st wkt	C White (100*)	and M J Wood (57*)	v. Surrey at Leeds	2002 +
167	1st wkt	M D Moxon(64)	and A A Metcalfe (116)	v. Middlesex at Lord's	1991 $
167	1st wkt	M J Wood (65)	and S P Fleming (139*)	v. Warwickshire at Leeds	2003 $
166	1st wkt	M D Moxon (82*)	and A A Metcalfe (70)	v. Northamptonshire at Leeds	1988 #
165	1st wkt	M D Moxon (80)	and D Byas (106*)	v. Derbyshire at Chesterfield	1993 $
165	1st wkt	M D Moxon (70)	and D Byas (88*)	v. Northamptonshire at Leeds	1993 $
164*	2nd wkt	G Boycott (91*)	and C W J Athey (79*)	v. Worcestershire at Worcester	1981 $
164	3rd wkt	A McGrath (105*)	and J A Rudolph (82)	v. Scotland at Leeds	2008 +
164	3rd wkt	J A Rudolph (84)	and A McGrath (73)	v. Glamorgan at Scarborough	2008 $
161	1st wkt	M D Moxon (74)	and A A Metcalfe (85)	v. Wiltshire at Trowbridge	1987 +
160*	1st wkt	G Boycott (70*)	and M D Moxon (82*)	v. Cheshire at Oxton	1985 +
160*	5th wkt	G M Fellows (80*)	and C White (73*)	v. Surrey at Leeds	2001 +
160*	3rd wkt	A Lyth (60*)	and G S Ballance (103*)	v. Unicorns at Scarborough	2012 $
160	1st wkt	G Boycott (67)	and J H Hampshire (84)	v. Warwickshire at Birmingham	1973 $
159	2nd wkt	G Boycott (92)	and D B Close (96)	v. Surrey at The Oval	1969 +

399

LIST A PARTNERSHIPS OF 150 AND OVER *(Continued)*

157	2nd wkt	K Sharp (71)	and R J Blakey (79)	v. Worcestershire at Worcester 1990 $
155	*1st wkt	A Lyth (67*)	and A Z Lees (69*)	v. Derbyshire at Scarborough 2014 +
154*	2nd wkt	J H Hampshire (111*)	and B Leadbeater (57*)	v. Sussex at Hove 1973 $
153	4th wkt	Younus Khan (100)	and A W Gale ((69*)	v. Nottinghamshire at Nottingham 2007 +
150*	5th wkt	S N Hartley (67*)	and J D Love (82*)	v. Hampshire at Middlesbrough 1983 $

LIST A HIGHEST PARTNERSHIPS FOR EACH WICKET

1st wkt	242*	M D Moxon (107*)	and A A Metcalfe (127*)	v Warwickshire at Leeds	1990 +
2nd wkt	202	G Boycott (87)	and C W J Athey (115)	v. Kent at Leeds	1980 +
3rd wkt	184	M P Vaughan (70)	and D S Lehmann (119)	v. Durham at Leeds	1998 #
4th wkt	207	S A Kellett (107)	and C White (113)	v. Ireland at Leeds	1995 +
5th wkt	190	R J Blakey (96)	and M J Foster (118)	v. Leicestershire at Leicester 1993 $
6th wkt	167*	M G Bevan (95*)	and R J Blakey ((80*)	v. Lancashire at Manchester 1996 #
7th wkt	149 *	J D Love (118*)	and C M Old (78*)	v. Scotland at Bradford	1981 $
8th wkt	89	R J Blakey (60)	and R K J Dawson (41)	v. Leicestershire at Scarborough 2002 $
9th wkt	88	S N Hartley (67)	and A Ramage (32*)	v. Middlesex at Lord's	1982 $
10th wkt	80*	D L Bairstow (103*)	and M Johnson (4*)	v. Derbyshire at Derby	1981 #

ALL LIST A 5 WICKETS IN AN INNINGS 1963-2014 (55)

C W J ATHEY (1)

5-35	v	Derbyshire	at Chesterfield	1981 $

AZEEM RAFIQ (1)

5-30	v	Sri Lanka A	at Leeds	2013

M G BEVAN (1)

5-29	v	Sussex	at Eastbourne	1996 $

P CARRICK (2)

5-22	v	Glamorgan	at Leeds	1991 $
5-40	v	Sussex	at Middlesbrough	1991 $

H P COOPER (2)

6-14	v	Worcestershire	at Worcester	1975 $
5-30	v	Worcestershire	at Middlesbrough	1978 $

D GOUGH (4)

5-13	v	Sussex	at Hove	1994 $
7-27	v	Ireland	at Leeds	1997 +
5-25	v	Surrey	at Leeds	1998 $
5-30	v	Yorkshire C B	at Harrogate	2000 +

G M HAMILTON (2)

5-16	v	Hampshire	at Leeds	1998 $
5-34	v	Sussex	at Scarborough	2000 $

P J HARTLEY (4)

5-36	v	Sussex	at Scarborough	1993 $
5-38	v	Worcestershire	at Worcester	1990 $
5-43	v	Scotland	at Leeds	1986 #
5-46	v	Hampshire	at Southampton	1990 +

M J HOGGARD (3)

5-28	v	Leicestershire	at Leicester	2000 $
5-30	v	Northamptonshire	at Northampton	2000 $
5-65	v	Somerset	at Lord's	2002 +

R A HUTTON (1)

7-15	v	Worcestershire	at Leeds	1969 $

R ILLINGWORTH (1)

5-29	v	Surrey	at Lord's	1965 +

P W JARVIS (3)

6-27	v	Somerset	at Taunton	1989 $
5-18	v	Derbyshire	at Leeds	1990 $
5-29	v	Northamptonshire	at Northampton	1992 $

J A LEANING (1)

5-22	v	Unicorns	at Leeds	2013 $

A C MORRIS (1)

5-32	v	Young Australia	at Leeds	1995

M D MOXON (1)

5-31	v	Warwickshire	at Leeds	1991 #

A G NICHOLSON (4)

6-27	v	Minor Counties	at Middlesbrough	1972 #
6-36	v	Somerset	at Sheffield	1972 $
5-17	v	Nottinghamshire	at Hull	1972 $
5-24	v	Derbyshire	at Bradford	1975 #

C M OLD (2)

5-33	v	Sussex	at Hove	1971 $
5-38	v	Northamptonshire	at Sheffield	1972 $

S OLDHAM (1)

5-32	v	Minor Counties	at Scunthorpe	1975 #

S A PATTERSON (1)

6-32	v	Derbyshire	at Leeds	2010 $

A U RASHID (1)

5-33	v	Hampshire	at Southampton	2014 +

A SHAHZAD (1)

5-51	v	Sri Lanka A	at Leeds	2007

C SHAW (1)

5-41	v	Hampshire	at Bournemouth	1984 $

A SIDEBOTTOM (2)

5-27	v	Worcestershire	at Bradford	1985 #
5-27	v	Glamorgan	at Leeds	1987 +

R J SIDEBOTTOM (2)

6-40	v	Glamorgan	at Cardiff	2003 $
5-42	v	Leicestershire	at Leicester	2003 $

C E W SILVERWOOD (1)

5-28	v	Scotland	at Leeds	1996 #

G B STEVENSON (4)

5-27	v	Berkshire	at Reading	1983 +
5-28	v	Kent	at Canterbury	1978 #
5-41	v	Leicestershire	at Leicester	1976 $
5-50	v	Worcestershire	at Leeds	1982 #

S STUCHBURY (1)

5-16	v	Leicestershire	at Leicester	1982 $

N D THORNICROFT (1)

5-42	v	Gloucestershire	at Leeds	2003 $

F S TRUEMAN (1)

6-15	v	Somerset	at Taunton	1965 +

C WHITE (2)

5-19	v	Somerset	at Scarborough	2002 $
5-25	v	Lancashire	at Leeds	2000 #

D WILSON (2)

6-18	v	Kent	at Canterbury	1969 $
5-25	v	Lancashire	at Bradford	1972 #

ALL LIST A PLAYERS WHO HAVE TAKEN 4 WICKETS
IN AN INNINGS 1963-2014 (158) AND BEST FIGURES

11	C M Old	4-9	v	Durham M C	at Middlesbrough	1978 +
10	C White	4-14	v	Lancashire	at Leeds	2000 $
		4-14	v	Surrey	at The Oval	2005 $
9	A Sidebottom	4-15	v	Worcestershire	at Leeds	1987 #
8	P W Jarvis	4-13	v	Worcestershire	at Leeds	1986 $
8	D Gough	4-17	v	Nottinghamshire	at Nottingham	2000 $
8	G B Stevenson	4-20	v	Essex	at Barnsley	1977 #
7	S D Fletcher	4-11	v	Kent	at Canterbury	1988 $
6	C E W Silverwood	4-11	v	Leicestershire	at Leicester	2000 $
6	H P Cooper	4-18	v	Leicestershire	at Leeds	1975 +
5	S Oldham	4-13	v	Nottinghamshire	at Nottingham	1989 $
5	R M Pyrah	4-24	v	Netherlands	at Rotterdam	2010 $
4	P Carrick	4-13	v	Derbyshire	at Bradford	1983 $
4	R K J Dawson	4-13	v	Derbyshire	at Derby	2002 #
4	T T Bresnan	4-25	v	Somerset	at Leeds	2005 $
4	G M Hamilton	4-27	v	Warwickshire	at Birmingham	1995 $
3	R A Hutton	4-18	v	Surrey	at The Oval	1972 $
3	A G Nicholson	4-15	v	Kent	at Leeds	1974 $
3	P J Hartley	4-21	v	Scotland	at Glasgow	1995 #
3	A L Robinson	4-25	v	Surrey	at The Oval	1974 $
3	R D Stemp	4-25	v	Gloucestershire	at Bristol	1996 $
3	M P Vaughan	4-27	v	Gloucestershire	at Bristol	2000 $
2	M K Bore	4-21	v	Sussex	at Middlesbrough	1970 $
		4-21	v	Worcestershire	at Worcester	1970 $
2	J D Woodford	4-23	v	Northamptonshire	at Northampton	1970 $
		4-23	v	Warwickshire	at Middlesbrough	1971 $
2	G J Kruis	4-17	v	Derbyshire	at Leeds	2007 $
2	D Wilson	4-22	v	Nottinghamshire	at Bradford	1969 $
2	V J Craven	4-22	v	Kent	at Scarborough	2003 $
2	M A Robinson	4-23	v	Northamptonshire	at Leeds	1993 $
2	S N Hartley	4-32	v	Derbyshire	at Leeds	1989 #
2	A U Rashid	4-38	v	Northamptonshire	at Northampton	2012 $
2	A McGrath	4-41	v	Surrey	at Leeds	2003 $
1	R Illingworth	4-6	v	Middlesex	at Hull	1983 $
1	M Johnson	4-18	v	Scotland	at Bradford	1981 $
1	G S Blewett	4-18	v	Lancashire	at Manchester	1999 +
1	G M Fellows	4-19	v	Durham	at Leeds	2002 $
1	A P Grayson	4-25	v	Glamorgan	at Cardiff	1994 $
1	C J Elstub	4-25	v	Surrey	at Leeds	2001 $
1	D S Lehmann	4-26	v	Devon	at Exmouth	2002 +
1	S A Patterson	4-28	v	Worcestershire	at Worcester	2011 $
1	C Shaw	4-29	v	Middlesex	at Leeds	1988 +
1	A G Wharf	4-29	v	Nottinghamshire	at Leeds	1996 #
1	F S Trueman	4-30	v	Nottinghamshire	at Middlesbrough	1963 +
1	J D Batty	4-33	v	Kent	at Scarborough	1991 $
1	P M Hutchinson	4-34	v	Gloucestershire	at Gloucester	1998 $
1	A K D Gray	4-34	v	Kent	at Leeds	2002 $
1	A Shahzad	4-34	v	Middlesex	at Lord's	2010 $
1	P M Stringer	4-35	v	Derbyshire	at Sheffield	1969 $
1	C S Pickles	4-36	v	Somerset	at Scarborough	1990 $
1	M J Hoggard	4-39	v	Surrey	at Leeds	2000 #
1	R J Sidebottom	4-39	v	Bedfordshire	at Luton	2001 +
1	K Sharp	4-40	v	Wiltshire	at Trowbridge	1987 +
1	T L Best	4-46	v	Essex	at Chelmsford	2010 $
1	A C Morris	4-49	v	Leicestershire	at Leicester	1997 $
1	D B Close	4-60	v	Sussex	at Hove	1963 +

Player	M	Inns	NO	Runs	HS	Av'ge	100s	50s	Runs	Wkts	Av'ge	Ct/St
Ashraf, M A ...	22	6	4	3	3*	1.50	0	0	895	23	38.91	4
Athey, C W J ...	140	129	14	3662	118	31.84	2	25	431	19	22.68	46
Azeem Rafiq ...	15	11	4	116	34*	16.57	0	0	483	17	28.41	4
Bairstow, D L ..	403	317	71	5180	103*	21.05	1	19	17	0	—	390/31
Bairstow, J M .	34	30	4	708	114	27.23	1	3	0	0	—	26/1
Baker, T M	4	1	0	3	3*	3.00	0	0	89	4	22.25	3
Balderstone, J C	13	11	2	173	46	19.22	0	0	38	2	19.00	3
Ballance, G S ..	30	29	6	1320	139	57.39	2	9	0	0	—	14
Batty, J D	38	16	7	50	13*	5.55	0	0	1297	42	30.88	18
Berry, P J	1	0	0	0			0	0	28	0	—	0
Best, T L	5	1	1	8	8*	—	0	0	166	10	16.60	1
Bevan, M G	48	45	12	2110	103*	63.93	2	19	540	28	19.28	11
Binks, J G	30	21	3	247	34	13.72	0	0	0	0	—	26/8
Blain, J A R	15	8	3	34	11*	6.80	0	0	462	14	33.00	3
Blakey, R J ...	373	319	84	7361	130*	31.32	3	35	0	0	—	369/59
Blewett, G S ...	17	17	0	345	77	20.29	0	2	196	11	17.81	7
Booth, P A	5	2	1	7	6*	7.00	0	0	147	3	49.00	1
Bore, M K	55	24	10	90	15	6.42	0	0	1600	50	32.00	15
Boycott, G ...	264	255	38	8699	146	40.08	7	63	1095	25	43.80	92
Bresnan, T T ..	142	97	26	1236	61	17.40	0	3	4983	156	31.94	41
Broadhurst, M..	1	0	0	0			0	0	27	0	—	0
Brooks, J A ..	8	2	0	0	0	0.00	0	0	323	11	29.36	2
Brophy, G L ..	68	57	12	1240	93*	27.55	0	9	0	0	—	67/14
Byas, D	313	301	35	7782	116*	29.25	5	44	659	25	26.36	128
Callis, E	1	1	0	0	0	0.00	0	0	0	0	—	0
Carrick, P	304	206	53	2159	54	14.11	0	2	7408	236	31.38	70
Chapman, C A ..	10	7	4	94	36*	31.33	0	0	0	0	—	7
Claydon, M E ..	7	2	0	15	9	7.50	0	0	293	8	36.62	0
Cleary, M F ...	4	3	1	50	23*	25.00	0	0	159	2	79.50	0
Close, D B	32	31	2	631	96	21.75	0	3	475	23	20.65	14
Coad, B O	7	3	3	3	2*	—	0	0	282	3	94.00	3
Cooper, H P ...	142	74	34	483	29*	12.07	0	0	4184	177	23.63	26
Cope, G A ...	37	20	13	96	18*	13.71	0	0	1020	24	42.50	9
Coverdale, S P .	3	3	2	18	17*	18.00	0	0	0	0	—	3
Craven, V J ...	42	39	5	580	59	17.05	0	2	353	21	16.80	14
Dalton, A J	17	16	1	280	55	18.66	0	1	0	0	—	7
Dawood, I	25	20	4	260	57	16.25	0	1	0	0	—	18/4
Dawson, R K J .	92	58	12	431	41	9.36	0	0	2784	91	30.59	31
Dennis, S J	56	24	11	114	16*	8.76	0	0	1736	42	41.33	7
Elliott, M T G ..	6	6	3	394	128*	131.33	3	0	0	0	—	0
Elstub, C J	10	4	4	6	4*	—	0	0	290	12	24.16	0
Fellows, G M ..	95	79	15	1342	80*	20.96	0	4	836	22	38.00	27
Fisher, I D	28	12	3	68	20	7.55	0	0	708	29	24.41	6
Fisher, M D ...	5	1	0	10	10	10.00	0	0	186	3	62.00	0
Fleming, S P ...	7	7	1	285	139*	47.50	1	1	0	0	—	3
Fletcher, S D ...	129	32	18	109	16*	7.78	0	0	4686	164	28.57	34
Foster, M J ...	20	14	1	199	118	15.30	1	0	370	6	61.66	6
Gale, A W ...	122	113	11	3200	125*	31.37	2	17	0	0	—	23
Gibson, R	5	4	1	19	9	6.33	0	0	158	5	31.60	1
Gilbert, C R ...	5	4	0	55	37	13.75	0	0	199	8	24.87	2
Gillespie, J N ..	18	4	1	29	15*	9.66	0	0	601	18	33.38	6
Gough, D	214	120	33	1280	72*	14.71	0	1	6798	291	23.36	43
Gray, A K D ..	31	19	7	130	30*	10.83	0	0	843	25	33.72	8
Grayson, A P ..	66	49	8	587	55	14.31	0	1	1441	39	36.94	19
Guy, S M	32	23	4	282	40	14.84	0	0	0	0	—	35/11
Hamilton, G M .	101	70	18	1059	57*	20.36	0	2	2803	121	23.16	15
Hampshire, A W	4	3	0	3	3	1.00	0	0	0	0	—	1

Player	M	Inns	NO	Runs	HS	Av'ge	100s	50s	Runs	Wkts	Av'ge	Ct/St
Hampshire, J H .	234	223	24	6296	119	31.63	7	36	26	1	26.00	69
Hannon-Dalby, O J	5	1	1	21	21*	—	0	0	202	5	40.40	3
Harden, R J	19	16	2	230	42	16.42	0	0	0	0	—	1
Hartley, P J	219	145	49	1609	83	16.76	0	4	7476	283	26.41	40
Hartley, S N . . .	171	154	31	2815	83*	22.88	0	13	2153	67	32.13	52
Harvey, I J	28	27	2	637	74	25.48	0	3	950	30	31.66	8
Hodd, A J	**13**	**9**	**2**	**186**	**69***	**26.57**	**0**	**1**	**0**	**0**	**—**	**18/3**
Hodgson, D M .	**12**	**10**	**1**	**272**	**90**	**30.22**	**0**	**3**	**0**	**0**	**—**	**10/2**
Hodgson, L J . .	6	2	0	9	9	4.50	0	0	161	4	40.25	1
Hoggard, M J . .	83	28	19	41	7*	4.55	0	0	2682	118	22.72	7
Hutchison, P M .	32	11	8	18	4*	6.00	0	0	844	43	19.62	3
Hutton, R A	107	80	25	1075	65	19.54	0	4	3000	128	23.43	27
Illingworth, R . .	41	15	11	171	45	42.75	0	0	793	40	19.82	14
Ingham, P G	12	10	4	312	87*	52.00	0	2	0	0	—	2
Inzamam ul Haq .	3	3	0	69	53	23.00	0	1	0	0	—	0
Jaques, P A	43	42	2	1588	105	39.70	1	13	0	0	—	16
Jarvis, P W	144	74	28	529	42	11.50	0	0	4684	213	21.99	33
Johnson, C	129	102	22	1615	73*	20.18	0	4	28	2	14.00	33
Johnson, M	14	6	3	34	15*	11.33	0	0	455	12	37.91	2
Katich, S M	3	3	2	79	40*	79.00	0	0	0	0	—	2
Kellett, S A	56	51	3	1207	118*	25.14	2	4	16	0	—	13
Kettleborough, R A	10	6	3	71	28	23.66	0	0	72	3	24.00	4
Kirby, S P	29	12	3	38	15	4.22	0	0	1061	24	44.20	6
Kruis, G J	55	22	11	138	31*	12.54	0	0	1793	62	28.91	9
Lawson, M A K .	4	4	0	30	20	7.50	0	0	141	3	47.00	1
Leadbeater, B . .	105	100	19	2245	90	27.71	0	11	95	5	19.00	26
Leaning, J A . . .	**14**	**13**	**4**	**342**	**111***	**38.00**	**1**	**2**	**141**	**7**	**20.14**	**7**
Lee, J E	4	0	0	0	0	—	0	0	116	7	16.57	0
Lees, A Z	**17**	**17**	**2**	**651**	**102**	**43.40**	**1**	**6**	**0**	**0**	**—**	**4**
Lehmann, D S . .	130	126	20	5229	191	49.33	8	38	1990	79	25.18	41
Lester, E I	1	1	0	0	0	0.00	0	0	0	0	—	0
Love, J D	220	203	33	4298	118*	25.28	4	18	129	5	25.80	44
Lucas, D S	5	2	0	40	32	20.00	0	0	187	3	62.33	1
Lumb, M J	104	98	8	2606	92	28.95	0	18	28	0	—	31
Lumb, R G	137	123	13	2784	101	25.30	1	16	0	0	—	21
Lyth, A	**84**	**78**	**7**	**2245**	**109***	**31.61**	**1**	**11**	**172**	**2**	**86.00**	**36**
McGrath, A	275	253	39	7220	148	33.73	7	44	2514	79	31.82	91
Metcalfe, A A . .	194	189	15	5584	127*	32.09	4	36	44	2	22.00	44
Middlebrook, J D	18	11	3	61	15*	7.62	0	0	530	13	40.76	5
Milburn, S M . .	4	2	1	14	13*	14.00	0	0	118	2	59.00	1
Miller, D A	3	3	0	45	44	15.00	0	0	0	0	—	3
Morris, A C	27	17	5	212	48*	17.66	0	0	464	21	22.09	5
Moxon, M D . . .	237	229	21	7380	141*	35.48	7	49	1202	34	35.35	77
Nicholson, A G .	120	46	22	155	15*	6.45	0	0	2951	173	17.05	16
Nicholson, N G .	2	2	1	1	1*	1.00	0	0	0	0	—	2
Old, C M	221	169	38	2572	82*	19.63	0	10	5841	308	18.96	56
Oldham, S	106	40	21	192	38*	10.10	0	0	3136	142	22.08	17
Padgett, D E V .	57	54	3	1069	68	20.96	0	2	25	1	25.00	13
Parker, B	73	61	8	965	69	18.20	0	1	18	0	—	12
Patterson, S A .	**57**	**22**	**15**	**136**	**25***	**19.42**	**0**	**0**	**2075**	**70**	**29.64**	**8**
Pickles, C S	71	48	20	375	37*	13.39	0	0	2403	63	38.14	23
Plunkett, L E . .	**6**	**5**	**2**	**136**	**53**	**45.33**	**0**	**1**	**249**	**8**	**31.12**	**3**
Pyrah, R M . . .	**110**	**72**	**20**	**971**	**69**	**18.67**	**0**	**2**	**3494**	**133**	**26.27**	**34**
Ramage, A	34	17	8	134	32*	14.88	0	0	1178	30	39.26	3
Ramsden, G	1	0	0	0	0	—	0	0	26	2	13.00	0
Rana Naved -ul-Hasan	17	16	1	375	74	25.00	0	3	681	26	26.19	5
Rashid, A U . . .	**82**	**57**	**18**	**799**	**71**	**20.48**	**0**	**1**	**2822**	**101**	**27.94**	**24**
Rhodes, S J	2	1	0	6	6	6.00	0	0	0	0	—	3

Player	M	Inns	NO	Runs	HS	Av'ge	100s	50s	Runs	Wkts	Av'ge	Ct/St
Rhodes, W M H	7	6	1	53	19*	10.60	**0**	**0**	**133**	**4**	**33.25**	**2**
Richardson. R B	28	28	6	993	103	45.13	1	8	0	0	—	5
Richardson, S A	1	1	0	7	7	7.00	0	0	0	0	—	0
Robinson, A L	92	36	19	127	18*	7.47	0	0	2588	105	24.64	14
Robinson, M A	89	30	16	41	7	2.92	0	0	2795	91	30.71	7
Robinson, O E	3	2	2	16	12*	—	0	0	66	0	—	4
Robinson, P E	135	123	15	2738	78*	25.35	0	14	0	0	—	47
Root, J E	**16**	**15**	**2**	**443**	**63**	**34.07**	**0**	**2**	**222**	**7**	**31.71**	**9**
Rudolph, J A	65	62	10	3090	132*	59.42	9	19	37	0	—	32
Ryan, S A	3	2	1	7	6*	7.00	0	0	149	5	29.80	3
Sadler, J L	1	1	0	19	19	19.00	0	0	0	0	—	0
Sanderson, B W	10	2	1	14	12*	14.00	0	0	247	8	30.87	5
Sayers, J J	31	30	2	594	62	21.21	0	5	79	1	79.00	5
Scofield, D	3	1	0	0	0	0.00	0	0	111	2	55.50	1
Shahzad. A	30	22	7	243	59*	16.20	0	1	1182	34	34.76	7
Sharp, K	206	191	18	4776	114	27.60	3	28	48	4	12.00	68
Sharpe, P J	91	86	4	1515	89*	18.47	0	8	11	0	—	53
Shaw, C	48	20	10	127	26	12.70	0	0	1396	58	24.06	8
Sidebottom, A	236	131	47	1279	52*	15.22	0	1	6918	260	26.60	51
Sidebottom, R J	**113**	**51**	**22**	**303**	**30***	**10.44**	**0**	**0**	**3631**	**124**	**29.28**	**24**
Silverwood, C E W	166	94	33	892	61	14.62	0	4	5212	224	23.26	25
Smith, N	7	2	1	5	5	5.00	0	0	0	0	—	2
Smith, R	3	2	0	17	17	8.50	0	0	0	0	—	1
Squires, P J	56	48	5	708	79*	16.46	0	3	4	0	—	10
Starc, M A	4	2	2	5	4*	—	0	0	181	8	22.62	1
Stemp, R D	88	28	10	118	23*	6.55	0	0	2996	100	29.96	14
Stevenson, G B	217	158	23	1710	81*	12.66	0	2	6820	290	23.51	38
Stott, W B	2	2	0	30	30	15.00	0	0	0	0	—	0
Stringer, P M	11	8	6	29	13*	14.50	0	0	256	15	17.06	0
Stuchbury, S	22	8	4	21	9*	5.25	0	0	677	29	23.34	2
Swallow, I G	8	5	3	37	17*	18.50	0	0	198	2	99.00	5
Swanepoel, P J	3	2	2	9	8*	—	0	0	100	3	33.33	0
Tattersall, J A	**1**	**1**	**0**	**0**	**0**	**0.00**	**0**	**0**	**0**	**0**	**—**	**0**
Taylor, C R	6	5	0	102	28	20.40	0	0	0	0	—	0
Taylor, K	10	10	0	135	30	13.50	0	0	168	11	15.27	3
Taylor, N S	1	0	0	0	0	—	0	0	45	1	45.00	1
Tendulkar, S R	17	17	2	540	107	36.00	1	1	167	6	27.83	3
Thornicroft, N D	14	7	4	52	20	17.33	0	0	591	17	34.76	3
Townsley, R A J	5	4	1	81	34	27.00	0	0	62	0	—	1
Trueman, F S	11	9	1	127	28	15.87	0	0	348	21	16.57	5
Vaughan, M P	183	178	13	4966	125*	30.09	3	29	1860	60	31.00	56
Wainman, J C	**1**	**1**	**0**	**33**	**33**	**33.00**	**0**	**0**	**51**	**3**	**17.00**	**0**
Wainwright, D J	48	21	13	150	26	18.75	0	0	1427	38	37.55	16
Waite, M E	**1**	**1**	**0**	**12**	**12**	**12.00**	**0**	**0**	**52**	**0**	**—**	**0**
Wardlaw, I	17	10	4	56	18	9.33	0	0	686	24	28.58	3
Waring, J	1	1	1	1	1*	—	0	0	11	0	—	1
Warren, A C	1	1	0	3	3	3.00	0	0	35	1	35.00	0
Wharf, A G	6	1	1	2	2*	—	0	0	176	8	22.00	1
White, C	292	266	39	6384	148	28.12	5	28	6120	248	24.67	84
Whiteley, J P	6	4	0	19	14	4.75	0	0	195	2	97.50	1
Widdup, S	4	4	0	49	38	12.25	0	0	0	0	—	2
Wigley, D H	1	1	0	0	0	0.00	0	0	38	0	—	0
Williamson, K A	**10**	**9**	**0**	**229**	**70**	**25.44**	**0**	**1**	**42**	**1**	**42.00**	**4**
Wilson, D	61	47	8	430	46	11.02	0	0	1527	76	20.09	22
Wood, G L	1	1	0	26	26	26.00	0	0	0	0	—	0
Wood, M J	145	134	14	3270	160	27.25	5	14	76	3	25.33	57
Woodford, J D	72	57	14	890	60	20.69	0	2	1627	77	21.12	25
Younus Khan	11	8	0	248	100	31.00	1	0	144	2	72.00	5
Yuvraj Singh	9	9	0	196	50	21.77	0	1	197	3	65.66	1

T20 RECORDS SECTION
TROPHY WINNERS 2003-2014

		Yorkshire's *Position*			*Yorkshire's* *Position*
2003	Surrey	Group N 2 (6)	2009	Sussex	Group N 5 (6)
2004	Leicestershire	Group N 5 (6)	2010	Hampshire	Group N 6 (9)
2005	Somerset	Group N 4 (6)	2011	Leicestershire	Group N 6 (9)
2006	Leicestershire	Quarter-Final	2012	Hampshire	Final
2007	Kent	Quarter-Final	2013	Hampshire	Group N 6 (6)
2008	Middlesex	Group N 3 (6)	2014	Warwickshire	Group N 5 (9)

SEASON-BY-SEASON RECORD OF ALL T20 MATCHES
PLAYED BY YORKSHIRE 2003-2014

Season	Played	Won	Lost	Tie	N R	Abd	Season	Played	Won	Lost	Tie	N R	Abd
2003	5	3	2	0	0	0	2011	15	6	7	0	2	1
2004	5	2	3	0	0	0	2012	12	9	2	0	1	1
2005	8	3	5	0	0	0	2012/13	6	2	3	0	1	0
2006	9	4	4	0	1	0	2013	10	2	7	1	0	0
2007	8	4	4	0	0	1	2014	11	6	5	0	0	3
2008	9	5	3	1	0	1							
2009	10	4	6	0	0	0		124	56	60	3	5	7
2010	16	6	9	1	0	0							

Abandoned matches are not included in the list of matches played.

ANALYSIS OF T20 RESULTS V. ALL TEAMS 2003-2014
DOMESTIC MATCHES

Opponents	Played	HOME Won	Lost	Tied	N. R.	AWAY Won	Lost	Tied	N. R.	Abd
Derbyshire	19	6	5	-	0	7	0	0	1	0
Durham	22	6	4	1	0	5	5	0	1	0
Essex	1	0	0	0	0	0	1	0	0	0
Hampshire	1	0	0	0	0	0	1	0	0	0
Lancashire	19	6	2	1	0	4	6	0	0	3
Leicestershire	17	4	4	0	0	3	6	0	0	1
Northamptonshire	5	0	2	0	0	2	0	1	0	1
Nottinghamshire	22	4	6	0	1	3	8	0	0	0
Sussex	2	0	0	0	0	1	1	0	0	0
Warwickshire	5	0	3	0	0	0	1	0	1	1
Worcestershire	5	3	0	0	0	0	2	0	0	1
Total	**118**	**29**	**26**	**2**	**1**	**25**	**31**	**1**	**3**	**7**

OTHER MATCHES

Opponents	Played	Won	Lost	Tied	N. R.	Won	Lost	Tied	N. R.	Abd
Uva	1	0	0	0	0	1	0	0	0	0
Trinidad and Tobago	1	0	0	0	0	1	0	0	0	0
Sydney Sixers	1	0	0	0	0	0	1	0	0	0
Mumbai	1	0	0	0	0	0	0	0	1	0
Highveld	1	0	0	0	0	0	1	0	0	0
Chennai	1	0	0	0	0	0	1	0	0	0
Total	**6**	**0**	**0**	**0**	**0**	**2**	**3**	**0**	**1**	**0**
Grand Total	**124**	**29**	**26**	**2**	**1**	**27**	**34**	**1**	**4**	**7**

ABANDONED T20 MATCHES (7)

2007	v. Lancashire at Leeds	2014	v. Warwickshire at Birmingham
2008	v. Leicestershire at Leeds		v. Lancashire at Leeds
2011	v. Northamptonshire at Leeds		v. Worcestershire at Worcester
2012	v. Lancashire at Manchester		

T20 HIGHEST TEAM TOTALS

BY YORKSHIRE

213:7	v.	Worcestershire at Leeds	2010
212:5	v.	Worcestershire at Leeds	2012
211:6	v.	Leicestershire at Leeds	2004
210:3	v.	Derbyshire at Derby	2006
207:7	v.	Nottinghamshire at Nottingham	2004
200:5	v.	Nottinghamshire at Leeds	2014
198:4	v.	Durham at Leeds	2003
198:4	v.	Derbyshire at Leeds	2005
196:5	v.	Nottinghamshire at Leeds	2003
187:7	v.	Worcestershire at Worcester	2010
186:5	v.	Derbyshire at Leeds	2003
186:8	v.	Durham at Chester-le-Street	2014
183:4	v.	Derbyshire at Chesterfield	2014
181:3	v.	Northamptonshire at Northampton	2014

AGAINST YORKSHIRE

222:6	for Derbyshire at Leeds	2010
221:3	for Leicestershire at Leeds	2004
215:6	for Nottinghamshire at Nottingham	2011
215:6	for Durham at Chester-le-Street	2013
210:7	for Nottinghamshire at Nottingham	2004
208:7	for Worcestershire at Worcester	2010
207:6	for Lancashire at Manchester	2005
201:5	for Nottinghamshire at Leeds	2014
195:4	for Nottinghamshire at Nottingham	2006
195:8	for Derbyshire at Leeds	2005
193:5	for Sussex at Hove	2007
191:4	for Leicestershire at Leeds	2011
184:4	for Nottinghamshire at Leeds	2005
183:6	for Worcestershire at Leeds	2012

T20 HIGHEST INDIVIDUAL SCORES

BY YORKSHIRE

109	I J Harvey	v.	Derbyshire at Leeds	2005
108*	I J Harvey	v.	Lancashire at Leeds	2004
102*	J M Bairstow	v.	Durham at Chester-le-Street	2014
101*	H H Gibbs	v	Northamptonshire at Northampton	2010
96*	M J Wood	v.	Nottinghamshire at Nottingham	2004
92	P A Jaques	v.	Leicestershire at Leeds	2004
91	A W Gale	v.	Nottinghamshire at Leeds	2009
89	A J Finch	v.	Nottinghamshire at Leeds	2014
88	A J Finch	v.	Lancashire at Manchester	2014
84*	M J Lumb	v.	Lancashire at Leeds	2006
79*	A W Gale	v.	Derbyshire at Chesterfield	2009
78	A Lyth	v.	Derbyshire at Leeds	2012
77	I J Harvey	v.	Leicestershire at Leicester	2005

AGAINST YORKSHIRE

111	D L Maddy	for	Leicestershire at Leeds	2004
101	S G Law	for	Lancashire at Manchester	2005
100*	G M Smith	for	Derbyshire at Leeds	2008
97	B J Hodge	for	Leicestershire at Leicester	2003
96*	A M McDonald	for	Leicestershire at Leeds	2011
94	L E Bosman	for	Derbyshire at Leeds	2010
91	M A Ealham	for	Nottinghamshire at Nottingham	2004
91	P Mustard	for	Durham at Chester-le-Street	2013
85	A Flintoff	for	Lancashire at Leeds	2004
83	J Moss	for	Derbyshire at Leeds	2005
82*	A C Voges	for	Nottinghamshire at Leeds	2009
80*	P J Hughes	for	Worcestershire at Leeds	2012
80*	C D Nash	for	Sussex at Cardiff	2012

T20 BEST BOWLING

BY YORKSHIRE

5-16	R M Pyrah	v.	Durham at Scarborough	2011
5-21	J A Brooks	v.	Leicestershire at Leeds	2013
4-18	M A Ashraf	v.	Derbyshire at Derby	2012
4-20	R M Pyrah	v.	Durham at Leeds	2008
4-20	A U Rashid	v.	Leicestershire at Leeds	2010
4-21	R M Pyrah	v.	Worcestershire at Leeds	2011
4-21	B W Sanderson	v.	Derbyshire at Derby	2011
4-21	J A Brooks	v.	Derbyshire at Leeds	2013
4-23	Rana Naved	v.	Nottinghamshire at Leeds	2009
4-24	A U Rashid	v.	Nottinghamshire at Nottingham	2008
4-25	R J Sidebottom	v.	Durham at Chester-le-Street	2012
4-26	A U Rashid	v.	Lancashire at Leeds	2011
4-30	S A Patterson	v.	Lancashire at Leeds	2010
4-33	C J McKay	v.	Derbyshire at Leeds	2010

AGAINST YORKSHIRE

4-9	C K Langeveldt	for	Derbyshire at Leeds	2008
4-19	K H D Barker	for	Warwickshire at Birmingham	2010
4-19	J S Patel	for	Warwickshire at Leeds	2014
4-21	J Needham	for	Derbyshire at Leeds	2009
4-23	A J Hall	for	Northamptonshire at Northampton	2011
4-25	J A Morkel	for	Derbyshire at Chesterfield	2013
4-25	I G Butler	for	Northamptonshire at Leeds	2014
4-31	Shakib al Hasan	for	Worcestershire at Worcester	2011
4-38	S J Harmison	for	Durham at Leeds	2008
3-3	J K H Naik	for	Leicestershire at Leeds	2011
3-6	B J Hodge	for	Leicestershire at Leicester	2003
3-6	J N Snape	for	Leicestershire at Leicester	2007
3-9	J J Cobb	for	Leicestershire at Leicester	2013
3-10	D M Benkenstein	for	Durham at Leeds	2005
3-10	D G Cork	for	Lancashire at Manchester	2005
3-10	D L Maddy	for	Warwickshire at Leeds	2011

T20 ECONOMICAL BOWLING

BY YORKSHIRE

4-0-12-2	T T Bresnan	v.	Lancashire at Manchester	2008

AGAINST YORKSHIRE

4-0-9-4	C K Langeveldt	for	Derbyshire at Leeds	2008

T20 MOST EXPENSIVE BOWLING

BY YORKSHIRE

4-0-65-2	M J Hoggard	v.	Lancashire at Leeds	2005

AGAINST YORKSHIRE

4-0-58-0	G Welsh	for	Derbyshire at Leeds	2003

T20 HIGHEST AND LOWEST SCORES BY AND AGAINST YORKSHIRE
PLUS INDIVIDUAL BEST BATTING AND BOWLING

The lowest score is the lowest all-out score or the lowest score at completion of the allotted overs, five-over matches not included.

Yorkshire versus:

Derbyshire

		By Yorkshire		Against Yorkshire	
Highest Score:	In Yorkshire	198:4	at Leeds 2005	222:5	at Leeds 2010
	Away	210:3	at Derby 2006	158:6	at Chesterfield 2008
Lowest Score:	In Yorkshire	119:8	at Leeds 2013	124	at Chesterfield 2014
	Away	109	at Derby 2012	119:7	at Leeds 2007
Best Batting:	In Yorkshire	109	I J Harvey at Leeds 2005	100*	G M Smith at Leeds 2008
	Away	79*	A W Gale at Chesterfield 2009	68	G M Smith at Chesterfield 2008
Best Bowling:	In Yorkshire	4-21	J A Brooks at Leeds 2013	4-9	C K Langeveldt at Leeds 2008
	Away	4-18	M A Ashraf at Derby 2012	4-25	J A Morkel at Chesterfield 2013

Durham

		By Yorkshire		Against Yorkshire	
Highest Score:	In Yorkshire	198:4	at Leeds 2003	159:7	at Leeds 2008
	Away	186:8	at Chester-le-Street 2014	215:6	at Chester-le-Street 2013
Lowest Score:	In Yorkshire	95	at Leeds 2014	116:8	at Leeds 2009
	Away	90:9	at Chester-le-Street 2009	98	at Chester-le-Street 2006
Best Batting:	In Yorkshire	76*	H H Gibbs at Leeds 2010	54	D A Miller at Scarborough 2011
	Away	102*	J M Bairstow at Chester-le-Street 2014	91	P Mustard at Chester-le-Street 2013
Best Bowling:	In Yorkshire	5-16	R M Pyrah at Scarborough 2011	4-38	S J Harmison at Leeds 2008
	Away	4-25	R J Sidebottom at Chester-le-Street 2012	3-17	D M Benkenstein at Chester-le-Street 2005

Essex

		By Yorkshire		Against Yorkshire	
Highest Score:	Away	143:7	at Chelmsford 2006	149:5	at Chelmsford 2006
Best Batting:	Away	43	G L Brophy at Chelmsford 2006	48*	J S Foster at Chelmsford 2006
Best Bowling:	Away	2-22	A Shahzad at Chelmsford 2006	2-11	T J Phillips at Chelmsford 2006

Hampshire

		By Yorkshire		Against Yorkshire	
Highest Score:	Away	140:6	at Cardiff 2012	150:6	at Cardiff 2012
Best Batting:	Away	72*	D A Miller at Cardiff 2012	43	J H K Adams at Cardiff 2012
Best Bowling:	Away	2-20	R J Sidebottom at Cardiff 2012	3-26	C P Wood at Cardiff 2012

T20 HIGHEST AND LOWEST SCORES BY AND AGAINST YORKSHIRE
PLUS INDIVIDUAL BEST BATTING AND BOWLING (Continued)

The lowest score is the lowest all-out score or the lowest score at completion of the allotted overs, five-over matches not included.

Yorkshire versus:

		By Yorkshire	Against Yorkshire
Lancashire			
Highest Score:	In Yorkshire	180:6 at Leeds 2012	168 at Leeds 2004
	Away	180:5 at Manchester 2014	207 at Manchester 2005
Lowest Score:	In Yorkshire	111:8 at Leeds 2009	131:9 at Leeds 2004
	Away	97 at Manchester 2005	104:3 at Manchester 2003
Best Batting:	In Yorkshire	108* I J Harvey at Leeds 2004	85 A Flintoff at Leeds 2004
	Away	88 A J Finch at Manchester 2014	101 S G Law at Manchester 2005
Best Bowling:	In Yorkshire	4-26 A U Rashid at Leeds 2011	2-10 K W Hogg at Leeds 2006
	Away	3-15 Azeem Rafiq at Manchester 2011	3-10 D G Cork at Manchester 2005
Leicestershire			
Highest Score:	In Yorkshire	211:6 at Leeds 2004	221:3 at Leeds 2004
	Away	177:5 at Leicester 2005	175:4 at Leicester 2010
Lowest Score:	In Yorkshire	134 at Leeds 2006	113:9 at Leeds 2013
	Away	105 at Leicester 2013	147:9 at Leicester 2012
Best Batting:	In Yorkshire	92 P A Jaques at Leeds 2004	111 D L Maddy at Leeds 2004
	Away	77 I J Harvey at Leicester 2005	97 B J Hodge at Leicester 2003
Best Bowling:	In Yorkshire	5-21 J A Brooks at Leeds 2013	3-3 J K H Naik at Leeds 2011
	Away	2-19 R M Pyrah at Leicester 2010	3-6 B J Hodge at Leicester 2003
		2-19 M A Starc at Leicester 2012	
Northamptonshire			
Highest Score:	In Yorkshire	162:7 at Leeds 2014	165:7 at Leeds 2014
	Away	181:3 at Northampton 2014	180:5 at Northampton 2010
Lowest Score:	In Yorkshire		151:7 at Leeds 2010
	Away	144 at Northampton 2011	132:7 at Northampton 2011
Best Batting:	In Yorkshire	36 L E Plunkett at Leeds 2014	43 D J Willey at Leeds 2014
	Away	101* H H Gibbs at Northampton 2010	76 R E Levi at Northampton 2014
Best Bowling:	In Yorkshire	3-23 A U Rashid at Leeds 2010	4-25 I G Butler at Leeds
	Away	2-18 R J Sidebottom at Northampton 2011	4-23 A J Hall at Northampton 2011

T20 HIGHEST AND LOWEST SCORES BY AND AGAINST YORKSHIRE
PLUS INDIVIDUAL BEST BATTING AND BOWLING (Continued)

The lowest score is the lowest all-out score or the lowest score at completion of the allotted overs, five-over matches not included.

Yorkshire versus:

		By Yorkshire		Against Yorkshire	
Nottinghamshire					
Highest Score:	In Yorkshire	200:5	at Leeds 2014	201:4	at Leeds 2014
	Away	207:7	at Nottingham 2004	215:6	at Nottingham 2011
Lowest Score:	In Yorkshire	141:8	at Leeds 2008	155:6	at Leeds 2009
	Away	112:7	at Nottingham 2010	136:6	at Nottingham 2008
Best Batting:	In Yorkshire	91 A W Gale	at Leeds 2009	82* A C Voges	at Leeds 2009
	Away	96* M J Wood	at Nottingham 2004	91 M A Ealham	at Nottingham 2004
Best Bowling:	In Yorkshire	4-23 Rana Naved-ul-Hasan	at Leeds 2009	3-38 J T Ball	at Leeds 2014
	Away	4-24 A U Rashid	at Nottingham 2008	3-17 S R Patel	at Nottingham 2013
Sussex					
Highest Score:	Away	172:6	at Cardiff 2012	193:5	at Hove 2007
Lowest Score:	Away	155	at Hove 2007	136:8	at Cardiff 2012
Best Batting:	Away	68* J M Bairstow	at Cardiff 2012	80* C D Nash	at Cardiff 2012
Best Bowling:	Away	2-22 T T Bresnan	at Cardiff 2012	3-22 S B Styris	at Cardiff 2012
Warwickshire					
Highest Score:	In Yorkshire	161:8	at Leeds 2011	164:5	at Leeds 2011
	Away	131	at Birmingham 2010	145:8	at Birmingham 2010
Lowest Score:	In Yorkshire	121:9	at Leeds 2010	155:8	at Leeds 2010
Best Batting:	In Yorkshire	54 A W Gale	at Leeds 2011	64 W T S Porterfield	at Leeds 2011
	Away	31 A Lyth	at Birmingham 2010	49* J O Troughton	at Birmingham 2010
Best Bowling:	In Yorkshire	3-22 R M Pyrah	at Leeds 2010	4-19 J S Patel	at Leeds 2014
	Away	3-25 S A Patterson	at Birmingham 2010	4-19 K H D Barker	at Birmingham 2010

413

T20 HIGHEST AND LOWEST SCORES BY AND AGAINST YORKSHIRE PLUS INDIVIDUAL BEST BATTING AND BOWLING (Continued)

Yorkshire versus:

		By Yorkshire		Against Yorkshire	
Worcestershire					
Highest Score:	In Yorkshire	213:7	at Leeds 2010	183: 6	at Leeds 2012
	Away	187:7	at Worcester 2010	208:7	at Worcester 2010
Lowest Score:	In Yorkshire	152:7	at Leeds 2011	109	at Leeds 2010
	Away	142	at Worcester 2011	183:7	at Worcester 2011
Best Batting:	In Yorkshire	65 J E Root	at Leeds 2012	80* P J Hughes	at Leeds 2012
	Away	39 A McGrath	at Worcester 2010	56	at Worcester 2011
Best Bowling:	In Yorkshire	4-21 R M Pyrah	at Leeds 2011	3-30 G M Andrew	at Leeds 2011
	Away	3-30 A Shahzad	at Worcester 2011	4-31 Shakib al Hasan	at Worcester 2011
Chennai					
Highest Score:	Away	140:6	at Durban 2012	141:6	at Durban 2012
Best Batting:	Away	58 G S Ballance	at Durban 2012	47 S Badrinath	at Durban 2012
Best Bowling:	Away	3-23 I Wardlaw	at Durban 2012	2-12 J A Morkel	at Durban 2012
Highveld					
Highest Score:	Away	131:7	at Johannesburg 2012	134:5	at Johannesburg
Best Batting:	Away	31 P A Jaques	at Johannesburg 2012	32 Q de Kock	at Durban 2012
Best Bowling:	Away	2-21 S A Patterson	at Johannesburg 2012	2-23 A M Phangiso	at Johannesburg
Mumbai					
Highest Score:	Away			156: 6	at Cape Town 2012
Best Batting:	Away			37 D R Smith	at Cape Town
Best Bowling:	Away	2-36 Azeem Rafiq	at Cape Town 2012		
Sydney Sixers					
Highest Score:	Away	96:9	at Cape Town 2012	98:2	at Cape Town 2012
Best Batting:	Away	25 J E Root	at Cape Town 2012	43* M J Lumb	at Cape Town 2012
Best Bowling:	Away	1-21 Azeem Rafiq	at Cape Town 2012	3-22 M A Starc	at Cape Town 2012
Trinidad and Tobago					
Highest Score:	Away	154:4	at Centurion 2012	148:9	at Centurion 2012
Best Batting:	Away	64* G S Ballance	at Centurion 2012	59 D Ramdin	at Centurion 2012
Best Bowling:	Away	3-13 R J Sidebottom	at Centurion 2012	1-16 K Y G Ottley	at Centurion 2012
Uva					
Highest Score:	Away	151:5	at Johannesburg 2012	150:7	at Johannesburg 2012
Best Batting:	Away	39* D A Miller	at Johannesburg 2012	29 S H T Kandamby	at Johannesburg 2012
Best Bowling:	Away	2-29 M A Ashraf	at Johannesburg 2012	3-32 E M D Y Munaweera	at Johannesburg 2012

T20 MAN OF THE MATCH AWARDS (56)

A W Gale	7	D A Miller	3	H H Gibbs	2
A McGrath	6	Azeem Rafiq	2	P A Jaques	2
R M Pyrah	5	J M Bairstow	2	A Z Lees	2
I J Harvey	3	T T Bresnan	2	M J Lumb	2
A Lyth	3	A J Finch	2		

One each: G S Ballance, J A Brooks, M E Claydon, S P Fleming, D S Lehmann, A U Rashid, J E Root, J A Rudolph, B W Sanderson, J J Sayers, A Shahzad, D J Wainwright and C White.

T20 PARTNERSHIPS OF 100 AND OVER 2003-2014 (12)

137*	2nd wkt	A W Gale	(60*)	and H H Gibbs	(76*)	v. Durham at Leeds	2010
131	1st wkt	A Lyth	(78)	and P A Jaques	(64)	v. Derbyshire at Leeds	2012
129	2nd wkt	A W Gale	(91)	and M P Vaughan	(41*)	v. Nottinghamshire at Leeds	2009
124	2nd wkt	I J Harvey	(109)	and P A Jaques	(37)	v. Derbyshire at Leeds	2005
121	3rd wkt	J A Rudolph	(56)	and A McGrath	(59)	v. Leicestershire at Leicester	2008
116	1st wkt	A W Gale	(70)	and P A Jaques	(48)	v. Leicestershire at Leeds	2012
108	2nd wkt	I J Harvey	(108*)	and P A Jaques	(39)	v. Lancashire at Leeds	2004
108	2nd wkt	A Lyth	(59)	and H H Gibbs	(40)	v. Worcestershire at Leeds	2010
104	1st wkt	A W Gale	(43)	and J A Rudolph	(61)	v. Leicestershire at Leicester	2009
103*	5th wkt	G S Ballance	(64*)	and A U Rashid	(33*)	v. Trinidad & Tobago at Centurion	2012/13
103	1st wkt	A W Gale	(65*)	and J A Rudolp	(53)	v. Leicestershire at Leicester	2010
101	2nd wkt	M J Wood	(57)	and M J Lumb	(55)	v. Nottinghamshire at Leeds	2003

T20 HIGHEST PARTNERSHIPS FOR EACH WICKET

1st wkt	131	A Lyth	(78)	and P A Jaques	(64)	v. Derbyshire at Leeds	2012
2nd wkt	137*	A W Gale	(60*)	and H H Gibbs	(76*)	v. Durham at Leeds	2010
3rd wkt	121	J A Rudolph	(56)	and A McGrath	(59)	v. Leicestershire at Leicester	2008
4th wkt	93	P A Jaques	(92)	and T T Bresnan	(42)	v. Leicestershire at Leeds	2004
5th wkt	103*	G S Ballance	(64*)	and A U Rashid	(33*)	v. Trinidad & Tobago at Centurion	2012/13
6th wkt	65	A McGrath	(39)	and A U Rashid	(34)	v. Worcestershire at Worcester	2010
7th wkt	68*	T T Bresnan	(45*)	and A U Rashid	(29*)	v. Warwickshire at Leeds	2014
8th wkt	43*	R M Pyrah	(22*)	and C J McKay	(21*)	v. Worcestershire at Worcester	2010
9th wkt	33*	A U Rashid	(5*)	and D Gough	(20*)	v. Lancashire at Leeds	2008
10th wkt	28*	A U Rashid	(28*)	and G J Kruis	(12*)	v. Durham at Chester-le-Street	2009

ALL WHO HAVE TAKEN 4 WICKETS IN AN INNINGS (14)

R M PYRAH (3)

5-16	v. Durham	at Scarborough	2011
4-20	v. Durham	at Leeds	2006
4-21	v. Worcestershire	at Leeds	2011

A U RASHID (3)

4-20	v. Leicestershire	at Leeds	2011
4-24	v. Nottingham	at Nottingham	2008
4-26	v. Lancashire	at Leeds	2011

J A BROOKS (2)

| 5-21 | v. Leicestershire | at Leeds | 2013 |
| 4-21 | v. Derbyshire | at Leeds | 2013 |

M A ASHRAF (1)

| 4-18 | v. Derbyshire | at Derby | 2012 |

B W SANDERSON (1)

| 4-21 | v. Derbyshire | at Derby | 2011 |

RANA NAVED-UL-HASAN (1)

| 4-23 | v. Nottinghamshire | at Leeds | 2009 |

R J SIDEBOTTOM (1)

| 4-25 | v. Durham | at Chester-le-Street | 2012 |

S A PATTERSON (1)

| 4-30 | v. Lancashire | at Leeds | 2010 |

C J MCKAY (1)

| 4-33 | v. Derbyshire | at Leeds | 2010 |

CAREER AVERAGES FOR YORKSHIRE

ALL t20 MATCHES 2003-2014

Player	M	Inns	NO	Runs	HS	Av'ge	100s	50s	Runs	Wkts	Av'ge	Ct/St
Ashraf, M A ...	17	1	0	4	4	4.00	0	0	462	17	27.17	1
Azeem Rafiq ...	60	27	17	131	21*	13.10	0	0	1,510	62	24.35	27
Bairstow, J M ..	49	44	9	887	102*	25.34	1	3	0	0	—	14/6
Ballance, G S ..	45	40	7	912	68	27.63	0	3	0	0	—	27
Best, T L	8	3	2	10	10*	10.00	0	0	243	7	34.71	4
Blakey, R J	7	5	1	119	32	29.75	0	0	0	0	—	5/1
Bresnan, T T ..	60	44	17	587	45*	21.74	0	0	1,490	60	24.83	20
Brooks, J A ...	11	0	0	0	—	—	0	0	271	13	20.84	4
Brophy, G L ...	54	46	9	717	57*	19.37	0	2	0	0	—	25/7
Claydon, M E ..	7	2	2	14	12*	—	0	0	188	5	37.60	2
Craven, V J	6	6	4	76	44*	38.00	0	0	67	0	—	3
Dawood, I	11	8	3	44	15	8.80	0	0	0	0	—	5/2
Dawson, R K J .	22	8	3	71	22	14.20	0	0	558	24	23.25	7
Finch, A J	10	10	0	256	89	25.60	0	2	0	0	—	14
Fleming, S P ...	4	4	0	62	58	15.50	0	1	0	0	—	1
Gale, A W	92	85	7	1972	91	25.28	0	15	0	0	—	28
Gibbs, H H	15	15	3	443	101*	36.91	1	2	0	0	—	8
Gilbert, C R	13	9	2	107	38*	15.28	0	0	0	0	—	7
Gillespie, J N ..	17	4	2	14	8*	7.00	0	0	422	17	24.82	5
Gough, D	17	7	3	42	20*	10.50	0	0	416	16	26.00	2
Gray, A K D ...	8	3	0	17	13	5.66	0	0	211	9	23.44	4
Guy, S M	10	6	1	44	13	8.80	0	0	0	0	—	2
Hamilton, G M .	3	3	1	41	41*	20.50	0	0	0	0	—	1
Hannon-Dalby, O J	2	0	0	0	—	—	0	0-	58	3	19.33	0
Harvey, I J	10	10	1	438	109	48.66	2	2	258	10	25.80	4
Hodd, A J ...	6	5	2	29	11	9.66	0	0	0	0	—	2/1
Hodgson, D M .	16	14	2	213	52*	17.75	0	1	0	0	—	9/1
Hodgson, L J ...	2	1	1	39	39*	—	0	0	59	2	29.50	1
Hoggard, M J ..	15	2	1	19	18	19.00	0	0	472	13	36.30	4
Jaques, P A	34	32	3	907	92	31.27	0	6	15	0	—	5
Kirby, S P	3	0	0	0	—	—	0	0	119	4	29.75	1
Kruis, G J	20	5	3	41	22	20.50	0	0	486	19	25.57	6
Lawson, M A K .	2	1	1	4	4*	—	0	0	87	3	29.00	1
Leaning, J A ...	4	3	0	14	8	4.66	0	0	30	0	—	0
Lees, A Z	12	12	2	348	67*	34.80	0	2	0	0	—	4
Lehmann, D S ..	9	9	3	252	48	42.00	0	0	180	8	22.50	4
Lumb, M J.....	26	26	3	442	84*	19.21	0	4	65	3	21.66	8
Lyth, A	61	52	2	939	78	18.78	0	2	56	3	18.66	25
McGrath, A	66	61	12	1403	73*	28.63	0	8	698	23	30.34	26
McKay, C J	8	6	3	54	21*	18.00	0	0	258	10	25.80	1
Miller, D A	14	13	4	457	74*	50.77	0	4	0	0	—	7
Patterson, S A ..	27	5	3	5	3*	2.50	0	0	801	26	30.80	4
Plunkett, L E ..	12	10	1	137	36	15.22	0	0	322	12	26.83	3
Pyrah, R M ...	95	65	20	558	42	12.40	0	0	2,086	101	20.65	35
Rana Naved-ul-Hasan	8	8	2	63	20*	10.50	0	0	159	11	14.45	2
Rashid, A U ...	70	47	11	498	36*	13.83	0	0	1,785	71	25.14	20
Rhodes, W M H .	2	2	0	13	13	6.50	0	0	14	0	—	0
Robinson, O E ..	7	3	0	5	3	1.66	0	0	162	6	27.00	3
Root, J E	28	24	4	423	65	21.15	0	1	224	4	56.00	9

Player	M	Inns	NO	Runs	HS	Av'ge	100s	50s	Runs	Wkts	Av'ge	Ct/St
Rudolph, J A ...	39	35	5	710	61	23.66	0	3	145	6	24.16	7
Sanderson, B W	4	0	0	0	0	—	0	0	74	6	12.33	0
Sayers, J J	17	14	0	253	44	18.07	0	0	0	0	—	5
Shahzad, A	22	16	4	129	20	10.75	0	0	576	17	33.88	5
Sidebottom, R J	**40**	**16**	**10**	**87**	**16***	**14.50**	**0**	**0**	**1,069**	**42**	**25.45**	**9**
Silverwood, C E W	9	5	2	32	13*	10.66	0	0	264	7	37.71	4
Starc, M A	10	2	1	0	0*	0.00	0	0	218	21	10.38	1
Swanepoel, P J .	2	1	1	2	2*	—	0	0	60	3	20.00	1
Taylor, C R	2	2	1	10	10*	10.00	0	0	0	0	—	0
Vaughan, M P ..	16	16	1	292	41*	19.46	0	0	81	1	81.00	2
Wainwright, D J	26	9	6	23	6*	7.66	0	0	551	21	26.23	9
Wardlaw, I	10	1	1	1	1	—	0	0	179	5	35.80	0
Warren, A C ...	2	0	0	0	—	—	0	0	70	4	17.50	0
White, C	33	31	0	570	55	18.38	0	2	132	2	66.00	8
Williamson, K S	5	5	0	93	41	18.60	0	0	37	3	12.33	1
Wood, M J	15	15	3	328	96*	27.33	0	2	32	2	16.00	11
Younus Khan ...	2	2	0	55	40	27.50	0	0	32	2	16.00	0
Yuvraj Singh ...	5	5	0	154	71	30.80	0	1	51	5	10.20	0

SECOND ELEVEN RECORDS
in the
SECOND ELEVEN CHAMPIONSHIP 1959-1961 AND 1975-2014

SUMMARY OF RESULTS BY SEASON

Season	Played	Won	Lost	Drawn	Tied	Abandoned	Position in Championship
1959	10	4	1	5	0	0	7
1960	10	1	3	6	0	0	14
1961	9	2	2	5	0	1	11
1975	14	4	0	10	0	0	4
1976	14	5	5	4	0	0	5
1977	**16**	**9**	**0**	**7**	**0**	**1**	**1**
1978	15	5	2	8	0	1	4
1979	16	5	0	11	0	0	3
1980	14	5	2	7	0	1	5
1981	16	2	3	11	0	0	11
1982	16	2	3	11	0	0	14 =
1983	11	5	1	5	0	3	2
1984	**15**	**9**	**3**	**3**	**0**	**0**	**1**
1985	14	3	3	8	0	1	12
1986	16	5	1	10	0	0	5
1987	**15**	**5**	**2**	**8**	**0**	**1**	**1 =**
1988	16	4	1	11	0	0	9
1989	17	2	3	12	0	0	9 =
1990	16	1	6	9	0	0	17
1991	**16**	**8**	**1**	**7**	**0**	**0**	**1**
1992	17	5	2	10	0	0	5
1993	17	6	1	10	0	0	3
1994	17	6	2	9	0	0	2
1995	17	7	1	9	0	0	5
1996	17	6	3	8	0	0	4
1997	16	8	5	3	0	1	2
1998	15	4	2	9	0	0	9
1999	16	3	8	5	0	1	14
2000	14	5	2	7	0	1	5
2001	12	8	2	2	0	1	2
2002	12	5	1	6	0	0	3
2003	**10**	**7**	**1**	**2**	**0**	**0**	**1**
2004	7	2	0	5	0	1	8
2005	12	2	4	6	0	0	10
2006	14	6	4	4	0	0	3
2007	12	4	5	3	0	0	10
2008	12	4	4	4	0	2	5
2009	9	5	0	4	0	0	(Group A) 2
2010	9	2	4	3	0	0	(Group A) 8
2011	9	0	4	4	1	0	(Group A) 10
2012	7	1	2	4	0	2	(North) 9
2013	9	3	4	2	0	0	(North) 4
2014	9	2	1	6	0	0	(North) 4
Totals	575	187	104	283	1	18	

Matches abandoned without a ball being bowled are not counted as a match played.
The Championship was divided into two groups from 2009, each team playng each other
once. The two group winners play for the Championship

ANALYSIS OF RESULTS AGAINST EACH OPPONENT

County	Played	Won	Lost	Drawn	Tied	Abandoned	First Played
Derbyshire	54	12	8	34	0	3	1959
Durham	29	11	5	13	0	2	1992
Essex	13	9	2	2	0	0	1990
Glamorgan	40	11	3	26	0	2	1975
Gloucestershire	10	3	3	4	0	0	1990
Hampshire	12	4	1	7	0	0	1990
Kent	26	5	4	17	0	1	1981
Lancashire	66	14	18	34	0	3	1959
Leicestershire	28	11	6	10	1	1	1975
MCC Young Cricketers	5	3	1	1	0	0	2005
MCC Universities	2	1	0	1	0	0	2011
Middlesex	18	7	2	9	0	0	1977
Northamptonshire	46	13	6	27	0	2	1959
Nottinghamshire	57	17	11	29	0	2	1959
Scotland	2	1	0	1	0	0	2007
Somerset	18	9	3	6	0	0	1988
Surrey	36	9	9	18	0	2	1976
Sussex	16	6	5	5	0	0	1990
Warwickshire	59	21	12	26	0	0	1959
Worcestershire	38	20	5	13	0	0	1961
Totals	575	187	104	283	1	18	

Note: Matches abandoned are not included in the total played.

Highest Total

By Yorkshire: 538 for 9 wkts dec v. Worcestershire at Stamford Bridge, 2007
Against Yorkshire: 567 for 7 wkts dec by Middlesex at RAF Vine Lane, Uxbridge, 2000

Lowest Total

By Yorkshire: 67 v. Worcestershire at Barnt Green, 2013
Against Yorkshire: 36 by Lancashire at Elland, 1979

Highest Individual Score

For Yorkshire: 273* by R J Blakey v. Northamptonshire at Northampton, 1986
Against Yorkshire: 235 by O A Shah for Middlesex at Leeds, 1999

Century in Each Innings

For Yorkshire:	C White	209* and 115* v. Worcestershire at Worcester, 1990
	K Sharp	150* and 127 v. Essex at Elland, 1991
	A A Metcalfe	109 and 136* v. Somerset at North Perrott, 1994
	R A Kettleborough	123 and 192* v. Nottinghamshire at Todmorden, 1996
	C R Taylor	201* and 129 v. Sussex at Hove, 2005
	A W Gale	131 and 123 v. Somerset at Taunton, 2006
	J J Sayers	157 and 105 v. Lancashire at Leeds, 2007
Against Yorkshire:	N Nannan	100 and 102* for Nottinghamshire at Harrogate, 1979
	G D Lloyd	134 and 103 for Lancashire at Scarborough, 1989
	A J Swann	131 and 100 for Northamptonshire at York, 1998
	G J Kennis	114 and 114 for Somerset at Taunton, 1999

Best Bowling in an Innings

For Yorkshire: 9 for 27 by G A Cope v. Northamptonshire at Northampton, 1979
Against Yorkshire: 8 for 15 by I Folley for Lancashire at Heywood, 1983

Best Bowling in a Match

For Yorkshire: 13 for 92 (6 for 48 and 7 for 44) by M K Bore v. Lancashire at Harrogate, 1976
Against Yorkshire: 13 for 100 (7 for 45 and 6 for 55) by N J Perry for Glamorgan at Cardiff, 1978

Totals of 450 and over

By Yorkshire (26)

Score	Versus	Ground	Season
538 for 9 wkts dec	Worcestershire	Stamford Bridge	2007
534 for 5 wkts dec	Lancashire	Stamford Bridge	2003
530 for 8 wkts dec	Nottinghamshire	Middlesbrough	2000
514 for 3 wkts dec	Somerset	Taunton	1988
509 for 4 wkts dec	Northamptonshire	Northampton	1986
502	Derbyshire	Chesterfield	2003
501 for 5 wkts dec	MCC Young Cricketers	Stamford Bridge	2009
497	Derbyshire	Chesterfield	2005
495 for 5 wkts dec	Somerset	Taunton	2006
488 for 8 wkts dec	Warwickshire	Harrogate	1984
486 for 6 wkts dec	Glamorgan	Leeds	1986
480	Leicestershire	Market Harborough	2013
476 for 3 wkts dec	Glamorgan	Gorseinon	1984
475 for 9 wkts dec	Nottinghamshire	Nottingham	1995
474 for 3 wkts dec	Glamorgan	Todmorden	2003
474	Durham	Stamford Bridge	2003
470	Lancashire	Leeds	2006
469	Warwickshire	Castleford	1999
462	Scotland	Stamford Bridge	2007
461 for 8 wkts dec	Essex	Stamford Bridge	2006
459 for 3 wkts dec	Leicestershire	Oakham	1997
459 for 6 wkts dec	Glamorgan	Bradford	1992
457 for 9 wkts dec	Kent	Canterbury	1983
456 for 5 wkts dec	Gloucestershire	Todmorden	1990
456 for 6 wkts dec	Nottinghamshire	York	1986
454 for 9 wkts dec	Derbyshire	Chesterfield	1959
452 for 9 wkts dec	Glamorgan	Cardiff	2005

Against Yorkshire (12)

Score	For	Ground	Season
567 for 7 wkts dec	Middlesex	RAF Vine Lane, Uxbridge	2000
555 for 7 wkts dec	Derbyshire	Stamford Bridge	2002
525 for 7 wkts dec	Sussex	Hove	2005
493 for 8 wkts dec	Nottinghamshire	Lady Bay, Nottingham	2002
488 for 8 wkts dec	Warwickshire	Castleford	1999
486	Essex	Chelmsford	2000
485	Gloucestershire	North Park, Cheltenham	2001
477	Lancashire	Headingley	2006
471	Warwickshire	Clifton Park, York	2010
458	Lancashire	Bradford	1997
454 for 7 wkts dec	Lancashire	Todmorden	1993
450 for 7 wkts (inns closed)	Derbyshire	Bradford	1980

Completed Innings under 75

By Yorkshire (3)

Score	Versus	Ground	Season
67	Worcestershire	Barnt Green (1st inns)	2013
68	Worcestershire	Barnt Green (2nd inns)	2013
69	Lancashire	Heywood	1983
74	Derbyshire	Chesterfield	1960
74	Nottinghamshire	Bradford	1998

Against Yorkshire (10)

Score	By	Ground	Season
36	Lancashire	Elland	1979
49	Leicestershire	Leicester	2008
50	Lancashire	Liverpool	1984
60	Derbyshire	Bradford	1977
60	Surrey	Sunbury-on-Thames	1977
62	MCC YC	High Wycombe	2005
64	Nottinghamshire	Brodsworth	1959
66	Leicestershire	Lutterworth	1977
72	Sussex	Horsham	2003
74	Worcestershire	Barnsley	1978

Individual Scores of 150 and over (60)

Score	Player	Versus	Ground	Season
273*	R J Blakey	Northamptonshire	Northampton	1986
238*	K Sharp	Somerset	Taunton	1988
233	P E Robinson	Kent	Canterbury	1983
221*	K Sharp	Gloucestershire	Todmorden	1990
219	G M Hamilton	Derbyshire	Chesterfield	2003
218*	A McGrath	Surrey	Elland	1994
212	G S Ballance	MCC Young Cricketers	Stamford Bridge	2009
209*	C White	Worcestershire	Worcester	1990
205	C R Taylor	Glamorgan	Todmorden	2003
204	B Parker	Gloucestershire	Bristol	1993
203	A McGrath	Durham	Headingley	2005
202*	J M Bairstow	Leicestershire	Oakham	2009
202	M J Wood	Essex	Stamford Bridge	2006
201*	C R Taylor	Sussex	Hove	2005
200*	D Byas	Worcestershire	Worcester	1992
200*	A McGrath	Northamptonshire	Northampton	2012
192*	R A Kettleborough	Nottinghamshire	Todmorden	1996
191	P E Robinson	Warwickshire	Harrogate	1984
191	M J Wood	Derbyshire	Rotherham	2000
191	M J Lumb	Nottinghamshire	Middlesbrough	2000
189*	C S Pickles	Gloucestershire	Bristol	1991
186	A McGrath	MCC Universities	York	2011
184	J D Love	Worcestershire	Headingley	1976
183	A W Gale	Durham	Stamford Bridge	2006
174	G L Brophy	Worcestershire	Stamford Bridge	2007
173	S N Hartley	Warwickshire	Edgbaston	1980
173	A A Metcalfe	Glamorgan	Gorseinon	1984
173	B Parker	Sussex	Hove	1996
173	R A Kettleborough	Leicestershire	Oakham School	1997

Individual Scores of 150 and over *(Continued)*

Score	Player	Versus	Ground	Season
172	A C Morris	Lancashire	York	1995
170*	R A J Townsley	Glamorgan	Harrogate	1975
169	J E Root	Warwickshire	York	2010
168	M J Wood	Leicestershire	Oakham School	1997
166	A A Metcalfe	Lancashire	York	1984
166	C A Chapman	Northamptonshire	York	1998
165*	A Lyth	Durham	Stamford Bridge	2006
165	J J Sayers	Sussex	Hove	2006
164*	A W Gale	Leicestershire	Harrogate	2002
164	J C Balderstone	Nottinghamshire	Harrogate	1960
163*	J E Root	Leicestershire	Oakham	2009
163	A A Metcalfe	Derbyshire	Chesterfield	1992
162*	D Byas	Surrey	Scarborough	1987
160	A A Metcalfe	Somerset	Bradford	1993
157	J J Sayers	Lancashire	Headingley	2007
155	S M Guy	Derbyshire	Chesterfield	2005
154*	C R Taylor	Surrey	Whitgift School	2005
153*	A A Metcalfe	Warwickshire	Bingley	1995
153	C White	Worcestershire	Marske-by-the-Sea	1991
153	R A Stead	Surrey	Todmorden	2002
152	A A Metcalfe	Gloucestershire	Bristol	1993
151*	P E Robinson	Nottinghamshire	York	1986
151*	S J Foster	Kent	Elland	1992
151*	J J Sayers	Durham	Stamford Bridge	2004
151	P J Hartley	Somerset	Clevedon	1989
151	A McGrath	Somerset	Elland	1995
151	V J Craven	Glamorgan	Todmorden	2003
150*	K Sharp	Essex	Elland	1991
150*	G M Fellows	Hampshire	Todmorden	1998
150*	S M Guy	Nottinghamshire	Headingley	2005
150*	J A Leaning	Worcestershire	Worcester	2011
150	K Sharp	Glamorgan	Ebbw Vale	1983
150	S N Hartley	Nottinghamshire	Worksop	1988
150	C R Taylor	Derbyshire	Chesterfield	2003

7 Wickets in an Innings (30)

Analysis	Player	Versus	Ground	Season
9 for 27	G A Cope	Northamptonshire	Northampton	1977
9 for 62	M K Bore	Warwicshire	Scarborough	1976
8 for 53	S J Dennis	Nottinghamshire	Nottingham	1983
8 for 57	M K Bore	Lancashire	Manchester	1977
8 for 79	P J Berry	Derbyshire	Harrogate	1991
7 for 13	P Carrick	Northamptonshire	Marske-by-the-Sea	1977
7 for 21	S Silvester	Surrey	Sunbury-on-Thames	1977
7 for 22	J A R Blain	Surrey	Purley	2004
7 for 32	P W Jarvis	Surrey	The Oval	1984
7 for 34	P Carrick	Glamorgan	Leeds	1986
7 for 37	P M Hutchison	Warwickshire	Coventry	2001

7 Wickets in an Innings *(Continued)*

Analysis	Player	Versus	Ground	Season
7 for 39	G M Hamilton	Sussex	Leeds	1995
7 for 40	M K Bore	Worcestershire	Old Hill	1976
7 for 44	M K Bore	Lancashire	Harrogate	1976
7 for 44	J P Whiteley	Worcestershire	Leeds	1979
7 for 51	J D Middlebrook	Derbyshire	Rotherham	2000
7 for 53	J P Whiteley	Warwickshire	Birmingham	1980
7 for 55	C White	Leicestershire	Bradford	1990
7 for 58	K Gillhouley	Derbyshire	Chesterfield	1960
7 for 58	P J Hartley	Lancashire	Leeds	1985
7 for 63	M J Hoggard	Worcestershire	Harrogate	1998
7 for 65	M K Bore	Nottinghamshire	Steetley	1976
7 for 70	J D Batty	Leicestershire	Bradford	1992
7 for 71	J D Batty	Hampshire	Harrogate	1994
7 for 81	K Gillhouley	Lancashire	Scarborough	1960
7 for 84	I J Houseman	Kent	Canterbury	1989
7 for 88	I G Swallow	Nottinghamshire	Nottingham	1983
7 for 90	A P Grayson	Kent	Folkestone	1991
7 for 93	D Pickles	Nottinghamshire	Nottingham	1960
7 for 94	K Gillhouley	Northamptonshire	Redcar	1960

12 Wickets in a Match (6)

Analysis		Player	Versus	Ground	Season
13 for 92	(6-48 and 7-44)	M K Bore	Lancashire	Harrogate	1976
13 for 110	(7-70 and 6-40)	J D Batty	Leicestershire	Bradford	1992
13 for 111	(4-49 and 9-62)	M K Bore	Warwickshire	Scarborough	1976
12 for 69	(5-32 and 7-37)	P M Hutchison	Warwickshire	Coventry	2001
12 for 120	(5-39 and 7-81)	K Gillhouley	Lancashire	Scarborough	1960
12 for 162	(5-78 and 7-84)	I J Houseman	Kent	Canterbury	1989

Hat-tricks (4)

Player	Versus	Ground	Season
I G Swallow	Warwickshire	Harrogate	1984
S D Fletcher	Nottinghamshire	Marske-by-the-Sea	1987
I G Swallow	Derbyshire	Chesterfield	1988
M Broadhurst	Essex	Southend-on-Sea	1992

ANNUAL REPORT
and
Statement of Account
for the year ended
December 31, 2014

CHAIRMAN'S STATEMENT

It is hard to put into words quite what Yorkshire winning the Championship means to me. It is a fantastic achievement, and to see what we have done this year is beyond my wildest dreams. When you look back over the past 13 years there have been a lot of low points, but winning the Championship made it all worthwhile.

A lot of people have asked me why I got involved in the first place. Purely and simply I love Yorkshire cricket. I have been a cricket fan all my life, and I enjoy every minute of being involved in this wonderful game.

COLIN GRAVES

Our Championship success is for you the members, as Yorkshire is a members' club and it always will be. To win the Championship was one of the proudest days I have had in my life, and to support the team is what it's all about. We are a cricket club, and cricket is at the heart of everything we do, but we have to be a commercial business that pays its way within the game.

On the pitch is where we continue to make great strides. I would like to personally thank the players and support staff for their continued efforts, and under the guidance of Martyn Moxon, Jason Gillespie and Andrew Gale we are heading in the right direction. I've said to them all that I believe it could be the start of an exciting new era for the next 10 years, and that is the target I'm setting them – for this team to dominate county cricket and one-day cricket over the next decade. We now have got the coaching staff, the players and the Academy structure for us to achieve this.

I seriously believe we can recreate the success of the great side from the 1960s, so we need to breed a habit of winning trophies year in and year out like the great sports teams around the world. It's not just the senior players performing. The Academy showed their rich potential by winning the Yorkshire League cup and League double. They dominated the competition against players with more experience. They are hungry for more success, and with the players coming through the system we can continue to dominate at regional level.

We are also now in a stronger position financially, as off the field we are making positive steps. Under the guidance of Mark Arthur there is a great unity among the office staff, and they are working tirelessly to enable the Club to prosper at the same pace as our achievements on the field.

With that in mind, the Headingley stadium complex is continually being upgraded. Permanent floodlights, the first phase of development, will be in place for the start of the 2015 season, and we are embarking on a long-term Masterplan to change and upgrade the facilities. This is the most ambitious project the Club and the venue will have undertaken since the ground was first established 125 years ago.

Our ambitions are clear. We want to create a stadium that is among the finest in the world and enable Yorkshire to continue to stage major international fixtures over the long term. As other venues around the country continue to invest in their facilities we cannot afford to stand still and expect that Headingley will always host international cricket without providing first-class facilities.

The stark reality is that if our stadium fails to evolve we will lose our international match status, which would be a devastating blow to the region and YCCC. It is essential that we fill the ground for international matches and make Headingley a leading venue.

More importantly, we are doing this without incurring any more debt. To stay ahead of the pack we have to continually upgrade the stadium and ensure Headingley remains an international venue of choice. We have an *Ashes* Test Match in 2019 and a number of World Cup matches, too.

I would like to thank Harold 'Dickie' Bird for his first year in office as President. He has had a fantastic year, and is a great President. His passion for the Club and all things Yorkshire is unrelenting. Dickie is a superb role model and ambassador. He is respected by the players, and his representing the Club at every game has given us kudos. Everyone wants to meet him, and he is always positive promoting the region. The nominations committee and the board are recommending him for a second term, and we had no hesitation in doing that. He thoroughly deserves another year.

Finally, to my fellow Board members, I would like to thank you for your efforts and resolute support over the years. It has been a challenging period for us all, but we are moving in the right direction and this is underpinned by the Club's efforts on the field. The next few years will continue to be inspiring as we aim for more success but in turn set ourselves some ambitious objectives of redeveloping the ground, eliminating the debt and commercially seeing the Club prosper.

To safeguard the future of Yorkshire cricket it is vital that we continually work to achieve our objectives for the long term. This is a fabulous time to be part of the greatest cricket club in the world, and I hope we have many more years like 2014.

May I wish you all a very enjoyable 2015 season, and I look forward to seeing you all throughout the campaign.

COLIN GRAVES
Executive Chairman
The Yorkshire
County Cricket Club

FINANCE DIRECTOR'S REPORT

PAUL HUDSON

It has been a busy time since I joined the Club in May 2014. I have witnessed a highly successful season on the pitch, and have taken over the financial reins from my predecessor, who I must thank for the good order in which the accounting records were left.

The Club faces many financial challenges, and at the same time is greatly indebted to Colin Graves for his ongoing financial support of the Club. I have met many members and supporters of the Club, and have received a very warm welcome from all. I am delighted to report that the Club has achieved an improvement in income and underlying Earnings Before Interest, Tax, Depreciation and Amortisation (EBITDA).

Income at £7.3m represents a 7.9 per cent growth over 2013, and EBITDA at £484,000 shows a significant improvement over £150,000 in the preceding year. These represent small but significant steps in the right direction. The increase in revenues over prior year of £533,000 is a result of a combination of factors. On the negative side the Test match ticket sales were £178,000 lower than the prior year. This was despite a June date, compared to May in 2013, and reasonable weather, again compared to 2013 when the first day was lost to rain. The One Day International against India was practically a sell-out on a hot September day, and proved a success with ticket sales, showing a small increase on the corresponding fixture last year.

Commercial income has shown a significant move forward, at £1,798,000 being a 10 per cent increase on 2013 as a result of increased sponsorship of the Club, including the support of our new principal partner Mazars, along with our other partners. The newly launched online shop has proved highly successful since its launch in August. This has helped us to leverage the success of performances on the pitch and allow us a far greater reach with sale of Club merchandise.

Income from the ECB also showed an increase over 2013, in part due to prize money for winning the County Championship and in part due to increased payments in respect of the Development of England players and their representation for the country. Overheads incurred by the Club are extremely well managed, and costs are very tightly controlled, year on year. Cricket expenses and overheads have together shown a 2.9 per cent decrease year on year. This is a creditable achievement at a large venue which is constantly subject to ongoing maintenance and upkeep. This is despite the removal of booking charges for international tickets, which have traditionally been included as a reduction in overhead costs. During the year the club received a £1,000,000 payment from the ECB, which was used to repay the short-term loan taken out in 2013. This was referred to in last year's accounts and in 2013 was used specifically to repay £500,000 of the Leeds City Council loan and to fund capital projects. This £1,000,000 of income received in 2014 has been recognised in the accounts as £500,000 of exceptional income on the face of the Income and Expenditure Account and £500,000 of grant income, held on the balance sheet and released in line with the depreciation charge on the related capital projects. Cash flows of the Club remain tight, with the improved surplus of income over expenditure being used to help service the financing costs of the Club.

A further loan of £1,000,000 was also received from Colin Graves during the year to support the ongoing cash flow of the Club. At the same time the interest rate on these loans was reduced to four per cent. We are, of course, grateful for both these actions to support the Club. As part of the ongoing development of the stadium we are in the process of erecting floodlights. These will enable us to stage our *T20* matches with a later start time, thus providing people more time to arrive at the stadium. They are also a requirement for staging World Cup matches in 2019. For both reasons this is another positive step forward for the stadium.

The total cost of the floodlights is in the region of £1,400,000. This is being financed in two components. There is a loan of £700,000 from the ECB, which will be repayable from four performance-related payments from the ECB of £175,000 each. These payments are received at the time of staging the first four televised floodlit matches. At 31 December 2014 £450,000 of this loan had been drawn down. The balance is the subject of a lease-finance arrangement which will incur small payments over the next three and a half years, and the balance will be settled in 2018 funded directly out of a one-off payment due from the ECB.

The Club understands that Stephen Willis is leaving Leeds Beckett University, and as such will stand down from the Board in April 2015. I would like to thank him for his service to the Club. The Club has been informed that Leeds Beckett University intend to nominate Professor Paul Smith as his replacement in due course. Finally, I would like to reiterate my thanks to members, supporters, the Yorkshire Taverners, partners and staff who continue to support the Club and have made my first term with Yorkshire County Cricket Club an enjoyable one.

PAUL HUDSON
Director of Finance
Yorkshire County Cricket Club

DIRECTOR OF PROFESSIONAL CRICKET'S REPORT

I said in my report last year that we were disappointed to finish second in the LVCC, as we felt we were in an excellent position ahead of the match against Durham at Scarborough. Everyone was determined to go one better this year. I am delighted to report that we did.

It was fantastic for everyone involved with the Club, and I was particularly pleased for our Chairman, Colin Graves. Without his support the Club may well have gone out of existence, so it was important that he was rewarded with some

MARTYN MOXON

success. Great credit must go to the players, not only with the brand of cricket they played, but for the desire they showed to win the title. The hard work started in November 2013 in the gym and on the 3G pitch at Weetwood. The work ethic of the players was phenomenal, and this continued throughout the summer. The squad's high levels of fitness shone through in the last few weeks of the season. I'm certain that this was instrumental in our winning four of the last five Championship games.

We nearly pulled off a remarkable win in the last game, too, and for me that last afternoon epitomised what we were all about. The players could easily have thought, "OK, we've already won the Championship, so what does it matter?" As it transpired, not only did they not want to get beaten, they wanted to win. The fact that the bowlers found the energy to put in that performance on the last afternoon showed the huge benefit of all that pre-season training. We pride ourselves on managing the players' workloads and achieving a balance between work and recovery. The aim is to ensure that the players are as fresh as possible for the run-in, because the competition is so intense that you cannot afford to let your standards slip for one minute.

Great praise goes to Ian Fisher, Kunwar Bansil and Blaine Clancy for the work they do with the lads to give Andrew Gale and Jason Gillespie as many fit players as possible to pick from during the whole season. The players were a team in every sense of the word. Their support for each other and the enjoyment of each other's achievements was a huge contributory factor to the success. They were extremely well led by the captain, Andrew Gale, who I believe is growing in the role each year. His management of the players last season was outstanding, and tactically he was excellent. Along with Jason Gillespie, he forms a strong management team which sets high standards but also encourages enjoyment of the game. We have a strong team ethic running throughout the Club now both on and off the field. It is an environment in which players and staff can thrive and hopefully continue to deliver positive results.

Obviously, there were some outstanding individual performances over the season, and this has been reflected in the various England team selections for the winter. At the time of writing we have had seven players involved in the England Performance Programme as well as Joe Root in the England ODI squad in Sri Lanka. We also have seven out of 14 in the England Lions squad that tours South Africa in January 2015. Add to that seven in the provisional England World Cup squad of 30 and it gives Yorkshire cricket supporters something of which to be very proud.

There is, however, a potential challenge for us around the corner. If these players perform to their capabilities during the winter I can foresee at least six of them making the England squad for the West Indies tour in April/May. This will test the strength of our squad in the early part of the season, but it will give opportunities to some of our younger players. Hopefully, they will rise to the challenge and put themselves forward as the next generation of Yorkshire cricketers.

We need to keep the production line flowing because there is a real possibility that we could lose a number of players to international duty. With that in mind, I would like to express my gratitude to Richard Dawson, Ian Dews and Richard Damms for this excellent work with our younger players. Richard was moulding the Second Eleven into a very competitive team by mid-summer, and they were producing some positive results. This was disrupted a little by the fact that five players were selected for the England Under-19 series. As a result we fielded a very young side, and results were more difficult to achieve. It did, however, enable us to challenge the replacements at a higher level, and eventually their performances began to improve.

Following on the theme of developing young players, the Academy, under Ian Dews and Richard Damms, also had an outstanding season. Winning both the Yorkshire League and Yorkshire League Knockout Cup was a magnificent achievement, and great credit must go to the players and coaches. Hopefully, these players will continue to develop and become successful Yorkshire cricketers in the future. Despite our success in the four-day game we still have work to do in the one-day formats. Although our performances in 2014 were an improvement on the previous year we were disappointed not to reach the quarter-finals of the *T20* Blast and the semi-final of the Royal London Cup. We had an opportunity to achieve both, but weren't able to close out the games from potential winning positions. We have identified areas for improvement, and will work hard this winter and during our pre-season to develop our skills even further. We want to be competitive in all forms of the game, and we have a desire to build on the County Championship success. However, we are under no illusion. It will be even harder next season to repeat the achievement. Once again, thank you for your continued support, and I hope 2015 will be another exciting and successful season.

MARTYN MOXON
Director of Professional Cricket
Yorkshire County Cricket Club

MEMBERS' COMMITTEE
CHAIRMAN'S REPORT

The following served on the Members' Committee during the year.

Chairman:	**Mr S J Mann**
Elected Members:	**Mrs C Evers**
	Mr R Levin
	Mr S J Mann
	Mr E Stephens
Appointed Members:	**Mr G Clark (to March 31, 2014)**
	Mr A Kilburn
	Mr R W Stott
In Attendance:	**Mr R Smith,** Board Director
	Mr M Arthur, Chief Executive
	Mr A Dawson, Commercial Director

There were seven full meetings during 2014. The minutes of these meetings are passed to the main Board and included in Board papers for meetings immediately thereafter. There were no changes to the list of participants and attendees during the year other than the resignation of Graham Clark for business reasons early in the year.

STEPHEN MANN

Two Member Forums were held during the year. While the content of some of the issues raised has left much to be desired the forums have proved to excellent opportunity for members to communicate with Club management. A change of venue helped to ensure uninterrupted debate, but the numbers attending were somewhat reduced. For 2015 the same venue in the old Pavilion will be used, but greater efforts made to communicate just where and when the meeting is being held. The committee and Club will seek to provide specific presentations on matters of member interest such as that during the year on proposed ground improvements.

Test match staging and attendance levels were subjects of debate at many of the committee meetings. The number of members buying tickets for Tests continues to be disappointing. While there are some justifiable reasons such as the county side playing elsewhere on the same dates it is hoped that in 2015 many, many more members will seek to watch at least one day of the Test. Test match attendance levels help to finance the Club in general and in particular help to ensure that the Academy is run and maintained at the current high standards.

The Club deserve considerable credit for the way Tests and ODI games are now staged and managed. The improvements over recent years are substantial with the 2014 Test a most enjoyable spectator experience, a view expressed by the majority of those attending.

Test match and ODI pricing were given much attention in the year. The committee and the Club have sought innovative ways to maximise attendances and this important income stream. The objective has been to price people into the ground and not have a pricing structure that drives spectators away. The Test Match "season ticket" looks, at the time of writing, to be proving the much-hoped-for attraction for the 2015 Test.

The committee provide feedback and comment to the Club on the numerous issues raised by the membership. Commercial activities through the shop and website have been subjects of particular discussion, and it is anticipated that a number of improvements will be evident in 2015.

The committee have continued to raise member dissatisfaction with the poor state of some facilities and general staging of games at Scarborough. That Scarborough is a much-loved venue is beyond doubt, but there really does need to be an improvement in the management and preparedness by the host club. Facilities need to be tried, tested and in full working order well in advance of the opening day.

In conclusion, I would like to express my sincere appreciation to all on the Members' Committee for their support and work throughout the year. They all give a significant amount of personal time and expense to work for the Club and the membership. Graham Clark was a fine example of these dedicated volunteers. Due to pressures of work Graham had to reluctantly step down from the committee early in the year. His work for the committee and the Club on operational matters is greatly appreciated.

STEPHEN MANN,
Chairman,
Members' Committee
Yorkshire County Cricket Club

INDEPENDENT AUDITORS' REPORT

TO THE MEMBERS OF THE YORKSHIRE
COUNTY CRICKET CLUB

We have audited the financial statements of The Yorkshire County Cricket Club for the year ended 31 December, 2014, set out on Pages 439 to 448. The financial reporting framework that has been applied in their preparation is applicable in law and UK Accounting Standards (UK Generally Accepted Accounting Practice).

This report is made solely to the Club's members, as a body, in accordance with Section 87 of the Co-operative and Community Benefit Societies Act 2014. Our audit work has been undertaken so that we might state to the Club's members those matters we are required to state to them in an auditor's report and for no other purpose. To the fullest extent permitted by law, we do not accept or assume responsibility to anyone other than the Club and the Club's members, as a body, for our audit work, for this report, or for the opinions we have formed.

Respective responsibilities of directors and auditor

As more fully explained in the Statement of Directors' Responsibilities set out on Page 438 the Club's directors are responsible for the preparation of financial statements which give a true and fair view. Our responsibility is to audit, and express an opinion on, the financial statements in accordance with applicable law and International Standards on Auditing (UK and Ireland). Those standards require us to comply with the Auditing Practices Board's Ethical Standards for Auditors.

Scope of the audit of the financial statements

A description of the scope of an audit of financial statements is provided on the Financial Reporting Council's website at www.frc.org.uk/auditscopeukprivate.

Opinion on financial statements

In our opinion the financial statements:

- give a true and fair view, in accordance with UK Generally Accepted Accounting Practice, of the state of the Club's affairs as at 31 December 2014 and of its deficit for the year then ended; and
- comply with the requirements of the Co-operative and Community Benefit Societies Act 2014.

435

Matters on which we are required to report by exception

We have nothing to report in respect of the following.

Under the Co-operative and Community Benefit Societies Act 2014 we are required to report to you if, in our opinion:

- the Club has not maintained a satisfactory system of control over its transactions; or
- the financial statements are not in agreement with the Club's books of account; or
- we have not received all the information and explanations we need for our audit.

A J SILLS (Senior Statutory Auditor) for and on behalf of KPMG LLP, Statutory Auditor
Chartered Accountants,
Leeds   FEBRUARY 10, 2015

CORPORATE GOVERNANCE

The Board is accountable to the Club's members for good corporate governance, and this statement describes how the principles of governance are applied.

THE BOARD

The Board is responsible for approving Club policy and strategy. It meets monthly, or more frequently if business needs require, and has a schedule of matters specifically reserved to it for decision, including all significant commercial issues and all capital expenditure.

The Executive Management Team supply the Board with appropriate and timely information, and the Board Members are free to seek any further information they consider necessary.

NOMINATIONS COMMITTEE

The Nominations Committee is formally constituted with written terms of reference, which are defined in the Club Rules and reviewed regularly. It consists of the President, Secretary and two other Board members, currently C J Graves and R A Smith.

RELATIONS WITH MEMBERS

The Club encourages effective communication with its members, and a specific Committee, as defined in the Club Rules, is appointed for that purpose.

INTERNAL CONTROL

The Board acknowledges its responsibility to maintain a sound system of internal control relating to operational, financial and compliance controls and risk management, to safeguard the members' interests and the Club's assets, and will regularly review its effectiveness. Such a system, however, is designed to manage and meet the Club's particular needs and mitigate the risks to which it is exposed, rather than eliminate the risk of failure to achieve business objectives, and can provide only reasonable and not absolute assurance against material mis-statement or loss.

The Club considers its key components to provide effective internal control and improve business efficiency are:

- Regular meetings with senior management to review and assess progress made against objectives and deal with any problems which arise from such reviews.
- A financial reporting system of annual budgets, periodic forecasts and detailed monthly reporting which includes cash-flow forecasts. Budgets and forecasts are reviewed and approved by the Board.
- A defined management and organisation structure with defined responsibilities and appropriate authorisation limits and short lines of communication to the Executive Chairman.

DIRECTORS' RESPONSIBILITIES

The directors are responsible for preparing the Annual Report and the Club's financial statements in accordance with applicable law and regulations. Co-operative and Community Benefit Society law requires the directors to prepare financial statements for each financial year. Under that law the directors have elected to prepare the financial statements in accordance with UK Accounting Standards.

The financial statements are required by law to give a true and fair view of the state of affairs of the Club and of its income and expenditure for that period. In preparing the Club's financial statements the directors are required to:

- select suitable accounting policies and then apply them consistently;
- make judgements and estimates that are reasonable and prudent;
- state whether applicable UK Accounting Standards have been followed, subject to any material departures disclosed and explained in the financial statements, and
- prepare the financial statements on the going concern basis unless it is inappropriate to presume that the Club will continue in business.

The directors are responsible for keeping proper books of account that disclose with reasonable accuracy at any time the financial position of the Club and enable them to ensure that its financial statements comply with the Co-operative and Community Benefit Societies Act 2014. They have general responsibility for taking such steps as are reasonably open to them to safeguard the assets of the Club and to prevent and detect fraud and other irregularities.

The directors are responsible for the maintenance and integrity of the corporate and financial information included on the Club's website. Legislation in the UK governing the preparation and dissemination of financial statements may differ from legislation in other jurisdictions.

INCOME AND EXPENDITURE ACCOUNT
for the year ended 31st December, 2014

	Note	2014 £	2013 £
Income			
International ticket and hospitality revenue		2,181,135	2,239,656
Domestic ticket and hospitality revenue		538,131	442,126
Subscriptions		564,990	520,234
England and Wales Cricket Board		2,194,791	1,832,574
Commercial income		1,797,563	1,633,442
Other income		30,588	105,975
		7,307,198	6,774,007
Cost of sales			
International match and hospitality expenditure		1,202,876	1,096,811
Domestic match and hospitality costs (home fixtures)		348,286	153,975
Retail		163,483	107,131
Catering		31,678	41,053
		(1,746,323)	(1,398,971)
Cricket expenses			
Staff remuneration and employment expenses		2,205,459	2,242,983
Match expenses (away fixtures)		215,808	301,606
Development expenses		317,529	357,089
Other cricket expenses		26,664	36,085
		(2,765,460)	(2,937,763)
Overhead			
Infrastructure and ground operations		807,500	846,013
Commercial		672,324	691,477
Administration		685,077	592,537
Ticket and membership office		146,568	156,972
		(2,311,469)	(2,286,999)
Earnings before interest, tax, depreciation and amortisation		483,946	150,274
Below the line expenditure:			
Loan Interest		(1,050,437)	(478,106)
Depreciation		(438,532)	(457,794)
Release of Capital Grants		178,265	146,195
		(1,310,704)	(1,316,258)
(Deficit) before taxation and exceptional items		(826,758)	(1,165,984)
Exceptional items *1		500,000	526,554
(Deficit) before taxation		(326,758)	(639,430)
Taxation	4	—	81,720
(Deficit) for the year after taxation		(326,758)	(557,710)

*1 A one-off amount of £500,000 was received from the ECB, and used to clear down part of the outstanding loan balance with the ECB. 2013 exceptional item, one-off interest rebate of £526,554 in respect of an interest-rate hedge.

BALANCE SHEET

as at 31st December, 2014

	Note	2014 £	2014 £	2013 £	2013 £
Assets employed:					
Fixed Assets	5		28,335,785		28,493,029
Current assets:					
Stocks		87,753		68,628	
Debtors	6	1,311,146		1,865,416	
Cash at bank and in hand		—		—	
		1,398,899		1,934,044	
Creditors: amounts falling due within one year	7	(3,764,065)		(3,521,551)	
Net current liabilities			(2,365,166)		(1,587,508)
Total assets less current liabilities			25,970,619		26,905,521
Funded by:					
Creditors: amounts falling due after more than one year	8		24,165,569		25,095,448
Deferred income — capital grants	9		5,019,668		4,697,933
			29,185,237		29,793,381
Capital and Reserves					
Called-up share capital	11		199		219
Capital redemption reserve	12		691		671
Income and expenditure account	12		(3,215,508)		(2,888,750)
			(3,214,618)		(2,887,860)
			25,970,619		26,905,521

These accounts were approved by the Board on 10th February 2015

C J GRAVES, Chairman

R A SMITH, Director

The accompanying notes form an integral part to these accounts. There were no other gains and losses in the current or preceding year other than those stated above.

CASH FLOW STATEMENT

for the year ended 31st December, 2014

	Note	2014 £	2013 £
Cash (outflow) / inflow from operating activities	13	**1,471,490**	(519,886)
Returns on investments and servicing of finance	14	**(1,050,437)**	(1,004,660)
Capital expenditure and financial investment	14	**(281,289)**	(300,708)
Cash inflow / (outflow) before financing		**139,764**	(1,825,254)
Financing	14	**(143,284)**	2,804,311
Increase in cash in the period		**(3,520)**	979,057

Reconciliation of net cash flow to movement in net debt		
Increase in cash in period	**(3,520)**	979,057
HSBC loan repayment	**200,000**	200,000
Leeds City Council loan repayment	**200,000**	200,000
Additional C J Graves loan	**(1,000,000)**	(1,000,000)
Additional Graves' Trust loans	**—**	(2,000,000)
Additional Debentures	**(13,617)**	(40,783)
Other loans - ECB net repayment	**559,296**	(899,296)
New finance leases	**—**	
Capital element of finance lease repayments	**197,585**	235,723
	139,744	(1,825,299)

ANALYSIS OF NET DEBT

	At 1 Jan 2014 £	Cash flow 2014 £	Other changes 2013 £	At 31 Dec 2013 £
Cash at bank and in hand	—	—	—	—
Overdraft - current	(301,249)	(3,520)	—	(304,769)
	(301,249)	(3,520)	—	(304,769)
Debt due within one year:				
HSBC loan	(200,000)	200,000	(200,000)	(200,000)
Leeds City Council loan	(200,000)	200,000	(200,000)	(200,000)
Other loans ECB	(70,000)	(380,000)	—	(450,000)
Finance leases less than one year	(197,692)	197,585	(126,586)	(126,693)
Debt due after one year:				
HSBC loan	(3,069,014)	—	200,000	(2,869,014)
Leeds City Council loan	(7,407,000)	—	200,000	(7,207,000)
Other loans ECB	(939,296)	939,296	—	—
Pride Appeal loan	(5,000)	—	—	(5,000)
Graves Family Trusts loans	(5,600,000)	—	—	(5,600,000)
C J Graves loan	(4,500,000)	(1,000,000)	—	(5,500,000)
Debentures	(366,679)	(13,617)	—	(380,296)
Finance leases more than one year	(1,212,655)	—	126,586	(1,086,069)
	(23,767,336)	143,264	—	(23,624,072)
Total	(24,068,585)	139,744	—	(23,928,841)

441

NOTES TO THE ACCOUNTS

for the year ended 31st December, 2014

1. Accounting policies

The accounts have been prepared in accordance with applicable accounting standards and under the historical cost convention. The principal accounting policies of the Club have remained unchanged from the previous year.

(a) Income

All income is accounted for on an accruals basis, except for donations which are accounted for in the year of receipt.

Income represents amounts receivable from the Club's principal activities. Income is analysed between international-ticket and hospitality revenue, domestic ticket and hospitality revenue, subscriptions, England and Wales Cricket Board, commercial and other income.

Subscriptions

Subscription income comprises amounts receivable from members in respect of the current season. Subscriptions received in respect of future seasons are treated as deferred income.

Domestic-ticket and hospitality revenue

Relate to amounts received from gate charges, ticket sales, hospitality and guarantees directly attributable to staging domestic cricket matches in Yorkshire.

International-ticket and hospitality revenue

Relate to amounts received from gate charges, ticket sales, hospitality and guarantees directly attributable to staging international cricket matches in Yorkshire.

England and Wales Cricket Board (ECB)

Income relates to fees receivable, including performance-related elements, in the current season distributed from central funds in accordance with the First Class Memorandum of Understanding. ECB fees received in respect of future seasons are treated as deferred income. ECB distributions receivable to fund capital projects are treated as deferred income, and are released to the Income and Expenditure Account by equal installments over the expected useful lives of the relevant assets in accordance with accounting policy (b) Fixed assets and depreciation, as set out belowe.

Commercial and other income

Relates to amounts received, net of related expenditure, from ground advertising, catering guarantees, box lettings, facility hire, dinners and other events. Advertising income received in respect of future seasons is treated as deferred income. Other income relates to amounts received, net of related expenditure, from retail, Cricket Centre bar, Taverners Club, fundraising activities and other sundry items.

(b) Fixed assets and depreciation

All expenditure in connection with the development of Headingley Carnegie Cricket Ground and the relates facilities has been capitalised. Finance costs relating to and incurred during the period of construction were also capitalised. Depreciation is only charged once a discrete phase of the development is completed.

Depreciation is calculated to write down the cost of fixed assets by equal annual installments over their expected useful lives.

The periods generally applicable are:

Headingley Carnegie Cricket Ground and Cricket Centre

Buildings	Carnegie Pavilion	125 years
	Other buildings	50 years
Fixtures		4 years
Plant & Equipment	Between 4 and 10 years	
Office equipment		
— telephone system		4 years
Computer equipment		2 years
Freehold land is not depreciated.		

All other expenditure on repairs to Headingley Carnegie Cricket Ground and other grounds is written off as and when incurred.

(c) Carnegie Pavilion

The Club's contribution towards the design and build cost of the Carnegie Pavilion is £3m, of which £1.5m is payable over 20 years under a 125 year lease agreement. The £3m, together with the associated legal, professional and capital fit-out costs of the areas within the Pavilion that the Club occupies have been capitalised and depreciated over the 125-year lease term. The £1.5m payable under the lease agreement has been treated as a finance lease within the financial statements with the capital element reported within Creditors (Finance leases), and the interest element charged to the Income and Expenditure Account on a straight-line basis over the 20-year term.

(d) Stocks

Stocks represent goods for resale, and are stated at the lower of cost and net realisable value.

(e) Grants

Capital grants relating to the development of Headingley Carnegie Cricket Ground (including the Yorkshire Cricket Museum) and Cricket Centre are included within the Balance Sheet as deferred income, and are released to the Income and Expenditure Account by equal installments over the expected useful lives of the relevant assets in accordance with accounting policy (b) Fixed asets and depreciation, as set out opposite.

Grants of a revenue nature are credited to the Income and Expenditure Account in the same period as their related expenditure.

(f) Disclosure of information to Auditor

The members of the Board who held office at the date of approval of the Annual Report and Accounts confirm that, so far as they are aware, there is no relevant information of which the Club's auditor is unaware; or each member has taken all the steps that he ought to have taken as a member to make himself aware of any relevant audit information or to establish that the Club's auditor is aware of that information.

2. Financial Position

The Club is in a net current liability position of £3.2m (2013: £2.9m). This includes deferred income of £1.8m (2013: £1.6m). Details of the loan and overdraft maturity analysis which impact on the financial position can be found in Note 8.

The Club is not expecting to generate a cash surplus in 2015, and therefore Mr C J Graves has agreed to provide such cash-flow support as the Club requires for at least 12 months from the date of the accounts to allow the Club to pay creditors as they fall due. Due to this support the Board considers it appropriate to prepare the financial statements on a going-concern basis.

3. Directors' remuneration

	2014 £	2013 £
Wages and salaries	—	—
Social security costs	—	—
Pension costs	—	—
	—	—

	2014 £	2013 £
4. Taxation		
UK corporation tax	—	—
Total current tax	—	—
Deferred tax (see Note 10)	—	(81,720)
Tax on (deficit) on ordinary activities	—	(81,720)
(Deficit) on ordinary activities before taxation	(326,758)	(639,430)
Current tax at 21.5% (2013: 23.25%)	(70,253)	(148,667)
Effects of:		
Expenses not deductable for taxation purposes	61,864	27,992
Non taxable income	(104,958)	(78,168)
Depreciation for the period		
in excess of capital allowances	2,366	(27,456)
Losses not utilised	110,981	226,299
Total current tax (see above)	£ —	£ —

5. Fixed assets (See next page)

6. Debtors		
Trade debtors	304,543	194,341
Deferred tax asset (see Note 10)	840,306	840,306
Other debtors	166,297	830,769
	1,311,146	1,865,416

7. Creditors: amounts falling due within one year		
Leeds City Council loan	200,000	200,000
Bank Loan	200,000	200,000
Bank overdraft (secured)	304,769	301,249
ECB loans	450,000	70,000
Trade creditors	175,157	252,503
Finance leases	126,693	197,692
Social security and other taxes	368,925	272,162
Other creditors	58,358	203,808
Accruals	111,774	245,825
Deferred income	1,768,389	1,578,312
	3,764,065	3,521,551

| | Cricket Centre | | Headingley Carnegie Cricket Ground | | | | | |
	Freehold Land and Buildings £	Plant & Equipment £	Freehold Land and Buildings £	Plant and Equipment £	Improvements to Leasehold Property £	Assets in the Course of Construction £	Office Equipment £	Total £
Cost								
At January 1, 2014	601,124	773,176	25,293,079	4,916,178	4,584,662	—	395,179	36,563,398
Additions	—	—	36,137	5,565	11,741	370,828	—	424,271
Adjustments	—	—	—	—	(142,982)	—	—	(142,982)
At December 31, 2014	601,124	773,176	25,329,216	4,921,743	4,584,662	370,828	395,179	36,844,687
Depreciation								
At January 1, 2014	122,826	761,182	2,376,134	4,287,149	157,893	—	365,185	8,070,370
Provided in the year	16,413	1,457	239,358	126,528	39,237	—	15,539	438,532
At December 31, 2014	139,239	762,639	2,615,492	4,413,677	197,130	—	380,725	8,508,902
Net book value								
At January 1, 2014	461,885	10,537	22,713,724	508,066	4,256,291	370,828	14,454	28,335,785
At December 31, 2014	478,298	11,994	22,916,945	629,029	4,426,769	—	29,993	28,493,028

Improvements to Leasehold Property consist of the Club's share of the costs associated with the design and build of the Carnegie Pavilion. This cost includes a £3m base capital contribution (£1.5m of which has been treated as a finance lease, with the outstanding capital balance shown within creditors). The remaining £1.3m represents costs associated with fit-out, structural amendments, legal and consultancy fees. The total cost is depreciated over 125 years, which represents the term of the lease. Assets in the Course of Construction represent the expenditure incurred by the end of 2014 relating to the installation of the floodlights at Headingley Cricket Ground.

445

	2014	2013
	£	£

8. Creditors: amounts falling due after more than one year

	2014	2013
Leeds City Council Loan	7,207,000	7,407,000
Bank Loan	2,869,014	3,069,014
ECB Loan	—	939,296
Pride Appeal Loans	5,000	5,000
CJ and J Graves Accumulation and Maintenance Trusts Loans	5,600,000	5,600,000
C J Graves Loan	5,500,000	4,500,000
Debentures	380,296	366,679
Finance Leases	1,086,069	1,212,656
Deferred income	1,518,190	1,995,803
	24,165,569	25,095,448

Loan and overdraft maturity analysis:

	2014	2013
In one year or less or on demand	1,281,462	968,941
In more than one year but not more than two years	6,075,000	1,465,986
In more than two years but not more than five years	6,925,000	7,625,000
In more than five years	9,647,379	14,008,659
	23,928,841	24,068,586

The Leeds City Council loan is repayable by December 15, 2025, at an interest rate of 4.5 per cent per annum. The Club has given a First Legal Charge over the freehold property known as Headingley Cricket Ground, St Michaels Lane, Leeds, to Leeds City Council in respect of this loan. Mr C J Graves has provided a shortfall guarantee in respect of this loan. The Club has also given a First Legal Charge to HSBC Bank plc over the Cricket Centre known as 41/43 St Michaels Lane, Headingley, Leeds, and a Second Legal Charge over the property known as Headingley Cricket Ground, St Michaels Lane, Leeds, in respect of the bank loan and overdrafts. HSBC Bank plc also has a fixed and floating charge over all the assets of the Club, subject to the Legal Charges referred to above. This loan is repayable by April 30, 2020, and bears an interest rate of 4.0 per cent over the Bank's base rate. Mr C J Graves has also provided a personal guarantee in respect of the indebtedness to HSBC Bank plc. The loan from Mr C J Graves bears interest at the rate of 3.5 per cent plus the Bank of England Base Rate. This was reduced from 4.0 per cent plus the Bank of England Base Rate during the year. The loan is repayable on demand with 12 months' notice. The Club has given Mr CJ Graves a Fourth Legal Charge over the property known as Headingley Cricket Ground. The C J Graves Accumulation and Maintenance Trust and J Graves Accumulation and Maintenance Trust each bear interest at the rate at the higher of 4.0 per cet above the Bank of England Base Rate, and 4.5 per cent per annum. However, interest is capped at 7.0 per cent. These loans are repayable in October 2016, and the Club has given a Third Legal Charge over the property known as Headingley Cricket Ground. The ECB loan outstanding at the end of 2013 represents a loan which was made available to all 18 First Class Counties with the purpose of supporting capital improvements and accerating capital-debt repayments. £939,296 had been drawn down by the end of 2013 and a further £60,704 was drawn down in 2014. The £1m loan was repaid towards the end of 2014 using a £500,000 one-off fee payment from the ECB and a £500,000 grant from the ECB towards capital improvements. An additional loan was made available by the ECB towards the cost of installing the floodlights at Headingley Cricket Ground. The total available loan is £700,000, of which £450,000 had been drawn down by the end of 2014. It is expected that this loan will be repaid by a series of one-off fee payments from the ECB following each of the first four floodlit televised games at Headingley Cricket Ground.

9. Deferred income -capital grants

	2014	2013
At January 1, 2013	4,697,933	4,844,128
Received in year	500,000	—
Released to Income and Expenditure Account	(178,265)	(146,195)
At December 31, 2013	5,019,668	4,697,933

	2014 £	2013 £
10. Provision for Liabilities		
— Deferred Taxation Asset / (Liability)		
At January 1, 2013	**(840,306)**	(758,586)
(Credit) to Income and Expenditure Account for the year	**—**	(81,720)
At December 31, 2013	**(840,306)**	(840,306)
The elements of deferred taxation are as follows:		
Difference between accumulated depreciation		
and capital allowances	**219,690**	219,690
Tax losses	**(1,059,996)**	(1,059,996)
	(840,306)	(840,306)

11. Share capital

	2014	2013
Allotted, called up and fully paid Ordinary shares of 5p each	**199**	219

During the year there was a net reduction in qualifying members of 401. The total number of qualifying members as at December 31, 2014, was 3,973 (2013: 4,374). Each member of the Club owns one Ordinary share, and the rights attached thereto are contained within the Club's rules which can be found on the Club's website, or from the Secretary on request.

12. Reserves.

	Income and Expenditure Account	Capital Redemption Reserve
At January 1, 2013	(2,888,750)	671
Deficit for the year	(326,758)	—
Shares in respect of retiring members	—	20
At December 31, 2013	(3,215,508)	691

13. Reconciliation of operating profit to cash flow

(Deficit) for the year before taxation	**(326,758)**	(639,430)
Loan interest and similar amounts payable	**1,050,437**	1,004,660
Operating (Deficit)	**723,679**	365,230
Depreciation of tangible assets	**438,532**	457,794
Capital grants received	**500,000**	—
Release of capital grants	**(178,265)**	(146,195)
(Increase) / decrease in stock	**(19,125)**	(4,430)
(Increase) / decrease in debtors	**554,270**	(607,155)
Increase / (decrease) in creditors	**(260,065)**	183,652
(Decrease) / increase in deferred income	**(287,536)**	(403,552)
Cash (outflow) / inflow from operating activities	**1,471,490**	(519,886)

14. Analysis of cash flows

Returns on investment and servicing of finance		
Loan interest and facility fees	**(1,050,437)**	(1,004,660)
	(1,050,437)	(1,004,660)
Capital expenditure and financial investment		
Purchase of tangible fixed assets	**(281,289)**	(300,708)
	(281,289)	(300,708)

447

	2014	2013
	£	£
Financing		
Other loans received in year:		
ECB	**510,704**	1,009,296
Debentures	**13,617**	40,783
C J Graves	—	1,000,000
Graves' Trusts	**1,000,000**	2,000,000
ECB loan repayment	**(1,070,000)**	(110,000)
HSBC loan repayment	**(200,000)**	(200,000)
LCC Loan repayment	**(200,000)**	(700,000)
Capital element of finance-lease rental payments	**(197,585)**	(235,723)
Issue of ordinary share capital	—	—
Repurchase of ordinary share capital	**(20)**	(45)
	(143,284)	2,804,311

15. Leasing commitments

Operating lease payments amounting to £41,700 (2013: £40,163) are due within one year. The leases to which these amounts relate expire as follows:

	2014 Land and buildings £	2014 Other £	2013 Land and buildings £	2013 Other £
In one year or less	—	—	—	221
Between two and five years	—	11,704	—	9,142
In five years or more	30,000	—	30,000	—
	£30,000	£11,704	£30,000	£10,163

16. Related party transactions

During the year Mr R A Smith was a Board Member and Trustee of the Yorkshire Cricket Foundation (YCF). During 2014 the YCF awarded non-capital grants of £20,083 (2013: £13,294).

17. Pensions

The Club operates defined contribution pension schemes for the benefit of certain employees. The amounts paid during the year were £236,334 (2013: £195,075). The assets of these schemes are administered in funds independent from those of the Club.

18. Audit Fee

The Club paid its auditors £16,750 (2013: £16,500) in respect of the audit of its Financial Statements.